# DICTIONARY OF MARKETING TERMS

SECOND EDITION

by

Betsy-Ann Toffler
Information Officer/Corporate Staff Writer
International Medical Corps

Jane Imber
Director of Marketing
Neodata Services

BARRON'S

All inquiries should be addressed to:
Barron's Educational Series, Inc.
250 Wireless Boulevard
Hauppauge, New York 11788

Library of Congress Catalog Card No. 93-23235

International Standard Book No. 0-8120-1783-8

**Library of Congress Cataloging-in-Publication Data**

Imber, Jane.

Dictionary of marketing terms / by Jane Imber, Betsy-Ann Toffler.
—2nd ed.
p. cm.
Rev. ed. of: Dictionary of advertising and direct mail terms.
©1987
ISBN 0-8120-1783-8
1. Marketing—Dictionaries.  I. Toffler, Betsy-Ann.  II. Imber,
Jane. Dictionary of advertising and direct mail terms.  III. Title.
HF5803.I46   1994
380.1'03—dc20                                          93-23235
                                                               CIP

PRINTED IN THE UNITED STATES OF AMERICA

4567  9692  987654321

# CONTENTS

# PREFACE

The codfish lays ten thousand eggs,
The homely hen lays one.
The codfish never cackles
To tell you what she's done.
And so we scorn the codfish,
While the humble hen we prize,
Which only goes to show you
That it pays to advertise.

Anonymous

"It pays to advertise" has been a part of our vocabulary and a part of our collective consciousness far longer than such terms as VCR or Social Marketing. But advertising is really only one component of the broader concept—*Marketing*. This concept encompasses the entire process involved in the transfer of goods and services from the producer of those goods and services to the consumer. The process includes the visualization of the product, the research and development of the product, the measurement of the product's relative value, the perception of the consumer of the product, the legal ramifications of the product, and the methods and avenues for promoting the product. As such, effective marketing calls upon skills in a wide variety of areas.

Marketing plays a major role in our daily lives, both as providers of goods and services and as consumers. From the time of birth through retirement, marketing has a major effect on a great many of our decisions. What doctor our parents select, what style baby furniture we grow up with, where we live, how we live, what brand of toothpaste we use, what schools and colleges we attend, what car we drive, how we consider travel options, where we retire—all these things are influenced by marketing. As providers of goods and services, marketing affects such things as what prices we charge, where and how to sell our products, what features we promote, how we select a client base, and what services we offer.

Our intention in writing this book is to provide you with the vocabulary you need to employ the tools of the trade as well as to provide a comprehensive resource. The definitions here touch upon all facets of marketing, including product planning, consumer analysis, public relations, sales promotion, marketing philosophies, and advertising. Recognizing the growing popularity of direct marketing techniques, we have been careful to include many terms relevant to that particular discipline. Whether you are a student, novice, specialized advertiser, marketing expert, or someone who works in a related field such as communications or development, the lexicon of marketing is an active part of your vocabulary.

In one easy to use source, *The Dictionary of Marketing Terms* provides functional, lucid definitions of the terms particularly applicable to the field of marketing. Bearing in mind that the language is constantly evolving, the authors have compiled this book as a practical, working reference for anyone interested in practicing or understanding effective marketing. Quality and integrity have been the passwords for our research in our efforts to define the world of marketing in a comprehensive, convenient, and clear fashion.

# HOW TO USE THIS BOOK EFFECTIVELY

**Alphabetization:** All entries are alphabetized by letter rather than by word, so that multiple-word terms are treated as single words. For example, **BUMP EXPOSURE** follows **BUMPER STICKER,** and **RUNAROUND** follows **RUN** and precedes **RUN CHARGE.** In unusual cases (such as **ABEND, ACORN,** or **FIM MARK**), abbreviations or acronyms (initialized nomenclature that are often a dominant factor in the language of advertising and direct mail) appear as entries in the main text, in addition to appearing in the back of the book in the separate listing of abbreviations and acronyms. This occurs when the short form, rather than the formal name, predominates in the common usage of the the field. For example, **ACORN** is more commonly used in speaking of "A Classification of Residential Neighborhoods" than the name itself; thus, the entry is at **ACORN.** Numbers in entry titles are alphabetized as if they were spelled out.

Many words have distinctly different meanings, depending upon the context in which they are used. The various meanings of a term are listed by numerical or functional subheading. Readers must determine the context that is relevant to their purpose.

**Abbreviations and Acronyms:** A separate list of abbreviations and acronyms follows the Dictionary.

**Cross-References:** To add to your understanding of a term, related or contrasting terms are sometimes cross-referenced. The cross-referenced term will appear in SMALL CAPITALS either in the body of the entry (or subentry) or at the end. These terms will be printed in small capitals only the first time they appear in the text. Where an entry is fully defined by another term, a reference rather than a definition is provided—for example: **BASHER** *see* SCOOP.

**Italics:** Italic type is generally used to indicate that another term has a meaning identical or very closely related to that of the entry. Occasionally, italic type is also used to highlight the fact that a word or phrase used has a special meaning to the trade. Italics are also used for the titles of publications.

**Parentheses:** Parentheses are used in entry titles for two reasons. The first is to indicate that an entry's opposite is obvious from a single discussion of the term; for example ZOOM IN (OUT). The second reason is to indicate that an abbreviation is used with about the same frequency as the term itself; for example, FEDERAL TRADE COMMISSION (FTC).

**Special Definitions:** Organizations and associations that play an active role in the field are included in the Dictionary along with a brief statement of their mission. They are also listed by initials in the Appendix under Abbreviations and Acronyms.

## AUTHOR'S NOTE

We recognize that this dictionary cannot possibly represent the ultimate and definitive language of our business for all time. Terms change or become obsolete. New technologies spawn new terms. Consequently, we invite the reader to submit suggestions that may be incorporated into the next edition.

# A

**AAAA SPOT CONTRACT** standardized contract prepared by the AMERICAN ASSOCIATION OF ADVERTISING AGENCIES and used by a national advertiser in the purchase of radio or television commercial time on a market-by-market basis (as compared to a NETWORK BUY). The contract is generally drawn between the advertising agency and the SPOT TELEVISION supplier and specifies the terms of the purchase, such as the number of SPOTS (commercials), the times they'll be shown, the cost, and the specific time period (i.e., a week, a month, 6 weeks, or 13 weeks). *See also* MARKET-BY-MARKET BUY.

**AA RATING** *see* AVERAGE AUDIENCE RATING.

**ABANDON RATE** percentage of the calls made by an automatic dialing device to prospective customers or by customers to a telemarketer that are not intercepted by a live operator before the prospect/customer disconnects. High abandon rates indicate that the telemarketer is not properly managing resources such as personnel and phone lines. Most telemarketers strive to maintain an abandon rate of less than 2%. *See also* AUTOMATIC DIALER; CALL BLOCKAGE; NO-OP; PREDICTIVE DIALER.

**ABC (ANALYZED) ISSUE** issue of a periodical used by a publisher to supply statistical information for the required biannual ABC STATEMENT and presumed to be representative of all issues during that 6-month period. The BUSINESS PUBLICATIONS AUDIT OF CIRCULATIONS organization requires that the May and November issues be used. The AUDIT BUREAU OF CIRCULATIONS, on the other hand, allows publishers to select two issues of their choice, enabling them to choose issues that are expected to sell in a quantity closest to the RATE BASE. The information reported on each analyzed issue includes both subscription and newsstand sales data. *See also* VERIFIED AUDIT CIRCULATION CORPORATION.

**ABCD COUNTIES** designations of the A. C. NIELSEN COMPANY used to indicate counties in the United States by size of population (based on the most recent Census) and proximity to a central city or metropolitan area. All counties in the United States have only one designation. These designations are used in all of the Nielsen Syndicated Services and serve as a guide to advertisers and advertising agencies in the preparation of media plans.

*A County:* any county located in the 25 largest United States cities or their consolidated statistical urban areas.

*B County:* any county not designated as an A County that has population over 150,000 or is part of a consolidated statistical area with population over 150,000.

*C County:* any county or consolidated statistical area not designated as an A or B County that has population over 40,000.

*D County:* any county not designated as an A, B, or C County. The consolidated statistical areas are determined by the Federal Government Office of Management and Budget and are considered to be standard.

**ABC STATEMENT** statement filed twice yearly by a periodical publisher to report statistical information about the periodical as required by either the AUDIT BUREAU OF CIRCULATIONS (ABC) or the BUSINESS PUBLICATIONS AUDIT OF CIRCULATIONS (BPA); also called *publisher's statement.* The statement must report information regarding the paid CIRCULATION on an issue-by-issue basis for a 6-month period. ABC requires that the statement show circulation by SOURCE, type, location, and selling price relative to BASIC RATE. BPA requires additional DEMOGRAPHIC information, such as the readers' occupations and the industries of employment in terms of the STANDARD INDUSTRIAL CLASSIFICATION (SIC) code. Used by advertisers when selecting periodicals in which to place advertisements, the publisher's statement identifies readers who would be exposed to their ads. The ABC consumer magazine statement is printed on pink paper and is sometimes referred to as the *Pink Sheet.* It is in use months before it is actually audited by ABC or BPA.

Publishers choose to file either an ABC statement or a BPA statement depending upon the type of advertiser they hope to attract. ABC statements are used primarily by consumer goods advertisers; BPA statements, by industrial goods advertisers. While it is possible to sell advertising space without publishing a statement, most advertisers prefer to do business only with publications that do provide an audited statement. *See also* ABC (ANALYZED) ISSUE; VERIFIED AUDIT CIRCULATION CORPORATION.

**ABEND** acronym for *ab*normal *end*ing or termination of a COMPUTER PROGRAM. An abend can result from a computer program error, an operator error, or a machine malfunction.

**ABEYANCE ORDER** order for commercial television time in a time period that is not available when the order is placed.

**ABOVE-THE-LINE COST** accounting term used by a commercial production company referring to initial budgeted expenses for the producer, director, cast, and scriptwriter working on the production of a specific commercial. This cost relates to nontechnical personnel and creative elements, such as artwork or graphics, in the commercial production. *See also* BELOW-THE-LINE COST.

**ABSORPTION** varying property of paper allowing it to soak up liquid. The degree of absorption of paper affects the quantity of ink needed to achieve a desired effect. For example, it is difficult to print a permanent address directly on the surface of glossy COATED PAPER, such as the cover of a magazine or catalog, since that type of paper does not absorb ink well. Address labels are usually attached to the covers of magazines and catalogs in lieu of directly printing the address.

**A-B SPLIT** method of random sampling that splits a list of names into two equal groups on an every-other-name basis. One group can then be used as a CONTROL group and the other as a TEST PANEL. The method is widely used for direct mail promotion testing as well as for most other types of research measuring the response of groups of people to various stimuli, such as advertisements, television shows, and new food products. This type of split eliminates the possibility of sampling errors that might occur from taking whole sections of a list—such as the selection of people who live near each other or of people who share a common ethnic heritage. For example, selecting names that start with "O" would heavily bias the sample toward people of Irish descent. *See also* NTH NAME SELECTION; SPLIT TEST.

**ACCEPTANCE**
1. in advertising, formal written approval typically issued by a seller of network radio and television commercial time to an advertiser agreeing to the terms of the purchase.
2. in consumer behavior theory, the degree to which a message is absorbed into an individual's consciousness, unchanged from what was intended by the sender. Acceptance can be blocked by strong contradictory opinions or bolstered by complementary opinions. For example, an individual with strong antismoking sentiments would not accept, recall, or retain quality of life claims made in a cigarette advertisement, or may recall a distorted version of those claims. For example, a phrase such as "strong flavor" may be recalled as "lethal." Conversely, an individual predisposed toward a political candidate may not recall specifics of the candidate's platform but will recall an effective speech that reaffirms the individual's choice. *See also* SELECTIVE ATTENTION; SELECTIVE RECEPTION.

**ACCESS**
1. in television programming, time segment in Eastern and Pacific time zones from 7:30 P.M. to 8:00 P.M., just prior to PRIME TIME. Monday through Saturday. On Sundays, prime time is extended one hour to include access time. (Access time in the Central and Mountain time zones is one hour earlier.) *See also* DAYPART.
2. in computer programming, time taken by the system to retrieve information from the storage unit.

**ACCORDION FOLD** zigzag type of fold in which a sheet of paper has two or more parallel folds that open in the manner of an accordion, permitting the paper to be extended to its full breadth with a single pull. Travel folders, for example, are often arranged in an accordion fold. Frequently used in the preparation of direct mail literature, the accordion fold allows the imprinted matter to be divided into more than four contiguous pages. It also saves on both the expense of binding and the bulk of stapling (making a difference in the weight and therefore the cost of mailing). The decision to use an accordion fold for a piece of advertising literature depends in large part upon the advertiser's budget and upon whether the copy lends itself to this format.

**ACCORDION INSERT** advertising pamphlet, CIRCULAR, or leaflet that has been folded in an ACCORDION FOLD and prepared for binding into a magazine or for enclosure in an envelope as a piece in a direct mail campaign. *See also* FANFOLD INSERT.

**ACCOUNT**
1. business relationship between an agent and a principal—for example, between an ADVERTISING AGENCY and an ADVERTISER.
2. CLIENT (individual or company) of an advertising agency.
3. customer of a supplier or tradesperson—for example, a purchaser of printing supplies or art materials needed for advertising production.

**ACCOUNT CONFLICT** problem that arises when two directly competing products or services are handled by the same ADVERTISING AGENCY. Because of the confidential nature of the client-agency relationship, clients are generally disapproving of an agency servicing competitive companies or products, since agencies would be privileged to information that might be either damaging to an advertiser if known by a competitor or useful in planning competitive advertising campaigns. Typically, this situation will result when agencies merge or when an advertiser acquires another company whose product competes with one the agency is already handling. An advertiser might choose to withdraw the account if a competitor is a client of one of the newly merged agencies.

**ACCOUNT EXECUTIVE (AE)**
**In general:** executive assigned by a service bureau or other supplier to act as a liaison for each customer and to assist the customer in utilizing the services available. See also customer service representative.
**Advertising:** ADVERTISING AGENCY person responsible for maintaining a liaison with designated agency CLIENTS. The account executive supervises the planning and preparation of advertising for one or more clients, depending on the size of the agency. It is the account executive's job to analyze the advertising and merchandising problems of the advertiser; to offer solutions to these problems; to transmit the plans of the agency for client approval; to bring to the agency's attention any suggestions or criticisms made by the client; and, generally, to service the client's advertising and merchandising reports to the ACCOUNT SUPERVISOR, who in turn reports to the vice president of

account services. In a smaller agency, the AE reports directly to the VP or might even serve to fill the VP position.

**Broadcast:** broadcast-station time salesperson who is paid a commission on the amount of money spent by a SPONSOR on the purchase of COMMERCIAL TIME.

**Printing:** account executive assigned by some printing houses to contact prospective customers and to service accounts that obtain their printing needs from the company.

**ACCOUNT REPRESENTATIVE** *see* ACCOUNT EXECUTIVE.

**ACCOUNTS RECEIVABLE**

**In general:** unpaid balance on a credit sale. Unpaid accounts receivable are a BAD DEBT expense.

**Advertising:** amount due the agency on client billings.

**Magazines:** amount due the publisher on unpaid credit order subscriptions.

**ACCOUNT SUPERVISOR** person to whom the ACCOUNT EXECUTIVE (AE) reports. The account supervisor is responsible for the overall review of account handling. He or she answers to the vice president of account services and directs the work of the AE. *See also* MANAGEMENT SUPERVISOR.

**ACETATE**

1. thin, clear or translucent and flexible plastic sheet or strip that will accept printing ink. Acetate is used for the production of OVERLAYS, CAMERA-READY PROOFS, and other types of GRAPHICS. The material is also used in the preparation of animated sequences in animated films. Each strip of the sequence is printed on a separate strip of acetate, called a *cel.*
2. material from which a phonograph disc is made.

**ACETATE PROOF** printer's PROOF made on transparent ACETATE. By use of a special press technique, the same material is printed in perfect REGISTER on both sides, giving greater OPACITY to the impression. Acetate proofs are usually prepared by the creative staff of an advertising agency to be used along with other collateral material in an advertising campaign. Frequently, they are used for sales presentations in charts and other displays. For example: In a presentation about a company, one acetate proof can be laid over another as speech support to demonstrate graphically a company's growth over a period of time. The opacity allows each OVERLAY to add a new dimension to the picture.

An acetate proof is sometimes called a *bronze proof* because bronze powder is dusted on the inked impression to make the printed matter completely opaque (*see* BRONZING).

**ACKNOWLEDGEMENT (ACK)** letter, postcard, or form sent to a customer confirming the receipt of an order, payment, or inquiry. It is frequently used in response to credit orders to encourage fast payment or to offer an opportunity to increase the order. The latter use is referred to as a COLLECTION EXTENSION, RENEWAL-AT-BIRTH, STEP-UP, or UPGRADE. *See also* CASH ACKNOWLEDGEMENT,

**A. C. NIELSEN COMPANY** research and marketing service firm, owned by Dun & Bradstreet, which provides (1) MARKETING RESEARCH information to CONSUMER GOODS manufacturers; (2) MEDIA RESEARCH syndication services (best known as the NIELSEN RATINGS) to manufacturers, advertisers, and MEDIA PLANNERS; and (3) coupon-redemption services to manufacturers and retailers. The NIELSEN FOOD INDEX and the NIELSEN FOOD AND DRUG INDEX report specific consumer-product purchases in food, drug, and mass merchandise outlets on a bimonthly basis; the NIELSEN TELEVISION INDEX and the NIELSEN STATION INDEX report audience size and composition for national and local television and offer a host of reports and services on a bimonthly, monthly, or quarterly basis. The consumer-product data provide advertisers with comprehensive information about sales volume, distribution, and pricing, as well as evaluations of MARKET SHARE and effectiveness of promotions, all of which benefit the advertiser in the planning of marketing strategy. The television and station indexes provide media planners with a basis for determining the time and placement of television commercials for network buyers and purchasers of commercial time on a local basis. All of Nielsen's syndicated and specialized reports are offered on a subscription basis to advertisers, media planners, and advertising agencies.

**ACORN** (acronym for *A Classification Of Residential Neighborhoods*) market SEGMENTATION provided by a company named CACI in Arlington, Virginia, that classifies all United States and United Kingdom households into geographic, socioeconomic, and DEMOGRAPHIC segments based on neighborhood of residence. In the U.S., there are 44 market segments a household can be classified into, and 13 groups of similar market segments. Assignment to each market segment is based on some part of the household address, such as BLOCK GROUP, CENSUS TRACT, ZIP CODE, or CARRIER ROUTE. For example, all the households in Zip code area 06905 might be assigned to a high-income, suburban segment and everyone in a 10021 Zip code to a high-income, urban, professional segment. Assignment based on carrier route provides the greatest degree of accuracy. Zip code assignment is the next most accurate. *See also* CLUSTER ANALYSIS; LIFE-STYLE-LIST ENHANCEMENT.

**A COUNTY** *see also* ABCD COUNTIES.

**ACQUISITION COST** all promotion costs associated with securing a new subscriber or customer, such as LIST RENTAL fees, design and production of a direct mail PACKAGE, and postage for the package and the reply.

**ACROSS-THE-BOARD** phrase indicating a program scheduled to be broadcast at the same time, on the same radio or television station, for five consecutive days every week (usually Monday through Friday)—for example, a television soap opera or the XYZ morning radio show. The name derives from the fact that the weekday program schedule is sometimes referred to as the *board*. Programs that are shown across-the-board generally appeal to the same audience every day and are therefore excellent vehicles for advertisers who wish to reach their current or prospective customers with this frequency in the belief that frequent repetition of commercials will best sell their product. Often, broadcast media representatives will offer special prices for COMMERCIAL TIME that is scheduled in across-the-board programming, making the commercial package economically attractive. Across-the-board programming is also called *strip programming*, because the program fills in a strip in the broadcast schedule.

### ACTION
**Advertising:** impelling function of advertising. Almost all advertising is based on some action that the advertiser wants individuals to take. The desired action may be to move people directly to the purchase of a product *(direct action)*, or it can be more subtle—for example, to move individuals toward a new thinking pattern in which the product or service is seen in a favorable light. Some examples of action-oriented advertising are the political advertisement, where the immediate desired objective is to generate positive feelings about the candidate and where the longer range desired action is to move the public to vote for the candidate. Two other examples are the price-off coupon offer in a print advertisement, where the desired action is the clipping of a coupon by the consumer and his or her subsequent purchase of the product, or the retail store sale advertisement designed to motivate the consumer to come to the store and shop.

**Film or television production:**
1. any motion by performers on the viewing screen that is intended to be transmitted or recorded.
2. order to begin movement in filming, as in "Lights, camera, action."

**ACTION DEVICE** component of a direct marketing promotion designed to generate reader involvement through performing a physical action, such as pasting on a stamp or placing a token in a slot; also called *involvement device*. The theory is that a greater involvement will bring a higher response from the reader. A good example of this type of device is PUBLISHERS CLEARING HOUSE sweepstakes packages designed by Henry Cowan, a major proponent of the involvement device theory; these packages often utilize a STAMP SHEET. *See also* PULL TAB; SCRATCH OFF.

### ACTION PROGRAM
1. precise details of a company's marketing strategy that spell out the specific tactics it will use to achieve its marketing objectives; also called MARKETING PLAN.

**2.** plan or strategy adopted to best position and sell the goods and services of a particular CLIENT. The program must have three primary objectives: (a) to satisfy the needs of the marketplace; (b) to secure an advantage over the competition; and (c) to create profit.

**ACTION SHOT**
1. photograph showing someone or something in motion.
2. *see also* MOVING SHOT.

**ACTIVE** customer who is considered active because, for example, he or she has made a purchase within a specified period of time (active buyer), or is eligible to receive one or more issues of a magazine (active subscriber), or has recently made a donation, or is currently fulfilling a MEMBER purchase commitment (active member).

**ACTIVE BUYER** *see* ACTIVE.

**ACTIVE MEMBER** *see* ACTIVE.

**ACTIVE SEARCH** information-gathering process by a consumer *interested* in purchasing something but lacking adequate information to make a purchase decision. The consumer will actively seek out magazine and newspaper articles and advertisements as well as expert opinions and other sources to collect the needed information, rather than just be exposed to the information by accident. The consumer who is engaged in an active search process is highly receptive to advertising messages.

**ACTIVE SUBSCRIBER** *see* ACTIVE.

**ACTIVITIES, INTERESTS, AND OPINIONS** (AIO) characteristics of an individual used by researchers to create a PSYCHOGRAPHIC profile of the individual; also called ATTITUDES, INTERESTS, and OPINIONS. When combined with quantifiable characteristics such as age, income, or education level, an AIO profile provides great insight into an individual's likes and dislikes as a consumer. Product specific AIO's, rather than general AIO's, may be used in NEW PRODUCT DEVELOPMENT or COPYWRITING to predict consumer response.

   Measurement of the AIO is used by marketers as a research tool to determine influences on consumer behavior and appropriate consumer markets. Researchers will ask respondents to state how strongly they agree or disagree with a series of statements about their activities, interest, and opinions. Answers are linked to DEMOGRAPHICS. Questionnaires are typically quite lengthy and contain statements such as:

I would rather stay home than go out for fun.

I dress for comfort rather than fashion.

I enjoy watching talk shows on television.

I am the kind of person who loves to make impulsive purchases.

I always plan very carefully.

Evaluation of the AIO is most useful in planning marketing strategy because it will help to identify the lifestyle group toward which a product will be targeted. *See also* LIKERT SCALE, VALS.

**AD**  *see* ADVERTISEMENT.

**AD-A-CARD**  trademark for a printed tear-off coupon attached to advertisements that are usually found in a supplement or comic section of selected Sunday newspapers. Ad-A Cards are tools to induce READER RESPONSE.

**ADD**  new RECORD placed in a computer or HARD-COPY file. A DIRECT MARKETING file usually requires a minimum of name, street address, city, state, and ZIP code. A great variety of additional information may also be retained in the record, depending upon the purpose of the file.

**ADD-ON-SALE**  promotion and sale of additional goods or services to a recent buyer, such as selling head cleaners and blank videocassettes to someone who recently purchased a VIDEOCASSETTE RECORDER (VCR); also called *loading.*

**ADDRESS CHANGE SERVICE (ACS)**  U.S. Postal Service program that provides the mailer with address change information on MAGNETIC TAPE. Using magnetic tape to process address changes is faster and more accurate than key entering (*see* KEY ENTRY) the same information from a 3579 FORM. Mailers participating in the ACS must print an identifying code on their mailing labels. This code is used by the USPS to identify the mailer who should receive the change information. There is no difference in the cost of using the ACS and in receiving 3579 forms.

**ADDRESS CODING GUIDE (ACG)**  directory listing the beginning and ending house numbers and street names contained in various geographic units, such as a BLOCK GROUP, CARRIER ROUTE, CENSUS TRACT, or ZIP CODE. The guide is used to segment (*see* LIST SEGMENT) and SORT mailing lists and to perform CLUSTER ANALYSES. Although many large mailers maintain their own address coding guide, the U.S. BUREAU OF THE CENSUS publishes its version, listing BLOCK GROUPS and ENUMERATION DISTRICTS.

**ADDRESS CORRECTION**  transaction changing an address currently on file to a new or corrected address. The corrections may be made individually by KEY ENTRY or through a computer program that compares old records to new. Addresses are corrected in response to individual or U.S. Postal Service notification of changes or just prior to a mailing. Address change information can also be purchased from private sources, such as other mailers or LIST COMPILERS. *See also* ADDRESS CHANGE SERVICE; NIXIE.

**ADDRESS CORRECTION REQUESTED**  inscription used on HOUSE list mailings, printed on the OUTER ENVELOPE, indicating the mailer's willingness to pay the U.S. Postal Service for providing new address information if the addressee has moved. This inscription is used only on first-, third-, and fourth-class mail. (The U.S. Postal Service automatically provides this information for second-class mail.) Regular use of the Address Correction Requested inscription helps to keep lists free of incorrect addresses.

Variations include Forwarding Requested (for forwarding, but no address correction) or RETURN POSTAGE GUARANTEED for Return to Mailer. Another type of endorsement used by mailers who prefer that the mail not be forwarded is Or Current Resident. The charge in 1986 for forwarding or address correction service is 30 cents per item. *See also* CENTRAL MARKUP SYSTEM; 3579 FORM.

**ADDRESS HYGIENE** accuracy of the name and address information on a mailing list. The greater the hygiene, the greater the deliverability of the mail produced. Factors affecting address hygiene include keeping up with address changes, assigning correct ZIP codes, and including necessary directionals (north, south, east, west) and apartment or suite numbers. Address hygiene can be improved by computer analyzing the list against the U.S. Postal Service produced NATIONAL CHANGE OF ADDRESS (NCOA) system. Address hygiene is usually higher on lists involving requested mailings (ex., magazines) than on lists used solely for sending direct mail promotions because the requestors will more readily notify the mailer of corrections or changes.

**ADDRESSING** process of applying the addressee's name and address on an order form, envelope, or other mailing piece. Addressing is usually accomplished by applying preaddressed labels or by using IMPACT PRINTERS, INK-JET PRINTERS, or LASER PRINTERS to add the name and address directly onto the mailing piece. Mail can also be addressed with a form visible through a window envelope. Ink-jet or laser-printed addresses appear more personalized than label addresses, but can be more costly.

**ADDRESSOGRAPH** printing machine that operates by means of pressure applied to embossed metal plates against an inked ribbon, thus producing printed material. Its principal use is for the reproduction on envelopes of names and addresses from a frequently used mailing list. Higher-volume models are capable of transcribing 5000 words or 30,000 figures per minute and are additionally used for payroll recordings, billing, and other repetitious business operations. *See also* CHESHIRE LABEL; ELLIOTT ADDRESSING MACHINE; IMPACT PRINTER; INK-JET PRINTER; LASER PRINTER.

## ADEQUATE SAMPLE

**In general:** statistical term used to indicate that a test group is large enough to achieve satisfactory precision and thus minimize the element of chance as a factor affecting the data obtained.

**Advertising:** test group of people used in compiling audience data selected so that the group adequately represents the market to be tested. For example, if the desired market for a product is an upscale male audience 35 years old plus, these characteristics will be reflected in the sample.

**ADJACENCY**
   **Broadcast:** scheduled radio or television program immediately preceding or following another scheduled program on a particular station.
   **Broadcast advertising:** time period (usually 2 minutes) that precedes or follows network programs; also called COMMERCIAL BREAK position. It is offered for sale for local or SPOT advertisers. COMMERCIAL TIME is sold on the basis of the ratings of adjacencies: the higher the RATING, the greater the listening or viewing audience, and therefore the greater the cost of the time period. The audience potential of an adjacency is greater than that of a program commercial position because of the fact that many people keep their television or radio tuned in to the following program after hearing or viewing the preceding adjacency. Similarly, many who want to see or hear a program will tune in early and are thus exposed to the commercials in the break position.

**ADJUSTMENT**   in fulfillment, change made to a computer file record. An adjustment to a customer file record is usually made in response to a complaint or clarification from a customer. *See also* ADD; ADDRESS CORRECTION; DELETE.

**ADNORM**   term indicating the percentage of readers of a particular publication who remember a particular advertisement in that publication; used in the Starch Reports published by the research firm of DANIEL STARCH AND ASSOCIATES. The research is based on the size of the ad, the use or nonuse of color, the type of product, and experience with the publication. The adnorm represents a proportion of an established norm for similar advertisements. An adnorm of 10 would mean that 10% of the readers of a particular publication who remember ads of a particular type recalled the ad in question.

**AD-NOTER**   designation used by the research firm DANIEL STARCH AND ASSOCIATES to indicate a reader who recalled seeing a particular advertisement in a particular issue of a publication. An ad-noter only recalls noticing the ad, without necessarily associating it with a product or advertiser. *See also* NOTED SCORE.

**ADOPTER CATEGORIES**   classification of consumers according to their readiness to purchase a product. There are five adopter categories: innovators, early adopters, early majority, late majority, and laggards. The innovators are the first users of a product, representing 2.5% of the TARGET MARKET. Innovators are considered to be venturesome people willing to take risks. Early adopters, who enjoy leadership, prestige, and tend to be opinion leaders, represent 13.5% of the TARGET MARKET. The first part of the mass market to purchase are the early majority. Although rarely leaders, these consumers usually adopt new ideas before the average person and they represent 34% of the TARGET MARKET. The late majority also represents 34% of the TARGET MARKET. This group of people is usually skeptical of change and will adopt an INNOVATION only after a majority has tried it. The laggards represent 16% of the TARGET MARKET and are the last to purchase. They are usually price-conscious, suspicious of change, tradition bound, and conservative by nature. *See also* DIFFUSION OF INNOVATION.

**ADOPTION PROCESS** sequence of events beginning with consumer AWARENESS of a new product leading to TRIAL USAGE and culminating in full and regular use of the new product. Over time the adoption process resembles a bell curve formed by INNOVATORS, EARLY ADOPTERS, the majority of consumers, late adopters, and laggards. *See also* DIFFUSION; INNOVATION.

**ADRMP** (Automatic Dialing and Recorded Message Player) *see* AUTOMATIC DIALER.

**ADVANCE CANVASS** technique used in retail advertising whereby retailers in a specific area are visited in advance of a new promotional CAMPAIGN in order to generate excitement about the campaign and to gain their support. The aim is to arouse the retailers' enthusiasm so that they will work to sell the product.

**ADVANCE RENEWAL** renewal of an individual magazine subscription received prior to the start of the publisher's regular renewal promotion. It may be in response to the publisher's own advance renewal promotion or other promotion vehicle such as a BIND-IN or a SUBSCRIPTION AGENT promotion. An advance renewal may be a COLLECTION EXTENSION promoted along with the first bill on a credit subscription order.

**ADVANCE START** new subscription that begins with an issue later than the CURRENT ISSUE being served; also called *preferred start* or *delayed start*. An advance start may be done at the subscriber's request, or at the publisher's convenience as a RATE BASE management tool. Advance starts are frequently assigned to Christmas gift orders, so that they will begin in January and expire during end-of-year renewal promotions. *See also* BACK DATING.

**ADVERTISE** appeal to a mass audience through the communications media for the purpose of calling attention to a product, service, idea, or organization so as to arouse a desire to purchase or patronize, to give information or to modify the thinking about, to promote the concept of, to motivate behavior toward, or otherwise to persuade the general public to buy, approve, or support the product, service, idea, or organization. *See also* ADVERTISEMENT; ADVERTISING AGENCY; COMMERICAL.

**ADVERTISED PRICE**
1. in broadcast, the established price for an advertiser, based on the

FREQUENCY of COMMERCIALS and the total amount of time purchased (volume); the cost to advertise a product.

**2.** cost to the purchaser of a product or service announced or stated in a commercial or an ADVERTISEMENT.

**ADVERTISEMENT** sponsored informational public notice appearing in any of the print communications media that is designed to appeal to a mass audience in order to persuade, inform, promote, motivate, or otherwise modify behavior toward a favorable pattern of purchasing, supporting, or approving a particular product, service, idea, or organization. When the advertiser's message appears in the BROADCAST MEDIA, it is called a COMMERCIAL. The first advertisement on record in an American newspaper appeared in the *Boston News Letter* on May 8, 1704. It described an estate for sale in Oyster Bay, Long Island.

**ADVERTISER** organization or person who pays for the production, execution, and placement of an ADVERTISEMENT. *See also* ACCOUNT; CLIENT.

**ADVERTISING** paid form of a nonpersonal message communicated through the various media by industry, business firms, nonprofit organizations, or individuals. Advertising is persuasive and informational and is designed to influence the purchasing behavior and/or thought patterns of the audience. Advertising is a marketing tool and may be used in combination with other marketing tools, such as SALES PROMOTIONS, PERSONAL SELLING tactics, or publicity.

**ADVERTISING AGE** ADVERTISING industry trade publication. Issued weekly in a slick, illustrated tabloid format, it reports the latest advertising and MARKETING news, including information on government actions affecting advertisers, ADVERTISING AGENCIES, MEDIA, and suppliers. It also covers advertising CAMPAIGNS for new and established products, as well as agency appointments and personnel changes, in addition to supplying data on radio, television, newspapers, magazines, and other media. Sold at newsstands and through subscription. *Advertising Age* employs 70 full-time reporters and approximately 50 correspondents worldwide. It has a wide readership throughout the advertising and marketing industry, with a circulation of almost 90,000. *See also* ADWEEK.

**ADVERTISING AGENCY** independent service organization that contracts with advertisers (firms or individuals attempting to find customers for their products and services) to manage their advertising. Historically, advertising agency services are of a creative nature, but the agency concept has expanded to include research services and media planning and buying. Agencies are typically classified by the type of business they handle (e.g., financial, industrial, or consumer packaged goods) or the range of services they offer (e.g., creative, media, or full service).

Compensation for services is derived from three different sources: (1) 15% commissions from the media on the rate charged for media space or time; (2) fees charged for services (usually noncommissionable, such as a market survey); however, situations will occur when the price-value relationship between media placement and creative services is out of balance (e.g., when a client uses the same broadcast commercial for a long period of time, incurring no creative costs, but incurring millions of dollars in broadcast billing), and agencies will be compensated by the substitution of a fee system in place of the 15% commission; and (3) percentage charges on materials and services used in the preparation of advertisements; in this area, clients are charged cost plus 17.65%.

## STRUCTURE OF A FULL-SERVICE ADVERTISING AGENCY

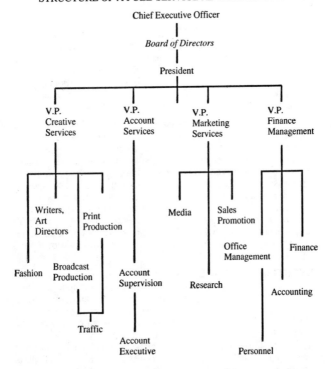

SOURCE: Thomas Russell/Glenn Verrill, *OTTO KLEPPNER'S ADVERTISING PROCEDURE*, 9th ed., ©1986, p. 102. Reprinted by permission of Prentice-Hall, Inc., Englewood Cliffs, New Jersey.

The structure of a typical full-service advertising agency is shown in the table on the previous page. In smaller agencies, many of these jobs will be combined or be filled by free-lancers. Additionally, some smaller agencies will hire outside companies to supply the services that are provided by entire departments in the larger agency. *See also* FULL-SERVICE AGENCY.

**ADVERTISING ALLOWANCE**  funds allocated by the provider of a service or the manufacturer of a product to be paid to a merchant for advertising that service or product. The advertising allowance may be in the form of a deduction from the wholesale price of a product to allow for the cost of advertising, or a reimbursement to the merchant for advertising costs already incurred. The Robinson-Patman Act (1936), which requires a seller to treat all competitive customers equally (proportionately) with respect to advertising allowances, has influenced the use of these allowances. *See also* CO-OP ADVERTISING.

**ADVERTISING APPROPRIATION**  part of an advertiser's income that is allocated for advertising purposes for a specific period of time. The advertising appropriation is generally established after administrative costs, manufacturing costs, direct-selling costs, and acceptable levels of profits have been calculated. The amount of the allocation may be based on any of the following: (1) percentage of estimated sales, (2) task to be accomplished, (3) assessment of the number of units sold in the previous budget period, (4) competitors' expenditures, or (5) arbitrary decision. The allocation is applied to a program over a specific time period (3 months, 6 months, 12 months, or longer-term).

**ADVERTISING ASSOCIATION OF THE WEST**  association of advertising clubs (which had been formed to provide a forum for the exchange of information and ideas) located on the West Coast; abbreviated AAW. In 1967, it merged with the Advertising Federation of America to become the AMERICAN ADVERTISING FEDERATION.

**ADVERTISING CHECKING BUREAU (ACB)**  nationwide service organization that issues reports on advertising and provides tear sheets of advertisements appearing in daily, Sunday, or weekly newspapers published in the United States. The service is provided free of charge to advertisers and their agencies and is paid for by the newspapers. The reports are tailormade by client or product category, depending on the request of the advertiser. This service is particularly important in providing proof of performance in compliance with retail cooperative advertising agreements. *See also* CO-OP ADVERTISING.

**ADVERTISING CLUB OF NEW YORK**  association of professional persons in advertising, publishing, marketing, and business, affiliated with the AMERICAN ADVERTISING FEDERATION. Membership is open to interested industry personnel. Founded in 1906, the club sponsors educational and public-service activities and also holds an annual advertising and marketing course, with classes in all phases of advertising. The club presents the annual ANDY AWARDS for excellence in all phases of advertising.

## ADVERTISING CONTRACT

**1.** agreement drawn between a supplier of advertising time or space, such as a communications media representative or the communications medium itself, and an advertiser, which specifies in detail the content, cost, and placement of the ADVERTISING and binds both parties to the stated terms. This agreement may be drawn between an ADVERTISING AGENCY, on behalf of a CLIENT, and said supplier, or directly between the supplier and the advertiser.

**2.** agreement between a retailer and a supplier of goods (i.e., manufacturer, sales representative, wholesaler) stating that the retailer will advertise the goods for a specific consideration of money or goods.

**ADVERTISING COUNCIL, INC. (ACI)** committee of prominent advertising figures representing the advertising industry and the media, and supported by the entire industry. Established during World War II, sometime between 1941 and 1942, as the War Advertising Council, it was started in part to counter negative criticism of advertising, and it functioned to secure public support for such causes as blood donations, purchase of war bonds, and enlistment of women in the armed services. It is a nonpartisan, nonpolitical, volunteer organization devoted to the public interest, whose members work together to plan, create, and distribute public service advertising programs on a national basis. Its operating budget depends entirely on contributions from businesses, advertising firms, and the media. The total value of time and space donated since inception exceeds 10 billion dollars. Some familiar campaigns are "A Mind Is A Terrible Thing To Waste" (United Negro College Fund), "It Works For All Of Us" (The United Way), and "Drinking And Driving Can Kill A Friendship" (United States Department of Transportation).

**ADVERTISING FEDERATION OF AMERICA** association of professional advertising organizations (abbreviated AFA), which, in order to provide a broader base of membership for the exchange of information and ideas, merged with the Advertising Association of the West in 1967 to become the AMERICAN ADVERTISING FEDERATION.

**ADVERTISING MANAGER** executive in an advertiser's company who is responsible for the review and approval of advertising plans as well as the maintenance of the advertising budget. The advertising manager maintains liaison with the advertising agency (usually through the ACCOUNT EXECUTIVE) and reports to the marketing manager or director of marketing at his or her own company.

**ADVERTISING RECORD SHEET** work sheet used to monitor (without computer assistance) the daily and monthly volume of orders received per advertisement. Information commonly included would be the cost of the advertisement, the offer made, the daily and monthly volume of orders received, and any identifying KEY CODES.

**ADVERTISING REGISTER** *see* STANDARD ADVERTISING REGISTER.

**ADVERTISING RESEARCH FOUNDATION** organization sponsored by the AMERICAN ASSOCIATION OF ADVERTISING AGENCIES and the ASSOCIATION OF NATIONAL ADVERTISERS that oversees MEDIA RESEARCH and works toward the advancement of scientific practices in advertising and marketing. Current member organizations of the foundation, which was chartered in 1936, consist of advertisers, advertising agencies, media, universities, and the two founding associations.

**ADVERTISING RESERVE** sum of money earmarked by the advertiser to be used if an unforeseeable contingency—one that could not have been anticipated when the original budget was drawn—occurs, requiring the expenditure of additional advertising dollars. For example: When a pharmaceutical company's advertised product was found to have been tampered with and some people died as a result of using this product, the company used its advertising reserve to finance an advertising campaign to counteract the damaging effects of this unfortunate incident.

**ADVERTISING WEIGHT**
**Advertising:** measure of the number of EXPOSURES planned or achieved via an advertising CAMPAIGN.
**Direct mail**: portion of a periodical that consists of advertising, calculated by dividing the number of advertising pages by the total number of pages, including editorial content. The advertising portion of a publication is charged additional postage if the periodical is mailed SECOND CLASS, and is the only portion on which postage due is based upon the number of ZONES traveled from entry point to destination.

**ADVERTISING WOMEN OF NEW YORK** association of women executives or administrators in advertising, publicity, marketing research, or promotion. Founded in 1912, the association currently has approximately 850 members, most of whom are concentrated in the New York City area. Advertising Women of New York sponsors professional development courses, seminars, and a career clinic for personal job counseling.

**ADVERTORIAL** word derived from a combination of the words *advertisement* and *editorial,* describing an advertising message presented in an editorial format. This form of advertising is used to offer information about sources or services of public interest and to communicate opinion about social, economic, political, or personal issues (ADVOCACY ADVERTISING), as well as to lobby for legislative changes. By law, an advertisement of this sort must be labeled as an advertisement so as not be confused with an actual editorial.

**ADVOCACY ADVERTISING** advertising used to espouse a point of view about controversial public issues. Advocacy advertising can be directed at either specific targets, or general targets, such as political activists, the media, consumer groups, government agencies, or competitors. It can be sponsored by any type of advertiser (businesses, consumer groups, special interest groups, political parties, or even individuals). An extreme example occurred in the 1960s, when a private citizen bought a two-page advertisement in the *New York Times* at a cost of $12,000 to offer his peace plan for ending the war in Vietnam.

In 1974, Mobil Oil Company began advocacy advertising concerning the need for offshore oil drilling to alleviate the energy crisis that existed at the time. NBC accepted the television commercial, but ABC and CBS did not, because of the controversial nature of the topic. As a result, Mobil Oil Company took out full-page newspaper ads, which reproduced in print the VISUALS and text for the commercial.

**ADWEEK** national advertising industry TRADE MAGAZINE published as a network of seven weekly regional editions, utilizing the combined resources of a 75-person editorial staff throughout the United States. *Adweek's* editorial content covers all phases of the advertising industry as well as the marketing and communications industries and is of primary interest to advertising agencies and advertisers. Readership exceeds 75,000.

**AFFIDAVIT OF PERFORMANCE** signed and notarized form that is legal proof of service rendered. It is usually enclosed with the invoice sent by a broadcast company to an advertiser. The affidavit documents the content, cost, and timing of the advertiser's commercials after those commercials have been on the air. It was developed by the ASSOCIATION OF NATIONAL ADVERTISERS and the RADIO AND TELEVISION ADVERTISING BUREAU as a control to prevent fraud.

**AFFILIATE** independently owned radio or television station that has a contractual agreement with a NETWORK to devote a portion of its broadcast time to programs originated by that network. The network offers the programming in exchange for COMMERICAL TIME, which can then be sold to a national advertiser. With a string of affiliates strategically positioned throughout the country, a network can offer advertisers wider viewing audiences and thus attract national corporations with large advertising budgets.

**AFFILIATED CHAIN** group of noncompeting retail stores throughout the United States whose association affords an economic advantage in large-scale purchasing. When a group of small stores get together to form such a chain, they can purchase advertising time and space as if it were a national advertiser.

**AFFILIATED RETAILER**
1. member of an AFFILIATED CHAIN.

**2.** independent retailer who affiliates with other independent retailers under a common trade name for merchandising purposes. A group of such independent retailers will advertise under this common trade name. *See also* AFFILIATED WHOLESALER.

**AFFILIATED WHOLESALER**
  **1.** WHOLESALER who sponsors or owns a group of AFFILIATED RETAILERS.
  **2.** wholesaler who affiliates with other wholesalers under a common trade name for merchandising purposes.

**AFFINITIES** groups of stores in close proximity to each other where each store offers the same merchandise as the other. For example, in many large metropolitan areas one can often find entire blocks where there are several stores side by side selling consumer electronic products or jewelry. Affinities allow consumers to comparison shop with relative ease.

**AFFORDABLE METHOD** procedure used to set advertising budgets, based on what the advertiser thinks it can afford to spend. This method lacks consideration for the objectives of the advertising and how those objectives can best be met. The advertiser may spend less than necessary to achieve a sales target or fail to provide the necessary support to a new or declining brand. *See also* PERCENTAGE-OF-SALES METHOD; OBJECTIVE-AND-TASK METHOD; COMPETITIVE PARITY.

**AFTERNOON DRIVE** in radio broadcasting, the time segment from 3:00 P.M. to 7:00 P.M. Monday through Friday. Afternoon drive time combined with *morning drive* time (6:00 A.M. to 10:00 A.M.) is considered radio's PRIME TIME, because these time periods together account for the largest listening audience.

**AGAINST THE GRAIN** feeding paper into a printing press against the GRAIN of the paper or folding paper at right angles against the grain. The grain is the direction in which the paper fibers run. Folds made against the grain are more bulky than folds made with the grain (i.e., in the direction of the paper fibers). Folding against the grain is not recommended when excess bulk may be a problem. *See also* CROSS DIRECTION.

**AGATE LINE** in newspapers and magazines, standard unit of area used to calculate the cost of advertising space. An agate line measures 1/14" in depth (height) by one column in width. There are 14 agate lines to a COLUMN INCH. The cost of a line is indicated on the publication's rate card. (Most newspaper columns are 2" in width, and magazine columns measure from 2" to 3" or more.) *See also* CONSUMER MAGAZINE AND AGRI-MEDIA RATES AND DATA.

**AGE & LIFE-CYCLE SEGMENTATION** marketing concept that utilizes different marketing approaches for different age categories or different life-cycle segments of the population. The concept is based on the fact that consumer needs and desires change with age.

According to the age and life-cycle segmentation, consumers' age categories are divided into four segments: child, young adult, adult, and older adult. Some companies offer similar products in different versions according to the age and life-cycle segmentation. For example, a vitamin manufacturer may offer a children's formula for ages 4–12, a vitamin specially formulated for young teenagers, an adult version for adult men and women, and a high energy formula for people over age 50. Some marketers will offer a product designed particularly for one specific segment of the age cycle, such as a shampoo developed for women over 40 to help with age-related hair changes.

**AGENCY** *see* ADVERTISING AGENCY; SUBSCRIPTION AGENT.

## AGENCY COMMISSION
**Advertising:**
1. fee that an advertising agency charges a client for time and effort spent in selecting and supervising production work done by another company (e.g., printing, photoengraving, photography, commercial recording, filming, and film editing). The amount charged the client is usually 17.65% of the gross production cost.
2. compensation paid to advertising agencies by the media (broadcast or print) for purchases of time or space made on behalf of clients. Since the ad agency saves the media the expense of direct sales and billing, the media allows the agency a 15% discount (16 2/3% for outdoor advertising), based on the gross advertising rate billed to the client. (The discount also serves as incentive to the agency.) For example: If XYZ Corporation spends $1 million on advertising placed through a recognized ad agency, the agency commission is $150,000 and the balance of $850,000 is paid to the media. The agency commission system represents the basic financial structure of the ad agency business. *See also* FEE BASIS.

**Magazines:** amount paid a SUBSCRIPTION AGENCY for its efforts in selling a subscription, based upon a percentage of the price paid by the subscriber. Agents are usually paid 80% to 90% of the selling price, depending on the expected impact of that magazine on the agent's total sales goal. Some magazines are featured in order to draw attention to other titles the agent sells, and the publishers of the featured magazines are rewarded with lower commission payments.

**AGENCY GROUP** *see* AGENCY NETWORK.

**AGENCY NETWORK** affiliation of independently owned, noncompeting advertising agencies throughout the world organized to help each other in unfamiliar markets. The network concept offers member agencies the opportunity to exchange ideas, experiences, and facilities, as well as translation services and production assistance for the more effective servicing of clients. The idea was the brainchild of Lynn Ellis, an advertising management consultant in the U.S., who formed the Lynn Ellis Group as the first network in 1929. With today's trend toward advertising agency mergers and international-ization, the agency network is not as necessary as it once was.

**AGENCY OF RECORD**  advertising agency that coordinates the pur-chase of MEDIA time and space for a large corporation that is likely to have a number of different agencies handling the various divisions and products. Appointed by the advertiser, this agency makes all the corporate media contracts and receives payment from the other agen-cies involved (usually 15% of their 15), for the media placement of their advertising.

**AGENCY-PRODUCED PROGRAM**  radio or television program produced by an advertising agency as compared to one produced by a LOCAL STATION NETWORK, or independent production company. The program is sold as a complete PACKAGE to the network or local station and allows the advertising agency to place its client's commercials in the commercial time slots.

**AGENCY RECOGNITION**  *see* RECOGNITION.

**AGENT**  organization or individual authorized to operate on behalf of another organization in exchange for a fee or commission. *See also* ADVERTISING AGENCY; CASH FIELD AGENT; CATALOG AGENCY; DIRECT MAIL AGENCY; PAID IN ADVANCE; PAID DURING SERVICE; SUBSCRIPTION AGENCY; TELEPHONE AGENCY.

**AGENT REINSTATE**  *see* AGENT'S REINSTATEMENT.

**AGENT'S CANCELLATION**  cancellation of an agent-sold order, either at the request of the customer or at the request of the agent if payment was not received. Cancellations must be applied against com-missions paid. *See also* AGENT'S REINSTATEMENT.

**AGENT'S CLEARANCE**  *see* AGENT'S ORDER.

**AGENT'S ORDER**  single order or group of orders submitted by a SUB-SCRIPTION AGENCY for FULFILLMENT prooessing; also called *agent's clearance*. The order may be in HARD COPY format or on MAGNETIC TAPE. *See also* AGENT'S SUMMARY.

**AGENT'S REINSTATEMENT**  previously canceled magazine sub-scription that is being reactivated, usually because a late payment has been received; also called *agency reinstate*. The AUDIT BUREAU OF CIRCULATIONS requires that reinstated subscribers receive continu-ous service by being sent any back issues they would have received between the time of cancellation and the time of reinstatement. *See also* REINSTATEMENT.

**AGENT'S SUMMARY**  document submitted with an AGENT'S ORDER that summarizes the subscription orders submitted in regard to quantity, selling price, term, and total dollar amount remitted net of commission.

**AGGREGATION** marketing strategy designed to appeal to a broad base of consumers. Aggregation focuses on the universal desires of a population, and when used by marketers, assumes that consumers in a particular market all want the same thing and are all alike. Mass product distribution and mass marketing campaigns are key elements of an aggregation strategy. When a shampoo product is mass marketed as the lowest price shampoo on the market in the belief that low price is universally sought by consumers of shampoo, the marketing decisions are based on an aggregation strategy.

**AGRICULTURAL PUBLISHERS ASSOCIATION (APA)** co-operative, nonprofit media association representing the farm press. The primary concentration of the APA is to gain acceptance for the farm press as the superior advertising forum for advertisers who want to reach this audience. The association also recommends advertising agencies for RECOGNITION for the benefit of its members. *See also* CONSUMER MAGAZINE AND AGRI-MEDIA RATES AND DATA.

**AID ANALYSIS** *see* AUTOMATIC INTERACTION DETECTOR ANALYSIS.

**AIDED RECALL** research technique used to test audience memory retention of advertisements. The respondents are prompted by being shown a particular advertisement and then asked to remember their previous exposure to it. Verbal aids are also used to prompt recall. This technique is used by research services to test readership, viewership, and listenership. *See also* UNAIDED RECALL.

**AIR** present a program on the air waves, as to broadcast; for example, "The XYZ Comedy Hour will air at 6:00 P.M."

**AIRBRUSH** drawing instrument shaped like a pencil that operates as a small pressure gun to apply watercolor pigment in a very fine spray by means of compressed air. Used to correct and obtain tone or graduated tone effect, the instrument gives a very smooth finish to artwork. It is widely employed for retouching of drawings and photographs. Airbrushed artwork may be used for reproduction by any printing process as well as for sign and poster displays.

**AIR-BUBBLE PACKING** protective, cushioning packing material made of plastic with air pockets covering the surface. The air pockets absorb shock, preventing damage to the material being shipped. Air-bubble packing can cost 20% less than other packing materials because less material and labor is required to fill the spaces surrounding the merchandise in the carton. *See also* BLISTER PACK.

**AIR CHECK** recording of an actual radio or television broadcast as it is presented on the air. The recording shows an ADVERTISER or SPONSOR exactly how the commercial or program appeared on the air. It serves as a file copy and is often used by the sponsor or advertiser to evaluate talent, program, or commercial appeal, or production techniques.

**AIR DATE** date on which a radio or television commercial or program will be broadcast.

**AIRMAIL FIELD** *see* AIRPORT MAIL FACILITY (AMF).

**AIRPORT MAIL FACILITY (AMF)** U.S. Postal Service facility located at or near an airport to receive, sort, and distribute mail; also called *airmail field.*

**ALL-INCLUSIVE STUDY** audience data report distributed by A. C. NIELSEN COMPANY. The study tabulates data over a four-week period and estimates the percentage of all persons or households who were exposed to television programming (REACH) and the average number of exposures for each (FREQUENCY).

**ALLOCATION**
**Broadcast:** range of wavelengths assigned to a broadcast system by the FEDERAL COMMUNICATIONS COMMISSION. *See also* AM STATION; FM STATION.
**Merchandising:** quantity of merchandise designated for a particular prospect or MARKET.

**ALLOWABLE ORDER COST** amount that can be spent on persuading a prospect or customer to make a purchase, without eroding the desired profit margin. The LIFETIME VALUE of the customer may be considered in determining the allowable order cost, or the marketer may simply look at the expected revenue from a single order. To be truly accurate, all costs and all revenues over the customer lifetime should be considered in the equation. For example, a magazine publisher designing a promotion to sell first-time subscribers should consider not only the revenue for this subscription, but also future renewal revenue and ancillary sales revenue as well as the costs of fulfilling the order, sending bill and renewal notices, and supplying product. A customer expected to renew a subscription several times at full price would be assigned a higher allowable order cost than one expected to respond only to highly discounted offers.

**ALLOWANCE**
**In general:** reduction in price.
**Merchandising:** reduction in price offered to a retailer by a manufacturer or wholesaler that is contingent upon some special arrangement. It usually compensates the retailer for expense incurred in marketing the product. *See also* ADVERTISING ALLOWANCE; BROKERAGE ALLOWANCE; DISPLAY ALLOWANCE; RETAIL DISPLAY ALLOWANCE.

**ALPHA ERROR** in marketing research, an attitude, opinion, or probable reaction, incorrectly found, that does not truly exist in the TARGET MARKET. For example, a researcher using FOCUS GROUP INTERVIEW techniques may erroneously conclude from the comments made that consumers consider lost toothpaste tube caps to be a significant problem when this is actually a minor issue. The marketer may be persuaded by this alpha error to market a redesigned tube with an attached cap, but fail to attract market interest. *See also* BETA ERROR.

**ALPHANUMERIC** describing a CODE or string of characters that includes both letters and numbers and/or punctuation marks or mathematical symbols. Most MATCH CODES, unique codes assigned to computer records as an identifier, are alphanumeric. For example, a match code might include the first, third, and fourth letters of the last name, the ZIP code, and the house number. The match code for Albert Becker at 761 Brentwood Road in Stamford, Connecticut, would be BCK06905761. *See also* KEY CODE.

**ALTERNATE-BUNDLES RUN** method used in newspaper or magazine advertising whereby two different versions of an advertiser's message are printed in separate phases of a press run and then alternately comingled when bundled for circulation delivery. Since bundles are distributed in the same geographic area, the method is used to test the effectiveness of one message against the other. *See also* SELECTIVE BINDING; SPLIT RUN.

**ALTERNATE DELIVERY** mail delivery service other than the U.S. Postal Service; also called *private delivery.* Alternate delivery is available for first-class mail only through certain carriers, because federal statutes grant a limited monopoly to the U.S. Postal Service on delivering this mail. Alternatives to first-class mail include Federal Express, and other express delivery services, and some major airlines. However, none of these carriers has access to mailboxes. Many alternatives exist for second- and third-class mail delivery, such as independent carriers who deliver door-to-door, leaving catalogs, brochures, magazines, and product samples at the addressee's front door. As much as 80% of fourth-class mail (parcel post) is handled by such alternate delivery services as United Parcel Service and Emery Air Freight. Alternate delivery of second- and third-class mail can be accomplished via a label attached to the mailing piece or a set of addressed cards given to the carrier and indicating the addressees. *See also* ELECTRONIC COMPUTER-ORIGINATED MAIL.

**ALTERNATE SPONSORSHIP** method of reducing costs of sponsorship of a television or radio program whereby two or more advertisers alternate as SPONSORS on a program-by-program, day-by-day, or week-by-week basis. This is often done for daytime SOAP OPERAS, which run for five consecutive days every week; each day's programming is sponsored by a different advertiser. Alternate sponsorship allows exclusivity for the time period of sponsorship.

**ALTERNATE WEEKS** instructions given to a radio or television station or to a newspaper to run a commercial or advertisement for a period of one week, skip a week, and then run it again for a week; abbreviated A/W. Under this method the advertiser pays for a two-week exposure, although the advertising message will actually run over a three-week period.

**ALTERNATIVE MEDIA** advertising media that does not fit into what are considered standard categories of broadcast, print, transit, and outdoor media. Examples of alternative media are supermarket video displays, shopping cart advertisements, video kiosks in shopping malls, business publications, trade journals, flyers, and telephone directories.

**AMBIGUOUS STATEMENT** advertising technique using a statement that can be interpreted in different ways to mean different things. Advertisers will sometimes deliberately use ambiguous statements in their advertising so that the message will mean different things to different people. This is particularly true when the product does not have a well-defined TARGET AUDIENCE. Studies indicate that consumers who do not have any strong belief about a brand are more likely to accept an ambiguous message. In this way they can project their own image and needs onto the brand.

**AMERICAN ADVERTISING FEDERATION (AAF)** nationwide association of advertising people, such as MEDIA owners, advertisers, advertising agencies, suppliers of advertising materials, and any organization otherwise concerned with advertising. Headquartered in Washington, D.C., the federation was formed in 1967 through the merger of the ADVERTISING FEDERATION OF AMERICA and the ADVERTISING ASSOCIATION OF THE WEST, although its origins go back to 1905, when various local advertising clubs formed a national association. This association launched a campaign for truth in advertising and established vigilance committees, out of which grew the BETTER BUSINESS BUREAU. The AAF also helped establish the FEDERAL TRADE COMMISSION and continues to maintain standards for truthful and responsible advertising.

**AMERICAN ASSOCIATION OF ADVERTISING AGENCIES (AAAA)** one of the major associations that helped to regulate advertising; also called *Four A's*, 4 A's. Established in 1917 and headquartered in New York City, AAAA is the national association of leading United States advertising agencies. Members are elected after filing application, and any agency judged to be unethical is denied membership. Represented in three regions—Eastern, Central, and Western—the organization functions as a great force in monitoring industrywide advertising practices and improving the standards of agency business. Its members place more than 80% of all national advertising. Additionally, this organization represents the advertising agency business in the public-service work of THE ADVERTISING COUNCIL, INC., and sponsors the AAAA Educational Foundation, which offers a program of grants and fellowships for graduate schools. It also operates a group of insurance plan and a group pension/profit-sharing plan for the benefit of personnel in member agencies. *See also* AAAA SPOT CONTRACT.

**AMERICAN BROADCASTING COMPANY (ABC)** one of the three major national television networks. Originally called the Blue Network, the system was formed in 1927 as the second member of the National Broadcasting Company, along with the Red Network. In the 1940s, the Federal Communications Commission imposed regulations that forced the sale of the Blue Network. It was purchased in 1943 by Edward J. Noble, chairman of Life Savers, Inc., and in 1945, the name was changed to American Broadcasting Company. In 1986, ABC was acquired by Capital Cities Communications, Inc., for approximately $3.5 billion and the new corporation became Capital Cities/ABC, Inc.

In addition to its television network, ABC also operates seven radio networks, comprising more than 1900 affiliated stations. The corporation also owns nine AM stations and eight FM stations, serving nine markets throughout the United States.

The ABC television network is composed of approximately 214 primary affiliates and 17 secondary affiliates throughout the country. Eight affiliates are owned by Capital Cities/ABC.

**AMERICAN BUSINESS PRESS, INC.** association of specialized business publications, such as industrial, trade, and professional magazines. Abbreviated ABP, it was incorporated in 1965 as a result of the consolidation of Associated Business Publications and National Business Publications. The corporation maintains financial information about advertising agencies that use the business press and reports this information to its members. It also provides sales tools for use by business publication space sales personnel as part of a public relations effort to help sell the idea of business publication advertising as the preferable medium for reaching the business market.

**AMERICAN FAMILY PUBLISHERS (AFP)** one of the largest DIRECT-MAIL AGENCIES that market CONSUMER MAGAZINE subscriptions to the public on behalf of magazine publishers. AFP is a chief competitor of PUBLISHERS CLEARING HOUSE, using a similar SWEEPSTAKES promotion.

**AMERICAN FEDERATION OF MUSICIANS OF THE U.S. AND CANADA** labor union for professional musicians; abbreviated AFM. The AFM is an international organization serving the needs of instrumentalists in the United States and Canada, with international headquarters in New York City. Founded in 1896, it is affiliated with the AFL-CIO.

**AMERICAN FEDERATION OF TELEVISION AND RADIO ARTISTS (AFTRA)** union organized for the protection and benefit of all persons performing on live radio and television and on videotaped programs. AFTRA was established as the American Federation of Radio Artists (AFRA) in 1937 to help radio performers fight the objectionable industry conditions that existed for performers at the time. In 1952, the American Federation of Television and Radio Artists was created through the merger of AFRA and the television performers union, the Television Authority. An affiliate of the AFL-CIO, AFTRA maintains national headquarters in New York City and acts as the collective bargaining agent for the on-air and on-camera personnel of commercial radio and television.

**AMERICAN GUILD OF MUSICAL ARTISTS (AGMA)** labor union representing ballet and modern dancers, opera singers, and stage managers for those groups, founded in 1936 and headquartered in New York City.

**AMERICAN MARKETING ASSOCIATION (AMA)** national professional society of MARKETING and MARKETING RESEARCH executives, sales and promotion managers, advertising specialists, and marketing teachers, headquartered in Chicago. Founded in 1915 by the merging of the American Marketing Society and the National Association of Marketing Teachers, to encourage and uphold sound, honest marketing practices and to keep marketing work on a high ethical plane. The association publishes *Marketing News*, the *Journal of Marketing*, and the *Journal of Marketing Research* for the benefit of the public. It also offers marketing bibliographies and various books and pamphlets on marketing.

**AMERICAN NEWSPAPER PUBLISHERS ASSOCIATION** trade association for daily and nondaily newspaper publishers in the United States and Canada; abbreviated ANPA. Founded in 1887 and headquartered in Washington, D.C., the association has a current membership of 1,400 publications. It serves as a clearinghouse for member newspapers on all phases of the newspaper business, and operates a technical training and research facility, as well as a library of 5,000 volumes on journalism, the newspaper business, and mass communications. The association also provides members with credit ratings of more than 1,200 advertising agencies.

**AMERICAN RESEARCH BUREAU, INC**. *see* ARBITRON RATINGS COMPANY.

**AMERICAN SOCIETY OF COMPOSERS, AUTHORS AND PUBLISHERS (ASCAP)** voluntary, nonprofit association of composers, lyricists, and music publishers, founded in 1914. Headquartered in New York City, ASCAP has as its primary concern the protection of members' copyrights. The society enforces the 1897 copyright law, which grants exclusive public performing rights to the copyright owner, and also functions as a clearinghouse, in that it issues performance licenses, and collects and distributes royalties for such performances on behalf of its members. *See also* BROADCASTING MUSIC INC.

**AMERICAN STATISTICAL ASSOCIATION (ASA)** professional society of statisticians and other persons interested in the application of statistics to human behavior, founded in 1839 and headquartered in Washington, D.C. ASA studies on economic, business, and social statistics are of primary interest in marketing and advertising research. The association also publishes the *Journal of the American Statistical Association.*

**AMERICAN TELEVISION AND RADIO COMMERCIALS FESTIVAL** annual worldwide competition established in 1960 to honor excellence in advertising and to stimulate higher standards in the advertising industry. Broadcast commercials are entered in various product or campaign categories and are judged by a panel of advertising creative executives and groups of technical specialists on a panel of 450 members representing 16 cities in 10 countries from 5 continents. Winners are awarded a gold statuette called a *Clio.*

**AMPLITUDE MODULATION (AM)**
1. method of transmitting radio signals by varying the size (amplitude) of the radio wave while the speed (frequency) of the radio wave remains constant. Signals transmitted in this manner carry great distances, particularly at night, but are susceptible to interference.
2. broadcast system using amplitude modulation. *See also* FREQUENCY MODULATION.

**AM STATION** any radio station in the amplitude modulation (AM) system. The FEDERAL COMMUNICATIONS COMMISSION has assigned to this system the range of wavelengths from 0.535 to 1.605 MHz (megahertz), or 53 to 160 on the radio dial. Any station within this spectrum is called an AM station. Currently, there are approximately 4,750 AM commercial stations in the United States, with a 1% annual growth rate to the system.

**ANALOGY ADVERTISING** style of broadcast commercial using an extraneous example of one product in a comparison to explain the advertised product. An example of analogy-advertising style would be the following commercial for XYZ vitamins: "Just as motor oil is important to the proper maintenance of your car's engine, XYZ vitamins are vital to your body's health."

**ANALYSIS OF VARIANCE** statistical technique used to determine the degree of difference or similarity between two or more groups. The method is based on a comparison of the average value of some characteristic of both groups. For example, the level of BAD DEBT expense that will be incurred by mailing to an untried list can be predicted by comparing a sample of that list to a sample of the CUSTOMER LIST—that is, by performing an analysis of variance calculation against the average bad debt expense of a sample of the untried list and a sample of the customer list. A shortcut formula for the analysis of variance calculation follows:

$$\text{Total sum of squares} = \sum_j \sum_i \chi_{ij}^2 - C,$$

$$\text{where } C = T^2/rc \text{ and } T = \sum_j \sum_i \chi_{ij}.$$

$$\text{Between-column sum of squares} = \frac{\sum_j T_j^2}{r} - C$$

$$\text{Between-row sum of squares} = \sum_j \sum_i \chi_{ij}^2 - \sum_j \frac{T_j^2}{r}$$

**ANALYTICAL MARKETING SYSTEM** type of MARKETING INFORMATION SYSTEM where research data is interpreted using computerized analytical techniques. The data base in such a system is composed of a statistical bank of information, which enables marketers to draw conclusions from data using statistical procedures such as MULTIVARIATE ANALYSIS, and a model bank of information, which enables marketers to make better marketing decisions using MODELS. An analytical marketing system is used primarily in planning marketing strategy.

**ANCHORPERSON** *see* NEWSCASTER.

**ANDY AWARDS** annual awards presented by the Advertising Club of New York for the best radio commercial, best television commercial, and best overall commercial from among the entrants. Seventy-five judges chosen from the advertising community select the winners, based on the commercial COPY and GRAPHICS as well as the selling concept. The award is a sculptured pewter head along with $1000 for the best radio and television commercials and $5000 for the best of show.

**ANIMATIC** unfinished television commercial produced by photographing STORYBOARD sketches on a film strip and synchronizing the audio portion on tape. An animatic is prepared by the advertising agency creative department at the discretion of the account executive to be shown to the client in order to help the client visualize the advertising concept. It can also function as a guide for the actual shooting of the commercial.

**ANIMATION** in television or motion picture filming, movement added to static objects, whereby inanimate objects appear to come to life. Animation is very useful in a situation where live action is not possible. Because the process of filming requires that each frame be shot individually, animation is very costly. A typical 30-second commercial may require more than 1000 drawings or movements of objects, making the cost of materials and labor very expensive. Animation may be accomplished through the use of ANIMATION CAMERAS or supercomputers. The computers delete the process of individual *cel* (*see* ACETATE) preparation, but they are still very costly to use, ranging from $2000 to $5000 per second.

**ANIMATION CAMERA**  camera designed for use when the desired result is animated film. An animation camera shoots drawings or objects one frame at a time as those drawings or objects are moved on a table designed for this purpose (*animation stand*). The camera has a registration of art cells so that each frame will be in perfect REGISTER. There are many different types of animation cameras specific to the needs of the animator, from a simple 16-millimeter camera that shoots on one plane, to the highly sophisticated instruments used for the familiar Walt Disney animations. Recent advances in the development of computer technology have created a process of computer imaging where images are done digitally without a camera and transferred directly to film or videotape. The Walt Disney Film *Tron* is an example of this new technology. *See also* ANIMATION.

**ANIMATION STAND**  *see* ANIMATION CAMERA.

**ANNOUNCEMENT**  brief message (typically 10 seconds) that advertises a product or service or offers public-service information. It is usually delivered in the interval between programs to capture the attention of the audience of both programs.

**ANNOUNCER V.O.**  *see* ANNOUNCER VOICE-OVER.

**ANNOUNCER VOICE-OVER**  voice of an announcer recorded off camera and played over the visual action on camera; abbreviated *announcer v.o.* In television COMMERICAL production, the voice-over is the spoken portion of a commercial delivered by an announcer who is heard but not seen. This is particularly effective when using a CLOSE-UP technique in the filming. For example, a fast-food chain commercial will feature a close-up of a hamburger cooking, while an announcer reads the copy. In this way the viewer's visual attention is directed exclusively at the product, as the audio portion offers information about the product. Generally, a voice-over costs less than an on-camera announcer.

**ANSWER PRINT**  finished COMPOSITE PRINT of a filmed commercial along with all the required OPTICAL effects and TITLES. The answer print is presented to the client for optical approval, after which it is corrected for color, quality, and synchronization, and a FINAL PRINT is made. *See also* WORK PRINT.

**ANTIHALATION BACKING**  coating applied to the back of film that prevents the formation of a halo or blurring around bright objects in the photograph.

**ANTIMERGER ACT**  1950 consumer protection amendment to Section 7 of the CLAYTON ACT that applied federal legislative barriers to corporate mergers that may impair or impede market competition, including mergers involving the acquisition of assets as well as stock; also called *Celler-Kefauver Act*. Section 7 of the Clayton Act had been previously limited to mergers involving only the acquisition of stock and therefore left a loophole that was closed by the Antimerger Act. *See also* ANTITRUST ACTS; SHERMAN ANTITRUST ACT.

**ANTIOFFSET SPRAY**   spray used on printing presses to prevent wet ink from the top of one sheet from rubbing off on the bottom of the next sheet.

**ANTIQUE FINISH**   rough surface texture of some papers. Antique-finish paper is usually used for book pages and book or booklet covers.

**ANTITRUST ACTS**   federal statutes that regulate trade in order to maintain competition and prevent monopolies. Many common business practices are governed by these statutes. The SHERMAN ANTI-TRUST ACT of 1890 made price-fixing (the setting of prices in cooperation with competitors) illegal. The CLAYTON ANTI-TRUST ACT of 1914 outlawed price discrimination (charging different prices to different buyers), as did the ROBINSON-PATMAN ACT of 1936. Under these Acts, advertising and promotional ALLOWANCES are permitted only if they are offered to all dealers on equal terms. If a 10% discount for promotion expense is awarded to one dealer and a 20% discount to another, a charge of price discrimination could be made by the first dealer.

**APPEAL**   advantages gained from purchasing a product, as described in the promotional copy. Appeals generally cater to our most basic instincts and needs such as health, security, beauty, and pride of accomplishment. Much of the theory on this subject stems from Abraham H. Maslow's "hierarchy of needs," which states that the basic, instinctual needs of man are naturally prioritized so that a high-level need, such as accomplishment, is not felt unless a low-level need, such as food, is satisfied. Therefore, it is easier to excite interest in a product by appealing to lower-level needs.

**APPLAUSE MAIL**   correspondence that is received by a radio or television station and is favorable toward a program, personality, or commercial.

**ARB**   American Research Bureau, Inc. *See* ARBITRON COMPANY.

**ARBITRON INFORMATION ON DEMAND (AID)**   computer-based system, owned by ARBITRON COMPANY and available to subscribers, which produces customized reports providing a multitude of ways to examine radio audience measurement results. Examples of AID reports are *Arbitrends*, an updated monthly estimate of station ratings; *Maximizer*, formerly *Radio AID*, an analysis of the radio station audience by specific demographics, geography, or time periods; and *Scarborough Reports*, a report providing local market qualitative information combining retail, life-style, product, and media data. The AID system can be accessed through personal computer applications (linking Arbitron databases with information from other advertising and marketing databases) to help marketers observe trends and make marketing decisions. *See also* ARBITRON COMPANY.

**ARBITRON RATINGS COMPANY** *see* THE ARBITRON COMPANY.

**ARBITRON COMPANY, THE** media information company that provides radio audience measurement data in a variety of formats to broadcasters, advertisers, and advertising agencies in approximately 99 local markets throughout the United States. Owned by the Ceridian Corporation, The Arbitron Company began doing business in Washington D.C. in 1949 as the American Research Bureau, Inc. (ARB), providing a television audience ratings service in the cities of Washington D.C., Philadelphia, and Baltimore. The company entered the radio measurement field in 1965 as a result of a special contract with RKO General to do a listener survey in Detroit. The name was changed to Arbitron Ratings Company in 1982 and then to The Arbitron Company in 1990. In 1993, The Arbitron Company announced plans to discontinue its 44-year tradition of providing syndicated local market television (and cable) ratings by January 1994, in favor of providing local market qualitative information for local television, cable, and radio broadcasters. Arbitron continues to offer its syndicated radio audience measurement services, producing more than half a million local market reports annually. *See also* ARBITRON INFORMATION ON DEMAND.

**ARC LIGHT** high-intensity light that uses as a source of illumination the arc made when a current passes between two electrodes. Also called a *carbon-arc light*, the arc light is used to throw light over wide areas. It will flood an area with brilliant light and can be used to simulate sunlight.

**AREA-BY-AREA ALLOCATION** method of allocating the advertising budget, in which the advertising dollars are assigned to be spent in areas (markets) in proportion to the advertiser's current or projected product (or service) sales in those areas; abbreviated ABA; also called *market-by-market allocation*. *See also* ADVERTISING APPROPRIATION.

**AREA DISTRIBUTION CENTER (ADC)** U.S. Postal Service facility located in a high-mail-volume area that distributes mail to other facilities within the system, such as post offices, but not to mail addressees. *See also* AUXILIARY SERVICE FACILITY; BULK MAIL CENTER.

**AREA OF DOMINANT INFLUENCE (ADI)** geographic area made up of all the counties influenced by originating stations in a particular television market. For example, the New York ADI comprises all the counties in New York and New Jersey where the New York City television stations are viewed. The concept was introduced by ARBITRON, a television research company, to be used in the measurement of audience data. Each county in the United States (excluding Alaska) is allocated exclusively to one ADI; there is no overlap. *See also* DESIGNATED MARKET AREA (DMA).

**AREA SAMPLE** in statistics, probability sample, also called *area selection*. The total geographical area under study is divided into a number of smaller areas, and then the areas or respondents to be used in the study are chosen by random selection. The result is an area sample. *See also* ADEQUATE SAMPLE; RANDOM SAMPLE.

**AREA SELECTION**  *see* AREA SAMPLE.

**ARMY AND AIR FORCE POST OFFICE/FLEET POST OFFICE (APO/FPO)**  U.S. Postal Service facilities handling the mail of active members of the armed forces. Some mailers offer special courtesy rates to APO/FPO customers.

**ARREARS**  *see* GRACE.

**ART**  drawings, photographs, layouts, decorative designs, as well as all other creative, illustrative matter that is not typeset, that is used in advertisements and commercials; also called *artwork.* Usually created by commercial artists, advertising art differs from noncommercial art in that it will be reproduced, and therefore when creating the work, the artist must consider the reproductive process to be used.

**ART AND MECHANICAL (A&M)**  term generally used in accounting to indicate costs of both the artwork and its layout in the production of a print advertisement; written as *A&M costs. See also* ART; MECHANICAL.

**ART BUYER**  individual knowledgeable in the various forms of photographic and illustrative technique who functions as the art purchasing representative for an advertising agency or commercial art studio. He or she must be knowledgeable about available talent and capable of making the necessary business arrangements with model agencies, photographers, illustrators, photo labs, and the like. The art buyer must work in close association with the ART DIRECTOR of an art agency or studio.

**ART DIRECTOR (AD)**  artist employed in an executive capacity by art advertising agency or any other organization that requires the preparation of artwork. This individual usually works directly under the vice president of creative services and side by side with the COPYWRITER on a project. The AD supervises a staff of artists and LAYOUT PERSONS and maintains an up-to-date listing of FREELANCE specialists (e.g., artists, graphic designers, photographers, camera personnel). The AD is responsible for the artistic development as well as the total look of all advertising programs. *See also* GRAPHIC DESIGN.

**ART DIRECTORS CLUB**  organization of art directors, visual information specialists, and graphic designers founded in 1920 and headquartered in New York City. Associate memberships are available to artists, cinematographers, photographers, copywriters, journalists, critics, and educators. The purpose of the Art Directors Club is to provide a format for the exchange of ideas and to provide knowledge of and stimulate interest in art direction. The Art Directors Club publishes the *Art Director's Annual,* which features the best of advertising and graphics. The club also sponsors educational, professional, and entertainment programs, and awards scholarships and monies to art students and art schools.

**ART SERVICE** outside supplier hired by art advertising agency to design and produce the artwork for advertisements. The art service can supplement the work of an art department or, in the case of a small advertising agency, can fulfill the functions of an art department.

**ASCENDER**
1. on lowercase letters, the stroke that rises above the body of the letter: b, d, f, h, k, 1, and t all have ascenders.
2. any capital letter, and any lowercase letter with an ascender. *See also* DESCENDER.

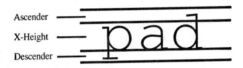

Ascender
X-Height
Descender

**ASPECT RATIO** ratio between the width and the height of a television or motion picture screen. This ratio is important to the person responsible for photographing products to be shown in a commercial, so that these products may be shown in their most flattering perspective.

**ASSEMBLY DAILIES** in film and television production, film footage from which the best take of each scene shot on a given day has been selected, cut, and spliced in correct sequence by an editor; also called *dailies* or *rushes,* Assembly dailies are used for review on a daily basis to check technique, CONCEPT, and continuity.

**ASSIGNED MAILING DATE** date a list user is authorized by the list owner to send a mailing to persons on the list. List owners control the MAIL DATE to prevent persons on a list from being overexposed to direct-mail promotions in a time period. In practice, the assigned mailing date often is loosely enforced, since many factors, particularly LETTERSHOP performance, can affect the actual mail date.

**ASSISTANT ART DIRECTOR** assistant to the ART DIRECTOR. The assistant art director usually works on one account at a time and is responsible for the artistic development of that account. He or she functions as liaison between the artistic staff on the account and the agency art director.

**ASSOCIATE CREATIVE DIRECTOR** assistant to the CREATIVE DIRECTOR. The ACD usually works on one account at a time and is responsible for the preparation of advertising concepts and production of advertisements for the media. In a large advertising agency, the associate creative director is assisted by a staff of writers and artists, either FREELANCE or on salary. In a smaller agency, the copywriting and art production become the responsibility of the associate creative director.

**ASSOCIATED BUSINESS PUBLICATIONS** *see* AMERICAN BUSINESS PRESS, INC.

**ASSOCIATION OF NATIONAL ADVERTISERS (ANA)** trade association of approximately 500 major manufacturing and service companies that advertise nationally. Founded in 1910 to improve the effectiveness of advertising, the organization is also actively involved in monitoring industrywide advertising practices, to protect the interest of its members. It also sponsors studies and issues reports on advertising effectiveness and techniques for the benefit of its members.

**ATMOSPHERICS**
1. (Retail Marketing) elements such as store lighting, temperature, noise level, scents, wall coverings, architecture, and display fixtures that can be studied and/or manipulated by retailers to produce an effect on consumer buying habits. Atmospherics are thought to influence the customer's shopping moods and time spent in the store and are used to create or reinforce the customer's desire to buy a product.
2. (Broadcast) phenomena that produce disturbances in broadcast reception creating static, such as lightning in a storm.

**ATTACHED MAIL** incidental first-class attachment that travels with a second-, third-, or fourth-class piece, at the postage rate of the host piece. The attached piece can be inside or outside the host piece, but must be secondary in purpose to the host mailing. For example, a bill that accompanies a magazine will be charged at the lower advertising pound rate. Third-class attached mail excludes most merchandise samples, although perfume and cosmetic samples embedded into the surface of a paper bind-in are permitted.

**ATTENTION** act of noticing an advertisement or commercial; a component of information or perceptual processing. Since consumers will usually take note of things relevant to their needs, attitudes, or beliefs, attention is selective. There have been cases in advertising history where attention was drawn to the advertising but, unhappily, not to the product being advertised. *See also* INTERPRETATION.

**ATTITUDES** mental position or emotional feelings about products, services, companies, ideas, issues, or institutions, Attitudes are shaped by DEMOGRAPHICS, social values, and personality. As the consumer attempts to evaluate a product, service, or the like, he or she will develop an attitude about the thing being evaluated. In advertising, the desire is to generate favorable perceptions toward the thing being advertised, and to promote positive consumer attitudes. *See also* ATTITUDE STUDY.

**ATTITUDES, INTERESTS, AND OPINIONS** *see* ACTIVITIES, INTERESTS, AND OPINIONS.

**ATTITUDE STUDY** study conducted by advertising researchers, advertisers, or their agencies in an attempt to assess the effectiveness of advertising or to determine consumer evaluations of a company, idea, issue, product, or service. Attitude studies are often done before and after exposure to an advertising campaign to determine the change (if any) in ATTITUDE on the part of the consumer. The results of a before and after study will also reflect the success of the campaign.

**ATTRIBUTION THEORY** the theory that consumer assumptions about a product or situation are derived from the consumer's experience, personality, or attitudes. For example, a consumer who has had poor experiences with domestic automobiles and a good experience with an import might attribute the quality of the import to the fact that it is not U.S. made. Such a consumer will be predisposed toward products that emphasize their foreign origin. Similarly, a product endorsement by a celebrity who is perceived to be unethical will be attributed to the money being paid for the endorsement and not to the celebrity's honest assessment of the product.

**AUDIENCE**
**In general:**
1. group of people assembled in a studio, theater, or auditorium to witness a presentation or performance.
2. personal meeting of a formal nature, as an audience with the Pope.
**Advertising:** total number of people who may receive an advertising message delivered by a medium or a combination of media.
**Communications:** total number of readers, viewers, or listeners reached by the appropriate medium.

**AUDIENCE ACCUMULATION** total net AUDIENCE reached by an advertising campaign, including newspaper, magazine, and outdoor advertising, as well as broadcast commercials. If an advertising campaign for a product runs for a six-week period and uses a combination of media, the audience accumulation would be the total number of people who were exposed to an advertisement or commercial at least once.

**AUDIENCE COMPOSITION**
**Advertising:** proportion of various types of people, classified by DEMOGRAPHIC or PSYCHOGRAPHIC characteristics, reached by an advertising medium or message.
**Broadcast:** breakdown by program of the listening and viewing AUDIENCE according to gender and age. The number in each category is compared against the total number of the listening or viewing audience for that program. (For example, 10% of a viewing audience for a specific television show might be adult women, while 20% might be adolescents.) This information allows the advertiser to position the message in or around a program that appeals to the people most likely

to utilize the product or service. Since different time periods (DAYPARTS) in programming have different costs, knowledge of audience composition permits the advertiser to select economically those hours during which a specific audience can be reached. *See also* AUDIENCE PROFILE.

**AUDIENCE DUPLICATION** measurement in terms of percentage of the amount of persons in a listening, reading, or viewing AUDIENCE who are reached more than once by the same commercial or advertisement appearing in different media as reported by the rating and measurement services. If an advertiser desires to reach as many different people as possible, then a low audience duplication percentage is necessary in the MEDIA PLAN. Many advertisers feel that their product or service will sell best if they concentrate their efforts on the same people, in which case, a high audience duplication percentage is desirable.

**AUDIENCE FLOW**
1. gain or loss of the audience during a broadcast program through turning on or off the television or through changing channels.
2. measurement of the traffic behavior of the TELEVISION HOUSEHOLD audience or the radio audience as reported by the rating and measurement services. Every program has an audience flow that indicates where the audience came from before the program and where they are going after the program. There are three audience options: (a) the listening or viewing audience who came from a preceding program on a competing broadcast station, (b) the audience who came from a preceding program on the same station, and (c) the audience who turned on their radios or televisions for a specific program. At the conclusion of a program these audience options are reversed, becoming (a) the audience who will turn off their sets, (b) the audience who will remain to watch or listen to the next program on the same station, and (c) the audience who will switch to another station. Audience flow data are important to the advertiser whose message is positioned in the time period between two shows. The fact that both shows have a high audience rating is not sufficient to assure that the message will be seen or heard. It is also important to know if both programs share the same audience.

**AUDIENCE FRAGMENTATION** division of AUDIENCES into small groups due to the wide spectrum of MEDIA outlets. This is a situation that becomes increasingly baffling to advertisers as the specialization of publications and broadcast opportunities become even more diverse. In addition, the advent of CABLE TELEVISON has made a vast number of television stations available to viewing audiences as well as confusing the geographic locations of viewers. For example: New York audiences can now watch programming of Atlanta, Philadelphia, or Boston stations, and Southern California receives programming from New York. This leaves a fragmented viewing audience in that consumers in California usually cannot avail themselves of services delivered in New York. Additionally, viewers now have the opportunity to watch two or three times as many television stations as in the past, so that audience size for any one local station is likely to be smaller than in the past. This situation creates an economic problem for advertisers who need to reach large audiences to make their advertising dollars cost effective. In addition, since the number of viewers determines the advertising rates, audience fragmentation will affect the networks' revenues as the audience size diminishes. As audiences become more fragmented, the major networks will need to create new revenue sources.

**AUDIENCE-HOLDING INDEX**   guide to how well a program holds its audience, measured on a minute-by-minute or quarter-hour basis by the research service companies. Many times a large audience will turn on a program, but will not stay tuned for the duration of the program. This is particularly true for sporting events, news broadcasts, and some MINISERIES. It is important, therefore, for an advertiser to be aware of the audience-holding index of a show before buying commercial time in that show.

**AUDIENCE-PARTICIPATION PROGRAM**   radio or television show in which members of the audience take part and whose participation is an integral part of the entertainment value of the show—for example, a radio show whose format calls for members of the listening audience to phone in and talk to the host, or a television show where the host conducts interviews with members of the studio audience or offers prizes for their ability (or lack of ability) to perform some task.

**AUDIENCE PROFILE**   socio-economic characteristics of a readership, viewership, or listenership; not to be confused with AUDIENCE COMPOSITION, which merely tells the makeup of the audience by age and gender. The profile gives some indication of the spending habits of a particular AUDIENCE. Among the factors taken into consideration are income, car and home ownership, leisure time activities, and geographic location. This information is provided by the MEDIUM based on its own research or on that of the syndicated research services, and is then supplied to the advertiser or advertising agency. In order to reach the logical buying market for a particular product or service, it is important to know the audience profile of the medium.

**AUDIENCE SHARE**   portion of the group of people who might receive an advertising message, or who are of interest to the advertiser, and who actually do receive the message.

Audience share can be calculated electronically, as with the NIELSEN RATINGS, or through personal, telephone, or direct mail survey, as is commonly done by magazine publishers. For example, a SAMPLE of 2000 skiers might be sent a survey by a skiing magazine publisher asking which magazines they read and the frequency with which they read them. If 1000 respond by saying they read a skiing magazine, and if 500 of those respondents read the publisher's skiing magazine, then the publisher's audience share is 500/1000 (50) or 500/2000 (25), depending upon how the audience is defined. *See also* SHARE.

**AUDIMETER** brand-name electronic device developed in 1936 and used by the A. C. NIELSEN COMPANY as a means of measuring broadcast audience data. Placed on the television receiver in people's homes, the device records the time the set is turned on, the channel to which it is tuned, and the length of time it is tuned to each channel. (It cannot record whether anyone is sitting in front of the television.) This information is then assimilated with other collected data into the NIELSEN TELEVISION INDEX. Originally, the Audimeter was designed to record radio listening. In early 1950 it was first used for television audience estimates as well. The Nielsen Company discontinued the radio measurement service in 1964.

**AUDIO** portion that is heard of a radio or television program or commercial or of an audiovisual presentation. It includes spoken narrative and dialog, sound effects, and music. A television script page is divided vertically into two halves: all information on the right side pertains to the audio portion of the script; information on the left pertains to the VIDEO portion.

**AUDIT**
**In general:** official examination and verification of accounts and records, as in a tax audit.
**Publishing:** examination of a publisher's records by an outside auditing firm to ascertain the validity of the publisher's statements regarding the circulation figures of a publication. An audit is done in an official capacity on an annual basis. The circulation figures are important, because the cost of advertising is based on circulation. The greater the circulation, the larger the reading audience, and, therefore, the greater the cost of advertising. Also audited are the publisher's methods of arriving at the circulation figures, with separate notations for reduced rate subscriptions, free copies, or subscriptions in arrears. *See also* AUDIT BUREAU OF CIRCULATIONS; AUDIT TRAIL; BUSINESS PUBLICATIONS AUDIT OF CIRCULATIONS; VERIFIED AUDIT CIRCULATION CORPORATION.

**AUDIT BUREAU OF CIRCULATIONS (ABC)** independent nonprofit auditing organization formed in 1914 whose membership is composed of advertisers, advertising agencies, newspapers, magazines, business publications, and miscellaneous publications. Its purpose is to AUDIT and validate circulation figures for the benefit of its members. Relied upon as a principal informational source by media planners, the bureau publishes annual AUDIT REPORTS that detail the findings of its auditors, as well as semiannual Publisher's Statements (*see* ABC STATEMENT).

**AUDIT BUREAU OF MARKETING SERVICES** nonprofit organization established in 1966 as an affiliate of the AUDIT BUREAU OF CIRCULATIONS (ABC). The Audit Bureau of Marketing Services (ABMS) audits services outside of publishing that are not eligible for ABC membership but that do have auditable data—for example, direct mail lists or trade show attendance.

**AUDITION**
1. method by which an advertiser decides on the feasibility of sponsoring a particular radio or television program. The advertiser listens to or views a trial performance, noting the format, talent, direction, style, and pace, and then decides if the program would be a beneficial association for the product or service.
2. trial performance by a radio, television, stage, or screen performer to demonstrate ability, talent, and suitability for a particular vehicle. Auditions are held by the PRODUCER. When auditioning talent for an advertisement or commercial, the advertiser has the final say.
3. in television production, a separate audio circuit in the control room that allows the sound engineer to preview sounds that originate outside the production studio before mixing them with the production in progress, such as music from an outside recording and playback source.

**AUDIT REPORT** annual report issued by the AUDIT BUREAU OF CIRCULATIONS (ABC) providing audited verification of the published circulation figures of newspapers and magazines. Audit Report will show any variances found in the circulation figures claimed by a publication and explain the reasons for these differences. The detailed information found in the Audit Report makes it possible for media planners to make decisions based on verified data.

**AUDIT TRAIL**
**In general:** verifiable evidence of a series of transactions that affect a file record.
**Magazines:** requirement of the AUDIT BUREAU OF CIRCULATIONS showing, for each paid SUBSCRIPTION record, all transactions made against that file record and the backup documents supporting each transaction.

**AUTHOR'S ALTERATION (AA)** change made to typeset copy not due to a typesetting error. It frequently derives from the author's desire to change wording. Printers charge a premium for author's alterations. *See also* EDITORIAL ALTERATION; PRINTER'S ERROR.

**AUTHOR'S CORRECTION** *see* AUTHOR'S ALTERATION.

**AUTOMATED BUSINESS MAIL PROCESSING SYSTEM (ABMPS)** method of automatically sorting BULK MAIL by FIVE-DIGIT ZIP CODE destination. The system, which is no longer used by the U.S. Postal Service, was a precursor to the NINE-DIGIT ZIP CODE system, which utilizes an AREA CODE on the lower right-hand corner of the REPLY ENVELOPE.

**AUTOMATIC DIALER**  device used by telemarketers to dial a predetermined list of phone numbers and play a recorded message when calls are answered, without operator involvement. Automatic dialers can greatly increase the productivity of an OUTBOUND TELEPHONE operation. Unfortunately, the device cannot distinguish between playing the message to a child, an answering machine, a business, or a physician's office. Some automatic dialers do not disconnect until the message has ended, even if the called party hangs up. Concern about tying up phone lines has resulted in state and federal legislation restricting the use of automatic dialers. An automatic dialer may be an integral part of the telephone system or a stand-alone device. *See also* PREDICTIVE DIALER; TELEPHONE CONSUMER PROTECTION ACT.

**AUTOMATIC INTERACTION DETECTOR ANALYSIS (AID ANALYSIS)**  statistical technique for MULTIVARIATE ANALYSIS. It can be used to determine the characteristics that differentiate buyers from nonbuyers. It involves a successive series of analytical steps that gradually focus in on the critical determinants of behavior, creating clusters of people with similar demographic characteristics and buying behavior. This technique is explained in John A. Sonquist and James N. Morgan, *The Detection Of Interaction Effects*, University of Michigan, Monograph No. 35, 1969.

**AUTOMATIC MERCHANDISING**  vending machine sales; called *automatic merchandising*, because it is impersonal retail merchandising, where the purchase is not influenced by sales personnel. Vending machines allow for round-the-clock sales in heavy traffic locations inside or outside retail stores, colleges, office buildings, factories, hospitals, and the like. Cigarettes and beverages account for 70% of all sales. Vending machines are very important sales channels in some product categories, particularly soft drinks.

**AUTOMATIC RENEWAL**  method of renewing magazine subscriptions without requesting the subscriber's permission after the initial order. The subscriber is frequently charged for each renewal by credit card number. There are complex legal issues to consider when doing automatic renewals to prove that subscribers are not being billed or charged for something they did not order. Publishers using this technique must retain written proof that the subscribers, permission was obtained at the time they first ordered the magazine, and must carefully word all invoices sent.

**AUTOMATIC REORDER**  vendor marketing tool effected by a Blanket Purchase Order (BPO), whereby a company will order supplies to be restocked by the vendor on a regular basis without the necessity of placing a new order each time. An automatic reorder may take place at periodic intervals or when supplies have reached a specific predetermined minimum quantity. Periodically the company buying the supplies will become involved with the reorder process to assess and possibly revise the quantities, the automatic reorder items, or the intervals between reorders. Automatic reorders may be handled through the computer by preset data entries or manually by reorder clerks.

**AUTOMOBILE INFORMATION DISCLOSURE ACT** 1958 federal consumer protection legislation that requires automobile manufacturers to post suggested retail prices on all new passenger vehicles.

**AUXILIARY SERVICE FACILITY (ASF)** U.S. Postal Service BULK MAIL processing facility that operates as a satellite facility to one of the 21 BULK MAIL CENTERS (BMCs) throughout the country. The ASF handles mail that enters and leaves the postal system within the same BMC service area.

**AVAILABILITY** broadcast time period available for purchase for a commercial message. When it has been determined by the MEDIA PLANNER (who is frequently the MEDIA BUYER as well) where an advertiser will best profit from commercial placement, he or she will contact the station or the station's sales representative and ask for *Avails* (the time periods that are available). The station or rep will then supply the buyer with a list of these TIME SLOTS, together with prices and estimated RATINGS of the shows in or around the available times. The ratings, and thus the prices, are based on the most recent ratings of the shows, as reported by the rating services.

**AVAILS** *see* AVAILABILITY.

**AVERAGE AUDIENCE RATING** one of several different kinds of ratings used by the A. C. NIELSEN COMPANY in the NIELSEN TELEVISION INDEX; also known as *AA rating*. It reflects the average size of the audience on a minute-by-minute basis (average size at minute 1, minute 2, minute 3, and so on) throughout the length of a program. This rating is very valuable to an advertiser because it tells most accurately the size of the audience for the advertiser's commercial. The AA Rating plays an important role in negotiations between the MEDIA BUYER and the NETWORKS. It is also the number used in computing a program's share of the audience or the cost of reaching 1000 homes (*see* COST PER THOUSAND, abbreviated CPM) with a specific advertising message. *See also* CUMULATIVE AUDIENCE RATING; RATINGS; SHARE; TOTAL AUDIENCE RATING.

**AVERAGE FREQUENCY** average number of times a consumer has been exposed to a commercial in any medium that is part of an advertising CAMPAIGN. If an advertiser runs a six-week campaign for a product, using radio, television, newspapers, magazines, and outdoor advertising, it would be hoped that the average consumer would be exposed to the advertising many times through the various media and that the average frequency rating for that product would be high.

**AVERAGE NET PAID CIRCULATION**  accounting term used by publishers and their auditors to indicate the average number of copies of a publication sold per issue. This term is used by the AUDIT BUREAU OF CIRCULATIONS in their publisher's statements (see ABC STATEMENT) and AUDIT REPORTS. The figure is arrived at by dividing the total number of subscription and newsstand-sold copies for all issues of the period by the total number of issues. For example: Magazine Z, a monthly, sold 14 million copies in a six-month period. The average net paid circulation is $14,000,000 \div 6$, since there were 6 issues in the time period or 2.3 million copies sold per issue.

**AVERAGE PAID CIRCULATION**  *see* AVERAGE NET PAID CIRCULATION.

**AVERAGE PROFIT MARGIN**
1. method of calculating the profit margin per item sold by applying an equal proportion of the total expenses of the seller against each item sold. It can be used to determine the benefit to be gained from advertising. For example, assume a $100 advertisement will generate 100 sales. Each item sells for $5 and costs $3 to produce and deliver, leaving a profit margin of $2. Since advertising will cost $1 per item sold, the average profit margin of $1 indicates that the item will be profitable after advertising expense.
2. GROSS PROFIT margin of a business enterprise averaged over a period of time. The gross profit margin is the annual net sales or revenues less the cost of goods sold

**AWARENESS**  first stage in the process of learning about a new product, service, or idea in which the consumer has received information about the existence of the INNOVATION but has not yet formed an opinion. For example, in the early stages of a political campaign, we become aware of the candidates but do not immediately have an opinion or interest in each of them. Building awareness is extremely important in industrial marketing because a prospect may not agree readily to see a salesperson representing an unknown company or product. *See also* AWARENESS, INTEREST, DESIRE, ACTION (AIDA).

**AWARENESS, INTEREST, DESIRE, ACTION (AIDA)**  model of consumer behavior that traces the sequence of cognitive events leading to a purchase decision or other action; also called HIERARCHY OF READINESS. For example, in a political campaign, one first becomes aware of the candidates. After receiving additional information, an interest develops in one or more candidates, eventually resulting in a desire to see one candidate elected, and the act of casting a vote for that candidate. The AIDA model is used by marketers as a guideline for creating communications. This requires an understanding of where the market for a product currently lies along the AIDA continuum.

Marketing of an INNOVATION requires building AWARENESS. Marketing of an established product may require building desire. Recipes that present new ways to use established brands are one way often used to build desire for an existing product.

**AWARENESS-TRIAL-REPEAT (ATR)** product-specific pattern of three key steps followed by consumers toward adopting a product. Awareness takes place as a result of the consumer learning of a particular product brand or a product's availability and its attributes. After learning of the product, consumers may make a trial purchase to test the product. If use of the product has favorable results, consumers will repeat their purchase of the product. ATR is used to demonstrate the product adoption process. *See also* BAIT-AD; BAIT AND SWITCH ADVERTISEMENT.

# B

**BABY BILLBOARD** *see* CAR CARD.

**BABY BOOMERS** individuals who were born during the years immediately following World War II. This group of people represents a sizable portion of the consuming public, and their spending habits and life-style have a powerful influence on the economy. They represent a TARGET AUDIENCE for many advertisers.

**BACK COVER** outside back of a magazine, called the *fourth cover*. Because this cover is more likely to be seen and read by more readers, it is usually sold at a premium. Often there is a waiting list for advertisements to be placed here. The price of advertising on the fourth cover always includes use of color whether or not the advertisement will be in color. The back cover is also usually the most expensive of all the covers. For example: In 1985, the cost, on a one-time basis, of the INSIDE FRONT COVER (second cover) or the INSIDE BACK COVER (third cover) in *U.S. News & World Report* was $38,365; the fourth cover cost $48,965.

**BACK DATING**
**In general:** writing a check or other document with a date prior to the date on which the document is actually written. Back-dated checks are sometimes written accidentally in January, because the writers have forgotten the year has changed. Most banks will allow a GRACE period for accepting these checks.
**Magazines:** starting a magazine subscription with an issue prior to the CURRENT ISSUE being served; also called *back start*. Back dating is used by the publisher as a RATE BASE management tool or to reduce an excessive back issue inventory. Back dating may also be done at

the request of the subscriber who wants a particular back issue. *See also* ADVANCE START.

**BACK END**
1. FULFILLMENT functions performed after a customer orders, including servicing the customer, delivering the product or service, and analyzing the response in terms of PAY UP and RENEWAL.
2. behavior of a customer after the initial order is received. Through back end analysis, the seller examines pay up, cancellation rates, and renewal or reorder rates.

**BACKER CARD**   poster space on the back of a large DISPLAY. Backer cards are used to achieve public awareness of a product or to motivate sales at point of purchase. They are often found in supermarkets or discount variety stores, where displays and DISPLAY BINS are used for merchandising. They offer a low-cost advertising MEDIUM in places where traffic is great and impulse purchasing can be stimulated.

**BACKGROUND**
1. anything used to support the message of a radio or television commercial or print advertisement—for example, sound effects, music, location, special scenery, or colors. These elements are used for a realistic effect and add to the emotional appeal of an advertisement or commercial. The background (abbreviated *BG*) also provides a subliminal message about the user of the product. For example: in an automobile advertisement where the car is displayed with prominence against a background of young people at a high school football game, there is the subliminal message that the car is for young people who want to have a good time; or for older people who want to feel young. Similarly, a soft-drink commercial where the canned beverage is passed from hand to hand at a local town parade featuring happy, smiling people conveys the subliminal message that everyone who drinks this beverage will be happy.
2. compilation of facts, figures, and past experience upon which decisions for future advertising and marketing are made.

**BACKGROUND MUSIC**   in motion picture or broadcast production, live or recorded music played behind the spoken dialogue or announcements to establish mood or to influence the emotional impact of a scene.

In advertising, background music will sometimes work to affect the disposition of the potential consumer of a product or service. Studies indicate that background music will favorably influence consumers when the appeal is emotional and/or simple. However, when the appeal is complicated and/or practical, background music does not work in favor of the product being advertised and is seldom used.

**BACKGROUND PLATE**   *see* REAR-SCREEN PROJECTION.

**BACKING UP** printing the other side of a printed sheet.

**BACK ISSUE** magazine issue prior to the CURRENT ISSUE. *See also* BACK DATING.

**BACKLIGHTING** production technique that lights a performer, object, or poster from behind rather than from above, below, or in front, in order to create a dramatic effect. Backlit outdoor displays are becoming increasingly popular. Using an outdoor display concept that originated in Canada, words and pictures are reproduced on a sheet that has a filmlike texture. This sheet is then mounted in a special frame and lighted from behind twenty-four hours a day, creating a display with brilliant color and no shadows. In high-traffic-volume areas, these signs have great visibility, and they appear from the roadway as a giant 35mm slide.

**BACK OF BOOK** in advertising, the section of a magazine (book) that follows the main body of editorial matter. According to direct response advertisers, this section has the lowest reader response of all the sections in a magazine, even though the advertising rates throughout the body of the magazine are usually the same. However, some publishers allow an advertiser to reserve a PREFERRED POSITION at a premium rate.

**BACK ORDER** seller's order for goods from a supplier that have been requested by the seller's customer but are not in the seller's current INVENTORY. A back order is an open obligation (of the supplier to ship and of the buyer to accept) until the merchandise becomes available and the transaction can be completed.

**BACK START** *see* BACK DATING.

**BACK-TO-BACK COMMERCIALS** two COMMERICALS in succession. Stations and networks will not air commercials for two competing products back to back. Often, back-to-back commercial time is purchased by a company that wants to sell two similar or companion products that it manufactures, such as floor wax and furniture polish. *See also* COMPETITIVE SEPARATION.

**BACKUP SPACE** advertising space in a magazine that adjoins an INSERT (such as a coupon, return card, or recipe book that has been bound into the magazine). If advertisers wish to use any of these inserts, they must purchase backup space. Magazines never sell inserts without backup space.

**BACKUP TAPE** duplicate MAGNETIC TAPE maintained for security. Some organizations utilize a previous-RUN tape (also called *father tape* or *grandfather tape*) plus all subsequent transaction tapes so that a duplicate of the current file can be reconstructed if necessary. Backup tapes should be kept in a secure location separate from the actual file tape.

**BACKWARD INTEGRATION** strategy employed to expand profits and gain greater control over production of a product whereby a company will purchase or build a business that will increase its own supply capability or lessen its cost of production. For example, a clothing manufacturer may purchase one of its suppliers of fabrics to lessen the cost of raw materials and have more control over the delivery schedules of the finished product. *See also* FORWARD INTEGRATION; HORIZONTAL INTEGRATION.

**BAD BREAK** problem or error in typesetting, such as the first line of a page or column beginning with a WIDOW or an improperly divided word at the end of a line of type.

**BAD DEBT** customer failing to pay for the merchandise or service received; also called *bad pay*. In the case of magazines, two to three issues are usually sent before service is suspended because of nonpayment. *See also* BAD DEBT ALLOWANCE; DEADBEAT.

**BAD DEBT ALLOWANCE** deduction from the RATE BASE guarantee based on an estimate of the number of credit subscriptions that will cancel or be canceled prior to payment; also called *bad pay allowance*.

**BAD PAY** *see* DEADBEAT.

**BAD PAY ALLOWANCE** *see* BAD DEBT ALLOWANCE.

**BAD-PAY LIST** list of DEADBEATS (individuals with a poor credit history); also called *bad-pay file*. This list serves as a purge file in a MERGE/PURGE to delete these individuals from the promotion list, thus reducing the probability of incurring BAD DEBT expense. Bad-pay lists may be maintained by a single marketer for his use or may be maintained by a supplier who accumulates bad-pay data from several marketers and sells the information to others.

**BAD-RISK FILE** *see* BAD-PAY LIST.

**BAFFLE** movable partition used in broadcast and film, that is constructed of materials that absorb sound and light. A baffle will prevent reverberation of sound and undesirable light reflection.

**BAGGING** process of placing outgoing BULK MAIL into a canvas SACK with the appropriate SACK TAG. For large-volume mailers, this method is gradually being replaced by palletization: entering mail into the postal system on a PALLET or wooden skid, instead of in a sack.

**BAG TAG** *see* SACK TAG.

**BAIT-AD** advertisement that offers retail merchandise at an alluringly low price to entice buyers to a store; also called *bait* and *switch advertisement*. In actuality, the customer may find it difficult, if not impossible, to purchase the advertised merchandise because it is the retailer's intention (1) to get the buyer to the store and then (2) to switch him or her to something more costly. Retailers that consistently use bait advertising are subject to legal action by the FEDERAL TRADE COMMISSION, as this practice is considered to be false or DECEPTIVE ADVERTISING.

**BAIT AND SWITCH** *see* BAIT-AD.

**BALANCE**
**Advertising**: blending of sounds, such as music and dialogue in television or radio, to achieve the desired proportion of volume; also, the artful blending of copy, drawings, illustrations, photographs, and other decorative material used in print advertisements to effect a pleasing aesthetic appearance.
**Fulfillment:** process of matching an updated file against the previous file, together with all subsequent transactions that should have been applied against it, to ensure that processing was done correctly. *See also* BATCH BALANCE.
**List rental:** names remaining on a list after a SELECTION has been made for rental or HOUSE promotion.

**BALLOON COPY** in copywriting (*see* COPYWRITER), a visualizing device borrowed from early comic-strip artists, where textual matter representing dialogue is circled and a continuous line is drawn to the speaker's mouth. The name is derived from the balloonlike appearance. However, today artists frequently dispense with the balloon, although any copy surrounded by an ellipse is still called balloon copy.

**BALOP** slide used with a BALOPTICON.

**BALOPTICON** trademark of a machine used to project images onto a reflecting surface so that they can then be traced for drawings or photographed. The machine is made by Bausch & Lomb, who are well known for their innovations in the field of optics. *See also* BALOP.

**BANGTAIL** promotional envelope with a perforated flap that can be removed and used as an order form. Bangtail envelopes are frequently used for film development promotion INSERTS in newspapers or magazines. *See also* WALLET FLAP.

**BANK** temporary computer file used to hold ADJUSTMENTS that have been made to file records until those adjustments are made to the mainfile during the scheduled UPDATE. A bank is necessary only to BATCH systems, which periodically update the mainfile, in contrast to ON-LINE systems, which continuously update the mainfile.

**BANNER**
1. display poster designed to look like a flag, with an imprinted advertising message. It is usually draped over a cord or wire and flown overhead. A banner is used generally as a customer awareness tool in high traffic areas in retail stores, such as supermarkets or discount variety stores, where it will have good visibility.

**2.** *see* BANNERHEAD.

**BANNERHEAD** newspaper headline usually announcing something spectacular. A bannerhead is set in somewhat larger type than the rest of the text and is printed in BOLDFACE. In advertising copy, a bannerhead works as an attention-getting device.

**BAR CODE** series of horizontal or vertical parallel lines representing a code that can be optically read and interpreted by a bar code SCANNER. Bar coding is used on envelopes and forms to speed data entry and for automated postal sorting. *See also* DELIVERY POINT BAR CODE; OPTICAL CHARACTER RECOGNITION; UNIVERSAL PRODUCT CODE.

**BAR CODE SORTER** OPTICAL CHARACTER RECOGNITION equipment used primarily by the U.S. Postal Service to sort mail by BAR CODES printed on the envelope that identify the destination ZIP code. The bar code may be printed one envelope at a time by the Postal Service, using high-speed machines operated by clerks, who read handwritten ZIP codes on the envelopes and key them into the machine. Large-volume mailers preprint the bar codes on their reply envelopes and cards, using a print template provided by the USPS.

**BAR GRAPH** *see* GRAPH.

**BARONIAL ENVELOPE** large envelope with a deep flap, normally used for official announcements and formal invitations (e.g., to charity balls or to banquets). Baronial envelopes are used in direct-mail promotions because the recipient will expect something important and worth reading inside. Standard baronial-size envelopes range in size from $3^{5}/8" \times 4^{11}/16"$ to $5" \times 6"$.

**BARTER** system of trading goods and services for advertising time or space. Long before broadcast advertising came into being, hotels would offer transferable documents called "due bills," each of which had the value of one day's stay per room, to newspapers and magazines in return for advertising space. The newspapers or magazines would then use the due bills for their own personnel or sell them at a discount to anyone desiring a reduced hotel rate. The cost of the advertising space was figured on the basis of the net price of the due bills. In other words, if the rate card for the advertising space was $20 per column inch, and if hotel rooms were rented at $20 per day, but the due bills each sold for $10, the barter arrangement would be at a rate of two-to-one, or two due bills for each column inch of space.

In the early days of radio, cash was tight and studio needs often exceeded budgets; thus much advertising time was sold through barter. This system continues today throughout the broadcast industry, and barter has become a highly competitive business. There are companies called *barter brokers*, who handle only barter business. There are also companies who have become wholesalers of broadcast time by building inventories of time accumulated through various barter situations (called *barter time*).

**BASE LINE** line upon which the body of lowercase letters and the base of all capital letters rest.

**BASE RATE** one-time rate charged by an advertising medium before any DISCOUNTS are offered; also called *open rate*. Discounts are offered on the basis of FREQUENCY (how often the ADVERTISEMENT or COMMERCIAL will run) and volume (the amount of money being spent). *See also* BASIC RATE; CARD RATE.

**BASE RECORD** component of a customer file with information pertaining to that customer and not to a particular order. Name and address are the primary components of the base record.

**BASHER** *see* SCOOP.

**BASIC NETWORK** minimum amount of stations on which an advertiser can purchase commercial time and still be availed of the network facilities, as determined by the network.

**BASIC PRICE** *see* BASIC RATE.

**BASIC RATE** standard published price of a periodical; also called *basic price*. There is usually a basic rate for single copies as well as for 1-, 2-, and 3-year term subscriptions. Special rates not available to everyone at all times cannot be considered basic rates, according to AUDIT BUREAU OF CIRCULATIONS rules. The Bureau also requires that the selling price of a periodical must be at least half the basic rate to be considered paid CIRCULATION. This assures advertisers in the periodical that persons included in paid circulation counts really want to read the periodical. *See also* ABC STATEMENT; ADVERTISED PRICE.

**BASIC WEIGHT** *see* BASIS WEIGHT.

**BASIS WEIGHT** pound weight of a ream (usually 500 sheets) of paper cut to a standard size and varying according to the grade of paper; also called *basic weight*. For example, the basis weight of a ream of one type of 25" × 38" BOOK PAPER is 80 pounds. The basis weight of BOND PAPER would be based on the weight of five hundred 17" × 22" sheets.

**BATCH**
1. mode of data processing that accumulates transactions for periodic file updating. *See also* BANK; ON-LINE
2. group of documents or transactions that require similar handling, are from the same time period, and/or are grouped for efficient processing—for example, all cash orders received in one day for the same product.

**BATCH BALANCE** checking some quantitative aspect of a processed BATCH to verify that the batch was processed correctly. For example, computer-generated batch quantities can be compared to manual batch counts. *See also* BALANCE.

**BATCH HEADER** document fed into a computer at the beginning of each BATCH and indicating common characteristics of the batch. For example, an order batch header may indicate that a certain product was ordered on credit and that the orders listed were all received on a particular day. Entering this information via a batch header eliminates the need to repeatedly enter the same information along with each order in the batch.

**BATCH IDENTIFICATION** code assigned to a BATCH to identify it for processing, balancing, storage, and audit LOOKUP; also called *batch number*.

**BATCH MODE** *see* BATCH.

**BATCH NUMBER** *see* BATCH IDENTIFICATION.

**BATCH PROCESSING** *see* BATCH.

**B COUNTY** *see* ABCD COUNTIES.

**BEARERS** metal devices that reduce the pressure on printing surfaces. One type uses flat surfaces or rings at the end of printing press CYLINDERS to determine the thickness of the packing that applies pressure on the printing surface. Another type consists of metal scraps left around an ENGRAVED printing plate to reduce wear on the plate when additional plates are molded from it.

**BEAT**
1. underlying rhythm in music.
2. pause for a count of one; terminology used by a director when shooting or overseeing the editing of a commercial.
3. pulsations of amplitude produced by radio waves of different frequencies. *See also* FREQUENCY MODULATION.

**BEAUTY SHOT** in a television commercial, the moment when the camera moves in, pauses, and focuses on the product. A beauty shot is a type of CLOSE-UP.

**BEHAVIOR SEGMENTATION,** MARKET SEGMENTATION strategy whereby the division of the TARGET MARKET is made according to the patterns in which the people in the market live and spend their time and money. Buyers in a market will differ in their wants, resources, locations, buying attitudes, and buying practices, and any of these variables can be used to divide a market. In behavior segmentation, potential buyers of a product are divided into groups based on their knowledge, attitude, uses, or responses to a product. *See also* DEMOGRAPHIC SEGMENTATION, GEOGRAPHIC SEGMENTATION, PSYCHOGRAPHIC SEGMENTATION.

**BELIEVABILITY** plausibility, as it relates to advertising COPY. In terms of effectiveness, believability is actually more important than truth. The commercial or advertisement must be written within the range of possibility. In order to effect believability, the COPYWRITER should convey the feeling of being a trusted friend. Of course, as a legal and ethical matter, the copywriter must tell the truth about the product, without overstatement or exaggeration.

**BELL COW** popular-selling retail item whose selling price far exceeds its cost of manufacture; also called *blue chip*.

**BELOW-THE-LINE COST** accounting term for production costs incurred for equipment, props, special effects, rentals, location fees, and anything else of a technical nature needed for a specific COMMERICAL shoot. This also includes any insurance or taxes that must be paid as a result of the production requirements of the commercial. *See also* ABOVE-THE-LINE COST.

**BENCHMARK** something that serves as the standard by which all other similar items can be measured or compared. In advertising, this can refer to the creative aspect of a COMMERICAL or ADVERTISEMENT, a particular advertising CAMPAIGN, a type of product presentation, a MEDIA PLAN, or the manner in which a particular agency represents a particular client.

**BENDAY PROCESS** (Ben Day) method of photoengraving that provides some variations in shading in a LINE CUT, which is usually reproduced without shading. The process involves the use of special screens, plates, patterns, and the machine, all named after its inventor, Benjamin Day. It was used particularly in newsprint reproductions, to add variation to a one-color illustration. This process was at one time cost effective, but with today's advanced computer technology, it has become obsolete.

**BENEFIT** satisfaction or need fulfillment that the consumer receives from a product or service. *See also* BENEFIT SEGMENTATION.

**BENEFIT SEGMENTATION** method of determining a TARGET AUDIENCE for a particular product in terms of those people who want the BENEFITS the product offers. If the product is a fast sports car, for example, the TARGET AUDIENCE will be the segment of the population that wants the benefit of a fast sports car.

There are different audiences for different perceived benefits. As an example: Dentifrice or toothpaste offers three distinct benefits, each of which will appeal to a different audience segment. One benefit relates to a tooth decay deterrent; the second, to a tooth whitener; and the third, to a mouth freshener. By segmenting the audience according to these benefits, through the copywriting the advertiser can position the product in three different markets to achieve maximum advertising effectiveness.

**BEST TIME AVAILABLE** instruction given by an ADVERTISER, or by an ADVERTISING AGENCY on behalf of a CLIENT, to a radio or television station to schedule a commercial SPOT, at the discretion of the broadcast station, in the best possible available time slot for the particular COMMERCIAL; that is, where it is most likely to capture the largest audience of potential users.

**BETA ERROR** in marketing research, failure to find an attitude, opinion, or probable reaction in the TARGET MARKET. For example, a researcher using FOCUS GROUP INTERVIEW techniques may fail to discover that a new product's PACKAGING is extremely distasteful to consumers and will depress sales. For example, a new brand of first-aid cream in a gray package may look dirty to consumers who, as a result, will not buy it. *See also* ALPHA ERROR.

**BETA TEST (BETA TEST SITE)** second-phase test of a new computer system or program in a live operating environment. Beta testing helps to identify flaws in the system prior to a full-scale introduction. The first test, conducted by the system developer, outside the production environment, is called the alpha test; the second is called the beta test and requires participation by the user. If results are not good, a third test, the gamma test, is conducted.

**BETTER BUSINESS BUREAU** organization that works to protect consumers against fraudulent and deceptive business practices, including those used in advertising and sales, by answering and investigating consumer complaints. It was established in 1916 as an outgrowth of the early vigilance committees of a national association later called the AMERICAN ADVERTISING FEDERATION. The agency operates as a system of local offices, financed by the local business community, and of national offices, funded by dues from more than 100,000 member companies. Membership is composed of business interests in a community, such as retailers, manufacturers, advertising agencies, and media representatives. The Better Business Bureau is a major influence on truth and accuracy in advertising. Its parent organization, Council of Better Business Bureaus, Inc., functions to help new industries develop standards for ethical and responsible advertising and also provides information about advertising regulations and recent court decisions and administrative rulings that affect advertising.

**BETTER OFFER COMPLAINT** complaint made by a customer who has seen a special offer of a lower price than the customer paid for the same item. Many sellers honor these complaints by refunding or adjusting the order appropriately even though they are not legally required to do so.

**BEVEL** edge of a printing plate that has been trimmed on an angle so that it can be more easily gripped by a clamp when used in the printing process.

**BIAS**

**In general:** outlook or point of view.

**Consumer research:** systematic error that comes about because the wording of a questionnaire or the attitude of the interviewer or leader appears to encourage one answer over other possible answers.

**BILLBOARD**

**Advertising:** 12' × 25' structure used for OUTDOOR ADVERTISING. The billboard, or poster panel, is usually anchored in the ground, although it may be affixed to a wall or roof, in an area of high traffic volume. In the advertising industry, a billboard is actually termed a POSTER because the advertiser's message is printed on large sheets of poster paper, which are then mounted by hand on the panel. Poster sizes are referred to in terms of sheets. Originally, a structure of this size required 24 of the largest sheets a printing press could hold, thus a billboard is often called a *24-sheet*. This term is still used today, although press sizes have changed and most poster sizes are larger. Today there are two basic sizes:

30-sheet poster: 9'7" × 21'7" printed area surrounded by a border.
bleed poster: 10'5" × 22'8" printed area extending all the way to the frame.

**Broadcast:** ten-second announcement at the beginning or end of a broadcast that identifies the sponsor or lists cast of a program.

*See also* PAINTED DISPLAY.

**BILLBOARD ALLOWANCE** amount of money in an advertising budget allocated for OUTDOOR ADVERTISING. *See also* BILLBOARD.

**BILL ENCLOSURE** see BILL INSERT.

**BILL GROUP** group of CREDIT ORDERS controlled, billed, tracked, and canceled for nonpayment, as a group. Most bill groups represent orders received during a particular period of time. *See also* BILL KEY.

**BILLING**

1. total charges to a client or advertiser by an agency, including MEDIA costs, production costs, and other noncommissionable agency charges.
2. amount of gross business done by an advertising agency in a given year as stated in terms of its billing, which is considered to be an indication of the agency's growth from year to year.
3. *see* ACCOUNTS RECEIVABLE.

**BILLING SERIES** direct mail promotion CAMPAIGN that attempts to collect payment for goods delivered prior to payment, as in the case of a magazine subscription or a catalog order. The COPY on each EFFORT in a billing series is progressively harsher in tone. The first effort usually thanks the buyer for his order and gently invites him to pay. The last effort is colloquially termed a "pay or die" message. At the conclusion of the billing series, the unpaid accounts are turned over to a COLLECTION AGENT or written off as BAD DEBT expense. *See also* ACKNOWLEDGEMENT; RENEWAL SERIES.

**BILL INSERT** secondary document, usually of a promotional nature, mailed along with an invoice to make optimal use of the mailing expense already incurred; also called *bill enclosure, bill stuffer*, or *statement stuffer*. For example, a telephone service bill might include an insert advertising an encyclopedia or a local car wash.

**BILL KEY** code assigned to a group of CREDIT ORDERS received during the same period. It is used to track and select that BILL GROUP and to control billing, suspension, and cancellation of unpaid orders. *See also* SUSPEND.

**BILL ME** *see* CREDIT ORDER.

**BILL OF MATERIALS** document used by a manufacturer or other business to authorize a set of purchases to be made or to request materials to be pulled from inventory in order to fulfill a customer order. The bill of materials indicates the specifications for each item and the company representative to whom delivery should be made. Marketers of industrial goods and raw materials can gain insight into the buying habits of their customers from the information in the bill of materials, including who is authorizing the purchase and/or selecting the vendors and what product characteristics drive their decisions. A bill of materials is also used to provide input to cost accounting systems in order to calculate the cost of goods produced.

**BILL STUFFER** *see* BILL INSERT.

**BILL TO/SHIP TO** order requesting the invoice be sent to a different address than the merchandise. This type of order is frequently used by business people who want to receive a magazine or other merchandise at their home address or at a warehouse but want to handle payment through a main business office.

**BIMETAL PLATE** PRINTING PLATE used in LITHOGRAPHY; it has a printing image base of copper or brass and a nonprinting area of aluminum, stainless steel, or chromium. The bimetal plate is used for long runs of several million images because it is much more durable than other plates. Copper and brass are used for the image areas of the plate because these metals attract ink and repel water. Conversely, aluminum, steel, and chromium are ink repellent and attract water.

Bimetal plates produce an image of equal quality to DEEP-ETCH PLATES but bear up better to the wear and tear of long runs.

**BIMODAL DISTRIBUTION** phenomenon that occurs in audience data research when in a list of questions there are two different answers which appear with equal frequency and they are also the answers which appear most frequently. When results of the questions are charted on a graph, the curve will have two high points, in place of a typical curve with only one high point. For example: A sports car manufacturer may wish to find out what appeals to prospective buyers about sports cars, in order to target advertising toward those desires. Researchers investigate a RANDOM SAMPLE of 500 people who have expressed an interest in sports cars. One hundred fifty respondents indicate that status is the appealing factor, and another 150 indicate that speed is the appealing factor. The others indicate various factors. Status and speed are then the most frequent factors given, and they appear with equal frequency. When these results are charted, they will show a bimodal distribution.

**BINDER ALLOWANCE** reduction in the gross selling price of a BULK magazine subscription order given, for example, to airlines to compensate them for the cost of plastic binders used to protect cabin copies distributed to passengers.

**BINDERY LINE** finishing process that collates and either staples or glues SIGNATURES together into a finished print product; also called BINDING.

**BIND-IN** promotional piece with a reply or order form, frequently on CARD STOCK, bound into a magazine. The RESPONSE DEVICE portion of the bind-in is usually perforated for easy removal from the binding. Most bind-ins are designed according to U.S. Postal Service size requirements, so that the reply form portion, if any, can be mailed. Some are the same size as a page and include several perforated reply forms. Although bind-ins can somewhat obscure the page they are bound on top of, they also make that page or advertisement more visible to anyone casually flipping through the magazine. Some bind-ins serve as the reply form for a SPACE AD. *See also* BLOW-IN.

**BINDING**
1. covering that holds together the pages of a book, booklet, catalog, or magazine. *See also* CASE; SPINE
2. process used to collate and join pages; also called BINDERY LINE. *See also* PERFECT BINDING; SADDLE STITCHING; SIDE WIRE; SPIRAL BINDING.

**BIND-IN ORDER CARD** *see* BIND-IN.

**BINGO CARD** insert bound into a periodical and used by readers as a return card to request information, literature, or samples from companies who either advertise in the periodical or are mentioned in the editorial content; also called *reader service card.* The insert has the appearance of a bingo card in that it is distinguished by rows of numbers each of which correspond to a company. To receive information, readers need only to mark off the numbers corresponding to the materials in which they are interested. Although bingo cards may be found in some consumer magazines, they are primarily used in trade publications.

**BIPAD NUMBER** Bureau of Independent Publishers and Distributors code assigned to magazines for identification on the newsstand. In the near future, it will probably be replaced by the ISSN (INTERNATIONAL STANDARD SERIES NUMBER) and/or the UPC (UNIVERSAL PRODUCT CODE).

**BIT**
**Advertising:** piece of comic or dramatic business such as a gesture, speech, or sound, which often stylistically identifies itself with the performer through repetitive use, such as Johnny Carson's golf swing or Rodney Dangerfield's "I get no respect."
**Data processing:** binary code used to represent data in a computer memory; acronym for *bi*nary dig*it.* Eight bits equal one BYTE of information. A computer word is 32 bits, or 4 bytes. Information is stored electronically in terms of the presence or absence of an electrical impulse or the polarity of the charge. In a binary system, an impulse is described by a "1" if *on* (positive) and a "0" if *off* (negative). Combinations of 1's and 0's, or bits, are used to represent information, depending upon the sequence in which they appear. A bit is, therefore, the smallest unit of information in a computer.

**BIWEEKLY**
**In general:** every other week.
**Magazines:** periodical with an every-other-week frequency of publication.

**BLACK AND WHITE (B&W)**
  1. advertisement (including ARTWORK, photographs, and type copy) printed in black ink on white paper. Reproduction of black-and-white copy is considered a one-color process (*monochrome* copy) and is less expensive than color advertisements, which have more than one color (*polychrome* copy) and are therefore more costly.
  2. photograph with an absence of colors other than black and white. Abbreviated b&w, B&W, B/W.

**BLACK BOOK** *see* CREATIVE BLACK BOOK.

**BLACK BOX CONCEPT** idea that consumer decision processes are not completely understandable or predictable. The black box concept attempts to mark the pattern followed by consumers when making purchasing decisions. The concept lists the components involved in the reception of marketing messages and the influences they have on consumers, taking into account external forces and consumers' personal characteristics. The factors considered in black box concept are environmental, such as economic conditions; personal, such as the ideas that guide the consumer's desire for a product; and the buyer's responses, such as the process by which the consumer makes a decision about a particular brand or quantity of a product. Although the black box concept is used as a model to demonstrate the influence of the MARKETING MIX in concert with other external variables, no one can actually pinpoint the definitive formula that results in the consumer's decision; hence the name, black box.

**BLACKOUT** exclusion of a live event from local telecasting. This happens most frequently with sporting events because of contractual arrangements with any one of the sport's authorities, such as the local team owner(s), the players' association, or the league management. A blackout is used to heighten ticket sales. If the sports arena or stadium is sold out by a certain date in advance of the event, the ban may be lifted.

**BLACK PRINTER** black-ink PRINTING PLATE that enhances neutral tones and details; also called *black plate*.

**BLANKET** rubber-coated fabric blanket used in OFFSET printing that is wrapped around a CYLINDER and transfers the print image from the plate cylinder to paper.

**BLANKET CONTRACT** agreement negotiated between a communications MEDIUM and an advertiser covering all products to be advertised; also called *master contract*. This contract supersedes any arrangements the advertiser may have with an advertising agency.

**BLANKET PURCHASE ORDER AGREEMENT (BPO)** *see Automatic Reorder.*

**BLANKING PAPER** white paper used on OUTDOOR ADVERTISEMENTS to surround the perimeter of a POSTER. Blanking paper acts as a border and sets off the poster in much the same way that matting sets off a piece of artwork.

**BLEED** reproduce a drawing or photograph so that it covers the entire page (or poster), leaving no margin. An advertisement that runs to the edge of a page is called a *bleed ad*. It may bleed on three sides, two sides, or one side, leaving the white space on the other side(s) open for copy. Whether the ad bleeds on one, two, three, or four sides, most magazines charge a 15% premium for its use, since the size of the plate needed to print a bleed ad is necessarily larger than that for typical advertisements. Designed to get attention, a bleed ad allows the artist greater flexibility in expressing the advertising concept, because the printing space is larger. *See also* BILLBOARD; BLEED IN THE GUTTER.

**BLEED AD** *see* BLEED.

**BLEED IN THE GUTTER** phrase describing an advertisement whose artwork and copy run uninterrupted through the center margin of a magazine (GUTTER) across the two facing pages. *See also* BLEED.

**BLEED POSTER** *see* BILLBOARD.

**BLIND EMBOSSING** stamping a blank impression onto paper, producing a raised or etched image without ink; also called *blind stamping*. Blind embossing is sometimes used to prepare the surface for the application of gold leaf or foil. It gives an expensive, official look to booklet covers and stationery. *See also* EMBOSSED FINISH.

**BLIND HEADLINE** HEADLINE having no discernible meaning to the reader unless the copy that follows is read. For example, "Roses Are Red" could be intended to advertise anything from lipstick to garden tools but fails to communicate its intention to the reader. Good copy usually avoids blind headlines, unless a special effect is desired.

**BLIND IMAGE** lithographic printing image that will neither hold ink nor print as a result of exposure to excess moisture.

**BLIND OFFER** *see* HIDDEN OFFER.

**BLIND PERF** PERFORATION that doesn't show through the reverse side of a sheet of paper. It is used to avoid interfering with printed images on the reverse side, such as in the case of a coupon printed on a page in a newspaper PREPRINT that has another advertisement on the other side.

**BLIND PRODUCT TEST** method of research in which people in a sample are asked to test various products that are not identified by brand name—for example, Brands X, Y, and Z. Products are tested in this manner so that respondents will be more likely to answer questions without bias or partiality toward the product because of its name or reputation, or because of previous experience with it.

**BLISTER PACK** packaging term describing an item mounted on a card and encased under a plastic dome; also called *bubble wrap*. Usually, small items that can easily be held in one hand are packaged in this manner to prevent theft. Also, items that do not conform to a uniform size or that have odd shapes can be packaged in a blister pack so that the packages will be of uniform size and can be stacked, stored, or displayed easily. Thus small and odd-shaped pieces will not be lost or damaged.

**BLOCK**
  **Broadcast:**
  **1.** time segment of consecutive hours in a daily broadcast schedule, such as the block of time from 1:00 P.M. to 4:00 P.M. Tuesday; or a strip of time on each of several days during the week, such as the block of time from 10:00 P.M. to noon Monday through Wednesday.
  **2.** in production, to plan the actors' movements or the camera movements throughout the course of the script.

**Direct marketing:** *see* BLOCK GROUP.
**Printing:**
1. wood or metal base on which a PRINTING PLATE is mounted. A mounted plate is "blocked."
2. in England, term for photoengraving.

**BLOCKBUSTER**
1. broadcast program that far exceeds expected or estimated RATINGS and thus brings in a much larger than expected AUDIENCE to advertisers whose commercials aired during the program.
2. feature movie whose box-office success has been extraordinary. When a blockbuster movie is planned for showing on television, the audience estimates are high and thus the estimated ratings are high.

**BLOCKFACE** U.S. Bureau of the Census term for one side of a city block between two intersections.

**BLOCK GROUP** U.S. Bureau of the Census term denoting a cluster of blocks in which 800 to 1000 people reside. Block groups are a subset of CENSUS TRACTS. *See also* ADDRESS CODING GUIDE.

**BLOCK GROUP SELECTOR** computer instruction that breaks a list of name and address records into segments by BLOCK GROUP and selects only the desired block group segments from the list for OUTPUT. This selection process may be used after an analysis has shown that particular block group segments have a history of responding better to promotions, or it may be used to test whether certain block group segments will respond better than others.

**BLOCK LETTER** *see* GOTHIC.

**BLOCK OUT**
**Art or photographic reproduction:** areas from a print or a photograph by masking over them and then rephotographing.
**Broadcast:** assignment of time periods on the broadcast schedule so that they are not available for sale, usually because they are to be used for public-service announcements or programs.

**BLOCK PROGRAMMING** airing radio or television programs of a similar mood, which also have common DEMOGRAPHIC appeal, one after the other for a 2-, 3-, or 4-hour time segment. In this manner, it is hoped that the audience will remain the same throughout the BLOCK. Usually there is an abrupt change of programming at the beginning and end of a block, which causes a loss of audience for those time periods.

**BLOOMING** in filming, a black rim, halo, or multicolored outline that may form around a bright, shining, or highly reflective object focused on by the camera. Sometimes blooming is used as a special effect, particularly when the projected image is a fantasy sequence, but usually this is an annoying distraction and steps must be taken by the camera technician to reduce its occurrence.

**BLOW-IN** promotional piece, usually on card stock, that is blown by machine between the pages of a magazine and held in place by pressure until the magazine is opened. Most blow-ins serve as REPLY FORMS or have a perforated reply form attached. Since it is not bound into the magazine, the blow-in can get the reader's immediate attention by falling into his or her lap. Unfortunately, blow-ins, unlike BINDINS, are frequently removed and disposed of by the first reader rather than remaining in place until they have delivered their sales message to an interested reader.

The cost of producing a blow-in depends upon the type of paper, the amount of color used, the size of the blow-in, and the quantity ordered. Average costs range from $5 to $30 per thousand. Most advertisers order a two-to-three-months' supply to keep the per piece cost at a minimum. Sizes vary depending upon the space advertising rates of the carrier publication but must conform with U.S. Postal Service postcard size regulations. An average blow-in measures $4'' \times 5^{3}/4''$. There is usually no charge for inserting blow-ins, in contrast to the insertion charges for bind-ins, which average $1 per thousand. Blow-ins are an important source of magazine subscription sales.

**BLOWUP** enlargement of written, printed, or pictorial materials by a photographic process. An advertiser may request a blowup of a print advertisement to be used as a poster in a point-of-purchase display or as a part of the television CAMPAIGN. This technique lends continuity to the series of campaigns.

**BLUE CHIP** *see* BELL COW.

**BLUELINE** *see* BLUEPRINT.

**BLUE PAN** quick camera movement that produces a blurred image; also called *swish*; whipshot; whiz pan. Blue pans are frequently used as a transition from one scene to another in a commercial or other motion picture film.

**BLUEPRINT**
1. photographic print where lines and solid shapes are developed in white on specially prepared blue paper; also called *blue*(s). A blueprint of drawings or photographs to be included in a publication serves as a guide for positioning them in a DUMMY copy of the magazine or other publication. It also assists the printer when making plates for the completed work.
2. plan of action.

**BLUES** *see* BLUEPRINT.

**BLUE SKY** *see* SYNECTICS.

**BLURB** brief mention of a company, its personnel, its product, or its advertising CAMPAIGN in an editorial column of a TRADE MAGAZINE or the press.

**BMC** *see* BULK MAIL CENTER.

**BOARD FADE** in recording or broadcast production, using the equipment in the control booth to fade out the sound rather than fading it out directly in the studio.

**BODY COPY** main copy block of an advertisement as distinguished from headings, subheadings, coupons, logo, captions of illustrations, and the like; also called *body text, text*. The body copy tells the sales story and is usually written as a personal one-on-one conversation. It explains how the product will satisfy the customer's need and appeals to the reader's self-interest. The length of copy will depend on the copywriter's technique, the product being sold, and the sales idea being presented. In some cases it will be a simple sentence; in others, a long paragraph. Generally shorter is better, but the only rule of thumb is that the body copy must sell the product.

**BODY TEXT** *see* BODY COPY.

**BODY TYPE** primary TYPEFACE used for the main body of text in an advertisement, mailing piece, or catalog. Body type should be easy to read and as large as possible, given the space available and the number of words required. Difficult-to-read typefaces, such as ITALICS or script generally should not be used for body type. *See also* DISPLAY TYPE.

**BOILERPLATE COPY** standard sections of BODY COPY that can be used again and again in print communications and/or advertising COPY. An example of boilerplate copy is a paragraph or two detailing the history of a company, which can be used in correspondence, advertising proposals, company reports, newsletters, etc.

**BOLDFACE** type that is darker than the rest of the text with which it is used; abbreviated *bf* or *bold*. Sometimes used for a paragraph heading or for a heading between paragraphs, boldface type draws attention to itself and adds emphasis to a specific idea. It also adds "color" to a page of type through the contrast of dark and light, breaking up the monotone of printed matter. *See also* WEIGHT OF TYPE.

**BOND BORDER** ornamental frame design, similar to that used on formal financial documents such as stocks and bonds, printed on CENTS-OFF COUPONS or direct-mail package COMPONENTS to give the impression of monetary value. Bond borders are especially effective in promotions involving finances, such as insurance or investment advice.

**BOND PAPER** high-quality grade of paper used for letterheads, envelopes, typed reports, and similar office applications. Bond paper is relatively expensive but durable and attractive. *See also* BASIS WEIGHT; BOOK PAPER; NEWSPRINT.

**BONUS CIRCULATION** CIRCULATION of a periodical above the circulation figure guaranteed by the publisher to advertisers. The advertisers are not charged for the additional readership achieved. *See also* CIRCULATION; RATE BASE.

**BONUS PACK** package containing two items that sells for the price of only one of the items. Bonus packs are used frequently to introduce a new product by the same manufacturer (for example, a new fabric softener included in a package with a laundry detergent made by the same company) or to make buyers aware of a companion product to one they already use (for example, a hair conditioner included in a package with shampoo). In addition, manufacturers will sometimes use a bonus pack as an incentive to purchase by attaching a sample size of a product to a full size of the same product. *See also* TWIN PACK.

**BONUS PLAN** promotional technique used primarily by CONTINUITY marketers that provides an incentive for multiple purchases, such as one free book (or record, etc.) for every three books purchased. The buyer is usually billed for shipping and handling charges on the free item.

**BOOK CLUB** direct-mail book marketing device that invites consumers to buy books (usually at reduced rates). NEGATIVE OPTION book clubs send books periodically unless the member instructs the club otherwise, according to a set procedure. POSITIVE OPTION book clubs require the buyer's permission to send a book. Most book clubs have a minimum purchase requirement (usually within a stipulated time frame), known as a *member commitment*. Book clubs were originally created when bookstores were less numerous and mail-order book buying was, in some rural areas, the only option. Many of today's book clubs are geared toward cooking, business, science, or some other particular interest. The best known and biggest of the genre, however, are the general-interest Book-Of-The-Month Club and The Literary Guild. Book clubs pay a royalty to publishers and must produce and sell their own printing of each book. Publishers generally view book clubs as a source of publicity more than as a source of revenue.

**BOOKENDS** 30-second television broadcast commercial split into two 15-second segments, where the two segments are aired in a given time frame but are separated by commercials for other advertisers' products. An example of bookends might be a commercial where the first segment demonstrates a woman taking a pain relief medicine because she has a severe headache, and the second segment demonstrates the same woman feeling energized and ready for action after her headache has been relieved by the product. Each segment is called a bookend. Bookends are sold as 30-second SPOTS and programmed into the same COMMERICAL BREAK.

**BOOKLET** series of printed pages bound together, in some cases by SADDLE WIRE stitching, and covered with the same paper used for inside pages. The contents may be an advertising message, instructions for product use, or detailed information concerning an advertiser's services. Manufacturers of household appliances, automobiles, computers, and stereo equipment all make use of booklets.

Booklets are used most often as sales tools or direct-mail pieces when the sales story is complicated or highly technical, and the item is costly (such as a computer). Colorful booklets provided by the manufacturer can aid in making the sale. They are also used for sales promotion—for example, recipe books are often attached to various liquor products, or books on lawn care or planting may be given away with garden equipment.

**BOOK PAPER** various grades of highly durable paper suitable for use in books. The standard size of a sheet is 25" × 38". Book paper can be either coated or uncoated. *See also* BASIS WEIGHT; BOND PAPER; COATED PAPER; NEWSPRINT.

**BOOK RATE** *see* FOURTH CLASS.

**BOOM**

**In general:** marked increase or upsurge, as an economic boom or a baby boom.

**Television production:**

1. movable, adjustable mechanical arm that acts as a support for the performers' microphone when telecasting. The boom keeps the microphone just above and in front of the speaking performer and out of sight of the camera. In this way, the volume is maintained at an even level and extraneous noise is shut out. The boom is telescopic and rests on a vertical stand. It can move forward, backward, or sideways. It can also be moved up or down, by means of a crank on the stand, and thus cover the entire stage area as required by the action on the set.
2. raise or lower the mechanical arm (boom) as in "boom up" or "boom down."
3. raise or lower a camera that has been mounted on a camera crane, as in "boom up" or "boom down."
   **Theater production:** stationary vertical pipe used for mounting spotlights on a stage.

**BORAX** in retailing, merchandise that appears to be of high quality but in fact is not. This type of merchandise is sometimes used in advertisements as a lead to bring customers into the store.

**BORDER** continuous design around the edge of a printed advertisement. It serves to set the ad apart from other ads on a page and also pulls together the elements of the advertisement. The border can be anything from a simple line to an elaborate, detailed, or highly decorative design. Depending on the talent and time available, the border can be drawn by the artist and submitted to the printer along with the LAYOUT, or the printer can set the border as part of the process of typesetting the ad copy.

**BOSTON BOX** *see* GROWTH SHARE MATRIX.

**BOSTON CONSULTING GROUP APPROACH** *see* GROWTH-SHARE MATRIX.

**BOTTLE HANGER** piece of heavy paper imprinted with an advertising message, and cut and folded so that it appears as a kind of collar when hung around the neck of a bottle. Often found in supermarkets or grocery stores, bottle hangers are an economical way to attract new customers and to reach known consumers of a product with information about a special sale of that product or about a new or companion product. Bottle hangers are also sometimes hung on supermarket items during a political campaign to reach large numbers of people in a local shopping area.

**BOTTOM-UP PLANNING** strategy used in corporate planning whereby information is gathered from sales personnel, product managers, advertising personnel, and other members working in the organizational unit to set goals and create a MARKETING PLAN. Bottom-up planning is considered good for morale because it fosters employees to participation in corporate planning. However, the strategy is sometimes difficult to coordinate because many different assumptions about the same concept must be considered. For example, there may be conflicting ideas about the impact of advertising on the sales of a particular product, making the establishment of a consistent and integrated plan quite difficult. *See also* TOP-DOWN PLANNING.

**BOUNCE BACK** promotion included in a merchandise shipment that asks the buyer to make another purchase from the same seller. A CATALOG HOUSE might include another copy of the same catalog from which the order was made.

**BOUTIQUE AGENCY** agency that specializes in the creative aspects of advertising. Boutique agencies offer only those services that have to do with the creation of advertisements. The staff is usually small and is composed entirely of COPYWRITERS and artists. Generally, the talent is very high caliber, and the services are purchased on a fee basis by the job. Often, a boutique agency will call in independent or FREE-LANCE writers and artists.

**BOXTOP OFFER** manufacturer's offer to a consumer of a free gift, or reduced-price item, or some kind of premium or refund, in exchange for a boxtop or other proof of purchase of the manufacturer's product. The offer is a sales promotion technique used to attract a potential user and to induce him or her to purchase the product right away. The various cereal brands offer premiums very often. Some manufacturers offer premiums on an ongoing basis, such as the flat silverware from General Mills.

**BPA STATEMENT** *see* ABC STATEMENT.

**BRAINSTORMING** idea-generating technique often used in advertising by a creative team to spark creativity. The team will gather in a group and throw out spontaneous ideas without evaluation until they hit upon something that may be useful. In this process nothing is too silly or farfetched to be suggested. The process helps to make the leap from the visualization of an idea to the concrete words and pictures that will actually form the basis of the advertising CAMPAIGN.

**BRANCH POST OFFICE**  U.S. Postal Service facility linked to a main post office in a city or town and located outside the corporate limits of that city or town. *See also* COMMUNITY POST OFFICE.

**BRANCH STORE**  retail store that is auxiliary to a larger store owned and operated by the same person, persons, or company. Usually a branch store is smaller and carries a less extensive line of merchandise than its larger counterpart. It may be located in the same region, but in a suburban setting rather than in any urban setting like the main store, or it may be located in an entirely different geographic area.

**BRAND**  identifying mark, symbol, word(s), or combination of same that separates one company's product or services from another firm's. *Brand* is a comprehensive term that includes all BRAND NAMES and TRADEMARKS.

**BRAND ASSOCIATION**  degree to which a particular BRAND is associated with the general product category in the mind of the consumer (*share of mind*). Often a consumer will ask for a product by the specific brand name rather than the general name—for example, a person wanting facial tissues may ask for Kleenex. When this happens, the consumer is making a brand association.

**BRAND ATTITUDE**  opinion of consumers toward a product determined through market research. The BRAND ATTITUDE will tell what people think about a product or services, whether the product answers a consumer need, and just how much the product is wanted by the consumer. Knowledge of brand attitude is very helpful in planning an advertising CAMPAIGN.

**BRAND AWARENESS**  having knowledge of the existence of a BRAND. Because brand awareness is considered the first step in the sale, the primary goal of some advertising CAMPAIGNS is simply to make the TARGET MARKET aware that a particular brand exists. Often, this effort alone will sell the product (or service).

**BRAND CATEGORY**  generic classification of products or services. Similar and competing products (or services) all fall into the same brand category. For example, all the different perfumes fall into the brand category of perfume because they all satisfy the same consumer need.

**BRAND DEVELOPMENT**  measure of the infiltration of a product's sales, usually per thousand population. If 100 people in 1,000 buy a product, the product has a brand development of 10. *See also* BRAND DEVELOPMENT INDEX.

**BRAND DEVELOPMENT INDEX (BDI)**  percentage of a brand's sales in an area in relation to the population in that area as compared to the sales throughout the entire U.S. in relation to the total U.S. population. For example, if Brand X has 15% of its U.S. sales in Area A, in which 20% of the U.S. population lives, the BDI for Area A is 75. The BDI allows the media planner to see the concentration of current customers of a brand on a market-by-market basis and thus concentrate advertising dollars in the markets where the brand enjoys the most usage.

**BRAND EXTENSION** addition of a new product to an already established line of products under the same BRAND NAME. Brand extension allows the new product the benefit of the older product's established reputation. For example, at its introduction to the marketplace, Ivory Shampoo already enjoyed the reputation of Ivory Soap, "the clean, pure soap." In addition, if consumers considered the brand name Ivory to mean a trusted product, they would already consider the new shampoo in a favorable light. *See also* DIFFERENTIATION STRATEGY; LINE EXTENSION.

## BRAND FRANCHISE
1. arrangement between a brand name manufacturer and a wholesaler or retailer that gives the wholesaler or retailer the exclusive right to sell the brand manufacturer's product in a specific territory. This arrangement is usually done by contractual agreement over a period of time. A brand franchise allows the wholesaler or retailer to sell the product in a noncompetitive market and therefore to set price limitations as the traffic will bear.
2. loyalty toward a brand by consumers. *See also* BRAND LOYALTY.

**BRAND IMAGE** qualities that consumers associate with a specific BRAND, expressed in terms of human behavior and desires, but that also relate to price, quality, and situational use of the brand. For example: A brand such as Mercedes Benz will conjure up a strong public image because of its sensory and physical characteristics as well as its price. This image is not inherent in the brand name but is created through advertising.

**BRAND LOYALTY** degree to which a consumer repeatedly purchases a BRAND. For advertisers to achieve their ultimate goal of brand loyalty, the consumer must perceive that the brand offers the right combination of quality and price. Many factors influence brand loyalty, such as consumer attitudes (see BRAND ATTITUDE), family or peer pressure, and friendship with the salesperson. The advertiser must consider all such factors. The degree of brand loyalty—that is, the brand's MARKET SHARE—is known as the brand franchise. Brand loyalty is stronger on established products than on new products. *See also* BRAND SWITCHING.

**BRAND MANAGER** marketing manager for a BRAND; also called *product manager*. This person makes most of the advertising decisions for that brand. Often in a company with many different brand name products, each product will have a brand manager compete with the others as if the products were competitive. Each may use a different advertising agency, and each will have a separate advertising budget. This system is advantageous for the company because all products within the company should receive equal attention. Any problems that arise for individual products should receive prompt responses, and advertising opportunities for the products will be quickly seized.

**BRAND NAME** that part of a BRAND, TRADEMARK, or SERVICE MARK that can be spoken, as distinguished from an identifying symbol. A brand name may consist of a word, letter, or group of words or letters.

**BRAND NAMES FOUNDATION, INC.** nonprofit business organization founded in 1943 and composed of BRAND NAME manufacturers, advertising media, and consulting retailers. Organized for the purpose of maintaining a favorable opinion toward brand names and brand name marketing practices among consumers, the foundation sponsors programs and public-service announcements designed to develop consumer and trade understanding of how brand name competition stimulates progress and how the purchase of brand name products is an assurance of maximum return for the dollars spent. Abbreviated BNF.

**BRAND POTENTIAL INDEX (BPI)** relationship between a brand's MARKET DEVELOPMENT INDEX and BRAND DEVELOPMENT INDEX (BDI) in a particular market area. The brand potential index is used to predict future sales and to aid in planning future advertising budget allocations.

**BRAND PREFERENCE** selective demand for a company's brand rather than a product; the degree to which consumers prefer one brand over another. In an attempt to build brand preference advertising, the advertising must persuade a TARGET AUDIENCE to consider the advantages of a brand, often by building its reputation as a long-established and trusted name in the industry. If the advertising is successful, the target customer will choose the brand over other brands in *any* category. *See also* BRAND SWITCHING.

**BRAND SHARE** amount of dollars spent by consumers on a particular brand as compared to the amount of dollars spent by consumers on all competitive brands in the same category, figured in terms of percentages; also called *market share*, *share of market*. Companies set marketing goals to achieve a specific brand share, and plan their strategies to meet those goals.

**BRAND SWITCHING** consumer decision to purchase a product brand different from that previously or usually purchased. Brand switching can be instigated by price promotions, in-store displays, superior availability, perceived improvements or innovations in competitive brands, desire for NOVELTY, number of available brands, perceived risk, frequency of purchase, changes in quality, or level of satisfaction with the most recent purchase. Brand switching is most common with products that have no great perceived variation in quality across brands such as bottled water, dairy products, or paper towels. *See also* BRAND LOYALTY.

**BREAK-EVEN ANALYSIS**   financial analysis that identifies the point at which expenses equal gross revenue for a zero net difference. For example, if a mailing costs $100 and each item generates $5 in revenue, the break-even point is at 20 items sold. A profit will be made on items sold in excess of 20. A loss will result on sales under 20. The break-even point may be analyzed in terms of units, as above, or dollars.

**BREAK FOR COLOR**   printing process that involves breaking an image into its component primary colors. *See also* FOUR-COLOR PROCESS; TWO-COLOR PROCESS.

**BRIDGE**
**Broadcast:** sound effect, narration, music, DISSOLVE (*see* FADE IN; FADE OUT) between two scenes in a television or radio program or commercial, used to indicate a transition and link from one scene to the other.
**Print advertising:** run an advertisement across the center margin of two facing pages (GUTTER) in a magazine or newspaper.

**BRIGHTNESS**   degree to which paper reflects light. Generally, the higher the grade of paper, the greater the brightness. Brightness can impact the scan capability of optical scanning equipment. *See also* OPTICAL CHARACTER RECOGNITION.

**BROADCAST ADVERTISERS REPORTS**   organization that monitors television commercials in 75 markets. It issues reports (called BAR reports) concerning advertised products and brands and their positioning in the broadcast schedule. The reports are offered by subscription to advertisers, advertising agencies, stations, and NETWORKS as a record of commercial activity.

**BROADCASTER**
**1.** one who delivers or sponsors an announcement, commercial, or program on a radio or television station or network, including station and network owners or operators, performers, and advertisers.
**2.** owner or operator of a radio or television station or network.

**BROADCAST MEDIA**   electronic instrumentation of radio and television, including local radio and television stations, radio and television NETWORKS, and CABLE TELEVISION systems. Because of their ability to reach vast numbers of people, broadcast media play a very important role in any advertising CAMPAIGN that needs to reach a broad market base. The broadcast media wield a very pervasive influence in most Americans' lives.

**BROADCAST MUSIC, INC.**   nonprofit organization of music publishers that functions to protect the performance rights to musical compositions copyrighted by its members. It grants licenses to radio and television stations, hotels, nightclubs, amusement parks, restaurants, and other public places to play their copyrighted music. Abbreviated BMI. *See also* AMERICAN SOCIETY COMPOSERS; AUTHORS AND PUBLISHERS.

**BROADCAST RATING COUNCIL** *see* ELECTRONIC MEDIA RATING COUNCIL (EMRC).

**BROADSIDE** tool often used in direct mail when the advertiser's message is lengthy or requires illustration and needs hard-hitting impact. Larger than a typical folder in a business envelope, a broadside can also be used as a store poster or window display. The advertising message is printed in bold type in one or more colors on one side of heavy stock paper, and by virtue of its size delivers a forceful impression. In DIRECT MAIL ADVERTISING, the broadside is folded to a compact size, which can be mailed or delivered personally.

**BROCHURE** fancy BOOKLET that differs from an ordinary booklet in that it is constructed of heavier quality paper, uses extensive color and expensive type, and is generally put together with special care. The name originates from the French verb *brocher*, meaning "to stitch," indicating a booklet bound by stitching, although today other binding methods are also used. Brochures are frequently part of a retail advertising campaign and are sometimes distributed with the Sunday papers. They are also enclosed in direct mail and considered to be the "workhorse" of the direct-mail package.

**BROKER** AGENT authorized to buy or sell for another organization or individual. *See also* DEALER; LIST BROKER; MANUFACTURER'S REPRESENTATIVE.

**BROKERAGE ALLOWANCE** commission paid by the seller in a transaction to the broker who arranged the sale, based upon some percentage of the selling price. For example, a LIST BROKER is paid a brokerage allowance for list rentals he or she arranges. A brokerage allowance usually refers only to transactions in which the broker does not take possession of the goods sold—for example, a list rental.

**BRONZE PROOF** *see* ACETATE PROOF.

**BRONZING** printing method that applies bronze powder to paper, producing a metallic sheen. Bronzing is frequently used for booklet covers and invitations.

**BROWN GOODS** audio/visual and consumer electronic products such as televisions, radios, and stereo sets. Originally this merchandise was manufactured in brown wooden or simulated wooden cabinets, hence, brown goods. However, with advancements in technology and changes in decorating styles, the term has come to be considered antiquated and is seldom used. *See also* ORANGE GOODS, RED GOODS, YELLOW GOODS.

**BUBBLE WRAP**  *see* BLISTER PACK.

**BUCKEYE**  advertisement with an obviously unsophisticated LAYOUT and lacking unity and balance. Visually, a buckeye appears crude and is characterized by artless copy and overdone graphic elements.

**BUCKSLIP**  small INSERT added to a mailing package; it is usually about the size of a dollar bill. Buckslips are an easy way to add information that supports the primary purpose of the mailing (such as an incentive for early replies known as an "early bird"offer) or that supports a secondary purpose (such as an advertisement for another product that can be used in conjunction with the primary product being sold—e.g., golf clubs and club covers). Buckslips can be created at much less cost than other package components and can serve as a last-minute addition if new or different information must be provided.

**BUFFALO PLAN**  computer program originally developed in Buffalo, New York, that is utilized by wholesalers and newsstand distributors to track magazine sales and return data.

**BULK**
**Direct mail:** second-, third-, or fourth-class mail, sent in large volumes at special postage rates. *See also* BULK MAIL.
**Magazines:** subscriptions or single-copy orders sold in quantities greater than one per issue to a single buyer; also called *bulk* order.
**Printing:** measurement of the thickness of paper.

**BULK CIRCULATION**  *see* CIRCULATION.

**BULK DISCOUNT**  reduction in per unit selling price made to reward buyers of bulk (large) quantities and to encourage future bulk purchases. The postage discounts offered by the U.S. Postal Service are available only for BULK MAILINGS. Advertisers may receive bulk discounts for purchasing bulk quantities of media space or time. *See also* FLAT RATE.

**BULKING**  process used to increase the BULK (thickness) of less costly paper stock to that of more costly higher-bulk stock. Bulking is used to make a book with few pages appear thicker, and to achieve the paper thickness required by the U.S. Postal Service for postcards (at least 0.007 inches), at a lower cost than using higher-bulk STOCK. Bulking does not affect the BASIS WEIGHT of paper.

**BULK MAIL**  second-, third-, or fourth-class mail, including magazines, catalogs, and parcels, mailed in large quantities, of identical pieces for which the mailer can get significant quantity discounts on postage, depending upon the class of mail and whether the mailer is a profit or nonprofit organization, and also upon how the mail is sorted before entry into the postal system (e.g., by carrier route or by five-digit ZIP code). The discounted postage rate for presorted bulk mail is called bulk rate. *See also* CONSOLIDATION LEVEL; PRESORT.

Bulk mailing requires an application fee as well as an annual fee. For third class, the mailing must contain a minimum of 200 pieces, which must be bundled separately according to state and broken down by zip code. In a direct-mail advertising campaign, where the advertiser is attempting to reach thousands of prospective buyers, the savings can be considerable.

**BULK MAIL CENTER (BMC)** U.S. Postal Service facility for processing BULK MAIL, including second-, third-, and fourth-class mail. There were 21 BMCs throughout the country in the mid-1980s. *See also* BULK MAIL SYSTEM.

**BULK MAILING** *see* BULK MAIL.

**BULK MAIL SYSTEM** U.S. Postal Service distribution network, including BULK MAIL CENTERS and AUXILIARY SERVICE FACILITIES, dedicated to handling bulk second-, third-, and fourth-class mail.

**BULK ORDER** *see* BULK.

**BULK RATE** *see* BULK MAIL.

**BULLDOG EDITION**
1. edition of a daily morning newspaper that is distributed and sold at newsstands the night before the date it bears. The actual origin of the name is uncertain, although some say it originated in New York City at a time when there were three morning newspapers—the *World*, the *Herald*, and the *Journal*—who "fought like bulldogs" to be the first to get their edition on the street. (Loosely, the term has come to mean the earliest edition of any daily paper, including afternoon papers.)
2. sections of the Sunday newspaper printed and distributed early in the week throughout the cosmopolitan area and in outlying rural areas, which are usually placed on sale prior to Sunday.

**BULLET** in print production, a heavy mark, sometimes in the shape of a bullet (but more often a boldface dot), that is used to indicate an item of special interest or some special features on a page of copy.

**BULLETIN**
1. brief account or statement, as of an important news event, issued for the information of the public.
2. information sheet circulated in an organization.
3. see PAINTED DISPLAY.

**BULLPEN** art studio within an ADVERTISING AGENCY where all creative ARTWORK as well as special techniques or special effects can be done. The bullpen staff consists of artists, hand-letterers, retouchers, PASTEUP personnel, and artists who specialize in a particular area, such as fashion illustrators or photographers. The availability of a bullpen relieves the ART DIRECTOR of the responsibility of maintaining a list of freelancers, who may prove unreliable or unavailable. It also lends continuity to the creative package offered by the agency and serves as a training ground for personnel working toward promotion to art director.

**BUM** bundle of empty canvas mail SACKS.

**BUMPER STICKER** display poster, with a message imprinted on one side and a sticky substance applied to the other, so that it can be affixed to the bumper of a motor vehicle. Most frequently, bumper stickers are used to advertise places that are reachable by motor vehicle, such as amusement parks, beaches, restaurants, motels, and resorts. They are also used by private interest groups for special messages, or are featured in political campaigns or public-service campaigns ("Don't Drink and Drive," sponsored by MADD—Mothers Against Drunk Drivers) or in public relations announcements ("Virginia Is for Lovers," sponsored by the Virginia Bureau of Tourism).

**BUMP EXPOSURE** in halftone photography, process in which the CONTACT SCREEN through which the artwork is shot is removed for a short time to reduce the size and number of DOTS and to increase the white areas of the image by increasing the exposure of the film to light.

**BUNDLE**
1. in marketing, selling more than one product together for a single price. For example, several software packages might be bundled and included in the purchase of a personal computer. Bundling is used by marketers to take advantage of the high demand for one product and sell another simultaneously or to increase the demand for both products through a perceived synergy between the products offered. *See also* TYING AGREEMENT.
2. in direct mail, two or more mail PACKAGES tied together prior to entry into the U.S. Postal Service system. *See also* CONSOLIDATION; PALLET; SACK.

**BUREAU OF ADVERTISING (B OF A)** nonprofit service division of the American Newspaper Publishers Association responsible for promotion of the newspaper press as a vehicle for advertisers. The bureau conducts research in specific markets and in newspaper readership, and provides advertisers and advertising agencies with the results of this research and with various statistical information gleaned from the research.

**BURIED OFFER** *see* HIDDEN OFFER.

**BURKE TEST** research tool to measure audience recall, administered by Burke Marketing Research, Inc., a TV-commercial for the benefit of television advertisers. This information is used by advertisers to evaluate the effectiveness of their COMMERCIALS.. On the day after a commercial is aired, Burke personnel conduct telephone interviews with a previously chosen SAMPLE audience, asking questions about the selling points the advertiser hoped to communicate through the commercial. As a result of these interviews, the extent of communication and BRAND NAME recognition can be assessed. *See also* DAY-AFTER RECALL.

**BURN**
**Film production:** filming, image that remains after the camera has focused on a shining object and then withdrawn. The picture tends to retain an after-ghost of the original image, which actually burns into the camera's picture tube.
**Printing:** term used for the part of the printing process when the image is imprinted on the PLATE (*plate exposure*).

**BURNISH** darken an area of a PRINTING PLATE which area would otherwise reproduce a lighter tone. This is done by rubbing the desired section with a polished steel tool that flattens the tops of the metal so that the section will absorb more ink.

**BURST**
1. *see* BURSTER.
2. graphic device in the shape of a jagged circle, containing a brief, attention-getting sales message—for example, "Free sample inside" or "New and improved"—that is set off from the main BODY COPY. Bursts are most often used on product packages and labels but are also used in direct mail on OUTER ENVELOPES and letters.

**BURST ADVERTISING** *see* SATURATION.

**BURSTER** machine that separates CONTINUOUS FORMS after printing.

**BUSINESS CYCLE** recurrent periods (about $2^1/2$ years on the average) in which the nation's economy moves in and out of recession and recovery phases. There is much controversy over whether money should be spent on advertising during the recessionary phase of the cycle, but there seems to be some evidence that companies who do not cut back on their advertising budgets fare slightly better than those who do. However, although there are several studies, they are essentially inconclusive.

**BUSINESS DATE** date assigned to DOCUMENTS by a firm's FULFILLMENT department to enable the documents to be processed according to a schedule. Business dates are also used to track and control batches of documents after processing. The business date usually corresponds to the date the document was received by the fulfillment department or the date money received with the document was deposited in a bank. Business dates are also part of the audit process. *See also* AUDIT BUREAU OF CIRCULATIONS; AUDIT TRAIL.

**BUSINESS ECONOMICS AND CORPORATE RESEARCH** type of research activity that seeks to evaluate the most common corporate marketing practices, such as short-range forecasting, long-range forecasting, business trend studies, pricing studies, acquisition studies, location studies, and export or internal studies, to gain information that can be used to identify and define marketing opportunities or problems.

**BUSINESS LIST** list of persons at business addresses, or of individuals who buy business-related products, maintained for the promotion of business products. *See also* BUSINESS-TO-BUSINESS ADVERTISING.

**BUSINESS PAPER ADVERTISING** *see* BUSINESS-TO-BUSINESS ADVERTISING.

**BUSINESS/PROFESSIONAL ADVERTISING ASSOCIATION (BPAA)** organization headquartered in New York and founded in 1922 as the National Industrial Advertisers Association to enhance professionalism for all business communicators and to further the development of business, industrial, and professional advertising. In 1959, the name was changed to Business/Professional Advertising Association. Its membership includes business and professional marketing communicators representing advertisers, agencies, and publishers. BPAA members have access to the Association's marketing data library, employment service, professional development seminars, newsletters, publications, and special studies.

**BUSINESS PUBLICATIONS AUDIT OF CIRCULATIONS (BPA)** nonprofit organization whose purpose is to audit the circulation of business publications. Its membership is composed of leading trade and industrial publishers. The BPA circulation-audit reports; provide the business advertiser with statistical information that is very useful in selecting the most appropriate publications for advertising. *See also* ABC STATEMENT; BUSINESS-TO-BUSINESS ADVERTISING.

**BUSINESS REPLY CARD (BRC)** promotion reply postcard preaddressed to the mailer and usually sent as PERMIT MAIL, requiring no

‖‖‖

NO POSTAGE
NECESSARY
IF MAILED
IN THE
UNITED STATES

**BUSINESS REPLY MAIL**
FIRST CLASS  PERMIT NO. HAUPPAUGE, NY

*POSTAGE WILL BE PAID BY:*
**BARRON'S EDUCATIONAL SERIES, INC.**
**250 WIRELESS BLVD**
**HAUPPAUGE, NEW YORK 11788**

postage payment by the responder. Mailers pay a fee of approximately $300 per year for a business reply permit. Business reply cards, which are mailed at first-class postage rates, make it easy for people to respond to a promotion. *See also* BUSINESS REPLY MAIL; INDICIA.

**BUSINESS REPLY ENVELOPE (BRE)** promotion reply envelope, for orders, payments, or inquiries, preaddressed to the seller. BREs are usually PERMIT MAIL, requiring no postage payment by the responder. Business reply envelopes mail at first-class rates. *See also* BUSINESS REPLY CARD; BUSINESS REPLY MAIL.

**BUSINESS REPLY MAIL (BRM)** preaddressed cards, envelopes, labels, or cartons that can be mailed without prepayment of postage. After delivery of the mailing piece, the U.S. Postal Service collects the postage due, based upon a printed permit number on the envelope that identifies the addressee. The addressee pays an annual fee of approximately $300 for the permit. *See also* BUSINESS REPLY CARD; BUSINESS REPLY ENVELOPE; PERMIT MAIL.

**BUSINESS-TO-BUSINESS ADVERTISING** advertising intended to communicate among businesses, as opposed to CONSUMER ADVERTISING. Business-to-business advertising is directed at business people or companies who buy (or *specify*—such as architects, engineers, or contractors) products for business use. Businesses advertise in their own trade publications (a practice called *business paper advertising*), of which there are three times as many as CONSUMER MAGAZINES. Business-to-business advertising accounts for approximately $3 billion annually in advertising revenue. *See also* AMERICAN BUSINESS PRESS, INC.; BUSINESS PUBLICATIONS AUDIT OF CIRCULATIONS.

**BUSY** descriptive term for a print layout where the elements are excessive and seem to be fighting each other, thus detracting from the advertising message.

**BUYER** one who purchases goods or services; also called *customer*. A consumer makes purchases for her own use or purpose. A professional buyer makes BULK purchases on behalf of a retailer or wholesaler. A MEDIA BUYER purchases media space or time for an advertiser.

**BUYER READINESS STAGES** *see* BUYER READINESS STATES.

**BUYER READINESS STATES** also called *buyer readiness stages*, the six decision-making stages through which consumers normally pass on their way to making a purchase. To be effective, the marketer must know at which stage of readiness the consumers in the TARGET AUDIENCE stand and to what stage the consumer must be moved so that the marketer can select correct communication objectives for the marketing plan.

These stages are (1) awareness—the marketer must be able to gauge the consumer's awareness of the product and be prepared to launch a campaign to build consumer awareness; (2) knowledge—consumers may be aware of a product but know very little about it, making product knowledge the focus of the marketing campaign; (3) liking—if consumers know the product, how do they feel about it? (4) preference—consumers may like the product but not prefer it to others, thus the product's positive qualities must be promoted; (5) conviction—consumers might prefer the product but not have any conviction about purchasing it, thus the marketer must build conviction that purchasing the product is the right thing to do; (6) purchase—some consumers may have conviction about the product but might not actually get around to buying it, thus marketers must lead consumers to take this last step with marketing strategies such as trial purchases, premium offerings with purchase, or offering the product at a low price.

The buyer readiness states are important considerations in any marketing plan, and the marketing plan must remain flexible so that it can be adjusted to keep pace with the changing distribution of buyer readiness.

**BUYING COMMITTEE** group of individuals who represent both wholesalers and the retail chains that act as outlets for the wholesalers' merchandise and who decide by committee upon products to be carried (especially new products), store sales promotions, special offers, and other such matters affecting retail sales in the stores or chains represented. The buying committee functions in the spirit of FAIR TRADE.

**BUYING CRITERIA** standards by which prospective purchasers of a product evaluate the product. These standards might relate to a product in terms of its technical specifications, the manufacturer of the product in terms of the manufacturer's reputation for quality or the lack thereof, or the person selling the product in terms of the salesperson's credibility, expertise, or trustworthiness.

**BUYING DECISION** series of choices made by a consumer prior to making a purchase that begins once the consumer has established a willingness to buy. The consumer must then decide where to make the purchase, what brand, model, or size to purchase, when to make the purchase, how much to spend, and what method of payment will be used. The marketer attempts to influence each of these decisions by supplying information that may shape the consumer's evaluation process. *See also* BUY PHASES.

**BUYING INCENTIVE** premium in the form of extra merchandise, a DISCOUNT, or a gift, offered to the prospective purchaser of an item or service in the hope that this bonus will motivate the purchase of the item. This incentive is used successfully in retail clothing chains and generally works very effectively as an advertising technique to bring traffic into the store. Familiar examples of buying incentives are "Buy One, Get One Free" or "Buy One For The Regular Price, Get The Next One For $1.00."

**BUYING LOADER** gift offered to a retailer by a manufacturer as a bonus for purchasing the manufacturer's merchandise; also called DEALER LOADER. This gift can be in the form of a PREMIUM or of a discount on inventory. *See also* DISPLAY LOADER; LOADING.

**BUYING POWER INDEX (BPI)** source for DEMOGRAPHIC data used by the *Survey of Buying Power* published annually by *Sales and Marketing Management* magazine. The *Survey of Buying Power* reports current data by metropolitan area, state, and region. Statistics such as retail sales by merchandise category, personal disposable income, and five-year projections are included in the survey. The BPI identifies these market factors and correlates them with the area's potential for these factors, and then combines the factors and their potential into a weighted index. The index is based on the area's share of the nation's disposable personal income, retail sales, and population.

Using the BPI a manufacturer would look up a particular metropolitan area, state, or region to find out what percent of the nation's disposable income is in this market along with the percent of the nation's retail sales and the percent of the nation's population. The buying power index for that particular area would then be calculated by multiplying each factor by a weighted value from a prescribed formula and then adding all three factors together. The result will tell the manufacturer the percentage of total national buying power in that particular area.

**BUY-OR-DIE MESSAGE** promotional copy directed toward INACTIVE direct-mail customers stating that they will be removed from the mailing list unless they make a purchase. For example, the message may state, "Although we value you as a customer, our costs have increased to the point where we'll be unable to send you future issues of this catalog unless we receive an order from you soon." The marketer is betting that the customer enjoys receiving the catalog, wishes to remain on the list, and will make a purchase from which the marketer can more than recover the cost of mailing catalogs to that customer. Customers who respond to a buy-or-die message may become more frequent buyers in the future.

**BUYOUT** one-time payment to talent appearing in a television or radio commercial, which purchases all rights to the performance in that commercial. Talent new to the profession is usually purchased on a buyout basis, since the performers lack the buying power to negotiate a residual arrangement; which would require payment every time that commercial appears. Given the life of most commercials, a buyout is usually more economical for the advertiser.

**BUY PHASES** series of stages that individuals or groups go through when making purchasing decisions. Generally there are eight buy phases: need recognition, need description, product specification, seller identification, proposal solicitation, proposal evaluation and selection, ordering procedures and order route specifications, and performance review.

**BYLINE**  line that precedes the text of a story or article and names the writer of the piece. It is called a byline because it tells by whom the piece is written. The term normally applies to journalism, although bylines have been used in advertising copy when the endorser is well-known.

**BY-PRODUCT**  merchandise sold by periodical publishers that is incidental to the publication itself, such as back issue binders, calendars, tote bags, and books.

**BYTE**  binary data stored on a computer consisting of a group of eight consecutive BITS (binary digits) that usually constitute one character.

# C

**CABLE TELEVISION**  independent service, purchased by subscription, whereby television signals are carried to households by direct wires (cables). Begun in the late 1940s as *Community Antenna Television (CATV)*, cable television was a method of improving over-the-air television broadcasting, particularly in remote areas where reception was difficult. Essentially, CATV operated by means of a huge master antenna, which picked up over-the-air television signals and then transmitted the signals to subscriber homes by cable.

As the years have passed, cable television service has grown, and with the launching of the Satcom satellite in 1975, a great many more stations and services have become available for subscribers. Satellite transmission has made possible the development of cable-exclusive networks such as ESPN and the Cable News Network, which have been incorporated into the cable system's basic service. It is estimated that by the year 2000 every home will have access to cable service.

Because cable is now available in large and small markets and delivers local, regional, and faraway stations, as well as cable-exclusive networks, the advertiser's media options for delivering commercials have been greatly expanded. In addition to the traditional networks —ABC, CBS, NBC—and their local stations, the advertiser can now consider *superstations*, which send their signals via satellite to subscribing cable systems throughout the country; *basic cable networks*, such as ESPN, MTV, or Cable News Network; and *local cable systems programs* offering programs such as the local high school football game. Cable television does not yet rely on advertiser support in the same way that over-the-air networks and stations do, but cable ad revenue is growing. At present, approximately 6% of the amount spent in regular network and SPOT TELEVISION advertising is spent on cable—approximately $600 million in 1985.

In addition to basic cable service, most cable systems offer noncommercial movie channels for an additional fee to subscribers, for example, Home Box Office (HBO), Showtime, or Cinemax; also called PAY TV. These movie channels create a problem for advertisers, because generally the audience for this noncommercial alternative is the same upscale viewing audience that advertisers are trying to reach through traditional television outlets.

*See also* AUDIENCE FRAGMENTATION; INTERACTIVE TELEVISION.

**CAD** *see* CAD/CAM.

**CAD/CAM (COMPUTER-AIDED DESIGN/COMPUTER-AIDED MANUFACTURING)** class of computer that electronically produces and modifies graphic images utilized in mechanical design or drafting tasks and manufacturing processes. CAD/CAM devices can bring a new design concept from prototype to product by interfacing with manufacturing machines. For example, an auto part can be designed on a CATHODE-RAY TUBE (CRT) DISPLAY screen utilizing a CAD/CAM device. That same device can pass on instructions to machines that mill, cut, and lathe steel in conformance with design specifications, to produce a finished product. CAD/CAM devices can also be used in PACKAGE DESIGN and a variety of other design applications.

**CAGE** part of the FULFILLMENT operation that receives, opens, and sorts mail and prepares bank deposits from all monies received. The name is derived from old-time fulfillment operations that were enclosed by metal fences or gates for security. This level of security was necessary when cash, rather than checks or money orders, was frequently sent through the mail. *See also* CASHIER.

**CALENDER ROLLS** cast-iron rollers sometimes used in papermaking. To make the surface of the paper smooth, paper is pressed between the calendar rollers of a papermaking machine prior to being wound on reels. Most papers other than ANTIQUE FINISHED papers are calendered. The degree of smoothness achieved is controlled by the amount of pressure applied to the rollers. Calendering produces an eggshell finish, VELLUM FINISH, or ENGLISH FINISH. *See also* FINISH; SUPERCALENDER.

**CALL-BACK**
1. second or subsequent call made to a performer asking him/her to audition or interview again. Talent is usually eliminated in rounds, and several call-backs may be needed before any role is actually filled.
2. subsequent call made by an interviewer in a survey to reach a previously unavailable respondent or as part of a continued survey project.

**CALL BLOCKAGE** in telemarketing, failure to receive a call made to an INBOUND TELEPHONE center because the caller receives a busy signal. Blockage rates are usually expressed in terms of calls blocked as a percent of calls offered. Sophisticated telephone systems called switches can be used to place a prescribed number of callers on hold before producing busy signals. It is up to the telemarketer to manage the length of time spent on hold against the number of calls blocked. Most telemarketers strive to maintain a call blockage rate of less than 5% with no more than 25 seconds average hold time. *See also* ABANDON RATE.

**CALL LETTERS** combination of letters assigned by the FEDERAL COMMUNICATIONS COMMISSION that identify any broadcast station. The initial call letter is W for stations east of the Mississippi and K for all those west of the Mississippi. (There are a few exceptions to this rule, because some stations were licensed before FCC regulations came into being.) The additional letters may represent an abbreviation such as WABC (ABC representing American Broadcasting Company) or may form a word that describes or advertises the station's format, such as WNEW or WJOY. The FCC requires that all stations must identify themselves by their call letters on a regular schedule throughout the broadcast day as well as at the beginning and end of programming every day.

**CALLOUT** phrases or sentences used to identify or call attention to elements in a LAYOUT, photo, or drawing. Placed outside the margin of the layout, photo, or drawing and connected by a straight line to the feature it describes, a callout is used to emphasize or explain the various elements depicted. Callouts can be used in the finished advertisement to note features of special interest, or they can work as aids to printing personnel to call attention to particular printing directions.

**CALL REPORT** report kept by an advertising agency of conferences between agency representatives and current or prospective advertiser clients; also called *conference report*, *contact report*. The call report tells when the meeting took place, who was present, and what was discussed.

**CALL TO ACTION** statement usually found near the conclusion of a commercial message that summons the consumer to act. A call to action will implore the consumer to "run right out" and purchase, "call now, while supplies last," write a letter, return a coupon before a deadline, or call an 800 phone number to place an order. Many clever commercials have failed to sell a product because, although they were entertaining, they lacked a clear call to action.

**CAMERA ANGLE** angle from which the camera photographs a subject or scene. There are a great variety of camera angles, any of which can add an interesting perspective to that which is being pictured. Sometimes the camera angle can greatly influence the audience interpretation of what is happening on the screen. Among the many variations are *normal angle, high camera angle, low camera angle, canted angle* (on a slant), *reverse angle, subjective camera angle* (from the point of view of the subject; the way the subject sees things), and *objective camera angle* (the way an objective party or outsider sees things). *See also* TILT SHOT.

**CAMERA LUCIDA**   optical device invented in 1831 that is used in making LAYOUTS. Nicknamed *lucy*, the instrument works on the principles of reflected and deflected light through a prism and enables the artist to enlarge or reduce an image and then to copy it by hand.

**CAMERA-READY**   term describing a LAYOUT, including artwork and copy that is ready to be photographed or otherwise reproduced in the printing process. All work must be camera-ready before it goes to the printer. In an advertising agency, this preparation is done by the art department.

**CAMPAIGN**   series of related advertising communications or promotional pieces, scheduled for a given period of time and related by verbal and/or visual themes and common objectives. Ideally, each succeeding element in the campaign adds to the cumulative impact. For example, an advertising space sales campaign might include a mailing to prospective advertisers supported by advertisements in trade publications and followed up by a salesperson's call. Each element would center around a theme featuring the major benefit of advertising in that publication.

**CANADA POST**   Canadian equivalent of the U.S. Postal Service with similar rules for consolidating, packaging, sacking, and labeling various classes of mail. Details on Canadian mail preparation requirements are given in the CANADIAN NATIONAL DISTRIBUTION GUIDE. As in the United States, both second- and third-class mail may be presorted to similar PACKAGE and SACK consolidation levels, including directs, CITY, DISTRIBUTION CENTER FACILITY, FORWARD CONSOLIDATION POINT, PROVINCE, and MIXED PROVINCE. Canadian package FACING SLIPS and SACK TAGS are orange for second class and green for third class. Sacks must weigh at least 20 pounds to qualify for a postage discount. If there are 6 pieces of second-class mail, or 10 pieces of third-class mail, for a CONSOLIDATION LEVEL they each must be packaged together. Mail destined for Canada that is mailed from the U.S. must be labeled with the entry point city, a contents identifier such as 2C, 3C, or NEWS (for *second class, third class,* or *news value,* respectively), and a routing code that is determined by the entry point city and the destination city.

**CANADIAN BROADCASTING CORPORATION (CBC)**   Canadian radio and television NETWORK. The CBC is operated by the Crown in Canada. It has both English- and French-language service and covers all regions throughout the country.

**CANADIAN NATIONAL DISTRIBUTION GUIDE**   Canadian equivalent of the U.S. Postal Service's DOMESTIC MAIL MANUAL, providing guidelines for preparing mail to enter the CANADA POST system; abbreviated NDG.

**CANADIAN POSTAL CODE (CPC)** Canadian equivalent of a ZIP+4 code. It consists of 6 ALPHANUMRIC characters in ANA-NAN sequence, where *A* represents one of 20 alphabetic characters and *N* represents a number from 0 to 9 (for example, HOA-9Z0). The first 3 characters represent a *Forward Sortation* Area (FSA); the last 3 characters, a *Local Delivery Unit* (LDU). The first character of the FSA represents a province, a group of small provinces or, together with the second character, a subdivision of a large province. The province codes run from east to west, with A being the most eastern province, Saint John. If the second digit is the number 0, the last character must also be 0, and the entire code represents a small, single-coded town. If the second digit is a number from 1 through 9, then the FSA code represents part of a large, multicoded city and the LDU represents a BLOCKFACE within that city. For example, the province of Toronto is represented by an *M* or *L* in the first position. The second position would be a number from 0 to 9, and the third position could be any of 20 alphabetic characters. The FSA, therefore, could be MIA, M2A, M3A, M2B, and so on. Following these rules, there are a total of 180 codes possible for Toronto, including the various LDUs representing blockfaces within Toronto.

The CPC was created to facilitate mail handling and delivery, but it is used by direct marketers the same way the ZIP CODE is used in the United States to group, characterize, and select name and address records.

**CANADIAN TV NETWORK** television network in Canada that is independently owned.

**CANCEL**

**Advertising:** terminate an advertisement or contract.

**Fulfillment:** customer request to cancel an order or stop service on a CONTINUITY or a subscription; also called *kill*. If it was a paid account, a refund is generated. Canceled magazine subscriptions generate a refund equal to the value of the remaining service. *See also* CREDIT CANCELLATION.

**CANDLER** light-sensitive device used on mail-opening equipment to detect material left in an envelope thought to be empty.

**CANNIBALIZATION** a negative consequence resulting from the LINE EXTENSION of a product. Although generally line extensions do not compete with each other, there are occasions when the new product will take the MARKET SHARE away from the older brand, as in the addition of a diet soda product to a previously existing brand line of soda. The diet soda product will compete with and eventually eat away at the profits of the previously existing product, hence the name cannibalization.

Cannibalization may also be said to occur when product sales fall at a particular sales outlet or set of outlets as the result of the opening of a new outlet, because sales at the new outlet are eating away at sales at the older ones.

**CANS**
1. colloquial expression used to describe the headphones worn by the technical staff in a radio or television control room or on a television set; so named because the earpieces look like tin cans.
2. circular metal containers for film storage. Movie production personnel use the phrase "in the can" to refer to films that have been completed and are stored in their libraries.

**CAN'T FIND** rejected transaction intended to be applied against a computer file record that was not located on the file.

**CAP** abbreviation for *capital letter*.

**CAPITAL LETTER** any alphabetical letter written in uppercase.

**CAPLES AWARD** award presented annually by the Direct Marketing Creative Guild to individuals rather than agencies or clients for outstanding direct-marketing advertising. The award is named after John Caples, who wrote one of the most famous HEADLINES in direct-mail history for the U.S. School of Music: "They laughed when I sat down at the piano—But then I started to play!"

**CAPTION** word, phrase, or sentence positioned above an illustration or photograph that describes, identifies, or clarifies the illustration or photograph. If this textual matter is found *beneath* the illustration or photograph, it is properly called a LEGEND, although in common usage both are called a caption. Captions may also be used as advertisement headings or chapter, section, and page headings in a book. The word originates from the Latin *caput*, meaning "head" or "top."

**CAPTIVE MARKET** potential consumers in an area where there are no competitive sources for products, and the only choices are to purchase what is available or to make no purchase at all. Generally a captive market is the victim of higher product pricing. Hotel shopping arcades, airport restaurants, and sports arenas are examples of captive market environments.

**CAPTIVE PRODUCT PRICING** the pricing of supplies, such as razor blades, staples, computer software, or camera film, which cannot be used without a companion product. Often producers of these products will use a product mix pricing strategy wherein they will set a low price on the companion product with a high mark-up on the supplies. *See also* CAPTIVE MARKET, PRODUCT BUNDLING, TYING AGREEMENT.

**CARBON TISSUE** light-sensitive paper used in printing for transferring an image from a POSITIVE to a copper printing CYLINDER or PLATE.

**CAR CARD** form of TRANSIT ADVERTISING designed for display inside public conveyances, such as buses, trains, subway cars, and ferryboats, sometimes called *baby billboards*. There are two basic types: *overhead,* located above the windows, standard size 11" × 28" (although the width may be any multiple of 14), and *bulkhead,* found along the doors (usually in subways), standard size 21" × 33". Cards are sold in packages by *full, half,* and *quarter showings*—that is, the message is shown in all, half, or one-quarter of the vehicles in the particular transit system.

**CARD DECK**
**In general:** collection of punched computer cards. *See also* KEYPUNCH.
**Direct mail:** *see* CARD PACK.

**CARD PACK** cooperative mailing of postage paid BUSINESS REPLY CARDS returned to advertisers who share the costs of mailing the card pack to potential buyers; also known as *card deck.* Card pack advertisers share a common TARGET MARKET such as housewives or retirees. The response rate is usually less than 1%. *See also* CO-OP MAILING.

**CARD PUNCHING** conversion of data onto cards designed for use in INPUT of information for a computer. With the modern advances in technology, data can now be inputted through the KEYBOARD, and the punchcard system is used less and less. Today the punchcard is most frequently used for billing purposes.

**CARD RATE** cost for advertising in a publication or on a broadcast station or network as published on the RATE CARD (or in Standard Rate and Data Service) for that publication, station, or network. *See also* EARNED RATE.

**CARD STOCK** paper meeting U.S. Postal Service weight requirements for postcards. Card stock is used for many purposes requiring a durable paper stock but is most often used for BIND-INS and BLOW-INS.

**CARRIER ENVELOPE** *see* OUTER ENVELOPE.

**CARRIER ROUTE** households served by an individual mail carrier within a FIVE-DIGIT ZIP CODE area. The carrier route is used to divide mailing lists into segments. Mail presorted by the mailer according to carrier route before entry into the postal system earns a substantial postage discount. The number of households within a carrier route ranges from 100 to more than 2500, based on whether the carrier serves a high-density area, such as an apartment building, or a low-density rural area. There are approximately 180,000 carrier routes in the United States. *See also* ADDRESS CODING GUIDE; CARRIER ROUTE CODING; CARRIER ROUTE INFORMATION SYSTEM; CARRIER ROUTE PRESORT; CARRIER ROUTE QUALIFIED; LIST ENHANCEMENT; LIST SEGMENT.

**CARRIER ROUTE CODING** process of adding a CARRIER ROUTE code to each name and address RECORD on a mailing LIST, SO that the mailing pieces can be sorted by carrier route to earn postage discounts. Depending on the number of individuals from the list living in each carrier route, not all of the records coded will be qualified for a CARRIER ROUTE PRESORT discount.

**CARRIER ROUTE INFORMATION SYSTEM (CRIS)** file maintained by the U.S. Postal Service that lists all of the approximately 180,000 CARRIER ROUTES by street name or ranges of street numbers. It is used by large-volume mailers to append the carrier route to the name and address records on their mailing lists so that mailings can be presorted accordingly, thereby earning a postage discount. *See also* ADDRESS CODING GUIDE; CARRIER ROUTE CODING; CARRIER ROUTE PRESORT; CARRIER ROUTE QUALIFIED.

**CARRIER ROUTE PRESORT** mail preparation process used by mailers that sorts mail by CARRIER ROUTE to earn PRESORT discounts on postage. *See also* CARRIER ROUTE QUALIFIED.

**CARRIER ROUTE QUALIFIED** CARRIER ROUTE sorted mail that qualifies for the highest postal discount offered by meeting the minimum volume requirements for presorted mail set by the U.S. Postal Service. The discount (in 1986, $0.018 on first class) varies by CLASS of mail and by whether the mailer qualifies as a not-for-profit or profit organization. Nonprofit mailers pay slightly lower postage rates. The discount changes frequently, as the Postal Service's revenue needs change. The minimum volume requirements vary by class of mail and by whether the mail is placed in SACKS or on PALLETS. Most carrier-route-sorted mail is second or third class. The following volume requirements must be met to qualify for a discount on second and third-class mailings.

*Second Class in Sacks:* The minimum is 6 or more pieces per PACKAGE to the same carrier route. The sack may be directed to a single carrier route or may contain packages destined for different carrier routes within the same FIVE-DIGIT ZIP CODE area.

*Second Class on Pallets:* The minimum is 6 or more pieces per pallet to the same carrier route. Packages on the pallet may be directed to any carrier route.

*Third Class in Sacks:* The minimum requires 10 or more pieces per package and a minimum of 125 pieces or 15 pounds of mail per sack. All the packages in a sack must be sorted to the carrier route level. The sacks may have mail packages for different carrier routes within the same five-digit or THREE-DIGIT ZIP CODE area.

*Third Class on Pallets:* The minimum is 10 or more pieces per carrier route per pallet. Within this limit, all pieces on the pallet qualify.

*See also* CONSOLIDATION.

**CARRIER ROUTE SACK** SACK of outgoing mail destined for one CARRIER ROUTE. The sack must contain a minimum number of pieces to qualify for carrier route discounts. *See also* CARRIER ROUTE QUALIFIED.

**CARRIER ROUTE SPLIT** separation of a LIST into groups through an A-B SPLIT of names by CARRIER ROUTE. Direct-mail experts believe that a carrier route split will produce two TEST PANELS of equal geographic variation, eliminating the possibility of geographic selection bias.

**CARRIER WALK SEQUENCE**  mail sorted by the sender according to the sequence followed by a mail carrier on his delivery route. Also called DELIVERY SEQUENCE. No postage discount is offered, but this type of sorting reduces mail handling time and speeds delivery. *See also* DELIVERY POINT BAR CODE.

**CARTOUCHE**  French word for a design, usually oval or oblong in form, drawn by an artist in a scroll-like pattern and used as a border for copy. It is intended to add a look of elegance or importance to the copy. Frequently, a cartouche is used to encompass a trade name or as part of a TRADEMARK.

**CASE**
### Merchandising:
**1.** *see* DISPLAY CASE.
**2.** container used for a standard quantity of goods sold at wholesale rates, such as a case of canned goods.
**Printing:** hard cover of a book attached to the SIGNATURES. The case consists of two boards, covering material, and lining material. The case is attached to the pages with an adhesive in a process termed *casing in*. Case bindings are usually used for high-priced publications intended to survive long periods of time, such as most textbooks, encyclopedias, and library copies of books.

**CASE ALLOWANCE**  discount offered to a retailer by a wholesaler or manufacturer when merchandise is purchased by the CASE; the greater the number of cases, the greater the discount.

**CASH ACKNOWLEDGEMENT**  notice sent to a CASH BUYER acknowledging receipt of the order. The ACKNOWLEDGEMENT may include an offer inviting the buyer to increase the purchase order. Cash acknowledgements are frequently used if delivery of the item ordered is delayed to reinforce the buyer's positive feelings about the purchase and to encourage future orders. Acknowledgements are also used to request additional information or to offer a substitution for an out-of-stock item. Like all good direct-mail pieces, the cash acknowledgement is a sales tool.

**CASH BUYER**  customer who pays by sending cash, check, or money order with his order. *See also* CREDIT ORDER.

**CASH CANCELLATION**  request to cancel a cash order. It requires a refund. Canceled subscriptions require a refund of only the unserved value of the subscription. Cash cancellations usually occur because of customer dissatisfaction with the product or the service.

**CASH COW** *see* GROWTH-SHARE MATRIX.

**CASH DISCOUNT** percentage reduction in the gross price given by a seller to a buyer who pays within a set period of time. Cash discounts are given to shorten the length of time the seller must wait to collect the amount due. Cash discounts are offered to buyers in most industries, including MEDIA BUYERS.

A common business phrase for a cash discount is "2/10, net/30," meaning that a 2% discount is offered if the amount due is paid within 10 days; otherwise 100% of the amount due is payable in 30 days. For example, if the amount due is $100, the buyer may pay $98 within 10 days or $100 within 30 days.

**CASH FIELD AGENT** SUBSCRIPTION AGENT that sells magazines door-to-door. There are two types of cash field agents. "Crew team" agents (so named because they utilize teenage salespeople transported in groups from town to town) are the least desirable type, with a reputation for deceiving and abusing the teenagers hired to sell magazines. Some crew team agents have also been accused of collecting payments for subscription orders that are never passed on to the publisher. The other type of cash field agent is a "mom and pop" operation that sells only in the local community and often successfully renews subscriptions for individuals, libraries, and reception rooms in the same community, year after year.

Because of the small volume they sell, cash field agents generally pass on their orders to a larger agent, such as a direct-mail agency, who deals directly with the publisher. The large agents take a 10% commission in addition to the cash field agent's commission. Cash field agencies usually sell subscriptions at the BASIC RATE, unlike most other types of agencies, who sell at discounted rates.

Since cash field agents offer publishers only a small volume of orders at some risk of lost revenue and subscriber goodwill, most publishers will authorize only a few, if any, cash field agents to represent them. In any case, cash field agents are a very minor subscription order SOURCE.

**CASHIER** FULFILLMENT function that includes the receipt of and the accounting for monies received for cash and CREDIT ORDERS in preparation for a bank deposit. The cashiering function in some organizations includes all CAGE functions as well but is usually limited to the preparation of bank deposits.

**CASH INCENTIVE** promotion technique that encourages customers to pay when they order in return for some compensatory gift. The gift costs the seller significantly less than sending bills. A frequent magazine cash incentive is an extra issue of the magazine.

**CASH ORDER** order accompanied by the required payment. *See also* CASH BUYER.

**CASH REFUND OFFER** rebate offered by a manufacturer to a consumer. After the consumer has purchased the manufacturer's merchandise, the manufacturer will return a portion of the purchase price in exchange for a label or some other proof of purchase.

**CASH WITH ORDER** *see* CASH ORDER.

**CASSETTE** recording tape threaded on two reels and self-contained inside a compact closed plastic case. There are two kinds, audio and video. The cassette functions as a recording or playback unit when placed in a cassette recorder or player. Advertising agencies, creative personnel (such as artists or photographers), or PRODUCTION companies will often store copies of commercials in which they have participated, or which they have created and produced, on videocassettes. These can be shown to prospective clients with relative ease.

**CAST-COATED** COATED PAPER with a smooth and glossy finish. Cast-coated paper is expensive and heavy, but attractive. The coating is applied by covering the paper on one side with a pigment mixture that is dried and polished with a heated metal cylinder. The cylinder surface is called a casting surface because it acts as a smooth cast for the paper. Cast coating works best with heavy paper because of the amount of water used in the process. It is frequently used for booklet covers and book jackets. *See also* DULL-COATED; FINISH; MACHINE-COATED.

**CASTING OFF** estimating either the amount of space needed for a BLOCK of COPY or the amount of copy needed to fill a block of space; also called *copy casting*. The type must fit the space designated for it in the layout; thus, before the type can be specified (in terms of size and style), the number of CHARACTERS in the copy must be determined, or *cast off*. There are two methods of casting off: the *word count method*, which results in a close estimate; and the *character count method*, which is more time-consuming but results in an exact count.

**CATALOG** list of items available for purchase, with the description and price of each item. Usually, a BIND-IN order form is included with the catalog. Toll-free telephone numbers are frequently given for ease of phone-in orders. Catalogs are normally mailed third class.

There are many types of catalogs. Some industries are dominated by catalogs—for example, more than 50% of gardening-supply sales are made through catalogs. Catalogs are also widely used for industrial and office supplies, such as computer accessories, stationery, and educational services. Some industrial catalogs are intended for use by sales representatives and contain a complete listing of all products sold by that company. This type of catalog does not have strong promotional copy or design relative to consumer catalogs. Some CATALOG HOUSES go to great extent to attractively present their goods, using elaborate photographic techniques and settings.

Retailers such as department stores are getting into the catalog business because it enables them to reach a larger market and to sell without the OVERHEAD COSTS of a store. In addition, store credit cardholders are an inexpensive source of individuals to whom mailings can be sent. Some retail outlets sell exclusively from catalogs without keeping any inventory on site.

The life of a catalog varies, depending upon the seasonality of the items sold. Christmas card and seed catalogs have a shorter life than stationery or jewelry catalogs.

*See also* CATALOG ORDER FORM; CATALOG REQUEST; ELECTRONIC CATALOG.

**CATALOG AGENCY** SUBSCRIPTION AGENCY that sells magazine subscriptions, via a CATALOG, to libraries, schools, and institutions. Catalog agents usually offer a relatively high REMIT RATE of 50% to 70% of the BASIC RATE. These subscriptions also renew at a very high rate; once a library begins receiving a magazine, it usually continues to do so indefinitely. As a result, catalog agencies are a highly profitable subscription SOURCE.

**CATALOG BUYER** customer who has made a purchase from a particular CATALOG. A catalog buyer is believed to be a good prospect for other catalog marketers.

**CATALOG HOUSE** seller who utilizes a mail-order CATALOG as the primary means of presenting merchandise to potential buyers. Some catalog houses have successfully opened retail outlets, in contrast to traditional retailers who begin with a store and branch out to catalogs. In the mid-1980s one of the most successful catalog houses to open retail stores was Banana Republic.

**CATALOG MARKETING** merchandising of products through catalog sales. Formerly the domain of huge general merchandise retailers, such as Sears, Roebuck & Company or Spiegel, catalog marketing has become a field with thousands of specialty books, so that consumers can now buy just about anything from a catalog. Over 12.4 billion copies of 8,500 different catalogs are mailed out in the United States annually, and the average household receives at least 50 catalogs a year.\* Many catalog marketers are now even selling their catalogs at book stores and magazine stands. Some are also experimenting with videotape catalogs, called videologs.

**CATALOG MERCHANDISING** promotion of goods for sale through a CATALOG.

**CATALOG ORDER FORM** form that is usually bound into a CATALOG and provides room for listing the items being ordered and their price, along with any necessary descriptions regarding size, color, or quantity. The order form also includes space for the buyer's name and address (both billing and shipping if different) and identification of method of payment. Additional charges can be calculated on

---

\*Miller, Ann, "Up to the Chin in Catalogs," *Newsweek*, November 20, 1989, pages 57-8.

the form, such as shipping and handling costs and sales tax. Money-back guarantees are usually printed on the order form. To maximize customer response, catalog order forms should be easy to use.

**CATALOG REQUEST**  request from a potential buyer for a catalog to review. Some companies charge a small fee for catalogs, which may then be credited against the first purchase made from the catalog.

**CATALOG SALES PROJECTION**  estimate of the total sales to be made based upon partial sales results. The *half-life method* bases the projection on the amount of actual sales made midway through the period after publishing a catalog that orders are normally received. For example, if XYZ company mails its catalog on October 1 and usually receives most of the orders from that catalog by December 1, it would use its actual dollar sales as of November 15 ($35,000) as the basis for its estimate of what total sales will be as of December 1 ($70,000). The projection must take into account factors that may affect sales from year to year. Elaborate computer models, using both historical sales data and current sales-to-date, are also used to forecast sales.

**CATCHING-UP**  lithographic printing problem concerning nonimage areas of a printing plate that attract ink and cause the printed image to spread; also called *scumming* or *dry-up*.

**CATHODE-RAY TUBE (CRT) DISPLAY**  computer INPUT device that produces an electronic image on a screen similar to a television picture tube. The CRT has become an essential office tool; direct marketers use it routinely in order entry, customer service, and BACK END analysis.

**CATV**  community antenna television. *See* CABLE TV.

**CAUSE-RELATED MARKETING**  marketing strategy linking purchases of a company's product with fundraising for a worthwhile charity, project, or cause. Cause-related marketing is an effective marketing tool that builds a more positive image for the company or manufacturer while helping a charity gain greater visibility and new sources of funding. In the mid-1980s, for example, American Express offered to donate one cent to the restoration of the Statue of Liberty for each use of its card. According to public record, American Express gave $1.7 million to the restoration, and the campaign produced a 28% increase in card usage.

**C COUNTY**  *see* ABCD COUNTIES.

**CEASE-AND-DESIST ORDER**
**In general:** order by a court or government agency to end an unfair or unlawful practice.
**Advertising:** order issued by the FEDERAL TRADE COMMISSION to stop a particular advertising practice or unfair method of competing that

commission feels is in violation of any of the acts that govern commerce and that fall under the agency's jurisdiction.

**CEASE ORDER** U.S. Postal Service Prohibitory Order; an official order by the USPS instructing a mailer not to mail additional promotions to an individual who has complained to the USPS about receiving those particular promotions. Most mailers will voluntarily remove people from their mailing lists upon request. *See also* DMA MAIL PREFERENCE SERVICE DELETE FILE.

**CEL** *see* ACETATE.

**CELL**
**Layout production:** single frame on a STORYBOARD.
**Motion picture or television production:** single FRAME on a roll of film or videotape.
**Research:** component of a SAMPLE group used in research.

**CENSUS COUNTY DIVISION (CCD)** subdivision of a county, in one of 20 states, with physical borders such as a river or highway. Used by the U.S. Bureau of the Census for the presentation of statistical data, the CCD covers a population of approximately 5500 people. It is similar to a MINOR CIVIL DIVISION, which is a subdivision of a more densely populated county. Census data is used in LIST ENHANCEMET to add demographic information to the records on a file, based on address criteria (such as CCD of residence). *See also* CENSUS-DESIGNATED PLACE.

**CENSUS DATA** DEMOGRAPHIC information gathered by the U.S. BUREAU OF THE CENSUS. This data is used by marketers to make predictions about the buying behavior of the residents of a census area who share common demographic characteristics. The Census Bureau makes this data available to the public in print and/or via computer access. Standard census tabulations are available free of charge in libraries. Custom tabulations and data in magnetic tape format are available for a fee.

**CENSUS-DESIGNATED PLACE (CDP)** U.S. Bureau of the Census subdivision of a county in a less-populated area than a CENSUS COUNTY DIVISION or a MINOR CIVIL DIVISION. The population of a CDP averages 3400 people.

**CENSUS TRACT** U.S. Bureau of the Census subdivision of a densely populated city. Census tracts are jointly defined by the Census Bureau and local groups. The specifications are that census tracts have uniform social and economic characteristics, have identifiable boundaries, and be defined so that all census tracts within a county cover the entire county. The average population of a census tract is 43,300. *See also* ADDRESS CODING GUIDE; BLOCK GROUP; CENSUS COUNTY DIVISION; CENSUS-DESIGNATED PLACE; MINOR CIVIL DIVISION.

**CENTER SPREAD** pair of facing pages at the center of a periodical. The center spread can be sold at a premium because it gives the advertiser two continuous pages in a prominent position for a high-impact advertisement. *See also* DOUBLE-PAGE SPREAD.

**CENTRALITY** degree to which an individual's attitude is tied to ego or the individual's sense of self-worth. The greater the centrality of an attitude, the more resistant that attitude is to change. For example, a U.S. Marine's attitude toward his country has a high degree of centrality and that marine would be highly resistant to antipatriotic PROPAGANDA. However, his attitude toward a brand of toothpaste has a low centrality and would be much less resistant to change. *See also* COGNITIVE CONSISTENCY.

**CENTRALIZED POSTAGE PAYMENT** option offered by the U.S. Postal Service that allows mailers with multiple ENTRY POINTS to pay all postage due with a single payment instead of sending payment to each entry point with each mailing. An estimated postage amount is paid at the beginning of the mailing period and is adjusted according to actual postage usage at the end of the mailing period. To qualify for centralized postage payment, the Postal Service must be satisfied that the mailer's method of calculating the postage due is accurate.

**CENTRAL MARKUP SYSTEM** computer-supported function of the U.S. Postal Service that applies a new address, if known, to an UNDE-LIVERABLE-AS-ADDRESSED mailing piece. *See also* ADDRESS CORRECTION REQUESTED; COMPUTERIZED MARKUP.

**CENTRAL PROCESSING UNIT (CPU)** main processing unit of a computer. The CPU executes COMPUTER PROGRAMS and performs arithmetic functions.

**CENTS-OFF COUPON** coupon that entitles the bearer to a discount on an item at the time of purchase. The coupon is given by the buyer to the retailer, who submits it to the manufacturer, wholesaler, or clearing house (e.g., NIELSEN CLEARING HOUSE) for reimbursement. Some retailers offer their own "store" coupons and assume the cost of the discount themselves in order to bring more customers into the store. Coupons are used to entice consumers to try new products, to increase the frequency with which they purchase a product, to increase the quantity they purchase at any one time, or to persuade them to buy a BRAND other than the one they usually buy. Some coupons employ an expiration date or minimum purchase quantity requirement to ensure the coupon issuer's objectives are met. Coupons are distributed via mail, in newspaper and magazine inserts, and in newspaper and magazine SPACE advertisements. The coupon should be designed to stand out prominently from the rest of the advertisement with a bold outline or different background color. Some are found in or on packages, and these are redeemable either for a repurchase of the same product or for the purchase of a companion product (for example, a coupon for a cheese spread enclosed with a package of crackers). The latter practice is called *cross-couponing*.

It is estimated that approximately 150 billion coupons are distributed annually. However only a small percentage of them are actually redeemed. The highest rate of redemption is from those offered in or on packages, since people who have already purchased a product are likely to repurchase.

**CERTIFIED MAIL** option offered by the U.S. Postal Service that provides the mailer with a receipt and requires the destination post office to record delivery of the piece. This service is available at a surcharge for domestic first-class mail only. Certified mail is too expensive for use in direct mail, but is commonly used when mailing something valuable to assure the mailer it was delivered. For an additional fee, the receipt will show the signature of the person who received the piece and the receipt date. For another fee, the address of delivery will also be shown, along with the signature and date.

**CHAIN SCHEME** illegal (according to U.S. Postal Service and Federal Trade Commission regulations) direct-mail promotion that sells advice on how to make money by selling the same advice, in the same way, to other people; also called *pyramid scheme*. A chain letter, suggesting that each recipient send money to previous recipients, and then send the letter to others with the same instruction, is a classic example.

**CHAIN STORE** individual retail store that is a part of a group of similar retail stores with the same management and ownership.

**CHALKING** problem with printed material on which the ink has dried and formed dust that falls off the paper.

**CHANGE** transaction against a computer file that ADDS, DELETES, or changes information in a record. *See also* CHANGE OF ADDRESS.

**CHANGE OF ADDRESS** modification of a record on a list or computer file to change or correct an address in the record; also called *C/A* or *CHAD*. A change of address might include a name or title change if that is considered by the file owner to be part of the address record. An address change will also result in a change of MATCH CODE, preventing the file owner from maintaining the identity of each record over time for historical reporting. Some marketers have overcome this problem by assigning a permanent record identifier number.

**CHANNEL COMPETITION** efforts by the marketers within a CHANNEL OF DISTRIBUTION, or by channels as a whole, to establish dominance over the others. For example, the restaurants in a downtown district compete with each other for customers as well as for the best locations and suppliers. The same restaurants also compete as a group against home/office meal delivery services. A restaurant can gain an advantage by differentiating itself from the rest of the competitors in the channel. For example, it might offer a formal lunch club open to members only or guaranteed 15-minute service for informal lunches. It can be difficult for a marketer to determine when a company that used to be part of a different distribution channel becomes a competitor within the same channel, such as in the case of Sears versus Wal-Mart or Continental versus Southwest Airlines.

**CHANNEL MANAGEMENT** process by which a marketer ensures the effectiveness of its MIDDLEMEN in terms of product knowledge, sales volume, and profitability. Marketers must provide their middlemen with the tools they need to promote and sell the product effectively as well as adequate incentives to do so. The middleman is not an employee of the marketer and will not share the same objectives unless given some incentive to do so.

**CHANNEL MARK** blocks printed on rolls of 1-up labels (*see* -UP) signifying a break in the material being labeled. The break may signify a change in SCF (SECTIONAL CENTER FACILITY), ZIP code, publication, edition, or some other division that requires labels to be applied to separate groups of mailing pieces. For example, a channel mark might be used to divide the labels for a student edition of a news magazine from the regular edition. Some channel marks can be read by OPTICAL CHARACTER RECOGNITION equipment.

**CHANNEL OF DISTRIBUTION** means used to transfer merchandise from the manufacturer to the end user. An intermediary in the channel is called a MIDDLEMAN. Channels normally range from two-level channels without intermediaries to five-level channels with three intermediaries. For example, a caterer who prepares food and sells it directly to the customer is in a two-level channel. A food manufacturer who sells to a restaurant supplier, who sells to individual restaurants, who then serve the customer, is in a four-level channel. Intermediaries in the channel of distribution are used to facilitate the delivery of the merchandise as well as to transfer title, payments, and information about the merchandise. For example, a manufacturer may rely upon the workforce employed by a distributor to sell the product, make deliveries, and collect payments. The channels used by a marketer are an integral part of the marketing plan and play a role in all strategic marketing decisions. *See also* CHANNEL COMPETITION; CHANNEL MANAGEMENT; DISTRIBUTION.

**CHANNEL OF SALES** SOURCE of subscription orders, such as DIRECT-MAIL ADVERTISING, AGENCY, or NEWSSTAND. Source analysis is the focus of circulation management activity. Channels of sales must be reported on the ABC STATEMENT or BPA statement. *See also* DEPLETION METHOD; MAINTENANCE METHOD; STEADY-GROWTH METHOD.

**CHARACTER** single letter, number, or other symbol used to represent information. The number of character spaces in a FIXED FIELD computer record controls the amount of information that can be stored in the file. *See also* ALPHANUMERIC.

**CHARGE BUYER** one who makes a purchase on credit to be billed at a later date; also called *credit buyer*. *See also* CREDIT ORDER.

**CHARGE GRACING** deleting the number of issues served beyond EXPIRE (the end of a subscription term) from the term of a magazine subscription renewed after gracing has begun. (Post-expire issues sent are graced issues.) *See also* GRACE.

**CHARGE REJECT** credit subscription order that cannot be entered to a computer file because a matching credit order already exists; also called *credit-on-credit reject*. Publishers will not allow subscribers to submit new credit orders until previous credit orders are paid, so computers are programmed accordingly.

**CHECK DIGIT** character added to a string of characters and based on a formula applied against the original group of characters. Check digits are used to verify the accuracy of data entry by comparing the check digit calculated after entry with the check digit actually entered. For example, a KEY CODE such as OA34 might have a check digit of 8. The KEY ENTRY clerk will enter OA348. The computer will then follow the appropriate formula to calculate a check digit and determine whether the resultant check digit matches the character in the fifth position of the key code. If not, one of the four key code characters was presumably entered incorrectly. In an on-line system, the computer will prompt the clerk to reenter the information. In a batch system, the entry transaction vill be rejected during UPDATE. *See also* TIEBREAKER.

**CHECKERBOARD** direction given for utilization of space for the placement of a magazine advertisement. The space is sold at the half-page rate, but the ad is designed in two quarter-page (or four eighth-page) BLOCKS placed in diagonal opposition to each other on the page, so that the advertising has the appearance of a checkerboard.

Checkerboard Layout

**CHECKING COPY** copy of a magazine forwarded by the publisher to an advertiser or agency to show that the advertiser's ad (or ads) appeared in the publication as ordered, in terms of LAYOUT, position in the book, and utilization of space. A checking copy is sent before billing usually at the request of the advertiser or agency. Most agencies will not pay bills before seeing a checking copy.

**CHECKOUT COUNTER** place where purchases are checked and paid for in a supermarket or other self-service store. For the advertiser, this is a good place for displays of items that lend themselves to impulse buying (called *point-of-purchase displays*), since the customer has money out and is already in a frame of mind to make a purchase. *See also* POINT-OF-PURCHASING ADVERTISING.

**CHECKPOINT** point in a production process at which progress can be evaluated. For example, the checkpoint may involve a count of orders received eight weeks after a mailing goes out.

**CHEMICAL PULP** pulp for papermaking made from wood chips treated with chemicals to remove impurities. *See also* MECHANICAL PULP.

**CHESHIRE LABEL** mailing label that has been computer printed on a page in groups and then cut by a CHESIRE MACHINE into individual labels. Cheshire labels are applied with glue to the mailing piece. They are approximately one half the cost of PRESSURE-SENSITIVE labels. *See also* CHESIRE PAPER; -UP.

**CHESHIRE MACHINE** machine that cuts pages of CHESIRE LABELS into individual labels and applies them to mailing pieces.

**CHESHIRE PAPER** BOND PAPER used for printing CHESIRE LABELS. The paper stock used is usually 15- to 20-pound white offset paper stock.

**CHINESE WHITE**
  **1.** white paint with a bluish tint used to retouch photographs.
  **2.** white pigment, with a bluish tint, that is added to colored inks to improve their intensity. *See also* OPAQUE INK.

**CHI-SQUARE TEST** statistical calculation that determines whether a test value is significantly different from a CONTROL value. For example, if a test mailing list generates a 3.5% response and the control list generates a 3.0% response, is the test list response significantly higher than the control list response or is the difference too small to matter? A chi-square test can answer this question. The chi-square, symbolized by $X^2$, is calculated from the test sample and control sample results and is then compared to a table of values that lists the probability, for each range of values, that the results of the two samples are significantly different. In this case, probability refers to the likelihood that the *null hypothesis* (that there is no difference) is false. An example, follows:

|  | Test Sample | Control Sample | Total Samples |
|---|---|---|---|
| Positive response | A | C | A + C |
| No response | B | D | B + D |
| Total sample mailed | A + B | C + D | N |

The calculation for this example is:

$$X^2 = \frac{N[((A \times D) - (C \times B)) - N/2]^2}{(A + B) \times (C + D) \times (A + C) \times (B + D)}$$

$(A = 35) + (C = 30) = 65$

$(B = 965) + (D = 970) = \underline{1935}$

$2000 = N$

$$X^2 = \frac{2000[((33950) - (28950)) - 1000]^2}{1000 \times 1000 \times 65 \times 1935}$$

$X^2 = 0.25$

Referring to a chi-square probability table, 0.25 has a probability of about 74%. Therefore, the test list has a 74% probability of performing better than the control.

**CHOP-AND-NEST** folding and cutting a single sheet of paper in order to produce two or more direct-mail package COMPONENTS. It is generally less expensive to produce components via chop-and-nest than to print the components separately.

**CHROMA** composition of color that defines its HUE, depending on the amount of black and white it contains. *See also* SATURATION.

**CHROMA KEY** television production technique effected by video engineers using a scanning system whereby a color is used as a "key" to alert the scanning system to insert an image from one source into a picture from another source. Technically, two separate video signals are being keyed into each other. Chroma key was originally used only to produce unique special effects, but its use is now quite commonplace. A familiar chroma key example is that of the football sports announcer appearing in front of the playing field. Actually, the announcer is in the control booth in front of a blue or green screen. The blue or green color acts as the key and is picked up by the chroma key scanning system, which then replaces everything in that blue or green color with the picture of the football field. Sometimes, if the announcer has eyes that match the key color, the background will also appear in the eyes of the announcer. If this is the case, the key color can be changed.

**CHROME**
>    **Photography:** transparent piece of photographic film with a positive
>    color image, as a 35mm slide; also called *color transparency*.
>    Common chrome sizes are 35mm slides, $2^1/4" \times 2^1/4"$, $4" \times 5"$, and
>    $8" \times 10"$.
>
>    **Printing:** apply chromium to a printing plate, to protect the plate from
>    corrosive action and allow the surface to require less ink. If there are
>    a great many pieces to be printed, the application of chromium will
>    give the plate longer printing life.

**CIRC** *see* CIRCULAR.

**CIRCULAR** advertisement printed on a single sheet of paper and circulated either by third-class mail or by hand; also called *circ*, FLIER.
The advertisement may be printed in one or more colors, and the paper
may be of any color stock. Usually a circular is folded so that the
edges are parallel and it can fit in an envelope. Circulars are used as
PACKAGE inserts, as retail over-the-counter handouts, and in direct-
mail packages. They work best if they are relatively large with colorful illustrations and exciting HEADLINES. They are often used by
business salespeople to provide prospective customers with technical
information.

**CIRCULAR SCREEN** circular, rotating HALFTONE screen. In FOUR-
COLOR PROCESS printing, each color must be photographed through
a halftone screen placed at precise angles that differ for each color. A
circular screen can rotate to the desired angles. Shooting at angles
keeps the various color dots aligned properly in the printed image. See
also SCREEN ANGLES,

**CIRCULATION** readership of a periodical or other printed advertising medium. Since the cost of advertising in a periodical is based upon
the number of readers deemed to be of interest to advertisers, the periodical's circulation is of prime concern. CONSUMER MAGAZINES base
advertising rates on paid circulation; TRADE MAGAZINES base advertising rates on the number of readers with the DEMOGRAPHIC characteristics of the periodical's TARGET AUDIENCE. The circulation claims
of publishers are audited by the AUDIT BUREAU OF CIRCULATIONS, the
Verified Audit of Circulation Corporation, or by the BUSINESS PUB-
LICATIONS AUDIT OF CIRCULATIONS. Total circulation counts sometimes
include PASS-ALONG CIRCULATIONS.
>    The following are some specialized terms regarding circulation:
>    **1.** bulk circulation—distribution of a publication by BUNDLES as dis-
>    tinguished from distribution by individual pieces. For example:
>    Schools will often subscribe to a local newspaper in bulk to be dis-
>    tributed to students and used as a tool in the classroom. This is con-
>    sidered part of the bulk circulation of the newspaper.

   **2.** CONTROLLED CIRCULATION—copies of a periodical distributed free of charge to readers of interest to the advertisers; also called *qualified circulation* or *nonpaid circulation*. The Business Publications Audit of Circulations has specific rules for qualifying the readers as being part of the advertiser's TARGET MARKET. Generally, the reader must be in a particular industry or profession to qualify. For example, *Circulation Management* magazine readers must work in publishing or a related field.

   **3.** effective circulation—readership of a publication that is part of the advertiser's TARGET MARKET.

   **4.** franchise circulation—readership of a periodical obtained by sending copies free of charge to the customers of a business organization.

   **5.** PAID CIRCULATION—total copies sold of a periodical consisting of net paid subscription copies and single copy sales. Paid circulation is usually calculated on an issue-by-issue basis or as an average over a six-month audit period. *See also* ABC STATEMENT; AVERAGE PAID CIRCULATION.

   **6.** request circulation—recipients of a periodical that is sent free of charge upon request. According to Audit Bureau of Circulations rules, recipients must be part of the advertiser's TARGET MARKET to be counted as qualified circulation. According to Business Publications Audit of Circulations rules, recipients must have completed a request form that also includes survey questions qualifying the recipient as being of interest to the advertiser. *See also* BONUS CIRCULATION; FREE CIRCULATION.

**CIRCULATION COUNCIL** branch of the DIRECT MARKETING ASSOCIATION serving the training needs of magazine circulation management professionals. The Circulation Council conducts seminars and workshops on CIRCULATION, publishes a newsletter describing industry trends and events, and participates in the semiannual DMA conferences. The Council provides a channel for sharing circulation management ideas and experiences.

**CIRCULATION MODELING** computerized system for forecasting the results to be expected from various scenarios regarding periodical CIRCULATION. The user asks "What if?" questions—for example, "If a direct mail campaign generates 200,000 subscription orders with a January start, what will the total circulation be in January, February, and March?" The model predicts how many of these new subscribers will pay, cancel, or renew. This system is used to predict circulation over time as a RATE BASE management and SOURCE EVALUATION tool. *See also* FINANCIAL MODELING.

**CITY**
**In general:** subdivision of a state, with its own local government. According to the U.S. Bureau of the Census, the average population of a city is 5000. Several cities can constitute a COUNTY. A city is usually chartered by the STATE.

**Direct mail:** classification of a SACK of mail destined for a non-unique THREE-DIGIT ZIP CODE prefix area within a multi-ZIP-coded city. A non-unique three-digit ZIP code prefix is one that is shared by areas in several cities. CITY SACKS are an optional mail CONSOLIDATION, according to U.S. Postal Service regulations, and are eligible for a postage discount. *See also* CITY MAIL.

**CITY DELIVERY** ZIP code designation that indicates delivery within a city of at least 2500 people, as distinguished from a RURAL ROUTE. City delivery mail is distributed by a postal carrier and requires a street name and unit number. *See also* NONCITY DELIVERY.

**CITY MAIL** mail sorted to the THREE-DIGIT ZIP CODE level, destined for a non-unique THREE-DIGIT ZIP CODE area. (A non-unique three-digit ZIP code is shared by more than one city.) A three-digit ZIP sort uses the first three digits of the ZIP code, which represent a group of contiguous cities. Mail sorted to the city mail level is eligible for a postage discount, which varies by class of mail and method of preparation, such as sacked mail. *See also* CITY SACK; UNIQUE THREE-DIGIT CITY.

**CITY SACK** sorted and sacked CITY MAIL destined for a city with a non-unique THREE-DIGIT ZIP CODE. *See also* UNIQUE THREE-DIGIT CITY.

**CITY-STATE MASTER** listing of all valid mailing cities and common alternate or incorrect spellings used to verify mailing addresses added to a file. A city-state master is created and maintained by each mailer as suits his or her needs. For example, a mailer who markets outside the U.S. will include foreign countries and cities in the city-state master.

**CLAIM** statement that is used in advertising a product and that addresses some positive aspect of the product's performance or a BENEFIT to be gained from use of that product—for example, "XYZ Soap is 99% pure!" or "XYZ Beer is less filling - - and - - tastes good!"

**CLAIMS-PAID COMPLAINT** customer complaint about receiving a bill, or bills, after payment has been sent to the seller. Most magazine publishers send a series of six to seven bills, at four-week frequencies, until payment is made. It is possible for one or two EFFORTS of a billing series to cross in the mail with a customer's payment. When the claims-paid complaint is received, the customer's record is checked to see if a payment was recorded shortly after a bill was mailed. If so, an apology is usually sent to the customer, explaining the situation and asking the customer to disregard any additional bill(s) already in transit. If a claims-paid complaint is received in response to the first bill, it is ignored.

Publishers have different policies on whether claims-paid complaints should be considered legitimate. Some require a photocopy of the canceled check. Others ask for the check number and deposit date. Other sellers require no evidence of payment. These policies are based largely on the relative value of subscription revenue versus advertising revenue that is based upon the number of subscribers.

**CLAPSTICK** small chalkboard with a hinged top, used in filming, that records the scene number, the TAKE number, the sound level, and all other points pertinent to the scene being filmed. At the start of a scene, as the board is clapped, the camera shoots a close-up of it and the audio engineer holds a microphone to it to register the clapping sound. In this way, film and sound begin at the same time. Although use of a clapstick may seem to be a Hollywood affectation to people not working directly with the production, it is actually very helpful in the editing process in locating and marking the scenes to be used in the final production, and in synchronizing the sound and picture.

**CLASS**
1. U.S. Postal Service designation for a level of service and priority given a type of mail; also called *mail classification*. First-class mail is typically used for personal-letter mail and invoices. Second-class mail is used primarily for publications, such as magazines. Third-class mail is used by bulk mailers for promotional mail (catalogs, etc.). Fourth-class mail is used for books and parcels. Each class of mail has its own regulations for preparation, postage, and delivery standards. First class has the highest delivery standards (including delivery in one to five days) as well as the highest postage rates; fourth class has the lowest delivery standards and rates.
2. in print media, grouping of people by their interests. For example, people whose interest is photography will be classified as individuals likely to purchase magazines dealing with photography.
3. sociological grouping of people, by income, education, life-style, residence, and occupation, as lower class, middle class, or upper class. *See also* UPSCALE.

**CLASSIFICATION DATA** facts by which an AUDIENCE, a geographic location, or BROADCAST MEDIA and PRINT MEDIA can be organized into data applicable for research, as, for example, by age, income, education, or occupation.

**CLASSIFIED ADVERTISING** advertising appearing in newspapers (although some magazines now also feature classified advertisements) that is arranged according to specific categories or classifications. The text of the advertisements is set in the same size and style of type and the ads are usually without illustration. The three major headings are Employment, Real Estate, and Automotive, although there are many additional categories (e.g., Business Opportunities, Lost and Found, Pets, Personals, and Legal Notices). Classified advertising is usually located in its own separate section of the publication and has its own RATE CARD. It is responsible for a major portion of the publisher's revenue. Rates are based on the amount of space (words or lines of COPY) and the length of time the ad will run. The longer the run, the cheaper the per diem rate will be. Since PRINT ADVERTISING is divided into two basic categories, classified and DISPLAY ADVERTISING, classified advertising is sometimes called *undisplay advertising*.

**CLASS MAGAZINE**  CONSUMER MAGAZINE intended for a special interest audience, as *Photography Today* is a magazine intended for those whose interest is photography; also called *special interest magazine*. Sometimes the expression is misused to mean a slick magazine directed at a high-income audience; this is totally in error. The word *class* in this case refers to a specific group (or class) of readers who share a common interest.

Manufacturers of specialized products will reach a more interested audience when they advertise in a class magazine. The manufacturer of a unique new camera lens, for example, will fare much better if the lens is advertised in *Photography Today* than in a more general publication. The information about the lens will be read by the select audience most likely to purchase the product. Class magazine advertising offers the advertiser a minimum of waste circulation.

**CLAYTON ACT**  1914 federal consumer protection legislation that prohibits certain monopolistic practices and other impediments to free market competition, includes price discrimination, mergers that may lessen competition, TYING AGREEMENTS and exclusive dealings. The Clayton Act also holds corporate officials personally liable for damages resulting from activities in violation of the Act's rulings. The Clayton Act was designed to be more effective in preventing threats or potential threats to competition than the 1890 SHERMAN ACT. The Sherman Act does not come into play until after a violation is committed and has impeded competition. The Clayton Act is enforced by the FEDERAL TRADE COMMISSION in conjunction with the Department of Justice. *See also* ANTITRUST ACTS; ROBINSON-PATMAN ACT.

**CLEARANCE**
**In general:**
**1.** permission or authorization received—such as the approval given by a LIST OWNER to mail a promotion to the people on his list. Many list owners require that they be shown the promotion PACKAGE before such approval or clearance is given.
**2.** permission granted to use copyright-protected material.
**Merchandising:** special offer by a retailer who is selling merchandise at reduced prices. This type of promotion may be used to clear out excess or off-season inventory.

**CLIENT**
**In general:** person, company, or organization who uses the professional services of another.
**Advertising:** manufacturer, owner, or provider of a product or service who desires to advertise that product or service utilizing the help of a qualified specialist; also called ACCOUNT. The client is the customer for whom the advertising agency works.

**CLIO**  *see* AMERICAN TELEVISION AND RADIO COMMERCIALS FESTIVAL.

**CLIPPING BUREAU**  service whose primary function is to read newspapers and periodicals and to clip articles and other information from these sources to send to customers who pay for this service. Subscribers to a clipping bureau include public relations firms who want to demonstrate and keep track of their ability to get their clients' names in print; advertisers and advertising agencies, who want to keep track of their advertising as well as the competitors'; individuals such as political figures, who want to keep track of their publicity; or research groups, who want to be aware of all that is printed about a particular area in which they are working. Some clipping services specialize in particular CLASSES of publications; others cover the wide general area of publications in a specific region. All of them read hundreds of publications daily and send their findings on a contractually specified basis.

**CLOSE** in personal selling, to acquire agreement from the prospect or customer to make a purchase or take a desired action. Closing may involve an exchange of goods for money, as in a real estate closing; a contract signature, as in a service agreement; or a verbal agreement to buy repeatedly over time. Each successful step in the sales process may be considered a type of close, including gaining agreement to meet with a salesperson to hear a pitch or agreeing to test a product, or just to accept a phone call from the salesperson. In some sales organizations, the more experienced salespeople specialize in closing sales initiated by other salespeople. This is often seen in automobile showrooms where the manager is brought in for the final negotiation and signatures.

**CLOSED-CAPTION TELEVISION** television for the hearing-impaired that features captions with the programming so that viewers can read what is being said. To receive closed-captioned television, viewers must subscribe to a providing service.

**CLOSED-CIRCUIT TELEVISION** television programming transmitted by cable to specific receivers intended for a select audience. Political groups or candidates will often take advantage of a closed-circuit television system and plan fund-raising events around programs to be shown only to invited guests. Also, live sporting events, such as boxing matches—particularly title bouts—will frequently be televised only on closed-circuit television and shown in specific locations. Tickets are sold to prospective viewers, who will be able to see the event on a television monitor at the location. Some large companies now conduct business meetings on closed-circuit television.

**CLOSE-UP** camera perspective in which the principal subject dominates the picture; a very close shot of a person or an object. There are two types of close-ups, extreme and medium. An *extreme close-up*, sometimes called a *tight shot*, is, as its name implies, a more extreme version of a close-up—for example, when the camera closes in on the face of a person and then comes in even closer to focus on an eye. A *medium close-up* emphasizes the principal subject but includes other objects that are nearby. Abbreviated CU in scripts.

**CLOSING DATE/CLOSING HOUR**  day and hour when all advertising material, including COPY, PLATES or prints, LAYOUT instructions, and MECHANICALS, must be in the hands of the publisher if the advertisement is to be included in a given issue; the "deadline" for copy. Information concerning the closing date and closing hour can usually be found on the publications RATE CARD

The closing date is also the deadline for all broadcast materials to be delivered to the station or network if a commercial is to be included in the broadcast schedule for a particular time period. (All materials for broadcast must be submitted to the station or network management for approval before they may be aired.)

**CLUBSORT**  mail preparation according to U.S. Postal Service sortation requirements in order to qualify for postage discounts. This is an old term that has been replaced in common usage by PRESORT or CONSOLIDATION.

**CLUSTER ANALYSIS**  method of statistical analysis that groups people or things by common characteristics of interest to the researcher. Can be used to characterize the behavior or interests of various customer clusters such as YUPPIES, so that promotion copy and design can be specifically targeted to them. Cluster analyses are frequently based upon geographic criteria so that mailings can be sent to the best clusters.

**CLUSTER BOX**  group of individually keyed mailboxes serving a group of households. Usually located near a curb in front of the houses, it acts as a *delivery center,* enabling mail carriers to leave mail for several households in one place. Cluster boxes usually provide a special shared box for parcels and a slot for outgoing mail. The U.S. Postal Service hopes to replace house-to-house delivery with clusterbox delivery wherever possible.

**CLUSTER SAMPLE**  multiple-step method of selecting test samples from a population by first dividing the population into mutually exclusive and exhaustive groups and then randomly selecting some of the groups for testing. For example, one-step cluster sampling takes two samples of 5000 from a population of 100,000, by dividing the population randomly into 20 groups and then selecting 2 of the 20 groups as a whole for testing. This technique ensures that both samples equally represent the characteristics of the population. Any difference in response between the samples will be due to the difference in the promotions sent to each group. Cluster sampling is considered a two-step process if only some of the individuals in the selected samples are chosen (at random) for testing. An AREA SAMPLE is a type of cluster sample. *See also* A-B SPLIT.

**CLUSTER SELECTION**  method of selecting names from a list by assigning each name to a group with common characteristics, called a cluster, and selecting only the clusters most likely to buy. For example, a group of pre-law students might be identified from a list of college undergraduates if a law school preparatory course is the item being sold. *See also* CLUSTER ANALYSIS; CLUSTER SAMPLE.

**CLUTTER** mass of commercials and promos (short messages about upcoming programs) broadcast in a time period as short as two minutes, all of which compete for the listener's or viewer's attention and the combination of which lessens the impact of any single commercial message. Any one commercial can get sandwiched in with as many as six or eight other commercials. Advertisers or their agencies will sometimes run clutter tests to measure the ability of their commercials to get the listener's or viewer's attention in this clutter situation. *See also* COMMERCIAL TIME; COMPETITIVE SEPARATION.

**COARSE SCREEN** type of screen used in a photoengraving printing process which requires that the reproduced copy (ARTWORK) have contrast in the form of light, medium, and dark tonal qualities (called HALFTONE copy). In order to accomplish this halftone printing process, a screen must be used, because a metal plate alone cannot reproduce the necessary contrast. A coarse screen is one of several different kinds of screens that can be used, depending on the nature of the copy and the paper. It consists of 100 or fewer ruled lines per linear inch, although the most commonly used screens have 60, 65, or 85 lines, making the reproduction suitable for printing on coarse paper. *See also* FINE SCREEN.

**COATED PAPER** type of paper with a smooth and sometimes glossy surface FINISH; also called *coated stock*. It is frequently used for high quality HALFTONE printing. Both color and black-and-white photographs are better reproduced on coated paper. Uncoated paper is better suited to type and to line drawings and is less costly than coated paper. Coated paper stock can be covered on one or two sides, one or more times, with either white or colored pigments. The finish can be glossy, semidull, or dull. Various techniques are used for coating the paper with pigments (*see* CAST-COATED; DULL-COATED; MACHINE-COATED).

**COATED STOCK** *see* COATED PAPER.

**COAXIAL CABLE** heavy-duty electrical wire made up of an inner conductor, consisting of several copper tubes about $1/4$" in diameter, and an outer conductor, used for transmission of impulses from one point to another. Most commonly, coaxial cables are used to transmit telephone conversations, but this same cable also carries CABLE TELEVISION programming to subscribers. Fiber optic cable is rapidly emerging as the state-of-the-art in cable transmission and is expected to supplant coaxial cable.

**CODE** symbolic representation of a piece of information, such as a social security number that represents a U.S. citizen in various file systems. Used for many purposes, codes store information efficiently in computer files and help to organize OUTPUT from those files in a meaningful way. Codes assigned to various types of promotions such as direct mail packages, CENTS-OFF COUPONS, SPACE ads, and CATALOG ORDER FORMS are used as the basis for organizing the results of those promotions in RESPONSE ANALYSIS reports. *See also* ALPHANUMERIC; KEY CODE; MATCHCODE.

**COEFFICIENT OF CORRELATION**   statistical measure of the relationship between two VARIABLES—that is, the extent to which one variable is affected by a change in another variable. The correlation coefficient indicates both the magnitude and the direction of that relationship. It ranges from + 1.0 to – 1.0. A perfect positive relationship is indicated by +1.0, and a perfect inverse relationship by –1.0; 0 means there is no relationship. *See also* COEFFICIENT OF DETERMINATION; CORRELATION ANALYSIS.

**COEFFICIENT OF DETERMINATION**   statistical measure of relative variation that describes the variation in one value that occurs in proportion to variations in another value. The coefficient of determination is symbolized as $R^2$. *See also* COEFFICIENT OF CORRELATION; VARIABLE.

**COGNITIVE CONSISTENCY**   innate human tendency to seek out stimuli that are consistent with one's beliefs and attitudes and to censor or limit one's exposure to stimuli that are inconsistent with beliefs and attitudes. For example, a Detroit autoworker is likely to read articles that extol the virtues of U.S. built cars and will avoid reading articles that are critical of U.S. cars or that praise foreign cars. By doing so, uncomfortable feelings associated with contradictory information, known as COGNITIVE DISSONANCE, are avoided. *See also* CENTRALITY; SELECTIVE ATTENTION; SELECTIVE RECEPTION.

**COGNITIVE DISSONANCE**   in general, psychological theory of human behavior. The theory suggests that conflicts between behavior and beliefs create a sense of discomfort, or cognitive dissonance, that the individual subconsciously attempts to eliminate by modifying his or her beliefs. For example, a man who believes in nonviolence may strike someone in anger. The theory states that the man will either modify his beliefs about nonviolence to justify the violent behavior or will believe his action to be something other than violence. He may convince himself that he was acting out of instinct or self-protection rather than a desire to inflict harm, or that the provocation was so extreme that even a nonviolent person like himself would have no choice but to respond. Individuals often seek reassurance from external sources that their behavior is not in conflict with their beliefs. Nazi war criminals defended their actions to themselves and others by claiming they were "only following orders" and were not responsible for behavior that was in conflict with social mores.
**Advertising:** theory that a consumer may use a particular product because he or she believes the advertising for that product, which claims that the product is the most effective of its kind in the job that it does. The consumer may then see a competitor's advertisement that

seems to prove conclusively that this competitive product is better. This creates dissonance. The consumer must now relieve the uncomfortable feeling that the dissonance brings about and will often do so by switching products. The theory acts as a double-edged sword, though, because while advertisers want to create dissonance for nonusers of their product, they do not want to create it for those who do use their product.

Cognitive dissonance most often occurs after the purchase of an expensive item such as an automobile. A consumer who is experiencing cognitive dissonance after his or her purchase may attempt to return the product or may seek positive information about it to justify the choice. If the buyer is unable to justify the purchase, he or she will also be less likely to purchase that brand again. An advertiser of high-priced durable goods has said that half of their advertising is done to reassure consumers that in purchasing their product the right choice was made.

**COGNITIVE MAPPING**  graphic representation of consumer perception of the distance to be traveled and time that would be spent getting to a store or other business. The consumer's perception is affected by the desirability of the products sold and the extent to which it is convenient and pleasant to shop there. When asked to draw a map showing the locations of various stores relative to their home, consumers tend to overestimate the distances to stores they don't like or that have inadequate parking or unfriendly sales staff. Consumers will underestimate the distance to stores they like. The well-known "New Yorker's View of the World" poster is a good example of cognitive mapping in that the area of New York City is much larger relative to all other cities and is pictured as being closer to desirable cities than it is in reality.

**COLD COLOR**  family of colors with a bluish tinge, such as blue, turquoise, or green. Cold colors are believed to evoke a calmer feeling than warm colors such as red or orange. Cold colors are considered appropriate to promotions for banks, hospitals, and insurance companies. Warm colors are held to be better suited to youth-oriented products such as record clubs and sports equipment.

**COLD LIST**  LIST not previously used by the mailer or consisting of names of people who are not currently customers of the mailer.

**COLD MAIL PROMOTION**  promotion sent by a mailer to people who are not current customers. *See also* COLD LIST.

**COLD TYPE**  several methods of composition, in offset lithography and gravure, not utilizing metal, used for a flat plate direct-impression method of printing; also called *nonmetallic composition*. Examples include PHOTOCOMPOSITION, Varityper, typewriter, Photon, Linofilm, STRIKE-ON COMPOSITION, Monophoto, and Fotosetter, or preprinted characters arranged by hand. Cold-type composition is less expensive than metallic-type composition but is not as durable for long runs and varies in quality. *See also* HOT TYPE.

**COLLATERAL MATERIAL** ancillary material used to support and reinforce a MEDIA advertising CAMPAIGN, such as sales kits, technical specification sheets, presentation charts, news releases, letters, films, catalogs, booklets, TRADE SHOW exhibits, point-of-purchase displays (*see* POINT-OF-PURCHASE advertising), and annual reports.

**COLLECTION AGENT** agency commissioned by the seller to attempt to collect on CREDIT ORDERS that have not been paid in response to the seller's own collection attempts. Collection agents usually receive 30% or more of the amount collected as compensation; therefore, they are used only as a last resort.

**COLLECTION EXTENSION** offer made with the invoice for a credit subscription order inviting the subscriber to extend the term of the original order for a special price. *See also* ADVANCE RENEWAL; RENEWAL-AT-BIRTH.

**COLLECT ON DELIVERY (COD)** sale that requires payment upon delivery of the merchandise; also called *cash on delivery*. The payment may include shipping and handling charges. COD selling offers the buyer the advantages of CREDIT ORDERS while offering the seller protection from BAD DEBT expense. However, it is more expensive to collect payment in this way, and these costs are frequently passed on to the consumer in the form of higher prices.

**COLLOTYPE**
1. screenless LITHOGRAPHIC printing process using CONTINUOUS TONE negatives; also called *photogelatin*. Collotype printing is not widely used but has been utilized for both fine art reproduction and low-quality color reproductions such as movie posters. The printing image is transferred from a metal or glass sheet covered by a gelatin-base substance.
2. print made by using this process.

**COLOR-CODED ROUTING STICKER** small PRESSURE-SENSITIVE labels used by mailers, on which numbers or letters are printed. Each character is on a different color background. The stickers are manually placed by the mailer on top of mail PACKAGES to identify the package CONSOLIDATION level. *See also* OPTIONAL ENDORSEMENT.

**COLOR CORRECTION** various techniques for improving the color of a print, such as masking (*see* MASK), DOT ETCHING, and scanning. Masking is used to adjust the contrast level in COLOR SEPARATIONS. Dot etching is used to increase or decrease color. SCANNERS are used to color correct electronically and to transfer the corrections to photographic film.

**COLOR FILTER** colored screen—either blue, red, or green—used in photography to absorb certain colors and enhance others. By photographing an image through color filters, an image can be produced that reflects only one of the three primary colors that constitute the original image. These are called color separations and are used in FOUR-COLOR PROCESS printing. The blue filter is used to create the yellow negative, the green filter produces the MAGENTA negative, and the red filter produces the CYAN negative.

**COLOR OVERLAY** transparent sheet of material that ean be inked or painted on, used in the printing process when manually separating the colors in full-color originals for reproduction. The artist will use a separate OVERLAY for each color, which, when placed one on top of the other, will simulate the original artwork.

**COLOR PLATE** red, blue, or yellow PRINTING PLATE used in the reproduction of full-color original artwork. A printing plate can print only one color at a time. Therefore, if a piece of ARTWORK is to be reproduced in full color, the printer must prepare a separate plate for each of the three primary colors, as well as an additional plate for black (which prints the shadows and contrasts). These plates are known as color plates.

**COLOR PROOFS** *see* PROGRESSIVE PROOFS.

**COLOR SEPARATION** process of separating full-color originals into the three primary colors—red, yellow, and blue—by a photographic method (using color filters when making negatives) for the purpose of duplicating the original. *See also* FOUR-COLOR PROCESS.

**COLOR TRANSPARENCY** *see* CHROME.

**COLUMBIA BROADCASTING SYSTEM (CBS)** one of the major broadcasting networks; began in 1927 as United Independent Broadcasters, Inc., with a group of 16 independent radio stations. CBS was named by William S. Paley, who purchased the radio network in 1928. He instituted a contract relationship with the affiliated stations whereby CBS would provide them with free programming in return for free radio time to sell for advertising. This system is still the basis for radio and television networking today. The CBS Television Network was established in 1948. Currently, CBS employs more than 30,000 people worldwide and consists of a commercial broadcast television network, with upwards of 200 affiliated stations, and two nationwide radio networks, comprising almost 900 affiliates. CBS also owns five television stations, as well as six AM and seven FM radio stations.

**COLUMN**
1. area of COPY that runs vertically down the page of a newspaper or magazine and whose width is always the same dimension in a particular publication. *See also* AGATE LINE; COLUMN INCH.
2. regular feature appearing in a publication on a daily, weekly, biweekly, or some other orderly schedule. A column is sometimes syndicated from one publication to another.

**COLUMN INCH**   unit of measure in a publication by which advertising space is sold. Magazines and newspapers are divided into so many COLUMNS wide and so many inches deep (depth = height). A column inch measures 1 inch deep by 1 column wide, whatever the standard width is for the particular publication. If an advertiser's message fits into space that measures 4 columns wide by 5 inches deep, the advertiser needs 20 column inches ($4 \times 5 = 20$). If the rate quoted by the publication is $20 per column inch, the space for the advertisement will cost $20 × 20 column inches, or $400. *See also* AGATE LINE.

**COMBINATION PLATE**   in photoengraving, a PRINTING PLATE where HALFTONE copy (ARTWORK characterized by variations of light and dark tones, or shading) and LINE COPY (solid line illustrations and/or type) are combined in one engraving.

**COMBINATION RATE**   reduced rate offered to advertisers for placing advertising in two or more publications owned by the same publisher. In order to take advantage of a combined rate, the advertisement must be the same for all publications in terms of copy and size, and the individual publications must be bought at the same time or within the same 24-hour period. Combined rate advertising appears most frequently in a morning and evening edition of the same paper or morning and evening editions of newspapers under the same ownership.

**COMBINATION SALE**   sale of two or more products together. This reduces the cost of promotion per dollar of revenue. The AUDIT BUREAU OF CIRCULATIONS has special requirements for combination-sold periodical subscriptions to protect advertisers from inflated CIRCULATION figures.

**COMBINED MAILING**   first- or third-class mail from several mailers presorted together to achieve higher postal CONSOLIDATION discounts than any individual mailer could achieve alone because of the minimum volume requirements.

**COMBO PROMOTION**   promotion offering two or more products together. *See also* CARD PACK; COMBINATION SALE; CO-OP MAILING.

**COMMERCIAL**   term for an advertising message that is broadcast on television or radio. An advertising message in print is called an *advertisement.* A broadcast message is structured by time rather than by space (as is an advertisement), and so must be creatively designed around words, sound, and music for radio, plus sight and motion for television. Commercials are produced on film or videotape which is then duplicated so that copies may be distributed to the various stations where they will be aired. *See also* ADVERTISEMENT; COMMERCIAL TIME.

**COMMERCIAL AUDIENCE**   actual audience that is actively viewing or listening to a particular television or radio commercial. *See also* COMMERCIAL DELIVERY.

**COMMERCIAL BREAK**  scheduled break in television or radio programming for the insertion of commercials.

**COMMERCIAL CODE NUMBER**  method of identifying a particular commercial print according to standardized industry practice so that stations will be able to distinguish one from another. Prints are labeled by the production company with a coded four-letter and four-digit number. If, for example, a company produced a COMMERCIAL for XYZ Company that aired December 1, 1986, the commercial code number might be XYZC1216.

**COMMERCIAL DELIVERY**  total AUDIENCE that has been "delivered" to the commercial or that has received delivery of the commercial; the part of the audience that is actually exposed to a particular commercial. *See also* COMMERCIAL AUDIENCE.

**COMMERCIAL EXPOSURE POTENTIAL**  number of possible receivers of a COMMERCIAL message, measured by comparing the number of television sets in the receiving area with the number of television sets tuned in to the commercial in the receiving area.

**COMMERCIAL INTEGRATION CHARGE**  fee charged an advertising agency or advertiser by a radio or television station or network to cover the clerical cost of including a commercial in the station or network broadcast schedule.

**COMMERCIALIZATION**  final step in NEW PRODUCT DEVELOPMENT when the product developer makes a major marketing commitment to the product. At this stage the product developer implements a total MARKETING PLAN and works toward production capacity. Commercialization procedures involve deciding the timeliness of the product introduction, the locations where the product should be introduced, the market to be targeted, and the budget and promotional strategies for the product introduction.

**COMMERCIAL MINUTE**  one minute (60 seconds) of broadcast time that has been set aside by the radio or television station or network for the airing of commercials. *See also* COMMERCIAL TIME.

**COMMERCIAL POOL**  at any particular given time, group of ready-for-air commercial prints from which an advertiser or advertising agency can select a commercial to be shown. Commercial prints in the commercial pool at the same time are said to be *pool partners*.

**COMMERCIAL PRINTER**  printer who provides various services necessary to prepare printed material. These services may include ART, BINDING, COMPOSITION, GRAPHIC DESIGN, LAYOUT, PASTEUP, PLATE making, PRESS PRODUCTION, or TRIM and fold. Other types of printers include in-house printers, who print for only one user, and government printers, who print government booklets and other publications.

**COMMERCIAL PROTECTION** *see* COMPETITIVE SEPARATION.

**COMMERCIAL REGISTER** degree of HALFTONE color-print image alignment in which the error allowance is +/– one row of DOTS. FOUR-COLOR PROCESS printing requires overlaying multiple images of one color each that, combined, produce a multicolor image. To get the correct coloration, each image must be overlaid in REGISTER (in precise alignment) with the rest. Each halftone color image consists of tiny dots of ink. To be commercially acceptable, the alignment of the COLOR SEPARATIONS should be off by no more than one row of dots. *See also* HAIRLINE REGISTER.

**COMMERCIAL TIME** as prescribed by the NATIONAL ASSOCIATION OF BROADCASTERS, allowable amount of time per hour of programming that can be used by a radio or television station or network to broadcast commercials. For example, a network television station must adhere to the following schedule:

|  | Prime Time (8–11PM) | Nonprime time |
|---|---|---|
| Network commercials | 6 min. | 12min. |
| Station commercials | 1 min. 10 sec. | 2 min. 20 sec. |
| Other (such as promos or public service | 2 min. 20 sec. | 1 min. 40 sec. |

Thus, during PRIME TIME, this station may show a total of 9 minutes and 30 seconds of commercials per hour of programming; during nonprime time, the station may air 16 minutes of commercial time per hour. Radio commercials are typically 60-second spots, and television commercials, 10- or 30-second spots. Recently, attempts have been made to use 15- and 20-second spots on television. An advertiser may purchase 60 seconds of commercial time and break it up into three 20-second spots, or purchase 30 seconds and break it up into two 15-second spots.

**COMMINGLE** send two pieces of mail of different classes to travel through the postal system together. Postage is charged on both pieces at the rate of the higher of the two classes if the mailer wants both pieces to receive the same level of service as the higher class of mail. They can also be charged individual class rates as if they were mailed separately and receive the service level of the lower class. However, invoices must be mailed at first-class rates regardless of the class of the partner mailing piece and the level of service desired by the mailer. Examples: An invoice might be enclosed with a magazine inside a POLY BAG; the magazine mails at second-class rates, but the invoice must be mailed at first-class rates. Or a renewal notice, which normally mails third class, may be attached with adhesive to the cover of a magazine and mailed at second-class rates along with the magazine.

**COMMISSION** *see* AGENCY COMMISSION.

**COMMISSIONABLE** term describing services provided by an advertising or other agency to a client for which the agency receives payment in the form of a commission from another source—for example, advertising time or space that is purchased by an advertising agency on behalf of a client and is subject to a commission. Recognized agencies (*see* RECOGNITION) are given a percentage discount from the RATE CARD by most of the MEDIA when placing advertising for clients. In these cases the rate charged for advertising time or space is said to be commissionable.

   *See also* AGENCY COMMISSION; FEE BASIS.

**COMMUNICATE** transfer information or a message from one person to another. The sender may communicate to the receiver via a verbal communication channel such as speech, or may use a nonverbal form of communication, such as body language that communicates feelings through gestures, or art that communicates ideas through visual images. The objective of advertising is to communicate the advertiser's message to consumers. *See also* COMMUNICATOR.

**COMMUNICATION CHANNELS** various sources used by marketers to send marketing messages to potential consumers. Communication channels may be personal, involving two or more persons communicating directly with each other, such as a customer/salesperson relationship, or impersonal such as BILLBOARD or OUTDOOR ADVERTISING or any other form of mass communication where there is no personal contact. *See also* MARKETING CHANNELS, TWO-STEP FLOW OF COMMUNICATION.

**COMMUNICATIONS SATELLITE CORPORATION (COMSAT)** first company to be licensed by the federal government to use communications satellites for commercial broadcast purposes. COMSAT is the U.S. representative on INTELSAT.

**COMMUNICATOR** source of a message that is transferred to a receiver. The communicator can affect how a message is received by the selection of the communication channel and by variations in tone or context. For example, a written message regarding over-the-counter drugs is believable when it comes from a perceived authority such as a famous physician. The same message is less believable, however, if it is communicated by the same physician, who appears on television with an unkempt look and a voice lacking confidence.

**COMMUNITY ANTENNA TV** *see* CABLE TELEVISION.

**COMMUNITY POST OFFICE** contractor-managed branch of a post office serving a community too small for a regular post office. It may be located in a grocery store or other public place.

**COMP**
   **Magazines:** short for *complimentary*; a free subscription to a magazine given by the publisher to individuals key to the success of the

magazine, such as advertisers, sales representatives, MEDIA BUYERS, and suppliers. *See also* COMP LIST.

**Printing:**

**1.** *see* COMPREHENSIVE LAYOUT.

**2.** short for *compositor*; a craftsman who assembles metal type by hand.

**COMPANY INDICIA**  INDICIA that identifies the mailer but not the ENTRY POINT. It enables a mailer with several entry points to use the same envelope stock for all of his mail. Mailers must have a bulk permit (*see* PERMIT MAIL) for each entry point, and the mailing piece must include a complete return address.

> BULK RATE
> U.S. POSTAGE
> **PAID**
> BARRON'S EDUC.
> SERIES, INC.

**COMPARATIVE ADVERTISING**  *see* COMPARISON ADVERTISING.

**COMPARISON ADVERTISING**  also called *comparative advertising*, a persuasive advertising technique that demonstrates the superiority of one brand in a product category by comparing it implicitly or explicitly to another brand in the category. Although advertisers may sometimes compare the advertised product to "brand X," the FEDERAL TRADE COMMISSION prefers naming competitors in advertisements. However, the advertiser must be careful to show its product in a favorable light and not to disparage or overexpose the competitive product.

**COMPETITIVE ANALYSIS**  *see* COMPETITOR ANALYSIS.

**COMPETITIVE BID**  price quote from a prospective supplier in response to a request from a buyer. Competitive bidding is most often used by government agencies who are required by law to periodically open all contracts to bid and must award business to the lowest bidder. This is intended to ensure impartiality in buying decisions. However, it also makes it more difficult for the supplier to communicate value or quality advantages that may justify a higher price. The supplier must attempt to predict how competitors will bid in order to be priced competitively. The supplier may bid relatively low if excess capacity is available to be filled, or it may bid relatively high if it has a significant competitive advantage. Competitive bids are also used to establish a market value for a product or service that cannot otherwise be priced. For example, a long-term customer of a service business may request competitive bids from other suppliers to find out if the price they pay for their uniquely tailored service is still competitive. Competitive bids sometimes have a mandatory deadline and may require a deposit to establish the financial stability of the bidder. *See also* REQUEST FOR PROPOSAL; SEALED-BID PRICING

**COMPETITIVE INTELLIGENCE** information acquired by a market competitor about the companies with which it competes. Competitive intelligence might include pricing, advertising strategies, names of clients, technical advantages and disadvantages, market strengths and weaknesses, and so forth. Competitive intelligence may be acquired from the competitor's customers (current and former), suppliers, former employees, stockholder meetings, industry associations and trade shows, trade journals, newspaper articles, research studies, or advertising copy. When gathering intelligence, the marketer must be careful to avoid unethical or illegal methods such as using a job interview or bribery to elicit information from a competitor's employee. The marketer's sales force is usually a prime source of competitive intelligence and should be trained to recognize and report this information. Competitive intelligence can be purchased from companies such as A. C. NIELSEN and MARKET RESEARCH CORPORATION OF AMERICA.

**COMPETITIVE PARITY** budget allocation for advertising based on the expenditures of competitors. The practice is sometimes called *defensive budgeting* or *defensive spending*, because it is based on the idea that one should defend against competition by spending as much (or as little) as one's competitor on advertising.

**COMPETITIVE-PARITY METHOD** competitive-based approach used to determine an advertising budget wherein an advertiser decides advertising dollars to be spent on the basis of competitors' spending. A problem with this method is that not only does it assume that all competitors' marketing objectives are the same but also that it leaves an advertiser subject to the same mistakes the competitor may make. Additionally, information concerning competitive-advertising expenditures is only available after the money has actually been spent; thus the advertiser who uses this method is always functioning on other companies' past results.

**COMPETITIVE POSITION** place in the market enabling a product or service to compete on a level with other competitive products or services. When a product or service has attained a noticeable percentage share of the market, it is said to be in a competitive position.

**COMPETITIVE SEPARATION** amount of space that separates competitive advertisements from each other. A competitive separation is included in the contract for advertising space drawn between the advertiser and the advertising medium. In broadcast, this separation, also a contractual agreement, is known as *commercial protection*, and is a time interval, usually 10 minutes, between competitive commercials. Even if there were no agreement, the media normally would honor this separation of competitors as standard industry practice. *See also* BACK TO-BACK COMMERCIALS.

**COMPETITIVE STRATEGY** promotional strategy used in an advertising CAMPAIGN that is designed to compete with rival brands. For example: A competitive strategy may try to discredit another brand or undercut another brand in terms of price, or may point out qualities and consumer benefits that are not present in another brand.

**COMPETITOR**
1. manufacturer or seller of a product or service that is sold in the same market as that of another manufacturer.
2. seller of a product or service whose product or service can be used to fill or satisfy a consumer need (real or imagined) in a market where other sellers offer products that will also fill or satisfy the same need.

**COMPETITOR ANALYSIS** also called *competitive analysis*, the process of identifying the performance and marketing strategy of competitive brands or products in the marketplace. In order to plan an effective marketing strategy, marketers need to know about the competitive environment and to find out all they can about competitors' products, prices, COMMUNICATION CHANELS, quality, and service so as to determine areas of competitive advantage and disadvantage.

**COMPILED LIST** list of names and addresses that is created specifically for renting to direct mail marketers and represents a particular TARGET MARKET. It differs from most other lists in that it does not necessarily consist of previous direct-mail buyers. Names are usually taken from directories, trade show rosters, public records, or other lists of people with common characteristics. For example, a list may be compiled of individuals in a medical field who are prospects for buying specialized types of equipment.

**COMPLEMENTARY COLOR REMOVAL** printing technique that removes color by shining a light in a complementary color on the image to be printed, thus canceling out the unwanted color. Color is the result of reflected and absorbed light. The color we see is complementary to the color that is absorbed by an object. Therefore, an object that is perceived to be red absorbs all green light. A blue object has absorbed yellow light. Shining a blue light on an image will cancel out the yellow.

**COMPLETED CANCEL** customer who has met his commitment to the seller prior to canceling, such as a book club member who has purchased the requisite number of books. *See also* MEMBER COMMITMENT.

**COMPLIMENTARY SUBSCRIPTION** *see* COMP LIST.

**COMP LIST** list of individuals or organizations (usually associates, suppliers, employees, or advertisers) receiving complimentary subscriptions to a periodical or being given other goods or services free of charge. Comp list RECORDS on a subscription file usually have no EXPIRE date and sometimes receive special editions or promotions directed specifically to them as advertisers or members of the trade.

**COMPONENT**  physical element of a direct-mail PACKAGE, such as a REPLY ENVELOPE, OUTER ENVELOPE, letter, LIFT LETTER, or ORDER FORM. Each component has an impact on the success of the promotion through the unique function it serves. Most components include copy and illustrations that support their particular function. The outer envelope for example, includes TEASER COPY that induces the recipient to open the envelope.

The profitability of a package is partially determined by the cost to produce each component and to INSERT all the components into the outer envelope. The more components used, the greater the inserting cost. Marketers experiment with different combinations of components and with various paper weights and printing techniques to keep costs as low as possible without negatively impacting response. Package design, LIST RENTAL, and postage costs also figure highly in the profitability of a package. *See also* COMPONENT TEST.

**COMPONENT TEST**  direct-mail PACKAGE test consisting of the addition or removal of one package COMPONENT to evaluate response to the modified package relative to response to the CONTROL package. For example, a LIFT LETTER might be added, with a resultant increase in response rates. Depending on the difference in response achieved and the value of that additional response to the marketer, a lift letter might then be added to all subsequent promotion packages.

**COMPOSING STICK**  tool used in hand composition to assemble and justify type. The stick can hold only a few lines at a time, so the type must be transferred to a GALLEY each time the stick is filled. The stick clamps the type firmly into the desired line length, ensuring that SPACING-IN and spacing-out of the words is done correctly. Hand composition has largely been replaced by automated methods.

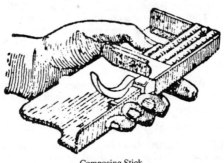

Composing Stick

**COMPOSITE PRINT** in the film production process (from filming to final print), the film print made between the WORK PRINT and the ANSWER PRINT; also called *optical print*. It is made after the work print has been approved by the client, and is the combination of sound and film tracks on one reel. Heretofore, the OPTICAL and sound tracks had been on separate reels. The composite print is the first synchronization of all tracks on the same reel. *See also* FINAL PRINT.

**COMPOSITE SHOT** picture displaying separate and distinct components but appearing as one entity—for example, a SPLIT SCREEN image, where one part of the screen shows one scene and another part of the screen shows another, allowing the viewer to watch both scenes at the same time; or a SPECIAL EFFECT, where one scene is superimposed over another.

**COMPOSITION** arrangement of type and/or art for printing. Composition may be a manual or computerized process. It includes all aspects of letter, word, and line spacing; line justification; indentation; hyphenation; type selection; and arrangement of all image elements on the page. *See also* COLD TYPE; COMPUTERIZED COMPOSITION; HOT TYPE.

**COMPOSITION HOUSE** in the printing industry, a shop specializing exclusively in the setting of type for advertising agencies, advertisers, and printers. Since the business specializes in typesetting, there is a vast array of typeface available and the facilities are far more expansive than those of a printer. Therefore the typography is generally of the highest quality. A composition house, which is an interim step between DESIGN concept and finished copy, will select or help to select the type, set it, and deliver CAMERA-READY PROOFS to the printer.

**COMPREHENSIVE** *see* COMPREHENSIVE LAYOUT.

**COMPREHENSIVE LAYOUT** LAYOUT of an advertisement, with all the type elements in place and the ARTWORK accounted for, used to give the client an idea of how the final copy will look; also called *comp*. Great attention is paid to detail in the preparation of this layout, and it is accurate in all dimensions. Usually the artwork is shown separately at one and a half times the size it will be in the actual ad, but it is also indicated on the comprehensive layout by precise boxes. After client approval, the layout will serve as a guide when making the final print or PLATE. *See next page.*

**COMPUTER-AIDED DESIGN/COMPUTER-AIDED MANUFACTURING** *see* CAD/CAM.

**COMPUTER-ASSISTED DESIGN** *see* CAD/CAM.

**COMPUTER-ASSISTED PICKING SYSTEM (CAPS)** computer-aided system for retrieving merchandise from warehouse storage. There are various types of CAPS, ranging from scheduling devices

Rough Layout

Comprehensive Layout

that coordinate warehouse picking trips, to devices that determine the best path through the warehouse depending on the items to be retrieved, to robotic devices that automatically retrieve merchandise from special storage bins. The most basic type of CAPS tracks stock locations and produces a *pull ticket* that lists the items needed and their location in the warehouse. In some cases, the computer-generated pull ticket is used to address a shipping package or to bill for an order.

**COMPUTER GRAPHICS** GRAPHICS designed from information put into a computer. There are many variations of computer graphics, based on the technology used, as well as the effects desired. Most of the results achieved by computer can also be drawn by an artist, but if properly programmed, the computer can accomplish more in a shorter period of time. Changes can readily be made and images can be manipulated with relative ease. In addition, computer technology makes possible a multitude of visual effects that can be played with over and over again until the desired result is achieved.

**COMPUTER INTEGRATED MANUFACTURING (CIM)** computer-based system of communication among all departments involved directly or indirectly in the manufacture of a product whereby all data concerning each department is entered into a data flow so that information from one department is available to all other departments. The goal of a CIM system is to maintain consistent product quality and to produce the product in an efficient time period.

**COMPUTERIZED COMPOSITION** computer-assisted process that drives typesetting machines that automatically hyphenate, JUSTIFY, and otherwise format pages for printing. *See also* COMPOSITION.

**COMPUTERIZED MARKUP** computer program of the U.S. Postal Service used to mark UNDELIVERABLE-AS-ADDRESSED mail with a new address, enabling the Postal Service to forward the mail to the new address. *See also* ADDRESS CORRECTION REQUESTED; CENTRAL MARKUP SYSTEM.

**COMPUTERIZED PAGE MAKEUP** computer-aided process that assembles film or type into finished page formats. Some systems can show, on a CATHODE-RAY TUBE DISPLAY, how the type size and face, line length, and so forth will look on the printed page, thus enabling the operator to change specifications and view results. Computerized page makeup systems that run on MICROCOMPUTERS have revolutionized publishing by making fast and inexpensive COMPOSITION capabilities available to small publishing businesses. *See also* HOT TYPE; LAYOUT.

**COMPUTER LETTER** computer-generated letter that appears to have been created especially for a particular reader. *Fill-in letters* are preprinted forms with blanks available for printing each recipient's name, address, and/or other information known about him. Another type of computer letter is created by printing concurrently on blank paper or letterhead the personalized information as well as the standard copy.

A type of computer-generated personalized letter draws paragraphs from a pool of paragraphs and combines them into a cohesive message while inserting information pertaining specifically to that customer. For example, the letter might have two paragraphs saying: "We have your complaint about not receiving the June issue and apologize for the inconvenience. Your subscription will be extended to August 1990 to adjust for the missed issue." In this example, the date of the missing issue and the new expiration date of the subscription were inserted into standard paragraph statements.

**COMPUTER PERSONALIZATION**  creating a personalized catalog or magazine by INK-JET PRINTING unique information on or in each copy. Personalization enables advertisers to create reader-specific editions of a catalog or magazine that include such information as the name of an outlet for the goods being advertised that is located near the reader. Computer personalization is also used to print the reader's name and address on a reply form inserted in the magazine or catalog. *See also* COMPUTER LETTER.

**COMPUTER PROGRAM**  set of instructions in a logical sequence interpreted and executed by a computer enabling the computer to perform a required function; also called *software*. Programs are the "thought processes" of computers, without which they cannot operate. Programs are written in various languages, to conform with the operating system of particular computers.

**COMSAT**  *see* COMMUNICATIONS SATELLITE CORPORATION.

**CONCENTRATED MARKETING** is a MARKET SEGMENTATION, and MARKET COVERAGE strategy whereby a product is developed and marketed for a very well-defined, specific segment of the consumer population. The MARKETING PLAN will be a highly specialized one catering to the needs of that specific consumer segment. Concentrated marketing is particularly effective for small companies with limited resources because it enables the company to achieve a strong market position in the specific market segment it serves without mass production, mass distribution, or mass advertising. *See also* DIFFERENTIATED MARKETING, NICHE MARKETING, UNDIFFERENTIATED MARKETING.

**CONCENTRIC DIVERSIFICATION**  *see* DIVERSIFICATION.

**CONCEPT**  idea (which may be a product, its benefits, and alternative uses), or its presentation as shown in an advertising LAYOUT or CAMPAIGN. Essentially, though, a concept is an unexecuted thought and must be tested among potential and current users of a product. Many ideas sound wonderful but do not work in practical reality. The road from concept to final result is a long one, but, in general, all successful advertising has been designed around a simple concept.

**CONCEPT TEST**  research whose primary objective is to test an idea or concept. Concept testing is done to assess the probability that an advertising CAMPAIGN will accomplish its objectives. MARKETERS use concept testing to determine which new product ideas are worth pursuing before a significant investment is made in development. *See also* NEW PRODUCT DEVELOPMENT.

**CONDENSED TYPE**  typeface that has been made narrower, so that it appears elongated. When type is condensed in this manner, a greater number of CHARACTERS can fit into the space that would be used by regular type. Thus, more copy can be used to describe the product or service featured in the advertisement. Advertisers will use condensed type when the amount of copy is greater than the available space.

**CONDITION** prepare the marketplace for acceptance of an advertising concept, product, or service. This is usually done by means of an advance advertising CAMPAIGN subtly designed to create a need or to draw attention to the product or service.

**CONFERENCE REPORT** *see* CALL REPORT.

**CONFIDENCE LEVEL** statistical measure of the number of times out of 100 that test results can be expected to be within a specified range. For example, a confidence level of 95% means that the result of an action will probably meet expectations 95% of the time. Most analyses of variance or correlation are described in terms of some level of confidence. *See also* CHI-SQUARE TEST.

**CONFIRMATION** written affirmation presented by a broadcast media representative to an advertising agency confirming verbal statements made concerning the AVAILABILITY of COMMERCIAL TIME on a particular station or network.

**CONGLOMERATE DIVERSIFICATION** *see* DIVERSIFICATION.

**CONJOINT ANALYSIS** statistical measurement of consumer attitudes that establishes the relative impact on the buying decision of one combination of product attributes compared to other combinations. Conjoint analysis provides a deeper understanding of consumer preferences than systems that rate product attributes individually. For example, consumers rating a fast-food establishment might indicate their priorities are taste, speed, price, cleanliness, and location. This would indicate to the marketer that taste and speed are of primary importance. However, when considered together, the combination of taste and location may rank significantly higher than taste and speed. This is a difficult technique to use when there are many product characteristics to consider.

**CONJUNCTIVE MODEL** this model of consumer attitude formation holds that the consumer requires a minimum level of satisfaction from every product characteristic or the product will not be purchased. A high degree of satisfaction from one or more characteristics does not compensate for a less than satisfactory rating on another. For example, if a brand of facial tissues meets the minimum for softness, price, and fragrance but is a color the consumer does not like, it will not be purchased. This is one of several noncompensatory models. *See also* DISJUNCTIVE MODEL; DOMINANCE MODEL; EXPECTANCY-VALUE MODEL; IDEAL POINT MODEL; LEXICOGRAPHIC MODEL.

**CONSIGNMENT** transaction that permits the return of unsold and undamaged merchandise. Consignment is widely utilized by newsstand retailers of magazines, who can return unsold copies to the wholesale distributors supplying them. Merchandise can be consigned by manufacturers to wholesalers or by wholesalers to retailers. Payment may be required in advance and subsequently refunded, based on returns.

**CONSOLE** stationary control panel utilized by the technical staff of recording and sound engineers. The console houses all the switches, levers, and buttons that control the electronic equipment being used in a studio, as well as television screens that display the picture transmitted from each and all cameras being used on a SHOOT.

**CONSOLIDATED METROPOLITAN STATISTICAL AREA (CMSA)** United States Bureau of the Census term for an area consisting of two of more overlapping and/or interlocking urban communities (known as PRIMARY METROPOLITAN STATISTICAL AREAS) with a total population of at least one million. CMSAs comprise the 20 largest metropolitan areas in the United States. The biggest CMSA, made up of 12 PRIMARY METROPOLITAN STATISTICAL AREAS, is New York-Northern New Jersey-Long Island, New York-New Jersey-Connecticut with a total population of 18 million. *See also* METROPOLITAN STATISTICAL AREA, PRIMARY METROPOLITAN STATISTICAL AREA.

**CONSOLIDATION** combining two or more computer records into one.

**CONSOLIDATION LEVEL** extent to which mailing pieces, sorted according to destination into BUNDLES, PACKAGES, SACKS, or PALLETS, have been sorted by ZIP CODE, SCF (SECTIONAL CENTER FACILITY), state, or other U.S. Postal Service destination segment. The higher the consolidation level, the greater the postage discounts available for the sortation. For example, CARRIER ROUTE is a high consolidation level, and mixed states, a low consolidation level. *See also* CANADA POST; PRESORT; SECOND CLASS; THIRD CLASS.

**CONSTANT** value that does not change in testing, so that the effects of changes in the values of other elements can be studied. For example, when a CONTROL PACKAGE is tested against a test package, one element, such as OFFER, COPY, or design, is changed and all other elements are held constant. Any difference in response to the control and test packages can be attributed to the element that changed.

**CONSUMER** ultimate user of a product or service. The consumer is not always the purchaser of a product. In the case of pet food, for example, the pet is technically the consumer because it is the ultimate user, although of course the advertising is aimed at the pet owner
Consumers are considered to be the users of the *final* product. For example, purchasers of building products are *interim users* of these products while constructing the finished product, which may then be purchased by a consumer. *See also* CONSUMER ADVERTISING; CONSUMER GOODS; CONSUMER SURVEY.

**CONSUMER ADVERTISING** advertising directed at the ultimate user of a product or service (*see* CONSUMER) in contrast to advertising directed at business and industry. Sometimes consumer advertising is directed toward a purchaser of a product or service who will then pass that product or service on to its ultimate consumer, as in the case of pet food advertising. Most radio, television, newspaper, and magazine commercials and advertisements are consumer advertising.

**CONSUMER CREDIT PROTECTION ACT** *see* TRUTH-IN-LENDING ACT.

**CONSUMER GOODS** merchandise made to be used by the CONSUMER for personal use; also called *consumer products*. Such items as food and clothing are considered to be consumer goods. Automobiles are likewise consumer goods, but the chrome sold to the automobile manufacturer for use on an automobile is not. (The chrome would come under the category of industrial goods.) Consumer goods are further classified as nondurables and durables, SOFT GOODS and HARD GOODS, and PACKAGED GOODS.

**CONSUMERISM** public concern over the rights of consumers, the quality of consumer goods, and the honesty of advertising. The ideology came into full focus in the 1960s after President John F. Kennedy introduced the Consumer Bill of Rights, which stated that the consuming public has a right to be safe, to be informed, to choose, and to be heard. Fuel was added to the fire in 1966 with the publication of Ralph Nader's book *Unsafe at Any Speed*, which attacked portions of the automotive industry. When corruption of government officials in the Watergate scandal of the seventies, and inflation and widespread consumer disenchantment with the quality of many American products were combined with the greater sophistication brought about by consumer advocates, consumerism became a powerful, action-oriented movement. The primary concern of this force is to fulfill and protect the rights of consumers articulated by President Kennedy more than three decades ago.

**CONSUMER LIST** list of people who have made inquiries or purchases that is maintained for future SALES PROMOTIONS.

**CONSUMER MAGAZINE** magazine that covers a broad or narrow interest and is directed to the general public, as distinguished from a TRADE MAGAZINE (professional magazine), which is geared toward the interests of a specific industry or occupation. A consumer magazine may be distributed free of charge or sold, according to the marketing goals of the publisher. *New York Woman* was introduced in 1986 as a free magazine sent to prestigious women in New York and was then converted to a paid magazine as it gained a reputation. Magazines are distributed free of charge to encourage advertisers to place ads in an untried publication going to individuals the advertiser wants to reach.

The publisher determines whether a magazine is classified as trade or consumer by defining the TARGET MARKET. For example, *Advertising Age* is a trade publication targeted to professionals and business organizations involved with advertising. *Business Week* is a consumer magazine—even though it deals with business-related topics and has a corporate audience—because it is marketed to the general public. Other consumer magazines cover a wide variety of interests that may be either narrowly targeted, such as *Ski* magazine, or broadly targeted, such as *Life* magazine. Most consumer magazines are audited by the AUDIT BUREAU OF CIRCULATIONS.

**CONSUMER MAGAZINE AND AGRI-MEDIA RATES AND DATA** directory of CONSUMER MAGAZINES and of agriculture industry-targeted MEDIA, used by advertisers when selecting media for advertisement placement. The directory lists the rates for each type of advertisement (including both SPACE [*see* CLASSIFIED ADVERTISING]) and classified advertisements according to the various sizes, and provides the name and telephone number of sales representatives for each magazine or other medium. The directory also indicates the size of the audience an advertiser could reach with each magazine or other medium. It is published monthly by Standard Rate & Data Service, Inc., 3004 Glenview Road, Wilmette, IL 60091.

**CONSUMER MARKET** all the individuals and households who purchase goods and services for personal use. The American consumer market consists of approximately 250 million people who consume more than $3 trillion worth of goods and services annually. This market grows by several million persons and more than $100 billion each year.\* Consequently, marketers find the American consumer market to be one of the most attractive markets in the world.

**CONSUMER PANEL** sample group of consumers in a TARGET MARKET whose buying behavior is believed to be representative of the entire market. By studying and defining the BRAND PREFERENCES, buying patterns, attitudes, and opinions of a consumer panel, marketers can extrapolate the behavior of the total market. For example, a marketer might use consumer panel research to determine whether TRIAL USAGE of a new product is leading to ADOPTION.

**CONSUMER PRICE INDEX (CPI)** federal government measure of the cost of living, also called the cost of living index. The CPI monitors monthly and yearly price changes for a wide range of consumer goods and services. The changes are expressed as measurements against a base period, and the base period in 1992 is 1982–1984. The price index for all items sold in that period is 100. For example, if a

---

\*Philip Kotler and Gary Armstrong, *Principles of Marketing*, Englewood Cliffs, NJ: Prentice Hall, 1991.

family's average monthly expenses for clothing were $100 in the base period 1982–1984, and $180 in 1992, the 1992 CPI for clothing would be 180 ($100 \times \$180/\$100$).

**CONSUMER PRODUCTS** *see* CONSUMER GOODS.

**CONSUMER PRODUCT SAFETY COMMISSION** independent federal regulatory agency, established in 1972 by the federal Consumer Product Safety Act, charged with reducing unreasonable risks of injury associated with consumer products. The commission establishes rules and guidelines for manufacturers and helps consumers identify safety risks. The commission was intended to compensate for previous legislation that provided for federal action only after an injury had occurred. The CPSC tracks injury statistics in order to identify products that require mandatory safety rules, such as the use of flame retardant fabric in children's sleepwear, or nonmandatory guidelines, such as those concerning playground surfacing. The five-person commission may be contacted by writing to the U.S. Consumer Product Safety Commission, Washington, DC 20207. Commissioners are appointed by the U.S. President with the advice and consent of the Senate.

**CONSUMER PROFILE** outline of significant demographic and psychographic details about the user of a particular product. The data include the user's age category, marital status, income level, education, occupation, sex, area of residence, and purchase behavior patterns. Knowledge of the consumer profile is very important in the determination of a creative advertising campaign. The advertising must appeal to both the user and the potential user of the product.

**CONSUMER PROTECTION** efforts to ensure that products purchased by consumers are safe to use, will meet all express or implied performance standards, that consumers will have adequate information to make safe purchase and use decisions, that marketers are prevented from using fraudulent methods to sell their products, and that marketers compete fairly in the marketplace. To achieve their objectives, consumer protection advocates, including individual consumers like Ralph Nader, and government agencies and businesses, use federal and state legislation, class action law suits, organized consumer actions like boycotts, and mass media tools like local newspaper columnists and "60 Minutes" type exposés. *See also* CLAYTON ACT; CONSUMERISM; CONSUMER PRODUCT SAFETY COMMISSION; FEDERAL TRADE COMMISSION; FOOD AND DRUG ADMINISTRATION; SHERMAN ANTITRUST ACT; TRUTH-IN-LENDING; WHEELER-LEA ACT.

**CONSUMER PROTECTION TELEMARKETING ACT** 1993 federal act passed to strengthen the Federal Trade Commission's ability to protect consumers from telemarketing fraud, deception and harassment, to require delivery of goods purchased by phone within a specified period of time, and to provide a cooling-off period during which the consumer may cancel an order. Many direct marketers opposed passage of this act, expressing concern that it would cover ground already covered by the 1991 TELEPHONE CONSUMER PROTECTION ACT and would lead to a morass of differing state and federal interpretations of the law.

**CONSUMER RESEARCH** research conducted through the use of various techniques and strategies, such as focus groups (*see* FOCUS GROUP INTERVIEW), in-depth interviews, INQUIRY TESTS, AIDED RECALL interviews, CONSUMER SURVEYS, and attitude testing, to obtain information about consumers. One of the major areas in advertising research (along with product research and market analysis), its purpose is to determine what influences consumer buying habits. Consumer research yields information concerning the motivations of consumers, their perceptions about advertising, the reason they buy a particular product, and the things that influence their brand choices. This type of research aids the advertiser in planning an advertising strategy and in defining the TARGET MARKET. For example: Suppose that a company is planning to introduce a unique new food processor. Consumer research would be conducted to learn people's feelings about cooking and the use of food processors, along with their desires for and their knowledge of the product, including any negative attitudes. Using this information, an advertising campaign can be tailored to the needs of the prospective purchasers of the product. The research will also identify the best prospects and the MEDIA they use, giving the company an idea of where to place advertising to best reach their target audience.

**CONSUMER RESEARCH DIRECTOR** executive responsible for defining marketing goals for an advertiser or advertising agency on the basis of CONSUMER RESEARCH and under whose auspices this research has been conducted; also called *director of research*, *marketing research director*, RESEARCH DIRECTOR. The consumer research director usually works directly under the vice president of marketing services and hand in hand with the head of the media department. Many agencies use outside research companies that provide syndicated research data, in which case it is the responsibility of the research director to interpret the outside input and coordinate with the MEDIA PLANNER.

**CONSUMER SURVEY** CONSUMER RESEARCH technique in which a questionnaire is used to gather information from a SAMPLE of consumers. The questionnaire may be sent directly to the sample group through the mail, or the information may be obtained through in-person or telephone interviews.

**CONSUMPTION** process of using consumer products in order to satisfy desires and real or imagined needs so that the products are used up, transformed, or deteriorated in such a manner as not to be either reusable or recognizable in their original form.

**CONTACT PRINT**  photographic print made when a negative or a positive comes in contact with sensitized paper.

**CONTACT REPORT**  *see* CALL REPORT.

**CONTACT SCREEN**  screen used in HALFTONE printing placed in direct contact with the film to obtain a halftone image from a CONTINUOUS-TONE original. *See also* CIRCULAR SCREEN; CROSSLINE SCREEN; DIRECT SCREEN HALFTONE.

**CONTESTS**  promotions, offering a prize, that may or may not require a purchase or demonstration of skill for prize eligibility. Contests that are judged to be LOTTERIES are illegal in most states. In-house lists of contest entrants can be used for additional promotions and can also be rented at different rates, based on whether the individuals are buyers or just entrants. Nonbuying entrants are referred to as *No's*. Contest lists must be DEDUPED to eliminate individuals who enter more than once. Contests can be used to accomplish secondary marketing objectives such as a recipe contest that increases usage. *See also* SWEEPSTAKES.

**CONTIGUITY**
**Broadcast:** particularly radio, a term describing two programs next to each other in time and sequence without interruption for commercials or announcements. For example, the XYZ Morning Show and the JKL Midday Show are said to share contiguity, since the morning show leads right into the midday show.
**Broadcast advertising:** a term describing commercial advertising time slots of equivalent value in terms of cost. For billing purposes, advertisers who purchase these time slots in several positions throughout the same day are said to have purchased on a *vertical contiguity*; those who purchase these time slots throughout the week purchase on a *horizontal contiguity*.
*See also* CONTIGUITY RATE.

**CONTIGUITY RATE**
1. special discount rate offered by the broadcast media to advertisers who sponsor contiguous programs.
2. special discount rate offered for contiguous commercial time slots. *See also* CONTIGUITY.

**CONTINGENCY TABLE**  method used in statistical analysis to define how one set of variables is controlled by variations in another set. For example, the effect of price on demand can be expressed by a contingency table that shows the number of units sold at various price levels.

**CONTINUATION**  *see* PYRAMIDING.

**CONTINUING DISCOUNT**  discount or reduced rate that has been given an advertiser by an advertising medium in a contract for a particular time period. and that continues to be in effect when the contract runs out and a new one is issued.

## CONTINUITY
### Advertising:
1. script for a television commercial.
2. use of a consistent theme throughout a promotional campaign, such as Pepsi's "choice of a new generation."
3. continuous, consistent use of an advertising media plan, such as Book-Of-The-Month Club's longstanding advertisement on the back of the *New York Times Review of Books*, alternating with the CENTER SPREAD. *See also* CONTINUITY ADVERTISING.

**Direct marketing:** type of sale that comprises a series of sales made over time. A closed-end continuity has a definite number of items to be delivered to the buyer. An open-end continuity has no fixed number of shipments and will continue until the buyer is canceled for non-payment or withdraws from the continuity program. Examples: Encyclopedias are usually sold as closed-end continuities; cookbooks are frequently sold as open-end continuities. Continuity subscribers can stop buying at any time, unlike club members, who must fulfill a MEMBER COMMITMENT prior to canceling. However, open-end continuity buyers are much more likely to cancel.

**CONTINUITY ACCEPTANCE DEPARTMENT** department at a broadcast station or network whose responsibility is to be certain that there is continuity between programming and the standards set for programming. It is the continuity acceptance department that will preview commercials to determine whether or not they are up to the broadcast standards of that station or network. Each station or network sets its own standards, although there is general agreement as to what is objectionable. Anything that makes an unsupported or false claim, is in bad taste, or expresses immoral language or concepts is considered unacceptable. If a commercial is rejected by the continuity acceptance department, the advertiser then has the option of changing the material and resubmitting it.

**CONTINUITY ADVERTISING** timing of media insertions (*see* INSERTION SCHEDULE) for the period of time an advertising CAMPAIGN will run. For example: In a campaign designed to run over a six-month period, 40% of the media budget may be allocated for time and space insertions in the first month, then 30% for the second month, no advertising at all in the third month, and 10% in each of the next three months. Since 70% of the budget in this particular plan is to be spent in the first two months, there will be some carryover effect in the third month, even though there will be no insertions during this time. The advertising insertions in the last three months will serve as reminders and will maintain the continuity of the plan. It is important to remember that continuity advertising has only to do with the timing of the advertising.

**CONTINUOUS AUDIT** type of Audit Bureau of Circulations or Business Publications Audit of Circulations audit that is conducted on samples drawn at regular intervals from the audited file. It usually samples the auditable transactions, such as payments of invoices, cash orders, and claims-paid complaints, processed into each file UPDATE. Noncontinuous audits are customarily conducted on an annual basis. Continuous audits replace the semiannual audits, reduce the amount of auditable documents that must be stored at one time, and can uncover problems, such as cashiering errors, before a large number of transactions are affected.

**CONTINUOUS FORMS**  forms produced on a WEB PRESS that are in continuous sheets separated by PERFORATIONS. They are used for computer printing and are perforated for easy bursting (*see* BURST). Continuous forms have PINFEED HOLES on either side to permit feeding through track-fed computer printers.

**CONTINUOUS-LOOP VIDEO**  advertising vehicle whereby a two- to three-minute commercial message is displayed over and over again on a video terminal. Continuous-loop videos are typically used at trade shows by exhibitors in individual display booths, but may also be used at retail outlets, particularly for new product demonstrations or promotional messages.

**CONTINUOUS TONE**  image, such as a photograph or painting, comprising all variations of color or shade from black to white and produced by varying concentrations of pigment. For example, watercolor paint can be applied thickly to produce a dark shade or thinly to produce a light shade. LINE COPY however, utilizes the same density of pigment, or ink, throughout the image. Because printers cannot reproduce a continuous tone image, a HALFTONE image must be created from the continuous tone image for printing.

**CONTRACT**
**In general:** legal agreement between two or more parties, such as that between an advertising agency and its clients, that describes the services to be performed and the price and payment terms.
**Direct marketing:** *see* TRAILER.

**CONTRAST**  tonal variations between the HIGHLIGHTS, MIDDLE TONES, and SHADOWS of an image.

**CONTRIBUTOR LIST**  names and addresses of individuals who have donated to a fund-raising organization.

**CONTROL**
**In general:** measure assuring conformity with an organization's policies, procedures, or standards, as in QUALITY CONTROL.
**Direct marketing:** standard against which test results are compared, such as a previously utilized direct-mail package that is being compared to test packages that have some variation in copy or offer or that employ new concepts in graphic design. The control package is usually mailed in larger quantities than the test packages. *See also* CHI-SQUARE TEST.

**CONTROLLED CIRCULATION** *see* CIRCULATION

**CONTROLLED CIRCULATION AUDIT** nonprofit group whose purpose is to audit the circulation figures of controlled CIRCULATION publications. *See also* AUDIT BUREAU OF CIRCULATIONS; BUSINESS PUBLICATIONS AUDIT.

**CONTROLLED DUPLICATION** computer process by which MULTI-BUYERS are identified and moved to a special list by searching two or more lists of buyers for interlist duplicates. Multibuyers are sent special promotions, and their names can be rented at high prices because of their strong purchase history.

**CONTROL PROGRAM** set of computer programs that control the activities and OUTPUT of a regular ongoing computer function, such as a file UPDATE.

**CONVERSION**
**Computer file maintenance:** process of converting data from one format or system to another, such as from HARD COPY to MAGNETIC TAPE; also called *reformatting*.
**Direct marketing:** transformation of a TRIAL OFFER buyer or catalog REQUESTOR into a customer through a first-time purchase.
**Magazines:** first-time renewal of a subscription. *See also* CONVERSION RENEWAL PERCENTAGE.

**CONVERSION RENEWAL PERCENTAGE** proportion of new magazine subscribers who renew their subscriptions. CONVERSION renewals are usually sold at a higher price than the subscriber paid for his initial order, which normally would have involved a discount available only to new subscribers.

**CO-OP ADVERTISING** *see* COOPERATIVE ADVERTISING.

**CO-OP COUPON PACK** *see* COOPERATIVE MAILING.

**COOPERATIVE ADVERTISING**
1. in retailing, an arrangement between a manufacturer and a retailer whereby the manufacturer will reimburse the retailer in part or full for advertising expenditures; also called *co-op advertising*. Ads and commercials are usually produced by the manufacturer and placed by the local retailer, using the store's name. Cooperative advertising is an important part of retailing and amounts to more than a billion dollars a year. It enables the manufacturer to advertise at the local rate for media, since all advertising is placed by the local retailer. This is usually cheaper than the national rate, and thus the manufacturer can buy more time and space for less money. Cooperative allowances are typically geared to sales, and the greater the sales, the greater the allowance given by the manufacturer to the retailer. Inevitably, co-op advertising means more advertising for everyone concerned, because more retailers will advertise if cooperative money is available. It is estimated that 75%

of all cooperative money is spent in newspaper advertising, while 12% is spent on broadcast (8% on radio and 4% on television).

**2.** individual advertisement sponsored by two or more manufacturers or retailers where the sponsors cooperate in the copy as well as the budget.

**COOPERATIVE MAILING** promotional mailing shared by several noncompetitive advertisers who target the same audience and are thus able to reduce mailing costs; also called *co-op mailing*. An example of a co-op mailing is the Carol Wright package of coupons sent out by Donnelley Marketing. Co-op mailings are growing in usage, particularly in BUSINESS-TO-BUSINESS ADVERTISING. *See also* CARD PACK; JOINT MAILING.

**CO-OP MAILING** *see* COOPERATIVE MAILING.

**COPY**
**1.** all written or textual material in an advertisement or direct-mail piece, including headlines, subheadings, and BODY COPY. The term is used in this context to refer to all such material *before* it is set in type, as well as *after* it appears in print. The term originates from the days when this material was received by the printer in handwritten form and would have to be copied into type for printing.
**2.** all material to be made into a PRINTING PLATE for duplicating. This includes artwork, photographs, illustrations, decorations, and typography. In this context, the term refers to the fact that all materials to be reproduced must be in LAYOUT form and copied by the photoengraver's camera before the printing plate can be made.

**COPYBOARD** frame that holds an original image while it is being photographed for reproduction.

**COPY CASTING** *see* CASTING OFF.

**COPY-CONTACT PERSON** advertising agency employee who has had both client experience and experience in the creation of copy for advertisements, and can function well enough in either area to represent the agency. A copy-contact person who works under the auspices of an ACCOUNT EXECUTIVE.

**COPYFITTING** selecting a typeface and typesize to best accommodate the amount of COPY that must be printed in a designated page area. Consideration must be given not only to the size of the type, but also to the style that best represents the spirit of the copy. If necessary, adjustments are made to the amount of space allotted to the copy.

**COPY PLATFORM** plan for use by the COPYWRITER that defines the basic theme of the advertising campaign and serves as a guide for writing an advertisement; also called *copy strategy*. Much the same as a political platform, the copy platform discusses the issues to be considered and describes the fundamental elements, such as slogans, visual symbols, and associations, to be built around the product (or service). It will also discuss the profile of the TARGET AUDIENCE, the product or service's claims, the kinds of appeals to be used, the customer needs that the product or service will satisfy, and the image to be created, as well as the style, tone, and implications of the finished advertisement. An agency will often use a copy platform in a client proposal, to give the client an idea of the creative work that will be done, before actually writing the advertisement. The platform can also be designed, after the advertising agency has been hired by the advertiser, as a kind of overview of the upcoming campaign.

## COPY PREPARATION
1. checking COPY before typesetting to ensure that it represents the final copy.
2. arrangement of copy elements and illustrations into a page format for printing. *See also* COMPOSITION; LAYOUT.

## COPY PRINT
1. original artwork or print from which a copy or copies will be made.
2. copy made from the original print or artwork.

**COPY RESEARCH** analysis and evaluation of the advertising message. Copy research is an aspect of advertising research and includes both the pretesting and the posttesting of advertisements or commercials in print or broadcast. Pretesting explores the product claims, technical aspects, TARGET AUDIENCE, and other areas affected by the copy, before or at the very beginning of the advertising CAMPAIGN. Posttesting will explore the effectiveness of the copy in communicating the advertising message and its meaning, at the conclusion of an advertising campaign. *See also* COPY TESTING.

**COPYRIGHT** form of protection granted by United States law to authors, artists, and musicians for their original work (including advertisements and commercials). A copyright protects the work from being copied, reprinted, sold, or used by someone else without the consent of the owner of the work. The Copyright Act of 1976, which became effective in January 1978, provides this protection for the period of the owner's lifetime plus an additional 50 years. (Previous to 1978, a copyright had been in force for 28 years and was subject to renewal for another 28 years, providing protection for a maximum of only 56 years.) Under this new law, a work is considered copyrighted immediately upon creation and need not be published or registered in order to be considered copyrighted. However, registration does offer certain advantages—for example, it establishes a public record and validity of the copyright, and if registration is made within three months after publication (or prior to an infringement), statutory damages and attorney fees will be available to the copyright owner. For this reason, it is advisable that advertisers copyright their advertisements and commercials.

When the copyright expires, the work comes into the category of public domain and can then be used by anyone. It is important to note that copyrighting protects the expression of an idea but not the idea itself. Also, names, titles, systems, and methods cannot be copyrighted.

**COPY STRATEGY** *see* COPY PLATFORM.

**COPY TESTING** measuring the effectiveness of the message in advertisements and commercials; often used when introducing a new product of repositioning a product, in order to test one kind of appeal over another, one product BENEFIT over another, or perhaps one price over another. There are many different methods of copy testing, such as HIDDEN OFFERS, consumer-jury panels, SPLIT RUNS in publications, or area testing, which is the running of a small campaign in a midsize town representative of the marketplace. Copy testing is also done before launching a campaign, in order to test CONCEPTS. The purpose of copy testing is to find and eliminate the negative elements in an advertisement or campaign so as to achieve maximum effectiveness from the advertising.

**COPYWRITER** creator of words and CONCEPTS for advertisements and commercials. Copywriters are usually employed by advertisers, advertising agencies, production companies, and other places where advertising is created. Generally, the copywriter works hand in hand with the ART DIRECTOR. Together, the two are responsible for the entire creative effort in an advertising campaign.

**COPYWRITER'S ROUGH** form in which the copywriter's work is first submitted, similar to a rough sketch, giving a general idea of the COPY text, its approximate length, and the basic conceptualization of the advertising idea or message. After the rough draft is approved by the creative team (the COPYWRITER, ART DIRECTOR, CREATIVE DIRECTOR, and assistants)—and sometimes by the client—the actual copy will be written in greater detail. The copywriter's rough is simply a rough idea of the work the copywriter will do.

**CORD FASTENER** cord with a metal SACK TAG holder attached that doubles as a fastener. The cord is used to close the mail sack; the fastener locks the cord to keep it from opening.

**CORNER CARD** colloquial term for the promotional GRAPHICS and COPY, as well as the return address, on an OUTER ENVELOPE; also called *teaser copy*. Many consider the corner card to be the most important element of a direct-mail piece because it entices the recipient to open and read the package. The copywriter should be careful not to use misleading corner card copy that doesn't truthfully represent the contents of the envelope. Widely used corner cards include "Valuable coupons inside" and "Dated Material."

**CORPORATE ADVERTISING** advertising whose purpose is to promote the image of a corporation rather than the sale of a product or service; also called INSTITUTIONAL ADVERTISING. This advertising is also used to create public awareness of a corporation or to improve its reputation in the marketplace.

**CORPORATE COMMUNICATIONS**  department in a corporation whose primary concern is to produce communication vehicles that promote understanding of and good public relations for the corporation. The corporate communications department is typically responsible for production of the annual report, promotional brochures, and employee communications. Often a public relations or marketing firm will offer corporate communications services for the benefit of those smaller companies that do not have such a department or for those companies that need to supplement their corporate communications departments.

**CORPORATE IMAGE**  consumer perception of the corporate entity behind a brand. In most cases, the corporation has no identity in the mind of the consumer, such as Con Agra, which owns the Healthy Choice foods brand, or CPC International, which produces Skippy peanut butter. In a few cases, the corporate entity is known and the image has a positive influence on brand sales, such as Heinz ketchup or Murphy's Oil Soap. In other cases, the corporate image acquires negative connotations such as Exxon did following the Valdez oil spill. A positive corporate image can greatly increase the speed of new product ADOPTION because of the CREDIBILITY of the manufacturer's claims.

**CORPORATION FOR PUBLIC BROADCASTING (CPB)**  nonprofit, nongovernmental agency founded in 1968, headquartered in Washington, D.C., and funded by the federal government along with contributions from the private sector. The purpose of CPB is to promote and finance the development of noncommercial broadcasting. The corporation offers grants to local public broadcast stations and works to provide long-range financing for public broadcasting.

**CORRECTION RUN**  second run of a computer file UPDATE to process transactions that rejected out of a prior run and have since been adjusted for entry. Rejects occur for different reasons, depending upon the system being used. For example, if the system edits KEY CODES, an incorrect key code will reject.

**CORRECTIVE ADVERTISEMENT**  advertisement whose purpose is to correct an advertised claim that has been found by the FEDERAL TRADE COMMISSION (FTC) to be deceptive. The corrective advertisement is used to counteract the earlier advertisement's effects. The FTC will require corrective advertising after sponsoring research whose findings indicate that lasting false beliefs have been created that can only be dispelled through this means. A corrective ad may be required even though the advertising in question has been discontinued. Each situation is decided on its own merits.

**CORRELATION ANALYSIS**  statistical analysis that defines the variation in one VARIABLE by the variation in another, without establishing a cause-and-effect relationship. The COEFFICIENT OF CORRELATION is a measure of the strength of the relationship between the variables; that is, how well changes in one variable can be predicted by changes in another variable. For example, correlation can be shown between the frequency with which a commercial is aired and sales volumes by plotting on a graph the values of each. A line drawn through the plotted points defines the correlation algebraically. The greater the density of the points around the line, the greater the strength of the correlation. In example I, the correlation is high; in example II, the correlation is low. Although the correlation may be high between advertising exposures and sales, other factors could be the cause, such as the supply of competitive products, availability of the product in stores, and so forth. *See also* ANALYSIS OF VARIANCE; CHI-SQUARE TEST; STANDARD DEVIATION.

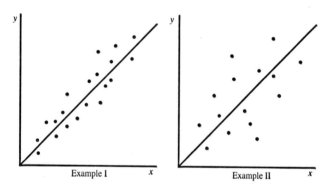

Example I          Example II

**CORRESPONDENCE COURSE**  educational course conducted through the mail by a correspondence school. Correspondence schools teach a variety of subjects, including professional trades. The schools must be careful not to make guarantees as to employment after completion of a course. Many correspondence courses are sold through SPACE ADVERTISING and INQUIRY-AND-FOLLOW-UP techniques. Correspondence schools frequently offer courses in areas where education in that subject is not otherwise available—for example, computer programming courses for people in rural areas. Various types of correspondence courses include high school- and college-accredited courses; self-improvement courses; and technical, scientific, and professional courses.

**COSPONSORSHIP**  shared sponsorship of a broadcast program by two or more noncompeting advertisers.

**COST-BENEFIT TRADE-OFF** desirability of a product or service in terms of the expected benefit relative to the cost; also called COST-BENEFIT ANALYSIS. For example, a homeowner might weigh the expense of a lawn care service against the benefit of more leisure time and a better looking lawn. A business weighs the expense of a new computer system against the benefit of reduced manual effort and errors. If the expected benefit exceeds the cost, the purchase is justified by a positive cost-benefit trade-off.

**COST EFFICIENCY** cost of reaching members of the TARGET AUDIENCE for a particular product or service as compared to the cost of reaching the entire audience of the medium in which the advertising has been placed; usually expressed in terms of COST PER THOUSAND.

**COST OF LIVING INDEX** *see* CONSUMER PRICE INDEX.

**COST PER GROSS RATING POINT (CPGRP)** measurement used in planning a television media buy based on the cost of a commercial time slot and the rating of the program where the time slot is positioned. If, for example, the cost of a commercial time slot during prime time was $1000 and the program rating for that time was 10 (which means that 10% of the total potential audience was tuned to that program), then the cost per gross rating point would be $1000 divided by 10%, or $100. The CPGRP measurement is a way of measuring the efficiency of media cost, as compared to measuring the COST PER THOUSAND and is generally used when making comparisons of the various broadcast vehicles. When the actual buy is made, the advertiser will still want to know the cost of reaching people on a cost-per-thousand basis.

**COST PER INQUIRY (CPI)** mathematical calculation of the promotion costs divided by the number of inquiries received. The CPI is used to evaluate the relative performance of a promotion. A promotion begins to be profitable at the point revenue expected from inquiry CONVERSIONS equals or exceeds promotion costs. *See also* COST PER ORDER; COST PER SUBSCRIPTION; COST PER THOUSAND.

**COST PER ORDER (CPO)** mathematical calculation of the costs incurred in selling an item divided by the number of orders received. It is used to examine the relative profitability of various promotions. The CPO ratio can be used to evaluate a single expense item, such as advertising, if all other expense items are excluded from the calculation. If the CPO exceeds the average sales value of each order, the promotion was not profitable. *See also* COST PER INQUIRY; COST PER SUBSCRIPTION; COST PER THOUSAND.

**COST PER SUBSCRIPTION (CPS)** mathematical calculation of the costs incurred in selling subscriptions divided by the number of subscriptions sold. Everyone has his or her own formula, but an example might be as follows:

$$\frac{\text{List rental} + \text{Package} + \text{Postage} + \text{Fulfillment}}{\text{Number of orders}} = \text{CPS}$$

The formula might also include BAD DEBT expense, cancellations, and/or overhead expense, and so forth. *See also* COST PER ORDER.

**COST PER THOUSAND (CPM)** cost of reaching an audience on a per-thousand basis. MEDIA PLANNERS use cost per thousand as a basis for comparison of the cost of advertising in various media. However, this comparison is only valid if the various media all reach the same TARGET AUDIENCE. The CPM is computed by multiplying the advertising cost times 1000 and dividing by the total audience.

**COST-PLUS PRICING** pricing method whereby a standard markup is added to the estimated cost of the product. The cost-plus price is computed by dividing the fixed costs of a product by the estimated number of units to be sold and then adding the variable cost per unit, or by adding the total variable costs and fixed costs and then dividing by the total number of units to be produced. This will determine the true unit cost. Once the true unit cost has been determined, that cost is divided by 1 minus the desired return on sales (a percentage) to determine the cost-plus price.

For example, if the fixed costs to produce an item are $300,000, the variable costs add up to $100,000, and the estimated number of units to be produced is 50,000. Add 100,000 to 300,000, divide by 50,000, and the true unit cost equals $8. If the desired return on sales is 20%, divide $8 by 1 minus .20, and the cost-plus price for this item will be $10.

**COUNTERMARKETING** efforts to permanently reduce demand for a product or service that may reflect poorly on the product itself, such as efforts by a group to discourage the use of a product the group deems unhealthy or bad for society. It is unlike DEMARKETING, in which one attempts to reduce demand without maligning the product. Political advertising targeted toward supporters of the opposing candidate uses countermarketing to reduce demand for that candidate.

**COUNTY** U.S. BUREAU OF THE CENSUS term for the largest geographic division of a state, with local government that represents the primary political and administrative subdivision within the state.

**COUPON** *see* CENTS-OFF COUPON.

**COURTESY REPLY ENVELOPE** preaddressed REPLY ENVELOPE that requires the sender to pay the postage. Although courtesy reply envelopes are frequently sent with invoices, most direct marketers prefer to pay the return postage on envelopes enclosed for orders, to avoid creating any additional obstacle to ordering on the part of the customer. When deciding whether to use a prepaid envelope or a courtesy reply envelope, the marketer must weigh the cost of the postage against the impact on response. Presumably, response to any type of promotion will be higher if the reply postage is prepaid, but testing sometimes proves the greater response does not bring in enough additional revenue to cover the cost of postage. However, response is always higher if a preaddressed envelope is used, with or without postage, saving the buyer the trouble of providing and addressing an envelope.

**COVER AD POSITION** advertisement placement on a cover of a magazine. The covers are named *first cover* (outside front), *second cover* (inside front), *third cover* (inside back), and *fourth cover* (outside back), and are considered to be very desirable positions in the magazine— particularly the fourth or BACK COVER for which there is often a waiting list. Because a cover ad position is a preferred position, it is almost always sold at a higher rate than any position inside the magazine.

**COVER LETTER** letter that is enclosed with other literature in a mailing and that introduces and explains the other literature.

**COVER PAPER** heavyweight, durable paper used for the covers of catalogs, booklets, and brochures; also called *cover stock*.

**CPU TIME** length of time the CENTRAL PROCESSING UNIT (CPU) of a computer is in operation while performing a function. Most functions are performed in segments interspersed by CPU activity related to other functions, allowing the computer to process several jobs concurrently. The cost of running a job is usually based on total CPU time instead of wall-clock (actual) time. The difference between wall-clock time and CPU time depends upon the complexity of the job(s) being run, the number of jobs being run, and the speed of the INPUT/OUTPUT devices being used.

**CRAWL** effect used in television production that is created by a device that moves credits or other graphic matter horizontally or vertically past the camera so that the information appears to crawl across or up the television screen. The device is actually a continuous strip of paper that is set between two rollers so that the paper can be moved past the camera either by hand or by mechanical means. The lettering used for the credits or other graphics is usually done in white on a black background so that the information can be superimposed over another picture.

**CREAMING A LIST**
1. selecting from a list only those key prospects most likely to buy, based on various selection criteria, such as HOTLINES or MULTIBUYERS.
2. making an offer that can't be refused, often at a loss, to individuals on a rented list in order to get those individuals onto a HOUSE list that can be used again without paying a rental fee or that can be rented to others.

**CREATIVE BLACK BOOK** annual two-volume worldwide directory of creative suppliers such as photographers, illustrators, directors, production facilities, and photofinishers. Sometimes called the *Black Book*, the Creative Book sells advertising space on an annual basis and contains approximately 22,000 listings in 10 categories. It is distributed throughout the United States, Canada, and Europe. The volumes are offered for sale to any interested persons but are sent free to those advertising agencies whose annual billing is at least $6 million.

**CREATIVE DIRECTOR** head of the creative department at an advertising agency. The creative director is responsible for all creative aspects of all advertising campaigns being handled by the agency from concept through production. The creative director sets the tone for the creative philosophy of an advertising agency and the standards for the quality of its workmanship, and thus is the key person responsible for the effectiveness of all advertising produced by the agency.

In a large agency, the creative director is assisted by a number of associates and a complete staff of artists, COPYWRITERS and LAYOUT personnel, and is directly responsible to the vice president of creative services. In a smaller agency, many of these jobs may be combined or the creative director may depend entirely on a free-lance staff. *See also* ASSOCIATE CREATIVE DIRECTOR.

**CREATIVE STRATEGY** outline of the development of the advertising message, as prepared by the creative team of an advertising agency, including the copywriter(s), art director, and creative director. Essentially, the creative strategy explains how the message will meet the advertising objectives. Included in the outline will be the product POSITIONING (how the product will be positioned in the marketplace, toward what audience) and the rationale for that positioning, such as the tangible or intangible BENEFITS of the product and the reasons for choosing those particular benefits. As the name suggests, the creative strategy deals only with the creative aspects of the advertising. Except perhaps on a very superficial level, it does not discuss the media, cost per thousand, gross rating points, or any other aspects outside the realm of the creative department.

**CREDIBILITY** degree to which a communicator or communication is believed by the recipient. Credibility is particularly important when the message to be conveyed varies substantially from the recipient's current beliefs or attitudes. The credibility of such a message will be increased if delivered by a communicator who is expert, trustworthy, and appealing. A message may be credible if only two of the three criteria for the communicator are met, provided the two criteria hold dominance in that context. For example, many voters will take political advice from a celebrity who is considered trustworthy and appealing despite the celebrity's lack of political expertise, but they would probably not take medical advice from that celebrity.

**CREDIT CANCELLATION** cancellation of an unpaid credit order; also called KILL; *kill bad pay*. Credit cancellations may be involuntary, as in the case of DEADBEATS, or voluntary. Future credit cancellation volumes must be estimated by magazine publishers, who then make plans to generate enough new subscriptions to replace the expected credit cancellations, thereby maintaining their RATE BASE. *See also* DIRECT CANCEL; PAID CANCEL

**CREDIT CARD ORDER** purchase paid for by credit card. 800-NUMBER PROMOTIONS frequently offer a credit card payment option. Credit card buyers are considered CASH BUYERS from a financial perspective but may be tracked separately for marketing information purposes, so that response to credit card promotions can be evaluated relative to other cash order promotions.

**CREDIT-ON-CREDIT REJECT** *see* CHARGE REJECT.

**CREDIT ORDER** order that is received without payment and that requires billing at a later date; also called *bill me* order. *See also* CASH ORDER; CREDIT CARD ORDER.

**CREDIT PRESCREENING** type of list PURGE that removes names matching those on a list of customers with a history of nonpayment. *See also* DEADBEAT.

**CREDITS**
1. *see* MAKEGOOD.
2. recognition of a person's contribution to a motion picture or television program presented on a CRAWL or as a VOICE-OVER CREDIT at the conclusion of the presentation; also called *credit line*, TITLE.
3. recognition of the sponsor of a broadcast program.

**CREDIT SUSPENSION** process whereby unpaid credit accounts are placed in inactive status so that customers no longer receive service but do continue to receive bills. For example, magazine subscribers would stop receiving issues after their accounts are suspended, but once payment is received, the accounts are reactivated. If the orders remain unpaid, the records are eventually canceled off the file. Most publishers serve two to three issues prior to suspending an account. *See also* CREDIT CANCELLATION.

**CREEP** forward movement of the print blanket during OFFSET printing; also called *blanket creep*. Blanket creep is caused by the normal printing process.

**CRISIS MANAGMENT** actions taken by a company to maintain its credibility and good reputation after a situation has occurred that may affect the company in a negative manner and therefore reduce sales of that company's product or service.

**CRITICAL PATH METHOD** scheduling technique used to manage complex tasks involving many steps. It describes the steps necessary to complete a project or achieve an objective, assigns a time estimate to each step, outlines the logical sequence of the steps, and identifies the longer paths from the beginning step to the end. The longer paths are more critical to the on-time completion of the project than the shorter path because the tasks on the shorter paths may be delayed without delaying the whole project.

For example, the steps in a direct mail promotion include choosing LISTS submitting LIST RENTAL orders, receiving the lists, performing a MERGE/PURGE, addressing labels, designing and printing the package components, inserting the mailing pieces, applying labels, and mailing the promotion. Some of these steps lie on the critical path, because completion of the entire project will be delayed if they are not finished on time. If, for example, it will take five days to print the package components and one day to address the labels, and if both steps are scheduled to begin the same day, the label addressing may be delayed up to four days without impacting the project. Therefore, label addressing does not lie on the critical path. If, however, the package components are not printed on time, the mailing will not go out on time and the project is therefore delayed. This step then is on the critical path.

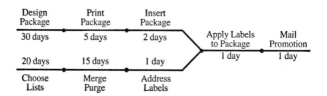

If it appears that a step on the critical path is running late, action can be taken to keep the project on schedule, such as hiring an additional printer to produce the package components. Another option is to reschedule steps on the critical path that have a history of delays to begin earlier. The marketer might, for example, switch to a printer with a better reputation for on-time delivery of package components or with more equipment, enabling him to deliver printed material in fewer days.

**CROP** trim part of an illustration, drawing, or photograph, so that undesired elements can be eliminated or so that the material will fit prescribed proportions.

**CROP MARK** line or lines drawn on a piece of artwork (including photographs), or on a transparent OVERLAY attached to the artwork, which will serve as a guide to cropping the material (*see* CROP). It is best to place crop marks on an overlay, in the event that the artwork is to be used again in some other context where the cropping may not be the same.

**CROSS-BOUNDARY MAIL**  mail shipped from one BULK MAIL CENTER or AUXILIARY SERVICE FACILITY to another, bypassing the parent bulk mail center at one end.

**CROSS DIRECTION**  direction running AGAINST THE GRAIN of paper. Paper is weaker and more susceptible to moisture damage in the cross direction than with the GRAIN

**CROSS ELASTICITY OF DEMAND**  degree to which DEMAND for one product is affected by the price of another product. Demand for frozen orange juice concentrate may increase when the price of fresh orange juice (a substitute product) increases. Demand for hotel rooms in a ski resort may decrease when the price of a lift ticket (a complementary product) increases. An increase that causes an increase is the result of positive elasticity. An increase that causes a decrease is the result of negative elasticity. Products with no impact on each other have zero cross elasticity. Marketers need to understand the cross elasticity factors that affect their products and competitor's products.

**CROSS FADE**  transition of two sounds. As one sound increases in volume (*see* FADE IN), another sound decreases (*see* FADE OUT). Together, the sounds create a cross fade. This same effect can be achieved with lighting instruments. As one lighting source fades in, a second source fades out. In video, however, the effect created by the simultaneous transition of two images is called DISSOLVE.

**CROSSLINE SCREEN**  screen consisting of an opaque grid pattern between two clear glass sheets through which images are photographed to produce a HALFTONE image. The crossline screen is mounted between a CONTINUOUS TONE image and the lens. DOTS produced by the crossline screen are square. *See also* CONTACT SCREEN; DIRECT SCREEN HALFTONE.

**CROSS MERCHANDISING**  setting up displays of complementary merchandise, usually in a supermarket, so that they are opposite each other; also called RELATED ITEM APPROACH (to merchandising). In this way, a customer may be tempted to "cross over" from one product to another. For example: A manufacturer's display of shampoo may be set opposite a display of hair conditioner made by the same company, to tempt the shampoo buyer to cross over to the hair conditioner as well.

**CROSS-PROMOTE**  promotion of a product to the buyers of another product sold by the same seller. This is a good way to generate additional business without incurring list rental expense. In book club operations, this kind of promotion is also called *Cross-Reenrollment.*

**CROSS-SELL**  also called Suggestive Selling, sales technique whereby complementary products are presented to a customer after the customer has demonstrated a desire and willingness to purchase a particular product. For example, when selling electronic equipment, a salesperson may attempt to sell a service contract for the extended maintenance of the equipment after the customer has decided to purchase the equipment. While cross-selling may make accessorizing more convenient for the customer, it also enables the salesperson to sell more products.

**CROSS TABULATION** statistical technique that establishes an interdependent relationship between two tables of values; but does not identify a causal relationship between the values; also called *two-way tabulation*. For example, a cross tabulation might show that cars built on Monday have more service problems than cars built on Wednesday. Cross tabulation can be used to analyze the results of a consumer survey that, for example, indicates a preference for certain advertisements based on which part of the country the consumer resides in.

**CRT** *see* CATHODE-RAY TUBE (CRT) DISPLAY.

**CUCALORUS** metal pattern, similar to that of a cookie cutter, that is inserted in front of the lamp in a spotlight; also called *cookie*. The cucalorus is used to produce a pattern on the wall of a set or on a curtain or other background piece to provide some visual variety or effect.

**CUE**
1. in advertising, a signal, either audible or visible, used to keep the elements of a production running smoothly. A cue may be a word or line spoken by another actor, a hand signal from a member of the stage crew, or an electronic beep or buzzer. Cues are given to signal actors to make an entrance or exit, speak a line, or take some action. They are also given to signal the beginning or end of a program, or for some other production activity, such as the changing of a set. A cue is also used to preset technical aspects of production, such as film, audiotape, records, or videotape so that any of these elements will be at the program director's fingertips.
2. in consumer behavior, a relatively minor influence on human behavior that, in concert with the more powerful influence of a PRIMARY DRIVE or LEARNED DRIVE, can control when, where, and how a response will be made; also called stimulus. For example, a restaurant patron driven by hunger will be cued by the time of day to respond to either the breakfast, lunch, or dinner items offered. Marketers can manipulate cues to influence behavior. Researchers have found that the color red stimulates appetite and might use red walls in a restaurant. Advertising can be a cue for purchasing a particular brand or for going to a particular restaurant.

**CUE CARD** large cardboard or oaktag strip (usually 14" × 22" in size) with the copy to be spoken by a performer written on one side in clear, legible print; also called *idiot card*. Used in television production, CUE cards serve as prompters for the talent in front of the camera. The cards are held by a member of the stage crew (usually the floor manager or assistant floor manager) near the camera lens, at a distance of about 8 to 12 feet away from the performer, so that it is not obvious to the home audience that the script is being read. Cue cards allow performers to make eye contact with the home audience and make it easier for them to deliver lines without mistakes.

**CUKALORIS** *see* CUCALORUS.

**CULTURAL ENVIRONMENT** *see* MACROENVIRONMENT.

**CUME** *see* CUMULATIVE AUDIENCE; HORIZONTAL CUME.

**CUMULATIVE AUDIENCE** audience accumulation for a medium over a specified time period. Individuals or households count only once in this measurement, no matter how many times they may have been exposed to the medium. Sometimes called the *cume* or *reach*, cumulative audience for the advertiser represents the *unduplicated audience* (the number of people who will be reached at least once) for a schedule over a specific time period. Therefore, the higher the cume, the larger the audience. *See also* CUMULATIVE AUDIENCE RATING.

**CUMULATIVE AUDIENCE RATING** rating used by A. C. NIELSON COMPANY in the NIELSON TELEVISION INDEX. It is based on the CUMULATIVE AUDIENCE, as compared to the average or total audience, and reflects the unduplicated audience size in 15-minute segments over a four-week period. For example, if a program has an average cumulative rating of 7 for its first quarter hour over the course of a four-week period, it means that 7% of the total potential audience tuned in to that program at least once during that quarter hour in the four-week period. *See also* AVERAGE AUDIENCE RATING; RATING; TOTAL AUDIENCE RATING.

**CURL** rippling effect on paper caused inadvertently by exposure to moisture or by coating one side of the paper. *See also* COATED PAPER.

**CURRENT ISSUE** issue of a periodical currently on sale at newsstands. New issues usually appear at the end of the prior issue period. For example, a monthly magazine's June issue would appear on the newsstands at the end of May. *See also* ON-SALE DATE.

**CURVED PLATE** plate used in printing that is curved to fit the CYLINDER of a ROTORY PRESS.

**CUSTOMER** buyer of a product or service.

**CUSTOMER DATABASE** collection of records of consumer purchasing patterns and histories stored in a computer system and organized so that it can be retrieved quickly to provide information for a variety of uses. Information contained in a customer database is obtained from store receipts, credit card purchases, mail-order requests, information inquiries, and other sources demonstrating customer preferences or predisposition to purchasing a product. Customer databases are useful to marketers when planning promotions for new products, repeat sales, or CROSS-SELLing techniques.

**CUSTOMER LIST** list of buyers maintained by a firm on a computer or in HARD COPY form for additional promotion.

**CUSTOMER PROFILE** description of a customer group or type of customer based on various DEMOGRAPHIC, PSYCHOGRAPHIC, and/or geographic characteristics; also called SHOPPER PROFILE. For example, magazine advertising salespeople provide advertisers with customer profiles describing the type of person who will be exposed to advertisements in that magazine. The description may include income, occupation, level of education, age, gender, hobbies, or area of residence. Customer profiles provide the knowledge needed to select the best prospect lists and to enable advertisers to select the best media.

**CUSTOMER SERVICE** department or function of an organization that responds to inquiries or complaints from customers of that organization. Customers may communicate in person or via written correspondence, toll telephone, or IN-WATS telephone.

Various techniques are used to generate correspondence back to the customer, including check lists, form letters, typewritten letters, COMPUTER LETTERS (fill-in type), or computer-generated personalized letters. For example, a check list may have three questions, with one question checked to indicate that it is the answer needed. Form letters accommodate a frequent and relatively standard situation. Typewritten letters are best for irate complaints or special situations. Computer letters combine the benefits of personalization with the efficiencies of automation.

Customer service correspondence may be in letterhead or postcard format. Customer service is an important part of the FULFILLMENT function, ensuring that customers will buy again and/or continue to be good customers.

**CUSTOMER SERVICE REPRESENTATIVE**
**In general:** employee responsible for maintaining goodwill between a business organization and its customers by answering questions, solving problems, and providing advice or assistance in utilizing the goods or services of the organization. *See also* CUSTOMER SERVICE.
**Postal service:** U.S. Postal Service employee responsible for assisting business mailers in utilizing and communicating with the USPS; abbreviated CSR. CSRs are assigned according to the location of the mailer's headquarters and will assist with the investigation and resolution of delivery problems nationwide, as well as provide information regarding postal procedures and regulations.

**CUSTOMIZED MARKETING** tailoring a particular product to the specific needs of an individual customer. Customized marketing is generally practiced by companies whose products are very expensive or unique, such as custom home builders or airplane manufacturers, because these products can be designed to suit the special needs of each customer. Since the company adapts its product and marketing program with such a high degree of specificity, customized marketing is considered to be the ultimate form of target marketing.

**CUT**
1. band on a long-playing record.
2. particular kind of photoengraving used as a PRINTING PLATE, derived from the term WOODCUT.
3. command given by a film or television director to stop action or production.
4. delete portions of filmed or videotaped material, or editorial and advertising copy, so that the material can fit into a particular time period or space.
5. immediate change from one scene to another, as distinguished from a fade (*see* FADE IN; FADE OUT) or DISSOLVE.

**CUTBACK**
**In general:** curtailment of production or expenditures provided for in a budget that has been adjusted.
**Advertising:** *see* FLASHBACK.
**Magazines:** reduction in the term of a magazine subscription because of UNDERPAYMENT It is usually calculated on a pro rata basis on the per copy value of the subscription order. *See also* PRORATE.

**CUT LINE** one-line copy that describes the illustration, drawing, or photograph next to which it appears. A cutline may also appear as a LEGEND or CAPTION.

**CUTOFF**
**Fulfillment:** point at which the processing of additional transactions is stopped prior to a file UPDATE. *See also* BUSINESS DATE CUTOFF.
**Printing:** printed-sheet length equal to the circumference of the PLATE CYLINDER used in a WEB PRESS.

**CUTSCORE** knife used to make a slight cut in the surface of paper or board to facilitate folding.

**CYAN** one of the inks used in FOUR-COLOR PROCESS printing. It produces colors with a blue hue.

**CYCLE** interval or unit of time specified within a contract, when the contract is for a longer time period. For example, an advertiser may have a television broadcast media purchase contract for a period of one year. Within that year contract, there may be specified four 13-week periods of television programming. Each 13-week period is considered a cycle. The advertiser may change or cancel the contract (with proper notice, of course) at the end of a cycle.
    A cycle is also used as a base for payment of talent fees in a commercial. Talent will be paid a fee for the specified length of a cycle.

**CYCLES PER SECOND (CPS)** *see* MEGAHERTZ.

**CYLINDER** cylindrical devices on a printing press, including PLATE CYLINDERS, BLANKET cylinders, and IMPRESSION CYLINDERS. In direct printing, the impression cylinder presses the paper against the plate cylinder. In offset printing, the blanket cylinder is pressed against the paper, transferring the image from one surface to another.

**CYLINDER GAP**  gap in printing press CYLINDERS housing the mechanism for PRINTING PLATE or BLANKET grippers and clamps.

# D

**DAILIES**
   **1.** newspapers published at least five times per week Monday to Friday.
   **2.** *see* ASSEMBLY DAILIES.

**DAILY RATE**  price of advertising space on a daily basis, usually in newspapers published Monday through Friday.

**DAMPENING SYSTEM**  printing mechanism that transfers dampening solution to the plate keeping the nonimage areas of an OFFSET plate moist and nonreceptive to ink. *See also* DESENSITIZER.

**DANDY ROLL**  wire cylinder used in papermaking that produces a smooth or ribbed surface. It is used to produce high-quality grades of paper.

**DANIEL STARCH AND ASSOCIATES**  market research firm located in New York which originated "recognition research" in periodical advertising. Each year, more than 30,000 advertisements in 1000 consumer and farm magazines, newspapers, and business publications are surveyed. Interviews are conducted to determine if a respondent has read a periodical. If the answer is yes, the periodical is opened to the advertisement in question. Further questioning is conducted to determine to what degree the advertisement was noted, read, and understood. Depending on their answers, readers are placed in one of three categories: *noted*, READ-MOST, SEEN/ASSOCIATED. *See* NOTED SCORE.

**DATA**  facts that become useful information when organized in a meaningful way or when entered into a computer. Marketing data on a customer include items like address and purchase history.

**DATA BANK**  information resources of an organization or business.

**DATA BASE**  collection of DATA stored on a computer storage medium in a common pool for access on an as-needed basis. The same pool of information can serve many applications, even those not anticipated at the time the data base was created. This is in contrast to traditional methods of data storage that hold a fixed amount of data retrievable in a predetermined format, often duplicating the storage of information in as many files as there are applications. For example, the name and address of the same customer may be in a marketing file, a billing file, and an ADDRESSING file. If any one of these applications changes, and the programs that access and use the customer record change, then the customer file must change. In data base systems, the customer information is retrievable for each application from a shared file that is not dependent upon the application programs for its structure.

**DATABASE MARKETING** collection, storage, analysis, and use of all available data about a prospect or customer; usually maintained on a computer file. Data may be collected from past purchases, such as items purchased, and the recency, frequency, and monetary value of purchases, or it may be nonpurchase related, such as income, education level, and age. Data can be generated by the marketer's activities (sales, surveys) and supplemented by data purchased from other sources. Database marketing assumes that the marketer can predict future purchase behavior through analysis of customer characteristics and past actions. Database marketing increases the cost effectiveness of promotions by segmentation of the customer list into clearly defined target groups with a high probability of purchase. Marketers can also use their understanding of the likes and dislikes of the market gleaned from analysis of the database to design or suggest new products. Although database marketing has been dominated by direct marketers, mass marketers are beginning to understand and use them as well. Some consumers have concerns about the privacy of the information maintained on databases. *See also* LIFETIME VALUE; PRIVACY LAW.

**DATA CARD** card published by a LIST OWNER that provides information needed by LIST USERS and LIST BROKERS about a list available for rental. The card includes, for example, a profile of the individuals on the list, the source of the names, the quantity, and the price based on the SELECTION CRITERIA used and the format of the output (LABELS or MAGNETIC TAPE). New data cards can be published as often as the list is UPDATED so that list quantities can be kept current. *See also* RATE CARD.

**DATA ENTRY** process of entering data into a computer system. Data may be converted to CODES prior to entry, that facilitate storage and retrieval of information. Data entry can be accomplished in several ways, including KEY ENTRY, TAPE ENTRY, and SCAN ENTRY. Tape entry is the most accurate and most efficient type of data entry, requiring the least amount of clerical involvement, followed by scan entry, then key entry.

**DATA OVERLAY** transfer of information from one list owner's file to another file lacking some information, by matching records on the receiving file to records on the file that already has the desired information. For example, DEMOGRAPHIC or LIFE-STYLE data can be added to a customer file by overlaying a demographic or life-style data file. The match may be accomplished on a geographic level, such as ZIP CODE or CARRIER ROUTE, or on a household level that matches by name and address.

**DATE LINE** in advertising, payment-due line on an order blank or contract.

**DAY-AFTER RECALL** research technique measuring the amount of audience recall one day after exposure to an advertisement or commercial. Results are usually gathered by telephone, with respondents being given the name of a product or brand and then asked what they can remember. *See also* BURKE TEST.

**DAY-GLO** brand name for a luminous paint that comes in brilliant colors and appears to glow in the dark. Although Day-Glo is often used for children's Halloween costumes, its primary use is on outdoor displays and advertisements, and wherever else eye-catching color is useful—for example, in a retail store window to call attention to a special sale.

**DAYPART** time segment in the broadcast day. Radio and television stations have divided the day into time segments to reflect broadcast programming patterns and audience composition throughout the day. Commercial time may be purchased by the daypart (rather than by the program), and its cost is based upon the average size of the audience for a specific daypart. PRIME TIME is an example of a television daypart where the programming is usually of a general nature with family appeal for a wide demographic range of viewers, and is usually the daypart with the largest viewing audience.

Dayparts are set by the individual stations, but they typically follow a standard pattern. Radio is typically divided into five dayparts as follows:

| | | |
|---|---|---|
| 6:00 A.M. – | 10:00 A.M. | MORNING DRIVE* |
| 10:00 A.M.– | 3:00 P.M. | Daytime |
| 3:00 P.M. – | 7:00 P.M. | AFTERNOON DRIVE* |
| 7:00 P.M. – | 12:00 A.M. | Nighttime |
| 12:00 A.M.– | 6:00 A.M. | All night |

*The combination of DRIVE TIMES accounts for radio's prime time.

Typical television dayparts may be as follows:

| | | | |
|---|---|---|---|
| 7:00 A.M. – | 9:00 A.M. | M–F | Morning |
| 9:00 A.M. – | 4:30 P.M. | M–F | Daytime |
| 4:30 P.M. – | 7:30 P.M. | M–F | EARLY FRINGE |
| 7:30 P.M. – | 8:00 P.M. | Sun–Sat | ACCESS |
| 8:00 P.M. – | 11:00 P.M. | M–Sat | Prime time (7:00 P.M.–11:00 P.M. Sun.) |
| 11:00 P.M. – | 11:30 P.M. | M–F | Late news |
| 11:30 P.M. – | 1:00 A.M. | M–F | Late fringe |
| 1:00 A.M. – | | Sun–Sat | Late night |

**D COUNTY** *see* ABCD COUNTIES.

**DEADBEAT** credit customer who, without just cause, has not paid for his order by the end of the BILLING SERIES; also called *uncollectible*.

Names of deadbeats are removed from the ACTIVE customer list and may be used later as a PURGE file against promotion lists. *See also* BAD DEBT; BAD DEBT ALLOWANCE; CREDIT PRESCREENING.

**DEAD EXPIRE** magazine subscription record that has expired without RENEWAL and is eventually removed from the ACTIVE subscriber list. Dead expire lists are usually maintained for two to three years for promotion purposes. Beyond three years, the names on the list are assumed to be of no value because the addresses may no longer be valid.

**DEAD LETTER** mailing piece that cannot be delivered as addressed or be returned to the sender. The U.S. Postal Service maintains a deadletter branch that aids in locating letters reportedly not delivered. The final disposition of dead letters depends upon the class of mail and the nature of the material. The retention period varies from 5 days to 30 days in most cases. Mail that is insured, or that is COD, is retained for 6 months. Unclaimed P.O. Box mail is kept as long as the box rental fee is paid. Registered mail is retained for 60 days. Foreign mail is turned over to the postal authorities of that country.

**DEAD MATTE** area surrounding a drawing, illustration, or photograph that has a dull finish so that it can be written on easily. Instructions for printing, or for other use, are written on the dead matte area.

**DEAD METAL** area of a metal PRINTING PLATE that is not TYPE HIGH and thus does not function in the reproduction process. The dead metal area is the blank area on the plate.

**DEAL** in marketing, sales promotion that enables a customer to save money on the purchase of a product or service. *Consumer deals* offer discounts or special purchases to the consumer for various products, usually within a time period. *Trade deals* offer special discounts to retailers for buying in large quantities, or special displays at reduced costs, or some other dollar incentive to purchase a manufacturer's goods or services. By law, trade deals must be offered on an equal basis to all retailers or dealers doing business with a manufacturer.

**DEALER** merchandise retailer. Dealers purchase and maintain an inventory of the merchandise to be sold and therefore share the costs of marketing and distribution with the manufacturer and wholesaler. Dealers differ from MANUFACTURERS REPRESENTATIVES AND BROKERS, who never take TITLE to the merchandise.

**DEALER IMPRINT** name and address of a local dealer, printed on a national advertisement, circular, pamphlet, or the like, after the piece has been designed and printed by the national manufacturer. The dealer IMPRINT may be handwritten, stamped, pasted, or professionally imprinted on the piece.

**DEALER LIST** list of local dealers appearing on a nationally presented advertisement in a regional publication. The advertisement will stay the same in all regional issues, but the dealer list will change from region to region.

**DEALER LOADER** *see* BUYING LOADER.

**DEALER TAG** local dealer identification at the end of a national broadcast commercial. Since the name is tagged on at the end of the commercial, it is called a dealer tag.

**DECAPPED** short for *decapitalized*; information OUTPUT from a computer, in upper/lower case format, that is stored in the computer in upper case. The conversion to upper/lower case format is usually for esthetic reasons.

**DECEPTIVE ADVERTISING** advertising that makes false claims or misleading statements, as well as advertising that creates a false impression. If retailers systematically advertise merchandise at low prices to get customers into their store and then fail to have the merchandise, they are guilty of deceptive advertising. Deceptive practices can take many other forms as well, such as false promises, unsubstantiated claims, incomplete descriptions, false testimonials or comparisons, small-print qualifications of advertisements, partial disclosure, or visual distortion of products. Anyone—including the manufacturer of a product, the advertising agency preparing the advertisement, the retailer, or even a celebrity who endorses a product—can be prosecuted for making unsubstantiated claims about a product or service. As a matter of fact, any advertising that leads the consumer to make purchase decisions based on false assumptions about the price and quality of competitive products is considered deceptive practice and is punishable by law. Responsibility for enforcement of the laws dealing with unfair and deceptive advertising comes under the jurisdiction of the FEDERAL TRADE COMMISSION.

**DECIBEL** unit measurement of the intensity of sound; abbreviated *db*.

**DECISION-MAKING UNIT** one or more individuals involved in a BUYING DECISION who share the same objectives and risks in making the purchase. The members of a household are a decision-making unit with regard to which television show to watch. Women are most often the decision-making unit for cosmetics and men for shaving cream. Marketers need to know who participates in a decision and the relative influence of each in order to create advertising that influences that decision. Auto manufacturers have only recently begun to target their advertising toward women, and some have initiated special sales training geared toward selling to women. Packaged food and household cleaning products manufacturers are now targeting some of their advertising to teenagers, who are increasingly participating in household responsibilities such as cooking and cleaning and consequently influence related purchases.

**DECISION MODELS** computer-based system used in making judgments about NEW PRODUCT DEVELOPMENT. Decision models employ scientific methodology to help understand, predict, or control marketing situations or problems. *See also* MODEL.

**DECKLE EDGE** feathery paper edge. Deckle edges are created by the process of making handmade paper. The paper tends to thin out around the edges underneath a wooden frame called a deckle. Contemporary machine-made paper does not have a deckle edge. However, moldmade paper used for fine stationery is still made with a deckle edge. In other grades of paper, the deckle edge is trimmed off.

**DECOY NAME** *see* SALT NAME.

**DEDICATED LINE** telephone or computer line that is reserved for one function or user, such as incoming customer phone calls.

**DEDUPE** process that uses matching logic to eliminate file records that are DUPLICATES (*dupes*); also called *dupe combine*. There are different strengths of dedupe computer PROGRAMS based on the objectives of the file user. For example, if a product being sold by the file user is inappropriate for apartment dwellers, then households with the same street address but different apartment numbers are dupes and are thereby eliminated from the list. If several rented lists are being deduped during a MERGE/PURGE a PRIORITY statement must be built into the dedupe program matching logic to indicate which lists dupes should be removed from. Random prioritization protects list owners from being disproportionately penalized for duplicate records by removing dupes from the lists on a random basis. Payment is made to the list owners for names remaining after the dedupe process, so the fewer dupes removed from their list, the more they are paid. For example, if List A and List B duplicate 8 records, 4 of the duplicates are removed from List A and 4 are removed from List B, thus reducing their rental revenue equally. *See also* DUPE CHECK; NET NAME ARRANGEMENT.

**DEEP-ETCH PLATE** in OFFSET lithography, PRINTING PLATE, used for long press runs, on which the inked areas to be printed are recessed slightly below the surface, making the plate more resistant to wear than *surface* plates. Even BIMENTAL PLATES are not as durable as deep-etch plates.

**DEFENSIVE SPENDING** *see* COMPETITIVE PARITY.

**DEFENSIVE WARFARE** competitive marketing strategies patterned after successful military defense strategies. Also called *marketing warfare*, defensive warfare is used by market leaders to protect their position in the marketplace against competitor attacks. There are six basic strategies: position defense, the most basic defense, which consists of building fortifications around the current market position; flanking defense, keeping careful check around the flanks and protecting the more vulnerable areas; preemptive defense, assumes that an ounce of prevention is worth a pound of cure and strikes out at competitors before they can make a move against the leading product; counter offensive defense, where the market leader studies the competitor's offense to find a gap and make counterattacks at this weak point; mobile defense, wherein the market leader stretches to new markets that can serve as future bases for defense and offense; contraction defense, a strategic withdrawal from the marketplace, giving up weaker positions and concentrating resources on stronger ones, or serving fewer markets but serving them much better. *See also* OFFENSIVE WARFARE.

**DEFERRED BILLING** delayed invoicing of a CREDIT ORDER buyer at the request of the seller. For example, billing may be deferred on a new subscription order so that the first issue of a magazine is received before the first bill arrives. This is especially important if the subscription promotion promised to send the first issue without obligation to pay. Deferred billing is also necessary for Christmas gift orders assigned a January ADVANCE START.

**DEFERRED SUBSCRIPTION INCOME RECOGNITION** accrual basis of periodical subscription accounting that recognizes income as earned when issues are served, as opposed to when the cash, check, or money order was received and banked. For example, if a magazine sells for $12 for 12 issues, on an accrual basis $1 is earned each time an issue is served, even though the full $12 was banked at the beginning of the subscription period. Accrual basis accounting offers the tax advantage of spreading revenue over time and is considered by some to be a better representation of revenue earned. Otherwise, adjustments must be made at a later date for cancellations and other changes.

**DEFINITIVE STAMPS** postage stamps issued by the U S. Postal Service for regular consumer mail usage, sold for an indefinite period of time. Commemorative and other special stamps are offered for a limited period of time and are frequently replaced by a new issue.

**DELAY CARD** announcement postcard sent to a customer advising of an expected delay in delivery of the merchandise ordered. Delay cards are sent to comply with the 30-DAY DELAYED DELIVERY RULE and as a courtesy to customers, to prevent complaints and cancellations.

**DELAYED BROADCAST** network program that is recorded when originally broadcast and is then broadcast from the recorded version at a later time or date by a local station in an area where the original broadcast was not received; abbreviated DB. This often happens in rural areas where the different networks share the same local station at various times.

**DELAYED DELIVERY RULE** *see* 30-DAY DELAYED DELIVERY RULE.

**DELAYED START**  *see* ADVANCE START.

**DELETE**
    **Computer file maintenance:** transaction that removes a record from a file; also called DROP.
    **Printing:** proofreader's instruction ("℘") to remove a portion of COPY set in type, or the printer's action in doing so.

**DELINQUENT**  *see* DEADBEAT.

**DELIVERABILITY GUARANTEE**  guarantee made by the LIST OWNER or LIST COMPILER to the LIST USER that either a certain percentage (usually 90% to 100%) of the list has valid (deliverable) addresses, or the postage expense of mailing to undeliverable addresses will be refunded to the mailer. Some exceptions to the guarantee may be made, such as excluding, for example, undeliverables that are complete except for an apartment number and could potentially be delivered. Some guarantees offer replacement names in lieu of cash compensation.

**DELIVERY CENTER**  group of individually keyed mailboxes serving a group of households; usually located in the lobby of apartment or office buildings. *See also* CLUSTER BOX.

**DELIVERY DATE**
    **1.** date the LIST OWNER agrees to deliver a list to the user.
    **2.** date a mailing piece is delivered to the recipient.
    **3.** date that merchandise is delivered to the customer.

**DELIVERY POINT BARCODE (DPB)**  11-digit, 62-bar, machine readable BAR CODE representing a NINE-DIGIT ZIP CODE plus two additional digits, used to address mail. The actual delivery point is represented by the last two digits, which indicate the last two numbers of a residential address, a P.O. box, rural route, or highway contract route. Substantial postal discounts are available to direct mail marketers who print a DPB on their mail. The DPB enables the U.S. Postal Service to use high speed scanners to sort mail down to the specific destination point so that it is in the proper sequence for the mail carrier without any manual sorting. The DPB may be printed in the address area or lower right corner of the envelope. If not preprinted by the mailer, the U.S.P.S. will use high speed document SCANNER/PRINTERS to read the address and apply a DPB. BULK MAILERS who apply the bar code themselves have greater latitude with regard to the selection of envelope colors and print styles without giving up postal discounts.

**DELIVERY SEQUENCE FILE**  computerized listing of all addresses served by the U.S. Postal Service. The U.S.P.S. issues a limited number of licenses (currently 11) to service companies that use the file to provide BULK MAILERS with list services such as improving ADDRESS HYGIENE, CARRIER WALK SEQUENCE CODING and application of NINE-

DIGIT ZIP CODES and CARRIER ROUTE CODES. These services increase the deliverability of the mailer's list. *See also* DELIVERY POINT BAR CODE.

**DELPHI TECHNIQUE** multi-step method used to estimate future demand for a product or service whereby a special group of experts in economic forecasting exchange views and then each individually submits estimates and assumptions to an analyst who reviews all the data received and issues a summary report. The summary report is then discussed and reviewed individually by the group members who each submit revised forecasts to the analyst, who then reviews the material again and issues a secondary report. This process continues until all participants reach a common ground.

**DEMAND** desire for a product or service that results in a purchase. Demand levels vary along a continuum from negative demand that leads to avoidance to excess demand that outpaces supply. Different marketing techniques are appropriate at different points along the continuum. For example, consumers are persuaded to donate blood by *conversional* marketing that changes their perception of it from a frightening to a positive experience. Some products for which there is no demand, such as tie-dye clothing in the '80s, came into demand again in the '90s through *stimulational* marketing. *Developmental* marketing creates a product to fill a previously unsatisfied demand or need. Other types of marketing increases demand for declining brands or may serve to maintain demand for a successful brand. At the far end of the demand continuum, DEMARKETING and COUNTERMARKETING are used to suppress demand. *See also* CROSS ELASTICITY OF DEMAND; DEMAND-ORIENTED PRICING.

**DEMAND-ORIENTED PRICING** method of establishing the price for a product or service based on the level of demand; also called *demand-based pricing*. For example, sellers of compact discs charge a higher price for recordings that appeal to a broad market, such as those of Garth Brooks or Madonna, than they charge for recordings of classical music. The manufacturing cost of the product and the required gross profit margin are of secondary importance to demand in setting the price. *See also* ELASTICITY; DEMAND; GOING-RATE PRICING.

**DEMAND STATES** various levels of consumer interest in the purchase of a product. At any given time there may be no demand, adequate demand, or too much demand for a given product, and marketers must be aware of these states of consumer demand in order to create a desired level of demand for their particular product. Marketers may face any of the following demand states: negative demand—a major part of the market dislikes the product, like dental work; no demand—consumers may be uninterested in the product; latent demand—consumers have a hidden want for a product that is not satisfied by any existing product, like unharmful cigarettes; falling demand—desire for a product declines; irregular demand—demand varies over a period of time, which may be seasonal, weekly, or even daily; full demand—

desire for the product is equal to the product manufacturer's ability to produce the product; overfull demand—the desire for the product is greater than the manufactuer's ability to produce the product.

**DEMARKETING** marketers attempt to reduce the demand for a product when the demand for the product is greater than the manufacturer's ability to produce it. Demarketing strategies involve raising prices, reducing advertising or promotion activities, or eliminating product benefits. Demarketing does not aim to destroy the demand but only to lower it to make it level with the ability to produce the product.

Marketers sometimes practice selective demarketing, which attempts to lower the demand for a product in a particular market, usually where one market is less profitable than other markets for the product. This is often done where the cost to manufacture, advertise, or promote the product is greater in one market than in other markets.

**DEMO** reel of broadcast programs, announcements, special projects, or commercials put together by an actor, director, production company, advertising agency, or the like, to demonstrate the ability and prestige of its owner; also called *sample reel. See also* CASSETTE.

**DEMOGRAPHIC EDITION** special edition of a periodical sent to a group of readers with common DEMOGRAPHIC characteristics. Demographic editions enable advertisers to reach better-targeted readers, although space advertising costs are higher than regular editions. For example, a special student edition, distributed to college students, would be of particular interest to beer and stereo advertisers.

**DEMOGRAPHIC ENVIRONMENT** *see* MACROENVIRONMENT.

**DEMOGRAPHICS** population or consumer statistics regarding socioeconomic factors such as age, income, sex, occupation, education, family size, and the like. Advertisers often define their TARGET MARKET in terms of demographics; thus, demographics are a very important aspect of media planning in matching the media with the market. Each demographic category is broken down (by the various research companies) according to its characteristics.

| CHARACTERISTIC | BREAKDOWN |
|---|---|
| Age | Preschool; 6–ll; 12–17; 18–34; 35–44; 50–64; 65+ |
| Income | Under $10,000; $10,000–$14,999; $15,000–$24,999; $25,000–$34,999; $35,000–$49,999; $50,000+ |
| Education | Grade school or less; high school; high school graduate; college; college graduate graduate school+ |
| Family size | 1–2; 3–4; 5+ |
| Sex | Female; male |

**DEMOGRAPHIC SEGMENTATION** MARKET SEGMENTATION strategy whereby the intended audience for a given product is divided into categories based on demographic variables (demographics). Demographic segmentation is the most popular basis for dividing groups, primarily because consumer usage and wants or needs usually match demographic categories, but also because demographic variables are easy to measure and obtain. age and life cycle segmentation is a form of demographic segmentation. See also behavior segmentation, geographic segmentation, psychographic segmentation.

**DEMONSTRATION COMMERCIAL** radio or television commercial used by a producer, production company, director, actor, advertising agency, technical representative, or the like, to demonstrate talent and ability for the purpose of securing new work. *See also* DEMO.

**DENSITOMETER** device used in printing to precisely measure the DENSITY of photographs and of color on a printed image to determine if the printing was consistent throughout the run.

**DENSITY**
**In general:** term used as a measure of population in proportion to a geographic area.
**Direct marketing:** measure of the proportion of customers or prospective customers in a geographic area compared to the total population of the area.
**Photography:** measure of the relative blackening of photographic images, which consist of silver particles spread in varying densities onto a surface. The particles create images of light, dark, and shadow. *See also* DENSITOMETER.

**DEPARTMENT STORE SALE**
**In general:** offering of merchandise at reduced prices in order to increase store traffic or otherwise promote sales.
**Magazines:** subscriptions sold through a department store, either via a catalog or via BILL INSERTS.

**DEPENDENT VARIABLE** *see* VARIABLE.

**DEPLETION METHOD** method of subscription SOURCE EVALUATION that measures the relative profit (or loss) over time of different SOURCES of new subscribers and that includes both the initial new order promotion expense and the RENEWAL PROMOTION expense as those new orders expire, but does not assume any additional new business promotion expense to replace subscribers that do not renew. Since the percentage of subscribers who renew is almost always less than 100%, the number of subscribers will decline over time.

**DEPTH** vertical length of a column in a newspaper, or magazine, measured in inches or AGATE LINES. *See also* COLUMN INCH.

**DEPTH INTERVIEW** research technique conducted in person in the field (rather than in the researcher's office) by a trained interviewer for the purpose of learning the motivation of consumers in the purchase decision process. In the unstructured home environment, the interviewer interacts with respondents and encourages them (usually in a one-on-one situation) to freely express their opinions, ideas, feelings, thoughts, and attitudes. The objective is to go beyond the superficial and to probe into consumer behavior. Depth interviews, along with FOCUS GROUP INTERVIEWS, are helpful in the evaluation of consumer reaction to a product or service. *See also* MOTIVATIONAL RESEARCH.

**DEPTH OF EXPOSURE** degree of penetration of the advertising message into the market. The greater the frequency of repetition of the advertiser's message, the greater the depth of exposure. In other words, the more frequently a consumer comes into contact with an advertiser's message (in any medium), the more likely it is that the consumer will purchase the product.

**DEPTH OF FIELD** in filming, videotaping, or photography, the area that surrounds the subject in a picture and is in acceptable focus. Whenever a camera lens is focused on a subject, an area in front of the subject and an area behind it will be in focus as well. The degree to which these areas are in focus denotes the depth of field. If there are a great many objects in focus surrounding the principal subject, the depth of field is said to be wide or deep. If there are almost no objects in focus surrounding the principal subject, then the depth of field is said to be narrow or shallow.

The depth of field plays an important role in the audience's perspective of a scene and is used as a visual technique to create an artificial perspective. For example: In a narrow depth of field, the audience attention is directed to the subject that is in focus, giving that subject a great deal of importance in the scene.

**DERIVED DEMAND** requirement for one product that is created due to the purchase of another product. Derived demand occurs for consumers who purchase goods for further production, because their purchases are based on the demand for their final product. For example, when the demand for automobiles is high, the derived demand for steel, and all other products used to make automobiles, is also high. Should the demand for automobiles drop, so will the demand for the products used to make the automobiles.

**DESCENDER**
1. that part of a lowercase letter that extends below the main body of the letter. The letters g, j, p, q, and y all have descenders.
2. any lowercase letter with such a descending stroke. *See also* ASCENDER.

**DESCRIPTIVE MODEL** MODEL used in CONSUMER RESEARCH to help set research objectives after a marketing problem has been defined.

The descriptive model is designed to describe things such as the market potential for a particular product or the DEMOGRAPHICS and attitudes of consumers who buy a particular product.

**DESENSITIZER**   printing process chemical that makes the nonimage areas of a PRINTING PLATE nonreceptive to ink and receptive to water. *See also* DAMPENING SYSTEM; FOUNTAIN SOLUTION; GUM ARABIC.

**DESIGN**   creation of an advertising campaign including any one of the individual elements, such as the illustrations, the package details, or the visual symbols, or all of the elements in the plan, as well as the plan itself.

**DESIGNATED MARKET AREA (DMA)**   geographic area defined by the A. C. NIELSEN COMPANY as a group of counties that make up a particular television market. These counties comprise the major viewing audience for the television stations located in their particular metropolitan area. For the most part, the metropolitan areas correspond to the standard metropolitan statistical areas (*see* METRO AREA) defined by the Federal Government Office of Management and Budget. The areas do not overlap, and every county in the United States belongs to only one DMA. DMAS are used in the evaluation of audience data as well as in the planning and buying of media. *See also* AREA OF DOMINANT INFLUENCE.

**DESIGN-FOR-RESPONSE**   introduction of a new product or INNOVATION to the market with a flexible design that can be quickly modified in response to consumer reaction. Design-for-response may be used in lieu of time-consuming, error-prone and costly market research prior to market introduction of a product. It is especially effective with products that are true innovations and therefore difficult for preintroduction consumer research to evaluate. For example, when "talking pictures" were first developed, the film industry thought they would be a passing fad. Design-for-response requires that the manufacturing process be able to respond quickly and cost-effectively to design changes. Hearst Publications uses design-for-response to develop new magazines that are introduced to the market as ONE-SHOTS and are then revised according to reader and advertiser response before being launched as regularly published titles.

**DESKTOP PUBLISHING**   creation of CAMERA-READY materials with a personal computer. Desktop publishing eliminates the need for manual preparation of mechanical art and is available to anyone with a personal computer and a high-quality printer. Computer software programs have been designed that make possible the creation of page layouts and cover designs for brochures, newsletters, or other ancillary printed materials that previously had to be produced by professional artists and layout personnel.

**DETACHED MAIL UNIT**   group of U.S. Postal Service employees assigned to work in a mailer's own facility to monitor the preparation of outgoing mail. Only major U.S. Postal Service customers receive this service on an ongoing basis. *See also* IN-PLANT LOADING.

**DETAIL PERSON**
  1. salesperson working as a MANUFACTURER'S REPRESENTATIVE who visits the manufacturer's customers and takes care of details. A detail person's primary responsibility is to promote goodwill by making sure that the manufacturer's customer is happy with the product. He or she will suggest merchandising ideas, take orders for delivery, check on the stock, and work with the customer in any way necessary to help with the sale of the manufacturer's product.
  2. salesperson whose primary job is to increase business from current and potential customers by providing them with product information and other personal selling assistance. The detail person's task is to persuade customers to buy the company's product from the local distributor; for example, detail persons are hired by liquor companies to visit bar owners and managers, and by pharmaceutical companies to call on doctors. Also called *missionary salesperson.*

**DEVELOPER**  chemical agent used in photography to make photographic images visible after exposure to light.

**DEX**  brand name of a transcribing machine that sends printed messages and documents over the telephone lines to specially designed terminals. *See also* FAX.

**DIARY TECHNIQUE**  method of collecting audience data (readers, viewers, listeners) used by the various research companies. Sent to sample audience members, the diaries are maintained over a specific time period for a fee paid by the research company. Respondents are asked to record some demographic information and also the viewing, listening, reading, and purchasing habits of each family member. Provided that the respondents keep accurate records, the diary technique yields very detailed information as to who comprises an audience, for how long, and to what extent. In some instances, the diary technique is being replaced by the use of a PEOPLE METER.

**DICK STRIP**  LABEL roll generated by an A. B. DICK label printing machine. The term is also commonly used to denote any 1-UP roll of labels used to address catalogs, magazines, or other high-volume mailing pieces.

**DIE CUT**  piece of cardboard, paper, or other material that has been cut into a special shape or design in a process similar to printing, except that a sharp steel die (*embossing plate*) is used in place of a PRINTING PLATE. Die cuts are used in the production of greeting cards; labels and tags; direct-mail promotional pieces, such as calendars; novelty items; cutouts; and folding boxes or displays.

**DIE-STAMPING**  GRAVURE printing process that produces a raised image by using intaglio plates that have the print image etched into their surface and filled with ink. The paper is forced into the engraved surface of the plate, picking up ink from the etched areas and being molded into the surface. Die-stamping is used primarily for printing letterheads and business cards.

**DIFFERENTIATED MARKETING** also called multisegment marketing. MARKET COVERAGE strategy whereby a company attempts to appeal to two or more clearly defined market segments with a specific product and unique marketing strategy tailored to each separate segment. Typically differentiated marketing creates more total sales than UNDIFFERENTIATED MARKETING, but it also increases the costs of doing business. *See also* CONCENTRATED MARKETING.

**DIFFERENTIATION STRATEGY**
1. marketing technique used by a manufacturer to establish strong identity in a specific market; also called *segmentation strategy*. Using this strategy, a manufacturer will introduce different varieties of the same basic product under the same name into a particular product category and thus cover the range of products available in that category. For example, a soda company that offers a regular soda, a diet soda, a decaffeinated soda, and a diet-decaffeinated soda all under the same brand name is using a differentiation strategy. Each type of soda is directed at a different segment of the soda market, and the full line of products available will help to establish the company's name in the soda category. This technique is quite costly to the advertiser because each individual product must be marketed independently, since separate marketing strategies are necessary for each market segment.
2. positioning a brand in such a way as to differentiate it from the competition and establish an image that is unique; for example, the Wells Fargo Bank positions itself as the bank that opened up the West. Also called PRODUCT DIFFERENTIATION.

**DIFFUSER**
1. in production, screen used as a filter and placed over a light to soften the light and eliminate harsh tones or shadows.
2. screen used over a camera lens to give the image a kind of fuzzy effect, as in a dream.

**DIFFUSION** process by which a new product or idea attracts the attention and interest of a market and is gradually adopted by the many individuals making up that market. Unlike individual adoption decisions, diffusion is influenced by communication about a product between an ever-widening group of consumers and is affected by the social dynamics of the group. *See also* ADOPTION PROCESS; INNOVATION; EARLY ADOPTER; INNOVATOR.

**DIFFUSION OF INNOVATION** describes the manner in which a product is disseminated in the marketplace. The diffusion of innovation spans an unspecified period of time from new product introduction through market saturation and affects the total sales level of a product. Diffusion of innovation relates to products such as the telephone answering machine, home computer, or microwave oven which had few users when initially introduced but became popular additions to American homes over time. *See also* ADOPTER CATEGORIES.

**DIFFUSION PROCESS** *see* DIFFUSION OF INNOVATION.

**DIFFUSION TRANSFER** photoprocessing method, exemplified by Polaroid film, consisting of a light-sensitive coating on a piece of film used to produce a NEGATIVE that is transferred to a paper sheet producing a POSITIVE image photograph.

**DIGEST-SIZE PAGE** advertisement that measures 5" × 7"; so named because this is the size of a page in the *Reader's Digest.*

**DIGITAL BROADCASTING** transmission of text or images to a group of people via personal computers. This gives viewers the option to access information or services at their convenience and allows interaction with a remote DATA BASE from home or office. Digital broadcasting has been used to book airline reservations, to provide stock quotations or sports results, and to sell real estate. *See also* ELECTRONIC CATALOG; TELETEX; VIDEOTEX.

**DIGITAL IMAGING CAMERA** camera that electronically relays, reads, or enters information by first converting it from HARD COPY to digital signals. This technology allows a direct marketer to relay orders received in various locations to a central location for KEY ENTRY of the orders to the FULFILLMENT system. Some digital imaging cameras also perform a SCAN ENTRY function, entering data directly to the fulfillment system. Digital imaging equipment is costly and would be economical only for large-volume operations.

**DIMENSIONAL MARKETING** direct mail approach to marketing in which the mailed materials are packages containing printed matter and three dimensional objects used as props to promote a product or service. Due to the bulk and weight of the promotional package, dimensional marketing is usually very costly and is thus done on a limited basis.

**DIMENSIONAL STABILITY** characteristic of paper that retains its size despite exposure to moisture.

**DIMINISHING MARGINAL UTILITY** economic theory that the perceived value of a product to a consumer declines with each additional unit acquired. For example, the first hot fudge sundae purchased by a consumer has a high degree of utility. A second or third sundae has a progressively lower marginal utility. Consumers attempt to maximize the utility derived from their dollars by purchasing a variety of products rather than multiples of the same product.

**DIORAMA**

> **Advertising:** elaborate display that is usually scenic and is almost always illuminated and three-dimensional; generally used in POINT-OF-PURCHASE ADVERTISING.
>
> **Television production:** setting built to scale in miniature that gives the impression of the actual larger setting.

**DIRECT ACCESS STORAGE DEVICE (DASD)** computer INPUT/OUTPUT device that stores information magnetically. Direct access means that the CENTRAL PROCESSING UNIT of a computer can directly access the information it requires without searching sequentially through the information stored. It is similar to playing a song on an album without playing all preceding songs first.

**DIRECT CANCEL**   request received from a subscriber to cancel a subscription; *also called* VOLUNTARY CANCEL. *See also* CASH CANCELLATION; CREDIT CANCELLATION.

**DIRECT COSTS**   expenses such as production materials and labor or sales force salaries that relate directly to the manufacture or sale of a product. Direct costs may be fixed or variable and may be charged against a product, a sales program, a customer account, or a marketing plan. *See also* INDIRECT COSTS.

**DIRECT HALFTONE PROCESS** method of making a HALFTONE print (a print that has varying tonal qualities) directly from the original, using a photographic process. The direct halftone process is used when making COLOR SEPARATIONS in the reproduction of color photographs or other color artwork.

**DIRECT-MAIL ADVERTISING**   form of advertising that uses person-to-person communication rather than mass media. The success of direct-mail advertising relies upon an efficient postal system, because the advertising reaches its audience by means of fliers, letters, BROCHURES, REPRINTS, CIRCULARS, and other such material sent directly through the mail. In direct mail, specific markets can be pinpointed with extreme selectivity and there is very little WASTE CIRCULATION.

Users of direct-mail advertising include manufacturers and retailers. Their objectives will vary, from prompting some desired action (such as a purchase) to providing information about a product or service (again, with a purchase in mind). Many formats may be used, depending upon both the objective and the advertiser's budget.

It is estimated that approximately 5% to 10% of the total overall retail advertising budget is spent on direct mail, which in 1984 amounted to $6 billion. Studies done between 1977 and 1983 reveal that 30% to 35% of all Americans respond to direct-mail advertising.

**DIRECT-MAIL AGENCY**   SUBSCRIPTION AGENT that sells subscriptions through the mail. Most direct-mail agencies use SWEEPSTAKES promotions offering high-value prizes, and can mail in larger quantities than any one publisher could afford. Promotion PACKAGES used by direct-mail agencies usually include STAMP SHEETS showing all of the magazines they sell and the price of each. The commission taken by agencies usually ranges from 75% to 95% of the selling price, and they typically offer the lowest price available from each publisher to the general public.

Publishers often use special RENEWAL PROMOTION offers and packages to renew subscriptions sold by direct-mail agencies, because these subscribers tend to be very price sensitive. Sweepstake promotions are especially effective in renewing sweepstake-sold subscriptions. Direct-mail agents tend to be the largest and most reputable subscription agencies. *See also* CASH FIELD AGENT, CATALOG AGENCY; SCHOOL AGENCY.

**DIRECT-MAIL LISTS, RATES, AND DATA (DMLRD)** directory of lists available for rental, including the price of selections from each. It is published semiannually by Standard Rate & Data Service, Inc., 3004 Glenview Road, Wilmette, IL 60091.

**DIRECT-MAIL MARKETING ASSOCIATION (DMMA)** *see* DIRECT MARKETING ASSOCIATION.

**DIRECT MARKETING** selling via a promotion delivered individually to the prospective customer. Direct marketing differs from general marketing in that the result of a promotion is measurable in terms of response; also, direct marketing is largely dependent upon the use of customer files and lists. Frequently associated with mail order, direct marketing also includes a variety of promotion media such as door-to-door selling, VIDEOTEX services, NEWSPAPER INSERTS, TELEMARKETING, TAKE ONE cards, and PACKAGE INSERTS. Direct marketing is a more personal type of promotion than advertising. The direct marketer selects the individuals who will receive the promotion, and is the direct recipient of the response, if any. The response may be a purchase, an inquiry, or a referral that can be traced directly back to the individual. Through the use of LISTS, computer files, and DATA BASES, the fourth "P" of MARKETING, *place*, is brought to the individual consumer. Direct marketing is utilized by virtually every type of business and organization. However, the primary users are magazine publishers, CATALOG HOUSES, political campaign organizations, and financial institutions.

**DIRECT MARKETING ASSOCIATION (DMA)** association of DIRECT MARKETING organizations and their suppliers. Its mission is to promote, through responsible self-regulation, the reputation of the industry and protect its freedom to operate unencumbered by legal restrictions, and also to provide its members with educational tools and a forum for sharing ideas. The DMA includes several special-interest councils, such as the LIST COUNCIL and the CIRCULATION COUNCIL.

It was previously known as the Direct Mail Marketing Association (DMMA). The DMA is headquartered in New York City.

**DIRECT MARKETING EDUCATIONAL FOUNDATION** organization that helps to provide sources of formal education in DIRECT MARKETING for those in the field and those hoping to join the field. It encourages universities and colleges to begin direct marketing programs of instruction.

**DIRECT MEDIA**  various communication channels (e.g., direct mail or telephone) utilized in DIRECT MARKETING to bring the promotion message to the individual prospect, as opposed to communication media that cannot be directed to a specific individual (e.g., television or radio).

**DIRECTOR OF RESEARCH**  *see* CONSUMER RESEARCH DIRECTOR.

**DIRECTORS GUILD OF AMERICA (DGA)**  independent union, founded in 1959 by a merger of the Screen Directors Guild of America and the Radio and Television Directors Guild; headquartered in Hollywood, California. The Directors Guild of America represents directors, assistant directors, floor managers, and some production assistants, in motion picture and television production. The union functions primarily in the negotiation of work agreements for its members. It also sets the minimum wage (scale) for directors and stipulates acceptable working and traveling conditions for its members. Additionally, the DGA has established clearly defined guidelines for the director's creative rights on a production.

**DIRECTORY ADVERTISING**  advertising that appears in a specialized directory classified according to some purpose. Although the most commonly known classified directory is the Telephone Yellow Pages, some 7000 classified directories of various types, are published in the U.S. each year—by real estate locators, trade associations, chambers of commerce, industrial groups, government agencies, newspapers and advertising services, and other organizations. Each directory features advertising aimed at the publisher's specialized field.

As compared to other forms of media, directory advertising is usually less expensive and provides advertisers with the opportunity to call attention to their product or service at a time when the customer is actively looking and prepared to buy.

**DIRECT PROMOTION**  sales communication delivered directly to the consumer without use of any intervening media. Examples of direct promotion are house-to-house selling, shop-at-home services, such as Avon or Tupperware sales, direct mail, and telemarketing. Direct promotion offers consumers the advantages of convenience and personal attention. *See also* DIRECT MARKETING, DIRECT MEDIA, INDIRECT PROMOTION.

**DIRECT RESPONSE**
1. *see* DIRECT RESPONSE ADVERTISING.
2. reply from a prospective customer to a DIRECT MARKETING promotion.

**DIRECT RESPONSE ADVERTISING** advertising whereby the only connection the consumer has to the product is the advertising and the only way a consumer can act on the advertisement or commercial is to return a coupon or make a phone call. Direct response advertising is geared to eliminate an intermediary in the purchase process. It can utilize a wide range of media, from matchbook covers to print or radio and television, although it is typically conducted through the mail.

In direct response advertising, the effectiveness of the advertising is directly related to the amount of sales. Thus people who specialize in it are very knowledgeable about the correlation between positioning an advertisement in a publication and the resulting audience responses.

**DIRECT RESPONSE AGENCY** ADVERTISING AGENCY, or division of a general advertising agency, that specializes in the creation of DIRECT MARKETING promotions. *See also* DIRECT RESPONSE ADVERTISING.

**DIRECT RESPONSE TELEVISION (DRTV)** broadcast advertising to which the consumer may directly respond by calling an 800 NUMBER or 900 NUMBER, or by mailing an order to the address given. DRTV advertisers try to buy time during programs that are complementary to their products. For example, a cooking magazine would advertise during a cooking show. Most DRTV advertisements run on cable networks because the time purchased is far less expensive than network television.

**DIRECTS** *see* DIRECT SACK.

**DIRECT SACK** sack of mail destined for the same delivery unit or post office. Direct sacks are usually destined for a FIVE DIGIT ZIP CODE area. *See also* FIVE-DIGIT DIRECT.

**DIRECT SALES** sources of magazine or other periodical subscriptions sold by the publisher without the use of a SUBSCRIPTION AGENT; also called *direct-to-publisher sales*. Direct-sold subscriptions require different renewal promotion copy, and direct-sold subscribers are generally less PRICE SENSITIVE than agency-sold subscribers. Renewal promotions for direct-sold subscriptions can be at higher prices and show less reliance upon the sweepstakes and premiums that agency-sold subscribers expect. Publishers use a variety of sources for direct sales, including DIRECT MAIL ADVERTISING, insert cards, and SPACE ADVERTISING.

**DIRECT SCREEN HALFTONE** HALFTONE NEGATIVE made by contact through a CONTACT SCREEN or CROSSLINE SCREEN.

**DIS**  *see* DISTRIBUTION AT.

**DISC JOCKEY (DJ)**  radio show host whose program consists of the playing of recorded music interspersed with light conversation and commercials or announcements; called *disc jockey.* Disc jockeys usually feature a particular type of music, such as jazz, rock and roll, or easy listening, and throughout the years, different DJ's have built up definite radio personalities specific to their particular brand of music—for example, Wolfman Jack and rock and roll music. With the advent of the discotheque and the video disk, the term has been widened to include anyone who plays popular recorded music for a group of listeners.

**DISCOUNT**  reduced price from a stated rate or LIST PRICE, usually offered to a customer as an incentive to make a purchase. There are many different kinds of commercial discounts, but generally they fall into four categories: (1) *trade*—given to intermediaries in exchange for services they perform (such as storage or handling); (2) *quantity* given to encourage bulk purchasing, whether in product or service, or in time or space; (3) *incentive*—given to encourage payment within a specific time period (for example, 2% off the bill if payment is made within 10 days); (4) *seasonal*—given to help level the production and marketing workload on seasonal merchandise (such as bathing suits, lawn furniture, gardening tools, or Christmas items) when the merchandise is out-of-season. Some discounts are offered in reaction to competitive advertising, as when a soda company offers increased volume discounts to retailers in response to a competitor's challenge campaign. Additionally, many gasoline companies offer discounts to consumers who pay with cash instead of credit cards.

**DISCOUNT HOUSE**  retail store that offers merchandise for sale at lower prices than conventional stores that sell merchandise at LIST PRICES or SUGGESTED RETAIL PRICES; also called *discount store.* Although most discount houses offer well-known national brands, they can afford to sell at a reduced markup because they are generally a "no-frills" operation. They reduce overhead costs by offering merchandise on a self-service basis, by providing a minimum of decor, fixtures, and facilities, and sometimes by operating in a low-rent area. The discount house may be a mass merchant, such as K-mart, or a specialty merchant, such as Toys "Я" Us for toys. The warehouse retailer and the catalog store (that sells primarily from a catalog—e.g., Consumers Distributing) are also considered variations of the discount house. Since the middle 1960s, discount house chains have accounted for more sales volume than all the conventional department stores combined.

**DISCOUNT STORE**  *see* DISCOUNT HOUSE.

**DISCRETIONARY INCOME**  spendable income remaining after the purchase of physical necessities, such as food, clothing, and shelter, as well as the payment of taxes. Marketers of goods other than necessities must compete for the consumer's discretionary dollars by appealing to various psychological needs, as distinguished from physical needs. When the economy weakens, goods normally purchased with discretionary income are the first to show reduced sales volumes. An expensive perfume will not sell during a depressed economic period, but people will continue to buy food and pay rent.

**DISCRIMINANT ANALYSIS** statistical analysis used to predict the probability of the occurrence of an event. For example, based on the DEMOGRAPHIC characteristics of the individuals on a promotion list, discriminant analysis can predict the probability of a positive response to a promotion by measuring the degree of similarity between the individuals on the list and current customers. Similarity can be defined across a variety of characteristics utilizing multiple discriminant analysis. *See also* MULTIDIMENSIONAL SCALING.

**DISJUNCTIVE MODEL** model of consumer attitude formation asserting that the consumer requires a minimum level of satisfaction on the most important product characteristics but not on every characteristic. A high degree of satisfaction with a less important characteristic will not compensate for a less than satisfactory rating on an important characteristic. For example, a car buyer may rule out all models that do not have the required price and fuel efficiency even though all other requirements are met or exceeded. This is one of several noncompensatory models. *See also* CONJUNCTIVE MODEL; EXPECTANCY-VALUE MODEL; LEXICOGRAPHIC MODEL; IDEAL POINT MODEL.

**DISK** computer storage device that magnetically stores data. On large computers, disks resemble a stack of phonograph records and the data can be accessed at any point by a movable arm just like the needle on a record player. Some microcomputers use floppy ("flexible") disks that are inserted into a disk drive that reads and writes data on the disks. *See also* DIRECT ACCESS STORAGE DEVICE.

**DISPATCH SCHEME** sequence in which mailing labels must be prepared by the mailer to coordinate with the order in which the mail must be loaded onto mail trucks for delivery to various U.S. Postal Service mail distribution facilities. The farthest zones are loaded first to facilitate truck unloading.

**DISPLAY**
**Marketing:** merchandise arranged to catch the eye and attract attention, in order to promote sales. Displays are differentiated by their placement and type—for example, window displays, in-store displays, floor displays, or POINT-OF-PURCHASE advertising displays. There are also ISLAND DISPLAYS or END-AISLE DISPLAYS, where the merchandise is stacked and readily accessible; upright displays especially made to hold the product; and cabinet displays (*see* DISPLAY CASE), where the product is readily viewable but not accessible. Displays are used most

frequently as collateral material in advertising campaigns, and show a relationship to the campaign through the use of an identifying mark as a visual symbol or logo.

**Printing:**
1. variety of type 18 points or larger in size. Display type is heavier and sometimes larger than textual type and is used in copy for emphasis, or for headlines in advertising, or for chapter titles, subheads, and the like in books or journals.
2. instruction to printer to set section of copy on a line apart from the rest of the copy.

## DISPLAY ADVERTISING
1. print advertising that is located throughout a publication and that utilizes size, color, illustrations, photographs, and various decorations and typography to attract the reader's attention. Display advertising is found among the editorial sections of a publication and is not grouped according to classification (as classified advertisements are). It further differs from CLASSIFIED ADVERTISEMENT in that it employs illustrations and varying type sizes and bases its rate structure on AGATE LINES, COLUMN INCHES, or fractions of a page.
2. freestanding advertisement designed for exhibition in traffic areas, such as retail stores, public buildings, terminals, and the like.

## DISPLAY ALLOWANCE  *see* RETAIL DISPLAY ALLOWANCE.

## DISPLAY BIN  one of the many varieties of displays used in POINT-OF-PURCHASE ADVERTISING. Usually constructed of cardboard or fiberboard, a display bin is an open container for small items. It is designed so that customers can handle and examine the merchandise contained within, in the belief that once a customer has the goods in hand, a purchase will result. Sometimes called *dump bin.*

## DISPLAY CARD  advertisement printed on a card or sheet of poster board and then attached to a store DISPLAY. Usually a display card will announce special sales, such as "two for one"; or special promotions, such as "buy now and win a free trip"; or special sale prices apart from regular prices.

## DISPLAY CASE
1. type of DISPLAY used in POINT-OF-PURCHASE ADVERTISING where the merchandise is in a closed container. A display case is usually a cabinet constructed of some sturdy material with glass panels so that the contents can be viewed. In order to handle the merchandise, the customer must ask a salesperson to open the case. Usually, large items and items of value, such as jewelry or stereo equipment, are displayed in a display case. Many of these cases are designed with lights, to create a setting for the merchandise within.
2. portable case carried by a salesperson and opened to display the merchandise within. For example, salespersons representing jewelry

manufacturers will carry their merchandise in a display case to show to the retailers and wholesalers in their various territories.

**DISPLAY LOADER** retailer or dealer premium included in a POINT-OF-PURCHASE ADVERTISING display, to be kept by the dealer when the promotion ends and the display is broken down. For example, some liquor companies will use a magnum of champagne or some decorative crystal glasses as part of a Christmas display. When the season is over, and the display is broken down, the store owner keeps the magnum or the glasses as a premium from the liquor company. *See also* BUYING LOADER.

**DISPLAY TYPE** *see* DISPLAY.

**DISSOLVE** visual effect, used most frequently in television production, in which one scene fades out to black as another scene fades in from black (*see* FADE IN; FADE OUT). The scenes appear to dissolve one into the other. A dissolve is used primarily to make a smooth transition between scenes in order to show the passage of time in a given situation, or to show simultaneous action in two different scenes. In audio, this simultaneous fading in and out is called a CROSS FADE.

**DISSONANCE** *see* COGNITIVE DISSONANCE.

**DISSONANCE ATTRIBUTION MODEL** in consumer learning theory, consumers will attempt to reduce COGNITIVE DISSONANCE after a purchase by gathering positive, reassuring information about the product, and ultimately attributing the purchase to good judgment, rather than the influence of peers, family members, or aggressive salespeople. *See also* ATTRIBUTION THEORY.

**DISTANT SIGNAL** television broadcast signal outside the local receiving area (as defined by the Federal Communications Commission), which is received by a cable operator and relayed to subscribers by cable; also called *imported signal.*

**DISTRIBUTING ROLLERS** rubber-covered CYLINDERS used in printing that transfer ink from the INK FOUNTAIN onto the ink drum of the printing press. *See also* PRINT DRUM.

**DISTRIBUTION**
**Magazines:** total number of copies distributed of a particular magazine issue. *See also* CIRCULATION.
**Merchandising:**
1. extent to which an item of merchandise is carried by retailers relative to the total number of retailers who could carry the item. *See also* EXCLUSIVE DISTRIBUTION; OPEN DISTRIBUTION; SELECTIVE DISTRIBUTION.
2. all elements of the system of delivery of merchandise to customers from the manufacturer or wholesaler, including retailers, brokers, transportation companies, advertising agencies, and so forth; also called *distribution channel. See also* CHANNEL OF DISTRIBUTION; MIDDLEMAN.

**DISTRIBUTION ALLOWANCE** price reduction offered by a manufacturer to a distributor, retail chain, or wholesaler, which allows for the cost of distributing the merchandise. A distribution allowance is frequently offered in a new product introduction.

**DISTRIBUTION AT (DIS)** designation used by the mailer to identify small quantities of SACKED mail destined for two or more post offices via one distributing office. Only the abbreviation "dis" is used in conjunction with the name of the distributing office.

**DISTRIBUTION CENTER FACILITY** Canadian version of a SECTIONAL CENTER FACILITY.

**DISTRIBUTION MODEL** program based on mathematical formulas or simulations of representative situations designed to assist management personnel in making decisions about distribution channels to be used for various products. A distribution model is helpful in determining locations for stores and warehouses as well as in the planning of marketing logistics.

**DISTRIBUTOR** firm or individual, particularly a wholesaler, who sells or delivers merchandise to customers, such as retail stores. Distributors act as intermediaries between manufacturers and retailers. They maintain a warehouse of merchandise, which is often purchased from many different manufacturers and then is sold (or distributed) among various retailers. By buying through a distributor, a retailer can have the advantage of one-stop shopping, rather than having to make individual stock purchases from each of the different manufacturers.

**DISTRIBUTOR BRAND** brand name owned by a retailer, wholesaler, or other distributor rather than by a manufacturer. For example: Kenmore is a Sears brand; Jane Parker, an A&P brand. All PRIVATE LABEL merchandise is sold as a distributor brand.

**DIVERSIFICATION** corporate growth strategy whereby a business builds its total sales by acquiring or establishing other businesses that are not directly related to the company's present product or market. There are three major diversification strategies: *concentric diversification*, where the new business produces products that are technically similar to the company's current product but that appeal to a new consumer group; *horizontal diversification*, where the new business produces products that are totally unrelated to the company's current product but that appeal to the same consumer group; *conglomerate diversification*, where the new business produces products that are totally unrelated to the company's current product and that appeal to an entirely new consumer group.

**DIVEST STRATEGY** plan whereby a product line (or a product division of a business) is liquidated or sold so as to limit either real or anticipated losses and to redirect the resources behind that product line or division to other company products or divisions.

**DIVISION MANAGER** *see* FIELD DIVISION MANAGER.

**DMA MAIL PREFERENCE SERVICE ADD-ON FILE** file previously maintained by the DIRECT MARKETING ASSOCIATION of people who have contacted the DMA to request that their names be included on promotional MAILING LISTS. This file is no longer made available, because mailers have found that the individuals on the list do not respond to direct mail promotions. *See also* DMA MAIL PREFERENCE SERVICE DELETE FILE.

**DMA MAIL PREFERENCE SERVICE DELETE FILE** file maintained by the DIRECT MARKETING ASSOCIATION of people who have contacted the DMA to request that their names be deleted from promotional MAILING LISTS. This file is available to all mailers on a subscription basis, as a PURGE file. Maintenance of this file is an important function of the DMA because it prevents consumer complaints about excessive "JUNK MAIL" volumes. The cost of a subscription varies by frequency (4 times/year, 2 times/year, 1/year) of use and by whether the user is a member of the DMA. Regardless, the price is a small fee that only covers the DMA's costs. The file can be ordered from the DMA's Washington, D.C. office. *See also* DMA MAIL PREFERENCE SERVICE ADD-ON FILE.

**DMLRD** *see* DIRECT MAIL LISTS, RATES, AND DATA.

**DMMA (DIRECT MAIL MARKETING ASSOCIATION)** *see* DIRECT MARKETING ASSOCIATION.

**DOCTOR BLADE** metal strip used in GRAVURE printing to wipe ink off the nonprinting areas of the printing CYLINDER or plate, leaving ink inside the printing areas of the plate.

**DOCUMENT** HARD COPY source of information, such as an order form, invoice, or complaint letter processed as part of the FULFILLMENT function.

**DOCUMENTARY** factual broadcast presentation of some authentic story, event, or situation, in contrast to a fictional account. A documentary is not usually presented for its entertainment value alone. It is supported by fact, and, as a rule, has a purpose or a theme, as well as a statement to make. Generally, documentaries take a journalistic approach to the material presented.

**DOGS** *see* GROWTH-SHARE MATRIX.

**DOLLAR VALUE PER ORDER** relative measure of the performance of a MAILING LIST or promotion, calculated by dividing the total gross revenue generated by the number of orders received.

**DOLLY**
   1. platform mount on wheels for a television camera so that the camera has easy access to all places in any scene being shot. A dolly

can be moved noiselessly throughout the set so that filming or taping can proceed with continuity.

**2.** command given by a director in television production to move a camera on a dolly: for example, "dolly in" (bring the camera closer); "dolly out" or "dolly back" (move the camera back for a longer shot).

**DOMESTIC MAIL MANUAL (DMM)** complete directory of U.S. Postal Service regulations concerning domestic mail services. It is published by the U.S.P.S. and utilized by all major mailers. The manual is available for a fee on a subscription basis from the Superintendent of Documents, Government Printing Office, Washington, DC 20402-0001. Updates are issued as necessary for changes in regulations. It has recently undergone a major revision to make it easier to understand.

**DOMINANCE MODEL** in this model of consumer attitude formation, the consumer rates a product according to the number of product characteristic expectations it satisfies relative to other brands. Unlike the LEXICOGRAPHIC MODEL, no characteristic takes a higher priority in the decision than another, and an unsatisfactory rating on just one characteristic can rule out a purchase. For example, a car buyer who is satisfied with a particular model in terms of every characteristic except the color of the interior will select another make that satisfies all requirements including interior color. *See also* CONJUNCTIVE MODEL; DISJUNCTIVE MODEL; EXPECTANCY-VALUE MODEL; IDEAL POINT MODEL.

**DOMINANT FIRM** company within a market that has the largest MARKET SHARE, such as McDonald's or Procter & Gamble. Dominant firms have a competitive advantage by virtue of their size, name recognition, and resources. They may hold onto their dominance through various strategies, including INNOVATION, BRAND EXTENSION, and PRICE WARS, that trailing firms do not have the resources to match. Dominant firms often have greater influence with distributors and can get their products into more retail outlets and in better display positions than trailing firms. *See also* CLAYTON ACT; ANTIMERGER ACT.

**DOMSAT** communications satellite system that allows for the transmission of broadcast programs or events throughout the U.S. *See also* COMSAT, INTELSAT.

**DONEE** recipient of a gift, such as a magazine subscription or book. Donees can be divided for mail promotion purposes into donee types, such as Christmas gift donees, non-Christmas gift donees, or donees of a trade gift given for business purposes. *See also* DONOR; DONOR CONTROL.

**DONOR**

**1.** person or organization who orders and pays for a gift, such as a magazine subscription or book. Donors can be divided into types, such as *recipient donors*, who themselves subscribe to the magazine being given, or *nonrecipient* donors, who do not subscribe to the magazine being given. Donors are sent promotions asking them to renew gift subscriptions they have given and are a good source of new business as well. *See also* CONTRIBUTOR LIST; DONEE; DONOR CONTROL; DONOR PROMOTION.

**2.** benefactor of a charity.

**DONOR CONTROL** record on a computer file used to control the billing and DONOR PROMOTION of a gift DONEE record. *See also* DONOR.

## DONOR PROMOTION

**1.** subscription RENEWAL PROMOTION sent to a DONOR listing all the DONEES to whom he gave a gift during one period of time. Gift subscription orders received from the same donor at different times are not renewal promoted together, because the subscriptions would not EXPIRE at the same time.

**2.** promotion sent to previous contributors soliciting another contribution.

**DONUT** prerecorded commercial with a blank time span in the center into which a special advertising message may be inserted. A donut is made by a production company and used by an advertiser who advertises on a regular basis and whose message is basically the same, but whose product will differ from time to time. For example: A retail chain may feature a different product for sale every week, although the theme of each sales promotion will be the same. Every week, their commercial will have the same opening and closing, and will use the same music and store LOGO. Thus, each week the production company will only have to shoot a new middle portion to feature the week's product(s), rather than having to shoot an entirely new commercial. The use of a donut saves the advertiser a great deal of money on production costs and guarantees continuity in the commercials. Further, DUBS of a donut can be sent to the networks and used over again each week, saving time, storage space, and effort. Only the middle section of the commercial will have to be trafficked on a weekly basis.

## DOOR OPENER

**In general:** any action or development that creates access to opportunity—for example, a gift offered by a door-to-door salesman in return for an opportunity to make a sales presentation.

**Direct marketing:** anything offered free by mail, or with a solicitation, that is reprinted from the publication being sold or consists of material related to the publication, and that is used to increase response to a promotion. According to AUDIT BUREAU OF CIRCULATIONS rules, door openers must not exceed 15 cents in value or else they are considered PREMIUMS. A door opener for a food magazine might be a collection of recipes; for a fishing magazine, a booklet of tips on fishing.

**DOT ETCHING** printing technique that alters the amount of color in a HALFTONE image by chemically reducing the size of the DOTS. Dot etching a NEGATIVE increases color. Dot etching a POSITIVE reduces color. *See also* COLOR CORRECTION; ETCH.

**DOT FORMATION**　arrangement of the individual elements (DOTS) on a HALFTONE printing plate or film.

**DOT GAIN**　HALFTONE printing error in which the DOTS print too large, producing an overly darkened image; also called *dot spread*.

**DOTS**　ink spots that, grouped in various levels of DENSITY and size, comprise HALFTONE images. When seen from a distance, a halftone image comprised of dots appears to be a CONTINUOUS-TONE image. The size of the dots created varies, depending upon the distance from which the printed image will be viewed. The closer the image will be to the viewer, the smaller the dots must be. The darkness of a printed area depends upon the density of the dots in that area. Billboards and posters utilize large dots; reading material utilizes small dots. *See also* DOT ETCHING; DOT GAIN; ELLIPTICAL DOT; HARD DOT.

**DOUBLE-DECKER**　two outdoor advertising displays built one on top of the other, usually seen in a high-volume traffic area.

**DOUBLE-PAGE SPREAD**　LAYOUT that covers two facing pages in a magazine or newspaper. If such a layout is featured in the center of the magazine or newspaper, it is called a CENTER SPREAD.

　　In advertising, double-page spreads are very costly and are usually used only when the advertiser is making some special announcement, such as the introduction of a new product, or a new brand promotion.

**DOUBLE POSTCARD**　direct mail promotion consisting of a form folded in half and usually sealed at one edge. One half of the form is a promotion addressed to the recipient and the other half is an order form or REPLY FORM addressed to the sender. The recipient tears off the order form to mail back to the sender. Double postcards must be printed on paper stock that meets U.S. Postal Service requirements for postcards. Different methods are used to seal the double postcard including SPOT GLUE, stickers, and tear strips. The REPLY FORM is usually postage paid and includes the prospect's preprinted name and address. Double postcards are a relatively inexpensive format for direct mail promotions but obviously limit the amount of sales copy and supportive materials that can be sent.

**DOUBLE SPOTTING**　two network or two local commercials aired one after the other during the same station break.

**DOUBLE TRUCK**　advertisement on a DOUBLE-PAGE SPREAD.

**DOUBLING DAY**　that point in a direct mail promotion life cycle at which you can anticipate half the expected returns to have been received. Depending on the class of mail used for the OUTER ENVELOPE and the REPLY ENVELOPE, doubling day will occur at different intervals, expressed as the number of days since the promotion was mailed. The number of responses received by doubling day are doubled to project total response. *See also* CATALOG SALES PROJECTION.

**DOWNSCALE** term used to identify the low-income segment of the population as distinguished from the high-income or UPSCALE segment.

**DOWNTIME** period during which a computer or equipment malfunction makes it inoperable.

**DRAGON'S BLOOD** powder applied to the relief portions of a metal PRINTING PLATE by using heat, so that the powder fuses with the plate's surface and protects the covered areas from damage caused by acid that is used during the printing process. Dragon's blood powder is made from the fruit of the rattan palm.

**DRAW**
  1. number of NEWSSTAND copies of a magazine issue taken by wholesalers, distributors, or retailers before return of unsold copies to the publisher. *See also* NEWSSTAND RETURNS.
  2. form of salesperson's compensation whereby the salesperson is paid in advance against expected future sales.

**DRAW-DOWN** technique used in ink preparation that tests the color of an ink mixture by spreading a thin film of ink on paper with a spatula. The term is taken from the movement of the spatula as it draws ink down the page.

**DRIER** chemical added to ink to speed drying.

**DRIOGRAPHY** print process, similar to lithography, utilizing PLATES that operate without water. Driography produces a high-quality print quickly and at low platemaking costs but requires special inks that make it a relatively expensive process.

**DRIVE STIMULUS** special sales promotion offered in the form of a DEAL to retailers, sales prospects, and consumers as a method of stimulating sales for the duration of the drive, the time period during which the product is being actively advertised. *See also* CUE.

**DRIVE TIME** one of the time designations used by radio advertising time sales departments or representatives to qualify the listening audience. Drive time represents those times of day when a majority of the audience are people listening to car radios on their way to or from work. There are two drive times: morning drive, generally from 6:00 A.M. to 10:00 A.M., and afternoon drive, from 3:00 P.M. to 7:00 P.M. These two periods together constitute radio PRIME TIME, the time periods with the largest listening audience. Commercial time is most expensive during this period because of the size of the audience to which the commercial will be delivered. *See also* DAYPART.

**DROP**

   **Direct marketing:** direct mail promotion entering the direct mail system; also called MAIL DATE. The drop date is usually planned to coincide with a buying season such as Christmas that has produced good results on prior mailings.

   **Fulfillment:** record to be removed from a computer file. *See also* DELETE.

**DROP DATE** date on which a direct mail promotion is due to enter the postal system, the date it is "dropped" in the mail.

**DROP IN** local television commercial aired during the broadcast of a nationally sponsored NETWORK show—for instance, a commercial for a local restaurant shown during a sporting event such as the Baseball Game of the Week or Monday Night Football.

**DROPOUT HALFTONE** reproduction of a photograph, drawing, or illustration that contains varying tonal qualities (called a HALFTONE) where some portion of the original copy has not been printed; also called HIGHLIGHT HALFTONE. The unprinted portion is usually a background area, which in reproduction will give greater contrast to the piece if it appears white or lets the printing paper show through. This effect is accomplished by dropping out the DOTS on the PRINTING PLATE or NEGATIVE, either by etching them away with acid or by opaquing the dot formation in the negative. The process is sometimes called *highlighting*, because the result is a reproduction with sharp, clear highlights.

**DROP-OUT PERCENT** relative proportion of customers who stop making purchases or donations or stop renewing subscriptions or memberships each year. *See also* RENEWAL RATES.

**DROP SHIPMENT** *see* DROP SHIPPING.

**DROP-SHIPPING**

   **Direct marketing:** trucking mail to various ENTRY POINTS to avoid U.S. Postal Service ZONE CHARGES.

   **Merchandising:** arrangement between a retailer and a supplier whereby the retailer can promote and sell merchandise that is stored and shipped by the supplier (*jobber*) directly to the retailer's customer. Ownership does not transfer until a purchase is made, enabling the seller to avoid tying up funds in inventory. However, drop-shipping suppliers usually charge a premium price to the retailer, who may pass this cost on to the customer. The retailer also loses the ability to control inventory quantities and the speed of delivery to the customer. Dropshipping is used by marketers selling a wide variety of expensive items (or heavy items) that would cost too much to keep in inventory economically (or ship). It is also useful when marketing a new item that may not sell.

**DRY MOUNT** mount artwork, posters, or photographs using a heat and pressure method, in contrast to a spray (or wet) adhesive. In the dry mount process, a thin, tissuelike paper is cut and placed between the piece to be mounted and the backing, and then all are placed in a special machine that applies pressure along with heat and seals the pieces together. Dry mount is a rather quick process that prevents the artwork from bubbling, while saving the time needed for adhesive to dry. It is used in advertising primarily for the making of posters or other display pieces.

**DRY-TESTING** promoting a product that is not yet available for delivery to the buyer in order to test response to the product before incurring the costs of producing or delivering the product. Dry-testing is usually done on a small scale to avoid customer complaints. Any cash orders received must be refunded. Dry-testing is not encouraged, but it is legal. It is used primarily by industries with very high product start-up costs, such as magazine publishers.

**DRY-UP** *see* CATCHING-UP.

**DUAL ADDRESSING** printing technology used by CATALOG houses that enables information, such as KEY CODES, printed on the mailing LABEL, to be printed simultaneously on the ORDER FORM inserted in the catalog.

**DUAL BRAND LOYALTY** tendency of a consumer to purchase either of two brands most of the time without exhibiting a consistent preference for one brand over the other. This differs from BRAND LOYALTY in that two brands share an equal degree of preference. Dual brand loyal consumers are easily influenced by brand availability, discount promotions, or special point-of-purchase displays. A dual brand loyal consumer may become brand loyal if perceived quality changes or other comparative factors change the balance. A perceived innovation by one brand, a permanent price change, or frequent stock-outs can have a strong impact as well.

**DUAL CHANNEL MARKET** geographic area that receives at least two television stations.

**DUAL OFFER** promotion technique that makes an "either-or" offer, such as the BOOK-OF-THE-MONTH CLUBS' offer of three books of one's choice for $1 or (as an alternative) the *Oxford English Dictionary* when an individual joins the club. A dual offer increases response because people enjoy choosing between two products, and because the offer enhances the perceived value of the products.

**DUB**
1. combine several sound tracks for recording on film or videotape.
2. add one television film to another; for example, to add the filmed version of a commercial to the film containing the regular entertainment program. This is called *dubbing* in.

**3.** duplicate of a commercial on videotape or audiotape made from a master print, usually for distribution among the stations and networks who will carry the commercial; sometimes called *dupe*. To *dub up* means to copy a videotape from a smaller format (i.e., 3/4") to a larger one (2" quad). To *dub down* means to copy a videotape from a larger format to a smaller one.

**DUCTOR ROLLER** roller on a printing machine that contacts both the INK FOUNTAIN roller and the PRINT DRUM roller, transporting ink from the fountain to the distributing system that prepares the ink for application to the plate or other image carrier.

**DULL-COATED** type of paper, used for artwork or in printing, that has a dull finish or surface, as compared to paper with a GLOSSY surface. The surface of the paper is referred to as its coating.

**DUMMY**
**Direct marketing:** *see* SALT NAME.
**Printing:** preliminary LAYOUT or set of blank pages created to show the planned format of the finished print product; it must be examined and approved by the printing buyer prior to the printing of multiple copies.

**DUMP** loosely formatted printout of some portion of the contents of a computer file, created for a quick review of the file. Dumps are frequently used by system programmers when working on a revision to a file or to review the contents of a MAGNETIC TAPE, such as a list rental tape.

**DUMP BIN** *see* DISPLAY BIN.

**DUOTONE** plate used in printing a monochrome (one-color) original as a two-color reproduction. In the duotone process, the artwork is photographed twice. The second time, the screen angle is changed so that the dots on the second color plate (the duotone plate) fall between the dots on the first plate, producing a rich effect.

**DUPE** *see* DUB; DUPLICATE

**DUPE CHECK** computer file maintenance program that detects the presence of DUPLICATES. *See also* DEDUPE.

**DUPE COMBINE** *see* DEDUPE.

**DUPLEX PAPER**
**1.** paper with a different color or finish on either side.
**2.** paper printed on both sides, like the pages of a book.

**DUPLICATE**
**In general:** copy or reproduction of a MAGNETIC TAPE, PRINTING PLATE, film, or photographic NEGATIVE; also called DUB if a film duplicate.
**Computer file maintenance:** two or more records on a file that can be combined into one record according to the matching logic being used; also called *dupe*.

**DUPLICATED AUDIENCE** listeners, viewers, or readers who are reached more than once by the same commercial or advertisement appearing in different media. *See also* AUDIENCE DUPLICATION.

**DUPLICATE ELIMINATION** *see* DEDUPE.

**DUPLICATING FILM** color film used for duplicating color TRANSPARENCIES. The transparencies can be STRIPPED together for color printing. *See also* FOUR-COLOR PROCESS.

**DUPLICATION** *see* AUDIENCE DUPLICATION; DUPLICATE.

**DUPLICATION FACTOR** degree to which DUPLICATES exist between two or more LISTS. If a rented list has a high HOUSE LIST MATCH rate, chances are that it is a good list to promote, once the duplicates are

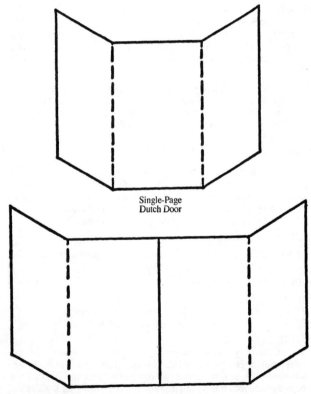

Single-Page
Dutch Door

Double-Page Dutch Door

eliminated. The assumption here is that people on a list share the same purchase habits and that, once promoted, noncustomers will become customers.

**DURABLE GOODS** long-lasting merchandise such as televisions, appliances, hardware, furniture, or recording equipment; also called HARD GOODS. *See also* SOFT GOODS.

**DUTCH DOOR** specially produced LAYOUT for a magazine advertisement. An ad with a Dutch door utilizes a double foldout that resembles a set of folding doors. A Dutch door is often used for new-product introductions, as the copy can readily lend itself to the format. *See also* CHECKERBOARD; GATEFOLD; HORIZONTAL HALF PAGE; JUNIOR PAGE; VERTICAL HALF PAGE. *See previous page.*

**DWELLING UNIT** place of residence not for business purposes. LIST SECTIONS can be made by type of residence, such as multiple-dwelling unit (apartment) or single-family dwelling, depending upon the product being promoted. For example, a promotion for lawn and garden care products would be sent to single-family homes, not apartments.

**DYE TRANSFER PRINT** color print made from a TRANSPARENCY or a NEGATIVE through a process of using specially treated photographic emulsions to transfer dye solutions to paper that has been coated with a gelatinous substance. The process allows for a great deal of retouching (*see* RETOUCH) and color correction. Although a dye transfer print is expensive, the end result is a very high-quality print.

# E

**EAR** space next to the MASTHEAD on either corner at the top of the front page of a newspaper. Often these spaces contain the paper's slogan, the weather forecast, or some announcement about the paper's content. In some papers, the ears are sold for advertising space.

**EARLY ADOPTER** consumer who is among the earliest within a market, after INNOVATORS, to adopt an INNOVATION. According to the bell curve model of DIFFUSION, early adopters are the next 13.5% of the consumers in a market, after innovators, to adopt an innovation. An advertiser can optimize the cost effectiveness of an advertising campaign for an innovation by targeting it toward innovators and early adopters. See also ADOPTION PROCESS.

**EARLY FRINGE** delineation of time made by the television broadcast media for the purposes of selling commercial time on the basis of audience size and DEMOGRAPHICS. Early fringe is the time period from 4:30 P.M. to 7:30 P.M. (When local time is purchased in the

Central Time Zone, early fringe is considered to be the time period from 3:30 P.M. to 6:30 P.M.) The name derives from the fact that the time period precedes PRIME TIME and is therefore on the early side (or fringe) of prime time. The cost of advertising in early fringe is less than in prime time, and the AUDIENCE COMPOSITION is similar (all-family). Thus, advertisers will purchase time in this segment in the hope of catching the prime-time viewer for less money than the cost of prime time. *See also* DAYPART.

**EARNED INCOME** revenue recognized on accounting ledgers as earned when the goods or services associated with the revenue are sold or delivered to the buyer. For example, in magazine income accounting, the pro rata value of all copies served, based on the subscription price divided by the total number of issues to be served, is earned income. The value of copies not yet served is *deferred income.*

**EARNED RATE** rate awarded to an advertiser based on the frequency with which an ad or commercial is run or the volume of advertising placed, or both, over a specific time period ranging from one month to one year. *See also* CARD RATE.

**EASTERN METHOD** method approved by the AUDIT BUREAU of CIRCULATIONS for estimating CREDIT CANCELLATIONS that will be applied against the outstanding gross credit business on an ABC STATEMENT, for a six-month audit period, by taking an average of the cancellations actually received during the period.

**EAST/WEST LABELS** name and address labels printed in sequence horizontally across the page. *See also* -UP.

**ECHO AWARD** award presented annually by the DIRECT MARKETING ASSOCIATION for excellence in direct marketing promotion. Awards are based on creativity, without consideration of actual response to the promotions.

**ECHO CHAMBER** studio room designed so as to cause sounds to reverberate. The sounds produced are used as SPECIAL EFFECTS in broadcast and can suggest a wide range of emotions or attitudes. For example, a hollow, echoing sound may suggest something sinister, thus arousing fear or uneasiness in the listening or viewing audience.

**ECONOMIC ENVIRONMENT** *see* MACROENVIRONMENT

**ECONOMIC INDICATORS** indices derived from data collected over long periods of time that represent business conditions and general economic activity. These indices may be maintained by government sources or private commercial groups. The CONSUMER PRICE INDEX, unemployment rate, gross national product, and Dow Jones Industrial Average are all types of economic indicators. Marketers use any number of different economic indicators in planning marketing strategies as a means to project demand for a particular product or service.

**ECONOMIC ORDER QUANTITY** most economically efficient amount of materials to order at a given time. Economic factors such as volume discounts, inventory receiving and storage costs, usage rates, and risks associated with running out of stock, as well as the average time from order to delivery, are factored into the determination of optimal economic order quantity. Industrial marketers attempt to persuade buyers to order more frequently or in larger quantities, using a variety of techniques including volume discounts and installment payment options. *See also* OPERATIONS RESEARCH.

**ECU** extreme close-up. *See* CLOSE-UP.

**EDIT**
   **Fulfillment:**
   **1.** in a computerized operation, to validate information entered into the system by utilizing programmed logic routines, such as checking the customer name FIELD for numeric characters; also called *edit check.*
   **2.** to prepare documents for KEY ENTRY to a computer system. The *editor* verifies that all information required by the key entry clerk, such as term and price, is clearly identified.
   **Photography:** to splice together film or audiovisual tapes, remove film segments, or otherwise rearrange film segments. *See also* CUT.
   **Publishing:** to correct or modify copy for preparation of a final draft.

**EDIT CHECK** *see* EDIT.

**EDIT CODE** FIELD in a computer file record used to further define the RECORD and to make selections from the file based on record definitions. An edit code might indicate, for example, whether a customer record is a business, personal, military, or foreign address.

**EDITING HOUSE** business specializing in the postproduction of film and videotape. After the actual shooting, an editing house will join the selected scenes together with titles, OPTICALS, and sound track, as directed by the production company, to produce the finished product. Some editing houses that specialize in editing commercials will also duplicate the master copy and send the DUBS to the various stations and networks on which the commercial is to appear.

**EDITORIAL** published or broadcast expression of opinion presented by the editor, publisher, manager, or owner of any medium.

**EDITORIAL ALTERATION (EA)** any change made after copy has been accurately set in type by the printer, at the request of the editorial staff of the advertising agency or advertiser where the copy was written. *See also* AUTHOR'S ALTERATION; PRINTER'S ERROR.

**EDITORIAL AUTHORITY** medium generally considered to be very credible by its audience because of its high journalistic standards and continuing efforts to report honestly, accurately, and objectively. Sometimes, advertisers will compose advertisements in an editorial format (ADVERTORIALS) for placement in media of this nature, in order to receive the same respect for their copy (and thus their product) as that enjoyed by the publication.

**EDITORIAL CLASSIFICATION** arrangement of various departments of a magazine or newspaper according to editorial content, such as the news department, fashion department, sports department, or fiction department.

**EDITORIAL COPY** all the reading matter in a publication that is not advertising. Editorial copy is written by the staff or contributing staff of the publication, whereas advertising copy is prepared by the advertiser or advertising company.

**EDITORIAL ENVIRONMENT** philosophical environment in which the editorial content of a medium is created. This environment encompasses the philosophy of the medium's management and ownership as well as the talents and attitudes of the creative and editorial staff. Many advertisers believe that the editorial environment of a medium will affect their advertising. Therefore, advertisers will carefully research the media to be certain of the appropriate vehicle for their product or service.

**EDITORIAL MENTION** promotional copy about a product that is inserted free of charge into a magazine because the editor feels it has some value to the reader relevant to the subject matter of the magazine. Editorial mentions are usually included as part of a magazine "shopping section" Editorial mentions are written by the seller and submitted to various publications in the hope of being accepted.

**EDITORIAL STYLE AD** *see* ADVERTORIAL.

**EDUCATIONAL BROADCASTING CORPORATION (EBC)** nonprofit, nonpartisan organization chartered by the New York Board of Regents and licensed by the Federal Communications Commission to operate WNET/Channel 13 in the public interest. In addition, EBC produces programs distributed by the PUBLIC BROADCASTING SERVICE (PBS) to noncommercial television stations in the U.S., Guam, and Puerto Rico. EBC depends on viewers, corporations, government, and its own revenues to achieve its mission of "producing and presenting quality television that advocates, enlightens, and entertains." In 1972, the EBC absorbed the National Educational Television organization.

**EDUCATIONAL CHANNEL** noncommercial television station that specializes in educational programs for classroom or home use.

**EFFECTS** *see* SPECIAL EFFECTS.

**EFFECTS TRACK** recording of sounds, used to simulate special conditions—for example, thunder, fire, screaming, sirens, and the like—in broadcast situations. *See also* SOUND EFFECTS (SFX).

**EFFICIENCY RATING** measurement of efficiency of advertising dollars in terms of how much money is spent on media to reach how many people. *See also* COST PER THOUSAND.

**EFFIE AWARD** bronze, silver, or gold awards presented annually by the New York Chapter of the American Marketing Association to advertising agencies and their clients (in various categories) in recognition of advertising campaigns that most effectively meet their own stated goals and objectives. Entries may be submitted in December, for a prescribed fee, for campaigns that ran some time during the previous 12-month period from October through September. The entries are judged by a panel of approximately 95 representatives of the advertising industry, drawn from agencies, advertisers, and other marketing associations. The awards are presented in June in New York City.

**EFFORT** one mailing in a series of promotional mailings with a common objective, such as renewing a subscription or collecting payment for a CREDIT ORDER. The results of a promotion are usually tracked on an effort-by-effort basis so that the copy can be varied and tested according to the effort. *See also* BILLING SERIES; CAMPAIGN; RENEWAL SERIES.

**800-NUMBER PROMOTION** DIRECT RESPONSE promotion that utilizes an 800 NUMBER as the RESPONSE DEVICE. The promotion is commonly used in conjunction with television advertisements that promise an operator is "standing by."

**800 PORTABILITY** technology required by the Federal Communications Commission, effective May 1, 1993, that enables telemarketers to retain their 800 NUMBER(s) when they change long distance carriers, enabling them to choose the best package of price and services without having to switch to a new 800 number. Portability also allows marketers to split their call volumes between two or more long distance carriers. This increased competition among carriers by removing a significant barrier to changing vendors.

**EIGHT MILLIMETER (8MM)** one of several sizes of motion picture film. (The other sizes are 16mm and 35mm.) Film size is determined by measuring the width of the film in millimeters. Eight-millimeter film is used primarily by amateur moviemakers for home movies. Some smaller stations and production studios use super 8mm as a low-cost alternative to 16mm. Although super 8 is exactly the same as that used by amateurs, the equipment used is more sophisticated, thus producing satisfactory results for broadcast. However, because of its size, 8mm film has less production flexibility in terms of splicing and editing.

**EKTACHROME** Eastman Kodak Company film that, developed, yields a color TRANSPARENCY that can be seen by projection on a screen or through transmitted light. The transparency (or CHROME) itself serves as original artwork for reproduction by COLOR PLATES. Ektachrome is very popular among professional photographers who work in advertising, primarily because it is available in formats larger than 35mm: $2^{1}/4$" × $2^{1}/4$", $4$"× $5$", and $8$"× $10$".

**ELASTICITY** degree to which supply or demand for a product or service will change as a result of a change in price. A price elasticity of 1.0, as demonstrated by actual sales history, means that demand (or sales) rises or falls in exact proportion to a decrease or increase in price. For example, if the price goes up 10%, sales go down 10%. Nonluxury items or services, such as emergency surgery in the extreme, have very little elasticity, because people will buy or pay for them regardless of cost.

**ELECTRICAL TRANSCRIPTION** archaic term used to describe the process of recording electrical impulses that represent sound waves and using them for broadcast; abbreviated *ET*. Simply put, electrical transcription is the recording of sounds to be broadcast. Today the term is commonly shortened to *transcription.*

**ELECTRONIC CATALOG** means for electronically presenting merchandise to consumers on a television screen on a selective basis. Electronic catalogs may be placed in public places such as shopping malls or may be made available privately on the consumer's own television set via cable access or via regular television broadcast. Electronic catalogs may be interactive, allowing the consumer to respond electronically, or noninteractive, requiring the use of some other means to respond, such as a telephone call to the seller. Some run automatically, not allowing the viewer to choose the sequence and duration of item viewing as does a printed catalog. Others are KEYBOARD controlled by the viewer. Electronic catalogs give sellers the dramatic capability of television (product demonstrations and so forth) together with the narrowly targeted exposure of a catalog. However, testing and refining an electronic advertisement is much more expensive than testing and modifying a printed catalog. *See also* DIGITAL BROADCASTING; INTERACTIVE TELEVISION; TELETEST; VIDEODISC; VIDEOTEX.

**ELECTRONIC COMPUTER-ORIGINATED MAIL (ECOM)** U.S. Postal Service program that enables users to transmit a message via computer link-up to a U.S.P.S. facility near the recipient, where it is converted to HARD COPY and delivered the next business day. *See also* ALTERNATIVE DELIVERY.

**ELECTRONIC DATA PROCESSING** use of computers to keep track of information and to process that information as needed, such as the keeping of accounts for billing purposes; abbreviated *EDP*.

**ELECTRONIC MAIL** message transmitted via telephone cables and a MODEM from one computer to another. The message may be displayed on a computer screen or printed on paper at the receiving end. Electronic mail is used to bypass regular mail delivery and speed communication. It is frequently used to relay LIST RENTAL orders to the LIST OWNER and to deliver rented lists to the user. Electronic mail ensures that list rental instructions are more accurately conveyed than they might be in a telephone conversation and in less time than would be required to send them through the mail. Electronic mail is also used to send press releases, announce sales promotions, explain price changes, describe product-line changes, update scripts, enter orders, and deliver direct-mail promotions. Electronic mail is especially useful in conjunction with TELEMARKETING; for example, in fund-raising it can get written confirmation of a pledge into the contributor's hands within 48 hours. It can also provide advance notice that a salesperson will be calling. Magazine publishers have used electronic mail to sell advertising space hours before an issue goes to press. *See also* ELECTRONIC MAILBOX.

**ELECTRONIC MAILBOX**   identifying code used to send and receive messages on an ELECTRONIC MAIL system. When sending a message the sender enters his mailbox code so the recipient knows the origin of the message. To identify the recipient of the message, another mailbox code is entered, similar to the address on an envelope. Mailbox codes differ based on the system used but are usually derived from the user's last name (e.g., WK for Workman).

**ELECTRONIC MARKETING**   marketing of products using electronic technology to determine the consumer market. Electronic marketing is a type of MICROMARKETING in which the retailer tracks consumer purchases using bar code scanner technology such as that found in many supermarkets. When making purchases, consumers fill out computer readable cards with demographic and other pertinent information. This information is logged into a database by the retailer who then uses it for: mailings of special promotions; direct mailing coupons for products in which the consumer has demonstrated interest; other special sales promotions of products already purchased by the consumer; or products that are complementary to those the consumer has already purchased.

**ELECTRONIC MEDIA RATING COUNCIL (EMRC)**   organization that sets the standards for electronic media ratings surveys and commissions audits of audience measurement services such as A.C. NIELSEN COMPANY and ARBITRON RATINGS COMPANY; formerly known as the Broadcast Rating Council, until 1982. Founded in 1964 and headquartered in New York City, EMRC is composed of members of broadcast trade associations, electronic media owners, and national networks. Its primary function is to monitor and accredit independent ratings services.

**ELECTROPHOTOGRAPHY**   PHOTOCOPY printing process that uses static electricity to transfer images from one surface to another.

**ELECTROSTATIC PLATES**   chemically coated plates used in high-speed laser printing *(see* LASER PRINTER).

**ELECTROTYPE** duplicate PRINTING PLATE made through electrolysis from a wax or metal mold of the original printing plate. Electrotypes serve as duplications of the original advertisement and are sent to the various magazines on the PRINT ADVERTISING schedule, who will use them to print the advertisement in their publications.

**ELITE** common type size used in typewriters. Elite type measures 12 characters to the linear inch. *See also* PICA.

**ELLIOTT ADDRESSING MACHINE** machine designed for the printing of names and addresses. The machine uses stenciled address cards that can be imprinted by any standard typewriter and that are guaranteed to print at least 10,000 times. The machine is used by direct-mail advertisers or other individuals or organizations when they use the same mailing list over and over again. *See also* ADDRESSO-GRAPH; CHESHIRE LABEL; IMPACT PRINTER; INK-JET PRINTER; LASER PRINTER.

**ELLIPTICAL DOT** elongated HALFTONE DOT that produces better gradations in tones. The best effects are achieved with MIDDLE TONE and VIGNETTES.

**EM** unit of measure of print type equal to the square of a type CHAR-ACTER. Most machine-set type characters are one-half an em (called an *en*). The term *em* is derived from traditional type sets that had a letter M cast on a square slug. The actual size of an em varies, depending on the point size of the type being used. In most cases, the term refers to a PICA or 12-point em. Each point equals 0.0138 inch (approximately $1/72$ of an inch).

Em-sized spaces are used to indent lines and to make line lengths equal in typeset copy. *See also* LETTERSPACING.

**EMBELLISHMENT** device used to give a larger surface area to an advertising display. Sometimes called an *extender* or *extension,* an embellishment fits over the frame and extends its borders. Embellishments are most frequently used in outdoor displays, and the standard size for this use is 5'6" at the top, 1' to 2' at the bottom, and 2' on either side.

**EMBOSSED FINISH** paper with a raised or depressed surface design that can resemble various textures such as cloth, leather, or wood.

**EMCEE** *see* MASTER OF CEREMONIES.

**EMOTIONAL APPEAL** type of advertising in which the copy is designed to stimulate one's emotions, rather than one's sense of the practical or impractical. When COPYWRITERS use emotional appeal in advertising, they are attempting to appeal to the consumer's psychological, social, or emotional needs. The copy is written to arouse fear, love, hate, greed, sexual desire, or humor, or otherwise create psychological tension that can best be resolved by purchase of the product or service. *See also* FANTASY COMMERCIAL; FEAR APPEAL; POSITIVE APPEAL.

**EMULSION SIDE** chemically treated light-sensitive side of photographic film that faces the lens during EXPOSURE of the film. *See also* DIFFUSION TRANSFER.

**EN** one half the width of an EM.

**ENAMEL** coating material on COATED TRANSFER that gives the paper a smooth finish and consists of solid pigments, water, and adhesives.

**ENAMEL PROOF** CAMERA READY proof on coated, glossy stock. *See also* REPRODUCTION PROOF; SLICK.

**ENCLOSURE** advertisement, photograph, brochure, graphs, charts, or any other matter that is placed in an envelope along with the principal content of the mailing; anything enclosed with other pieces in a mailing. *See also* ENVELOPE STUFFER; INSERT.

**ENCODE** check-processing technique that prints a computer-readable number on the check, representing the amount of the check. The encoded number is required for processing by the Federal Reserve banking system. The code is called "MICR" coding. Some direct marketers encode checks they receive from customers to save the cost of having the bank of deposit encode the checks for them.

**ENCUMBERED ROUTE** RURAL ROUTE assigned to a regular postal carrier.

**END-AISLE DISPLAY** POINT-OF-PURCHASE ADVERTISING display of merchandise, usually found in a supermarket or discount variety store and located at the end of a row of shelving. *See also* DISPLAY; ISLAND DISPLAY.

**END-OF-MONTH FREE (EOM FREE)** under AUDIT BUREAU OF CIRCULATIONS rules, publishers of weekly, biweekly, and bimonthly publications may allow all subscriptions to EXPIRE at the *end* of the month in which the term of the subscription lapses and still count all copies served as PAID CIRCULATION, even though payment has not been made for all copies served. *See also* EX-GRACING.

**ENDORSEMENT**
**Advertising:** statement by a perceived authority used in a promotion to recommend a product. That authority may be a satisfied customer, a celebrity, or someone with relevant professional credentials, such as a physician who endorses a brand of aspirin.
**Fulfillment:** signature on the back of a check or other negotiable instrument that transfers ownership of an asset (such as cash) from a *maker* to a *payee.*

**ENGEL'S LAWS** axioms noting differences in consumer spending patterns at different income levels, as observed by Ernst Engel in a paper published in 1857. Engel noted that the percentage of income families spent on food declined as their income level rose. The percentage of income spent on clothing and shelter remained constant, and the percentage of income spent on recreation, education, luxuries, and savings programs rose. Although written more than a century ago, Engel's Laws still apply today.

**ENGINEERING METHOD** method of cost-per-item accounting appropriate to a single-product business that tabulates all costs incurred in selling and delivering a product, divided by the number of items sold. All costs must be considered in the calculation, including BAD DEBT, shipping, handling, returned merchandise, and lost shipments.

**ENGLISH FINISH** various grades of uncoated paper with a smooth finish. The lower grades of English-finish paper are used for PACKAGE INSERTS, magazines, and catalogs. The higher grades are used primarily for books.

**ENGRAVE** cut, etch, or incise figures, letters, drawings, or other devices on a metal surface for personalizing, for decoration, or for reproduction by a printing process.

**ENGRAVER'S PROOF** first copy of a reproduction made from the printing plate that meets the engraver's satisfaction. The engraver's proof is printed on high-quality paper and submitted with the plate to the advertiser for examination and approval. The engraver's proof will give the advertiser an idea of how the print will look, provided, of course, that it is duplicated on the same quality paper.

**ENHANCEMENT** *see* LIST ENHANCEMENT

**ENTROPY MODEL** mathematical model of BRAND LOYALTY that estimates the probability that a brand will be purchased based on market factors such as the total number of brands available and the distribution of market share across brands. The entropy model assumes that due to the influence of other factors, BRAND LOYALTY provides less than 100% probability of purchase. The entropy model is used to forecast sales volumes when consumer-level data about brand loyalty is not available.

**ENTRY POINT** postal facility at which mail enters the postal delivery system. Mailers may truck mail to more than one entry point to reduce ZONE CHARGES. *See also* CENTRALIZED POSTAGE PAYMENT; COMPANY INDICIA; DROP-SHIPPING.

**ENUMERATION DISTRICT** U.S. Bureau of the Census term referring to a rural, little-populated area with approximately 800 to 1000 people.

**ENVELOPE** paper carrier used to transport mail. The standard No. 10 envelope measures 9 1/2" × 4 1/8" A No. 9 envelope, often used for BUSINESS REPLY MAIL, fits inside it. *See also* BARONIAL ENVELOPE; OUTER ENVELOPE. *See next page*.

**ENVELOPE STUFFER** advertisement, teaser *(see* TEASER AD), order form, announcement, or other informative printed matter that is stuffed into an envelope along with other material—for example, a special

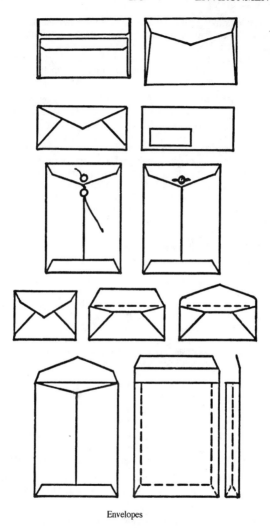

Envelopes

upcoming holiday sale announcement that a department store includes with its monthly billing statement. *See also* ENCLOSURE; INSERT.

**ENVIRONMENTAL ANALYSIS** study of all external factors that may affect a company or its marketing plan. Environmental analysis is a basic marketing function used to help marketers identify trends or outside forces that may impact upon the success or failure of a particular product. Marketers will look at the economy, political situation, cultural forces, social conditions, competitors, and legal and ecological factors when effecting an environmental analysis. *See also* MACROENVIRONMENT.

**ENVIRONMENTAL THREAT** any factor in the market, external to the marketing organization, that has the potential to negatively impact demand for the marketer's product or service. An environmental threat might be the entrance of a new competitor, the merger of two competitors, the introduction of a new brand, the development of new technology, legislative changes, or social and economic trends. For example, the tobacco industry has faced numerous environmental threats due to increased social, medical, and legislative pressure against smoking. The marketer must be positioned through COMPETITIVE INTELLIGENCE and other market trend research to respond quickly to environmental threats. The tobacco industry responded by deeply discounting some brands and redirecting its resources to non-tobacco products and to foreign markets where the environmental threats are not as great.

**EOM FREE** *see* END-OF-MONTH FREE.

**EPIDEMIC MODEL** mathematical model of product DIFFUSION based upon the theory that AWARENESS of a new product is spread from one consumer to another in a pattern that is mathematically similar to the spread of a disease. The number of EARLY ADOPTERS is normally used to project peak sales volume as well as sales volume levels over time. Epidemic models vary by the factors considered in the equation. One factor might be the impact of a negative experience with a product upon future purchase decisions. *See also* ADOPTION; PENETRATION.

**ESQUISSE** scaled-down, quickly sketched approximation of the LAYOUT of an advertisement, which gives the artist a basic idea of the ad's look and tone. Sometimes an esquisse is called a THUMBNAIL sketch.

**ESTABLISHING SHOT** in motion pictures and television production, opening shot that establishes the environment of a show or scene. The establishing shot usually has a wide field of view and serves to orient the audience to the surroundings of the situation they are about to see.

**ESTIMATOR** individual in a large advertising agency whose primary responsibility is to compute the cost of the advertising media schedules.

**ETCH**
1. printing process that produces an image on the PRINTING PLATE through a chemical or electrolytic process. *See also* COLOR CORRECTION; DOT ETCHING; FINE ETCHING; GRAVURE.
2. solution used to prevent the nonprinting areas of a print plate from holding ink. *See also* DESENSITIZER.

**ETCHED PLATE** metal PRINTING PLATE that has been etched with acid so that its surface may be used for printing. Technically, an etched plate is not an engraved plate, since its surface has been carved through the corrosive action of acid (or by electrolysis), whereas an engraved plate is one that has been carved through the use of a tool.

**ETHICAL DRUG COPY** advertising copy pertaining to drugs sold only by prescription; usually found in medical journals and other publications directed toward physicians.

**ETHNIC MARKETING** the direction of marketing activities in the United States toward members of a specific minority or nationality group that is a part of the larger community. Ethnic marketing efforts are presented in the language of the target group, and the media used for advertising or promotional purposes is typically that which is widely used by the group's members, such as Spanish or Asian television stations, or Hebrew or Russian language newspapers.

In the 1980s approximately 500,000 immigrants from various ethnic backgrounds accounted for 20% of the total United States population growth each year. This has created new outlets for marketers of clothing, food, furniture, and other products that can be specially designed to appeal to one or more of these groups.

**ETHNIC MEDIA** media directed toward a specific ethnic group and often written or broadcast in a language native to the group (e.g., foreign-language newspapers or Hispanic television stations). Some products or services are tied to a particular ethnic group, and the best way for an advertiser to reach this TARGET MARKET is through ethnic media.

**EURO-AD** advertisement specifically designed for the European market. Euro-ads are generic in design and take into account cultural differences among nations, individual nations' readiness for a particular product or service, and the economic, political, and legal climate in which the ad will be presented. Although Euro-ads may differ in the language spoken, they are similar in production standards, execution, and message.

**EUROBRAND** variations of consumer products that have been discontinued in the United States but that continue to be sold in the European market.

**EUROPEAN ECONOMIC COMMUNITY (EEC OR EC)** economic community, also known as the Common Market, originally formed in 1957 to work toward the regulation of international trade. The EEC is made up of 12 member nations, including Belgium, Denmark, France, England, Germany, Greece, Ireland, Italy, Luxembourg, the Netherlands, Portugal, and Spain. Its agreements call for the elimination of tariffs or other trade restrictions among members and the establishment of uniform tariffs for nonmembers. The EEC also encourages common standards for food additives, labeling, and packaging.

The EEC is of interest to marketers because it represents some 320 million consumers with a combined population that is roughly 1.4 times that of the United States and a combined gross national product that is nearly 90% of that of the United States.*

**EUROPEAN FREE TRADE ASSOCIATION (EFTA)** regional economic community formed to bring about free trade among members, who are Western European Nations that are not in the EUROPEAN ECONOMIC COMMUNITY.

**EVENTS MARKETING** marketing products through the sponsorship of events such as concerts, sports contests, or art exhibits. Sponsorship of an event affords the marketer an opportunity to establish good public relations among the members of the target market while also offering an opportunity for sales promotion. The event itself can create an environment attractive to the product's target market, and the marketer can give away free samples and special promotional material, while developing a positive image for the product.

**EXCHANGE** barter agreement between two parties that involves a trade of goods or services of equal perceived value without any monetary compensation. For example, an exchange may be an agreement between two LIST OWNERS to trade lists for one-time usage without a rental fee if the owners share a common TARGET MARKET but are not in direct competition—for example, a children's clothing manufacturer and a children's furniture manufacturer. An exchange might also be made by a magazine publisher and a BOOK CLUB in which book PACKAGE INSERT space is traded for advertising space on a page in the magazine.

**EXCLUSIVE DISTRIBUTION** retail selling strategy typically used by manufacturers of high-priced, generally upscale merchandise, such as cars or jewelry, whereby manufacturers grant certain dealers exclusive territorial rights to sell the product. The retailer benefits from the lack of competition, and the manufacturer benefits from a greater sales commitment on the part of the retailer. Additionally, exclusive distribution gives the manufacturer greater control over the way the product is merchandised. *See also* OPEN DISTRIBUTION.

**EXECUTION** way in which a COMMERCIAL or ADVERTISEMENT delivers or communicates the advertising message—for example, through EMOTIONAL APPEAL, FEAR APPEAL, or POSITIVE APPEAL. In some advertising circles, the execution is considered more important than the message, and many COPYWRITERS use this theory as a copywriting approach.

---

*John K. Ryans, Jr; *Marketing Strategies for the New Europe*. Chicago American Marketing Association, 1990.

**EX-GRACING** serving GRACED issues of a periodical after the EXPIRE issue has been sent. *See also* END-OF-MONTH FREE.

**EXPANSIBILITY OF DEMAND** degree to which the demand for a product can be stretched by changing the advertising or sales message. For example, promoting golf or tennis as healthy recreational activities may lead to more people taking up the sports and consequently increase demand for golf or tennis clothing and equipment.

**EXPECTANCY-VALUE MODEL** model of consumer attitude formation that asserts that the consumer rates a product according to the sum of the ratings given the product on a variety of product characteristics; also called FISHBEIN MODEL. Unlike the CONJUNCTIVE MODEL and the DISJUNCTIVE MODEL, there is no minimum rating on a particular characteristic that must be met, and a high rating on one characteristic can compensate for a low rating on another. This is one of several compensatory models. For example, a car buyer may not like the price of a car but will buy it anyway if it exceeds the consumer's expectations for fuel efficiency and braking performance. *See also* LEXICOGRAPHIC MODEL; DOMINANCE MODEL; IDEAL POINT MODEL.

**EXPENSE-TO-SALES RATIO** key indicator of the economic efficiency of a marketing organization, such as the ratio of advertising expense to product sales. A significant rise in the advertising expense-to-sales ratio may indicate that the advertising is less cost-effective than it could be. It may also represent a temporary fluctuation in demand, or it may be an early warning of a new ENVIRONMENTAL THREAT. Minor fluctuations in the ratio are normal and not cause for concern. If the ratio were plotted over time, variations from the average should resemble an automobile's path down a highway with slight variations from the midpoint without actually crossing into the next lane. Slight variations that build over time, either increasing or decreasing, should prompt action.

**EXPERIMENTAL METHOD** determining advertising effectiveness by manipulating the level or type of advertising in statistically similar markets and attributing any difference in demand to the difference in advertising. The experimental method relies upon the somewhat precarious assumption that two such similar markets can be identified and that the absence of other influences on demand can be controlled or assumed. The experimental method might also be used to measure the effect of different sales techniques or brand characteristics.

**EXPIRE**
1. used as a verb to indicate the completion of the term of a subscription: for example, after service of the LAST ISSUE on a periodical subscription, the subscription expires.
2. used as a noun to refer to a subscriber RECORD or group of records that have expired. Expires are usually maintained on the subscription file for six months after expire, enabling the seller to reactivate

the subscription if it is renewed after expire. Lists of expires are also kept on an EXPIRE FILE for several years after expire to be used as a promotion and LIST RENTAL file. After a few years, it is assumed that the addresses are no longer valid, and the lists are disposed of.

**EXPIRE ANALYSIS** report that shows the number of subscriptions expected to EXPIRE from a subscriber file by future month or ISSUE of expire. The expire analysis is used by periodical publishers to plan PRINT ORDERS and to manage RATE BASE by estimating the number of new or renewal orders that must be generated in order to maintain the desired subscription file size on an issue-by-issue basis.

**EXPIRE FILE** list of expired customer records maintained for promotion. Most marketers maintain customer records on an expire file for two to four years following EXPIRE, at which point the records are erased under the assumption that the addresses are no longer valid after that period of time. Expires frequently respond to promotions from the LIST OWNER at a higher than average rate but do not perform especially well for other marketers who rent the list. For example, the former subscribers to a magazine sometimes respond very well to a promotion for that magazine but not any better than other individuals to a promotion for another product.

**EXPOSITION**
1. explanation of the story line in a drama told by a narrator, announcer, or one of the characters.
2. public exhibition or show, such as a TRADE SHOW.

**EXPOSURE**
**Advertising:** presentation of a promotion piece or advertisement to an individual, such as a person viewing a television commercial or a reader opening a magazine to an advertisement page. The number of exposures achieved is an important measure of the effectiveness of an advertisement if it is measured in conjunction with the quality of the exposures achieved. For example, if a golf club advertisement is exposed to 1000 golfers, it has greater value than if it is exposed to 1 million nongolfers. *See also* MEDIA REACH.
**Photography:** point in the photographic process during which light-sensitive film is exposed to a light source. *See also* F STOPS.

**EXPRESS MAIL** class of mail delivery offered by the U.S. Postal Service that, with the exception of international mail, guarantees on-time delivery of mail received by 5:00 P.M. There are four different types of express mail services, including an overnight mail service, a same-day airport service, an international mail service, and a custom designed service. Express mail service is not available everywhere in the U.S. The cost of express mail is competitive with other overnight mail delivery services such as Federal Express and Purolator Courier.

**EXTEND**

**In general:** prolong the duration of a contract beyond the original term. For example, an extension might be granted on a special price offer or on the deadline for delivering advertising COPY and ART to a publication for printing.

**Magazines:** add additional issues to the term of a subscription. A subscription is usually extended to compensate the subscriber for issues missed because of some delivery or FULFILLMENT problem. *See also* GRACE.

**EXTENSION**

**1.** *see* EMBELLISHMENT.

**2.** *see* EXTEND.

**3.** period of time that exceeds the length of a given contract.

**EXTRACT** *see* SELECTION.

**EXTRAPOLATE** in statistical research, to estimate a value of a variable from known data. In the advertising industry, this analytical tool is used to project future experience on the basis of past experience. Advertisers extrapolate information from audience and COPY TESTING data so that they can anticipate trends when planning future advertising.

**EXTREME CLOSE-UP** *see* CLOSE-UP.

**EYEBROW** small LEAD-IN placed above the main HEADLINE, such as "HOT!" placed over "We're fired up to greet you!" or "NEVER AGAIN" over "The sale of a lifetime!"

**EYE CAMERA** device used by researchers to measure and observe eye movements of respondents reading advertising COPY. There are several types of eye cameras: one photographs a small spot of light reflected from the eye; another actually takes motion pictures of the eye, noting changes in the diameter of the pupil.

Eye cameras are used in COPY TESTING to discern what parts of the copy attract attention. The eye camera also indicates the holding power of the sales message. This information helps the COPYWRITER in placing headlines, and in making decisions about copy length and LAYOUT.

**EYE MOVEMENT ANALYSIS** tracking the movement of a research subject's eyes over advertising copy, or other images, to measure the level of attention and the sequence in which attention is paid to various components. Eye movement analysis is done with a camera designed for that purpose and requires a laboratory environment, which makes it a somewhat restrictive and artificial technique. Eye movement analysis assumes the subject will attend more to pleasing images than to unpleasant images. *See also* GALVANIC SKIN RESPONSE.

# F

**FACE**
1. printing surface that makes contact with the material to be imprinted.
2. style of type used for printing—that is, the TYPEFACE. *See also* BOLDFACE; GOTHIC; ITALIC; SANS SERIF; SERIF.

**FACED MAIL** pieces of mail arranged so that all addresses and stamps or METER imprints face the same way. Some mail-processing machines, such as BAR CODE and ZIP code SCANNERS require that mail be faced to accommodate a fixed SCAN HEAD. *See also* FIM (FACING IDENTIFICATION MARK).

**FACING**
**Outdoor advertising:** surface of a billboard. If two billboards are adjacent to each other, visible from the same direction and less than 25' apart, they are said to have a double facing; if there are three billboards, they are said to have a triple facing, and so on.
**Retailing:** way of describing the look of a DISPLAY on shelves. Each individual unit of a product is one facing wide, because its face takes up one space. The overall shelf display is measured in terms of the number of facings per product.

**FACING SLIP** label required by the U.S. Postal Service to be placed on top of mail PACKAGES showing the destination and CONSOLIDATION LEVEL of the package. It is similar to a SACK TAG or PALLET TAG.

**FACSIMILE TRANSMISSION** *see* FAX.

**FACTOR** third party who provides the marketer with cash by purchasing, or taking a lien against, the accounts receivable or inventories of the marketer. A factor who purchases the accounts receivable assumes all risk and responsibility for collection. Sale of accounts receivable to a factor is risky in that the factor is dealing directly with the marketer's customers and may antagonize them or be perceived as an indication that the marketer is having financial difficulties. Factors are most often used by industrial marketers.

**FACTOR ANALYSIS** mathematical procedure used to reduce a large amount of data into a structure that can be more easily studied. Factor analysis summarizes information contained in a large number of variables and condenses it into a smaller number of factors containing variables that are interrelated. For example: In a study about a group of women, their characteristics of height, weight, hobbies, activities, and interests might be summarized, using factor analysis, as *size* (height and weight) and *life-styles* (the combination of hobbies, activities, and interests). In so doing, five variables have been condensed into two separate factors.

**FACTORY PRICING** prices that are discounted to compensate the buyer for the cost of transportation from the seller's place of business to the buyer's. Factory pricing saves the seller from the expense and management of shipping and places the risk of loss during transport to the buyer. Marketers who are located close to their customers can better afford to sell with factory pricing than marketers who are located at a greater distance. For example, a metal bed frame manufacturer who sells a relatively heavy weight product at a low price could not compensate for the cost of transportation to a customer in a distant location. *See also* FREIGHT ALLOWANCE PRICING.

**FADE IN** in broadcast, to gradually increase the video or audio signal so that a picture emerges on the screen from black or blank space, or sound volume increases from an inaudible or low level to audible or loud sound. *See also* CROSS FADE; DISSOLVE; FADE OUT.

**FADEOMETER** instrument used in printing to measure the degree to which the colors of an ink sample will fade with exposure to light. The light fastness of an ink is important for print products that will be exposed to a lot of light, such as OUTDOOR ADVERTISING billboards. The acceptable degree of fading is determined by the length of time the printed product must last.

**FADE OUT** in broadcast, to gradually decrease the video or audio signal so that an image on the screen slowly changes to black or empty space, or the sound volume slowly diminishes so that it becomes completely or almost completely inaudible. *See also* CROSS FADE; DISSOLVE; FADE IN.

**FAD PATTERN** model of consumer buying practices of fad products. These products enter the marketplace quickly, are adapted with great enthusiasm, reach a sales peak very early, and decline in popularity almost overnight. Fad products typically attract a limited following, generally because they have a novel quality that does not really satisfy a strong consumer need. There are some fad products, such as the hula-hoop, that become popular once every few years, but after their initial appearance on the market, they maintain the same fad pattern.

**FAIR PACKAGING & LABELING ACT** 1966 federal legislation requiring that product packages and their labels provide consumers with accurate information as to the manufacturer and the quantity of the contents and that the labels help consumers make value comparisons between brands. The act is enforced by the Secretary of Health and Human Services and the Federal Trade Commission. *See also* NUTRITION LABELING.

**FAIR TRADE** term used in retailing that refers to an agreement between a manufacturer and retailers that the manufacturer's product be sold at or above an agreed-upon price. In many states, fair-trade agreements were incorporated into and enforceable by state laws. However, in

1975, Congress passed the Consumer Goods Pricing Act, which prohibits the use of resale price maintenance laws in interstate commerce. This Act has worked to effectively eliminate fair-trade arrangements.

**FAKE-COLOR PROCESS** manual color-reproduction process that creates color prints from a BLACK-AND-WHITE photograph or drawing. COLOR SEPARATIONS are created manually by an artist, who decides which colors should be used in each area of the original image. Fake-color is less costly than true FOUR-COLOR PROCESS printing.

**FALLING DEMAND STATE** *see* DEMAND STATES.

**FAMILY RESEMBLANCE** phrase used to describe a group of TYPE-FACES that bear a resemblance to each other in design but differ from each other in size or weight of stroke. Usually these groups share a common name, as, for example, the Caslon family: Caslon Bold, Caslon Old Style, Caslon Bold Italic, Caslon Old Style Italic.

**FANFOLD** method of folding brochures or forms like a fan; also called *accordion*. CONTINUOUS FORMS are also fanfolded. A fanfolded brochure fits inside a standard-size envelope, yet unfolds easily to an oversize piece. It is not as easy for the reader to refold and presumably ignore. Fanfold brochures are especially useful for product promotions using large colorful pictures that have great dramatic impact. *See also* ACCORDION INSERT.

**FANOUT** printing problem caused by moisture-damaged paper edges that produce a distorted print image. Fanout can also occur if the humidity of the air in the pressroom is lower than the natural moisture content of the paper, causing the paper edges to dry out.

**FANTASY COMMERCIAL** style of commercial that uses special effects or caricatures to create the idea of fantasy about the product, such as the Little Elves who make cookies, or Mr. Clean, or the Jolly Green Giant. The technique of a fantasy commercial is principally to appeal to the emotions to arouse interest in the product. In a fantasy commercial, the focus is the message itself, whereas in a testimonial commercial *(see* TESTIMONIAL ADVERTISEMENT), for example, the focus is the *source* of the message.

**FAST EVENING PERSONS REPORT (FEP)** report issued weekly from the NIELSEN TELEVISION INDEX by A. C. NIELSEN COMPANY, providing audience estimates and audience composition information for network evening television programs. The report is termed *Fast,* because it is mailed to subscribers just 9 days following the end of the reporting interval. For example: If the reporting interval should end on Sunday, the report will go out one week from the following Tuesday. Hence, in this example, intervals end on Sundays and FEP reports go out every Tuesday during the first 18 weeks, or more, of the television season, which begins in September.

**FAX** system for the electronic transmission of images over telephone lines from one fax machine to another. *Fax* is an abbreviated term for *facsimile*. Faxing is frequently used to send PRESS PROOFS from the printer to the customer for approval. International publishers sometimes fax LAYOUTS to various printers throughout the world for local printing and distribution of newspapers and magazines, getting them to readers faster than if they were printed at one location. *See also* DEX.

**FAX-ON-DEMAND** method of delivering information stored in a computer to a customer or prospect via facsimile, upon the request of the recipient. Usually, recipients call the computer via an 800 NUMBER or their own fax machine to request information be sent directly to their fax machine. Fax-on-demand gets information to customers when they want it and before their interest wanes. It also saves catalogers the expense of printing and sending more information than is of interest to the customer and allows for up-to-the-minute changes in pricing or product offerings. Because of its speed, fax-on-demand is gradually replacing the BINGO CARD as a means of generating requests for information. Some fax-on-demand systems are one-call—the recipient pays for both the request and the transmission call time. Others are two-call—the sender pays for the call time during transmission of the requested information.

**FEAR APPEAL** advertising that attempts to create anxiety in the consumer on the basis of fear, so that the consumer is encouraged to resolve this fear by purchasing the product or service. For example, an advertisement may use people's fear of offending or of rejection to influence them to purchase personal products such as mouthwash or deodorant. Another example of fear appeal is an advertisement for fire insurance that pictures a family devastated by the fire that has destroyed their home. *See also* EMOTIONAL APPEAL.

**FEDERAL CIGARETTE LABELING & ADVERTISING ACT** 1967 federal legislation requiring that a printed warning appear on cigarette packages to tell consumers that cigarette smoking "may be hazardous to your health." The warning was strengthened by a 1970 amendment that changed "may be" to "is." A 1971 amendment banned cigarette advertising on broadcast media.

**FEDERAL COMMUNICATIONS COMMISSION (FCC)** government administrative agency, established as a result of the Communications Act of 1934, that assigns wavelengths to radio and television stations, issues (and renews) licenses to radio and television stations, and regulates the broadcasting industry, including television, radio, telephone, and telegraphy. The commission reports directly to Congress and is composed of seven commissioners appointed by the President with Senate approval. Each commissioner serves a seven-year term, and no more than four commissioners may be from the same political party at any given time.

**FEDERAL FOOD AND DRUG ACT** *see* FOOD AND DRUG ADMINIS-
TRATION.

**FEDERAL INFORMATION PROCESSING STANDARDS CODE
(FIPS CODE)** National Bureau of Standards coding system covering various aspects of computerized information processing by the government, including, for example, geographic codes used to represent a
state, county, SMSA (STANDARD METROPOLITAN STATISTICAL AREA),
city, or town about which data has been collected. These universal
codes are used by various government agencies to facilitate the consolidation of data collected by different agencies. Marketers intending
to use census data or other government statistics should be familiar with
these codes and use them as standards in their own data files.

**FEDERAL TRADE COMMISSION (FTC)** government agency created in 1915, under the Federal Trade Commission Act of 1914, whose
purpose is to protect the system of free enterprise and competition
in the interests of a strong economy. In the words of the Federal Trade
Commission Act, Section 5, the FTC is responsible to "promote free
and fair competition in interstate commerce in the interest of the public through prevention of price-fixing agreements, boycotts, combinations in restraint of trade, unfair methods of competition, and unfair
and deceptive acts and practices." The commission consists of five
commissioners, each of whom serves a seven-year term. Not more
than three of the members may be from the same political party. The
FTC is empowered to investigate interstate and foreign commerce as
well as to take legal action to enforce the laws that fall under its jurisdiction. In the advertising industry, the FTC functions to prevent
fraudulent or deceptive advertising, and unfair trade practices.

**FEDERAL TRADE COMMISSION IMPROVEMENT ACT** *see*
MAGNUSSON-MOSS WARRANTY ACT.

**FEE BASIS** method of payment for advertising agency services
whereby the advertiser is charged a fixed monthly, bimonthly, semi-
monthly, semiannual, or annual sum for all the services provided by
the agency. *See also* AGENCY COMMISSION.

**FEEDBACK**
1. audience response from which advertisers can glean information
   about how well the advertising message is received, the environment in which it is received, and the temperament and attitude of
   the consumer upon its reception.
2. in video, effect created when the camera is focused on its own
   monitor. This will produce a series of random patterns on the television screen.
3. in audio, sound effect created whenever a microphone is held too
   close to its monitor speakers. At low levels, the sending of the audio
   signal back on itself in this way will produce an echo effect, which
   is sometimes used by recording artists to add another dimension to

a recording. At higher levels or when uncontrolled, feedback will produce a loud squeal or howl.

**FEEDER** mechanism that automatically feeds paper to the printing press. Feeders may handle individual sheets of paper or CONTINUOUS FORMS.

**FELT SIDE** side of paper exposed to a felt print blanket during the papermaking process. It is the smoother side of paper with less grain that is preferred for printing. The felt side is a normal byproduct of the papermaking process, but paper to be printed on both sides can be given a felt finish on the WIRE SIDE as well by pressing a felt blanket against the wire side before the water content is removed or by embossing dry paper.

**FIDELITY** accuracy with which an electronic recording device can reproduce the original sound or image. The primary value of all recording equipment lies in the exactness of its ability to reproduce the original sounds and/or images (in comparison, of course, to its price).

**FIELD**
**Data processing:** part of a computer file RECORD consisting of a set of continuous characters that represent a piece of information, such as a name field or an address field. *See also* FIXED FIELD; VARIABLE FIELD.
**Marketing:** geographic area in which a product or service is sold. Consumer research done via personal interviews with consumers is accomplished by sending interviewers into the field.

**FIELD AGENCY** agency that sells subscriptions through personal contact, such as door-to-door sales, telephone sales, or reception room sales. *See also* CASH FIELD AGENT; SUBSCRIPTION AGENT.

**FIELD DIVISION MANAGER** manager of one of the 74 U.S. Postal Service field divisions. The field manager reports to the Regional Postmaster General.

**FIELD STAFF** company employees whose work is in the marketplace outside of the company office and who are thus said to work in the field. In retailing, the field staff are the MANUFACTURER'S REPRESENTATIVES, also known as DETAIL PERSONS.

**:15** scriptwriter notation for 15 seconds

**FIFTY-FIFTY PLAN** plan used in COOPERATIVE ADVERTISING whereby 50% of the advertising costs incurred are paid by the retailer and the other 50% are borne by the manufacturer. *See also* COOPERATIVE ADVERTISING.

**FILE** group of RECORDS stored together for some common purpose. Large files are usually stored on computers. A file may consist of current customers, subscribers, or donors, or previous customers, subscribers or donors. Each individual name on a file is contained in a unique record with information pertaining to that person. *See also* FILE MAINTENANCE; MAINFILE; UPDATE.

**FILE MAINTENANCE** procedure that keeps computer files current by applying all necessary transactions (ADJUSTMENTS) against the file. A file maintenance procedure must be performed prior to generating any OUTPUT, such as LABELS, reports, or LIST RENTAL selections, from the file. Transactions include changes of address, addition and deletion of RECORDS, application of payments to CREDIT ORDERS, and so forth. In ON-LINE systems, file maintenance is performed continuously. In BATCH systems, it is scheduled according to the frequency with which output must be generated. *See also* UPDATE.

**FILE SEGMENT** group of RECORDS in a FILE. Customer records may be extracted at random from a file to create a promotion test segment that is representative of the entire file. Files may also be divided nonrandomly into segments that share common characteristics requiring different handling than other segments require. For example, a subscription file segment may include all magazine subscription DONORS who gave a Christmas gift subscription the preceding year and who will be sent donor renewal promotions this year. A record may be part of several file segments, depending upon the segmenting technique in use. For example, a donor record can be part of the donor segment and may also be selected for a test segment.

**FILLER** short item, typically not longer than 500 words, used in newspapers and magazines to fill in spaces between editorial matter or advertisements. The items are usually informational or humor pieces with no specific time parameters. Often, publicity releases are used as fillers.

**FILLING IN (FILLING UP)** printing problem that involves ink filling *in* the spaces between the halftone DOTS or plugging *up* the type slugs.

**FILL-IN LETTER** *see* COMPUTER LETTER.

**FILM**
1. strip of plastic or celluloid with a silver emulsion light-sensitive coating, available in a wide variety of formats and used for the production of photographs, motion pictures, or television video *(videofilm)*. In television production, a difference of opinion exists among producers and directors as to whether film is better than videotape. Those who favor film feel it offers greater creative capabilities, with a softer, more glamorous quality to the image. In addition, although film requires processing time, filming equipment is quite compact, as well as durable and highly reliable.
2. use film to record an event, performance, entertainment, or the like.
3. loosely, synonym for *movie*.

**FILM CLIP** short footage that has been clipped from a longer reel of film and then inserted into another film, or shown by itself to a live audience or used as part of another program or performance. Film clips are commonly used in instructional or educational programs and in news or documentary productions where the location or the activity cannot be duplicated or re-created in the studio or where such re-creation would lessen the effect or reality of the production. For example, a documentary about the Holocaust that uses film clips of the actual detention camps is more authentic and should have greater impact than one that simulates these scenes. Also called *film sequence.*

**FILM COMMERCIAL**  COMMERCIAL recorded on film rather than on videotape.

**FILM I.D.**  notation ("Film") marked on a container or on a broadcast schedule that identifies a filmed program or commercial, as distinguished from taped or live programming.

**FILM LIBRARY**
1. collection of films. Often, a film studio's film library is a valuable asset to the studio because the films in the collection can be marketed individually or in packages to television stations or networks for a considerable profit.
2. place where a collection of films is housed. These films are used for viewing (and sometimes production, as in stock footage—*see* STOCK SHOT), but they are not for sale. Film libraries are generally maintained by production companies, film studios, film owners, advertising agencies, or private citizens.

**FILM LOOP**
1. in television production, an electronic circle created by FEEDBACK.
2. continuous sequence of film created by splicing together the ends of the film so that it runs in a never-ending circle. Such a loop might be used to enhance a SPECIAL EFFECT, such as an explosion in a disaster film.

**FILM PICKUP**  transmission of film over the airwaves as compared to transmission of a live performance or situation. For example, a program may be a film pickup or a live pickup. Both types of transmission frequently appear in televised news programs.

**FILM PRINT**  reproduction of a film used for distribution to movie theaters, television stations, or the like.

**FILM SEQUENCE**  portion of a program or performance that appears on film. *See also* FILM CLIP.

**FILM SPEED**  indication of the amount of light needed to maximize the reproduction capability of film. *Fast film* is very sensitive to light and therefore can be used in situations where there is not a high level of illumination. *Slow film,* on the other hand, has a lower sensitivity to light and therefore needs a high level of illumination to produce an image. While fast film offers greater flexibility to the photographer, the resulting image will have a GRAINY quality, whereas slower film will produce a higher-quality picture. Film speed is expressed as an

ISO number, which refers to an internationally standardized exposure index that utilizes a numerical scale as a method of rating film; the higher the ISO number, the faster the film.

**FILMSTRIP** film that looks like motion picture film but is actually a series of SLIDES spliced together and shown sequentially in still projectors designed exclusively for this purpose. Typically, filmstrips are used as speech supports in speaker presentations or as visual aids in company training programs.

**FILM TRANSFER** transfer of VIDEOTAPE to FILM, using equipment designed for this purpose. Film transfers must be done for television stations lacking facilities for videotape broadcasting. The process of transferring film to tape is called a *tape transfer.*

**FILTER**
1. colored screen made of gelatin or glass placed between an image to be photographed and the film in order to selectively screen out certain colors while allowing other colors through, thereby creating COLOR SEPARATIONS. The green filter produces the MAGENTA separation; the blue filter, the yellow separation; and the red filter, the CYAN separation.
2. camera lens covering used to alter the image photographed by reducing or diffusing light or by adding a color tone. Filming a black-and-white motion picture through a sepia-colored filter gives it an old appearance. This can be used to create a turn-of-the-century look. Diffused light can be used to create a fantasy or dream atmosphere.
3. device that reduces or alters sound, such as one that makes ordinary speech sound as if it were being spoken into a stadium microphone; also called *filter microphone.* Sound filters can be applied to specific frequencies of sound.

**FIM (FACING IDENTIFICATION MARK)** machine-detectable series of vertical bars printed in the upper middle portion of an envelope that is used by the U.S. Postal Service for automatic FACING and cancellation of letter mail. The FIM code identifies regular zip-coded BUSINESS REPLY MAIL, business reply mail with a bar-coded ZIP+4 CODE imprint, and ZIP+4 coded courtesy reply mail. A FIM is required by the Postal Service on business reply letters and cards and on any bar-coded mail, but not on ordinary ZIP+4 mail. *See also* BAR CODE; FACED MAIL.

**FINAL PRINT** "ready-for-air" finished product that is the final stage in the film production process. The final print is the completed work after client approval and detail corrections (such as COLOR CORRECTION or synchronization) have been achieved. It is from this print that duplicates are made. *See also* ANSWER PRINT; COMPOSITE PRINT; WORK PRINT.

**FINANCIAL ADVERTISING** ADVERTISING geared to the world of finance, such as Wall Street brokerage firms, banks, or insurance companies. Typical products in financial advertising are publicly offered financial products such as Mutual Fund shares or limited partnership shares. The Securities and Exchange Commission (SEC) enforces strict legal regulations in regard to promotional advertising of public offerings of securities and requires some amount of MANDATORY COPY on most other products. A large part of financial advertising has to do with the promotion of the image of financial corporations with the hope that the corporation will become a trusted name that will appeal to investors.

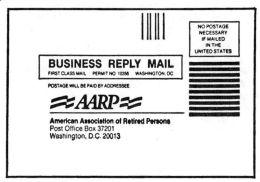

Business Reply with FIM

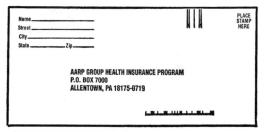

Courtesy Reply with FIM

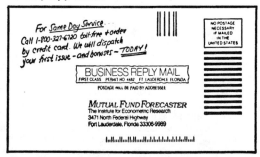

Business Reply with FIM

**FINANCIAL MODELING**  computer-assisted process that forecasts the financial results to be expected from changes in VARIABLES. The model user asks "What if?" questions to determine which scenario represents the best course of action to take. For example, a financial model might tell what the impact on pretax profit would be if 50% of the new subscription orders for a magazine were sold at a price lower than the BASIC RATE. The accuracy of a model's predictions depends upon the assumptions made about the relationship between variables. *See also* CIRCULATION MODELING.

**FINDER NUMBER**  sequential number assigned to each name on a MAILING LIST, and printed on each reply form, that is used to speed the DATA ENTRY of responses to a promotion by eliminating the need to enter a name and address; also called *instant number*. The finder number has fewer characters than a name and address and therefore takes less time to enter. Most marketers use a number with 15 or fewer characters. Finder numbers can be entered through KEY ENTRY or SCAN ENTRY from the reply form. After entry, the computer matches the finder number to the correct promotion file RECORD and transfers the name and address from the promotion file to the FULFILLMENT file. Most promotion designers prefer a short finder number because they believe that the more codes there are on a form, the lower the response will be.

**FINDER'S FEE**
**In general:** fee paid to an individual or company whose function is to bring together the parties involved in a business deal. The finder will often serve as an intermediary until the deal is consummated. The fee is usually based on either a percentage of the profit created by the deal or the value of the deal, but it may also be a flat rate paid by one or all of the parties involved.
**Advertising:** fee paid by an advertising agency to the individual or firm responsible for bringing a large account into the agency.

**FINE ETCHING**  DOT ETCHING on metal printing plates to fine tune the tonal values of the image to be printed; also called *re-etching*. Fine etching is a common technique in photoengraving and GRAVURE cylinder printing.

**FINE-GRAIN**  term describing the texture of prints (including photographs and drawings) that are relatively free from impurities on the surface of the material, in contrast to coarse-grain, which indicates a rough surface. Fine-grain artwork has a delicate quality in appearance.

**FINE SCREEN**  type of screen used in reproducing HALFTONE copy. A fine screen has more than 100 ruled lines per linear inch. The most commonly used have 110, 120, 133, 150, 175, or 200 lines, although very fine screens up to 400 lines have been used for the reproduction of fine artwork. A determination of the screen to be used is made according to the quality of paper to be used for the reproductions; the finer the grain of paper, the finer the screen must be. *See also* COARSE SCREEN.

**FINISH** surface texture of paper. There are many types of finishes, including coated *(see* COATED PAPER) or uncoated, dull *(see* DULL-COATED) through GLOSSY, and smooth or textured. Smoothness is important for the high-quality HALFTONE printing for which glossy COATED PAPER is most often used; generally, the smaller the halftone DOTS, the smoother the finish required. Textured paper with a ribbed, leatherlike or textilelike surface is popular for stationery and book covers. Uncoated or rough-finish paper is usually used for offset lithography printing.

While all coated papers have a smooth surface texture, uncoated papers vary greatly in degree of smoothness. Uncoated paper also has a natural difference in the finish on each side caused by the way paper is manufactured. These two surface finishes are called the FELT SIDE and the WIRE SIDE. *See also* CALENDER ROLLS; LAID PAPER; PLATE FINISH; SUPERCALENDER; WOVE PAPER.

**FINISHED ART** advertising artwork that is complete and CAMERA-READY.

**FIPS CODE** *see* FEDERAL INFORMATION PROCESSING STANDARDS CODE.

**FIRM BUNDLING** *see* FIRM PACKAGE.

**FIRM ORDER DATE** date after which an order for advertising time or space is no longer cancellable. Since advertising time or space is contracted in advance, it is cancellable for a period of time between the contract date and the firm order date. After the firm order date, the advertising will run, no matter what.

**FIRM PACKAGE** two or more pieces of identical mail going to the same address that are mailed at a single-piece postage rate. Firm packaging is useful and economical when several magazines, catalogs, or promotion PACKAGES are going to different individuals in the same office or household. There is no maximum limit other than what can be physically bundled with plastic strapping, rubber bands, or string. Metal strapping is not permitted by the U.S. Postal Service.

**FIRST CLASS** U.S. Postal Service designation for mail that receives the fastest delivery (2 to 5 days across the U.S.) and costs the highest postage rate of the four classes of mail (first, second, third, and fourth). Non-BULK MAIL letters and invoices must mail first class according to U.S.P.S. regulations. Invoices inserted into merchandise shipments must follow the regulations governing commingled mail *(see* COMMINGLE). First-class mail meeting minimum volume requirements may be presorted by FIVE-DIGIT ZIP CODE before being entered into the postal system and may be mailed at a PRESORT discount rate. Undeliverable first-class mail will be returned to the sender or forwarded to a new address without charge, with the exception of first-class postcards. Promotional mail is sometimes sent first class with a postage stamp instead of a METER imprint so that it won't look like promotional mail. This is especially effective for mailings going to professionals such as doctors and lawyers, who receive, and throw away, more promotional mail than most people. Because of the expense, first-class mail is the exception rather than the rule in DIRECT MARKETING.

**FIRST COVER** *see* FRONT COVER.

**FIRST-ISSUE FREE OFFER** subscription promotion offer that promises the new subscriber he can receive, review, and keep the first issue without any obligation to pay or to continue the subscription. One type of first-issue free offer deducts the first issue from the term of the subscription if the subscription is continued, but others add it on. *See also* HARD OFFER.

**FIRST-TIME BUYER** customer who has bought something from a seller for the first time. First-time buyers are considered good prospects for additional sales and are usually sent additional promotions while they are still in a buying mood. *See also* FORMER BUYER; HOTLINE.

**FIVE-DIGIT DIRECT** packages of presorted mail to be delivered to a single FIVE-DIGIT ZIP CODE. The U.S. Postal Service does not ordinarily require that such direct packages be marked, but mailers may print *DIR*, a CONSOLIDATION code, on the shipping label to instruct their own mail-handling personnel to apply a red "D" COLOR-CODED ROUTING STICKER to the package. This facilitates handling by the U.S.P.S. later on. Direct packages can also be identified in the OPTIONAL ENDORSEMENT line.

There are different sacking and palletizing rules for direct packages, based on the class of mail. If there are four or more direct packages for a five-digit ZIP code, they must be SACKED. In palletizing, a direct PALLET must be made up if there are 650 pounds or more of mail for the ZIP code. *See also* FIVE-DIGIT SACK.

**FIVE-DIGIT QUALIFIED** six or more pieces of mail presorted *(see* PRESORT) to the FIVE-DIGIT ZIP CODE level and prepared in conformance with U.S. Postal Service regulations governing five-digit ZIP SORT postage discounts. In 1986, first-class mail earned a discount of $.04 per piece; third-class mail earned a discount of $.024 per piece. The discount is slightly larger for nonprofit mailers.

**FIVE-DIGIT SACK** mail SACK containing presorted mail *(see* PRESORT) destined for one particular FIVE-DIGIT ZIP CODE area. *See also* FIVE-DIGIT QUALIFIED.

**FIVE-DIGIT ZIP CODE** ZIP (Zoning Improvement Plan) code instituted by the U.S. Postal Service to facilitate mail handling and delivery. The first digit represents one of ten areas of the country (0 = New England, 9 = West Coast). The first three digits together represent a SECTIONAL CENTER FACILITY or main post office. The last two digits further define the destination point in terms of a post office or DELIVERY CENTER area within a large city or in terms of a small city or town whose residents share the same ZIP code. Some large buildings or organizations that receive high mail volumes have their own five-digit ZIP code(s). Users of BULK MAIL are required by the Postal Service to sort their mailings by five-digit ZIP code. Mailers also use the ZIP code to SEQUENCE and SEGMENT lists by the DEMOGRAPHIC characteristics of the residents of each ZIP code area and to identify the best ZIP code areas to send future promotions. *See also* FIVE-DIGIT QUALIFIED; NATIONAL ZIP CODE AREA NINE-DIGIT ZIP CODE; ZIP SELECT.

**FIVE-LINE ADDRESS**  name and address record requiring five lines of space on a label or form. Five-line addresses are usually business addresses that include a company name and/or a title in addition to the individual's name. Most nonbusiness addresses have only three or four lines of information. BUSINESS PUBLICATIONS AUDIT OF CIRCULATIONS audit statements must include a count of active subscribers according to whether the address includes these other address elements, to help advertisers evaluate whether the appropriate business audience can be reached through that publication. Foreign addresses also frequently require additional space to accommodate country and other address elements. Computer files designed to hold business or foreign address records should be equipped to handle five-line addresses.

**FIXATIVE**  solution, generally of alcohol and shellac, that is applied to the surface of artwork by hand, atomizer, or airbrush and is used to protect the surface from smudging or being rubbed off. It also helps set the colors. Fixatives are typically applied to pencil, pastel, or charcoal drawings and form a permanent seal on the work.

**FIXED COST**  business expense that does not vary with the quantity of goods sold or manufactured, within the limits of current capacity. The cost of executive salaries, legal retainers, building occupancy, and office furniture are fixed. The cost of product packaging, shipping, raw materials, and sales commissions are variable with the quantity of goods sold. However, at certain levels of sales volume, fixed costs may have to be increased in order to add capacity. For example, additional manufacturing equipment and supervisory staff may be needed. The marketer must know that when operating at full capacity, a small-increase in sales volume could knock fixed costs into a higher plateau that is not justified by the increased revenue.

**FIXED FIELD**  computer file with predefined RECORD lengths. Each record is divided into segments called FIELDS that uniformly represent in each record the same information, in the same location, and with the same number of characters. For example, the first field in each record in a customer file might be the customer's five-digit ZIP code, the second field might be her last name, and so forth. Fixed-field files must be redesigned at considerable effort to add a new field or extend the size of an existing field. The amount of information included in a VARIABLE FIELD record is not the same across records.

**FIXING** photographic process that chemically renders the photograph permanent and insensitive to further EXPOSURE to light, by removing unexposed silver halide.

**FLAG**

1. notation placed on a HARD-COPY or computer file RECORD that marks it for special handling or indicates that some action has occurred, such as selection of the record for a mailing test PANEL.
2. title or LOGOTYPE of a publication printed on the cover page, such as "M" for "the magazine of the civilized male."
3. graphic device used on package labels and other promotional pieces to highlight a brief message such as "30¢ off regular price." Also called *pointer*.

**FLANKER BRAND** new brand introduced into a product category by a company that already markets an existing brand in that category. The flanker may be a different size, flavor, or type of the existing product but is a logical extension within the product category, such as the addition of other flavors to cranberry—Cranapple, Crangrape— by Ocean Spray.

**FLASHBACK** theatrical technique used in dramatic presentations where the chronological sequence of events is interrupted by a scene recalling an event or occurrence from an earlier time; also called *cutback*. Flashback technique is often used effectively in television commercial production, as, for example, in a commercial for a dishwashing detergent where a housewife flashes back to a time when she used another detergent and was embarrassed because her dishes were not clean and did not shine.

**FLASH COUNT** preliminary count of direct mail promotion responses usually made on a daily basis as returns are received. Flash counts provide a quick view of response rates without waiting until computer reports are issued at the end of the FULFILLMENT process. Flash counts are usually tabulated on a SOURCE KEY basis but may be calculated on a PACKAGE or CAMPAIGN basis. Flash counts relieve (or confirm!) some of the anxiety that surfaces after a promotion is mailed, but shouldn't be the basis for major decisions, because they are not as accurate as the counts received after processing has been completed and duplicates and other REJECTS have been deleted. They are sometimes used to decide whether to send out another mailing. *See also* MAIL COUNT; WEIGH COUNT.

**FLASH EXPOSURE**

1. photograph taken with the aid of a sudden bright light, produced by a flash bulb, that better illuminates the object to be photographed.
2. second EXPOSURE to light of a HALFTONE photographic NEGATIVE to darken the DOTS in shadow areas. Flash exposures are frequently necessary to achieve the desired shading effect.

**FLAT**

**Direct mail:** oversize piece of first- or third-class mail, such as an $8^{1}/2$" × 11" manila envelope. Flats are handled by the U.S. Postal Service separately from parcels and other mail. The actual postage due is based on the weight of the piece.

**Printing:**

**1.** descriptive term for a photograph or print with little contrast between light and dark areas. *See also* GAMMA; HIGH CONTRAST.

**2.** negatives or positives arranged on a GOLDENROD PAPER or other carrier surface, used to create a PRINTING PLATE.

**FLATBED CYLINDER PRESS** type of LETTERPRESS printing press that utilizes a moving flatbed that holds the type while a fixed rotating cylinder provides the pressure that makes the impression. The paper is secured to the cylinder and rolled over the printing surface as the bed passes under the cylinder. The flatbed cylinder press has not been manufactured in the United States since 1962 and is slowly becoming obsolete.

**FLAT ETCHING** process for chemically re-etching large areas of a print plate to reduce the DENSITY of the printed image. Flat etching is accomplished by placing the plate in a tray filled with etching solution. The areas not to be further etched are covered with a protective solution. If needed only on small areas of the plate, the re-etching is called "staging." In this process, the solution is applied manually with a paint brush.

**FLAT PROOF** in LETTERPRESS printing, a PROOF pulled before the PRINTING PLATE has been processed to print evenly (MAKEREADY process). The flat proof is proofread to check the accuracy of the copy and the overall look of the printed piece. The copy on a flat proof will be spotty in some areas and heavy in others, making the proof a poor-quality reproduction. However, it is necessary to pull a flat proof, because the makeready process is time-consuming and costly, and, therefore, all elements of the copy must be checked for accuracy and appearance before continuing the printing process.

**FLAT RATE**

**In general:** per unit price that remains the same regardless of the quantity purchased or other considerations. Many products are sold at variable rates that decline as the number of units purchased increases. Paper is usually sold at a variable rate. *See also* VARIABLE PRICING.

**Advertising:** fixed price of nondiscounted advertising space or time.

**Direct marketing:** fixed cost for a LIST RENTAL regardless of the number of names remaining after a MERGE/PURGE is performed. A flat rate is usually used only for small lists typically of fewer than 10,000 names. *See also* NET NAME ARRANGEMENT.

**FLIER** advertising medium that is usually a single, standard-size (8 ½" × 11") page printed on one or both sides with an advertising message; also, *flyer*. Fliers are most often used in direct-mail advertising and as HANDBILLS given to customers by local retailers. In direct mail, they often accompany a formal letter to expand information in the letter. For the local retailer, fliers offer market coverage at low cost with little waste and good flexibility. However, fliers have a high THROW-AWAY rate.

**FLIGHT**
1. term used in media scheduling that indicates the length of the advertising period. Typically, an advertising campaign runs for a specified number of weeks, followed by a period of inactivity, and then is resumed. Each activity period is known as a flight. This spacing prevents overexposure to the advertisement or commercial without allowing the message to be forgotten. It also reduces MEDIA expenditures.
2. part of a promotional CAMPAIGN conducted in segments over time, such as a DIRECT-MAIL ADVERTISING campaign with a series of DROPS.
    Each flight in a direct mail campaign is generally larger than the previous one and is not mailed until the success of the previous flight is confirmed. The final and largest mailing is called the ROLL OUT. *See also* FLASH COUNT; PYRAMIDING; WEIGH COUNT.

**FLIGHT SATURATION** heavy concentration of advertising during a FLIGHT, to the point where the media have become saturated with the advertising message and further advertising will have a negative effect on the marketplace. The saturation point is difficult to determine, and sometimes advertisers will unknowingly go beyond it. In the 1960s, for example, Anheuser-Busch, Inc., through a series of experimental studies, found data suggesting that the marketplace had become so saturated with Budweiser beer advertising that sales of Budweiser had actually fallen off, because consumers had become annoyed with the advertising.*

**FLIP CARD** individual card used in a sequence of CUE CARDS.

**FLIP CHART** tablet used in a presentation whose pages can be turned (flipped) at appropriate points to show illustrations, graphs, or overlays, or used for visual effect to add details and interest to the presentation.

**FLOAT**
1. variations in the placement of a label on a form. Float interferes with the SCAN ENTRY of the information on the label since the desired information does not move in front of the SCAN HEAD in a consistent manner. Float may also interfere with the deliverability

*Source: William M. Weilbacher, *Advertising*, (New York: Macmillan Publishing Company), p. 97-98.

of a mailing piece if the label must be seen through an envelope window. Float is usually the result of careless label application but may be created intentionally to make a mailing piece look as if a person, and not a machine, prepared it. Marketers have tested various degrees of float to identify the precise degree of individuality people respond to best. *See also* OPTICAL CHARACTER RECOGNITION.

**2.** addressing procedure that "right justifies" (aligns along the right edge) each line of COPY for a neat look. *See also* JUSTIFY.

**3.** placement of a SPACE advertisement in an area larger than necessary to accommodate the dimensions of the advertisement.

**4.** money given to an advertising agency by the advertiser that may be invested or otherwise used, prior to its delivery to the media owners for which it is intended.

**FLOODLIGHT** lighting instrument that emits a steady beam of soft, diffused light through a large opening over a widely spread area. Floodlights are used by photographers and in motion picture or television production to eliminate shadows.

**FLOOR PYRAMID** type of POINT-OF-PURCHASE ADVERTISING display used in retailing, in which items for sale are stacked in the shape of a step pyramid, usually no higher than eye level.

**FLOOR STAND**
**Advertising:** freestanding rack, frame, or mount used by retailers for merchandise in a POINT-OF-PURCHASE ADVERTISING display.
**Television production:**
**1.** device used for mounting lights that stand on the studio floor.
**2.** easel used for holding title cards or graphics to be displayed on camera.

**FLOP**
**In general:** (informal) effort that has failed, such as an unsuccessful advertising campaign or a show that has disappointed its audience.
**Copy reproduction:** develop a film negative on the reverse side of the original so that the finished product will be the opposite of the original. Sometimes, after the rough LAYOUT has been prepared, it can be seen that the copy will read or fit better if the elements face from right to left rather than the reverse. When this is true, the printer or photoengraver will be instructed to flop the negative made from the original photograph and then to make the reproduction from the flopped negative.

**FLOW** degree to which ink will spread over the surface of printing rollers; also called VISCOSITY, *body*. Thick inks are best for LETTER-PRESS and for LITHOGRAPHY. Thin inks are best for package printing and ROTOGRAVURE printing.

**FLOWCHART** diagrammatic representation of a system or process utilizing various symbols connected by arrows showing the step-by-step sequence. Flowcharts are universally used in the design of computer systems and programs and may also be used to describe manual processes. The following is a very simplified diagram of the conversion of HARD-COPY information to MAGNETIC TAPE.

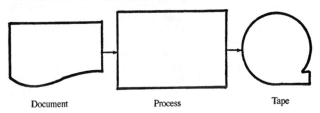

Document                    Process                    Tape

A more sophisticated flowchart would describe the "process" with a series of symbols that fully represent every step in the process.

**FLUSH** LAYOUT term indicating that type is not to be indented but is to be set flush with the margin. A flush cover of a book, magazine, catalog, manual, or other publication is cut to the same size as the pages within. In a flush paragraph, all the sentences (except perhaps the last one) are of equal width across the page, and there is no beginning paragraph indentation. FLUSH LEFT OR RIGHT indicates that type is to be set so as to line up at the left or right margin. To flush the margin in this manner is also called to *justify. See also* RAGGED LEFT OR RIGHT.

**FLUSH COVER** cover of a catalog or book that is the same size as the pages, forming an even edge. Most softcover books, brochures, magazines, and catalogs are inexpensively covered with a flush cover made from a slightly heavier paper stock than that used for the pages. Expensive publications, such as hardcover books, are given a CASE binding that is slightly larger than the pages and protects them from wear. Very wide hardcover books are given flush covers because it reinforces them and keeps them from sagging when they are set upright on a shelf.

**FLUSH LEFT OR RIGHT** COPY in which each line is "left justified" or "right justified," so that the characters are aligned evenly along the left or right edge. Virtually all copy is set FLUSH left and with either left-side indentations to mark the beginning of a paragraph *(paragraph indent),* or additional spacing between paragraphs *(see* FLUSH PARAGRAPH). *See also* RAGGED LEFT OR RIGHT.

**FLUSH PARAGRAPH** COPY that is set completely flush left, even at the start of each paragraph, without any indentations. Extra space must be left between paragraphs so that the beginning and end of each paragraph is clearly defined. *See also* FLUSH LEFT OR RIGHT.

**FLYER**  *see* FLIER.

**FLYING PASTER**  printing press mechanism that automatically pastes a new roll (WEB) of paper to the end of an almost exhausted roll while the press continues to run; also called *automatic paster*. The paster speeds up the printing process and reduces paper waste.

**FM STATION**  any radio station in the FREQUENCY MODULATION (FM) system. The FEDERAL COMMUNICATIONS COMMISSION (FCC) has assigned the range of wavelengths from 88 to 108 MHz (MEGAHERTZ), which appear as 88 to 108 on the radio dial, to this system. Any station within this spectrum is an FM station. Not including non-commercial stations, there are approximately 3550 FM stations in the United States, with an annual growth rate of almost 8%.

**FOCUS**
1. point where light rays converge to produce an image that is clear and sharp in definition.
2. see a clear and distinct image.
3. subject or issue that is the center of attention, as in a focus group.

**FOCUS GROUP INTERVIEW**  unstructured group interview technique where 8 to 12 people are brought together, under the guidance of a trained interviewer, to focus on a specific concept, product, or subject. Advertisers use the focus group during the advertisement development phase as an exploratory marketing tool. When the interview is led by a skilled moderator, the group dynamics will generate ideas and provide insights into consumer reactions and perceptions. The focus group interview requires a great deal of expertise on the part of the moderator, who will introduce the subject and encourage the group to discuss it. Groups are composed of users and potential users of products of all ages and both sexes.

**FOCUS IN**  bring a scene into FOCUS by beginning with the camera totally out of focus, so that the picture appears as little more than a blur, and slowly coming in on the scene until the image becomes clear. *See also* FOCUS OUT.

**FOCUS OF SALE**  primary issue, BENEFIT, or claim about a product or service that will be emphasized in the advertising and toward which the prospective customer will be directed by the advertising strategy.

**FOCUS OUT**  slowly defocus the camera so that the picture goes from a clear, sharply defined image to little more than a blur. To focus out will provide a dreamy quality that can be used effectively to show changes in time or place or to suggest an altered perception such as an hallucination. *See also* FOCUS IN.

**FOG**  photographic defect caused by a deposit of silver on the image areas creating a cloudy area. Fog is caused by incorrect exposure of the film or by a poorly balanced chemical developing solution. Photographs with fog are usually discarded.

**FOLDER** printed CIRCULAR used most often in direct mail although sometimes distributed by hand in an advertising campaign; also called leaflet. A folder is usually a sheet of paper of any color, imprinted on one or both sides, that has been folded so that each folded section reads as a single page and the printed matter does not cross the fold. Folders are usually designed to fit in a standard-size envelope, such as a #10 (4$^1/8$" × 9$^1/2$"). *See next page.*

**FOLIO**
**Magazines:** magazine for people in the magazine industry, published monthly by Hansen Publishing. It covers all aspects of magazine publishing from EDITORIAL to FULFILLMENT. *Folio* also sponsors several conferences and seminars each year.
**Printing:**
1. page numbers of a book or catalog, often placed at the outside top of a page. Right-handed pages are usually odd-numbered; left-handed pages are even-numbered. A *drop folio* is a page number printed at the bottom of a page.
2. brochure, magazine, or catalog comprised of SIGNATURES and consisting of four pages printed onto one sheet of paper that is folded once, forming two leaves with four surfaces or pages.
3. sheet of 17" × 22" paper.
4. (colloquial) book with exceptionally large pages.

**FOLLOWER** marketer whose product or brand did not get to market first or who does not maintain a dominant market share. It is extremely difficult for a follower to take market share from a LEADER. For example, Xerox, Coca-Cola, IBM, and McDonald's led their markets for many years, and their brands represented the standard for those products as perceived by consumers. Followers need to discover the leader's Achilles heel in order to compete successfully. The Avis "we try harder" campaign exemplified the marketing strategy of a follower establishing a competitive advantage that directly addressed a weakness of the leader.

**FOLLOWING, NEXT TO READING MATTER** order for placement of advertisements in a magazine. "Following, next to reading matter" specifies a position that is either completely flanked by reading (editorial) matter or located at the top of the page and alongside reading matter. This is a preferred position and usually costs more than a RUN-OF-PAPER position, which is wherever the publisher chooses. Within the publishing industry, the following, next to reading matter position is sometimes called the Campbell Soup Position, because the Campbell Soup Company often specifies the first right-hand page following the main editorial section of a magazine for placement of its advertising.

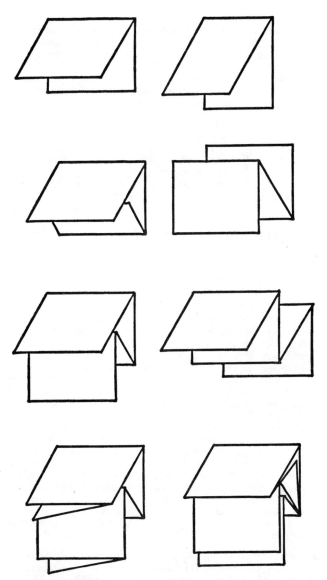

Folders

**FOLLOW-UP**
  **In general:** any letter, telephone call, or personal call subsequent to a contact or communication intended to continue or to further evaluate the earlier contact. *See also* FOLLOW-UP LETTER; INQUIRY AND FOLLOW-UP.
  **Marketing:** step in a marketing plan that follows the implementation of an advertising campaign or promotion or the introduction of a new product, in order to evaluate the results.

**FOLLOW-UP LETTER**  sales letter sent to someone who has made an INQUIRY inviting the inquirer to make a purchase; part of the INQUIRY CONVERSION process. This process is generally used for expensive items requiring a lot of information and thought before a purchase decision is made, such as an automobile or an insurance policy. Follow-up letters differ from other promotional mailings in that they are mailed in response to an inquiry on an individual basis in contrast to being mailed in BULK on a date determined by the mailer. The first follow-up letter in a series is usually the most detailed, while subsequent EFFORTS highlight individual benefits. *See also* INQUIRY AND FOLLOW-UP.

**FONT**  typographer's name for the complete selection of type of one size and FACE. A font will include all 26 letters in the alphabet (including uppercase and lowercase as well as small *caps),* the numbers from 0 through 9, punctuation marks, and some commonly used symbols, such as the ampersand (&) and dollar sign ($).

**FOOD AND DRUG ADMINISTRATION (FDA)**  federal government agency responsible for the protection of consumer rights in the administration of the Pure Food and Drug Act of 1906, which prohibits shipment of adulterated foods and drugs, and the Pure Food, Drug and Cosmetics Act of 1938, which attempted to clarify the legislation of 1906. The FDA functions as a division of the Department of Health and Human Services and has authority over the safety and purity of foods, drugs, and cosmetics, including the labeling of these products. The administration sets the standards, as put forth in the combined laws of 1906 and 1938, for food, drug, and cosmetic products, their packages and labels, and has the additional authority to ban these products as well as to regulate their contents. Although the jurisdiction of the FDA is actually in the area of content, packaging, and labeling—as distinguished from advertising—of foods, drugs, and cosmetics, the term *labeling* has been held to include advertising that appears in the places where these products are sold. Therefore, advertisers whose products are in these categories must pay careful attention to the packaging and labeling restrictions and requirements in their advertising.

**FOOD AND DRUG INDEX**  syndicated research service provided by A. C. NIELSEN COMPANY. The Food and Drug Index offers subscribers information on products in contractually specified categories. This information is most useful to advertisers in the analysis of the competitive situation in terms of marketshare *(see* BRAND SHARE), BRAND PREFERENCE, effectiveness of advertising, and other related factors. Offered to subscribers on a bimonthly basis, the index reports sales volume, distribution, and inventory levels of products by brand through the measurement of consumer purchases in retail food, drug, and mass merchandise stores.

**FOOD, DRUG, AND COSMETICS ACT** *see* FOOD AND DRUG ADMINISTRATION.

**FOOTAGE** length of motion picture film, expressed in running feet, that has been used to film a particular scene or episode, a group of scenes, or a full-length film.

**FORECASTING MODEL** model used to forecast market demand for a product. A forecasting model has three informational bases: (1) what people say; (2) what people do; and (3) what people have done in the past. The forecasting model is designed to anticipate what buyers are likely to do under certain circumstances.

**FOREIGN**
**In general:** outside the country, such as an advertisement placed in a MEDIUM outside the advertiser's country.
**Advertising:** newspaper advertisement placed by an advertiser located outside the area in which the newspaper is distributed.
**Direct mail:** in the U.S., an order, customer, or customer record that is not from a U.S., U.S. Possession, APO/FPO, or Canadian address. Some direct marketers include Canadian addresses as foreign orders or customers.

**FORGETTING RATE** in media research, measurement of the rate at which memory of advertising is lost from one advertising period to another without continued reinforcement. The forgetting rate can be very important in planning advertising strategies. In one experiment, two randomly chosen groups of women were mailed thirteen different newspaper advertisements for an ingredient food. One group received one advertisement a week for thirteen weeks; the other group received the same thirteen advertisements at intervals of four weeks throughout the year. The retention in the first group declined steadily, and by the 48th week, there was almost no recall, reflecting a high forgetting rate. The second group, on the other hand, showed strong retention of the advertising over the year, and although memory rate fell between mailings, it never fell below the level of awareness of the preceding mailing. Overall, there was a steady incline in the retention of the advertising, reflecting almost no forgetting rate.

**FORM**
**Direct mail:** order document, letter, invoice, or renewal notice that constitutes a mailing PACKAGE component. They are usually computerprinted CONTINUOUS FORMS.

**Merchandising:** physical state of a product such as solid, liquid, or aerosol.

**Printing:** set of type or film elements enclosed in a metal chase (frame) and ready for printing.

## FORMAT
### Broadcast:
1. style or content of the material aired by a radio station, such as all news, country-western music, or rock-and-roll music; also called PERSONALITY. Other common formats include classical music, easy-listening music, talk shows, general interest programs, or special interest broadcasts, such as religious or Spanish-language programs. The program format is part of the context in which an advertising message is received and affects how the message is perceived. *See also* COMMUNICATION.
2. style or content of a television program, such as a variety show, talk show, game show, situation comedy, police drama, and so forth. *See also* item 1 above.

**Direct marketing:** medium on which a LIST or FILE is produced, such as MAGNETIC TAPE, LABEL, or GALLEY. Magnetic tape is used when additional computer processing of the information is planned or when the information requires access only via computer. Labels are used when a mailing piece will be sent to the individuals on a list. Labels are produced in a variety of formats such as CHESHIRE LABELS, or PRESSURE-SENSITIVE LABELS, HEAT-ACTIVATED LABELS, and so forth. Galley formats are used when the information must be accessed manually—for example, by a CUSTOMER SERVICE REPRESENTATIVE.

**Fulfillment:** arrangement of FIELDS within a computer file or RECORD. *See also* FIXED FIELD.

### Printing:
1. general design of an original or printed image or of a completed print product, such as the arrangement of elements on a page or the size and shape of a book. *See also* COMPOSITION; GRAPHIC DESIGN; LAYOUT.
2. page size expressed in terms of the number of pages per SIGNATURE, usually in multiples of four.

## FORMATTING
1. creation of a PRINT TAPE that will computer-address labels or forms in a desired format and/or sequence. For example, a formatted print tape might be programmed to print the address within the amount of space available on a label in the required FIVE-DIGIT ZIP CODE sequence.
2. CONVERSION of computer file elements to a different format for processing on a different system, such as the rearrangement of FIELDS in each RECORD or the conversion of a MAGNETIC TAPE file to LABELS for mailing.

**3.** preparation of a floppy DISK as required for the SOFTWARE with which it will be used.

*See also* FORMAT.

**FORMER BUYER** customer who has not made any additional purchases within a specified period of time, usually a year. Former buyers are generally better prospects for additional sales than nonbuyers because they have already shown a willingness and ability to buy. However, lists of former direct-mail buyers decline in value over time because many of the customers will have moved to a new address. These lists are usually maintained no longer than two to three years. Lists of former buyers at business addresses also lose validity over time because individuals change jobs or move to different companies. *See also* EXPIRE; INACTIVE.

**FORM ROLLERS** inking or DAMPENING SYSTEM rollers applied against the PRINTING PLATE or other image carrier on a PRINTING PRESS; also called *plate rollers.*

**FORMS FLASH** LASER PRINTER technique that prints the same standard image, such as a letterhead, logo, or signature, on several forms, leaving room for additional, concurrent printing of a personalized or unique image; also called *forms overlay.* The forms flash, analogous to a stencil imprint, is laser printed on blank paper or partially preprinted forms as the variable images are also being printed. For example, when renewal notices are printed, the basic renewal format can be overlaid onto generic stock while special SOURCE KEYS, EFFORT numbers, messages, and/or offers can be printed on each document, depending upon the subscriber's PRIOR SOURCE or DEMOGRAPHIC cluster or other characteristic.

Forms flashing enables marketers to reduce the number of forms they must keep in INVENTORY and to pay less per form (because they are ordering larger quantities) without reducing their flexibility to change offers and messages. When these changes occur, existing stock is not wasted.

**FORWARD CONSOLIDATION POINT** Canadian version of a STATE DISTRIBUTION CENTER. *See also* CANADIAN POSTAL CODE.

**FORWARD INTEGRATION** acquisition of or expansion into a DISTRIBUTION CHANNEL. For example, a book publisher who acquires or launches a direct mail book club can increase profit margins and sales volumes on books sold through the club channel. *See also* BACKWARD INTEGRATION; HORIZONTAL INTEGRATION.

**FORWARD SORTATION AREA (FSA)** first three digits of the CANADIAN POSTAL CODE, which identify the area in which the addressee is located. Marketers use the FSA, just as they use the first three digits of the ZIP code, to categorize customers and identify prospects. *See also* FIVE-DIGIT ZIP CODE; SECTIONAL CENTER FACILITY.

**FOTOTYPE** (trademark) brand of specific FONTS imprinted on individual pads of white cardboard, with characters that can be peeled off separately and mounted as original copy to be reproduced by any printing process. Fototype is used when there is not a lot of type matter in the copy as a way of economizing, because it eliminates the need for a compositor. However, when the BODY COPY is extensive, this becomes a false economy, because the individual Fototype characters must be hand set, which can become a tedious and time-consuming process.

**FOUNDRY** printing plant that produces PRINTING PLATES called ELECTROTYPES or STEREOTYPES and utilizes them for the printing of books and magazines in a duplication process called the *electrolytic process.* A foundry also produces metal type characters (called *foundry type*), which can be sold to compositors and printers, and are set by hand. With the advancement of technology, foundry has become obsolete, since there now exist faster and more economical methods for duplication.

**FOUNDRY PROOF** proof pulled from original type matter and engravings before the electrolytic process of duplication (which can only be done in a FOUNDRY). Foundry proof is kept in the files as a record of the original copy. The foundry proof is characterized by heavy black borders made by the *foundry rule,* a piece of metal placed around the page to keep it in place during the process of making the ELECTROTYPE. This entire process has become obsolete.

**FOUNDRY RULE** *see* FOUNDRY PROOF.

**FOUNDRY TYPE** *see* FOUNDRY.

**FOUNTAIN SOLUTION**
  1. dampening solution used in LITHOGRAPHY to keep the nonimage areas of the plate from holding ink. Since OFFSET lithographic plates have a smooth surface, in contrast to PRINTING PLATES with a raised *(relief)* or recessed surface, the nonadherence of ink to the nonimage areas of lithographic plates must be chemically controlled. The fountain solution must be applied at intervals throughout the printing process as it is depleted. The solution is stored in a device called an INK FOUNTAIN, which automatically applies solution to the plate. *See also* GUM ARABIC.
  2. ink stored in an INK FOUNTAIN on the printing press for automatic application to the image carrier (PLATE).

**FOUR A'S (4 A'S)** *see* AMERICAN ASSOCIATION OF ADVERTISING AGENCIES.

**FOUR-COLOR** *see* FOUR-COLOR PROCESS.

**FOUR-COLOR PROCESS** HALFTONE printing process utilizing four ink colors (black, MAGENTA, CYAN, yellow) to produce a printed image that matches the coloring of the original image. Four-color process printing is more expensive than two-color printing but has a greater impact on the viewer. It is accomplished by creating a COLOR SEPARATION for each of the three primary colors perceived by the human eye: blue, red, and green. The image is photographed through blue, red, and green COLOR FILTERS, producing a negative for each color that effectively blocks out that color. The red filter produces a cyan positive; the green filter, a magenta positive; the blue filter, a yellow positive. The three positives are combined to produce a preliminary print that requires the addition of black and variations in the primary color proportions to achieve the desired effect. Four-color process is used in GRAVURE, LETTERPRESS, OFFSET, and SCREEN printing. *See also* COLOR CORRECTION; DUPLICATING FILM; PROGRESSIVE PROOFS; TWO-COLOR PROCESS.

**FOUR-LINE ADDRESS** *see* FIVE-LINE ADDRESS.

**FOUR P'S OF MARKETING** *see* MARKETING.

**FOURTH CLASS** U.S. Postal Service designation for parcels, books, records, and other nonletter mail that weighs at least one pound, receives a low delivery priority, and pays a low postage rate. Books are one of the most common items mailed fourth class, thus the frequent use of the term "book rate," for this class. The postage is based upon the type of material, the number of ZONES traveled, the weight of the mailing piece, and the BULK MAIL CENTER that receives the mail. There are no service guarantees regarding the delivery speed of fourth-class mail. However, the same forwarding rules apply to fourth-class mail as to SECOND-CLASS and THIRD-CLASS mail.

There are three subclasses within fourth class for different types of material. The *Special Fourth-Class Rate* is for bound books that are not advertisements but may contain "some" advertising, and for films, recordings, and scripts; a PRESORT discount is available on mailings of 500 or more pieces. The *Bound Printed Matter Rate* applies to books and catalogs that have advertising as their primary purpose and that weigh between one and ten pounds. The third subclass is the *Parcel Post Rate,* which applies to all other fourth-class mail and is most often used for merchandise and unbound printed matter. This subclass of mail service competes with ALTERNATE DELIVERY services such as Federal Express and Purolator.

*See also* ATTACHED MAIL; CLASS; RETURN POSTAGE GUARANTEED.

**FOURTH COVER** *see* BACK COVER.

**FOUR UP** *see* -UP.

**FRACTIONAL PAGE AD** print advertisement occupying part of a page ($1/8$, $1/4$, or $1/2$ of a page) as distinguished from a full-page ad.

**FRAME**
  **Layout:** single unit (or *cell*) of a STORYBOARD.

**Production:**
1. in video, complete television picture. In videotape reproduction, 30 frames are produced per second.
2. in film, single picture in a series of pictures on moving picture film; also called *cell.* In film, 24 frames are produced per second.
3. outline of a television or motion picture screen used by the director to determine which elements to include or exclude when setting a scene—"to frame a shot."

**Research:** reference source for a population universe that is to be sampled.

## FRANCHISE
1. license granted by a company (the *franchisor*) to an individual or firm (the *franchisee*) to operate a retail, food, or drug outlet where the franchisee agrees to use the franchisor's name; products; services; promotions; selling, distribution, and display methods; and other company support. McDonald's, Midas, and Holiday Inn are all examples of franchise operations.
2. right to market a company's goods or services in a specific territory, which right has been granted by the company to an individual, group of individuals, marketing group, retailer, or wholesaler. *See also* BRAND FRANCHISE.
3. specific territory or outlet involved in such a right.
4. right of an advertiser to exercise an option to sponsor a television or radio show, as well as the granting of such a right by the broadcast medium (as "to exercise a franchise" or "to grant a franchise").
5. right granted by a local or state government to a cable television operator to offer cable television service in a community.

**FRANKED MAIL** mail delivered by the U.S. Postal Service free of charge for members of Congress, the Vice President and President of the U.S., and former presidents. The intent of this privilege is to encourage these public officials to communicate with their constituents. Franked mail must be for a use related to the sender's official business and duties. It is not meant to be used for reelection campaigning. The sender's signature must be printed on the outer envelope or wrapper. *See also* PENALTY MAIL.

**FREE-ASSOCIATION INTERVIEW** research technique where respondents are encouraged by a trained interviewer to speak about the first thing that comes to mind after hearing or seeing a spoken or displayed stimulus. The free-association interview offers insight into the thought processes and motivations of consumers in the purchase decision-making process.

**FREE CIRCULATION** *see* CONTROLLED CIRCULATION.

**FREE LANCE**
1. artist, writer, producer, director, or advertising person who works independently on a job-by-job basis. (Such a person is known as a free-lancer.)
2. work as a free-lancer.

**FREE SHEET** high-quality paper free of GROUNDWOOD PULP or mechanical wood pulp fibers. Free sheet paper can be twice as expensive as mechanical pulp paper; it is also less absorbent and therefore not suitable for high-speed printing such as newspaper printing. However, free sheet paper is much more durable and resistant to aging from exposure to air and light, and accordingly is well suited for book paper and catalogs with a long useful life. Free sheet paper is heavy (60 to 100 pounds BASIC WEIGHT). Its clean white surface is appropriate for the high-quality FOUR-COLOR PROCESS printing used in magazines and merchandise catalogs. *See also* KRAFT.

**FREESTANDING INSERT** advertising material in any of several formats, including BROADSIDES or multiple-page booklets, enclosed in a newspaper (particularly the Sunday edition); also called *freestanding stuffer.* The advertisement is called freestanding because it is not printed by nor is it a part of the newspaper. The newspaper distributor will generally charge a fee for including the inserts, except, perhaps, in the case of a nonprofit charity group, where the distributor will often donate these services.

**FREEZE-FRAME** effect produced on videotape where the action on the screen appears to stop. The freeze-frame is achieved by continually repeating the same video FRAME. On film this effect is called a *stop motion.*

**FREEZER CASE** refrigerated closed DISPLAY CASE used in grocery stores and supermarkets (or other outlets where frozen food is sold) for the containment of frozen food products.

**FREIGHT ALLOWANCE PRICING** price that is high enough to compensate the seller for the cost of transportation from the seller's place of business to the buyer's. The seller may pay the carrier directly and thus assume the risk of loss during transportation (F.O.B. Destination) or may reimburse the buyer and not assume the risk of loss (F.O.B. Shipping Point). A third type of freight allowance pricing called *freight equalization* varies the freight discount according to the differential between the cost of shipping from that seller's location and the cost of shipping from a competitor located closer to the buyer. *See also* FACTORY PRICING.

**FRENCH FOLD** method of folding a sheet of paper that is printed on one side only, so that the printed side shows and the unprinted side does not. The result is a four-page folder. French folds are sometimes used for enclosures in direct-mail advertising but are most often used for printed invitations or announcements. *See also* ACCORDION FOLD: FANFOLD. *See next page.*

**FREQUENCY**
1. number of times an advertising message is presented within a given time period.

| | |
|---|---|
| Page 1 | Page 4 |
| Page 2 | Page 3 |

French Fold

2. average number of times a commercial or advertisement has been viewed per person (or per household) during a specific time period. The idea of frequency is the same throughout all of the possible advertising media choices. Frequency, along with REACH, is an important concept in the planning of an advertising media schedule. Frequency is calculated by dividing the total possible audience by the audience that has been exposed at least once (reach or CUMULATIVE AUDIENCE) to the particular time segment (in broadcast) or publication in which the advertising message appears.

3. wavelength allocations made by the Federal Communications Commission for broadcasting, including radio stations, television channels, amateur radio (ham) operators, citizens' band radios, police radios, and the like. *See also* MEGAHERTZ.

4. in general, number of times something occurs within a specified period of time. Frequency may refer to the issues of a periodical, the purchases made by a customer over time, or the number of times a commercial or an advertisement is aired or printed or reaches its audience.

## FREQUENCY MODULATION (FM)

1. method of transmitting radio signals by varying the FREQUENCY (speed) of the radio wave while the height (amplitude) of the wave remains constant. The FM wave is approximately 20 times wider than the wave in AMPLITUDE MODULATION (AM), accounting for the fact that the FM system has a finer tonal quality, However, FM signals do not carry for long distances.

2. broadcast system that uses frequency modulation. *See also* AMPLITUDE MODULATION.

**FRIEND-OF-A-FRIEND** promotion similar to MEMBER-GET-A-MEMBER that offers an incentive for referring a third party to the seller; also called *third-party referral*. It differs from member-get-a-member promotions in that the person making the referral is not necessarily a customer; however, most friend-of-a-friend promotions are directed to current or new customers. This is an inexpensive way for direct marketers to identify their best prospects, assuming that those receiving the promotion will only refer friends likely to be interested in the product or service being sold. CATALOG HOUSES frequently offer a discount on future purchases to individuals who request a catalog for a friend, although this offer might be contingent upon the friend's making a purchase. This type of promotion is also a popular technique of airline travel clubs that award mileage credits in exchange for referrals.

**FRINGE AREA** listening or viewing area on the periphery of broadcast reception for a particular radio or television station. For example, the outlying regions in the northwest corner of New Jersey are a fringe area for the New York City television stations.

**FRISKET PAPER** transparent, specially prepared paper that can be applied to a section of artwork to form a protective coating, allowing the artist to work on other sections of the piece without damaging the frisket-coated section. An artist, for example, may want to retouch a section of a drawing with an AIRBRUSH. Frisket paper will protect the sections that do not need retouching from any excess paint issuing from the airbrush.

There is also a clear liquid material, which can be applied to artwork with a brush, that will form a protective coating when it dries and that acts as frisket paper (even though its original substance was liquid).

Frisket paper is also used to cover DEAD METAL areas on a PRINTING PLATE, so that those areas will not print anything when the plate is used in the printing process.

**FRONT COVER** front outside cover of a magazine that states the name of the magazine and the date of issue, and sometimes indicates editorial content; also called *first cover.* In American CONSUMER MAGAZINES, this cover is not sold for advertising space. Some business periodicals will sell a portion of the front cover for an advertisement, but these are generally publications that are available only to a specific trade.

**FRONTLOAD** schedule the bulk of an advertising budget for a specific time period in the beginning days or weeks of the advertising campaign. For example: If a campaign is scheduled to run for 13 weeks, a type of frontloading would be to budget 70% of the advertising allocation to be spent on media in the first 5 weeks, and the remaining 30% to be spent in the subsequent weeks.

**FRONT OF BOOK** section of a magazine ("book") that comes before the main editorial content of the magazine ("book"). Although advertising space rates are usually the same throughout the book, most advertisers prefer to have their advertisements placed in the front of the book. Therefore, many publishers will charge a premium to guarantee a front-of-book position.

**FTC RULE** *see* 30-DAY DELAYED DELIVERY RULE.

**FULFILLMENT** processes necessary to receive, service, and track orders sold via DIRECT MARKETING. There are different types of fulfillment systems based on the product or service sold, including SUBSCRIPTIONS, BOOK CLUB memberships, CONTINUITIES, CATALOG merchandise, and FUND-RAISING. The differences among fulfillment services arise from whether the sale is a ONE-SHOT or involves continuous service over time, whether there is one product being sold at a time or many, whether the sale is on a cash or credit basis, the nature of the product being sold and its delivery requirements, and the type of statistical information that must be compiled.

The primary functions of fulfillment systems are (1) to respond quickly and correctly to an order by delivering the item ordered, (2) to maintain customer records, (3) to send invoices and to record payments, (4) to respond to customer inquiries and complaints and resolve problems, and (5) to produce purchase and payment information on an individual customer basis and on a group basis (usually by SOURCE or KEY CODE) to aid in developing marketing plans and strategies. The basic processes of fulfillment are mail opening, caging *(see* CAGE), ORDER ENTRY, CUSTOMER SERVICE, address label printing and presorting *(see* PRESORT), merchandise PICKING and PACKING, billing, promoting, and statistical analysis and reporting.

Additional information can be obtained from the Fulfillment Management Association in New York City.

**FULL-COVER DISPLAY** agreement between magazine publishers and retail NEWSSTAND dealers that their magazines will receive preferential and prominent display positions on the newsstand in return for a RETAIL DISPLAY ALLOWANCE (RDA) of 6% to 10%. Although the dealers', intentions may be honorable, their adherence to this agreement is inconsistent and almost impossible to enforce. In many cases, there is an unspoken agreement that the RDA is really being paid to provide an incentive to the dealer for allocating space to that magazine. This incentive has become necessary as the cost of retail space increases and the profit MARGIN on magazines (particularly for newsstand dealers in airports) declines. If a publisher is determined to audit full-cover display, he must send an auditor into the field to visually inspect each newsstand.

**FULL DEMAND STATE** *see* DEMAND STATES.

**FULLFACE ENVELOPE** envelope without a window; also called *closed-face envelope.* Fullface envelopes are about 35¢/M cheaper than WINDOW ENVELOPES and can be used with a variety of FORMS. Window envelopes must be designed to accommodate a particular form, so that the appropriate image, COPY, or address information shows through the window. Fullface envelopes are usually addressed with a CHESHIRE LABEL or PRESSURE-SENSITIVE LABEL. A fullface envelope has a more personalized appearance than a window envelope because it is the same type of envelope as is used for nonpromotional, personal mail.

## FULL RUN

1. order for advertising to be placed in all editions of a newspaper that are put out on any one day. Some regional daily newspapers publish different editions for each of the counties (or sections of county) in which they are distributed. Each of these editions has its own RATE CARD for advertising, but the publisher also sets a special rate for advertisers who wish to advertise in all the editions (to advertise on a full run).

2. *see* FULL SHOWING.

## FULL-SERVICE AGENCY   ADVERTISING AGENCY that is equipped to serve its clients in all aspects of communication and promotion, so that there is no reason for the client to use any other outside service agency. The full-service agency offers total service in both advertising and non-advertising areas. The advertising services concern preparation and placement of advertising and include the creating, planning, and production of advertisements and commercials as well as research services and media selection and purchase. The non-advertising services are in the area of production and include sales promotion materials, publicity pieces, annual reports, TRADE SHOW exhibits, and sales training materials.

Although a full-service agency can offer this wide range of services, all full-service agencies are not alike. They vary greatly in size, focus, and areas of specialization. Therefore, they also vary in the type of client they serve. When choosing a full-service advertising agency, it is important to the advertiser to be aware of the agency's expertise in the area that best serves the advertiser's product or service.

## FULL SHOT (FS)

1. camera shot that shows in full length the person or object featured in the scene/frame.

2. camera shot, sometimes called a LONG SHOT, that encompasses an entire scene equivalent to one the audience would see if the production were a live presentation in legitimate theater, in contrast to a CLOSE-UP shot, which excludes all elements from view except the principal subject.

## FULL SHOWING

1. purchase of all the outdoor advertising positions in a specific geographical area for an advertising display for a specific time period, usually 30 days. A full showing indicates that 100% of the population in a community will pass the advertising at least once on any given day. The term is also used to indicate that a particular outdoor advertising position will be passed by everyone in the

community at least once during a given 30-day period, thus affording the position a 100% SHOWING.

**2.** method of purchasing CAR CARDS or *posters* (*see* BILLBOARD) for advertising display in or on a transit system; also called *full run*. A full showing indicates car cards are to be displayed in all of the vehicles in a fleet. Usually, rates are for 1 month, although discounts are typically offered for 3-, 6-, and 12-month runs. *See also* QUARTER SHOWING.

**FULL-TEXT LETTER** personalized COMPUTER LETTER that is printed in one step in its entirety with the exception of the LETTERHEAD and/or signature, in contrast to a fill-in letter that has personalized elements printed within the blanks on a preprinted form letter; also called *full-out letter*. The visual merging of personalized text with standard text can be achieved more effectively with a full-text letter. Full-text letters can be more expensive than fill-in letters because computer printing tends to be more expensive than press printing and because full-text letters require more computer time to print. For small mailings of less than 50,000 pieces, or larger mailings split into small test PANELS, the additional cost can be negligible since the per piece cost of press printing small quantities of fill-in letters can be as high as the cost of computer printing.

**FUNCTIONAL MANUALS** group of six manuals published by the U.S. Postal Service, including the DOMESTIC MAIL MANUAL (DMM) and the INTERNATIONAL MAIL MANUAL (IMM) used by most MAILERS and the various administrative policy and procedure manuals used only by the U.S.P.S. The regulations described in the DMM and the IMM are subject to some degree of interpretation. When in doubt, you should contact your Postal Service CUSTOMER SERVICE REPRESENTATIVE or local postmaster, who can be very helpful in interpreting the regulations, frequently to the mailer's advantage.

**FUNCTIONAL TITLE** job title descriptive of the occupation or professional responsibilities of an individual, such as accounting manager, farmer, vice president sales, or advertising executive. Functional titles are included in each RECORD on a BUSINESS LIST so that promotions can be properly addressed and can be targeted to the professional interests of groups of individuals.

LIST RENTAL selections are frequently made by functional title. The classification of titles into groups is determined by the LIST OWNER as best meets her marketing objectives. For example, if the list is used for promoting farm goods, then "accounting manager" might be grouped under a miscellaneous category and "farmer" classified according to cattle, grain, dairy, and so forth. Conversely, if financial services are being promoted, then all types of farmers would fall under a miscellaneous category and "accounting manager" would be a unique category.

**FUND-RAISING** effort to solicit contributions from individuals or organizations for nonprofit organizations having educational, medical, religious, political, charitable, or other stated purposes. Fundraising is particularly well suited to DIRECT MARKETING techniques because efforts can be concentrated on individuals who have contributed before, and who tend to be willing to give again, or who have some demonstrated interest in the purpose of the organization—for example, Democratic politicians can send fund-raising solicitations to all registered Democrats in their jurisdiction. The most common techniques of fund-raising are DIRECT MAIL ADVERTISING and TELEMARKETING. Most state and local governments have laws concerning the conduct of fund-raising, such as reporting requirements, limits on organization salaries and commissions, or restrictions on when or where telemarketing may be used. Fund-raisers may rent or use their own CONTRIBUTOR LISTS for solicitation of the individuals on the list.

**FUND-RAISING LIST** contributors or potential contributors to a FUND-RAISING effort consisting of a list of DONORS to a single fundraising organization or a COMPILED LIST of donors to several related fund-raising organizations. The expected response rate of a list of contributors to a fund-raising solicitation is greater than that of other lists. Their response can be estimated based on the RECENCY/FREQUENCY/MONETARY VALUE RATIO of their prior contributions and the degree of similarity between the purpose of this solicitation and the solicitation(s) responded to previously.

**FUZZ** fibers or pieces of lint that stick out along the surface of paper. Paper with smooth finishes, such as COATED PAPER, has very little fuzz. Fuzz interferes with fine HALFTONE printing that requires small DOTS; therefore, this type of printing is usually done on coated paper.

# G

**GAFFER** in motion picture and television production, the head lighting electrician on the set.

**GAFFOON** in broadcast, informal term for the person responsible for SOUND EFFECTS. This term is used particularly in television production.

**GAG WRITER** writer (usually for television) who specializes in comical lines or situations.

**GALLAGHER REPORT** weekly newsletter published by The Gallagher Report, Inc., in New York City and sold by subscription for the benefit of executives in advertising, management, marketing, and media. The report offers news and comment on corporate acquisitions and mergers, advertising programs, marketing trends, executive decisions, media patterns, and advertising-budget allocations. It also issues a monthly supplement, the Gallagher President's Report, which is written by physicians in various specialties, and contains information concerning executive health problems, new medical technology, and the latest trends in health maintenance.

## GALLEY

**Data processing:** computer-printed HARD-COPY listing of selected RECORDS from a file. *See also* FORMAT.

**Printing:** shallow tray used in manual typesetting to hold composed metal type. *See also* GALLEY PROOF.

**GALLEY PROOF** preliminary print of typeset material, such as an advertisement or brochure, submitted by the typesetter for correction or approval by a proofreader prior to final page MAKEUP and printing; also called *galley*. *See also* AUTHOR'S ALTERATION; EDITORIAL ALTERATION; PROOFREADER'S SYMBOL.

**GALLUP AND ROBINSON, INC.** research organization that conducts syndicated and custom studies of advertising effectiveness in print and television.

**GALVANIC SKIN RESPONSE** in marketing research, clinical measurement of a subject's response to stimuli, such as an advertisement, in terms of changes in skin resistance to electrical current; also called PSYCHOGALVANIC SKIN RESPONSE or sweaty palms. Theoretically, the greater the change in resistance, the more positive the subject's reaction to the stimuli. The validity of this technique has been much disputed, particularly because there is no way of knowing for sure that the stimulus provided by the researcher (the advertisement) was the cause of the response. Its proponents argue that it is more objective than research that relies on voluntary responses like interviews or surveys. *See also* EYE MOVEMENT ANALYSIS.

**GAME SHOW** radio or television program with a contest format in which the participants selected are celebrities or members of the listening or viewing audience, or a combination of both, who compete against each other or against the house, according to a prescribed set of rules, for some kind of reward. *See also* GIVEAWAY.

**GAMMA** trigonometric unit of measure of the degree of contrast between the darkest and lightest areas in a photographic image. *See also* HIGH CONTRAST.

**GANG** *see* GANG RUN.

**GANG RUN** concurrent printing of two or more printing jobs in the same press RUN for purposes of saving labor and time. Since more than one job is printed at the same time, there will also be a cost savings for each job, which can then be passed on to the customer. The sheet printed in a gang run is called a *gang*.

**GATEFOLD** form of magazine advertisement where the cover or an inside page opens to reveal an additional page that folds out, giving the advertisement a much larger dimension than the regular-size page. Gatefolds are used most frequently for special occasions to make a spectacular presentation of a new product such as colorful new eye makeup products or a new car. Gatefolds are expensive, and not all magazines offer them since arrangements for their inclusion must be made well in advance of the closing date for an issue.

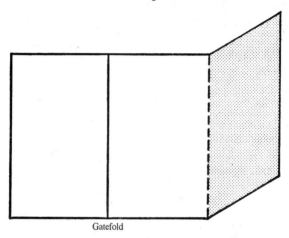

Gatefold

**GATEKEEPER** member of a DECISION-MAKING UNIT or social group who acts to prevent or discourage a purchase by controlling the flow of information and/or access to people in the buying center. A mother who does not allow her child to choose a presweetened cereal at the supermarket is acting as a gatekeeper. A secretary who does not put calls through to the decision maker is a gatekeeper. Marketers must direct their advertisements not only to the end user, but also to any potential gatekeepers.

**GATHERING**
**Direct mail:** collation of promotion PACKAGE components prior to inserting into an OUTER ENVELOPE. *See also* INSERTER.
**Printing:** BINDERY LINE process that collates and assembles folded SIG-NATURES into the appropriate sequence for BINDING. Technology now exists for computerized SELECTIVE BINDING that can create multiple versions of a print product in one production stream by gathering different signatures for each version, usually according to a code on the address label placed on the final product.

**GATT (GENERAL AGREEMENT ON TARIFFS AND TRADE)** institutional framework signed in 1948 by 23 nations, including the

United States, for the purposes of fostering multilateral trade agreements among members. A basic tenent of GATT is the most-favored nation principle, which allows every nation within the framework the best contract terms received by any single nation within the framework. GATT provides a set of rules and principles that are committed to the liberalization of trade between member nations, and the member nations meet every two years to negotiate new tariff agreements. As of 1991, 108 nations were participating in GATT, representing over 80% of the total volume of international trade.

**GEAR STREAKS**  parallel streaks that blemish the surface of printed material making it unusable. The streaks occur at intervals identical to the distance between the gear teeth on the printing CYLINDER.

**GEL**  colored transparent sheet attached to the front of a lighting instrument to produce colored light. The name originates from the fact that the gel was originally made of a gelatinous substance. However, other materials have been found to be better suited for this purpose, since gelatin deteriorates quickly under the hot lights and over long periods of use.

**GENDER ANALYSIS**  analyzing a list of names to determine which represent male or female individuals according to a list of typically male or female names. LIST SELECTIONS may then be made on the basis of gender to promote products suitable to only one gender. Some amount of error is inevitable in gender analysis since various names are given to both men and women. Gender analysis can also be used to add a *Mr, Miss, Ms,* or *Mrs* title to each record so that forms and mailing labels can be appropriately addressed. The choice of adding either Miss, Ms, or Mrs to a female name is made by the LIST USER based on the source of the names, DEMOGRAPHIC data available about the individual such as age or marital status, and the preference of the target market for a Miss versus a Ms title. For example, a list of high school students would be addressed as Miss or Ms, but a list of pregnant women would probably be addressed as Mrs. However, this leaves a lot of room for error, so the safest choice in all cases is Ms.

**GENERAL DELIVERY**  level of service provided by the U.S. Postal Service that requires mail to be picked up at the post office by the addressee. General delivery is mandatory in some sparsely populated areas or for households without a street address, such as a secluded mountain or beach home. General delivery may also be requested by individuals who travel frequently and do not want their mail to pile up at home. General delivery recipients represent an insignificant portion of most promotion mailings and should not be of special concern to the direct mail advertiser (see DIRECT MAIL ADVERTISING).

**GENERAL MAIL FACILITY (GMF)**  U.S. Postal Service processing centers used for handling mail not processed by BULK MAIL CENTERS.

**GENERAL MAIL SYSTEM (GMS)** U.S. POSTAL SERVICE mail distribution service consisting of various levels of service defined by mail CLASS, with varying postage rates based on class, type of material, distance traveled, PRESORT level, and the profit or nonprofit status of the mailer. *See also* ALTERNATE DELIVERY; CUSTOMER SERVICE REPRESENTATIVE; DOMESTIC MAIL MANUAL.

**GENERAL POST OFFICE (GPO)** main post office in a city with several BRANCH POST OFFICES. The GPO provides complete postal services not necessarily provided by branch offices. The GPO should be consulted about inquiries regarding mail delivery problems in that service area.

**GENERAL SCHEME** delivery plan for a state or section of a state describing the flow of mail to various local post offices. The general scheme could be consulted by your U.S. Postal Service CUSTOMER SERVICE REPRESENTATIVE to help identify the source of a delivery problem.

**GENERATION** term referring to the number of times a film, audiotape, or videotape has been reproduced since the original MASTER. *First generation* refers to a film or tape that has been duplicated directly from the master, *second generation* refers to a film or tape that has been reproduced from the first generation; and so on. The technical quality diminishes as the number of generations increases.

**GENERIC ADVERTISING** *see* PRIMARY ADVERTISING.

**GENERIC APPEAL** advertising appeal on behalf of a product category in which no mention is made of a specific BRAND NAME—for example, the advertising that encourages the drinking of milk, sponsored by the American Dairy Association. This type of advertising may be sponsored by an industry association representing all the individual producers of the product or service, or by a leading producer in the industry—for example, the Alcoa-sponsored advertising for aluminum products. Its purpose is usually to make the public aware of the product category.

**GEO CODE**
1. code assigned by a file owner to file RECORDS according to the owner's own coding system that identifies the geographic location of each individual's residence or business in terms of region, state, county, city, or other subdivision larger than a ZIP code area. Geo codes are used to analyze the concentration of customers in various areas or to select LISTS for promotion. The assumption is that people who live in the same geographic area as good customers will also be good customers because they share similar DEMOGRAPHIC characteristics and interests.
2. generic term for the various postal codes used throughout the world, such as the ZIP CODE or the CANADIAN POSTAL CODE.

**GEODEMOGRAPHY** attribution of DEMOGRAPHIC characteristics to a group of individuals residing in the same geographic area based on an OVERLAY of demographic survey data against a geographically segmented list. For example, geodemography might determine that Stamford, Connecticut, comprises a high proportion of affluent married people with young children. It would thus be appropriate to target Stamford for children's furniture promotions and so forth. *See also* U.S. BUREAU OF THE CENSUS.

**GEOGRAPHIC BALANCE** names remaining on a rented list after a GEOGRAPHIC SELECTION has been made. For example, if previous analysis has shown that residents of the southern U.S. do not respond to promotions for ski equipment, then the names of these individuals would be excluded from a LIST RENTAL for a ski equipment CATALOG and those excluded individuals would constitute the geographic balance.

**GEOGRAPHIC CENSUS DIVISION** U.S. Bureau of the Census term for a logical division of the U.S., made up of contiguous states, for which census data is attainable. The four main regions are the Northeast, the South, the Midwest, and the West. Each of these regions is further divided as follows: *Northeast:* Mid-Atlantic—NY, PA, NJ; New England—ME, VT, NH, MA, CT, RI. *South:* W. South Central—LA, AR, OK, TX; E. South Central—KY, TN, MS, AL; S. Atlantic—MD, DE, DC, WV, VA, NC, SC, GA, FL. *Midwest:* W. North Central—ND, SD, NE, KS, MN, IA, MO; E. North Central—WI, MI, IL, IN, OH. *West:* Pacific—CA, WA, OR, HI, AK; Mountain—MT, ID, WY, NV, UT, CO, AZ, NM.

CUSTOMER PROFILES can be analyzed in terms of geographic census divisions so that advertisements and direct mail promotions can be directed to the most appropriate regions and tailored to the characteristics of that population.

**GEOGRAPHIC SEGMENTATION** MARKET SEGMENTATION STRATEGY whereby the intended audience for a given product is divided according to geographic units, such as nations, states, regions, counties, cities, or neighborhoods. Marketers will tailor marketing programs to fit the needs of individual geographic areas, localizing the products, advertising, and sales effort to geographic differences in needs and wants. Marketers will also study the population density or regional climate as factors of geographic segmentation. *See also* BEHAVIOR SEGMENTATION, DEMOGRAPHIC SEGMENTATION, PSYCHOGRAPHIC SEGMENTATION.

**GEOGRAPHIC SELECTION** extraction of RECORDS from a list based on address criteria. Geographic selections are made so that direct marketing promotions can be targeted to the best prospects. The process begins with an analysis of files of current customers to determine where they reside. The theory is that good customers live near other people who share the same characteristics that made them good customers. For example, certain food preferences are demonstrated by Southerners (collard greens, grits, black-eyed peas) and by Northerners (clam chowder, hot chocolate), making the promotion of these foods (or products used to serve and prepare them) more profitable in specific areas. Geographic selections are made using a variety of address criteria, such as ZIP code, COUNTY, STATE, or GEOGRAPHIC CENSUS DIVISION. *See also* GEOGRAPHIC BALANCE; ZIP SELECT.

**GESTALT THEORY** psychological point of view that says it is necessary to consider the whole of something, since the whole has a meaning apart from its individual elements. In advertising, the implication of this theory is that a particular brand must be considered as an organized whole and not just as a total of its attributes. Therefore, if an attribute is altered in any way or if a new attribute is added, consumer perception of the brand may change radically, and consumers who have previously purchased the product may no longer continue to do so.

The idea of the organized whole implicit in the gestalt theory also applies to the advertising context for the product. If the context is changed, it is likely that the market for the product will change as well.

**GHOST**
1. old record maintained on a computer file after a change has been made that creates a new record from the old. It is kept as a pointer to the new record in case a transaction must be made involving both records. For example, a change of address creates a new MATCHCODE and a new record, and a customer inquiry written from the old address can only be matched to the ghost record.
2. television or printed image that is a pale duplication of the primary image. A ghost on a television screen is a reflection of the image transmission. A printed ghost may be caused by mechanical or chemical printing errors.
3. writer who allows her work to be published under another person's name.

**GIFT BUYER** *see* DONOR.

**GIFT CARD** card sent to the recipient of a gift or enclosed with the gift by the seller or sent directly by the DONOR. It is used to announce the gift and identify the donor. Gift cards are necessary in direct mail marketing because the gift is usually delivered directly to the recipient through the mail rather than being personally presented by the donor. Some gift cards are computer printed with the donor's name on the card and the recipient's name and address on the envelope or on the opposite side of a postcard. A gift card may also be hand inscribed with the donor's name and/or message. Gift cards range from expensive types such as are found in a greeting card store to simple postcards on white card stock. Many marketers who normally send gift cards directly to the donor will address and mail the cards to the recipients themselves during the Christmas/Chanukah holiday season to ensure that the cards are received before the holiday.

**GIFT ORDER** purchase made by a DONOR to be given to one or more DONEES. Direct mail campaigns are conducted during the holiday season to promote gift orders. These campaigns usually mail during the September through November time period. Gift orders are not heavily promoted other times of the year (although they are always accepted) except by sellers of gift items, such as gourmet foods or flowers. *See also* GIFT CARD.

**GIFT-WITH-PURCHASE OFFER** advertising incentive program in which a PREMIUM is given away with the purchase of a product or service. Gift-with-purchase offers are used frequently in DIRECT-RESPONSE promotions as well as in DIRECT-MAIL ADVERTISING. *See also* IN-PACK PREMIUM.

**GIMMICK** attention-getting device used in advertising a product or service, also called *hook.* A gimmick can be in the form of unusual or contrived words or expressions in the copy, a unique or novel display device, pictures or headlines that do not actually relate to the message, a novelty GIVEAWAY, or any other unusual form of promotion for a product or service.

**GIVEAWAY**
1. form of radio or television GAME SHOW where a prize or PREMIUM is given away to contestants or members of the listening or viewing audience.
2. premium, prize, or merchandise given free to prospective consumers for promotional and advertising purposes. *See also* GIMMICK.

**GIZMO** novelty item used as a GIMMICK.

**GLOBAL MARKETING** see INTERNATIONAL ADVERTISING.

**GLOSSY**
1. sheet of very smooth or COATED PAPER with a reflective finish that is used for photographs or proofs suitable for direct reproduction.
2. *see* REFLECTION COPY.

**GOING-RATE PRICING** establishing the price for a product or service based on prevalent market prices. This is most common with products that do not vary much from one supplier to another, like steel or fresh meat. *See also* DEMAND-ORIENTED PRICING.

**GOLDENROD PAPER** yellow or orange paper used as a support sheet for assembling groups of NEGATIVE and POSITIVE film strips for printing. Goldenrod paper requires less preparation but holds its shape less well than other support sheet materials such as vinyl, polyester, and glass. It is therefore used only for black-and-white or continuous-tone multicolor printing and not for fine HALFTONE or FOUR-COLOR PROCESS printing. *See also* STRIPPING.

**GONDOLA**   type of merchandise DISPLAY stand used in retailing. A gondola is a bank of freestanding shelves that are open on all sides.

**GOOD HOUSEKEEPING SEAL**   seal of approval of a product that meets standards established by the Good Housekeeping Institute as directed by *Good Housekeeping Magazine* in a policy designed for consumer protection. The magazine will license use of the seal by an advertiser but will set limits for the ways the seal may be used. Companies desiring a Good Housekeeping Seal of Approval for a product must advertise in the magazine, and the advertised product must be accepted by the magazine. (Advertising for tobacco products and certain alcoholic beverages will not be accepted.) A contract for licensing will also require a minimum volume and frequency of advertising in the magazine, and advertisers may use the seal in other advertising only according to contract terms. Since it is generally accepted that the Good Housekeeping Institute has become a recognized authority, trusted by the public, use of the seal provides a seemingly independent endorsement of a product's quality. Thus it is considered beneficial to include the seal in advertisements.

**GOTHIC**   group of TYPEFACES where the letters are without SERIFS (cross strokes at the ends of the main strokes) and are relatively uniform in weight. There are several different styles of gothic faces, which are also sometimes called SANS SERIF ("without serif") or *block letter.* Gothic typography should not be confused with faces referred to as Old English or text, since these fall into the classification of black letter typography.

**GO TO BLACK**   direction used in videotaping or filming to indicate that the picture should FADE OUT until the screen is empty of any image and appears to be black.

**GOUACHE**
  **1.** totally opaque type of watercolor paint that has a gumlike base; sometimes used to color in drawings.
  **2.** painting made with gouache.

**GOVERNMENT MARKET**   consumer group composed of federal, state, and local government units. The government market in total accounts for the greatest volume of purchases of any consumer group in the United States, spending hundreds of billions of dollars on goods and services each year. Although government purchases comprise a wide range of products such as food, military equipment, office supplies, buildings, clothing, and vehicles, selling to this market typically involves a great deal of paperwork, financial constraints, bureaucratic barriers, and awareness of specific political sensitivities. *See also* ORGANIZATIONAL MARKET.

**GOVERNORS** *see* U.S. POSTAL BOARD OF GOVERNORS.

**GRACE** serve issues of a periodical after the subscription has expired, usually in order to meet the RATE BASE, to use extra copies of an issue, or to further encourage renewals; also called *arrears*. Gracing is more economically advantageous for magazines that derive more of their revenue from advertising than from subscriptions.

The AUDIT BUREAU OF CIRCULATIONS has specific rules for gracing to which the publisher must adhere in order to count these issues as paid CIRCULATION. The most important rules are that gracing applies only to paid subscriptions that have not missed any issues since EXPIRE and that graced issues can be sent for only three months.

**GRAIN**
**Photography:**
1. relative size of the particles forming a photographic image, expressed in terms of FINE-GRAIN or COARSE-GRAIN images.
2. flaws in a photograph caused by excessive enlarging.
**Printing:** direction in which most fibers in paper run as a result of the papermaking process. Paper tears more easily with the grain than against the grain, and when the shape of paper is affected by moisture, or by a lack of humidity, it changes more in the direction of the grain. For some types of paper, folds made parallel to the grain will cause less damage to the paper and will be less bulky. Other types of paper must be folded AGAINST THE GRAIN.

The pages of a book or catalog turn more easily if the grain of every page runs parallel to the binding. However, advertisers often place BIND-INS so that the grain of the bind-in crosses the binding, causing the magazine or catalog to tend to open at that point. This works especially well if the bind-in paper stock is heavier than that of the pages.

For OFFSET printing, the grain should be parallel to the long edge of the printed image so that changes in the paper shape due to moisture will have less impact on the print REGISTER.

Many other rules apply to different types of paper and printing. Your printer or production manager should be consulted when choosing the appropriate paper for a job.

**GRAINING**
1. process that treats LITHOGRAPHY plates with abrasives to make them more porous and water retentive and less likely to pick up ink on the nonprinting areas.
2. process of embossing a decorative grain pattern onto paper that does not have a natural grain on the surface.

**GRAINY**
1. in audio, scratchy sound that is the result of inferior quality in either the recording or the PLAYBACK equipment.
2. in film, degree that the granules of silver (which make up the emulsion) appear in the print or on the screen. As a photograph is blown

up to larger proportions, the granules become more obvious; the greater the enlargement, the greater the degree of graininess. Also, the faster the film speed is, whether in still photography or moving pictures, the more likely it is that the grain will be visible. *See also* FILM SPEED.

**GRAMMAGE** metric system measure of paper weight representing the gram weight of one square meter of paper; expressed as $g/m^2$ or grams per square meter. The cost of paper and its appropriateness for various print products are a function of the weight. In the U.S., the pound system for paper weight is more often used. Forty-pound book paper equals approximately 60 $g/m^2$ paper. The conversion factor at various standard paper sizes is as follows:

| Paper Size | $g/m^2$ to lbs. | lbs. to $g/m^2$ |
|---|---|---|
| $17 \times 22$ | 0.266 | 3.760 |
| $20 \times 26$ | 0.370 | 2.704 |
| $24 \times 36$ | 0.614 | 1.627 |
| $25 \times 38$ | 0.675 | 1.480 |
| 1000 ft$^2$ | 0.205 | 4.831 |

*See also* BASIS WEIGHT.

**GRANDFATHER TAPE** *see* BACKUP TAPE.

**GRAPH** diagram that shows the changes in one VARIABLE in relation to the changes in one or more other variables. In a *line graph,* these changes are shown as a series of points, connected by a line or a curve, whereas in a *bar graph* or *histogram,* solid columns are used. Graphs are used to chart the results of research and to picture mathematical data, particularly that used by advertisers or MEDIA PLANNERS in designing advertising campaigns.

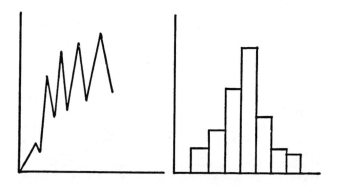

**GRAPHIC DESIGN** preparation of a visual representation of an idea or message, such as a print or broadcast advertisement or direct-mail-promotion PACKAGE, including all aspects of the final image/package desired, such as illustrations, set typefaces, colors, paper stock, or arrangement of elements on a page. The design of any promotion must incorporate the marketing objectives and strategy, the production capabilities, and the budget limitations of the advertiser.

Graphic design services can be provided by in-house staffs, advertising agencies, printers and lettershops, free-lance artists, and syndicated artwork services. An in-house staff is economical if large quantities of design work are needed but limits the advertiser to the style and skills of that pool of designers. Printer and lettershop staffs are usually adept at tailoring graphic designs to a client's printing and production capabilities. Art studios offer a diverse range of talent but at a relatively high cost. Freelancers can produce very good quality work at a more reasonable price but may not be available when needed. Syndicated services provide identical artwork and designs to many users, who must adapt them to suit their purposes.

## GRAPHICS

1. illustrations formed by hand design, engraving, drawing, or computer that represent the majority of visual elements in the production of advertising and audiovisual artwork, all of which work toward the clear visual expression of the finished product.
2. in television, all visuals prepared for a production, including cameracards, slides, titles, lettering, illustrations, diagrams, electronically generated symbols and letters, and all pictures, maps, charts, and graphs. Virtually every television program makes some use of television graphics.
3. *see* GRAPHIC DESIGN.

**GRAVURE** printing process, also called *intaglio,* where the matter to be duplicated is etched into the printing surface rather than raised from the surface as in letterpress printing. After etching, the incisions are then inked, and as the paper comes into contact with the printing surface, ink is deposited on it in varying amounts, depending on the depth of the incisions. Gravure (photogravure) printing has a soft, velvety quality with subtle gradations of tonal values that combine to produce a lovely illustrative effect, which can even be done on inexpensive paper. (Its reproduction of type, however, tends to be a bit fuzzy.) Gravure printing was used for the first time in an American newspaper in 1914 by the *New York Times* for its magazine supplement and is used today predominantly for the magazine sections of all newspapers.

**GRAY COMPONENT REPLACEMENT (GCR)** computer-supported COLOR SEPARATION process that replaces with black ink a colored ink that was initially used to create gray tones; also called *achromatic color;* INTEGRATED COLOR REMOVAL. In conventional FOUR-COLOR PROCESS separations, two primary colors of ink make

PRINCIPLE OF THE GRAVURE PRESS

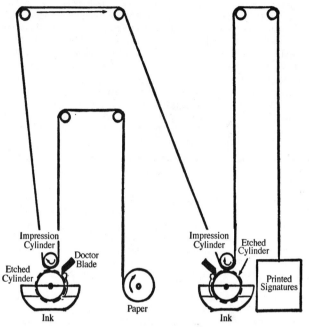

up the image and a third color is overlaid to create shadows, gray areas, and muted tones. With GCR, the use of black ink instead of a third color creates a sharper, less washed-out image. It is also easier to reach, through trial-and-error, the right amount of black ink needed, because a bit too little or too much of black ink won't change the color of an image the way that a third primary color will. Black only changes the lightness or darkness of the image.

GCR has been credited with more consistent print quality through a print RUN, less paper wasted getting the press ready to print, less ink usage and lower ink cost since black ink is cheaper than color ink, and better reproduction of the original image colors. *See also* UNDERCOLOR REMOVAL.

## GRAY SCALE
**Printing:** strip of gray tones, ranging from white to black, that is placed at the side of original copy when photographing, to measure the range and contrast of the tones.

**Television production:** seven- to ten-step chart progressing from television white to television black. (Since the television camera cannot accurately reproduce pure white or pure black, these tones are referred to as television white and television black.) The gray scale measures the reflective qualities (the percentage of light reflected by the tone) of the gray tones from approximately 60% reflectance (television white) to approximately 3% reflectance (television black). Average skin tone is about 35% reflectance, or number 3 on the ten-step scale. Number 5 on the ten-step scale is approximately 18% reflectance and is a standard photographic measure used to take average light readings.

**GREEK** meaningless symbols, designed to look like printed copy, that are drawn on a rough LAYOUT to show the size of the copy and where it will actually go when the layout is complete. A rough layout using Greek is usually done in the preliminary stages of development so that the artist (and sometimes account executive and client) can see the overall design of the piece.

**GREEN BOOK** directory of international market research firms, which is published annually by the New York Chapter of the American Marketing Association.

**GREEN MARKETING** promotion of environmentally safe or beneficial products. Green marketing began in Europe in the early 1980s when certain products were found to be harmful to the earth's atmosphere. Consequently new types of products were created, called "green" products, that would cause less damage to the environment. The movement quickly caught on in the United States and has been growing steadily ever since. The development of ecologically safer products, recyclable and biodegradable packaging, energy-efficient operations, and better pollution controls are all aspects of green marketing. Green marketing has produced advances such as packages using recycled paper, phosphate-free detergents, refill containers for cleaning products, and bottles using less plastic.

**GRID CARD** RATE CARD used in broadcast media sales, which indicates the fees for commercial advertising in the various DAYPARTS.

**GRIP** in filming and television production, a person who functions as a handyman on the set. The grip will assist wherever necessary and will help with moving scenery and lighting instruments or prop storage.

**GRIPPER EDGE**
1. leading edge of paper as it is fed through a printing press or folding machine. The devices that hold the paper in place on the long side and pull it through the press are called *grippers.* You cannot print on the 3/8"-wide gripper margin and must make some allowance for trimming them off when ordering paper for BLEED printing.
2. front edge of a lithographic or WRAPAROUND plate attached to the front clamp of a plate CYLINDER.

**GRIPPER MARGIN** *see* GRIPPER EDGE.

## GROSS AMOUNT

**In general:** total before deductions. The gross amount minus deductions equals the NET AMOUNT. *See also* GROSS PROFIT.

**Advertising:** total amount owed by an advertiser to an advertising medium for advertising space or time purchased prior to the deduction of the advertising agency's commission. *See also* GROSS AUDIENCE; GROSS BILLING; GROSS NIGHT HOUR; GROSS RATING POINT.

**Direct mail:** responses received from a promotion, including prepaid orders (CASH ORDERS) and CREDIT ORDERS. The NET RESPONSE is the total of all cash orders and paid credit orders. *Gross response* is an important early measure of a promotion's success, but net response is used to measure the promotion's profitability. Various aspects of response are measured in terms of a percent of gross, such as net paid orders, cash orders, credit orders, or orders received within a certain number of days following the MAIL DATE. The measurements are used to evaluate a promotion relative to other promotions and/or to forecast the results that can be expected from similar promotions. *See also* RESPONSE RATE.

**List rental:** total number of names on a list prior to a MERGE/PURGE. *See also* NET NAME ARRANGEMENT.

**Magazines:** selling price of a subscription prior to the deduction of AGENT commissions. *See also* GROSS CIRCULATION.

## GROSS AUDIENCE

total number of individuals (or households) in a listening, viewing, or reading audience without regard to duplication of audience members. For example, in television, a person is counted twice if that person appears in the audience of two of the programs in the broadcast schedule being counted. When gross audience is expressed in terms of percentage, it is often referred to as *homes per rating point* or GROSS RATING POINTS; when expressed in terms of numbers of individuals (or households), it is referred to as GROSS IMPRESSION.

## GROSS BILLING

1. *see* BILLING.
2. cost of advertising with a communications medium, including the advertising agency commission.
3. cost of a one-time insertion in a communications medium.

## GROSS CIRCULATION

1. maximum amount of people who pass an outdoor advertising display and have a reasonable opportunity to view the message. The gross circulation is calculated for a given display over a specific period of time (usually 30 days).
2. *see* CIRCULATION.

## GROSS CONTRIBUTION MARGIN *see* GROSS PROFIT.

## GROSS NIGHT HOUR

in television, one-time cost to sponsor one hour of PRIME TIME programming. The gross-night-hour (GNH) figure is used as a relative comparison to other costs for commercial advertising time. (In other words: If it costs X amount of dollars for an hour of prime time on a particular station, how will that figure compare to the cost for 16 minutes of 30-second commercials on the same station?)

**GROSS PROFIT** difference between revenue *(sales)* and the cost of goods sold. For example, XYZ Company sold through a newspaper advertisement 120 belts that cost XYZ $10 each. XYZ sold each belt for $18. The gross profit is calculated as follows:

$$120 \times \$18 = \$2160$$
$$120 \times \$10 = \underline{\$1200}$$
Gross profit $ 960

The gross profit as a percentage of revenue is termed the *gross profit margin*. Gross profit is different from NET PROFIT, which is gross profit net of other income or expenses, interest expense, and taxes. *See also* AVERAGE PROFIT MARGIN.

## GROSS RATING POINT (GRP)

1. sum of all rating points over a specific time period or over the course of a MEDIA PLAN; sometimes called *homes per rating point*. The rating of a show represents the percentage of people (or households) tuned in to a television program as compared to the number of television sets in the particular television universe (geographical location). Each rating point is equal to 1%. If a show has a rating of 7, that means that 7% of all persons (or households) who have a television were tuned in to that show (whether the other televisions were turned on or not). If there are two shows on a particular station during a particular time period, and the first show has a rating of 7 and the other a rating of 10, then the GRPs for that time period equal 17.

   MEDIA PLANNERS use gross rating points as a method of designing a media schedule in an attempt to deliver a maximum number of GRPs at minimum cost. In this instance, GRPs are calculated by multiplying the total REACH (the UNDUPLICATED AUDIENCE) of the schedule by the FREQUENCY (average amount of exposures) of the insertion in the proposed schedule. The gross rating points then will represent the product of reach and frequency and will express the "gross" duplicated percentage of audience that will be reached by the proposed plan. (It is important to note that GRPs are a percentage. Therefore, if a given market has 1000 television households, each GRP represents 10 viewing households, whereas in a market of 10,000 television households, each GRP represents 100 viewing households. Thus, the largest amount of GRPs does not necessarily mean the largest audience.)

2. in outdoor advertising, percentage of the population that passes an outdoor advertising structure on a daily basis. GRPs are the same as SHOWINGS.

**GROSS RESPONSE**  *see* GROSS AMOUNT.

**GROUNDWOOD PULP**  mechanically produced wood pulp used to make low grades of inexpensive paper for newspapers, SHOPPERS, magazines, and other disposable print products. It is especially well suited to high-speed printing, such as newspaper printing, because of its high ABSORPTION level. *See also* FREE SHEET; THERMO-MECHANICAL PULP.

**GROWTH-SHARE MATRIX**  graph, designed by the Boston Consulting Group and often called the Boston Box, that classifies all of a company's STRATEGIC BUSINESS UNITS and measures the performance of a company's products. The graph's vertical axis defines the market growth rate, or the degree of market attractiveness, and the horizontal axis defines the relative market share, or the degree of the company's strength in the market. The graph is divided into four sections: stars, cash cows, question marks, and dogs. SBUs and company products fall into any one of these four sections depending on their position between the two axes. Stars are high-growth businesses or products that typically need a lot of investment to secure their rapid growth; cash cows are low-growth businesses or products, usually established businesses or products that do not need high investment to maintain their market share; question marks are low-share business units in high-growth markets, and they require a lot of cash investment to hold thier position; dogs are low-growth, low-share businesses or products.

Companies use the growth-share matrix to determine the positions of SBUs and products and to determine whether or not to continue supporting them.

GROWTH-SHARE MATRIX

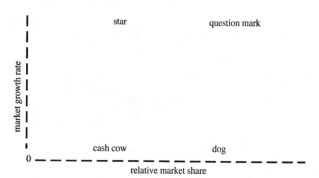

**GROWTH STRATEGY** tactic used in marketing management to expand the consumer market for a company's product. Growth strategies may follow any one of several courses: *Market penetration*, where the company will attempt to create more sales to existing customers without changing the product. This will be done by cutting prices or increasing advertising at the risk of short-term profits for greater market penetration. *Market development*, where the company will identify and develop new markets for the current product. *Product development*, where the company will offer a modified product or a new product to existing current markets. *Diversification*, where the company will develop or purchase products that are entirely different from the current product or market.

**GUARANTEE** *see* RATE BASE.

**GUERRILLA WARFARE** competitive marketing strategy typically followed by smaller companies challenging larger ones for a greater share of the consumer market. The market challenger will make small periodic attacks against the larger competitor, hoping to establish a permanent foothold in the market. Guerrilla warfare tactics include selective price cuts, executive raids on key personnel, intense bursts of promotional activities, or various legal actions. *See also* OFFENSIVE WARFARE.

**GUILLOTINE** machine that cuts large stacks of paper, before or after printing, to a desired size; also called *paper cutter; power cutter.* Oversized REPLY FORMS may be guillotined before being processed by a FULFILLMENT operation to make them easier for KEY ENTRY clerks to handle and store or to make them feed through OCR (OPTICAL CHARACTER RECOGNITION) SCANNERS faster. Printers and binders use guillotines to cut sheets prior to printing, to cut printed sheets prior to folding or die-cutting *(see* DIE CUT*)*, to cut folded sheets into individual pages for binding, and/or to separate printed 2-UP or 4-UP sheets. Guillotines are powerful and dangerous machines, and the safety of the operator is a crucial consideration in guillotine design and usage.

**GUM ARABIC** in OFFSET lithography, a substance made from acacia trees that is used to coat the nonprinting areas of a PRINTING PLATE to make them nonreceptive to ink. *See also* DESENSITIZER; FOUNTAIN SOLUTION; GUMMING.

**GUMMED LABEL** label that requires the application of moisture to activate the adhesive backing. Gummed labels are usually addressed by typewriting onto perforated label sheets. The sheets must be BURST and applied by hand. They are therefore advisable only for extremely small mailings where speed of preparation is not a priority and costs must be kept to a minimum. Gummed labels are not used by large-volume mailers. *See also* CHESHIRE LABEL; HEAT-SENSITIVE LABEL; PRESSURE-SENSITIVE LABEL.

**GUMMING** applying GUM ARABIC to the nonprinting areas of lithographic PRINTING PLATES to make them nonreceptive to ink.

**GUTTER** center margin or crease formed by a pair of facing pages in a book or magazine.

Gutter
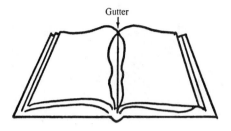

**GUTTER BLEED** *see* BLEED IN THE GUTTER.

# H

**HAIRLINE REGISTER** degree of alignments of an image, perforation, or mark on a page with an alignment error allowance less than or equal to the width of $^1/2$ row of DOTS. Hairline register is ideal when aligning halftone COLOR SEPARATIONS, in order to produce a high-quality FOUR-COLOR PROCESS image. However, hairline register cannot be maintained over long periods at press-running speeds that make economic sense. Therefore, COMMERCIAL REGISTER is considered the acceptable level of quality in printing industry practice.

**HALATION**
1. *see* BLOOMING.
2. blurred effect in a photographic image that results from light spreading beyond its normal boundaries. This effect can be achieved with special lighting techniques or through the developing process, although it sometimes results, unwanted, from a technical error.

**HALF-PAGE DOUBLE SPREAD** magazine advertisement or photo LAYOUT that is positioned on either the lower half or the upper half of two facing pages. Typically, this layout will cost the same as a full-page advertisement. Advertisers will choose it over a full page when the copy more readily lends itself to this format.

**HALFTONE** print reproduction with CONTINUOUS-TONE variations made by photographing the original image through a SCREEN (in the camera)

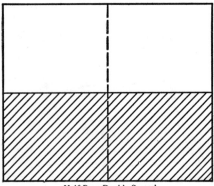

Half-Page Double Spread

that breaks up the image into a pattern of DOTS of varying size. The copy then serves as a pattern for making the PRINTING PLATE. (It is the dots that make the printing of tonal values possible.)

The screens used for halftone reproduction vary from 45 lines per linear inch up to 400. The lower numbers are called COARSE SCREENS and are used for reproductions to be printed on coarse-quality paper. Screens with more than 100 lines per linear inch are called FINE SCREENS and are suitable for use when fine detail is necessary in the finished product, but require very smooth paper. Most newspapers use a 65-line (coarse) screen whereas most magazines use a 120-line (fine) screen for halftone reproduction.

There are many variations of halftone copies, including a square halftone, where the corners are square and an overall screen is used; a silhouette halftone, where the background is removed; a VIGNETTE halftone, where the background fades away from the edges; a SURPRINT, where a line negative (no tonal variation) is superimposed over a halftone (or vice-versa); and a *highlight halftone* or DROPOUT HALFTONE, where the dots are removed from some areas to give the finished product greater contrast.

**HALO EFFECT** subjective reaction on the part of consumers noticed by researchers when attempting to analyze consumer attitudes and their relationship to the market structure, particularly in the area of advertising or brand evaluation. For example: In theory, an individual should be able to evaluate each feature of a given brand independently and should have no difficulty giving a high rating to one feature while giving another a low rating. However, in practice, researchers have noticed that respondents have a tendency to give a high rating to all the brand's features if they like the brand, and a low rating to all the features if they do not like the brand. This is known as a halo effect.

The halo effect makes it difficult to evaluate brands in terms of their strengths and weaknesses. However, if a BRAND NAME has a quality reputation in the marketplace, the halo effect may work to the brand's advantage, particularly when the company is introducing a new product into the line.

**HANDBILL** single sheet of paper, usually $8^{1}/2" \times 11"$, in any color stock, imprinted with an advertising message or announcement of a sale or special event, and distributed by a local retailer. Often, handbills will be left on the counter in a retail store or placed in the entrance lobby of a large store for customers to pick up while shopping. Frequently, they are distributed by hand on the street or left on parked cars. For the local retailer, the handbill offers a quickly produced and inexpensive form of advertising. Handbills are also called *throwaways* (for obvious reasons). *See also* FLIER.

**HAND-HELD ADDRESSING** hand tool for applying a name and address to a form or label. There are a great variety of these tools, but because their use is so time-consuming, few are still in use. Most require the application of water to a reusable address plate. The address is then applied to the paper with pressure or by rubbing the back of the plate by hand. Most large mailers use machine-applied labels such as CHESHIRE LABELS.

**HANDLING ALLOWANCE** discount or special price offered by a manufacturer to a wholesaler, distributor, or retailer when the manufacturer's product requires special handling. For example, grocery stores may be eligible for a handling allowance from a manufacturer if they redeem the manufacturer's discount coupons, since the coupons require extra work on the part of the store staff.

**HANDSETTING** setting type by hand rather than by machine. Originally, all type was handset. Even today, the resultant copy of hand set type has a distinguished, high-quality appearance. However, hand setting is both time-consuming and costly and is done only when there is not a large amount of text in the copy.

**HAND TOOLING** finishing of a PRINTING PLATE (or engraving) by hand so as to add finer detail or contrast and improve the quality of the reproduction. Hand tooling is a specialized trade and is charged for by the hour.

**HARD COPY** information printed on paper in contrast to being electronically displayed on a computer screen. This term is now used by many people to represent all paper documents, including memos, order forms, letters, print advertisements, books, catalogs, and so on. Hard copy has the advantage of being accessible to everyone everywhere, without the expense or inconvenience of a computer. In addition, even the best electronic images cannot duplicate an original image as well as a printed image can. However, hard copy is not easily modified or transmitted over distances and takes space and time to store and retrieve.

**HARD DOT** in a HALFTONE image, a DOT with a sharp, clean edge. A *soft dot* has a HALATION or fringe around it. Hard DOTS create a better image. Wear on some PRINTING plates eventually produces a soft-dot image. There are plastic plates in use that do not wear as much as metal plates.

**HARD EDGE** clearly defined boundary on a piece of artwork or a reproduction. Sometimes a hard edge is an element in the design, but sometimes it results from a flaw in the creative or printing process.

**HARD GOODS** *see* DURABLE GOODS.

**HARD OFFER** in DIRECT MARKETING, a promotion that asks for payment with an order, in contrast to a *soft offer,* which includes an option to review the goods first and then pay or return the goods as desired by the customer. Regardless of the offer made, the right of the consumer to return unwanted goods for a refund or prior to payment is honored by most marketers.

Soft offers almost always get a higher response but also increase the BAD DEBT expense incurred. They are commonly used in magazine subscription promotions that allow the subscriber to receive and/or keep an issue before he pays or cancels.

Typical wording of a hard offer is "Yes, send me your product at the rate of $12.00." Typical wording of a soft offer is "Please send me, without cost, obligation, or commitment of any kind. . ." A satisfaction guarantee may be added to either offer, such as "I understand if I am not delighted, I may return it for a full refund." *See also* FIRST-ISSUE FREE OFFER; TRIAL OFFER.

**HARD PROOF PAGE** PROOF in HARD-COPY form as distinguished from proof displayed on a computer screen. Hard proofs are the traditional means of reviewing typeset material before final printing, so that errors can be identified and corrected. Computer-generated proofs are a relatively new technology that makes corrections quicker and easier to implement.

**HARDWARE** mechanical and electronic parts that constitute a computer system, as distinguished from the COMPUTER PROGRAMS (SOFTWARE) that drive the system. The main hardware elements are the CENTRAL PROCESSING UNIT, DISK or MAGNETIC TAPE data storage devices, CATHODE-RAY TUBE DISPLAY terminals, KEYBOARDS, and PRINTERS.

**HAWTHORNE EFFECT** generally accepted psychological theory that the behavior of an individual or a group will change to meet the expectations of the observer if they are aware their behavior is being observed. In designing consumer research, this factor must be taken into consideration, by disguising or concealing the purpose or sponsor of the research. For example, if XYZ Company conducts a taste test and tells the subjects that XYZ Company produced beverage No. 1, most respondents will say they prefer beverage No. 1. Thus, it is not a true test. Similarly, if a TEST PANEL are told they are testing an appetite suppressant, they will begin to eat less. This behavior was documented by a research team led by Elton Mayo in the 1920s at the Western Electric Company Hawthorne plant. In studying the effect of lighting on productivity, the researchers found that, regardless of the lighting conditions introduced, productivity improved.

**HEADHUNTER**  independent employment service (or individual) that seeks out personnel for high-level executive positions; formally known as an executive search company (or consultant). Headhunters are generally used by companies that are looking outside their present staff to fill executive positions.

**HEADLINE**  sentence, phrase, word, or group of words set in large, bold type on a newspaper front page or above a body of text on any page of a newspaper or magazine, or in a printed advertisement (or featured as part of a broadcast commercial). The purpose of a headline is to attract attention and usually to encourage the reading of the following copy (or, in the case of broadcast, to encourage the listener or viewer to keep listening or viewing). In print advertising, the headline is considered to be the most important element, because it invites the reader into the advertisement. Therefore, it must arouse interest and curiosity about the advertised product or service. A variety of techniques are used in designing headline copy, such as the offer of a reward, the promise of a product BENEFIT, the asking of a question, or the use of key provocative words such as "new," "amazing," or "revolutionary." SPLIT-RUN research testing of headlines, where the headlines differ but the body text remains the same, has proven that the headline is the key factor in the effectiveness of an advertisement. *See also* BLIND HEADLINE.

**HEAD MARGIN**  empty space above the first line on a printed page. The size of the head margin is determined by the individual responsible for GRAPHIC DESIGN but is usually equal to three to five lines of type and may include a RUNNING HEAD.

**HEALTH AND BEAUTY AIDS**  (1) products in the categories of overthe-counter remedies and medicines; (2) personal care items, such as toothpaste, shaving cream, and mouthwash; (3) hair care items, such as shampoo, conditioners, setting lotions, and home permanents; (4) body care items, such as body lotion, skin moisturizer, and facial applications; and (5) cosmetics, including face makeup and perfume. In mass merchandise outlets and supermarkets, health and beauty aids are displayed in a department separate from other merchandise. Abbreviated *HABA* or *HBA*.

**HEALTH CARE MARKETING** marketing of health-related products and services. Health care promoters are often nonprofit organizations or associations such as the National Cancer Institute or the American Heart Association, and their advertising message is typically produced and presented to consumers as a community service by agencies and the media. Health care marketing is carried out by large associations, hospitals, and clinics and is primarily focused on preventive medicine and good physical or mental health.

**HEAT-ACTIVATED LABEL** label that requires the application of heat to activate the adhesive backing. Heat-activated labels are expensive to produce, require special equipment to apply, and are no longer in common usage, having been supplanted by CHESHIRE LABELS and PRESSURE-SENSITIVE LABELS.

**HEAT-SEAL LABEL** *see* HEAT-ACTIVATED LABEL.

**HEAT-TRANSFER LABEL** label with a reverse carbon image printed on the back. The carbon image can be transferred up to three times to an envelope or promotion form by the application of heat. Heat-transfer labels are inexpensive but are time-consuming to apply and produce a low-quality, slightly blurred image. Most mailers prefer to use CHESHIRE LABELS or PRESSURE-SENSITIVE LABELS.

**HEAVY-UP** heavy concentration of advertising for a short period of time in a media schedule. If an advertiser's product is more likely to be used at one specific time than at another, the advertiser may choose to heavy-up the advertising for that time period—for example, to heavy-up advertising cranberry sauce for the three weeks immediately preceding Thanksgiving.

**HEAVY USERS** that percentage of a population representing the majority of a product's users. Market research shows that in many product categories, a small percentage of consumers account for a very large percentage of the total sales. Advertisers in these categories typically direct their efforts to this heavy-user group.

**HEURISTICS** problem solving methodology that uses trial and error as well as rules of thumb to take shortcuts to a solution. Although a heuristic approach may not lead to the optimal solution, it is a faster, less expensive, and more practical technique than optimization techniques. For example, when choosing a dry cleaner, a consumer may limit the search to those within a convenient distance and those that the consumer has heard about from a friend. In contrast, an *optimization* approach would require careful study of every dry cleaner in the market on a variety of criteria including price, quality, turnaround time, and so forth.

**HICKEY** spot or imperfection on a reproduction that occurs during the RUN because of a speck of dust on the press, a paper particle, a dried ink stain, or some other factor that was overlooked in the preparation of materials for printing.

**HIDDEN CAMERA COMMERCIAL**  television COMMERCIAL showing unrehearsed genuine users of a product talking about or using the product while their actions are being recorded by a concealed camera.

**HIDDEN CAMERA TECHNIQUE**  technique of filming or videotaping action to be used in a HIDDEN CAMERA COMMERCIAL.

**HIDDEN OFFER**  technique used to measure readability of an advertisement or reader attention to an advertisement; also called *blind offer, buried offer.* A hidden offer calling for reader response is written inconspicuously into the text of an advertisement. The degree of response will indicate how closely the advertisement was read.

**HIERARCHY OF NEEDS MODEL**  theory of human behavior proposed by Abraham H. Maslow that people are motivated by five innate needs and that each of these needs has progressively greater priority. The five needs, in order of priority, are physiological (food, water, air), safety, social (status, sex), self-esteem, and self-actualization (achievement). According to Maslow, if a higher priority need has not been met, lower priority needs will have no motivational power. For example, a hungry man will be more motivated by a desire to eat than by a desire for social status. Marketers need to know which needs can best be met by their products and must design their marketing strategies accordingly. Some toothpastes are targeted toward satisfying social needs and others appeal to health and safety desires. A food product cannot be sold by appealing more to safety needs than to hunger abatement. Therefore a health-oriented appeal for a hamburger would not work as well as an appeal focused on taste and satisfaction of hunger. *See also* LEARNED DRIVES; PRIMARY DRIVES.

**HI-FI**  color advertisement preprinted on one side of a continuous roll of smooth COATED PAPER, so that the ad resembles a wallpaper pattern, which can be fed into a newspaper's printing press; sometimes called HI-FI INSERT. The newspaper can then print its own material on the reverse side. Also called a *preprint,* a hi-fi has been used for color advertising in newspapers because the use of high-speed PRESSES and the porosity of newspaper stock has until recently made high-quality color reproduction impossible. However, today new photographic development technologies exist that make color reproduction on newspaper stock more possible. Hi-fi is short for high-fidelity color.

**HI-FI INSERT**  *see* HI-FI.

**HIGH CONTRAST**  descriptive term for a photographic reproduction in which there is a greater difference in darkness (DENSITY) between the dark and light areas than on the original image; also called *high gamma. See also* GAMMA.

**HIGH-INVOLVEMENT MODEL**  advertising medium that requires active involvement on the part of the consumer. PRINT MEDIA are generally considered to be high-involvement models, since the consumer must be an active participant in the sense that he or she must read in order to gain information.

**HIGH-KEY LIGHTING** in filming or videotaping for television, the lighting of a scene to eliminate shadow areas. High-key lighting is usually associated with news, interview, or panel programs, which are basically not of a dramatic nature, thus the lighting director's attempt to give a bright, lively appearance to the scene. *See also* KEY LIGHT; LOW-KEY LIGHTING.

**HIGHLIGHT**
1. whitest area of an image, such as a HALFTONE print area with the smallest or the least number of DOTS, or the whitest area of a CONTINUOUS-TONE original.
2. call attention to an object by concentrating light on it.
3. call attention to a printed image through some graphic device such as an arrow, a BURST, a JOHNSON BOX, or a BULLET.

**HIGHLIGHT HALFTONE** *see* DROPOUT HALFTONE; HALFTONE.

**HIGHWAY CONTRACT ROUTE** service purchased on a contractual basis by the U.S. Postal Service whereby mail is carried from one U.S.P.S. specified starting point to another, via highway, by private carriers; also called *star route.* Highway contract routes are offered at the Postal Service's convenience and do not adversely impact delivery time.

**HISTOGRAM** *see* GRAPH.

**HIT** *see* MATCH.

**HITCHHIKE**
1. brief commercial mention at the tail end or immediately following the sponsor's final commercial in a broadcast program. The hitchhike advertises a product manufactured by the sponsor but heretofore unmentioned during the time period presented by the sponsor. It is so named because it "hitches a ride" with a commercial for another of the manufacturer's products.
2. ten- to twenty-second period for commercials or announcements immediately following a program and immediately preceding station identification.

**HOLDING FEE** additional payment made to talent in a commercial and giving the advertiser the right to hold the commercial after its initial airing and use it again in another advertising FLIGHT without having to renegotiate payment.

**HOLDOUT** characteristic of low absorbency paper *(see* ABSORPTION) that produces a glossy print image by allowing the ink to dry on the surface of the paper rather than be absorbed by the paper fibers. SET-OFF (the transfer of ink from the first printed side of a sheet to the second) can be caused by paper with too much holdout. Holdout is important for rotogravure printing and for any printing using glossy (shiny) inks.

**HOME OFFICE**
  1. main office of an organization; also called *headquarters.*
  2. workstation set up in a worker's home. The use of a home office is a growing trend among white-collar workers who utilize computers in their work and among creative people such as artists and copywriters. *See also* WORK-AT-HOME.

**HOME SERVICE BOOK**   name for a magazine, such as *Better Homes and Gardens,* that is directed at an audience whose interests lie in the areas of home and domesticity; also called a *shelter magazine.*

**HOMES PER RATING POINT (HPRP)**   *see* GROSS AUDIENCE; GROSS RATING POINT.

**HOME VIDEO RECORDER**   *see* VIDEOCASSETTE RECORDER.

**HOMOGENIZATION**   blending together of RESPONSE data so that variations in response by campaign components cannot be identified because the CAMPAIGN components were not properly key coded. For example, if three different packages are sent to three segments of the same list, but the KEY CODE on the packages is identical, response to the list can be identified, but not response to each package.

**HOOK**
  1. in advertising copywriting, thing that catches the reader's, listener's, or viewer's attention. *See also* GIMMICK.
  2. giveaway offer made in broadcast, such as a radio program offer of a free record album to the next ten callers. In this context, the hook is used as a device to incite audience response in order to be able to approximate the size of the listening or viewing audience by the number of phone calls and the speed with which they are received immediately following the announcement.
  3. in retailing, free gift offered along with the purchase of a product (as an incentive to purchase).
  4. premium given away as a result of the hook.

**HOOVEN PROCESS**   automatic letterwriting process using specially designed automatic electric typewriters. The Hooven process is used to prepare large quantities of individually typed form letters. The form letter is recorded and typed automatically; then the addresses and salutations are typed in by hand.

**HORIZONTAL CONTIGUITY**   *see* CONTIGUITY.

**HORIZONTAL CUME**   in broadcast, CUMULATIVE AUDIENCE RATING, or the REACH, for the same program on successive days.

**HORIZONTAL DIVERSIFICATION**   *see* DIVERSIFICATION.

**HORIZONTAL HALF PAGE**  magazine space offering for advertisements or the like. The horizontal half-page position is either the lower or the upper half of a page in the magazine.

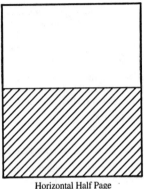

Horizontal Half Page

**HORIZONTAL INTEGRATION**  expansion via acquisition of a competitor or by adding outlets to a chain. For example, a book publisher might acquire another publishing house to increase its stable of editors and authors or to otherwise enhance its competitiveness. Horizontal integration is highly regulated by federal ANTITRUST ACTS to prevent unfair dominance of markets. See also ANTIMERGER ACT; FORWARD INTEGRATION.

**HORIZONTAL MARKETING SYSTEM (HMS)**  joining of two or more corporations on the same level for the purposes of pursuing a new marketing opportunity. Usually a horizontal marketing system is established so that the individual members can combine resources to make the most out of the marketing situation. Products from each member can be marketed and/or distributed together, such as a bottle manufacturer combining with a producer of dehydrated salad dressing preparations. The two products are marketed together, allowing the two companies to combine their marketing resources and accomplish much more than either one might accomplish alone. Corporations in a horizontal marketing system also have the option of combining their capital and production capabilities, in addition to their marketing and distribution resources, to produce synergistic benefits for all members. *See also* VERTICAL MARKETING SYSTEM.

**HORIZONTAL PUBLICATION**  TRADE MAGAZINE or paper whose editorial content is of interest to individuals in different business categories. For example, a trade publication that discusses trends and innovations in office equipment will be of interest to users of office equipment, no matter what category their own business falls into.

A horizontal publication cuts across industry classifications, in contrast to a VERTICAL PUBLICATION, which is directed toward a specific industry.

**HOTLINE** name of an individual who has recently made a purchase, inquiry, or donation. The notion of what constitutes a "recent" transaction varies between marketers but usually is within a range of one to three months. Hotlines are rented (*see* LIST RENTAL) at a premium rate, because these individuals are believed to be ready, willing, and able to buy.

**HOT POCKET** special POINT-OF-PURCHASE display offered by a wholesaler or distributor to retailers in selected locations for a limited promotion period in exchange for a fee. For example, a magazine normally distributed only on the east coast might purchase hot pocket displays on the west coast for an issue featuring a cover article about the film industry. Highly desirable retailers who can be selective about the titles they carry may accept a hot pocket promotion if they believe it will sell well. In addition to increased sales of that particular issue, it may be the push needed to convince the retailer to carry that title on an ongoing basis.

**HOT TYPE** automated COMPOSITION technique that utilizes a machine to create properly spaced metal type in one complete line at a time. This solves some of the problems of manual composition, such as the storage, retrieval, and composition of individual type SLUGS. Hot type is melted down after use rather than returned to storage. It is used for newspapers, print advertisements, business forms, and all types of promotions. Hot type is not as versatile as COMPUTERIZED COMPOSITION because word breaks at the end of each line must be operator controlled.

There are two types of hot-type composition. *Monotype* systems create individual slugs of metal type for each character of space. *Linecasting* machines create a solid line of metal type. *See also* LETTERSPACING; NONMETALLIC COMPOSITION.

**HOUSE**
1. internal product or possession, such as LIST that is controlled by the LIST OWNER and includes all of the owner's customers, or a house advertising agency that is owned by an advertiser, or a house advertisement that is placed at no cash cost in the advertiser's own medium. House advertisements are placed at the expense of lost advertising space sales revenue. *See also* HOUSE ORGAN.
2. residential unit as defined by the U.S. Bureau of the Census, sharing a common entrance and cooking facilities; also called *household.*
3. firm providing a product or service, such as a publishing house or a CATALOG HOUSE.

**HOUSE ACCOUNT** customer or prospect handled by the seller's management team rather than by a commissioned salesperson or agent. A house account might be a long-term customer with an established personal relationship with management or a prospect of especially great importance to the business. The seller must balance the desire to stay close to that customer against the salesperson's right to potential commissions. A salesperson cannot succeed with a territory that has had all the best prospects cherry-picked for house accounts.

**HOUSE AGENCY** type of advertising agency born in the early days of advertising when some large advertisers established their own agencies primarily for the purposes of saving media commissions and achieving total control of their advertising. These agencies were financially backed by the advertiser and were set up as independent FULL-SERVICE AGENCIES to perform all advertising functions on behalf of the advertiser. Some house agencies even took on additional clients. Advertisers discovered, however, that the outsider point of view was necessary to the creation of effective advertising and that advertising services were better with outside agencies. Thus, the house agency fell out of favor.

The concept of the house agency has changed over time, so that, today, many large advertisers utilize an *in-house agency* operation. This in-house service differs from the house agency in that it works internally and provides a kind of advertising administrative center with a minimum of staff that coordinates and directs advertising efforts to outside services. For example, an in-house advertising service may employ a creative service on a fee basis to create the advertising and then hire a MEDIA-BUYING SERVICE to place the advertising for less than the usual 15% commission rate.

**HOUSEHOLDS USING TELEVISION (HUT)** A. C. Nielsen Company term representing the percentage of households in a specific area and in a particular time period that have their television sets turned on as compared to the total number of television households in that area. If, for example, there are 1000 television households in a particular survey area and 500 of those televisions are turned on in a given time period, the HUT level for that area in that time period is 50. The HUT level can be figured as an overall number for the entire United States (a figure used for network programs) or for a local market, as in the case of local programming.

A program's SHARE of the audience is calculated on the basis of the HUT level. If a program carried a 20 share, that means that 20% of all households using television had their televisions tuned to that program. *See next page.*

**HOUSE-LIST MATCH** customer RECORD acquired from an outside source that duplicates a record on the house LIST. The usual practice is to PURGE house list matches from MAILING LISTS when the intention of the mailing is to bring in new business. A high house-list match rate indicates that the remaining names on the outside list probably represent excellent prospects for new business, assuming that all the

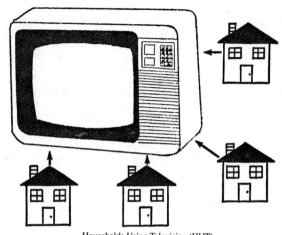

Households Using Television (HUT)

people on the list share a common interest or background that makes them buyers of similar goods or services.

**HOUSE ORGAN** magazine that is published by a company whose editorial content is relative to that company's business. There are two types of house organs, internal and external. The internal publication is designed primarily for company personnel and features articles and information concerning company activities and events that are of interest to the employees. Its purpose is to strengthen the relationship between management and staff and to heighten company morale. The external house organ is intended primarily for customers, potential customers, dealers, or other outside people who may have some interest in the company's affairs. Editorial content of the external house organ consists primarily of articles concerning the company's growth, technological advances, product development, and any other information that will help sell the company and its products. The purpose of the external publication is to present a picture of the company and its operations to outsiders.

**HOUSE-TO-HOUSE SAMPLING** distribution of a product sample to individual homes in a market area to induce trial and subsequent purchase. Many manufacturers use house-to-house sampling as a promotional tactic to stimulate word-of-mouth advertising. House-to-house sampling puts the product in the hands of individuals who may be likely to become spokespersons for it and help advertisers to establish credible user endorsements. For the most part today, house-to-house sampling is actually done with the aid of the postal system through the mail.

**HOUSE-TO-HOUSE SELLING** direct sale made by calling upon prospective customers at their homes with or without an appointment; also called *door-to-door*. House-to-house selling enables the marketer to gain wide distribution at no risk and little cost. However, this type of marketing is declining as more women join the workforce leaving fewer at home to receive the salesperson.

One of the largest house-to-house marketers was Avon, whose salespeople now make most of their sales at their fulltime workplace, such as offices and factories. Some types of sales in service industries, such as insurance and financial services, are still made house-to-house, but primarily on an appointment basis.

**HOUSEWIFE** archaic term used primarily in broadcast media research to denote any woman over 16 years of age who is head of a household.

**HOUSEWIFE TIME** broadcast media research indicating that part of the broadcast day when women over 16 make up the bulk of the listening or viewing audience. In both radio and television, HOUSEWIFE time is the daytime hours, generally between 10:00 A.M. and 3:00 or 4:30 P.M. Even though a large portion of women are in the working force, research shows that women still make up the largest share of the audience in these daytime hours.

**HUE** color. Red, blue, and green are the primary hues that, in varying proportions, produce all the colors we see. Variations on these primary colors plus black are the basis for FOUR-COLOR PROCESS printing that is able to duplicate all the colors of an image with only three colors of ink.

**HUT (LEVEL)** *see* HOUSEHOLDS USING TELEVISION.

**HYDROPHILIC** property of paper or other material that attracts and absorbs moisture. *See also* ABSORPTION.

**HYDROPHOBIC** property of paper or other material that repels water. *See also* ABSORPTION.

**HYPE** in broadcast, special promotional activities in programming presented by a station or network in order to attract a large audience and therefore generate higher audience ratings for a particular time period; also called *hypo*. For example: Traditionally, broadcast rating measurements are made for local stations in February, May, and November. Accordingly, local stations have been known to hype their audiences during these time periods.

**HYPERMARKET** variation of a supermarket that offers a variety of nonfood items, such as appliances, clothing, and services, in a vast space much larger than a regular supermarket, sometimes in excess of 200,000 square feet; also called SUPERSTORE. The grocery items are often priced below market to draw traffic into the store; however, the grocery selection is also more limited than in a regular supermarket.

Originated in France, the hypermarket has had limited success in the U.S. due to consumer resistance to the limited grocery selection and the warehouse atmosphere. Success in Europe is attributed to the fact that fewer alternatives are available. Compared to regular supermarkets, a large volume of goods must be sold to break even.

## HYPO
**Broadcast:** see HYPE.
**Photography:** short for sodium hyposulfite; a chemical fixative used in photography; also called *sodium thiosulfate, ammonium thiosulfate.* Hypo makes the nonimage areas of a photograph insensitive to further exposure to light.

# I

## I.D.
1. short form of the word *identification*. As in STATION IDENTIFICATION, I.D. refers to a broadcast station's CALL-LETTERS and location—for example, WTVJ-TV Miami.
2. eight- to ten-second station-break announcement that accompanies the station identification and is just long enough to identify a product.

**IDEAL POINT MODEL** model of consumer attitude formation asserting that the consumer rates a product according to the degree to which it resembles several ideal product characteristics defined by the consumer. In contrast to other MODELS, it is not enough to merely satisfy an expectation. The product must be rated close to the ideal point. For example, two brands of facial tissue might have a satisfactory price, fragrance, and texture, but the brand selected may have a fragrance similar to the buyer's favorite perfume. *See also* CONJUNCTIVE MODEL; DISJUNCTIVE MODEL; LEXICOGRAPHIC MODEL; EXPECTANCY-VALUE MODEL; DOMINANCE MODEL.

**IDENTIFIED RENEWAL** subscription renewal order made via the publisher's own renewal promotion form that carries a MATCHCODE identifying the subscriber. The matchcode, or KEYLINE, can be entered in less time and with greater accuracy than an entire name and address, regardless of whether it is entered by KEY ENTRY or SCAN ENTRY. Renewals coming from other sources, such as bind-in cards, are unidentified renewals.

**IDENTIFIED TRANSACTION** computer-file-maintenance transaction that utilizes a MATCHCODE printed on a document to identify the customer RECORD the document involves. By KEY ENTRY or SCAN ENTRY of the matchcode, the appropriate record can be automatically identified by the computer. Identified transactions are only possible when handling TURNAROUND DOCUMENTS (documents printed by the marketer to be returned by the customer) received from current customers. Therefore, invoices and renewal notices can be processed via an identified transaction, but orders from new customers not yet on the file cannot. Other transactions not received on a turnaround document, such as payment checks received without an invoice or renewal requests submitted on a BIND-IN card, must also be handled as *unidentified transactions*.

Without a matchcode, the entire name and address must be entered. This involves more entry time and the possibility of more entry errors. There is also a greater chance of being unable to locate the correct record, because the name and address given is illegible or varies significantly from that in the record.

*See also* FINDER NUMBER; IDENTIFIED RENEWAL.

**IDIOT CARD**  *see* CUE CARD.

**IDIOT TAPE**  MAGNETIC TAPE that provides input to computerized PHOTOTYPESETTING. The tape contains in an unformatted (unjustified and unhyphenated) mode all of the data to be typeset. The computerized typesetting program FORMATS the contents as necessary.

**ILLUSTRATION**  visual element in an advertisement. The illustration is an efficient way to represent an idea and works in concert with the HEADLINE to attract the reader to the advertisement. It is the illustration that helps to make the COPY believable.

**ILLUSTRATOR**  in advertising, artist who hand-creates pictures to be used in advertisements, without using mechanical means such as cameras or computers.

**IMAGE**
1. visual counterpart or likeness of an object, a person, or a scene produced by an optical device such as a mirror or a camera.
2. illusory conception created by advertising and projected by the media, that embodies emotions, perceptions, attitudes, and intellectual orientation group toward an entity.

**IMAGE ADVERTISING**  ADVERTISING directed at the creation of a specific IMAGE for an entity (such as a company, product, or brand), as distinguished from advertising directed at the specific attributes of the entity. The image may be one of sophistication, reliability, elegance, or luxury. For example, an image advertisement for dishes pictured a bride and groom sitting down to a table setting, with a line of copy indicating that the Queen of England had used similar dishes at her wedding dinner.

Image advertising is also frequently used in political campaigns to promote the idea of the candidate as "a person of the people," rather than to point out the candidate's qualifications.

**IMAGE ASSEMBLY**  *see* STRIPPING.

**IMPACT ADVERTISING** strategy of placing advertising messages in the media where they are likely to have the greatest impact. Some advertising messages have proven to be more effective in one medium than in another. The key to impact advertising is to position the advertising so that the greatest number of consumers will be exposed to it, remember it, and be motivated to acquire the advertised item or service.

**IMPACT PRINTER** computer-driven high-speed PRINTER that operates like a typewriter in that it strikes a type character against paper with an inked ribbon in between. The type may be encased in a PRINT CHAIN or PRINT DRUM. An impact printer automatically feeds CONTINUOUS FORMS through as it prints, one line at a time, in contrast to a LASER PRINTER that prints the entire page at once. Impact printing is slower than laser printing (2000 lines per minute versus two $8^1/2"$ × 11" pages per second). It also does not have as much flexibility with respect to type FONTS and image orientation (i.e., it can print only across the page, not from top to bottom). However, because of the low equipment cost, it is the most common type of printer used in DIRECT MARKETING. The print quality is dependent upon the quality of the machine and ink ribbon used but is typically not as consistent as the quality achieved by INK-JET PRINTERS or laser printers. Impact printers are used to print CHESHIRE LABELS, DIRECT-MAIL ADVERTISING letters and forms, renewal notices, invoices, and so forth.

**IMPOSITION** plan for arranging the images to be printed on a SHEET so that the printed pages will be in the appropriate sequence when the paper sheet is folded; also called *imposition layout*. The standard imposition patterns are *sheetwise, work-and-turn, work-and-tumble,* and *work-and-twist*. In sheetwise printing, both sides of the sheet are printed by rotating the sheet, between impressions, moving the left side to the right, keeping the top and bottom edges constant, and exposing the second side of the sheet to the image carrier. All four layout plans involve some variation of rotating and/or turning the sheet between impressions. *See next page.*

**IMPRESSION**
1. *see* GROSS AUDIENCE.
2. in printing, pressure of the type, PRINTING PLATE, or other printing apparatus as it comes into contact with the paper.
3. in printing, image created by the printing process.

**IMPRESSION CYLINDER** cylindrical device on a PRINTING PRESS that presses the paper against the PRINTING PLATE (*direct printing*), or against the BLANKET (OFFSET printing).

**IMPRINT**
1. anything that has been printed, such as advertising COPY or a company LOGO, by some sort of printing process.
2. *see* DEALER IMPRINT.

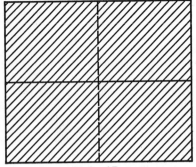

Work and Turn

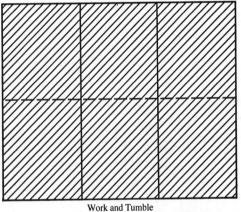

Work and Tumble

Imposition Patterns

**IMPULSE PURCHASE**  spontaneous, rather than premeditated, buying of something; also called *impulse buy*. The entire concept behind POINT-OF-PURCHASE ADVERTISING is to stimulate the impulse purchase.

**INACTIVE**
1. customer or list name that has not made a purchase or had a transaction within a set period of time, usually 12 months. *See also* FORMER BUYER.
2. customer file RECORD not currently receiving service, such as issues due but not being sent on a magazine subscription because the mailer knows the address in the record is not valid, or because past-

due charges on a credit order have not been paid, or because service on the record has otherwise been temporarily discontinued.

**IN-AD COUPON** COUPON positioned within an advertisement. Typically, in-ad coupons are used by retail stores as a method of getting customers into the store and thus can only be redeemed in the store sponsoring the advertisement.

**INBOUND TELEMARKETING** *See* TELEMARKETING.

**INCENTIVE PROGRAM** employee motivation technique that offers cash, gifts, special recognition, or other awards for exceeding performance goals. An incentive program may be a contest with a single employee or group of employees winning a prize, or it may be structured to reward as many employees as are able to achieve the defined performance goal. Many incentive programs are designed to support sales or piece work goals. To be effective, the rules of the incentive program must be clearly understood and fairly administered.

**INCOMING MAIL**
1. mail being received by the addressee. For direct mail marketers, the efficient processing of incoming mail is a priority, ensuring that orders are filled and money is deposited quickly. Processing can be faster if the mail is sorted by the type of processing necessary. Many large-volume incoming-mail operations pay (at $300 per year per box) for the use of several P.O. box numbers (referred to as phantom P.O. boxes) printed on various reply envelopes, depending upon the type of media expected to be returned. For example, three different P.O. boxes could be used for orders, payments, and renewals. The U.S. Postal Service will sort the mail by P.O. box number before sending it on to the addressee. *See also* MAILROOM.
2. mail received by a U.S. Postal Service SECTIONAL CENTER FACILITY (SCF) or city facility for delivery within that SCF or city.

**IN-COUNTY DISCOUNT** postage discount offered by the U.S. Postal Service on SECOND CLASS mail that enters the postal system and is also distributed within the county where the publisher/mailer is headquartered. Many large publishers with readers nationwide have made good use of this discount by taking an in-county discount at several points where the publication is printed throughout the country. The discount is primarily intended, however, to support local newspapers, and recent legislative changes now enforce that intention by limiting the discount to publications with a CIRCULATION of less than 10,000 or with 50% or more of their circulation within the county of publication.

**INCREMENTAL COST** additional business expense incurred as a result of taking a particular action. For example, acquisition of a new client might result in additional labor and equipment costs that would not otherwise have been incurred. When making a decision on a new account, service, product or capital expenditure, the focus tends to be on the incremental costs rather than the *sunk costs* (money already spent on sales and development). When pricing a product or service, both incremental costs and sunk costs should be considered.

**INCREMENTAL SPENDING** budget allocation that allows for increased or decreased spending on media for advertising in direct proportion to sales. The problem with allocating funds in this manner is that rarely is budget size tied in with the advertising objectives and, therefore, it is difficult to evaluate the success or failure of the advertising in terrns of expenditure. *See also* COMPETITIVE PARITY.

**INCUMBENT AGENCY** current tenured advertising agency for an advertiser's product or service, or advertising agency currently under contract for a particular client.

**INDEPENDENT**
1. *see* INDEPENDENT STATION.
2. business that is owned outright by an individual or group of individuals and is not a part of or a subsidiary of a larger conglomerate.

**INDEPENDENT NETWORK** any broadcast system that is not affiliated with the three major networks, ABC, CBS, or NBC.

**INDEPENDENT STATION** broadcast station that is not owned or controlled by or affiliated with a network; also called INDEPENDENT STORE. According to Federal Communications Commission regulations, any station that carries less than ten hours of PRIME-TIME network programming per week is considered independent. For the most part, independent stations are local stations, although there are currently four independent television stations, called "superstations," that operate locally and also transmit their signals throughout the country via satellite: WTBS in Atlanta, WGN in Chicago, and WOR and WPIX in New York. An independent station is also called an *indy*.

**INDEPENDENT STORE**
1. classification used by A. C. NIELSEN COMPANY in their retail indexes to indicate an individual store or a small chain store with no more than three branches.
2. individually owned and operated retail shop.
3. casual reference to an INDEPENDENT STATION.

**INDEPENDENT TELEVISION MARKET**
1. home market for an independent television station (*see* INDEPENDENT STATION).
2. television market area where the viewing audience is inconsistent with the typical NETWORK audience, because the local television stations pull the largest SHARE of the audience. Generally, where there is network programming at the same time as local programming, the network programs will draw the largest audience. In an independent television market, this is not the case.

**INDEPENDENT VARIABLE**

**Advertising research:** the independent variable is the element that is subject to arbitrary (not random) change, in order to test the results. For example: If the objective were to test audience response to headline copy, keeping all other factors equal, the sample audience would be subjected to different headline copy to determine the effectiveness of the various headlines. The audience response would be dependent on the stimulus provided—in this case the copy; therefore, the headline copy would be considered the independent variable when it came time to chart the results.

**Mathematics and statistics:** the factor that is not dependent for change on other factors. For example: if $y = 3x$, the value of $y$ is always dependent on the value of $x$, but $x$ can be anything and is therefore the independent VARIABLE.

**INDEX BASIS** comparative calculation that defines the relationship between two or more values by calling one value the standard with a value of 100 and all other values some percent over or under the base standard of 100. For example, if the standard is 20, a value of 30 would be expressed as 150.

Indexes are frequently used to define relative MARKET SHARE. For example, if a marketer sells 130 units to every 100 sold by a competitor, his relative market share is 130.

Indexes can also be used to compare cost trends over time. For example, if $100 is spent on advertising per 1000 units sold in the base year, and $80 is spent on advertising for every 1000 units sold two years later, the advertising cost index in the third year is 80.

**INDICIA** notation on a mailing piece or envelope, authorized by the U.S. Postal Service, that indicates postage has been prepaid by the mailer. It is used in lieu of a METER STRIP or postage stamp and indicates the CLASS of mail and permit number and either the entry post office or the permit holder's name, or both. It may also indicate the amount of postage paid. A typical CATALOG indicia statement is "Bulk Rate, U.S. Postage Paid, Permit No. 000, City, State." According to Postal Service regulations, the indicia may be preprinted in the upper right-hand corner of the mailing piece parallel to the length or in the upper right hand corner of the address LABEL. There is no size or color requirements other than that the indicia be legible; however, it must be printed, not handwritten or typed. *See also* BUSINESS REPLY MAIL; COMPANY INDICIA.

**INDIFFERENCE BARRIER** phenomenon that arises where purchases are made out of habit to save time and energy, without any regard to advertising. The indifference barrier presents a total absence of compulsion toward any product or service on the part of the consumer. Advertisers are constantly attempting new ideas and different approaches to neutralize the indifference barrier.

**INDIRECT COST** *see* FIXED COST.

**INDIRECT EXPOSURE**  consumer purchase of a product or service due to the personal influence of someone else who has been exposed to the advertising, rather than due to direct EXPOSURE to the advertising itself on the part of the consumer purchaser.

**INDIRECT PROMOTION**  sales communication delivered to the consumer through intervening media such as television, radio, or any other mass media vehicle. Indirect promotion offers consumers anonymity but allows marketers to reach a vast audience with each communication. *See also* DIRECT PROMOTION.

**INDUSTRIAL ADVERTISING**  field of advertising directed at commercial business customers. The advertised products are raw materials, components, or equipment needed in the production or distnbution of other goods and services. *See also* BUSINESS-TO-BUSINESS ADVERTISING; CONSUMER ADVERTISING.

**INDUSTRIAL BUYER**  individual in a business, government agency, or association who makes purchase decisions regarding services, raw materials, product components, or finished goods, also called ORGANIZATIONAL BUYER. Industrial buyers are more, but not solely, motivated in their buying decisions by profit objectives than by personal objectives and require different marketing strategies than consumer buyers. *See also* BUSINESS-TO-BUSINESS ADVERTISING; INDUSTRIAL ADVERTISING; INDUSTRIAL CONSUMER; INDUSTRIAL GOODS.

**INDUSTRIAL CONSUMER**  user of industrial products. (The actual term should be industrial *customer*, since a consumer is an *individual* purchasing or using a product or service for *personal* use. However, the term industrial consumer is used informally throughout the industry to distinguish one type of user of a product from another.) *See also* INDUSTRIAL ADVERTISING; INDUSTRIAL BUYER.

**INDUSTRIAL GOODS**  raw materials, equipment, or product components required by a business for the production or distribution of other goods or services. Industrial goods range from mineral, agricultural and forestry products to complex electronic equipment. *See also* BUSINESS-TO-BUSINESS ADVERTISING; INDUSTRIAL BUYER.

**INDUSTRIAL MARKET**  consumer group composed of companies or organizations that purchase goods and services for use in the production of other goods and services that are sold, rented, or supplied to others. For example, the clothing manufacturing industry purchases fabric that is used in the production of dresses and other apparel. Fabric manufacturers are also members of the industrial market because they purchase other raw materials for use in the production of the fabric. The industrial market is the largest and most diverse ORGANIZATIONAL MARKET, consisting of more than 13 million organizations that buy more than $3 trillion worth of products each year. Some of the major industries represented in the industrial market are construction, agriculture, mining, manufacturing, communication, public utilities, transportation, and finance.

**INDY** *see* INDEPENDENT STATION.

**INELASTIC DEMAND** desire for a product or service that does not vary with increases or decreases in price. Products that are daily necessities, and for which there are few alternatives, tend to exhibit inelastic demand. For example, the demand for bar soap, salt, and milk is relatively inelastic. In contrast, demand for vacation travel, premium ice cream, and entertainment tends to be elastic. *See also* ELASTICITY; PRICE SENSITIVE.

**IN-FLIGHT PUBLICATION** magazine distributed exclusively through the airlines and given free of charge to passengers. There are several different in-flight publications, published by private individuals or companies. Their EDITORIAL content consists of material that may be of interest to business people and frequent flyers.

**INFLUENCER** member of a DECISION-MAKING UNIT who has an impact on the BUYING DECISION but is not the decision maker. For example, a child may influence the choice of breakfast cereal, but the purchase decision is made by the parent. Influencers have varying levels of influence depending upon the product and their relative status in the decision-making unit. A small child will have no influence on an automobile purchase. A teenager may have some influence and a spouse usually has a lot of influence on an automobile purchase decision.

**INFOMERCIAL** 15–60 minute television commercial typically presented in a casual talk show format that is designed to appear as an ordinary television program. Infomercials (information + commercial) often feature celebrities talking about their successful experiences with a given product. Infomercials are often used when presenting a new product to the marketplace and the primary objective is to build consumer awareness of the product.

**INFORMED CHOICE** purchase decision made after acquiring information about a product. The amount of information required by a consumer is a function of the PERCEIVED RISK associated with a wrong choice. A high-priced, complex DURABLE GOOD has a higher perceived risk than a low-priced, consumable commodity. Therefore, a consumer purchasing a refrigerator will seek out more information before making a purchase than a consumer buying a quart of milk. Some consumers require more information than others depending upon their personalities and priorities, level of income, education, and sophistication. For example, health-conscious consumers read food product labels before buying to ascertain fat content. The marketer must meet the information needs of the target market without overwhelming consumers with excessive data. *See also* CONSUMER PROTECTION; FAIR PACKAGING AND LABELING ACT; NUTRITION LABELING; OPEN DATING; TRUTH-IN-LENDING ACT; UNIT PRICING.

**INGREDIENT LABELING** information printed on a product package describing the contents. The sequence of the ingredients listed indicates the relative proportion of each with the first ingredient being the largest component. *See also* CONSUMER PROTECTION; FAIR PACKAGING AND LABELING ACT; INFORMED CHOICE; NUTRITION LABELING.

**IN-HOME** term describing MEDIA that is seen, heard, or read in the home, as compared to "out-of-home" media such as BILLBOARDS or TRANSIT ADVERTISING, which can only be viewed out of the home. Radio, television, newspapers, and magazines are all considered in-home media. *See also* OUT-OF-HOME.

**IN-HOME SHOPPING** purchases made from the buyer's home, via mail, telephone, door-to-door sales, fax, computer, or INTERACTIVE TELEVISION. In-home shopping has grown significantly since the advent of DIRECT RESPONSE TELEVISION, interactive television, INFOMERCIALS, and cable network shopping channels. Product information is delivered to consumers at home via direct mail promotions, catalogs, print advertisements, broadcast media, and OUTBOUND TELEPHONE. The primary motivator for in-home shopping is convenience; however, entertainment and impulse are also motivators.

**IN-HOUSE (ADVERTISING)** *see* HOUSE AGENCY.

**INITIAL PURCHASE** first-time purchase of a product or service on the part of a consumer, or the first-time purchase of a media vehicle for advertising on the part of an advertiser.

**INK FOUNTAIN** printing press device that stores and supplies ink to the plate or other image carrier. A system of rollers transfers ink from the fountain to the plate. Some presses intended to be used for a single purpose, such as newspaper presses, are able to directly access ink storage tanks, but presses used for a variety of purposes must obtain ink from ink fountains that are manually filled with the correct ink for each print job. The amount of ink used to make each impression depends on the type of plate, the type of paper, and the quality of the ink. *See also* DUCTOR ROLLER; FOUNTAIN SOLUTION.

**INK-JET PRINTER** high-speed computer-driven PRINTER that sprays a row of fine streams of ink onto labels and/or forms to create a DOT pattern pnnt image. The dots can be small and dense enough to appear to form continuous lines. Ink-jet printers offer several advantages over IMPACT PRINTERS, such as speed, DUAL ADDRESSING, and personalization, but are not able to supply the greater personalization, image orientation, and type-FONT flexibility of LASER PRINTERS. *See also* MEAD.

**INK MIST** fine threads of ink that form during the printing process and form a messy cloud of ink filaments around the press that settle on the press equipment and paper; also called *ink flying*. Long ink that flows easily over the printing rollers and is used in newspaper printing tends to generate these threads more than other inks. *See also* INKOMETER.

**INKOMETER** instrument used by ink manufacturers to measure the stickiness or pulling capacity (*tack*) of ink that can damage the surface of paper; also called TACKOSCOPE. Ink with excessive tack pulls fibers off the surface instead of flowing smoothly onto the page. An inkometer can also measure the tendency of ink to produce INK MIST.

**INLINE** typography style characterized by a thin white line through the center of the letters, surrounded by a black border.

**INNOVATION** product, service, or idea that is perceived by consumers as new. There are differing magnitudes of innovation. Adding bran to an established brand of breakfast cereal is considered a *continuous innovation* in that it constitutes a small change to an existing product with little market impact, as opposed to *discontinuous innovations* like the personal computer, which caused great societal impact. The public outcry against the "new" Coca-Cola belied the relatively small continuous innovation that it was. An *innovative strategy* uses continuous innovation to stay one step ahead of the competition. *See also* ADOPTION PROCESS; DIFFUSION; EARLY ADOPTER; INNOVATOR.

**INNOVATOR**
  1. consumer who is among the first within a market to adopt an INNOVATION. According to the bell curve model of DIFFUSION, innovators are the first 2.5% of the consumers in a market to adopt an innovation. An advertiser can optimize the cost effectiveness of an advertising campaign for an innovation by targeting it toward innovators and EARLY ADOPTERS. *See also* ADOPTION PROCESS.
  2. Marketer who sells one or more product innovations.

**INOCULATION APPROACH** approach used in a comparative advertising campaign to build consumer resistance to competitive products. The name derives from the medical method of preventing disease by using inoculations of small weakened doses of the disease in order to stimulate the body's natural defense system. In advertising, in a similar fashion, consumers are subjected to weakened or ineffectual advertisements for a brand in order to build up their defense against that brand's advertising. For example, in a recent 30-second commercial, a fast-food chain advertises the hamburgers of its competitors, using one line from each of the competitive commercials, and then favorably compares its own product to all of the competitors. This advertiser is using an inoculation approach to build up a resistance to the competitors' commercials.

**IN-PACK COUPON** device used as a promotional technique to encourage the repurchase of an item or sometimes the purchase of another item made by the same company. The in-pack coupon is enclosed in the PACKAGE with a product and is redeemable in any outlet where the product named on the coupon is sold. Typically, it offers the next purchase of the named product at a reduced price.

By comparison with other types of COUPONS, the REDEMPTION rate for in-pack coupons is quite high, averaging almost 20%, whereas coupons placed in Sunday newspaper supplements average approximately a 3% redemption rate.

**IN-PACK PREMIUM** free gift (or COUPON redeemable for a gift, including a discount coupon) enclosed in the package along with a product. In-pack premiums offer instant gratification to the consumer and are designed to work as incentives to purchase a product. *See also* ON-PACK PREMIUM.

**IN-PLANT LOADING** service offered by the U.S. Postal Service allowing large-volume mailers to load outgoing mail directly onto U.S.P.S. trucks at the mailer's facility to save the time and expense of delivering mail to a postal facility. *See also* DETACHED MAIL UNIT.

**INPUT**

1. information fed into a computer from another source. In some computer systems this information must be coded on special cards, called *punch cards*, and then fed into the system through a scanning process. In other systems this information can be fed into the computer directly through the KEYBOARD. *See also* DATA ENTRY; OUTPUT.
2. (informal) individual's ideas on a given subject, as in "We need Ms. Jones' input on this problem."

**INQUIRY** request for information about a product or service. An inquiry from a prospective customer may be unsolicited, but many advertising dollars are spent attempting to generate inquiries as well as purchases. Inquiry promotions identify individuals with an interest in the product or service, provide leads for FOLLOW-UP sales calls or promotions, and measure both the effectiveness of various advertisements and also the demand for a product or service. It is important to answer all inquiries with a FOLLOW-UP LETTER or sales call to convert the inquirer to a buyer. In some cases, the marketer must follow up with questions that qualify (*see* QUALIFIED LEADS) the prospect, determining if he is ready, willing, and able to buy. For example, if the inquiry concerns computer equipment, the seller can ask about the computing requirements of the inquirer and determine whether the need is imminent. *See also* INQUIRY AND FOLLOW-UP.

**INQUIRY AND FOLLOW-UP** promotional techniques that involve an offer of information about a product or service and, when the offer results in an INQUIRY, subsequent attempts to sell that product or service to the inquirer. For example, the FOLLOW-UP may begin with a quick postcard announcing that additional information is on the way and giving the name of a local dealer. This card may also ask if the inquiry was for information only or for an immediate need. In the meantime, the literature is mailed and a salesperson may then be notified of the inquiry so that a personal call can be made. Quick follow-up is essential to making the most of the sales opportunity offered by inquiries. *See also* FOLLOW-UP LETTER.

**INQUIRY CONVERSION** CONVERSION of an inquirer to a customer through an INQUIRY AND FOLLOW-UP process. *See also* INQUIRY.

**INQUIRY RUN** computer process that extracts information from a file without altering anything on the file. For example, if a LIST SELECTION is going to be made on an nth-name basis (*see* NTH-NAME SELECTION), an inquiry run may first be done to determine the total size of the file. If there are 10,000 records on the file and 1000 are needed for a test mailing, then every 10th name will be selected in a subsequent run.

**INQUIRY TEST**
   1. technique used in advertising research where the advertising, brand, or product is tested through RANDOM inquiries of respondents. The information acquired is generally used to evaluate the various forms of advertising media. In some cases, the respondents are actually people who have written unsolicited comments to the advertiser. In other cases, the response has been stimulated by an advertiser's offer.
   2. test of the effectiveness of advertising based on the number of inquiries about an advertisement. For purposes of the test, inquiries are solicited by coupons or by hidden offers in the advertising.

**INSERT** enclosure that is used to relate information as part of an overall advertising campaign. Inserts can be found in all phases of advertising, such as direct-mail pieces, FREESTANDING INSERTS in newspapers, extra printed matter in magazines, or package inserts.

   In direct mail, inserts work as a part of the selling package and may take the form of informational material as well as return forms, including order forms, to be filled out, and even gift PREMIUMS, such as a calendar.

   Newspaper inserts are freestanding, preprinted pieces ranging in size from a single card to a 30-page (or more) TABLOID.

   In magazine advertising, inserts are bound into the pages of the magazine and sold as a form of advertising space in conjunction with an adjoining advertisement; they may take the form of return cards, coupons, recipe booklets, or order forms. Sometimes, advertisers will have to pay an extra charge for the binding, along with the extra charge for the insert. In both newspapers and magazines, printing costs are borne by the advertiser.

   Inserts also appear in some packages as redeemable coupons or bounce-back circulars telling about another of the advertiser's products. Additionally, there is a relatively new practice of selling space in packages, similar to the way other advertising space is sold. Inserts enclosed as a result of this type of contracted space are called *ride-alongs*.

**INSERT CARD** *see* BIND-IN; BLOW-IN.

**INSERTER** equipment necessary to prepare large volumes of mail that would take too long to prepare by hand. It inserts various mailing *package* components into an OUTER ENVELOPE at a rate of about 2500 envelopes an hour. Inserters are limited by the number of pockets they have that hold and feed each component to be inserted, averaging four to six pockets. The components are inserted in pocket sequence. The inserter can also seal and METER the envelope. It cannot fold components or put (*nest*) one component inside another. Each component must be ready for insertion prior to being loaded into the inserter. If more components are being used than there are pockets, some may be nested inside others before loading onto the inserter. However, the components must be thin enough to fit easily inside the outer envelope; inserters cannot insert tight-fitting components. Some inserters also have attachments for inserting special items such as miniature pencils.

**INSERT-IF-ABSENT** computerized customer file TRANSACTION that searches for a RECORD and creates a record if one is not found. This procedure is necessary to process a customer complaint that a product ordered has not been received. The complaint is considered an order regardless of whether an order already exists on the file. If the complaint states that the order was paid for, it is treated as a CLAIMS-PAID COMPLAINT. Otherwise, the new record goes on file as an unpaid CREDIT ORDER.

**INSERTION ORDER** instructions to a publisher detailing the placement of material for PRINT ADVERTISING. The insertion order is issued by the advertiser or advertising agency and will specify the size of the advertisement, the position, the quoted price, and the date (or dates) on which the ad is to appear. Usually a copy of the advertisement will be enclosed along with the insertion order.

**INSERTION SCHEDULE** schedule of insertions in the media for a particular advertising CAMPAIGN. *See also* FLIGHT.

**INSIDE BACK COVER** preferred position in magazine advertising for placement of advertisements; also called the *third cover*. *See also* BACK COVER.

**INSIDE FRONT COVER** preferred advertising position in a magazine; also known as *second cover*.

**INSIDE-OF-VEHICLE** form of transit advertising that is posted inside the transportation vehicle for exposure to riders. Advertisements may be placed inside buses, taxis, trains, and subways. *See also* CAR CARD.

**INSTALLMENT** credit-sales technique that divides the amount due into individual segments billed over time. It usually works best on purchases greater than $30. Installment billing is attractive to some buyers because it may solve a cash-flow problem and/or because the perceived price of the merchandise seems lower than if the price were charged all at once. The amount of each installment is usually highlighted on the promotion form, while the total cost is downplayed.

The amount of each billing segment is usually calculated by dividing the total selling price by the number of segments, resulting in equal payments. If there are unpaid prior segments, they will be added to current billing segments, or the current amount due will be recalculated based on the number of segments remaining.

Installment billing generally does not increase PAY-UP (the total percentage of credit buyers who pay) but does increase gross and NET response. A disadvantage of installment billing is that it increases billing costs and slows the receipt of cash, although, in many cases, 50% of installment buyers will pay in full on the first bill. The disadvantages of installment billing must be weighed against the added response.

Installment billing is the primary billing technique of DIRECT MAIL AGENCIES selling magazine subscriptions.

**INSTANT NUMBER** *see* FINDER NUMBER.

**INSTITUTE OF OUTDOOR ADVERTISING**   national marketing organization for the OUTDOOR ADVERTISING industry. The institute provides research data and other information to advertisers about the medium of outdoor advertising and works to promote the use of the medium by advertisers.

**INSTITUTE OF SURVEY RESEARCH**   research association affiliated with the University of Michigan that conducts studies about the economy and its effects on consumers. The organization will provide this information to clients on a subscription basis.

**INSTITUTIONAL ADVERTISING** *see* CORPORATE ADVERTISING.

**INSTITUTIONAL MARKET**   institutions such as houses of worship, museums, hospitals, prisons, libraries, and schools that purchase goods and services for people or things in their care. Members of the institutional market are generally not profit motivated, and their marketing objectives are usually different from those of traditional business organizations. *See also* ORGANIZATIONAL MARKET.

**IN-STORE DEMONSTRATION**   promotional technique whereby the use of a product is demonstrated in a retail outlet. The in-store demonstration is used most often in large department stores, supermarkets, or mass-merchandise outlets that exhibit a heavy consumer-traffic pattern. Often, manufacturers will offer product discounts to dealers who will do in-store demonstrations.

**INTAGLIO** *see* GRAVURE.

**INTEGRATED COLOR REMOVAL**   computerized method of COLOR CORRECTION that replaces with black or gray ink a primary color that was used in FOUR-COLOR PROCESS printing to create gray tones, in order to make a washed-out or overly darkened image clearer and better defined. *See also* GRAY COMPONENT REPLACEMENT.

**INTEGRATED MARKETING** coordination of a variety of promotional vehicles (e.g., print/broadcast advertising, public relations, direct marketing, in-store promotions) and multiple stages in a promotional campaign to ensure that the marketing message is consistently received by the greatest possible number of people in the target market.

**INTELSAT (INTERNATIONAL TELECOMMUNICATIONS SATELLITE ORGANIZATION)** nonprofit international organization, composed of more than 100 member countries, that operates a communications satellite system that allows for the transmission of broadcast programs or events throughout the world. Through the Intelsat network, people in the U.S. may watch an event such as the tennis matches at Wimbledon, England, as they are being played.

**INTERACTIVE FAX** retrieval of information via facsimile machine, involving active participation by the recipient, including FAX-ON-DEMAND, scheduled fax (transmission via PC at a scheduled time), and manual fax. Although interactive fax is limited in terms of the type of information it can send and the lack of confidentiality of the information once received, it excels in terms of speed. Fax transmission can be used to receive product and pricing information, to send and receive purchase orders, and for customer service correspondence.

**INTERACTIVE TELEVISION** television service that enables consumers to shop, vote, bank, play games, and so forth, via a television/telephone/computer combination. For shopping, merchandise is displayed on the television screen and may be ordered by hitting keys on a special keypad or on a touch-tone telephone dial that is linked electronically to the seller. *See also* DIGITAL BROADCASTING; ELECTRONIC CATALOG; TELETEXT; VIDEOTEX.

**INTERCUTTING** technique used in film editing to provide a particular emotional effect. The same scene is filmed from all possible angles, and then the best frames of each are chosen by the editor, who splices them together in rapid, sequential order to produce the desired effect in the finished product.

**INTERIOR MONOLOGUE** dramatic technique used by an actor to present a monologue of his or her character's thoughts. The monologue is done for the benefit of the audience and not for the other characters in a scene. The presentation can be in the form of a VOICE-OVER or as an actor's aside.

**INTER-LIST DUPLICATE** RECORD or name on a LIST that, according to the matching logic being used, matches one or more records on another list being used by the same LIST USER. Inter-list duplicates are usually MULTIBUYERS. A rented list showing a high rate of inter-list duplicates when matched against a HOUSE list in a MERGE/PURGE can be considered a good prospect list, provided that there are enough names remaining on the rented list to promote after the duplicates are eliminated. The assumption is that the nonduplicates on the rented list share the characteristics of the duplicates, including a demand for that product. A high rate of inter-list duplicates between two rented lists will result in one list being eliminated from future rentals by that user so that she is not paying twice to receive the same names. *See also* DEDUPE.

**INTERLOCK** phase in the film editing process during which the OPTICALS and sound track are synchronized with the WORK PRINT.

**INTERNATIONAL ADVERTISING** advertising conducted in foreign markets. International advertising traditionally has required different strategies than domestic advertising, because of the differences in culture, economic systems, government regulations, and consumer needs. However, in the 1980s the increase in the number of MULTI-NATIONAL CORPORATIONS has brought about the idea of the world as a common marketplace, where people desire the same life-styles and products, and, consequently, the same product is often advertised (and marketed) the same way in every country, regardless of economics, culture, politics, or media and language differences.

Because of the many countries in which products (particularly, American products) are now marketed, the term *global marketing* has begun to be associated with international advertising. Global marketing is a misnomer, however, since it literally implies the marketing of a product around the globe (worldwide). The actual reality of global marketing is not here, yet.

**INTERNATIONAL ADVERTISING ASSOCIATION** association of individuals involved in the advertising or marketing of goods and services in international markets, headquartered in New York City. Founded in 1938, the association conducts research on advertising trade practices, restrictions and taxes on advertising, and advertising expenditures in foreign markets. It also maintains a list of recommendations for international advertising standards and practices for the benefit of its membership, and sponsors an annual award "for distinguished services in the field of international advertising and marketing."

**INTERNATIONAL ADVERTISING FILM FESTIVAL (CANNES)** international competition, open to anyone in the advertising industry, for the best commercials in various consumer categories. The stated purpose of the festival is to see the "best in world creativity and technique." The competition and festival is sponsored by Screen Advertising World Associates Limited of London, England, and is judged by a panel of 20 representatives from the advertising industry throughout the world. The awards are presented annually in June in Cannes, France. Winners are chosen from among approximately 700 entries submitted by at least 400 entrants from almost 50 different countries.

**INTERNATIONAL ASSOCIATION OF BUSINESS COMMUNI-CATORS (IABC)** international information network of communications professionals representing more than 11,500 companies in over 40 countries throughout the world. IABC is "dedicated to fostering communications excellence worldwide, to helping communicators contribute to their organization's goals, and to being a model of communication excellence itself." Headquartered in San Francisco, IABC offers a wide range of member services including a program to become an *A*ccredited *B*usiness *C*ommunicator, workshops, conferences, publications, resources for research, career planning, and referrals, and attempts to promote better understanding of the professional communicator's role.

**INTERNATIONAL MAIL MANUAL (IMM)** directory of U.S. Postal Service regulations governing international mail services. The IMM should be used by all mailers sending significant volumes of mail to FOREIGN destinations, in order to ensure prompt, efficient handling of their mail. The manual describes for each CLASS of mail the physical requirements of mail pieces, mail preparation requirements, postage rates, methods of postage payment, and addressing requirements. It is available from the Government Printing Office in Washington, D.C., for an annual subscription fee of $14 and is updated whenever changes in regulations warrant a revised edition. *See also* DOMESTIC MAIL MANUAL.

**INTERNATIONAL NEWSPAPER ADVERTISING AND MAR-KETING EXECUTIVES (INAME)** professional organization of daily newspaper advertising and marketing executives, founded in 1911; formerly called *Newspaper Advertising Executives Association*. INAME is headquartered in Washington, D.C., and is primarily devoted to promoting the use of advertising in daily newspapers.

**INTERNATIONAL STANDARD BOOK NUMBER (ISBN)** *see* INTERNATIONAL STANDARD SERIAL NUMBER.

**INTERNATIONAL STANDARD SERIAL NUMBER (ISSN)** Library of Congress assigned number that identifies a serial publication (periodical), such as a magazine, newsletter, or newspaper, much the same as a license plate number identifies a car. It consists of eight digits, with a CHECK DIGIT at the end, in the following format: ISSN XXXX-XXXX. The ISSN is used by the Library of Congress, other libraries, and other organizations in the periodical publications industry to identify, catalog, order, and track periodicals. It is very similar to the International Standard Book Number (ISBN) used in the book industry to identify books. Retailers use ISSN and ISBN numbers to record what they have sold, what they need to order, and what they have ordered. The numbers are usually included in advertising to the publications industry so that periodicals and books can be ordered by number, making it easier for everyone involved to get the right publication to the right person. The ISSN also has an important application for the U.S. Postal Service, which uses it to identify publications granted SECOND-CLASS mail privileges. Per USPS regulations, the ISSN must be published somewhere in the first five pages of the periodical, preferably in the MASTHEAD. If the publication does not have an ISSN number, the USPS Office of Mail Classifications will assign a USPS identification number.

ISSN numbers can be requested by publishers of new and existing publications from the Library of Congress in Washington, D.C. Book publishers can request an ISBN number, to be assigned to the book of their choice, from the R. R. Bowker Company in New York.

**INTERNATIONAL SURFACE AIR LIFT (ISAL)** U.S. Postal Service program for the delivery of bulk printed matter to FOREIGN destinations at a speed and postage rate, between airmail and surface mail rates, based upon the weight of the mailing and the destination country. ISAL is used by mailers who are not able to fill an air shipment container (750 lb. is required by federal law) with their own mail volume alone. The USPS will combine their mail with that of other mailers to make up a full container. To utilize ISAL, the mailer must deliver his mail to one of ten AIRPORT MAIL FACILITIES (New York, Chicago, Boston, Philadelphia, Washington, D.C., Dallas, Houston, Los Angeles, San Francisco, or Miami), depending on the destination country. The mail is then shipped by air to the destination country, where it is further transported by surface mail. The USPS does not offer a delivery-time guarantee and will not ship in less than 14 days if it does not have enough mail to make up a full shipment. Once shipped, the mail is usually delivered in seven to ten days. The cost ranges from $1.80/lb. for Europe to $4.00/lb. for Asia/Australia, and averages $3.00/lb. of mail.

**INTERPRETATION** step in the process of consumer awareness of advertising as analyzed and isolated by researchers. The advertising industry conducts a great deal of research into the consumer communication system in order to discern the processes by which the advertising message is received, understood, and acted upon. This information is deemed necessary for successful advertising. The diagram that follows illustrates the process the advertising message must undergo in order for the consumer to gain knowledge of the item being advertised. Researchers call this the Perception Process. *See next page.*

**INTERVIEW**
1. formal consultation or meeting for the purpose of ascertaining and evaluating the qualifications of a person, group of people, or company to fill a particular job situation.
2. formal or informal meeting between two people or among a group of people for the purpose of obtaining information about something in particular. The interview is a successful tool in advertising research and may be conducted in any number of ways, including the DEPTH INTERVIEW and the FOCUS GROUP INTERVIEW.

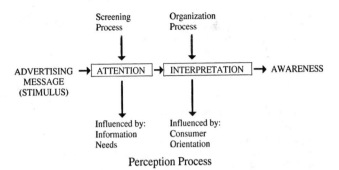

Perception Process

**INTERVIEWER BIAS** opinion or prejudice on the part of an interviewer, which is displayed during the interview process and thus affects the outcome of the interview. In research interviews, it is necessary that the interviewer conduct the interview with total objectivity, so that respondents are not influenced by any outside source in their responses. For this reason, interviews should be conducted by well-trained and qualified interviewers.

**IN-THEATER SAMPLING** distribution of product samples to movie theater patrons. In-theater sampling tends to be less expensive than direct mail, door-to-door, or shopping mall distribution of samples. Marketers can select an appropriate target for their products according to the type of film being shown. For example, the audience for *Wayne's World* would be a good target for a rock music magazine, while a children's film like *Aladdin* would provide a good target audience for a fast-food kid's club. Products already associated with the movie theater experience, like snack foods or beverages, could benefit from this type of exposure.

**INTRA-LIST DUPLICATE** RECORD or name on a list that matches one or more other records on the same list. Intra-list duplicates can occur when the addition of a new record to a file is made without an automatic or manual check for duplicates or when an entry or programming error changes the name and address elements of the record enough to bypass the DUPE CHECK system. Most list owners DEDUPE their lists periodically, if not continuously, using a COMPUTER PROGRAM similar to that used in a MERGE/PURGE process. Every list owner or user has his own definition of a DUPLICATE and therefore his own matching logic, based on the purpose of the list.

Intra-list duplicates can be a problem or an opportunity. They are a problem if the duplication results in customers' receiving and/or being billed twice for the same item or receiving duplicates of every promotion. They present an opportunity if customers who have made several different purchases can be identified for special promotions.

**INTRAPRENEURSHIP** innovative corporate management style that encourages employees within an organization to create new product ideas. If employee ideas are approved, management will finance research and development of the product while sharing an equitable partnership arrangement with the employee. Intrapreneurship is an independent and daring management concept and has worked very successfully in small and new business organizations.

**INTRODUCTORY OFFER** offer, such as a discount or free gift, made to interest consumers in the purchase of a new product, or a product that has been changed or improved, and is being reintroduced.

**INTRUSIVENESS** level at which advertising becomes an irritation to the consumer and thus begins to have negative impact. This phenomenon is particularly noticeable in television advertising, where the repetition of commercials can become an intrusion into people's homes. The number of repetitions needed to change advertising acceptance into consumer irritation is not easily discernible and depends on many factors, such as consumer brand preference, the similarity to competitive advertising, the intensity of the advertising campaign, and the entertainment value of the advertising.

**INVENTORY** supply of goods or materials on hand. In manufacturing, inventory consists of raw materials, work-in-process, and finished goods. In wholesaling and retailing, inventory is the stock of merchandise on hand. In direct marketing, inventory may refer to direct-mail PACKAGE components that are available for mailing when needed. In the broadcast and print MEDIA industry, inventory is the time or space available for sale to advertisers. In magazine publishing, inventory is the number of copies of each issue available for distribution.

An ample inventory ensures that sales will not be lost or deadlines missed but can require a substantial cash investment in both material and storage space. There are also risks associated with excessive inventory, such as a change in circumstances that reduces or eliminates demand for an item in inventory or that renders the item obsolete or illegal, or the risk of loss due to theft, fire, aging, and so forth. The costs and risks must be weighed against the cost of lost sales and missed deadlines to determine the optimal inventory level.

**INVOICE** bill or document showing the amount owed, the item(s) purchased, the price and quantity, and the billing date, and requesting payment for a CREDIT ORDER. In many businesses, particularly DIRECT MARKETING, invoices are accompanied by a letter and a REPLY ENVELOPE. *See also* BILLING SERIES; BILL INSERT; RENEWAL-AT-BIRTH.

**INVOLVEMENT DEVICE** *see* ACTION DEVICE.

## IN-WATS (INCOMING WIDE-AREA TELEPHONE SERVICE)

long-distance inbound telephone service that is billed directly to the receiver at no cost to the individual caller; also called *toll-free calling; 800-number calling*. The fee is usually paid on a monthly basis and, depending upon the telephone company used, is based upon the volume, duration, and distance of the calls received. Usually, the greater the number of calls, the lower the per-call price. In-WATS is used to receive orders, complaints, or inquiries from retail and wholesale customers.

Most, but not all, in-WATS numbers can be dialed from all continental U.S. locations with the exception of the receiver's local phone area. For that area, the receivers must provide a local telephone number for their customers to use. However, some marketers think that two telephone numbers clutter promotion forms and depress response to 800-NUMBER PROMOTIONS.

It is possible to take all calls (both long-distance and local) on one 800-number at additional cost. Marketers using this type of in-WATS service must weigh the additional cost against the value of the additional response. Instead of using an 800 number, marketers also have the option of accepting collect calls from customers on their regular telephone number, without encouraging and/or promoting this option to them.

Some 800 numbers, referred to as "vanity" numbers, spell out words related to the product or service being sold, such as 800-CAR-POOL.

In-WATS service is currently provided by AT&T and, to some extent, by MCI; other communications companies are also entering the field because of its attractive growth rate (about 20% annually).

*See also* CUSTOMER SERVICE; TELEMARKETING; TELEPHONE AGENCY.

## IRIS

1. component of a camera lens. The iris is an expandable circular opening through which light passes, thus making allowances for the varying levels of illumination. When the iris is open as far as it will go, a maximum amount of light is transmitted through the lens to the camera. Conversely, when the iris is closed, a minimum of light is transmitted to the camera. The size of the iris opening is measured in F-STOPS, ranging from f/1.4 to f/22, with f/1 .4 being the widest opening. The iris opening can be controlled either manually or automatically, depending on the sophistication of the camera.

2. elliptical masking device that blocks out a portion of the picture appearing on the motion picture or television screen. A scene may begin while the iris is completely closed and, as the iris is slowly expanded to an open position, the scene will seem to "grow" in an expanding circle from the center of the screen. When a scene closes from its boundaries in a slowly shrinking circle, the iris is being

contracted from an open to a closed position. These moves are respectively called *IRIS IN* and *IRIS OUT*.

**IRIS IN/IRIS OUT** *see* IRIS.

**IRREGULAR DEMAND STATE** *See* DEMAND STATES.

**ISLAND DISPLAY** retail store DISPLAY separated from all other displays in the store. An island display is a type of point-of-purchase display wherein the merchandise is arranged so as to be accessible from all sides. The display itself is freestanding and is typically located in an open area of the store.

**ISLAND POSITION** placement of advertising in media so as not to be surrounded by other competitive advertising. In print, the island position is one that is completely surrounded by editorial or textual matter. In broadcast, the island position isolates the commercial from other commercials by placing it so that program content immediately precedes and immediately follows. An island position is very favorable, since there are no other advertising messages to compete for audience attention.

**ISSUE** one of a series of regularly published periodicals, such as a magazine, newspaper, or newsletter, defined by the date of publication or the content. For example, a magazine published in January is the January issue. The last magazine published each year may be a special "End-of-Year" issue. *Sports Illustrated* has a "Bathing Suit" issue published each year, featuring swimsuit fashions and the models that show them.

Some special-content publications called *special editions* are actually different versions of an issue, such as a West Coast edition of a January issue, featuring advertisements from local West Coast retailers. The issue name, title, price, and some or all of the editorial content are the same, but the advertising content and distribution areas differ.

**ISSUE CODE** code used in subscription FULFILLMENT for tracking, controlling, and analyzing subscriber files by issue. The EXPIRE issue of a subscription is very important when planning new business (new customer) promotions to replace subscriptions that expire. Issue codes are also used to assign a starting issue to a new subscriber according to the publisher's issue INVENTORY and RATE BASE management requirements. For example, an issue code may consist of three digits corresponding to the day, week, or month of publication in a particular year—for example, *906* for the September '86 issue.

**ISSUES-TO-GO** number of issues remaining to be served on a magazine or newsletter subscription prior to EXPIRE. RENEWAL PROMOTION campaigns begin at a point determined by the issues-to-go. Most begin when there are six or seven issues remaining in the subscription term.

**ITALIC** type style with characters slanted upward to the right, used to emphasize a word or passage. The PROOFREADER SYMBOL for italics is a straight underline. The use of italics is not recommended for long passages of text because this typeface is not as easy to read as roman. Roman type, with upright, straight characters, is the more common typeface used for text. LASER PRINTERS have made the use of italic typeface in direct mail promotions easier than ever because these printers are able to print personalized (*see* PERSONALIZATION) promotion letters using a combination of type styles.

# J

**JINGLE** catchy repetitious sounds or words used in rhyming fashion and usually set to music to form a simple musical verse, which is featured in a commercial and used in conjunction with other advertising for a product. A popular example is the "plop, plop, fizz, fizz" jingle used in advertising for Alka Seltzer.

**JOBBER** *see* DROP-SHIPPING.

**JOB PRINTER** COMMERCIAL PRINTER equipped to do only small jobs. Typically, a job printer will produce resumes, letterheads and envelopes, business cards, invitations, and small pamphlets, folders, or brochures, but is not equipped to print larger materials such as books or periodicals.

**JOB TICKET** tag attached to an order that details the pertinent data about the work to be done as well as the data about the individual or firm for whom the job is being done. In advertising agencies, the job ticket will give the date, the name of the agency, the name of the client, and the printing or production instructions to be followed, and will also serve as a record-keeping document. If the work is to be processed through more than one department, such as art, layout, and typesetting, each department will check off its work upon completion, as well as its costs. Therefore, the job ticket will also function as a means of keeping track of the progress of the job and all the costs incurred. Sometimes, the envelope containing the work will serve as the job ticket, with all the information written on its face.

**JOG** align pieces of paper into an evenly edged pile, making them easier to box, bind, or insert. Automatic jogging machines gently shake a stack of papers held against an L-shaped cradle until they are aligned. Most LETTERSHOPS will place CONTINUOUS-FORM documents into a jogger after BURSTING, so that they are properly aligned for loading onto an INSERTER.

**JOHNSON BOX** graphic device often used in direct-mail sales letters consisting of a box-shaped outline made of asterisks. It is used to highlight a short message, such as a typewriter-face headline or a *sidebar* (message printed vertically along the edge of a page). *See also* BURST.

**JOINT MAILING** promotional mailing that combines two or more complete mailing PACKAGES from two or more direct marketers, including OUTER ENVELOPES, into a common envelope, in order to share the cost of postage and LIST RENTAL. It is more expensive to do a joint mailing than a COOPERATIVE MAILING because the cost of purchasing and inserting the common outer envelope is added to the cost of the two original outer envelopes. It is also difficult to find a MAILING LIST that will respond better to a joint mailing than to a cooperative mailing, generating enough additional orders to make this type of mailing more profitable. A few mailers who have tested joint mailings *have* succeeded because of the right combination of products, packages, offers, and lists.

**JOINT VENTURING** formal or informal agreement between two companies to join together to take advantage of a marketing situation, sometimes called a *strategic alliance*. In a joint venture companies share marketing or marketing expertise, costs, knowledge of important connections, and other resources, resulting in reduced marketing and distribution costs and favorable trade terms. In recent years, joint venturing has become very popular in the international marketplace and is often considered crucial for dealing with global markets. There are four general types of joint ventures: (1) licensing, wherein one firm gives the other the rights to a manufacturing process, trademark, or patent in exchange for a fee or royalty. Licensing allows a company entry into a foreign market with very little risk; (2) contract manufacturing, wherein an international company establishes a contract with a local company to have its products made locally. Contract manufacturing offers the advantage of being able to start up quickly in the new market, but affords the international company less control over the manufacturing process; (3) management contracting, wherein an international company supplies management knowledge to a local company and the local company supplies the capital; (4) joint ownership, wherein an international company joins with local investors to create a local business in which all share joint ownership and control.

**JUMBLE DISPLAY** point-of-purchase DISPLAY in which all items may be different but are priced the same. A jumble display is used primarily in retail and is an open display, typically a bin (*see* DISPLAY BIN) of some kind, where the customers can rummage through to see the variety of merchandise.

**JUMP CUT** in film, radical transition between two camera shots. Jump cuts will cause viewer disorientation and are sometimes used deliberately to create that effect. However, they are usually accidents that happen as a result of such factors as an extreme change in subject, size, camera angle, screen direction or position, or a camera shift from moving action to a stationary shot. If a jump cut happens too often, the viewer may become irritated and lose interest in the action on the screen.

**JUNIOR PAGE** space designation for magazine advertisements, so named because the space is the standard size of a page in a small magazine ($4^3/8" \times 6^1/2"$); also called *junior unit*.

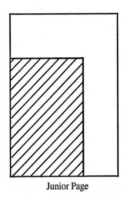

Junior Page

When an advertisement appears on two facing junior pages, it is called a *Junior Spread* or *Pony Spread*.

**JUNIOR SPREAD** *see* JUNIOR PAGE.

**JUNIOR UNIT** *see* JUNIOR PAGE.

**JUNK MAIL** derogatory term used colloquially for promotional mail. The term is most often used by persons who object to receiving unsolicited mail from someone they do not know or do business with. It is not considered an acceptable term in the direct-mail industry. However, one industry speaker, Coleman Hoyt of *Reader's Digest*, used it quite effectively by saying that junk mail represents all of the undeliverable incorrectly addressed mail that is sent.

**JUSTIFY** *see* FLUSH.

**JUST NOTICEABLE DIFFERENCE** minimal apparent difference between two products as observed by the consumer. *See also* WEBER'S LAW.

# K

**KERNING** typesetting technique that overlaps the edges of two type characters to provide the illusion of even spacing and to reduce the amount of white space between letters. Kerning is a phototypesetting technique. Ligature provides the same effect with metallic typesetting by casting two letters onto one body of type. The term *kerning* is derived from *kern,* that portion of a letter that extends into adjacent character space.

**KEY ACCOUNT** primary account, in terms of revenue, for a service business. In advertising, a key account would be a client who spends a great deal of money on advertising through one specific advertising agency, such as one of the leading automobile manufacturers.

**KEYBOARD**
1. computer input/output device that resembles a typewriter and is used for KEY ENTRY of data into a computer. A small version of a keyboard with only numeric keys is called a *keypad.* Keyboards are used to enter data to order FULFILLMENT systems and to interact with ELECTRONIC CATALOGS.
2. keys on a piano or similar instrument.

**KEY CODE** numeric or alphanumeric code used to represent a particular advertisement, CENTS-OFF coupon, catalog, mailing package, list, offer, test, EFFORT, and so forth. Key codes are an essential tool for tracking and controlling promotion response. Keys are the basis for statistical analyses that evaluate the relative profitability and effectiveness of the aforementioned promotion campaign components. For example, a key code may be used to identify several different direct-mail packages being mailed to segments of the same LIST; any difference in response between the groups can then be attributed to the particular package and not to the list, thereby enabling the marketer to identify the best package. As another example, a Christmas gift catalog with three different covers (A, B, and C) is sent to a HOUSE list of previous catalog buyers. The first digit of the key code (X) identifies it as the Christmas catalog. The second digit identifies the cover, and the third digit represents the list (H). Each catalog order form would have a key code printed on it as follows: XAH, XBH, and XCH. When the orders are entered into the FULFILLMENT system, the key code is also entered. Statistics can then be generated, indicating the number and average value of purchases generated by each version of the catalog. *See also* HOMOGENIZATION.

**KEY ENTRY** type of computer data entry accomplished by manually typing the information on a computer KEYBOARD. Key entry is much less efficient than other types of entry, such as SCAN ENTRY or TAPE

ENTRY, because it is slower and more prone to human error. However, the computer equipment required to key enter data is easily affordable by most business organizations. Scan entry equipment can be quite costly, and tape entry applies only to situations where orders are received from intermediaries, such as telephone agents, and not directly from consumers who submit their orders in HARD-COPY format or over the telephone.

## KEYLIGHT

**Theater production:** light that illuminates the actor's face.
**Television production:** primary source of illumination. The level of the key light is the level from which all other supporting light used in a scene is balanced. It also determines the F-STOP for the camera, which allows for the amount of light transmitted to the camera.

## KEYLINE

1. outline drawing used as a guide over finished artwork to show the position, shape, and size of the other elements that will appear in the LAYOUT. The keyline is sometimes referred to as the *type mechanical.*
2. code placed on an ORDER FORM or mailing LABEL used to identify the customer and reduce the amount of information that must be entered to the FULFILLMENT system. The keyline usually includes a MATCHCODE and other control information, such as the expiration date of a magazine subscription.

**KEY PLATE** one of the four printing plates used in FOUR-COLOR PROCESS printing that functions as a guide to correct color REGISTER. Good register requires very precise placement of all the plates on the paper. The key plate is printed first and becomes the standard by which the other three plates are positioned. The black ink plate is usually selected to be the key plate by which the CYAN, MAGENTA, and YELLOW plates are positioned.

**KEYPUNCH** type of DATA ENTRY that involves punching holes into 80-column computer cards in a code (Hollerith) that can be machine read by a computer. Keypunch has been replaced by KEY ENTRY in most order FULFILLMENT operations.

**KEY-TO-DISK** type of KEY ENTRY that stores data on a computer DISK storage device. Unlike KEY-TO-TAPE entry, key-to-disk entry permits fast access to the data on a random basis without taking time to load a MAGNETIC TAPE or waiting for the availability of a TAPE DRIVE. Key-to-disk entry is preferable when the MAINFRAME is in a remote location, because disk-stored data can be easily transmitted to the mainframe via satellite or communications cable.

**KEY-TO-TAPE** type of KEY ENTRY that stores data on a MAGNETIC TAPE. Key-to-tape entry requires less expensive HARDWARE than KEY-TO-DISK entry and is ideally suited to situations where the data does not have to be accessed often or quickly. Tape storage, however, is more prone than disk storage to data loss because of physical damage to the tape. Key-to-tape entry is most practical if the MAINFRAME is in the same location as the entry operation, because tapes can be easily delivered to the mainframe.

**KICKBACK** practice considered unethical whereby an advertising agency will secretly offer to split the media commission with an advertiser or someone representing the advertiser (as an employee of the advertiser) in order to get the advertiser's business.

**KICKER**
1. lighting instrument, located behind the subject and casting light behind the subject (*backlight*), the particular purpose of which is to add highlights to the head and hair. The kicker light is a variation of the backlight and is typically used for a glamour effect.
2. in the writing of COPY for advertisements, subheadline that actually appears above the headline for the copy.

**KILL**
**Publishing:** delete, as words or lines from the text of COPY or photographs, drawings, or illustrations from a story, or an entire story from a publication. A copy for publication that contains the markings of the work to be "killed" is called a *kill copy*. If a free-lance story has been accepted for publication in a magazine and then has been deleted, some publishers will pay the writer a *kill fee.*
**Printing:** break down a PRINTING PLATE after a RUN or when the plate is no longer necessary to reproduce the copy with which it was set. A client will issue a kill order to the printer when the plate is no longer required.
**Radio or television production:** turn off a light, cut a sound or picture, or delete words, lines, scenes, or entire programs from the broadcast schedule. *See also* CANCEL; CREDIT CANCELLATION; KILL BAD NAME.

**KILL BAD NAME** colloquial term for a computer file maintenance transaction that deletes RECORDS with undeliverable addresses from the file. The word KILL usually refers to the deletion of a record from a file for any of a number of reasons, such as expiration, inactivity, change in DEMOGRAPHIC status, and so forth.

**KINESCOPE** forerunner to the videotape recorder. The kinescope is a process whereby live television broadcasts were filmed from a television monitor, using 16-millimeter film. This was done primarily for programming that was on a time delay, particularly to accommodate the Western time zone. The kinescope process was not very efficient, since the film had to be developed and dried before it could be used for broadcast, and the reproduction was lacking in clarity. Today, with its speed of reproduction and portability, the videotape recorder has replaced the kinescope. The videotape quality is such that the reproduction is virtually indistinguishable from the live production.

**KISS IMPRESSION** clean print image created while applying the least amount of pressure possible (approximately .004 inch of pressure) against the paper with the print BLANKET or PLATE, or against the plate with the blanket. A harder impression might produce smudged ink around the edges of the printed areas. A lighter amount of pressure would not adequately transfer the image. It is therefore a delicate balance to achieve.

**KLIEG LIGHT** carbon arc lamp invented by John H. Kliegl and Anton T. Kliegl in 1919 and used in motion picture photography. The word *klieg* is often used to refer to any bright light used on a theater, motion picture, or television set.

**KRAFT** strong paper made from unbleached wood pulp that is naturally brown but may be dyed another color and is frequently used for large envelopes, paper bags, wrapping papers, and toweling. A lighter grade of kraft paper is used for newspapers and food packaging. Kraft, from a German word meaning sturdy, is inexpensive as well as strong. Kraft paper is sometimes used in DIRECT-MAIL ADVERTISING promotions for the OUTER ENVELOPE. Since the envelope is so inexpensive, the promotion must generate fewer responses to be profitable. Kraft paper is sometimes used to create envelopes that resemble those the government uses to mail tax refunds, in the hope of enticing recipients to open them quickly.

**KRYLON** type of FIXATIVE.

# L

**LABEL**
**Advertising:**
1. tag on a product PACKAGE that identifies the contents of the package but also serves as an advertising medium. For example, the label on a food package usually has an appetizing photograph of the product, shows the brand name and/or LOGO, and has various FLAGS, BURSTS, or other graphic designs highlighting its benefits—for example, "new great taste," "low in calories," "30¢ off," "microwave to table," and so forth. A CENTS-OFF COUPON is sometimes included on labels (for this particular purchase or for future purchases), as are recipes and other suggestions that encourage greater consumption.
2. descriptive term used to classify people according to a type, such as homemaker, single parent, or trendsetter.
**Direct mail:** small slip of paper, imprinted with a name and address, that is applied to a mailing piece in order to address it to the intended

recipient; also called *address label*; *mailing label*. A "fancy label" has colored lines underneath each address line and a colored border around the face. On order forms, labels are not as suited to SCAN ENTRY as are names and addresses printed directly on the envelope, because label placement tends to FLOAT, preventing the SCAN HEAD from reading all the characters correctly. PRESSURE-SENSITIVE LABELS are usually the most expensive, but the cost varies with the volume ordered. They require little or no equipment to apply and may be peeled off a base sheet by the recipient and applied to a REPLY FORM. CHESHIRE LABELS are inexpensive and are used most often. HEAT-ACTIVATED LABELS, HEAT-TRANSFER LABELS, and GUMMED LABELS are no longer used to any great extent.

**Merchandising:** brand name of a retailer, fashion designer, clothing manufacturer, or recording company, such as the Perry Ellis label or the RCA Records label.

**LABEL COPY** copy written exclusively for the labels of products. A great deal of label copy related to product ingredients, contents, and public health (e.g., cigarettes) is regulated by law and enforced by government agencies, such as the Food and Drug Administration.

**LABEL PANEL** *see* LABEL SET.

**LABEL PRINTER** equipment that prints names and addresses onto paper or LABELS used to address forms and envelopes. There are several computer-driven types of label printers in use today, including IMPACT PRINTERS, INK-JET PRINTERS, and LASER PRINTERS. *See also* -UP.

**LABEL SET** group of name and address records that are to be printed in LABEL format and that have been split off from the total list prior to printing; also called *label panel, label split*. Each record in a label set should be given a KEY CODE to identify it as a member of that set. The labels in a label set will most likely be applied to a common mailing piece or package.

**LABEL SPLIT** *see* LABEL SET.

**LABEL STRING** postal presorted segment of a LABEL SET, such as CARRIER ROUTE QUALIFIED records, FIVE-DIGIT QUALIFIED records, and non-presorted records. Label strings are printed in ZIP code and other PRESORT sequence so that as labels are applied to a mailing piece, the appropriate postal presort breaks in the mailing can be made. This may be accomplished manually by someone watching for BAR CODES on the labels signifying breaks, or it may be automated, utilizing a machine that reads the codes on labels and automatically separates mailing pieces from each label string.

**LACQUER** clear, shiny solution applied to paper to give it a protective coating. The glossy finish is both decorative and functional, enhancing the colors printed on the paper and making the paper more resistant to moisture and grease. *See also* COATED PAPER; VARNISH.

**LADY OF THE HOUSE** term used primarily in advertising copy to describe the female head of the household; abbreviated *loh.*

**LAID PAPER** paper with parallel watermark lines covering the surface creating a ribbed appearance. A laid finish is used in direct-mail letters and envelopes to connote elegance.

**LAMINATE** bond a plastic film to a printed sheet by means of heat and pressure for protection of the work or to improve the appearance of the work.

**LANHAM ACT** popular name for the Federal Trade-Mark Act of 1946 that became effective in 1947, properly called the Lanham Trade-Mark Act. The Lanham Act governs the registration of TRADEMARKS, trade names, and other identifying marks used in interstate commerce and protects registered trademarks from interference or infringement.

**LAPSE** interruption in, or cessation of, a continuous service, such as a subscription, insurance policy, or book club membership. The AUDIT BUREAU OF CIRCULATIONS (ABC) requires that service on a subscription be continuous without any lapses resulting in missed issues. If an issue is lost in the mail, ABC will still consider it paid circulation, provided that the missed issue is replaced or the subscription extended. However, publishers may not intentionally cause a lapse in service in order to inflate circulation for future issues.

**LASER COLOR SEPARATIONS** laser process for making COLOR SEPARATIONS from PASTEUPS. *See also* LASER PLATEMAKING.

**LASER PLATEMAKING** laser process for exposing PLATES *(see* EXPOSURE*)*. The great advantage of laser platemaking is that it can convert an image to electric impulses that can be transmitted over great distances to another location where the plate actually resides. *See also* LASER PRINTING.

**LASER PRINTER** computer-driven device that utilizes a laser beam to print forms, letters, and labels. *Laser* is an acronym for Light Amplification by Stimulated Emission of Radiation. Laser printers are high-speed, high-quality printers with unique flexibility as to combinations of type fonts and orientation of characters on the page. They can create personalized computer letters with a combination of type fonts such as boldface or italics, to highlight words or passages. With a laser printer, by rotating the printed image 90° or 180°, more forms can be printed on any given quantity of paper. Laser printing also allows for copy variations within a mailing without the expense of printing different CONTINUOUS FORMS for each variation. The laser printer is fast because it creates an image in its entirety at once, in contrast to a LINE PRINTER that prints one line at a time. This eliminates the need for line charges usually levied by printers for long letters. With current laserprinting technology, only black inks can be used.

**LAST COPY SENT** most recent issue of a periodical that has been sent to the subscriber, indicated by a FIELD in the subscription file RECORD. This field is checked when a subscriber complains that he has missed an issue.

**LAST ISSUE** final issue to be served on a subscription before expiration and prior to service of any GRACE issues. This issue can be split off from the rest of the LABELS so that a special RENEWAL PROMOTION can be sent along with it. Some magazine publishers attach a special cover (or enclose a special INSERT) to the last issue announcing that it is the last. *See also* WRAPPER.

**LATE FRINGE** segment of every broadcast day from 11:00 P.M. to 1:00 A.M. (on some stations until sign-off), which has been designated by the television broadcast media for the purpose of selling commercial time on the basis of audience size, composition, and demographics. Late-fringe time is charged at a lower rate than PRIME TIME or other DAYPARTS.

**LATENT DEMAND STATE** *See* DEMAND STATES.

**LATEST SOURCE** SOURCE of the most recent subscription order from an individual subscriber. Subscription RECORDS renewed at least once usually contain information about the original source *(see* ORIGINAL ORDER), the PRIOR SOURCE, and the latest source, so that source-to-source migration can be tracked. This helps the publisher discover how best to promote the renewal of subscriptions sold via different sources. For example, an agent-sold subscription renewed for the first time through the publisher's own RENEWAL PROMOTION has an agency original source and prior source, and a renewal latest source. If this subscriber renews again with an INSERT CARD, the prior source is a renewal and the latest source is an insert card. The original source (agency) does not change.

**LAUNCH** introduction of a new product to market often accompanied by heavy advertising and promotion expenditures to build AWARENESS and interest. *See also* ADOPTION; DIFFUSION; INNOVATION.

**LAYOUT**
1. diagrammatic drawing of a job prepared for TYPESETTING that indicates the arrangement of the COPY elements and the style of type to be used on the image carrier. There are three types of layouts, depending upon the extent to which they accurately and completely represent the finished product: a *rough layout,* a finished layout, and a COMPREHENSIVE LAYOUT. Space advertisements can be evaluated on the basis of a layout, but other print products, such as product packages, booklets, or brochures, that involve more than a two-dimensional image must be evaluated with a DUMMY in addition to a layout, to check the construction, binding, sequencing of pages, and so forth. *See also* IMPOSITION; STRIPPING.

2. sequence of printed matter, such as the pages of a catalog.
3. arrangement of SIGNATURES in sequence for BINDING.

**LAYOUT PAPER** strong, heavyweight paper with a smooth finish and a degree of transparency that is used in the preparation of an advertising LAYOUT; also called TISSUE OVERLAY. The layout paper is used as an overlay by the artist to trace accepted elements in the advertising copy. As new elements are approved or accepted, the artist retraces them onto new layout paper until eventually the layout is complete. In this way each new element can be changed without disturbing the other elements.

**LAYOUT PERSON** person responsible for the production of elements used in a LAYOUT, such as graphics, illustrations, drawings, or type elements. The layout person, who is usually a graphic artist, will arrange all the VISUALS used in the copy and is ultimately responsible to produce the finished layout.

**LEAD**
1. in typesetting, thin metal strip used as a ruler for spacing between lines of type; pronounced *led. See also* SLUG.
2. in stage, screen, or television production, primary player or players around whom the action generally takes place; the principal role.
3. in a vocal group, main singer, who usually sings the melody.
4. in journalism, story of primary importance, particularly a news story or the introductory portion of a news story.
5. prospective customer who has either expressed an interest in a product or service or who has been referred to the seller by a third party. It is essential that leads be followed up promptly so as to reach the prospect before interest wanes. *See also* BINGO CARD; FRIEND-OF-A-FRIEND; LEAD GENERATION; LEAD QUALIFICATION; MEMBER-GET-A-MEMBER.

**LEADER** marketer whose product or brand got to the market first or who maintains a dominant market share. The greatest advantage of being the market leader is that consumers tend to associate the product itself with the leader's brand name, making it extremely difficult for competitors to take market share away from the leader. McDonald's, IBM, Xerox, and Coca-Cola were all such leaders in their industries. Consumers tend to choose the leading brand because, among other things, it simplifies the decision process. The leading brand also gains wider distribution because it can demand priority from retailers and restaurateurs. Market leaders also tend to attract more investment capital. Coca-Cola's "It's the real thing" campaign exemplified the strategy of a leader who used its dominant position to maintain market share. *See also* FOLLOWER.

**LEADER PRICING** reduction in the price of a high-demand item to get people to come into a retail store or to encourage a direct-mail purchase that may inspire additional purchases; also called LOSS LEADER pricing. It is believed that once a decision to purchase an item is made, the customer's resistance to purchasing additional items at full price will be lower. Leader pricing can be at or below the seller's own cost. The loss leader is usually a moderately priced item that most people can afford and that has a well-known normal selling price. Supermarkets usually use a staple item such as soap or coffee as a loss leader. Leader pricing may involve a single product or a complete product line. *See also* CLEARANCE; MARKDOWN.

**LEADERS** series of evenly spaced dashes or dots used in print to guide the reader's eye across a page. Leaders are used in a table of contents, invoices, programs, tabular work, or the like.

**LEAD GENERATION** marketing activities focused on identifying prospective customers for a product or service. There are many techniques for lead generation, but a common method is to ask current customers for the name of someone else who may be interested in buying. Acquiring a list of the attendees of a trade conference or other public event is another method of generating leads. *See also* LEAD.

**LEAD-IN**
1. in broadcast, program directly preceding another program on the same station. The lead-in program is said to lead the audience to an advertiser's program on the same station. *See also* AUDIENCE FLOW; LEAD-OUT.
2. opening words in the copy text of an advertisement; said to lead the reader to the text.
3. in a dramatic presentation, opening monologue.

**LEADING NATIONAL ADVERTISERS, INC.** national service that offers monthly reports to subscribers about competitive advertising activity; abbreviated *LNA*. The service reports on approximately 24,000 brands, providing information as to the media budgets and combination of media used by each. This information is very valuable to advertisers when designing a MEDIA PLAN, particularly when deciding among alternative media (as broadcast or print).

**LEAD-OUT** in broadcast, program immediately following another program on the same station; said to lead the audience out of the advertiser's program on the same station. *See also* AUDIENCE FLOW; LEAD-IN.

**LEAD QUALIFICATION** marketing activities focused on evaluating the readiness, willingness, and ability of a LEAD to buy. Industrial marketers, who rely on personal selling, may use a telemarketing or direct mail effort to qualify leads before spending money on a personal call. *See also* LEAD GENERATION.

**LEAFLET** *see* FOLDER.

**LEARNED DRIVES** internal motivators of human behavior such as pride or greed that are acquired as the result of experience rather than being instinctual. Consumers make purchases to satisfy either learned drives or PRIMARY DRIVES. CUES affect how people respond to drives. Brand advertising cues a consumer to purchase a particular brand. If the purchase satisfies a drive, the purchase behavior will be reinforced and brand loyalty will begin to be established. *See also* HIERARCHY OF NEEDS MODEL.

**LEARNING THEORY** body of psychological research that describes how people modify their behavior patterns as a result of personal experience or the experiences of a role model. Internal needs, called *drives*, motivate consumers to seek products or services that will satisfy those needs. Consumers learn by experience that a particular brand will or will not satisfy those needs. Learned buyer behavior may be *generalized* across brands for a consumer with no brand preference who has had positive experiences with several brands, or it may be *discriminative* for a brand loyal consumer whose experience has been most satisfactory with a single brand. The greater the perceived similarity between brands, the greater the generalization. A negative experience with one brand may also be generalized across many brands. Marketers must use advertising to reinforce good experiences with a brand or to otherwise reward purchase of that brand. *See also* CUES; LEARNED DRIVES; PRIMARY DRIVES.

**LEASE-OR-BUY DECISION** business decision that compares the cost and benefits of a lease arrangement with the cost of a purchase. The customer may choose to lease a photocopy machine because leasing requires a smaller initial capital outlay and enables the lessee to upgrade, downgrade, or eliminate the copier as the lessee's business needs change. Thus, the lessor derives more profit over the useful life of the copier by leasing it than by selling it. A lease agreement is often easier to sell than an outright purchase because the risk to the customer is lower. Some lease agreements give the lessee an option to buy at a later time and to apply some lease payments to the purchase price. *See also* MAKE-OR-BUY DECISION.

**LEAST-EFFORT PRINCIPLE** theory among advertisers that consumers will make purchases based upon the least amount of effort possible and will tend to buy what is handy. This is one of the underlying theories of POINT-OF-PURCHASE ADVERTISING, whereby consumers will make a purchase because they do not have to expend any effort to do so.

**LEAVE BEHIND** *see* LEAVE PIECE.

**LEAVE PIECE** printed information used by salespersons that can be left with the prospective customer; also called *leave behind*. The leave piece is imprinted with the salesperson's name and telephone number as well as information about the merchandise or service, and is left behind with the idea that it will keep the product or service in the mind of the prospect.

**LED DISPLAY** *see* LIGHT-EMITTING DIODE DISPLAY.

**LEGEND**
1. textual matter appearing beneath an illustration, drawing, or photograph that titles, describes, identifies, or clarifies that which appears above it. *See also* CAPTION.
2. explanatory list of symbols on a chart or map, including the mileage scale on a map.
3. lettering or writing in an inscription, as on a coin or medal.

**LETTER CARRIER U.S.** Postal Service employee who delivers mail to its final destination within an assigned area known as a CARRIER ROUTE; also called *postman, mailman.* The letter carrier may also collect mail from various mail collection boxes along the route.

**LETTERHEAD** printed stationery. Business letterheads usually include a LOGO, a return address, and a telephone number. Direct marketers have found that the design of the letterhead can impact response to a promotion letter.
  For promotion letters, it is best to design a letterhead unique to each letter, one that is tailored to the style of the letter COPY varying the logo, color, or even return address. For example, a FUND-RAISING campaign letter for a nonprofit organization might utilize a simple black-and-white letterhead rather than the organization's usual two-color embossed, gothic-type letterhead that might look too rich. Some marketers have rented post office boxes in a location suitable to their product, such as a Washington, D.C., box to use as a letterhead address for a political fund-raising campaign or a Florida P.O. box to use for a cruise line. Some marketers believe that a color letterhead will generate a higher response than a black-and-white letterhead, regardless of the promotion type, because the color increases the reader's level of interest in the letter.

**LETTERING** drawing or inscribing copy by hand, as compared to the mechanical setting of metal type. Sometimes called *hand lettering,* lettering is done by an artist when the desired effect requires a quality that is not obtainable with type. It is also done to accommodate the space available when the required space prevents the use of type or as an economy measure to save on the cost of typesetting. Lettering is considered an art form and is also used for inscriptions on gold, silver, or other metal pieces.

**LETTERING PERSON** artist who specializes in LETTERING.

**LETTERPRESS** process of printing from an inked raised surface. Letterpress is the oldest printing method and is used primarily for jobs consisting mainly of reading matter (without illustrations), such as price lists, parts lists, timetables, rate schedules, and directories. *See also* GRAVURE; LITHOGRAPHY.

**LETTERSET** dry offset printing technique that uses a relief plate and an intermediate printing BLANKET; also called *dry offset; indirect relief printing*. It does not require a DAMPENING SYSTEM. Letterset derives from a combination of LETTERPRESS and OFFSET printing techniques.

**LETTERSHOP** clerical operation or service organization that prepares large-volume mailings; also called *mailing line*. Some lettershops offer creative services such as copywriting (*see* COPYWRITER, GRAPHIC DESIGN), list compilation (*see* COMPILED LIST), and LIST MAINTENANCE. However, their traditional functions are retrieving stock from a warehouse and collating mailing package components; ADDRESSING; bursting (*see* BURST), trimming (*see* TRIM), and folding components as needed; using a mechanical INSERTER to insert them into the OUTER ENVELOPE; sealing the envelope; preparing mail according to U.S. Postal Service regulations for entry to the mail system; and packaging and shipping merchandise.

**LETTERSPACING** modifying the distance between the letters within a word. Letterspacing is a COMPOSITION technique that helps to create lines of equal width on a page or to shorten or lengthen text. It is effectively used for COPY or HEADLINES in capital letters, but with lowercase or italic letters nonuniform spacing between the letters in body text is aesthetically unappealing and makes reading difficult. Uniform line lengths can also be created by SPACING-IN or spacing-out—that is, modifying the distance between words in a line; also called *wordspacing. See also* JUSTIFY.

No Letterspacing
## COPY OR HEADLINES

2 Point Letterspacing
## COPY OR HEADLINES

4 Point Letterspacing
## COPY OR HEADLINES

**LETTER TEXT** portion of COMPUTER LETTER that is constant for all recipients prior to personalized text being added. It usually constitutes most of the letter BODY COPY, with room for several insertions of the recipient's name or town. Depending on the quality of the printing, it can be difficult for the recipient to discern that his name and so forth were added to a standard letter. LASER PRINTERS usually do the best job of merging the personalized text with the letter text.

**LETTER TRAY** plastic or cardboard trays used to store and transport letter-size mail. Each tray holds 500 to 1000 pieces of mail, depending upon the thickness of the contents. Letter trays are widely used by the U.S. Postal Service, by large-volume mailers, and by recipients of large volumes of mail. FLASH COUNTS are sometimes done in terms of the number of filled letter trays received from the USPS, giving a quick estimate of the response to a direct-mail promotion. WEIGH COUNTS are almost always done by letter tray.

**LEVELER** term coined by researchers to distinguish a particular thinking pattern found among consumers. Levelers are people who tend to overlook details in an attempt to simplify their environment. Levelers want all experience to fit a familiar mold and have need for things to be clear and simple; therefore, they pay no attention to particulars, especially if those particulars make situations confusing. (Distinctions among thinking patterns are made by researchers attempting to learn how people come to know something. This information is used in designing promotional campaigns.)

**LEXICOGRAPHIC MODEL** model of consumer attitude formation that assumes the consumer evaluates product characteristics according to ranked priorities and will select the brand that best satisfies the highest priority characteristics. For example, a consumer may rank the price of a car most important, followed by fuel efficiency, braking, and headroom. If two cars are equally satisfying in terms of price, fuel efficiency, and braking, the car that has the most headroom will be chosen. Lower ranked characteristics such as color will not sway the decision. *See also* EXPECTANCY-VALUE MODEL; CONJUNCTIVE MODEL; DISJUNCTIVE MODEL; DOMINANCE MODEL; IDEAL POINT MODEL.

**LIABILITY**
**In general:** amount owed by an organization or individual, such as the amount owed by advertisers for space or time purchased.
**Magazines:** issues remaining to be served on all ACTIVE subscriptions. As copies are served, the liability on those subscriptions is reduced and earned income increases at a value equal to the per-copy value of the issues served. Adjustments must be made to the liability amount if a subscription is canceled prior to EXPIRE or if a canceled subscription is reinstated.

**LIBEL** defamatory statement about a person that is published and thereby exposes that person to public ridicule. Libelous statements are not the same as slanderous statements. Libelous statements are printed, malicious (i.e., printed without just cause), and may be true; however, slanderous statements are spoken, not printed, and are not true. A lawsuit charging a publisher or advertiser with libel may be lost if it can be proven that the allegedly libeled individual is a celebrity (in the public eye) and that the statement in question was published because of its newsworthiness, not because of malicious intent on the part of the publisher or advertiser.

**LIBRARY SHOT** *see* STOCK SHOT.

**LICENSING** contractual agreement between two business entities in which the licensor permits the licensee to use a brand name, patent, or other proprietary right, in exchange for a fee or royalty. Licensing enables the licensor to profit from the skills, expansion capital, or other capacity of the licensee. Licensing is often used by manufacturers to enter foreign markets in which they have no expertise. The creators of popular comic strip and movie characters often license the use of a character's likeness to manufacturers of lunch boxes, clothing, toys, and other children's products. The popularity or familiarity of the character helps otherwise undistinguished products to stand out from their competitors. The licensee benefits from the NAME RECOGNITION and creativity of the licensor. Licensing fees range from 5%–25% of the wholesale price.

**LIFE CYCLE** period of time during which a positive reaction to advertising is noticeable. An advertisement or an advertising campaign is said to have a life cycle that begins with the introduction of the advertising and ends when the advertising is worn out and no longer elicits a positive response.

**LIFESTYLE** individual pattern of living as reflected by interests, opinions, spending habits, and activities.

**LIFESTYLE OVERLAY** technique for LIST ENHANCEMENT that adds LIFE-STYLE data to each RECORD in a file by matching the name and address elements on the file against those on the lifestyle file. Most matches are done on a ZIP CODE level, as it is difficult to gather lifestyle data on a household or CARRIER-ROUTE level. For example, if the lifestyle file indicates that most people living in ZIP code area 06905 play golf and dine out frequently, then everyone on the overlaid file living in the 06905 area will be categorized as someone who plays golf and dines out frequently. The assumption must be made that most people living in the same neighborhood share the same basic lifestyle characteristics. CUSTOMER LISTS are broken into lifestyle groups to determine the characteristics of those who are the best customers and to enable marketers to select for promotion those individuals on prospect lists who share the same characteristics.

**LIFETIME PROCEEDS** in direct-mail marketing, total profit or loss estimated or realized from a customer over the ACTIVE life of the customer record; also called *lifetime value.*

**LIFETIME VALUE** total profit or loss estimated or realized from a customer over the ACTIVE life of the customer relationship; also called lifetime proceeds. *See also* ALLOWABLE ORDER COST; DATABASE MARKETING.

**LIFT** material used in one presentation, such as a film, recording, advertisement, or commercial, that is legally taken (or *lifted)* from that presentation and used in another. A lift is used to provide continuity, particularly in serialized programming such as a soap opera, or as a practical or economic measure, when a previously shot scene (or a previously made recording) will suffice in the new presentation.

**LIFT LETTER** letter added to a direct-mail promotion package to lift (increase) response; also called *publisher letter.* For example, it may be a note signed by the publisher and enclosed in a small envelope saying, "If you've decided not to order, please read this." This is a common technique that does not add significantly to the cost of the mailing.

**LIGHT BOX** instrument used for viewing CHROMES, or color transparencies. A light box is simply a box of any size that contains electric lamps and has a white translucent glass (or plastic) cover. When the box is electrified, diffused light is transmitted through the cover, and the box becomes a light source for the transparencies placed upon it.

**LIGHT-EMITTING DIODE DISPLAY** semiconductor diode made of gallium arsenide phosphide that emits light when voltage is applied; also called *LED display.* LED displays are used in calculators, clocks, watches, and other items to produce alphanumeric displays.

**LIKERT SCALE** attitude measurement used in research, where, in place of a numerical scale for answers, answers are given on a scale ranging from complete agreement on one side to complete disagreement on the other side, with no opinion in the middle.

**LIMBO**
1. in filming, any shot whose background has no identifying characteristics (e.g., showing time or place), therefore giving the illusion that time and space are endless.
2. in filming, lighting technique in which the scene is lighted so that the subject or object is displayed in the foreground and the background appears either gray or black.

**LIMITED DISTRIBUTION** distribution of a product only to specific geographic locations or to specific stores or a specific area within a geographic location.

**LIMITED-TIME STATION** broadcast station that is assigned a FREQUENCY or channel for broadcasting only during a specified time period. At other times, the frequency or channel is shared by other stations. Many local television stations operate on a limited-time basis.

**LINE COPY** drawing consisting of lines or solid areas that can easily be printed without conversion to HALFTONE IMAGE DOTS; also called *line drawing.* Line copy does not have contrasting tones or shadows other than those created by cross-hatched lines or lines of varying thicknesses.

**LINECUT** etched metal PRINTING PLATE suitable for reproducing LINE COPY.

**LINE DRAWING** *see* LINE COPY.

**LINE EXTENSION** adding of another variety of a product to an already established brand line of products. For example, when a coffee manufacturer adds decaffeinated coffee to the same brand line of coffee products already on the market (such as regular coffee and instant coffee), a line extension has been made. Line extensions do not compete with each other, since each answers different needs and thus appeals to a different market. *See also* BRAND EXPANSION; DIFFERENTIATION STRATEGY; FLANKER BRAND.

**LINE GRAPH** *see* GRAPH.

**LINE LENGTH** in magazines or other publications, horizontal width of a column. *See also* AGATE LINE; COLUMN INCH; DEPTH.

**LINE PRINTER** computer-driven machine that prints one line at a time in its entirety on CONTINUOUS forms. High-speed line printers print at about 1000–2000 lines per minute and are used for address labels, bills, renewals, statistical reports, and promotion letters. *See also* IMPACT PRINTER; LASER PRINTER.

**LINE RATE** cost of advertising in a publication on a per-line basis. *See also* AGATE LINE.

**LINESHOT** printing process that is used for LINE COPY.

**LINEUP**
1. in television, rundown of shows to be broadcast in a specific season—for example, the "fall lineup."
2. in broadcast, stations that will be carrying a particular network broadcast.

**LIP SYNC** *see* LIP SYNCHRONIZATION.

**LIP SYNCHRONIZATION** in television and film production, making the recording of the spoken dialogue (or singing) simultaneous with the visualization of the spoken dialogue (or singing); synchronizing the voice track with the video track. The name (short form: *lip sync*) derives from the fact that the movement of the lips is synchronized with the sound of the words.

**LIST**
1. collection of name and address RECORDS of individuals sharing a common interest, purchase history, demographic profile, membership, affiliation, or contribution history. There are many types of lists best described by the characteristics of the individuals or organizations on the list or by the SOURCE of the names on the list. For example, a list may consist of CATALOG HOUSE customers, or it may be a COMPILED LIST of medical professionals taken from various directories, a list of magazine subscribers, or a prospect list of people expected to be good customers once promoted. Lists are the lifeblood of the DIRECT MARKETING industry. *See also* entries following that begin with LIST.
2. *see* LIST PRICE.

**LIST BROKER** agent who arranges for the rental of LISTS by a LIST USER on behalf of the LIST OWNER in return for a commission on the rental fee. List brokers perform various marketing and list consultation services in the process of bringing buyer and seller together, such as researching and recommending lists to the list user and evaluating the performance of each list after mailing. List brokers are also responsible for controlling on-time delivery of the list to the list user and usually guarantee payment for the LIST RENTAL to the owner. A list broker may work exclusively with a HOUSE list or with several COMPILED LISTS or lists geared to specific target markets such as people over sixty, homemakers, or executives.

**LIST BUYER** direct marketer who pays a fee for the one-time use of a mailing list. The word *buyer* is a misnomer in the sense that the list is rented for one-time use but is not purchased. *See also* LIST USER.

**LIST CLEANING** process of removing names from a list that are not desirable to mail. These include undeliverable addresses, DEADBEATS, individuals on the DMA MAIL PREFERENCE SERVICE DELETE FILE, DUPLICATES, and various other poor prospects for a mailing. Some LIST OWNERS will compensate the LIST USER for sharing the results of a list cleaning. *See also* LIST MAINTENANCE.

**LIST CODE** KEY CODE used on direct mail PACKAGES to identify the list from which the names of the recipients were obtained. It is used to track response by list. *See also* HOMOGENIZATION.

**LIST COMPILER** organization that creates and markets COMPILED LISTS.

**LIST COUNCIL** organization within the DIRECT MARKETING ASSOCIATION that caters to the specific interests of DMA members who work primarily with MAILING LISTS.

**LIST CREDIT ROUTINES** computer-supported procedure for allocating a LIST RENTAL fee between two or more LIST OWNERS who have supplied the same name to the LIST USER. INTER-LIST DUPLICATES are not detected until a MERGE/PURGE process is performed.

**LISTENER DIARY** journal of radio/television programs heard/viewed that is kept by a participant in a market research study that measures AUDIENCE SHARE. *See also* MEDIA REACH; NIELSEN RATING; PEOPLE METER.

**LIST ENHANCEMENT** addition of data to a LIST, pertaining to each individual RECORD, that adds to the value of the list. For example, LIFESTYLE or DEMOGRAPHIC data added to a list enhance the user's ability to select individuals from the list that are the best prospects. *See also* DATA OVERLAY.

**LIST EXCHANGE** barter arrangement between two LIST OWNERS who agree to allow each other one-time use of a list without any fee paid except a LIST BROKER commission if a broker is involved. A list exchange may involve one list in exchange for some other type of compensation, such as advertising space in the list-user's magazine or catalog. Some list owners, who are reluctant to rent their list out of concern for the privacy of persons on the list, are willing to exchange lists with a similar organization. For example, a medical association might agree to exchange lists with another medical association but would not rent their list to a pharmaceutical company.

**LIST HOUSE**  *see* LIST BROKER; LIST COMPILER; LIST MANAGER.

**LIST MAINTENANCE**  process of making changes to a list to keep it current. Three basic types of *transactions* are possible: ADD, DELETE, and CHANGE. Some functions are performed in response to an event, such as receipt of an order or address change request. Other transactions occur automatically at predetermined intervals, such as the deletion of FORMER BUYERS. *See also* FILE MAINTENANCE.

**LIST MANAGER**  individual or organization responsible for marketing a LIST to LIST BUYERS. The list manager may be an employee or an agent of the LIST OWNER and may handle one list or several. List managers frequently place advertisements regarding lists in trade publications read by the direct-mail industry. A list manager may also be a LIST BROKER but frequently utilizes the services of a broker instead.

**LIST MARKETING**  *see* LIST MANAGER.

**LIST OWNER**  organization or individual who owns a LIST used for HOUSE promotions or other purposes and also made available to others via LIST RENTAL arrangements. *See also* LIST BROKER; LIST MANAGER.

**LIST PRICE**  in retail, price regularly quoted to customers before applying discounts. List prices are usually the prices printed on dealer lists, invoices, price tags, catalogs, or dealer purchase orders.

**LIST RENTAL**  purchase of a list for one-time use. Most list rentals are delivered to the LIST USER on CHESHIRE LABELS or in MAGNETIC TAPE format. List rental agreements are arranged for the LIST OWNER by LIST BROKERS. Most lists are rented on a NET NAME ARRANGEMENT at a rate of about $50/thousand.

**LIST ROYALTY**  *see* LIST RENTAL.

**LIST SEGMENT**  subset of a LIST that is selected by some common characteristic such as HOTLINES. Segments are selected for the promotion of goods or services expected to be of particular interest to that group.

**LIST SELECTION**  process of extracting a LIST SEGMENT from a list.

**LIST SEQUENCE**  order in which RECORDS are organized on a list. Most lists are in geographic sequence by ZIP CODE or are in alphanumeric sequence within ZIP code, to facilitate the preparation of mailings to the list in ZIP SORT sequence.

**LIST SORT** computer-assisted process that arranges the names on a list into a desired sequence. *See also* LIST SEQUENCE.

**LIST SOURCE**
1. directory, association membership list, conference roster, or other origin of names on a COMPILED LIST.
2. origin of a list as defined by the LIST OWNER, or the owner's means of collecting the names on a list, such as the *Ace Seed Company customer list* or the *Ace Seed Company summer catalog buyers list.* It is extremely important that DIRECT MARKETING firms track response to their promotions by list source, so that they can select for future promotions only those lists that respond well. This is usually accomplished by printing a SOURCE KEY on each REPLY FORM or label, identifying not only their own promotion but also the source of each name.

**LIST TEST** promotion sent to a small sample of a list to TEST the responsiveness of the list.

**LIST TRADE**
1. business of buying and selling LISTS. It is an essential component of the DIRECT MARKETING industry. *See also* LIST BROKER; LIST MANAGER; LIST OWNER; LIST RENTAL; LIST USER.
2. *see* LIST EXCHANGE.

**LIST USER** one who rents or otherwise attains the one-time use of a LIST for promotional purposes. *See also* LIST EXCHANGE; LIST RENTAL.

**LITHOGRAPHY** printing process in which the printing surface is neither raised *(see* LETTERPRESS) nor etched into the plate *(see* GRAVURE), but in which the printing and nonprinting areas exist on the same plane, and printing is effected by means of a chemical process that allows ink to adhere to only the parts of the surface to be reproduced. The process, which was developed in the late eighteenth century, depends on the fact that water and grease repel each other. Originally, the image to be reproduced was drawn on a slab of stone with a grease crayon. The stone was then dampened with water, but the grease from the crayon would repel the water so that, when a grease-base ink was rolled across the stone, the ink would adhere only to the drawing, and the stone would be ready for the application of paper to reproduce the drawing. Lithography ("writing on stone") is accomplished according to the same principle today, but the stone has been replaced by a metal plate and the technology of preparing the plate has become more sophisticated. Lithography is less expensive than either letterpress or gravure printing and is a reasonable alternative, particularly when an order calls for a short run.

**LIVE**
1. in broadcast, term used for a program that is presented as it is happening, in contrast to a prerecorded broadcast. A live broadcast is said to be happening in "real time."

2. in broadcast or stage production, term describing an instrument or device that is turned on, as a live electrical outlet or a live microphone.
3. in filming, concurrently recorded voice track and action, in contrast to a voice track recorded *after* the action has been shot.

**LIVE ANIMATION**  *see* ANIMATION.

**LIVE ANNOUNCER**  announcer broadcasting in real time. *See* LIVE.

**LIVE LIST**  list of HOTLINES or ACTIVE buyers.

**LIVE MATTER**
1. area of a PRINTING PLATE that carries the image to be printed.
2. printing materials, such as type COMPOSITIONS or PLATES, that have been prepared for use and are not to be broken down after that use because they are likely to be used again.

**LIVE TAG**  in broadcast, LIVE ending that has been added to a prerecorded message.

**LIVE TIME**  time on a broadcast schedule that has been set aside for a LIVE broadcast.

**LIVE TITLE**  title of a program filmed or videotaped directly from a source appearing on the set at the time of shooting, as distinguished from a title inserted during the editing process.

**LIVE TV**  live television broadcast; not prerecorded. *See* LIVE.

**LOADING DEAL**  *see* BUYING LOADER.

**LOCAL ADVERTISER**  private business or nonprofit organization that advertises in the media that are local to the immediate area in which the business or organization is located. Generally, local advertisers are retailers. Typical local advertisers include food stores, drugstores, appliance stores, shoe stores, specialty shops, hardware stores, clothing merchants, jewelry stores, and local eating places.

**LOCAL AGENT**  *see* CASH FIELD AGENT.

**LOCAL-CHANNEL STATION**  broadcast station licensed by the Federal Communications Commission to broadcast over a limited area (e.g., a college radio or television station). A local-channel station has a maximum of 250 watts of power, which is just enough power to be heard or viewed within a short radius of the station's point of transmission. Local channels are assigned on an airwave that has been set aside for all local-channel stations.

**LOCAL MAIL**  mail that enters the postal system at the same post office that services the area to which it is addressed.

**LOCAL MEDIA**  media vehicles, such as newspapers, radio stations, television stations, and cable stations, that function primarily to serve the communications needs of the communities or metropolitan areas in which they are located. The local advertiser is typically offered a special discount rate to advertise in local media.

**LOCAL PROGRAM** broadcast program that originates from a local broadcast station, in contrast to a network program.

**LOCAL RATE** special discount advertising rate offered by the media to local advertisers. The local rate is usually a noncommissionable rate lower than that offered to national advertisers.

**LOCAL STATION** broadcast station that functions as part of the LOCAL MEDIA.

**LOCAL TAG** *see* DEALER TAG.

**LOCKBOX** box in a U.S. Postal Service facility, opened with a key or combination lock, that is used for the delivery of mail to an addressee who rents the box. A group of lockboxes that constitute a CARRIER ROUTE is called a *lockbox section* or Post Office Box Station. Bill payment envelopes are often addressed to lockboxes, which, as part of an arrangement with the recipient's bank, accelerate the processing of deposits, thus helping cash flow.

**LOCK UP** in printing, to combine all the LETTERPRESS printing elements, including type and plates, in a single unit, called a *form,* and then to position the form in a rectangular metal frame, called a *chase,* so that the entire unit is ready for printing.

**LOGICAL APPEAL** advertising approach that appeals to the consumer's practical or functional needs in an attempt to appeal to the consumer's sense of logic. In a logical appeal, the product or service is positioned as the logical choice for the consumer. For example, if an individual on a diet wants to drink beer, then the logical choice would be a light beer or perhaps a beer that is "less filling."

**LOGICAL SACKING** computer PRESORT technique that prints PACKAGE/SACK MARKS on ADDRESS LABELS, solely according to U.S. Postal Service regulations for packaging and sacking, without regard for physical constraints; also called *physical sacking.* For example, if the USPS allows 75 packages of mail going to a particular destination to be placed in the same sack, a bar code indicating the end of a sack will be printed on the 75th label, even though a sack may physically be capable of holding only 50 packages. This enables the mailer to determine manually the physical sack or package breaks without overlooking the logical break requirements.

**LOGO** logotype; unique design, symbol, or other special representation of a company name, publishing house, broadcast network, or other organization, used as a TRADEMARK.

Logo

**LOGOTYPE** *see* LOGO.

**LONG PLAY (LP)** phonograph record that makes 33$\frac{1}{3}$ revolutions per minute.

**LONG SHOT** camera shot of a subject that is taken a long distance from the subject that usually includes a wide-angle field of view. *See also* ESTABLISHING SHOT.

**LOOKUP** process of accessing a RECORD on a computer, HARD-COPY, or microfilm file to analyze, adjust, or gather information in the record.

**LOOP**
1. *see* FILM LOOP.
2. to add a voice track to a film reel so that the action and sound are synchronized.

**LOOSE-PACK SACK** canvas SACK of untied but FACED MAIL ready for delivery to the U.S. Postal Service.

**LOOSE RENDERING** rough sketch of artwork that shows a representation of the elements in a LAYOUT. A loose rendering is drawn to scale and will be used to give an idea of the overall concept without specific details.

**LOSS LEADER** retail merchandise that is advertised and sold at a price representing a loss of profit for the retailer, but is used to draw *(lead)* customers into the store in the hope that they will make additional purchases. *See also* LEADER PRICING.

**LOTTERY** contest that requires a purchase be made in order to qualify for a random drawing. Lotteries—as opposed to SWEEPSTAKES, which do not require that entrants make a purchase—are not legal according to U.S. Postal Service regulations governing direct mail promotions, because they are considered a form of gambling.

**LOWERCASE** small letters of the alphabet, as compared to the capital or UPPERCASE letters.

**LOWER-INVOLVEMENT MODEL** example of an advertising medium where there is very little involvement on the part of the consumer. Broadcast media, particularly television, are examples of low-involvement models, since listening and viewing are rather passive activities and the consumer need not be actively involved in order to hear or view the advertising message. With a low-involvement model, the consumer is not usually seeking information on a conscious level; the information is merely absorbed and stored in the brain. When choosing broadcast as a vehicle for advertising, the advertiser should be aware that, because the broadcast media are lower-involvement models, the consumer must be repeatedly exposed to an advertising message in order for the advertising to be effective.

**LOW-KEY LIGHTING** in filming or videotaping for television, the lighting of a scene so that there is a great deal of contrast between dark and light areas, making artistic use of deep shadows. Low-key lighting is used effectively in dramatic presentations to create variety and establish mood, particularly in mysteries or thrillers.

**LOW-PRICE STRATEGY** establishing a relatively low price for a product or service, usually to stimulate demand and acquire market share. This makes the most economic sense for the seller when there are significant economies of scale achievable from high volume production, or when the buyers are price sensitive and the seller has few competitive advantages. *See also* PREEMPTIVE PENETRATION; PRICE LEADER; SKIM PRICING.

**LUCY** *see* CAMERA LUCIDA.

**LUDLOW** machine used in printing that casts type CHARACTERS from brass molds (which have been set by hand) into a metal one-piece line of type, called a SLUG.

---

# M

---

**M** abbreviation for one thousand. M is used after a slash mark to indicate a per-thousand price or rate. For example, the price of renting a LIST might be expressed as $50/M names. *See also* MM.

**MACHINE-COATED** type of COATED PAPER that is coated during the papermaking process by the same machine. It is relatively low cost compared with other coated papers and is generally good quality. Off-machine coated paper is more costly but is also the best quality coated paper. Coated-paper quality is important for HALFTONE and FOUR-COLOR PROCESS printing such as is used in magazines and CATALOGS.

**MACHINE COMPOSITION** in printing, the setting of type by machine rather than by hand.

**MACHINE DIRECTION** *see* GRAIN.

**MACHINE READABLE** *see* OPTICAL CHARACTER RECOGNITION.

**MACROENVIRONMENT** universe of sociological elements that affect a company's ability to serve its customers or sell its goods and services. There are six major macroenvironment forces: cultural, demographic, economic, natural, political, and technological. The cultural environment includes institutions and other forces that affect the basic values, behaviors, and preferences of the society—all of which have an effect on consumer marketing decisions. The demographic environment includes the study of human populations in terms of size, density, location, age, sex, race, occupation, and other statistical information. The economic environment consists of all factors—such as salary levels, credit trends, and pricing patterns—that affect consumer spending habits and purchasing power. The natural environment involves all the natural resources, such as raw materials or energy sources, needed by or affected by marketers and marketing activities. The political environment includes all laws, government agencies, and lobbying groups that influence or restrict individuals or organizations in the society. The technological environment consists of those forces that affect the technology and which can create new products, new markets, and new marketing opportunities. *See also* MICROENVIRONMENT.

**MADA (MONEY, AUTHORITY, DESIRE, ACCESS)** attributes assigned by marketers to members of a target population when attempting to devise a marketing strategy. The population is characterized by their ability to pay for a product (money), their power to make buying decisions (authority), their interest in making a product purchase (desire), and their accessibility to the product (access). Marketers use MADA attributes to measure the potential for product sales in a particular market.

**MADISON AVENUE** avenue in New York City that was once the address of many of the major advertising agencies. Some of these agencies are still located in New York City but have moved to other addresses as well as expanded to include offices in Chicago, Los Angeles, and other national and international locations. Additionally, advertising agencies in cities other than New York have grown to national recognition. However, the phrase *Madison Avenue* has come to be synonymous with the advertising agency industry, just as *Wall Street* (also in New York City) has come to stand for the financial industry.

**MAGAZINE**
1. publication issued periodically, containing miscellaneous editorial pieces, such as articles, short stories, interviews, photographic essays, or poems, of either a specific or general nature. Noted for their superior production quality, magazines are sold by subscription and at newsstands. They usually obtain the bulk of their revenue from the sale of advertising space. Often, newspapers, particularly Sunday editions, will feature a separate magazine section. *See also* SUPPLEMENT.
2. supply chamber, as a holder on a gun for cartridges or a lightproof compartment in or on a camera or projector for film.
3. *see* MAGAZINE FORMAT.

**MAGAZINE ADVERTISING BUREAU (MAB)** nonprofit organization of magazine publishers that functions as a branch of the MAGAZINE PUBLISHERS ASSOCIATION. The purpose of the MAB, which was organized in 1943, is to sell the concept of magazines as a vehicle for advertisers. Its sales efforts include industry and agency presentations, research projects concerning audiences and media, and promotional consumer and trade advertising.

**MAGAZINE COUPONS** CENTS-OFF COUPONS printed in a magazine. Magazine coupons can better reach a TARGET AUDIENCE than newspaper coupons and offer the advantage of FOUR-COLOR PROCESS printing that newspapers can achieve only with an INSERT. Magazine coupons should have a KEY CODE, so that the source of the coupons can be tracked. The coupon may be perforated for easy removal but, regardless, should be a simple square or rectangle that is easy to cut out. Some advertisers have created coupons in the shape of the product they are selling that are so difficult for consumers to cut out that almost no one does. *See also* NEWSPAPER INSERTS.

**MAGAZINE FORMAT** organization of a television program into different features, each with its own story, similar to the way a MAGAZINE is organized. A magazine format is often used for nonfiction news programs. Examples are "60 Minutes" and "20/20."

**MAGAZINE GROUP** variety of magazines appealing to different interests and published by the same publisher, such as, *Time, Life, People, Money, Fortune,* and *Sports Illustrated,* which are all published by Time, Inc. Some publishers of magazine groups will offer a special group advertising rate to advertisers.

**MAGAZINE PLAN** media plan for placing advertisements only in those magazines within the TARGET AUDIENCE'S geographic area. For example, if an advertiser wanted to reach people in the Northeast, the plan would include only those magazines with a circulation in the Northeast region.

**MAGAZINE PUBLISHERS ASSOCIATION (MPA)** organization headquartered in New York and founded in 1919 to promote magazines as an advertising medium; also known as Periodical Publishers Association. In addition, the MPA reports on legislative and regulatory issues and provides circulation marketing support to members. Members of the MPA are magazine publishers of publications issued not less than four times a year. The MAGAZINE ADVERTISER'S BUREAU assumes full responsibility for all MPA's marketing and sales activities.

**MAGAZINE SUPPLEMENT** section of a newspaper printed in a MAGAZINE format and included in the newspaper. Magazine supplements are usually featured as part of the weekend edition of a newspaper. *See also* SUPPLEMENT.

**MAGENTA** red used in FOUR-COLOR PROCESS printing.

**MAGNETIC TAPE** tape on which computer-readable data is electronically stored via magnetic particles embedded in the tape; also called *mag tape.* Most magnetic tapes in use today are $1/2$ inch wide, holding 800, 1600, or 6250 BYTES per inch (BPI). IBM mainframes usually require 9-track 6250 BPI tape. Magnetic tape is the most common medium used for LIST RENTALS, so that lists from a variety of sources can be fed into a computer in preparation for a MERGE/PURGE. Magnetic tape storage is less expensive than DISK but more susceptible to physical damage. *See also* KEY-TO-TAPE.

**MAGNUSSON-MOSS WARRANTY ACT** (also called the Federal Trade Commission Improvement Act) legislation enacted in 1975 for the protection of consumers that requires full warranties on products to meet very specific minimum standards. These standards include free repair of the product within a reasonable time period and a full refund or replacement if the product does not work after a reasonable attempt at repair has been made. If product manufacturers are unwilling to offer such a warranty, according to the act, they must be clear that they are only offering a limited warranty. This legislation has led some manufacturers to stop using warranties on their products as marketing tools.

**MAG TRACK** magnetic track; MAGNETIC TAPE with sprocket holes that appears as a strip on a reel of film. Film with a mag track is sound film and must be used in conjunction with a sound camera in filming and a sound projector in playback. A sound camera features a small audio head that records the sound as the action is being filmed; a sound projector contains a small playback head for the projection of the sound when showing a film.

**MAILBAG** *see* MAIL POUCH; SACK.

**MAILBOX** box mounted on a door or by a curb in front of a house or office, used to receive mail delivered by the U.S. Postal Service. It is illegal for ALTERNATE DELIVERY services to use this box. *See also* CLUSTER BOX; DELIVERY CENTER; LOCKBOX.

**MAIL CLASSIFICATION** *see* CLASS.

**MAIL COUNT** quantity of mail received by a direct-mail marketer on a daily basis. Mail count is determined by weighing batches of mail, counting LETTER TRAYS of mail, or counting individual pieces by KEY CODE. Mail counts are usually done on new-business promotions but not on other types of mail such as payments or customer complaints, for which postprocessing reports are adequate. The counts are used to project total response to a promotion and may also be the basis for a decision to send out another mailing. The time, money, and effort spent on planning a promotion create a level of anxiety that is soothed by these quick counts, but they are not as accurate as the counts available one to five days later as output from the ORDER ENTRY system. *See also* DOUBLING DAY; FLASH COUNT; WEIGH COUNT.

**MAIL DATE** DROP date planned for a mailing usually as agreed upon by the mailing LIST OWNER and LIST USER; also called *mailing date.* The number of returns received at various intervals following the mail date can be used to project total response. The projection is usually based upon previous experience with this product and promotion, as well as the time of year and any other factors that may impact demand. Some direct marketers believe that certain days of the week are better to mail than others, but time of year and proximity to holidays probably have more to do with response. *See also* DOUBLING DAY; MAIL COUNT; ORDER PLOW PATTERN.

**MAILER**
1. business that utilizes the mail as its principal means of contact with buyers or that uses the mail extensively for other purposes such as FUND-RAISING or LEAD generation. *See also* DIRECT MARKETING.
2. protective container for mail, such as a cardboard tube, box, or WRAPPER.
3. *see* LETTERSHOP.
4. *see* SELF-SEALER.

**MAILER'S TECHNICAL ADVISORY COMMITTEE (MTAC)** group of representatives of the direct mail business, including printers, catalog houses, magazine publishers, and FULFILLMENT service bureaus, who assist the U.S. Postal Service and protect the interests of the industry by making recommendations to the USPS concerning policies and procedures.

**MAIL FORWARDING** *see* ADDRESS CORRECTION REQUESTED.

**MAIL FRAUD** illegal promotion that is designed to deceive consumers and is delivered through the mail. For example, it would be fraudulent to advertise a "miracle weight-loss pill guaranteed to make an individual lose 10 pounds overnight." It is also considered mail fraud if a consumer orders merchandise through the mail without any intention to pay. Marketers who receive several orders from the same address but with different names, or orders with obviously bogus names and addresses, such as "Mickey Mouse, Planet Pluto," may report these individuals to the appropriate authority for investigation. Some mailers maintain a list of frequently used bogus names and reject all orders from them. Regulations governing mail fraud have been enacted by the FEDERAL TRADE COMMISSION, state and local governments, the U.S. Postal Service, local Better Business Bureaus, and trade organizations such as the DIRECT MARKETING ASSOCIATION. *See also* POSTAL INSPECTION SERVICE.

**MAILGRAM** message transmitted electronically by Western Union and delivered in HARD COPY to the recipient by the U.S. Postal Service. *See also* ELECTRONIC COMPUTER-ORIGINATED MAIL; ELECTRONIC MAIL; FAX.

**MAILING LINE** *see* LETTERSHOP.

**MAILING LIST** compilation of possible customers prepared as a list for use in direct-mail solicitation. There are many different kinds of lists, such as business lists that distinguish users of particular materials or supplies, zip-code lists that distinguish communities by affluence, credit card lists that distinguish those who buy on credit, magazine lists that distinguish special interests, or airline lists that distinguish those who travel. Through the use of these specially prepared lists, the directmail advertiser is able to pinpoint almost exactly the TARGET MARKET for the advertised product. Mailing lists can be purchased directly from some sources (e.g., magazine subscription lists) or bought or rented from companies that specialize in the preparation of such lists. *See also* LIST BROKER; LIST BUYER; LIST OWNER; LIST RENTAL; LIST SEGMENT; LIST SOURCE.

**MAILING MACHINE** various devices used in a LETTERSHOP to prepare mailings by inserting PACKAGE components, applying addresses or address labels, applying postage, sealing the envelopes, and so forth. *See also* INSERTER.

**MAILING PIECE** direct mail promotion typically consisting of at least an OUTER ENVELOPE, ORDER FORM, letter, and REPLY ENVELOPE, but it may also consist simply of a postcard; also called PACKAGE.

**MAIL-IN PREMIUM** gift offered as part of a special promotion by a manufacturer in exchange for some appropriate representation of purchase of the manufacturer's product, mailed in to the manufacturer.

**MAIL KEY** *see* KEY CODE.

**MAIL ORDER** DIRECT MARKETING business that utilizes the mail as its primary vehicle for promoting and delivering goods and for communicating with its customers *(mail-order buyers)*. Mail-order firms may also accept telephone orders utilizing an 800-NUMBER PROMOTION. Mail order differs from other types of direct marketing in that the buyer and seller do not make any face-to-face contact. CATALOGS and *space advertisements* are the most common tools for mail-order selling. *See also* MAIL-ORDER ADVERTISING.

**MAIL-ORDER ADVERTISING** advertising that creates orders for purchase through the mail. Mail-order advertising can utilize almost any form of media, although CATALOGS, such as the Spiegel catalog, are the most popular form. The catalogs are distributed through the mail, and then orders are likewise placed through the mail (although, as a convenience to customers, some mail-order houses or CATALOG HOUSES offer a telephone ordering service, through the use of an 800 or toll-free telephone number). The important characteristic of mail-order advertising is that there is no interaction between the consumer and the advertiser and that, except when using the telephone option, the only means of communication between consumer and advertiser is through the mail. *See also* DIRECT-MAIL ADVERTISING, DIRECT-RESPONSE ADVERTISING.

**MAIL PREFERENCE SERVICE** *see* DMA MAIL PREFERENCE SERVICE ADD-ON FILE DELETE FILE.

**MAILROOM** FULFILLMENT operation responsible for receiving, opening, cashiering *(see* CASHIER), and distributing INCOMING MAIL from customers. Mail must be opened and distributed quickly, so that money received can be deposited, orders received can be entered, complaints can be handled, and so on. Mailroom volume capacity must be flexible to cope with the highly seasonal nature of direct-mail marketing. January and July are the heaviest mail periods and may double or triple the volume of lower mail-volume months. Most high-volume operations utilize automated mail-opening equipment that slits envelopes on one to three sides and delivers each envelope on a conveyor belt to the mail-opening clerk, who extracts and sorts the contents.

**MAIL SACK** *see* SACK.

**MAINFILE** master record of customers or subscribers, members, or contributors, usually maintained on a computer, containing all relevant data pertaining to each customer; also called *masterfile.* Most OUTPUT, such as address labels, statistical reports, and invoices, is generated from the mainfile. *See also* BACKUP TAPE; FILE MAINTENANCE; UPDATE.

**MAINFRAME** main computer or CENTRAL PROCESSING UNIT in what is typically a full-size computer system. Computers have made it possible to handle large amounts of data quickly and accurately. The major drawbacks to the large mainframes are that they generally require climate-controlled rooms and a technically adept staff to run, maintain, and program them. Computers are omnipresent in marketing, used to maintain and MERGE/PURGE lists; to analyze consumer characteristics, promotion response, and product sales information, to fulfill orders, to compose type; and so forth. *See also* MICROCOMPUTER; MINICOMPUTER.

**MAIN HEAD** main HEADLINE primary or most important headline in a piece of editorial matter. It is the main head that catches the reader's eye and invites further examination of the copy that follows.

**MAINRUN** subscription FULFILLMENT computer function that produces address labels from the current mainfile that will be used to address the current magazine issue or other periodical issue to all ACTIVE subscribers. Supplemental runs are done between mainruns to produce labels for new or reactivated subscribers.

**MAINTENANCE METHOD** subscription SOURCE-EVALUATION technique for projecting the cost of maintaining a constant number of subscribers over time from a particular SOURCE, by projecting the renewal, EXPIRE, and cancellation rates to be realized from this source and by bringing in new subscribers to replace those that drop out. This is an especially useful technique when considering the acquisition of names from another publication that is going out of business. The additional names will commit the publisher to a higher RATE BASE, and the maintenance method technique will enable the publisher to ascertain the cost of meeting that rate base commitment. *See also* DEPLETION METHOD; STEADY-GROWTH METHOD.

**MAKEGOOD** credit given to an advertiser (or advertising agency) by a publication or broadcast medium for an advertisement or commercial spot to make up for an error or unavoidable cancellation on the part of the publication or broadcast medium. The credit is usually in the form of a rerun of the advertisement or commercial.

In print advertising, the publisher must agree that an advertisement was poorly run. Generally, print makegoods are given when an advertisement has been placed in a position in the publication other than the one contracted for or when there has been some mistake on the part of the publisher in the printing of the ad copy.

In broadcast, a makegood may be offered in the form of an extra run of a commercial when the broadcast medium did not deliver the audience size or composition promised for a previously contracted commercial. Broadcast makegoods are also given when transmission was poor, through some fault of the broadcast medium, or when the commercial did not run as scheduled, through some unforeseen circumstance.

All makegoods are subject to negotiation between the advertiser (or advertising agency) and the medium.

**MAKE-OR-BUY DECISION** business decision that compares the costs and benefits of manufacturing a product or product component against purchasing it. If the purchase price is higher than what it would cost the manufacturer to make it, or if the manufacturer has excess capacity that could be used for that product, or the manufacturer's suppliers are unreliable, then the manufacturer may choose to make the product. This assumes the manufacturer has the skills and equipment necessary, access to raw materials, and the ability to meet its own product standards. A company who chooses to make rather than buy is at risk of losing alternative sources, design flexibility, and access to technological innovations.

**MAKEREADY**
1. get a printing press ready to print a RUN, as filling the INK FOUNTAIN, adjusting the paper feeder, setting the side guides, and so on.
2. prepare a LETTERPRESS printing plate. This process takes a great deal of care and skill, because different-size image elements exert different pressures; thus, the plate must be built up to even out the impression so that the HIGHLIGHTS will print correctly and not puncture the paper.

**MAKEUP**
**Direct-mail advertising:** *see* PRESORT
**Printing:** preparation of a complete film or photoprint page, with all COPY and illustration elements, prior to printing. The page makeup will be identical to the final print product.

**MAKEUP RESTRICTION** limitation imposed by a publication on the size and layout of print advertisements, so that the publication does not end up with an odd-shaped space on any of its pages. Such an odd-shaped space would be unsuitable for editorial copy and unsalable for advertising space.

**MALL**
1. public promenade or concourse open only to pedestrian traffic.
2. public area containing a complex of shops with associated walkways and parking areas; also called *shopping mall.* Some malls are also covered, to provide the same climatic conditions year-round.

**MANAGEMENT**
1. collective administrative heads of a company, institution, business, etc., who are responsible for conducting the affairs of the company (institution, business, etc.) for meeting its short-range and long-range objectives, and for maintaining it as a profit-making organization and/or an ongoing enterprise.
2. leading or supervising of an organization, business operation, or the like.
3. wise use of means to accomplish a purpose.

**MANAGEMENT CONSULTANT** individual or firm with expertise in management procedures and practices. Management consultants are hired by businesses to analyze and provide solutions to existing problems or to conduct studies of the business operation, including its personnel structure, aimed at improving efficiency and profitability.

**MANAGEMENT SECTIONAL CENTER (MSC)** U.S. Postal Service facility whose manager has direct line responsibility for the post offices within the delivery area it serves.

**MANAGEMENT SUPERVISOR** employee of a large advertising agency who is in charge of all the ACCOUNT EXECUTIVES and who is ultimately responsible for the management of each account. This position exists only in large agencies where accounts are numerous and where each account is handled by a separate account executive. In some agencies this position is titled *account supervisor.* The difference in nomenclature is entirely dependent upon the structure of the company as determined by its owners and executive staff.

**MANDATORY COPY** copy that by law must be included in the advertising and/or on the labels of some products, such as alcoholic beverages, cigarettes, real estate developments, and some food and drug items. Messages such as "This is not an offering, which can only be made by prospectus" or "Warning: The Surgeon General has determined that cigarette smoking is dangerous to your health" are mandatory copy.

**MANUFACTURER'S BRAND** merchandise bearing a manufacturer's brand name, rather than a private label brand. The marketing effort of a manufacturer's brand is to attract customers loyal to the manufacturer's name. For example, many successful clothing designers, operating on this principle, have licensed their manufacturer's brand name outside the clothing category to include cosmetics, perfumes, and even jewelry.

**MANUFACTURER'S REPRESENTATIVE** salesperson whose line of merchandise represents a particular manufacturer. Some manufacturers maintain a salaried staff of sales representatives; others (usually smaller companies) offer their lines to independent salespersons, who are remunerated by commission. Thus the manufacturer's representative may be a salaried employee, or an independent broker, working on commission, who represents more than one manufacturer's line of merchandise. In the latter case, the various lines are usually compatible and may be distributed along the same channels or purchased by the same customers.

**MANUSCRIPT (MS)**
1. handwritten or typed copy of a text or document, as distinguished from copy that has been typeset and/or printed.
2. handwriting.

**MARGIN**
**Marketing:** *see* GROSS PROFIT; MARKUP.
**Printing:** space on a page between the COPY and the edge of the page. The four margins are called, clockwise from the top, head margin, front margin, foot margin, and inside or back margin. BLEEDS are produced by printing into the margin up to or slightly beyond the point at which the paper sheet will be trimmed to page size. The GUTTER is the area between the margins of two pages on an untrimmed sheet.

**MARGINAL RETURN** amount of sales of a product that will be generated by an increment in the cost of advertising.

**MARKDOWN** reduction in selling price to stimulate demand, take advantage of reduced costs, or force competitors out of the market. Markdowns are common for domestic goods sold in FOREIGN markets where incomes are lower, where wholesalers demand a larger piece of the revenue, and/or where surplus goods are disposed of. *See also* CLEARANCE; LEADER PRICING; MARKUP.

**MARKET**
1. economic system bringing together the forces of supply and demand for a particular good or service. A market consists of customers, suppliers, and CHANNELS OF DISTRIBUTION, and mechanisms for establishing prices and effecting transactions. For example, the softdrink market comprises the manufacturers, bottlers, distributors, retailers, restaurants, and consumers. *See also* MARKETING.
2. sell some good or service.

**MARKET ATTRACTIVENESS** measure of the profit possibilities that lie within the structure of a particular industry or market. There are many different factors that contribute to market attractiveness. These include: (1) market factors such as growth rate and size of the market; (2) economic factors such as investment potential and industry saturation or rates of inflation affecting consumers' purchasing power; (3) technological factors such as availability of raw materials; (4) competitive factors including the types of rival business and the bargaining power of suppliers; and (5) environmental factors such as the existing regulatory climate and the degree of social acceptance for a product within a particular market.

**MARKET BUILD-UP** method of estimating the revenue potential of an industrial market by identifying the number of potential buyers in the market and the purchase requirements of each. The source of the data may be published SIC coded data, primary research like questionnaires or surveys, or sales history. In the absence of actual purchase data, the annual revenue or number of employees of a buyer may be used to estimate their purchase requirements by assuming their requirements are the same as those of customers with similar revenues or numbers of employees. *See also* COMPETITIVE INTELLIGENCE.

**MARKET-BY-MARKET ALLOCATION**  *see* AREA-BY-AREA ALLOCATION.

**MARKET-BY-MARKET BUY** method of purchasing commercial time on broadcast stations, where the time is bought in one market (geographical area) at a time, as opposed to a NETWORK BUY, where the time is bought all at once on all the stations affiliated with the network throughout the region or country. Although a market-by-market buy is more time-consuming, advertisers will purchase commercial time on this basis when they want to direct the advertising only to specific markets. Also, a judicious MEDIA BUYER can often make a more economical purchase of time in a market-by-market buy.

**MARKET COVERAGE STRATEGY** method for evaluating the various segments of the marketplace and deciding which segments to cover in the marketing of a particular product. Marketers generally adopt one of the following three general market coverage strategies: (1) UNDIFFERENTIATED MARKETING, which focuses on what is common in consumer needs in the marketplace and is effected by presenting one product for all markets or presenting all of a company's products in one market; (2) DIFFERENTIATED MARKETING, wherein several market segments are targeted for marketing campaigns with separate promotional offers for each market; (3) CONCENTRATED MARKETING, which focuses on one small part of the marketplace and is effected by a concentrated marketing promotion that seeks to gain a large share of the small market.

Market coverage strategy can also be applied to product distribution, describing the number of distribution outlets in a given market through which the product is available. In this case market coverage would be the percentage of outlets where the product is available compared to the number of possible outlets where the product could be available. Strategies would apply to the methods of evaluating and deciding the distribution outlets for a particular product.

**MARKET DEMAND** total amount of consumer purchases of a particular product in a specific market over a specific period of time within a specific marketing environment under clearly defined levels of marketing expenditure and effort.

**MARKET DEVELOPMENT** manufacturer's attempt to identify and develop new markets for marketing current products. There are three general strategies applied in market development: (1) working within the demographic market to see if any particular demographic group can be encouraged to buy more of the product or if any new group within the demographics can be encouraged to purchase the product; (2) looking at the institutional market to see if these buyers can be increased; (3) attempting to develop markets in new geographical areas. To effect these strategies, marketers will attempt new distribution methods, change the design of promotional efforts, and attempt to discover and promote innovative uses for an existing product.

**MARKET DEVELOPMENT INDEX** relationship between potential and actual customers of a brand in a particular market (geographical area) compared to the relationship nationally (throughout the U.S.)

**MARKET ENTRY** initiation of efforts to sell a new or existing product to a group of consumers not previously targeted by that marketer. McDonald's entered the Moscow market by establishing a retail outlet in Moscow. Radio Shack entered the personal computer market by introducing its own brand. Entry may be achieved through INNOVATION, acquisition of another company already in that market, or expansion of current distribution channels. Entry might also be achieved through cooperation with other business entities in an arrangement called a *virtual corporation* in which the skills and assets of one company are combined with those of another to achieve a shared goal. The existence of strong competitors, patented technology, or the necessity for large initial capital outlays, act as barriers to market entry. *See also* FOLLOWER; LEADER.

**MARKET FORECAST** total level of demand for a product, across all brands, expected to result from a particular marketing effort by the competitors in the market. Environmental trends not under the control of the marketers, such as social trends or economic changes, can greatly impact the accuracy of the market forecast. *See also* ENVIRONMENTAL THREAT; MARKET BUILD-UP; SALES FORECASTING.

**MARKET GROWTH RATE** annual increase in product sales or population within a given market. The market growth rate is a factor to be considered when evaluating the performance of a particular product in a particular market. Sometimes marketers establish a marketing campaign based solely on increasing a specific market's growth rate. This can be done through generic advertising to make consumers more aware of the product or more conscious of their need for a particular product.

**MARKETING**  process associated with promoting for sale goods or services. The classic components of marketing are the Four Ps: product, price, place, and promotion—the selection and development of the *product,* determination of *price,* selection and design of distribution channels *(place),* and all aspects of generating or enhancing demand for the product, including advertising *(promotion). See also* DIRECT MARKETING; MARKET; MARKET PROFILE; TARGET MARKET.

**MARKETING AUDIT**  strategic tool used to review the effectiveness of a marketing program. A marketing audit is a comprehensive, systematic, periodic evaluation of a company's marketing capabilities. The audit examines the goals, policies, and strategies of the marketing function as well as the methods of the organization and the personnel who carry out the goals, policies, and strategies of the marketing function. Marketing audits are performed on a regular basis by an unbiased, independent company and are used to improve a company's overall marketing performance or to establish new marketing plans.

**MARKETING CHANNELS**  avenues used by marketers to make products available to consumers. Wholesalers, distributors, sales agents, retailers, and all other sources used in getting the product to consumers are included in the category of marketing channels. S*ee also* COMMUNICATION CHANNELS.

**MARKETING COMMUNICATIONS MIX**  the particular combination of marketing tools that work together to communicate the marketer's message, to achieve the marketer's objectives, and to satisfy the target market.

**MARKETING CONCEPT**  goal-oriented, integrated philosophy practiced by producers of goods and services that focuses on satisfying the needs of consumers over the needs of the producing company. The marketing concept holds that the desires and needs of the target market must be determined and satisfied in order to successfully achieve the goals of the producer.

**MARKETING CONTROLS**  procedures followed by companies to monitor and regulate marketing activities. The effectiveness and efficiency of a marketing program can best be determined by using marketing controls. *See also* MARKETING AUDIT.

**MARKETING DIRECTOR**  head of all marketing functions within the structure of an advertiser's company, including advertising, sales promotion, research, and all other marketing elements. A typical structure of the marketing department in a large company may look like the following:

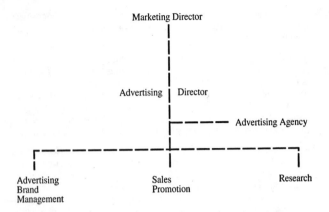

**MARKETING INFORMATION SYSTEM** processes associated with collecting, analyzing, and reporting MARKETING RESEARCH information. The system used may be as simple as a manually tabulated consumer survey or as complex as a computer system for tracking the distribution and redemption of CENTS-OFF COUPONS in terms of where the consumer got the coupon, where he redeemed it, what he purchased with it and in what size or quantity he purchased it, and how the sales volume for each product was affected in each area or store where coupons were available. Marketing information provides input to marketing decisions including product improvements, price and packaging changes, copywriting, media buying, distribution, and so forth. Accounting systems are a part of marketing information systems providing product sales and profit information. Marketing information may be gathered inhouse or purchased from outside services such as the A. C. NIELSEN COMPANY.

**MARKETING MIX** combination of marketing elements used in the sale of a particular product. The marketing elements center around four distinct functions, sometimes called the "four Ps": *product, price, place* (of distribution), and *promotion*. All these functions are considered in planning a marketing strategy, and any one may be enhanced, deducted, or changed in some degree in order to create the strategy necessary to efficiently and effectively sell a product.

**MARKETING MYOPIA** narrow-minded approach to a marketing situation where only short-range goals are considered or where the marketing focuses on only one aspect out of many possible marketing attributes. Because of its shortsightedness, marketing myopia is an inefficient marketing approach. *See also* MARKETING CONCEPT.

**MARKETING PLAN** plan that details a company's marketing effort; also called ACTION PROGRAM, *marketing strategy*. The marketing plan may be laid out for an individual product or for the entire company and all its products. In either case, the plan specifies the marketing goals and objectives to be achieved over a specific time period and then lays out the various strategies to be followed in achieving them. It will also delineate the responsibilities for carrying out the plan. The strategies will involve the proposed development of the product(s), the definition of the TARGET MARKET(S), and the types of media and SALES PROMOTIONS to be used.

**MARKETING RESEARCH** gathering and analysis of information about the moving of goods or services from producer to consumer. Marketing research covers three wide areas: market analysis, which yields information about the marketplace; product research, which yields information about the characteristics and desires for the product; and consumer research, which yields information about the needs and motivations of the consumer. The results of marketing research will supply facts needed to make marketing decisions and will determine the extent and location of the market for a product or service.

**MARKETING STRATEGY** *see* MARKETING PLAN.

**MARKETING WARFARE** *See* DEFENSIVE WARFARE, OFFENSIVE WARFARE.

**MARKET-MAPPING STUDY** any study conducted concerning attitudes of consumers, product comparisons, or marketing evaluations, or any combination of marketing factors, where the results are charted on a graph to show a correspondence among VARIABLES (wherein one variable is dependent on another and a change in one will effect a change in the other).

**MARKET NICHE** small segment of a market that is particularly suitable as a target audience for a specific product. Generally a market niche offers significant potential for sales of the product and is often free of competitors for the particular product. For example, an automobile manufacturer may produce a car that is substantially less expensive than its competitors and that appeals only to those consumers in the vast automobile market who are interested in purchasing an inexpensive automobile. Although the target audience for the inexpensive auto represents only a small percentage of the total number of automobile buyers, the audience is still substantial enough to allow the auto manufacturer to carve out a niche and make a profit.

**MARKET PENETRATION** depth of sales of a particular product in a given market. The deeper the penetration, the higher the volume of product sales. In order to expand the sales of current products in markets where their products are already being sold, marketers utilize market penetration strategies such as cutting prices, increasing advertising, obtaining better store or shelf positions for their products, or innovative distribution tactics.

**MARKET POSITIONING** *see* POSITION.

**MARKET PROFILE** outline of the characteristics of the inhabitants of a particular consumer region. Used primarily in developing marketing strategies, a market profile will describe DEMOGRAPHICS, geographical data, lifestyle patterns, consumer needs and preferences, and socioeconomic conditions within a particular market.

**MARKET RESEARCH CORPORATION OF AMERICA (MRCA)** national organization that sponsors a consumer panel of more than 6000 families who report their purchases to the organization on a weekly basis. These reports are then analyzed, and the results of the analysis are compiled into syndicated reports that detail the purchasing habits and usage patterns of consumers. The reports are offered to interested parties on a subscription basis.

**MARKET RESEARCH DIRECTOR** *see* CONSUMER RESEARCH DIRECTOR.

**MARKET SEGMENTATION** process of dividing the market according to similarities that exist among the various subgroups within the market. The similarities may be common characteristics or common needs and desires. Market segmentation comes about as a result of the observation that all potential users of a product are not alike, and that the same general appeal will not interest all prospects. Therefore, it becomes essential to develop different marketing tactics based on the DIFFERENCES among potential users in order to effectively cover the entire market for a particular product. There are four basic market segmentation strategies: behavior segmentation, demographic segmentation, geographic segmentation, and physiographic segmentation.

**MARKET SHARE** *see* BRAND SHARE.

**MARKET TARGETING** choosing an appropriate market for a given product. Marketers of a given product need to evaluate the different market segments and decide which and how many to serve. To do this effectively, they must examine three general factors: (1) segment attractiveness (i.e., the impact of competitors); (2) segment size and growth; (3) company objectives and resources.

Market targeting differs from TARGET MARKETING in that a product is already established and decisions must be made as to which market is most appropriate for it. In target marketing, a company finds a market it wants to serve and then develops a product appropriate for that market. *See also* MARKET COVERAGE STRATEGY, POSITION, TARGET MARKET.

**MARKET TEST** EXPOSURE of goods or services to a small sample of the entire market to test various marketing strategies. Some areas of the country are considered better barometers of demand than others, because the tastes of a particular area for certain products seem to resemble those of the whole country. These are most often areas that attract mobile people from all over the country, such as the Sunbelt states. The area chosen must be representative of the areas where that product is in demand. For example, swimwear would not be tested in North Dakota, nor snowshoes in Florida.

Some markets are used as the ultimate test of demand for a product, because consumers there are slow to accept a new brand or product. That's the meaning behind the theatrical phrase "Will it play in Peoria?"

**MARKOV-PROCESS MODEL**  model of brand loyalty that mathematically forecasts future market share based on current rates of purchase and repurchase. For example, upon establishing that the first 100 consumers to purchase a new product show a 70% rate of repurchase of that brand, 20% of brand X and 10% of brand Y, then the probability that each brand will be purchased again can be mathematically projected. This is a relatively simplistic view of market dynamics, and many variations on the Markov model attempt to introduce additional variables and assumptions.

**MARKUP**
**Marketing:**
1. *see* GROSS PROFIT.
2. determination of a retail selling price, based on some percentage increase in the wholesale cost; also called margin. For example, a 20% markup on an item wholesaling at $100 would be $20, resulting in a retail selling price of $120. Typical markups are 28% for cameras, 41% for dresses, 46% for costume jewelry, and so forth. The size of retail markups tends to vary inversely with the wholesale cost and with TURNOVER (the rate at which a quantity is sold). *See also* MARKDOWN.

**Printing:** written instructions for the typesetter on COPY—for instance, underlining words to indicate they should be set in italics.

**MASK**
**Photography:** piece fitted over the camera lens to modify the shape or size of the lens opening in order to create a visual effect such as a VIGNETTE.
**Printing:**
1. method of COLOR CORRECTION that modifies the color in a FOUR-COLOR PROCESS print by altering the color of individual COLOR SEPARATION negatives. This is accomplished by placing a different color POSITIVE over each separation NEGATIVE, changing the DENSITY of the image created by the negative.
2. opaque material that covers a portion of an OFFSET process PRINTING PLATE during EXPOSURE.

**MASK OUT**  in printing, block out a portion of a drawing, illustration, photograph, or layout so that it will not appear on the reproduction.

**MASLOW'S HIERARCHY**  *See* HIERARCHY OF NEEDS MODEL.

**MASS APPEAL** nondirected marketing approach designed to appeal to all possible users of a product. Because consumers differ, a mass appeal is usually not the best strategy for a product unless the product is one that crosses all DEMOGRAPHIC and PSYCHOGRAPHIC boundaries— for example, circus tickets or soft-drink products. There are some generic advertising campaigns designed for mass appeal, such as the one advertising milk, sponsored by the American Dairy Association.

**MASS CANCEL** subscription FULFILLMENT process of canceling groups of CREDIT ORDERS that remain unpaid at the end of the publisher's BILLING SERIES. Mass cancellation follows suspension *(see* SUSPEND) of the records. When credit orders are mass canceled, the publisher's ACCOUNTS RECEIVABLE and deferred liability are reduced at a value equal to the BAD DEBT expense. Mass-canceled records are sometimes maintained so that those individuals can be purged from any future promotions lists. *See also* MERGE/PURGE.

**MASS COMMUNICATION** medium that appeals to a mass audience in terms of DEMOGRAPHICS and PSYCHOGRAPHICS (e.g., television).

**MASS DISPLAY** in retail, large additional display of an item already on the shelf, positioned in a separate prominent place where the majority of store traffic will pass it.

**MASS MAGAZINE** magazine that is not targeted to appeal to a specific audience, but that has editorial content of a general nature, so that it appeals to a diversified readership—for example, the *Reader's Digest.*

**MASS MARKET** approach to advertising that attempts to reach every consumer, rather than targeting a particular market segment. A mass market strategy is effective for products that appeal to a broad cross-section of consumers, like aspirin or orange juice. It is not appropriate for products with limited appeal, such as a gold club or sewing pattern. Mass market media are usually more expensive than direct marketing media, because they are priced according to the number of consumers who will be reached, and must generate a larger return in order to justify the expense. *See also* TARGET MARKET; UNDIFFERENTIATED MARKETING.

**MASS MEDIA** broad spectrum of radio and television broadcast stations and networks, newspapers, magazines, and outdoor displays designed to appeal to the general public. *See also* MEDIA.

**MASTER** primary and usually most complete copy of a film, audio recording, file, document, tape, or other item that involves a significant effort to create or re-create, and from which all DUPLICATES are made. Copies of the master are made and placed in a safe and usually fireproof storage area, to be used should the duplicate be damaged, lost, or stolen. *See also* MAINFILE.

**MASTER CONTRACT** *see* BLANKET CONTRACT.

**MASTER FILE** *see* MAINFILE.

**MASTER FILM** *see* MASTER.

**MASTER OF CEREMONIES** host of a formal event, such as the Miss America Pageant, or host of an entertainment program who functions as leader of the ceremonies by introducing the various entertainments or acts and maintaining a running patter or commentary between them.

**MASTER TAPE** *see* MASTER.

**MASTHEAD**
1. name of a newspaper displayed at the top of the first page.
2. in a newspaper or magazine, printed section, usually located on the editorial page, that details the title and address of the publication, the owner and/or publisher, the staff, and the advertising and subscription rates.

**MAT** *see* MATRIX; MATTE FINISH.

**MATCH** RECORD on a file that DUPLICATES another record according to the matching logic being used; also called hit. *See also* DEDUPE; INTERLIST DUPLICATE; INTRA-LIST DUPLICATE.

**MATCHBOOK COVER** protective covering on a book of matches that is frequently used as an advertising medium. Advertising messages may be printed on the outside or inside cover and then distributed locally, regionally, or nationally as the matchbooks are distributed. Local institutions such as clubs, hotels, restaurants, or the like often use matchbook covers as a method of advertising. Usually in this case the institutions pay for imprinting the covers and will distribute the books themselves. A regional or national advertiser can purchase space on matchbook covers through a sales agent or service agency, who will then see to the distribution of the matchbooks through established trade channels. Advertising rates are based on the quantity of matchbooks ordered, with the minimum order typically one or two million. The space available on each standard-size cover is 96 agate lines—51 outside and 45 inside. Advertising on the outside cover may use up to four colors, but inside space requires the use of only one color. Studies indicate that 99% of all smokers carry matchbooks at one time or another and that 45% of those carrying matchbooks can name the advertisers on the books they are carrying.

**MATCHCODE** alphanumeric code used to sequence and identify RECORDS on a computer file; also called KEYLINE. Matchcodes are usually created from portions of the name and address FIELDS and typically include a CHECK DIGIT and/or a TIEBREAKER—that is, a randomly assigned number that prevents the assignment of a duplicate matchcode to two or more records with similar names and addresses. The matchcode is printed on customer-reply documents such as ORDER FORMS, INVOICES, and questionnaires, as well as on mailing LABELS, to make it easier to locate the correct record when the documents are returned for processing.

Matchcodes are a more reliable means of locating a record than name and address because people have a tendency to sign their names illegibly or to vary their name and address slightly when they correspond. For example, George W. Green at 123 Main Street could also be Dr. G. William Green at P.O. Box 456, and he may indiscriminately use one address or the other when ordering or corresponding. If his matchcode is also on the correspondence, the record can easily be identified.

A drawback to using a matchcode system is that the matchcode changes each time the customer's address or name is permanently changed. The marketer then loses the ability to track a customer's purchase history over long periods of time. For example, when Jane Doe marries and becomes Jane Green and submits an order to the marketer, she is assigned a new matchcode based on her new last name. The computer can't tell that they are the same person and treats Jane Green as a FIRST-TIME BUYER. This problem can be solved by assigning, instead of a matchcode, a random customer number (an account number) that can stay with the customer despite changes in name or address. This account number system will work only if customers diligently submit their customer number with all correspondence.

**MATCHED DISSOLVE** in film or videotape production, a DISSOLVE where the image that fades in closely resembles the image that has faded out (*see* FADE-IN; FADE-OUT). This is accomplished when each of the cameras to be used in the dissolve are set up so that their shots match. For example, if each camera is focused on an individual face, and each subject is in the same position, the matched dissolve will produce an effect where one person's face and features are slowly transformed into the other person's face and features.

**MATCHED SAMPLE** sample group for test purposes that is the same as another group in terms of size, DEMOGRAPHICS, and PSYCHOGRAPHICS. Matched samples are used in advertising research to reinforce results, as controls of one another, or to test variations of a product or communication. Two or more matched samples may be given different stimuli to test reactions, or they may be given the same stimuli to see if the groups will test the same way.

**MATRIX**
1. paper mold of a printing plate made from a type form; also called *mat*. A matrix is used primarily for newspaper reproductions where the advertiser needs an inexpensive duplicate and wants to preserve the original for future use. *See also* STEREOTYPE.
2. small brass mold of a type character, used in the machine casting of type.

**MAT SERVICE** business that specializes in the production of matrices (*see* MATRIX) and the supplying of them to newspapers.

**MATTE FINISH** paper finish that is dull, lacking luster or gloss.

**MATTE PRINT** *see* MATTE FINISH.

**MAXIMUM DEPTH REQUIREMENT** maximum height or depth a print advertisement may be to claim a fractional column rate, rather than be charged a full column rate.

**McKITTRICK'S DIRECTORY** directory of advertising agencies published four times a year that lists the agency, the names and positions of its staff, and accounts handled by the agency.

**MCU** medium close-up. *See* CLOSE-UP.

**MEAD** BRAND NAME of INK-JET PRINTER that produces 1-UP labels at approximately 180,000 LABELS per hour. Only four Mead printers had been built by late 1986. They are used by three of the largest magazine mailers: Time, Inc., Newsweek, and Neodata Services.

**MEAN** arithmetic average calculated by summing a set of values and dividing by the number of values in the set. The mean is frequently confused with the MEDIAN or MODE. The mean of $4 + 8 + 6 + 12$ equals $30/4$, or $7^1/2$. Mean is a good representation of quantitative data, such as the mean number of items purchased per catalog order or the mean dollar value of each order. Qualitative data, such as the item purchased most often from a catalog, is better suited to a mode calculation.

**MEASURE** width of a line of type defining the number of characters that may be set in the space available; usually expressed in PICAS (sixths of an inch). A typical book has 40 lines per page, with 50 to 75 characters per line.

**MECHANICAL** camera-ready *paste-up* of artwork and copy on a sheet of white cardboard or posterboard, which includes all the elements to be reproduced, such as set type, photographs, illustrations, drawings, and line art. The name refers to the fact that the production of the mechanical is a mechanical process that involves only the cutting, trimming, and pasting of previously prepared artwork and copy.

Mechanical

**MECHANICAL PULP**  *see* GROUNDWOOD PULP.

**MEDIA**  channels of communication that serve many diverse functions, such as offering a variety of entertainment with either mass or specialized appeal, communicating news and information, or displaying advertising messages. The media carry the advertisers' messages and serve as the vital link between the seller of a product or service and the consumer.

Available types of media include print, electronic, out-of-home, and direct mail. Print usually refers to newspapers and magazines but also includes directories, school and church yearbooks and newsletters, and programs at sporting events and theater presentations. Electronic media are usually referred to as broadcast media, or radio and television, including cable. Out-of-home media are designed almost exclusively to serve only an advertising function, and include billboards, transit advertising, and posters in public places such as stadiums, airports, and train stations, as well as flying banners (banners towed by airplanes) and skywriting. Direct-mail media are advertisements that are mailed directly to prospects. As technology advances, new forms of media are being discovered every day, such as movie-house advertising and special automatic telephone devices with prerecorded advertising messages. Any single form of communication is known as a *medium.*

**MEDIA ASSOCIATION**  organization whose membership consists of persons affiliated with a particular form of media, such as a daily newspaper, and whose purpose is to build acceptance for that medium. Media associations include the AMERICAN NEWSPAPER PUBLISHERS ASSOCIATION, AMERICAN BUSINESS PRESS, AGRICULTURAL PUBLISHERS ASSOCIATION, and Transit Advertising Association. There are a great many of these associations, with at least one for almost every form of media.

**MEDIA BUY**  purchase of time or space in an advertising medium, such as radio, television, or print space. The media-buy decision is based upon the amount of money available, the number of EXPOSURES desired, the TARGET MARKET the advertiser wants to reach, the FREQUENCY of exposure desired, the number of people each medium will reach, and the impact each medium will have on the MESSAGE— for example, the impact of a fashion advertisement in a fashion magazine versus one in a magazine about fishing. Since there is no one right way to spend advertising dollars, it is the MEDIA BUYER'S job to choose a reasonable optimum. *See also* MEDIA CLASS; MEDIA OPTION; MEDIA PLAN; MEDIA WEIGHT; MULTIMEDIA; ONE-SHOT; VEHICLE.

**MEDIA BUYER**  individual responsible for the purchase of time and space for the delivery of advertising messages in the media. A media buyer may be an employee of an advertising agency who specializes in such purchases, but, technically, a media buyer is any advertiser, advertising manager, or individual who buys the commercial time or the advertising space. In some large agencies, the purchase of advertising media has become quite specialized, and there are those who purchase only broadcast time *(time buyers)*, others who purchase only print space *(space buyers)*, and still others who purchase only outdoor space *(outdoor space buyers)*. In any case, the overall nomenclature is that of *media buyer*.

**MEDIA BUYING SERVICE** agency that specializes in media buying services. *See* ADVERTISING AGENCY; MEDIA BUYER.

**MEDIA CLASS** type of media, as compared to a particular VEHICLE. For example, magazines are a media class, whereas *Good Housekeeping* magazine is a vehicle.

**MEDIA FLIGHTING** practice of skipping intervals in the presentation of advertising in the media. Advertisers contract with the media to present advertising for a prescribed period of time, skip some time, and then present the advertising again for a prescribed period of time. Media flighting is generally done when advertising budgets are limited as a means of stretching the advertising campaign over a longer time period than would be possible given the limited budget. Suppose an advertising budget will only allow for six weeks of media advertising at posted rates. Advertisers can schedule one or two weeks of advertising at a time, and by skipping a week in between each week or two of advertising, the six-week campaign can be stretched to a nine-week campaign.

**MEDIA INSERTION SCHEDULE** *see* INSERTION SCHEDULE.

**MEDIA KIT** packet of materials put together by a specific advertising medium that contains information about the costs of advertising in the medium along with information about the medium's audience. In the case of print media, specifications for camera-ready artwork to be included with advertising are also included in the kit.

**MEDIAMARK RESEARCH, INC. (MRI)** market research firm that provides marketers with consumer statistics (DEMOGRAPHICS, LIFESTYLE, purchase habits) broken down by 2400 groups of residential neighborhoods across the country called "clusters." Data is collected annually from a sample of 20,000 households, using a combination of PERSONAL INTERVIEWS and QUESTIONNAIRES regarding print and broadcast viewing, demographics, and product and brand usage. The questions concern which magazines the respondents have read recently, which radio or television programs they have viewed recently, and which products they have purchased recently. MRI also provides an estimate of the number of times a reader is exposed to the same page of advertising in a publication he picks up to read more than once. In addition, MRI provides reader action measures, such as the number of readers who clip coupons or articles or return BINGO CARDS.

**MEDIA MIX** combination of media to be used in an advertising campaign. In the past, television and magazines dominated the media mixes of most national advertising campaigns because these media reached the broadest segments of the market. However, in recent years, CLUTTER, rising advertising costs, and smaller audiences have caused advertisers to seek more cost-efficient avenues for their advertising dollars. Consequently, media mixes may now include vehicles such as telephone directories, cable television, ballpark billboards, supermarket shopping carts, and other forms of media that may reach a narrower market segment but cost less and target more effectively.

**MEDIAN** middle value in a range of values arranged in sequence by size. For example, the median of 6, 3, 9, 2, 12, 3, 54 is 6, determined by arranging the numbers in the following sequence: 2, 3, 3, 6, 9, 12, 54. A median can give a good feel for the range of a set of values, such as a median value of $50 for catalog orders, indicating that half the purchases made were more (or less) than $50. *See also* MEAN; MODE.

**MEDIA OPTION** specific description of the characteristics of an advertisement or commercial excluding the copy and artwork. The media option will detail the size (full page, half page, etc.), color (black-andwhite, or four-color), and location (inside front cover, interior, etc.) of a print advertisement, or the length (60, 30, 10 seconds, etc.) and placement (morning drive, prime time, etc.) of a broadcast commercial. Media options are generally listed in a MEDIA PLAN.

**MEDIA PLANNER** advertising agency employee in the media department who is responsible for the planning of media to be used in an advertising campaign. The primary function of the job is to match the TARGET AUDIENCE in each campaign with the appropriate media. The media planner will identify the desired target audience (from the advertiser's or account executive's input) and then make media selections based on the profiles of the various available media while also evaluating the media in terms of cost. The planner will make client recommendations as to the medium or combination of media that will best reach the target audience and meet the media objectives. In a smaller agency, the media planner is also the MEDIA BUYER, but larger agencies will have a staff of buyers usually grouped according to MEDIA CLASSES.

**MEDIA PLANNING** process of designing the objectives and strategies for the use of media in a marketing program and selecting the media that will most effectively and efficiently reach the intended audience for an advertiser's product. *See also* MEDIA PLAN.

**MEDIA REACH** size of audience exposed (*see* EXPOSURE) to an advertisement through a particular MEDIUM. For example, the media reach of a television commercial could be millions of viewers, but the potential media reach of a local newspaper advertisement could be only hundreds of people.

Reach is difficult to measure precisely. There are usually many more readers per copy of a magazine or newspaper than the number of copies sold. Estimates go as high as 4.5 readers per copy for a particular publication. The A. C. NIELSEN COMPANY measures the number of television sets tuned to a program based on a sample, but many more or fewer people may actually be watching. Some marketers attempt to get a true measure of reach by asking people what they remember viewing or reading. *See also* DIARY TECHNIQUE; NIELSEN RATING; PEOPLE METER.

**MEDIA SURVEY** study conducted about the media, among the general public to determine the depth of PENETRATION of the communications media and to what extent the media reaches a particular market or audience.

**MEDIA WEIGHT** volume of audience delivered by an advertising campaign in terms of the number of commercials and advertisements, amount of insertions, time parameters, and budget; the total audience delivery.

**MEDIUM**
1. *see* MEDIA.
2. method, instrument, or material used by an artist in the creation of a work, such as a pen-and-ink drawing, or oil paints, or photography.

**MEDIUM CLOSE-UP (MCU)** *see* CLOSE-UP.

**MEDIUM SHOT** in photography, film, or videotape production, shot where the subject and background share equal dominance in the picture. A medium shot of an individual will take in the body from the knees or waist up.

**MEGAHERTZ** in radio transmission, frequency unit equal to one million hertz, which is a unit of frequency equal to one *cycle per second;* abbreviated MHZ.

**MEGATHON** large-scale FUND-RAISING campaign, usually national in scope, involving several INBOUND TELEPHONE operations receiving pledges—for example, the 1986 Hands Across America campaign. The term *megathon* was coined by George W. Smith of Telemarketing Corporation of America. A megathon differs from a telethon in that it involves more than one inbound telephone operation.

**MEMBER** one who is associated with an organization by virtue of payment of a fee, by profession, by expression of allegiance, or by participation in working toward the goals of the organization. Direct-mail club members usually commit to making a specified number or value of purchases over a specific period of time. *See also* BOOK CLUB; COMPLETED CANCEL.

**MEMBER COMMITMENT** terms that a new club member or a continuity MEMBER agrees to fulfill as a condition of membership, such as purchasing three books in two years; also called *customer* *commitment, commit.* This protects the marketer from losses incurred in selling the membership. For example, many book clubs will give new members three books for one dollar, at which point the new membership has cost the marketer the wholesale value of three books less one dollar. (Shipping and handling costs are typically paid by the new member.) The marketer begins to recover his costs and make a profit when the member purchases additional books at the full member price. *See also* BOOK CLUB; CONTINUITY; COMPLETED CANCEL.

**MEMBER-GET-A-MEMBER (MGM)** organization or customer recruitment technique that offers an incentive to current members for referring new members. For example, BOOK CLUB MGM promotions offer discounts on books to members who successfully recruit new members. *See also* FRIEND-OF-A-FRIEND.

**MEMBER LIFE** number of promotion cycles an average club MEMBER remains a member before cancellation of his membership. For example, a BOOK CLUB that sends an average of 60 monthly promotions to its members has a member life of 60. The length of the member life is a measure of the fiscal health of the club, as it is a primary determinant of sales revenue and profitability per member. *See also* MEMBER COMMITMENT.

**MEMORY UNIT** section of a computer where programmed information is stored.

**MERCHANDISING**
1. "The planning involved in marketing the right merchandise or service at the right place, at the right time, in the right quantities, and at the right price." (American Marketing Association)
2. promotional sales activities of an advertiser's sales force, retailers, wholesalers, or dealers, including advertising, point-of-purchase displays, guarantee seals, special sales, and in-store promotions, designed to show a product or service in a favorable light so that it will be purchased by the business community and/or the consuming public.
3. retail selling effort that is the principal task of in-store sales personnel through the use of promotions designed by a manufacturer, such as unique displays, giveaways, or discount and premium offers. In this case, merchandising is the act of managing and arranging the merchandise on display in a store so as to promote its sale.

**MERCHANDISING ALLOWANCE** reduction of the wholesale price as an incentive to retailers or middlemen. A promotional allowance compensates the retailer for expenditures made promoting the product. *See also* ALLOWANCE; BINDER ALLOWANCE.

**MERCHANDISING DIRECTOR** individual responsible for directing the merchandise sales effort for a manufacturer, retailer, wholesaler, distributor, dealer, or advertising agency. *See also* MERCHANDISING.

**MERCHANDISING SERVICE** merchandising help offered by any of the communications media. Such offer will include suggestions for optimum positioning of advertising, copy, and layout suggestions to best appeal to the medium's audience, and the sharing of information about the medium's market. A merchandising service is usually a normal function of most of the communications media and is typically offered to advertisers at no additional charge.

**MERGE**
1. combine two or more LISTS or files by combining duplicate RECORDS into single records. Merging is normally done in conjunction with a purging process that eliminates undesirable names. *See also* MERGE/PURGE.
2. financially combine two companies so that only one of the companies survives as a legal entity.

**MERGE/PURGE** process of combining two or more LISTS or files, simultaneously identifying and/or combining DUPLICATES and eliminating unwanted RECORDS such as DEADBEATS and NIXIES. The purpose of the merge/purge is to provide a mailer with the best possible list of names to which to mail a promotion. The INPUT to a merge/purge consists of all of the lists the mailer has rented and several other lists he has created or rented. A common practice is to use one's own customer list (HOUSE list) as a PURGE file, so that promotions intended to generate new customers are not sent to existing customers. Many mailers also maintain their own list of deadbeats and nixies they will purge from the list.

The merge/purge program describes how the mailer wishes to identify duplicates and how he wants to allocate deductions for duplicates to the various rented lists. LIST RENTALS are usually based on the number of names remaining after the merge/purge; thus, each LIST OWNER has an interest in having duplicates fairly allocated so that no one owner is excessively penalized.

The OUTPUT of the merge/purge is usually on mailing LABELS but may be on MAGNETIC TAPE, depending on how the LIST USER intends to promote the list. In addition to labels, reports are generated showing how many names were input and output by list, and sometimes by LIST BROKER. A FINDER NUMBER is sometimes assigned during the merge/purge process.

*See also* DEDUPE; LIST RENTAL; MULTIBUYER; NET NAME ARRANGEMENT; PRIORITY LIST.

**MESSAGE** primary element of the COMMUNICATION process, consisting of the information passed from the COMMUNICATOR to the RECEIVER, such as the message of a television commercial or magazine advertisement. For example, the message of an aspirin commercials is usually that the product will relieve pain quicker than other products.

Marshall McLuhan's phrase "The medium is the message" illustrates his thinking that the medium that delivers a message impacts how a message is perceived. For example, an advertisement appearing in the *New York Times* may he perceived as more credible than an identical ad in a small local newspaper.

**MESSAGE DEVELOPMENT**  process of creating the advertising message. Advertisers must first determine the desired audience response and then develop the advertising message to achieve that response. Desired audience response may be to heighten awareness of a product, service, or general situation, or to inspire an audience action such as voting for a candidate, placing a telephone order, or going out and purchasing a particular product. In the creation of the advertising message, message developers talk to competitors, dealers, and potential customers and then engage in brainstorming techniques to try to imagine using the product and determine the benefits sought. The advertising message is very important to the success of the advertising campaign. It must attract audience attention and communicate effectively.

**METER**

**Direct mail:** apply postage to a mailing piece through the use of a U.S. Postal Service authorized meter (or METER STRIP) that stamps an image onto the envelope identifying the mailer and the amount of postage due. It is faster and more efficient to machine-meter large volumes of mail than to apply a postage stamp to each piece. The Postal Service charges postage based on the number of meter impressions made, according to a count recorded hy the meter machine. A USPS auditor is sent periodically to personally inspect the meters and ensure that the usage quantities reported by the mailer are accurate. *See also* INSERTER, LETTERSHOP; METER STRIP.

**Market research:** device used to measure a behavior, such as television viewing, of research participants. *See also* DIARY TECHNIQUE; PEOPLE METER.

**METERED MAIL**  *see* METER

**METER STRIP**  adhesive-backed label roll upon which a postage-METER imprint is stamped. The roll is cut and pasted to mailing pieces, either mechanically or manually, in lieu of a postage stamp or direct meter imprint. Small advertisements are sometimes included on the meter strip.

**ME-TOO PRODUCT** tactic of a market FOLLOWER who attempts to avoid losing market share to a competitor by offering a product that is a copy of a competitor's product or INNOVATION. For example, many followers in the liquid dish detergent market have offered their own versions of a clear detergent in response to an innovator's clear product. It may cost more than the follower can reasonably afford to execute this strategy since heavy advertising expenditures are required to step out of the innovator's shadow.

**ME-TOO RESPONSE** tactic of a market FOLLOWER who attempts to avoid losing market share to a competitor by imitating the actions of a competitor. For example, the follower might respond to a competitor's price decrease by decreasing its own price. It is usually necessary to spend a considerable amount on advertising and promotion to draw attention to a me-too response in order to get some benefit from it. It is also a dangerous tactic to pursue because the follower may not have the same economic or budget justification as the competitor for the me-too response.

**METRIC SYSTEM** system of measuring size, weight, and volume, based upon decimal units. The basic metric system units are grams, meters, and liters. One gram = 0.035 ounce. One meter = 39.37 inches. One liter = 61.025 cubic inches (cubic capacity), 0.908 quart (dry measure), or 1.057 quarts (liquid measure).

All nations of the world with the exception of the United States and two very small countries use the metric system. The U.S. reluctance to conform with these worldwide standards makes it difficult to market packaged goods globally. For example, a consumer abroad accustomed to buying in liter or gram quantities will not understand a package label that uses quarts or ounces. Also, food package recipes cannot be easily translated from teaspoons and cups to grams and liters as required for non-U.S. cooking utensils. However, for international marketing, the expense of printing metric versions of labels and packages is a costly necessity.

**METRO AREA** metropolitan area that is the central core of a MARKET. The metro areas throughout the United States are based on designations of the federal government as prepared by the Office of Management and Budget from the most recent census. A metro area, named a METROPOLITAN STATISTICAL AREA by the government, always includes a city of 50,000 population or more as the central core (from whence all broadcast originates), the county in which it is located, and the surrounding counties that share a high degree of economic and social integration with the central core city. Metro areas are used by the various rating services, such as A.D. NIELSON COMPANY or Arbitron *(see* ARBITRON RATINGS COMPANY), in the computation of RATINGS and SHARES.

**METROPOLITAN STATISTICAL AREA (MSA)** United States Bureau of the Census term for an area consisting of one or more counties around a central urban area with 50,000 or more inhabitants and with minimal agricultural employment. An MSA contains either a city of 50,000 population or an urbanized area of 50,000 population with a total population of 100,000, although its population can exceed one-million. In 1992, there were 263 MSAs in the United States, excluding CONSOLIDATED METROPOLITAN STATISTICAL AREAS. The United States Bureau of the Census also classifies urban areas into Consolidated Metropolitan Statistical Areas (CMSAs) and PRIMARY METROPOLITAN STATISTICAL AREAS. *See also* METRO AREA.

**METRO RATING** TELEVISION HOUSEHOLDS in a METRO AREA tuned in to a particular station or program, computed as a percentage of all the television households in the metro area.

**MICROCOMPUTER** small- to medium-capacity computer that utilizes microchip technology to perform some of the functions of a large computer at a lower cost, uses a high-level programming language that is easy to learn, and is encased in a relatively small cabinet that does not require special temperature or antistatic controls; also called *personal computer* or PC. The scope and range of microcomputer capabilities broadens every day as SOFTWARE becomes more sophisticated, but are largely dependent upon the data-storage capacity of each computer. Microcomputers can be used to analyze response to promotions, to perform word processing and composition functions, to generate mailing labels, to assist with GRAPHIC DESIGN, and so forth. Microcomputers can also serve as remote TERMINALS providing access to a large computer. *See also* MAINFRAME; MINICOMPUTER.

**MICROENVIRONMENT** elements close to a company that impact the company's ability to serve its customers. There are six components of the microenvironment: the company's internal environment, composed of the management personnel and including the finance, purchasing, manufacturing, research and development, and marketing departments; the company's suppliers, who provide the goods and services necessary for the production of the company's products; the marketing intermediaries, composed of all the individuals or companies who help in the promotion, selling, and distribution of the company's products; the customers, consisting of the five types of markets in which the company may sell its products (consumer, industrial, reseller, government, and international markets); the company's competitors; and the company's various publics, which can be any individual or group that can affect the company's ability to achieve its objectives, such as citizen action groups, the media, or the government. *See also* MACROENVIRONMENT.

**MICROFICHE** HARD-COPY printout of a microfilm GALLEY. Microfiche must be read with a special magnifying screen. It is frequently used to store customer file data and/or to DUPLICATE customer files so that copies can be distributed to customer-service clerks.

**MICROMARKETING**   designing, creating, and manufacturing products, marketing strategies, and advertising campaigns for the benefit of very specific geographic, demographic, or psychographic segments of the consumer market. Micromarketing is a relatively new marketing trend created by the diversity of the consumer population and the difficulty in creating a single product that appeals to all the diverse groups in the population. Also, improved technological research abilities (such as supermarket scanners) have enabled marketers to pinpoint which specific market segments are buying what products, and retailers have come to prefer localized marketing promotions directed toward the characteristics of the population in the neighborhoods of their retail outlets.

**MICROPHONE**   instrument that causes sound waves to generate electric current, resulting in the amplification of the sounds; also called *mike*. Microphones are usually used for the transmission or the recording of sounds, such as music or voices.

**MIDDLEMAN**   intermediary within a CHANNEL OF DISTRIBUTION used to transfer products from the manufacturer to the end user. Those who actually take title to the products and resell them are *merchant middlemen*. Those who act as BROKERS but do not take title are agent *middlemen*. Merchant middlemen include wholesalers and retailers. Agent middlemen include MANUFACTURER'S REPRESENTATIVES, brokers, and sales agents. Middlemen expand the capacity of the manufacturer to distribute products to the end user, transfer title between channel levels, collect payments from middlemen and end users, and communicate product information to all channel participants. When the financial and expert resources are available in house, manufacturers can increase their profit margins by reducing the involvement of middlemen. *See also* FORWARD INTEGRATION.

**MIDDLE TONES**   gray areas in a photographic print that lend contours and dimension to an image otherwise consisting only of HIGHLIGHTS and SHADOWS.

**MILKING STRATEGY**   short-range marketing strategy planned to take the largest possible profit from an item in the shortest amount of time without regard to the item's long-range possibilities for sales. Milking strategies are adopted when budgets are low and the need for funds in other operational areas, such as research and development, is great. The idea behind a milking strategy is to use the profits from one item to develop other products that are believed to have greater profit potential.

**MILLER-TYDINGS FAIR TRADE ACT**   1937 amendment to the SHERMAN ACT that exempted from antitrust laws any interstate price-fixing agreements concerning trademarked or brand name products; also called FAIR TRADE LAW. The intent of the Miller-Tydings Act was to address concerns about big chains pushing out small retailers through LOSS LEADER pricing. The Miller-Tydings Act gave manufacturers control over the prices charged by retailers. The Miller-Tydings Act was repealed in 1975 by the Consumer Goods Pricing Act. Today, the only price protection the manufacturer has is the suggested list price, which can't be legally enforced. *See also* CLAYTON ACT; ROBINSON-PATMAN ACT.

**MILLINE RATE**   cost per milline *(milline is* equivalent to one agate line of space per 1,000,000 circulation) based on the circulation of a newspaper. Because it takes the circulation into consideration, the milline rate is used to compare the cost effectiveness of advertising in one newspaper over another. It is computed by the following formula:

$$\frac{\text{rate per agate line} \times 1,000,000}{\text{circulation}} = \text{milline rate}$$

**MIMEOGRAPH**   image duplication technique utilizing a porous image carrier through which ink is forced. Mimeograph machines were typically used for low-volume offset duplication and have been almost completely replaced by PHOTOCOPY machines. Special 20 lb. paper measuring 17" × 22" was used.

**MINICOMPUTER**   medium-capacity computer that is larger than a MICROCOMPUTER but smaller than most MAINFRAMES A minicomputer can handle a larger amount of data than a microcomputer and can perform most of the functions of a mainframe.

**MINIMUM DEPTH REQUIREMENT**   requirement of most newspapers that advertisements be in proportion. Generally, advertisements must be an inch in height (depth) for every column in width. Therefore, if an advertisement is four columns wide, it must also be four inches high.

**MINIMUM THICKNESS**   U.S. Postal Service requirement for postcard paper stock. It must be at least .007 inches thick to be accepted by the USPS for handling.

**MINISERIES**   television drama serialized for at least 2 episodes but for less than the standard 13-week season. One of the more famous miniseries was the dramatization of Alex Haley's book *Roots,* which night after night drew a very large audience SHARE and rewarded advertisers with a much larger than anticipated audience for their commercials.

**MINOR CIVIL DIVISION**   U.S. Bureau of the Census term for a governmental subdivision of a county, such as town or township, with a population of approximately 25,000 people.

**MISDIRECT**   FULFILLMENT industry term for a document that has been routed incorrectly during processing.

**MISLEADING SILENCE** subtle form of deceptive advertising where the advertising is silent about some aspect of the advertised product. The Federal Trade Commission may consider this type of silence to be incomplete disclosure that can lead to a misconception about the product, and will, therefore, frown upon its use.

**MISSIONARY SALESPERSON** *see* DETAIL PERSON.

**MIX**
1. in recording or broadcast, combination of different sound elements, such as music, direct voice, sound effects, announcer voice, or singing voice, into a sound track for radio and television commercials or programs or audio recordings.
2. in television broadcast, combination of programs in a television contract for a series. For example, a contract for a 13-week series may call for 13 original performances, or it may call for 9 original and 4 rerun performances, or any combination of originals and reruns.
3. in retailing, combination of merchandise in a retail package or the entire variety of inventory of a retailer, wholesaler, or distributor.
4. combination of products, including various sizes of the same product, for a particular brand in a given store.
5. *see* MARKETING MIX.

**MIXED PROVINCES** Canadian equivalent of a MIXED STATES sack. It contains presorted mail destined for several provinces that cannot be sorted to a finer level because of low volumes across a wide range of addresses. *See also* PRESORT.

**MIXED ROUTE FIVE-DIGIT SACK** SACK of presorted mail *(see* PRESORT) destined for a particular FIVE-DIGIT ZIP CODE area that has been sorted into CARRIER-ROUTE packages of 10 or more pieces.

**MIXED STATES** SACK of presorted mail destined for more than one state that cannot be sorted to a finer level because of low volumes across a wide range of destination addresses. *See also* PRESORT.

**MM**
1. abbreviation for 1 million; used after a slash mark to express a price or rate per million units. For example, 500/MM might indicate that 500 responses were received for every million surveys mailed. *See also* M.
2. abbreviation for one millimeter. *See also* METRIC SYSTEM.

**MOBILE UNIT**
1. television filming and recording facilities capable of moving or of being moved from location to location with relative ease and speed, used most frequently by the news departments of television stations.
2. research facilities, libraries, blood banks, and the like, built into trailers that can be pulled by truck or driven under their own power from place to place as the demand arises. Mobile units such as these are often located in shopping-center parking lots because of the high volume of traffic in these locations.

## MODE
1. statistical value equal to the most frequent value in a series of values. For example, the mode of 1, 2, 3, 4, 4, 5, 7 is 4. When evaluating product preferences reported by a PANEL of consumers, the mode is a more meaningful measure of preference than the MEAN. Assume, for example, that in a test of three muffins 20 out of 40 consumers prefer the taste (i.e., the amount of sugar) of muffin 1, and the other 20 consumers prefer the taste of muffin 3. By calculating the mean ( $(20 \times 1 \bullet 20 \times 3) /40 = 2$), you would arrive at the false conclusion that the amount of sugar in muffin 2 is preferred. Calculation of the mode provides the correct conclusion that muffins 1 and 3 have equal appeal but that muffin 2 does not appeal to anyone.
2. highest point in a bar GRAPH or histogram.
3. operating environment of a computer, such as OFF-LINE/on-line, BATCH, and so forth.

**MODEL** computer-based system that uses mathematical formulas to help marketers make better marketing decisions. A model represents some real system, process, or outcome and is used to answer hypothetical questions of "what if?" or "which is best?" Over the past 20 years, scientists have developed numerous models that are used by marketing managers to forecast new product sales and to determine MARKETING MIX combinations, the design of sales territories and sales call plans, the best sites for retail outlets, and the optimal advertising mixes. *See also* CIRCULATION MODULE; FINANCIAL MODELING.

**MODELED LIST** collection of name and address records that is segmented into groups of consumers, or *clusters*, with shared characteristics. Modeling breaks a list into segments via a computerized process that appends demographic, psychographic, and other data from other sources to each name and address record and then separates the resultant list into segments with similar data profiles. Segments from modeled lists are selected for promotions that are expected to appeal to consumers with that characteristics profile. For example, all single men earning more than $50,000 and living in an urban area might constitute a target list segment for *GQ* magazine. *See also* CLUSTER ANALYSIS; LIST; OVERLAY.

**MODEM** device that links computer systems via telephone lines enabling computers in different locations to exchange information; short for modulator-demodulator. Modems convert telephone impulses to computer-interpretable impulses. There must be a modem at each end of the communications link to either send or receive converted impulses. Modems can be used to transmit mailing LISTS or LIST RENTAL instructions, to access customer FILES from a remote location, to submit last-minute print advertisement copy to a publication, and so forth.

## MOIRE
**Printing:** undesirable effect found in a HALFTONE print caused by the conflict of the ruled lines on the halftone screen and some pattern in the original copy to be reproduced.

**Television production:** undesirable color patterns that appear on the television screen when certain designs, such as stripes or checks on fabrics or graphics, come into conflict with the television's scanning system.

## MOM AND POP STORE
**1.** small business owned and operated by one family.

**2.** any very small retail business.

**MONEY COPY**  paid-CIRCULATION copies of a periodical for which the publisher has actually received money, as distinguished from circulation considered paid but for which money is never received (for example, GRACE issues, END-OF-MONTH-FREE copies, or copies served in response to a CLAIMS-PAID COMPLAINT).

**MONEY ORDER**  negotiable instrument issued by a bank or post office for a specified amount of money. Since the financial responsibility of the bank or the U.S. Postal Service is behind the check, there is no question of its being good. Money orders are often included in direct-mail orders from individuals without checking accounts, who do not want to send currency through the mail.

## MONITOR
**1.** instrument used to audit something, as a RECEIVER used in a television studio to view the picture being picked up by the camera, or HARDWARE that displays the operations of a computer system.

**2.** using a RECEIVER to listen to or view a radio or television broadcast to check fidelity and quality, as well as content.

**3.** regulate or control, from a control booth, the production of a radio or television show or an audio recording session.

**MONOPOLY**  situation in which one and only one company produces and/or sells a particular product or service. Monopolies occur in the United States if a company has a patent on a product or a process it invented or if a company is a public utility. In the case of public utilities, all marketing plans and charges must be approved by the government. In privately owned companies where monopolies occur, the marketer's challenge is to maintain the uniqueness of the product while at the same time discouraging other companies from entering the market. *See also* MONOPSONY; OLIGOPOLY.

**MONOPSONY**  situation in which there is only one major buyer in a region for products supplied by a number of vendors. For example, the Federal Government is a monopsony in the United States for machine guns or F-16s. *See also* MONOPOLY, OLIGOPOLY.

## MONTAGE

**Art:** drawings, illustrations, photographs, or the like that have been cut in various shapes and sizes and pasted on an artboard at different angles to each other or overlapped so that the combination presents an individual impression or tells a story. Montages are used as murals and for special effects in print advertisements.

**Television production:** series of images shown in rapid succession, used to effect a particular mood or to suggest a chain of events or the passage of time.

**Radio production:** series of sounds blended together in sequence and used in the same manner as a television montage.

**MORNING DRIVE** radio-broadcasting time segment from 6:00 A.M. to 10:00 A.M. Monday to Friday. This time period, along with AFTERNOON DRIVE time (3:00 P.M. to 7:00 P.M.), is considered to be radio's PRIME TIME, the time segment that draws the largest listening audience. *See also* DAYPART.

**MORTISE** groove or slot cut out of a section of a PRINTING PLATE for the purpose of inserting another smaller plate (with type or engraved artwork or the like on it) into it so that both may be printed together. A mortise is often used in the reproduction of regional advertisements where the basic copy will remain the same but dates, locations, or prices will differ from region to region. If the opening is cut into a corner or side of the printing plate and is therefore not surrounded by the plate, it is more properly called a *notch.*

**MOTION PICTURE FILM** film used exclusively for the production of motion pictures. Generally, 35-millimeter film is used for feature films, but, in the case of wide-screen presentations, 70-millimeter film is used. *See also* EIGHT MILLIMETER; FILM; SIXTEEN MILLIMETER; THIRTY-FIVE MILLIMETER.

**MOTIVATIONAL RESEARCH** studies conducted in order to determine the motivations behind consumer purchases. The research is psychologically oriented and attempts to learn why people behave as they do, why they make certain purchases, and why they respond to specific types of advertising appeals. The resultant information is used by advertisers and advertising agencies to plan new products, develop advertising campaigns, and, in general, to create more effective advertising.

**MOTIVATION THEORY** psychological discipline that attempts to describe why people or animals behave as they do solely in terms of internal needs that drive behavior, rather than attributing any influence to external stimuli. For example, someone may choose to dine in an elegant restaurant because of an internal drive such as hunger or the need for self-esteem, but not because he saw a neon sign saying "Eat here." Marketers study motivation theory so that their promotions can be designed to appeal to the internal forces that presumably are a powerful influence on buying behavior—more powerful than external stimuli. For example, you wouldn't see an advertisement that says "Buy this perfume and smell good." You do see advertisements that say "Buy this perfume and have all your needs for love, sex, and romance [social interaction] fulfilled. DEPTH INTERVIEWS are used in MARKETING RESEARCH to probe into the hidden motivations behind people's behavior as consumers. *See also* APPEAL; MARKETING CONCEPT.

**MOTORIZED CARRIER**  residential mail carrier who travels along his route in a mail truck instead of on foot.

**MOTORIZED ROUTE**  *see* MOTORIZED CARRIER

**MOTTLE**
  1. splotchy pattern that can be printed on paper, usually in a single color of ink, for an aesthetic effect. It can be created manually by applying ink to paper with a sponge.
  2. splotchy pattern on a printed image caused by some error in the printing process.

**MOVIEOLA**  instrument used for editing film.

**MOVING SHOT**  in motion picture or television production, technique used to give the audience a feeling of motion by moving the camera along with the action, as a scene depicting a moving automobile, shot by a camera attached to the automobile and moving along with it. A familiar example of this technique is the famous chase scene in the movie *The French Connection,* in which the audience members actually felt as if they were in the chase because the scene was filmed through a camera inside the fast-moving car.

**MULLEN TESTER**  device used to measure the BURSTING strength of paper.

**MULTIBRAND STRATEGY**  sale of two or more competing brands by the same marketer. For example, the various dishwashing liquids made by Procter & Gamble to appeal to different segments of the market for that product. Marketers who use a multibrand strategy acquire greater market share than they could with fewer brands, even though one of their brands may somewhat CANNIBALIZE another. Multiple brands also enable marketers to acquire more shelf space and to respond to consumer demand for something new. In some companies, competition between their brand managers is believed to hone their skills. The key is to recognize the optimal number of brands that will deliver more benefit than it costs. There are diminishing returns as the number of brands increase. Cost efficiencies due to economies of scale decrease as production volumes are spread across a greater number of brands, and brand cannibalization increases.

**MULTIBUYER**  DUPLICATE record on two or more CUSTOMER LISTS, indicating that the person has made purchases from each LIST OWNER;

also called *multiple buyer.* Multibuyers may be moved to a special propensity to buy.

**MULTICODED CITY** large city with more than one FIVE-DIGIT ZIP CODE area.

**MULTICOLLINEARITY** existence of a relationship between the INDEPENDENT VARIABLES in a MULTIPLE REGRESSION—that is, a change in one variable causes a change in the other variable. Together, they cause a change in the DEPENDENT VARIABLE(S).

**MULTIDIMENSIONAL SCALING** popular survey research tool used to ascertain consumers' attitudes about the similarities of products and consumer preferences among those products. Respondents are asked to answer questions about various brands of a product while keeping in mind their ideal version of the product. Answers are charted on a scale with an X-axis and a Y-axis, where each axis represents a specific characteristic of the product. Analysis of the scale then enables the producer of the product to develop one single product through knowledge of the importance consumers place on different product features.

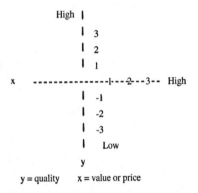

y = quality    x = value or price

**MULTIFAMILY DWELLING** residential building housing more than one household, such as an apartment building. *See also* DWELLING UNIT.

**MULTIGRAPH** LETTERPRESS printing machine that utilizes a cylindrical drum to create the impression. Special type characters are inserted into the cylinder, which is then inked with a roller or an inking ribbon (depending on the operator's requirements for the printing job). Reproductions are made when paper is passed under the revolving cylinder. The Multigraph can also print illustrations provided they are drawn on special forms curved to fit the cylinder. With the increased availability of PHOTOCOPY machines, use of the Multigraph is decreasing. It is primarily used today by small businesses, schools, churches, and rural libraries.

**MULTILITH** printing machine used primarily by small businesses. The Multilith operates on the same principle as LITHOGRAPHY, through the use of paper forms (on which the matter to be reproduced is prepared) placed on a cylinder and run off in a manner similar to the MULTI-GRAPH. Businesses use the Multilith for reproduction of business forms, letterheads, order blanks, or other related materials.

**MULTIMAGAZINE AGENCY** magazine SUBSCRIPTION AGENT selling more than one magazine, such as PUBLISHERS CLEARING HOUSE or AMERICAN FAMILY PUBLISHERS. *See also* CATALOG AGENCY; DIRECT MAIL AGENCY; PAID DURING SERVICE.

**MULTIMEDIA** advertising promotion that utilizes two or more MEDI-UMS. In many cases, a primary medium is supported by a secondary medium, such as a radio or television commercial that supports a Sunday newspaper INSERT. Most advertising campaigns utilize several mediums, including BILLBOARDS, television, radio, print, and so forth, taking advantage of the unique qualities of each medium and increasing the overall EXPOSURE rate of the campaign by reaching different people and also by reaching the same people more than once.

**MULTINATIONAL CORPORATION** corporation based in one country that maintains manufacturing facilities or operations offices in other countries and that markets its products or services on an international basis. A multinational corporation is able to take advantage of special economically advantageous opportunities that exist in the countries where it operates, such as a low labor cost or favorable rate of currency exchange.

**MULTIPLE REGRESSION** statistical analysis that describes the changes in a DEPENDENT VARIABLE, such as sunglass sales volumes, associated with changes in one or more INDEPENDENT VARIABLES, such as the average age of the residents of a market area. For example, a multiple-regression analysis might reveal a positive relationship between demand for sunglasses and various DEMOGRAPHIC characteristics (age, income) of the buyers—that is, demand varies directly with changes in their characteristics. Multiple regression thereby helps marketers to identify their best prospects. *See also* MULTICOLLINEARITY.

**MULTIPLE SOUND TRACK** tape of several different sound tracks recorded simultaneously for stereophonic or quadriphonic recordings.

**MULTIPLE-UNIT SALE** discount given for the purchase of a particular product in large quantities.

**MULTIPLEX** system enabling the transmission or reception of several messages simultaneously on the same circuit. A multiplex transmission system is needed to transmit stereophonic broadcast signals. In order for these signals to be received in stereo, the receiver must also be a multiplex system.

**MULTISEGMENT MARKETING** *see* DIFFERENTIATED MARKETING.

**MULTISUB INDEX** subscription FULFILLMENT computer FILE used to link DONOR records to DONEE records so that payments can be applied to both records and RENEWAL PROMOTIONS can be sent to the donor at the appropriate point in the term of the gift subscriptions. *Multi-sub* stands for *multiple-subscription.*

**MULTIVARIATE ANALYSIS** statistical procedure used in market research where more than one variable is analyzed at the same time. The goal of multivariate analysis is to identify statistical relationships between the variables, such as the relationship of home and family, or to gauge the dependence of the variables on each other through techniques such as CONJOINT ANALYSIS or MULTIDIMENSIONAL SCALING.

**MULTIZONE CITY** *see* MULTICODED CITY.

**MUSIC TRACK** sound track of background music played under the action in a film or videotape.

**MYLAR** trade name of a polyester material manufactured by DuPont and used to make recording tape, STRIPPING film, and boards that hold film for an IMPOSITION layout.

# N

**NAB** National Association of Broadcasters. *See* NATIONAL ASSOCIATION OF BROADCASTERS.

**NAB CODE** *see* NATIONAL ASSOCIATION OF BROADCASTERS.

**NAC** net advertising circulation. *See* NET CIRCULATION.

**NAME RECOGNITION** degree to which a brand or company name has meaning to a consumer. In industrial marketing, a company without name recognition will have difficulty getting into prospect offices and will not be sent a REQUEST FOR PROPOSAL. In consumer marketing, name recognition lends CREDIBILITY to product claims, helps a brand stand out from similar but lesser known brands, coaxes shelf space from the retailer, and is often the reason that brand is selected by the consumer. Consumers faced with too many choices will often purchase the brand they recognize. *See also* CORPORATE IMAGE; HEURISTICS.

**NARROWCASTING** alternative to *broad*casting wherein advertising messages are presented to relatively limited audiences by means of direct mail, local cable television, specialty publications, or other specifically targeted media. Although narrowcasting reaches a smaller audience than traditional mass media, the audience reached is more likely to be predisposed toward purchase of the advertised product or service. Consequently, narrowcasting can be very efficient, particularly when advertising budgets are limited.

**NATIONAL ADVERTISING REVIEW BOARD (NARB)** industry-sponsored organization that through self-regulation reviews complaints of questionable advertising. When a case involving false and deceptive advertising arises, it is initially investigated by the National Advertising Division (NAD) of the Council of Better Business Bureaus. If an advertiser or the party filing the original complaint disagrees with the decision of the NAD, the case is then appealed to the NARB. The NARB is composed of 50 members plus a chairperson, including 30 national advertisers, 10 agencies, and 10 lay persons. When an NAD decision is appealed, the NARB chairperson appoints a special five-person panel to evaluate the claim. If the NARB panel sides with the advertiser, the case is closed. If not, the advertiser is asked to change the challenged advertising, and informed that the case will be referred to an appropriate government agency if it refuses to do so. All the NARB'S findings are always publicly disclosed, along with a statement from the advertiser.

**NATIONAL ASSOCIATION OF BROADCASTERS (NAB)** association headquartered in Washington, D.C., and formed in 1922 to foster and promote the development of aural and visual broadcasting. The NAB works to uphold the American system of broadcasting, protect members from unjust actions, combat censorship and discriminatory legislative proposals, and obtain more agreeable acceptance of radio and television coverage of public proceedings. The NAB'S membership consists of radio and television stations, networks, and associate members.

**NATIONAL BRAND** brand name used by a manufacturer whenever that product is sold. For example, Del Monte is a national brand for food products. In contrast, many marketers offer products under a variety of brand names called PRIVATE LABELS, unique to each distributor or retailer. National brand marketing requires greater advertising expenditure on the part of the manufacturer to compete with lower-priced private label brands. If consumer preference for the national brand is strong, then pricing can be high enough to support the additional advertising and provide the desired profit margin. National brands are often perceived to be of higher quality and can therefore demand a premium price. Many national brands are now experiencing a loss of market share to private label brands as a result of the narrowing quality gap. *See also* MILLER-TYDINGS ACT.

**NATIONAL BROADCASTING COMPANY (NBC)** oldest of the four major radio and television NETWORKS founded in 1926 as a wholly owned subsidiary of the Radio Broadcasting,Company (RCA). NBC provides network television and radio services to nationwide station affiliates and produces live and recorded programming for television and radio. In addition, it owns and operates TV and radio stations under license from the Federal Communications Commission.

In 1926, RCA purchased radio station WEAF from AT&T to be operated by NCC. Since RCA already had its own minor network, it identified the old and the new by colors. The AT&T network became NBC Red and the RCA network became NBC Blue. The Red Network soon became the nation's first permanent network, consisting of 19 stations joined together for simultaneous broadcasting. In 1943, NBC was forced to sell its Blue Network by the FEDERAL COMMUNICATIONS COMMISSION (FCC), after being accused of keeping the network in operation to prevent competitive new networks from getting started. After the sale, the Blue Network became known as the AMERICAN BROADCASTING COMPANY (ABC).

To date, more than 500 stations are affiliated with the NBC radio network, and over 200 stations with its television network. In 1986, NBC became a wholly-owned subsidiary of the General Electric Company.

**NATIONAL BULK MAIL SYSTEM** group of 21 BULK MAIL CENTERS and 10 AUXILIARY SERVICE FACILITIES receiving and distributing BULK MAIL from postal facilities throughout the country.

**NATIONAL BUSINESS PUBLICATIONS** *see* AMERICAN BUSINESS PRESS, INC.

**NATIONAL CABLE TELEVISION ASSOCIATION (NCTA)** organization founded in 1952 to foster the development of the cable industry through research, discussion, and publications. In addition, the NCTA assumes an active role in legal, legislative, and regulatory matters affecting cable communications, and in representing the cable industry before Congress and the Federal Communications Commission. The NCTA's members include cable and equipment manufacturers, cable operators and franchisers, distributors, networks, satellite communications system owners, brokerage firms, financial institutions, and others interested in the cable industry.

**NATIONAL CHANGE OF ADDRESS** U.S. Postal Service system for providing change-of-address information to MAILERS on MAGNETIC TAPE, before the mailer has sent mail to an invalid address. This is accomplished by computer matching the USPS address-change file against the mailer's promotion LIST, and generating a tape-listing of all MATCHES with the new, valid address. This is an improvement on the ADDRESS CHANGE SERVICE that can provide address change information only after an undeliverable mailing piece has been sent.

**NATIONAL DISTRIBUTION GUIDE** Canadian version of the DOMESTIC MAIL MANUAL, published by Canada Post, outlining the regulations and services of the Canadian mail system, including various classes of service, postage rates, and mail preparation requirements. It is used by mailers in and to Canada.

**NATIONAL EDITORIAL ASSOCIATION (NEA)** *see* NATIONAL-NEWSPAPER ASSOCIATION.

**NATIONAL EDUCATIONAL TELEVISION** *see* EDUCATIONAL BROADCASTING CORPORATION.

**NATIONAL ENVIRONMENTAL POLICY ACT** (1970) federal law declaring that it is a policy of federal and state governments to use all means available to promote the general welfare of the natural environment. In practice, the NEPA requires that environmental impacts be fully understood and justified before action is taken. It also sets standards for the level of impact that is permissible. The NEPA added costs to doing business, in the form of environmental impact studies, and time lags to the process of securing government permits, approvals, and financing. The Environmental Protection Agency and numerous other environmental regulatory agencies and legislation, in both the U.S. and internationally, grew out of the NEPA. Senator Henry Jackson (Washington) is considered the father of the NEPA.

**NATIONAL INDUSTRIAL ADVERTISERS ASSOCIATION** *see* BUSINESS/PROFESSIONAL ADVERTISING ASSOCIATION.

**NATIONAL NEWSPAPER ASSOCIATION (NNA)** organization that represents the interests of newspapers at the federal level and is devoted to bettering newspapers in the U.S.; formerly called the *National Editorial Association*. Questions about the postal service, antitrust and libel matters, the Freedom of Information Act, advertising taxes, estate tax laws, and censorship are examples of issues that the NNA pursues.

**NATIONAL OPINION RESEARCH CENTER** *see* NORC: A SOCIAL SCIENCE RESEARCH CENTER.

**NATIONAL OUTDOOR ADVERTISING BUREAU (NOAB)** organization owned cooperatively and exclusively by general advertising agencies, founded in 1916 to provide contracting and administrative services for OUTDOOR ADVERTISING campaigns. The NOAB performs research support, display space consulting, billing consolidation, field service inspection, and other related activities to help users with the details of their outdoor promotions. For its services, a percentage of the usual agency compensation or billings is retained. All other income, after operating costs, goes to its participating agencies.

**NATIONAL ZIP CODE AREA** first digit of the FIVE DIGIT ZIP CODE, designating one of ten regions of the country. The digits and regions are:

| | |
|---|---|
| *0* MA RI NH ME VT CT NJ NY | *5* IA WI MN SD ND MT |
| *1* PA NY DE | *6* IL MO KS NE |
| *2* DC MD WV NC SC | *7* LA AR OK TX |
| *3* GA FL AL TN MS | *8* CO WY ID UT AZ NM NV |
| *4* KY OH IN MI | *9* CA HI OR WA AK |

**NATURAL ENVIRONMENT** *see* MACROENVIRONMENT.

**NBP** National Business Publications. *See* AMERICAN BUSINESS PRESS, INC.

**NEA** National Editorial Association. *See* NATIONAL NEWSPAPER ASSOCIATION.

**NEGATIVE** photographic image that reverses shadow and light areas so that light-sensitive paper exposed (*see* EXPOSURE) through a negative will show the correct POSITIVE image.

**NEGATIVE APPEAL** advertising copy approach that points out the negative aspects of life without the advertised product. The negative appeal attempts to increase people's anxiety about not using a product or service and stresses the loss they will experience if they do not purchase the product or service. *See also* POSITIVE APPEAL.

**NEGATIVE DEMAND STATE** *see* DEMAND STATES.

**NEGATIVE OPTION** DIRECT-MAIL ADVERTISING selling technique in which shipments of goods are made at regular intervals unless the customer sends a refusal notice in advance of each shipment. Most BOOK CLUBS operate on a negative-option basis, sending a new book each period unless the member tells them not to. Some state governments have attempted to ban negative-option programs, in accordance with laws that disallow billing for something that has not been ordered, but only Hawaii has actually done so. Most negative-option sellers mail the customer a reply form and envelope along with a product brochure or catalog describing the next item to be shipped and other items that can be purchased. The customer can either refuse the next shipment, order something instead of the next item to be shipped, or order items in addition to the next item to be shipped. Most marketers do not prepay the postage on the reply envelope, making it less appealing, and less economical, for the customer to send a refusal. *See also* POSITIVE OPTION.

**NEIGHBORHOOD DELIVERY AND COLLECTION BOX** *see* CLUSTER BOX.

**NEMO** distant television or radio broadcast signal origination point. When television or radio programs are aired, their signal points may originate outside the studio. An example of a faraway signal origination point would be a broadcast from a baseball game or a social affair.

**NEON**
1. sign with chemically inert gas in a transparent tube that illuminates when electrified; also called *neon lamp, neon light, neon tube.* Any roadside or on-premise PAINTED DISPLAY, poster panel, or nonstandardized sign may use neon gas for attention-getting impact and easy visibility during night or day. Neons are usually placed in highly trafficked day-and-night locations to attract the maximum number of passersby.
2. chemically inert gas used to illuminate outdoor advertising signs.

**NET ADVERTISING CIRCULATION (NAC)** *see* NET CIRCULATION.

## NET

**In general:** *see* NET AMOUNT,
**Broadcast:**
1. short for NETWORK.
2. abbreviation for National Educational Television.
3. spotlight diffuser, made of metal or gauze, used in broadcast production.

   *See also* NET CIRCULATION; NET COVERAGE; NET PROFIT; NET RATING POINT.

## NET AMOUNT

**In general:** quantity remaining after a deduction from the GROSS AMOUNT, such as the money remaining from a sale after the deduction of expenses. *See also* GROSS PROFIT
**Direct marketing:**
1. names remaining on a LIST after a MERGE/PURGE.
2. amount of subscription sales revenue remitted to the publisher after deduction of the agent's COMMISSION.

   *See also* NET RESPONSE.

## NET CIRCULATION

1. total number of persons viewing a BILLBOARD, PAINTED DISPLAY, or any other form of OUTDOOR ADVERTISING, within a given period of time. An outdoor advertiser's goal is to have a sign with maximum net circulation, given certain budgetary constraints.
2. *see* CIRCULATION,

**NET COVERAGE**  measure used to quantify audience REACH, representing the entire area or number of persons reached by a communications medium. High net coverage is desirable when introducing a new product, or when an advertising message does not require many repetitions.

**NET NAME ARRANGEMENT**  LIST RENTAL agreement whereby the LIST USER pays the LIST OWNER only for the names used, usually after a MERGE/PURGE has deleted undesirable names or after a SELECTION has been made from the total list. Most agreements include that a minimum of 85% of the gross names must be paid for, but this is subject to negotiation and in the mid-1980s was the subject of much debate by list owners, who wanted it raised to increase their revenue, and list users, who felt it should be lowered.

**NET NAME DISCOUNT**  *see* NET NAME ARRANGEMENT.

**NET NAME FILE**  names remaining on a FILE after a MERGE/PURGE is completed. *See also* NET NAME ARRANGEMENT.

**NET PER COPY**  publisher's profit or loss on a subscription expressed in terms of the number of copies served. *See also* GROSS AMOUNT; NET AMOUNT; NET PER SUB.

**NET PER SUB** publisher's net profit or loss on a subscription calculated by deducting all expenses from the gross selling price of the subscription. *See also* GROSS AMOUNT; NET AMOUNT; NET PER COPY.

**NET PROFIT** amount of money earned after all expenses, including overhead, employee salaries, manufacturing costs, and advertising costs, have been deducted from the total revenue.

**NET RATING POINT (NRP)** one percent of the CUMULATIVE AUDIENCE for a given broadcast program or commercial. The net rating points are totaled to arrive at a program's RATING.

**NET RESPONSE** gross RESPONSE (*see* RESPONSE RATE) to a mailing minus unpaid CREDIT ORDERS and cancellations. Net response may also be expressed as the total CASH ORDERS plus paid credit orders. The success of a sales promotion is measured in terms of net response, which is a more accurate measure than gross response. For example, assume that mailing A had a gross response of 100 orders and mailing B had a gross response of 75 orders. It would appear that mailing A was more successful. However, mailing A had a pay-up rate of 50%, for a net response of 50. Mailing B had a pay-up rate of 80%, for a net response of 60, making mailing B more successful than A. *See also* RESPONSE ANALYSIS.

**NETWORK**
1. group of affiliated stations interconnected for the simultaneous broadcast of the same programs. A network usually consists of a program-producing central administering organization, owned and operated stations, and independently owned and affiliated stations. The network produces or buys a program that is economically unfeasible for a single station to produce and sells it to national advertisers for an amount equal to program production costs plus the affiliates' air-time charges. With the network system, advertisers reach larger audiences at a lower cost per person than with a single station, and local stations get key programming to attract sponsors. *National networks* offer complete national coverage of an advertising message. *Regional networks* concentrate on a specific geographic area, providing a means to cater to regional preferences. *Tailor-made networks* are a group of stations joining together on a temporary basis for a special program. *Cable networks* deal with satellite-delivered programming. After the program is aired, the network is dissolved, although it may be reformed at a later time.
2. group of noncompeting agencies or executives who meet to exchange information or services and develop contacts; called *networking*.
3. group of newspapers spread over a wide geographic region, whose advertising space is sold as a unit under one billing.

**NETWORK BUY** purchase of commercial broadcast time made directly from the network, so that time on all the stations affiliated with the network is bought at once. A network buy is similar to "one-stop shopping" in that many geographic areas can be bought at the same time in the one order. Advertisers who wish to advertise throughout the country will purchase commercial time in this manner. The air dates for commercials in a network buy can be scheduled to run concurrently throughout the country or staggered according to the needs of the advertiser. For example, major motion picture companies will often use this method of purchase but will schedule their commercials to be aired at different dates, to correspond with the appearance of the movie at local theaters. *See also* MARKET-BY-MARKET BUY.

## NETWORKING

**In general:** *see* NETWORK.

**Broadcast:** television or radio stations and programs banded together for network broadcasting. Stations agree in affiliation contracts to broadcast the programs furnished by the network. Stations are provided with a varied program schedule, and advertisers are given the chance to tie their commercials to network programming. *See also* SPOT.

**NEW MEMBER MAILING** direct-mail promotion sent only to nonmembers and intended to recruit new club customers. New member mailings must be sent to individuals on rented lists and therefore cost more than mailings to individuals on a house list, for which there is no LIST RENTAL expense. *See also* COLD MAIL PROMOTION.

**NEW PRODUCT DEVELOPMENT** preparation for full-scale manufacturing of a product not previously offered by that marketer, including these activities: conceptualization; concept testing and approval; research and development; prototype testing; economic and market research; and decision making with regard to positioning, pricing, packaging, distribution, and promotion. A new product may be a minor or great variation on an existing brand, a true product INNOVATION, or an imitation of a product already on the market. New product development is necessary to maintain market share because demand for most brands or products tends to decline over time.New product development is also a necessary response to new technology and changing market conditions. New product development may be handled by a dedicated department within the company or may be part of each brand manager's responsibilities. *See also* DIFFUSION; PRODUCT LIFE CYCLE.

**NEWSCASTER** individual employed in a professional capacity by a broadcast or cable NETWORK or station to announce the news. A newscaster may work for a local station or a network, and his additional responsibilities may include news writing and research, film or tape editing, and the development of interviews and documentaries. An anchorperson is the key newscaster at a central station who is chiefly responsible for coordinating and integrating a broadcast that may involve specialized newscasters for sports, weather, traffic, stock market, and other news areas, with coverage coming from several different locations.

**NEWSLETTER** information sheet often styled in the format of a small newspaper. Newsletters generally contain information that is of interest primarily to a special group. For example, the "GALLAGHER REPORT" is a newsletter of interest to those who advertise or who are in the advertising business.

**NEWSPAPER ADVERTISING EXECUTIVES ASSOCIATION** *see* INTERNATIONAL NEWSPAPER ADVERTISING AND MARKETING EXECUTIVES.

**NEWSPAPER ADVERTISING SALES ASSOCIATION (NASA)** organization founded in 1943 as the American Association of Newspaper Representatives to promote newspapers as an advertising medium. NASA members include sales representatives of daily newspapers in the U.S. and Canada. Educational programs and information services to promote the standards of excellence in the industry are provided by NASA chapters.

**NEWSPAPER INSERT** printed promotional enclosure in a newspaper; also called *preprint*. Newspaper inserts vary from a response card to multiple-page INSERTS. Sunday newspapers are the primary carriers of inserts, particularly CENTS-OFF COUPONS. Newspaper inserts enable advertisers to target their advertisements to specific GEOGRAPHIC markets. *See also* HI-FI.

**NEWSPAPER SYNDICATE** organization that sells material to different newspapers for simultaneous publications, on a commission basis. Some newspaper syndicates specialize in editorial copy (columns, feature articles, news, etc.) and/or photography, art, puzzles, or cartoons. A newspaper syndicate usually pays a contributor 40% to 60% of the gross proceeds, although some firms pay by salary and others purchase material outright.

**NEWSPRINT** inexpensive, lightweight paper stock with visible wood pulp that is used to print newspapers and other print products or which the content is more important than the durability or appearance. *See also* TWIN-WIRE MACHINE.

**NEWSSTAND** retail outlet for single-copy magazine and newspaper sales; abbreviated N/S. Aside from the typical street corner and lobby newsstand, other outlets include bookstores, pharmacies, supermarkets, and convenience stores. Newsstand dealers buy publications from WHOLESALERS or DISTRIBUTORS, usually on a returnable basis, whereby unsold copies may be returned for a refund. The newsstands in some locations, such as airports, must pay a fee to the owner of the space occupied equal to a percentage of their gross revenue. This has discouraged some newsstands from selling magazines, because magazines offer a smaller profit margin than other items they could sell. Some airports have solved this problem by offering a tiered pricing structure that requires a smaller payment on magazine sales than other items (10% versus 15%), so that people using the airport will be able to buy magazines. In other locations, newsstand space may be allocated on the basis of who will pay the highest percentage of revenues to the landlord. The usual profit margin before deduction of the landlord's fee is 20% to the newsstand retailer and 40% to the wholesaler. The newsstand dealer may also get 6% to 10% more in the form of a RETAIL DISPLAY ALLOWANCE. *See also* FULL COVER DISPLAY; NEWSSTAND DRAW; NEWSSTAND RETURNS; NEWSSTAND SALES; NONRETURNABLE.

**NEWSSTAND CIRCULATION**   percentage of a publication's CIRCULATION that is accounted for by retail sales. Unsold publications are returned to the distributor on a weekly or monthly basis so that the number of issues sold can be calculated and measured against the subscription circulation. Newsstand circulation is an important percentage of a publication's total circulation, particularly in terms of advertising revenue, since the total circulation figures provide the basis for advertising rates.

**NEWSSTAND DRAW**   magazine copies taken by NEWSSTAND dealers in advance of sales; also referred to as *N/S draw*. Most magazine WHOLESALERS begin distributing copies 5 to 10 days prior to the ONSALE DATE. *See also* NEWSSTAND RETURNS.

**NEWSSTAND PRICE**   retail single-copy selling price of a periodical; usually printed on the cover. The newsstand price is the nondiscounted BASIC RATE.

**NEWSSTAND RETURNS**   unsold copies remaining from the NEWSSTAND DRAW, usually reported back to the WHOLESALER or DISTRIBUTOR for refund to the newsstand dealer; also referred to as *N/S returns*. Returns are reported either by a return of the front cover of each unsold copy or simply with a document stating the number of copies sold and remaining (*see* RETURN AFFIDAVIT). Returns range from an average of 30% to 60% but vary widely depending upon the publication, its competition, and its suitability to the customers patronizing each newsstand outlet. For example, *Good Housekeeping* will sell better in a suburban supermarket than in a camera store, whereas *American Photographer* will sell better in a camera store than in a supermarket. Also, when *U.S. News & World Report* was introduced in China, copies sold out as quickly as the publisher could print them, because competition was limited and interest was high. *See also* NONRETURNABLE.

**NEWSSTAND SALES**   periodical copies sold through NEWSSTAND outlets. The newsstand sales represent the difference between NEWSSTAND DRAW and NEWSSTAND RETURNS There is a great variance in the degree to which any one periodical depends for its revenue upon newsstand copy sales versus subscription copy sales (and advertising space revenue). Certain publications such as *American Heritage* derive more revenue from subscription sales, because the magazines are targeted to special interests and contain information of a nature that people like to receive regularly or save for reference or display in complete sets. Newsstand publications sold primarily, or entirely, on newsstands, such as *Woman's Day* are purchased by many consumers on an irregular basis, depending upon the buyer's interest in an article or item featured on the cover. Publishers maintain statistics on newsstand sales rates by cover subject and experiment with various covers to increase sales. Different covers are sometimes used on newsstand copies from those used on subscription copies to test reaction to them or because the cover subject will generate higher newsstand sales but is not as appealing to subscribers.

**NEXT-TO-LAST COPY**  issue sent to a subscriber prior to the EXPIRE issue; also called *next-to-last issue*. RENEWAL PROMOTIONS are sometimes enclosed in, or attached to, the next-to-last copy as well as the expire copy; however, renewal efforts generally begin six or seven issues prior to expire. *See also* WRAPPER.

**NFI**  Nielsen Food Index. *See* FOOD AND DRUG INDEX

**NICHE MARKETING**  marketing strategy whereby marketers devote 100% of their efforts toward a small segment of a market instead of the whole market. Niche marketing generally appeals to smaller companies with limited resources. Typically, the small market segment, or niche, has been overlooked or only casually served by other larger competitors but is still large enough to be profitable. There are several different niche marketing strategies: end user strategy, serving only one type of end user customer; vertical level strategy, specializing in one level of the production-distribution cycle; customer size strategy, selling products designed for only one size customer, such as petite or extra large clothes; service strategy, offering a service not available from any other company; and geographic strategy, selling only in one geographic area.

**NIELSEN FOOD AND DRUG INDEX**  *see* FOOD AND DRUG INDEX.

**NIELSEN MARKET SECTIONAL REPORTS**  reports distributed by A.C. NIELSON offering either market research or broadcast analysis, by geographic regions. Nielsen's Market Research Sectional Report indicates a breakdown of a product's sales, market share, and competition in a specific geographic area. Nielsen's Broadcast Sectional Report presents an overview of television ratings, audience DEMOGRAPHICS, and other pertinent data by geography. Nielsen Market Sectional Reports are used by marketers who need an in-depth analysis of a market in a certain geographical region, rather than a national overview.

**NIELSEN RATING**  generally conceived to be the number of people watching a particular television program (as calculated by the A.C. NIELSON COMPANY). The Nielsen rating is actually used to calculate the TOTAL AUDIENCE RATING of a program, rather than the AVERAGE AUDIENCE RATING, and refers to households whose television sets are tuned to a particular program for a minimum of six minutes.

**NIELSEN STATION INDEX (NSI)** audience measurement service of A.C. NIELSON COMPANY that provides information concerning the size of local television viewing audiences in approximately 220 markets. The NSI also breaks down the audience according to DEMO-GRAPHIC characteristics for the various DAYPARTS per market. This information is used by MEDIA PLANNERS as the basis of local broadcast-time buying decisions. The Nielsen Station Index is available to clients by subscription. *See also* NIELSON TELEVISION INDEX.

**NIELSEN TELEVISION INDEX (NTI)** syndicated national network television audience measurement service of the A. C. NIELSON COMPANY. The Nielsen Television Index provides audience estimates for all commercially sponsored network programs in the United States through approximately 1200 AUDIMETERS placed in homes and approximately 2400 viewing diaries (*see* DIARY TECHNIQUE) kept by persons in television households throughout the U.S. (However, diaries are slowly being replaced by PEOPLE METERS.) The NTI also includes television ratings for network programs, and information about the age and sex of network audiences. The information presented in the Nielsen Television Index helps to form the basis on which advertisers and media planners make their television media-buying decisions. The NTI is available to clients by subscription. *See also* NIELSON STATION INDEX.

**NINE-DIGIT ZIP CODE (ZIP+4)** extension of the five-digit zip code providing the U.S. Postal Service with even more precise destination information to facilitate mail handling. The nine-digit ZIP is based on a system of BLOCKFACE grids. The first two digits of the added four digits are a SECTOR; the last two digits are a SEGMENT within a sector.

The USPS intends the nine-digit ZIP to be used by business mailers, not by individuals, and offers a small discount for its use. Another benefit provided by the nine-digit ZIP is that it can serve as a basis for DEMOGRAPHIC and PSYCHOGRAPHIC selections from mailing lists.

**NIXIE** colloquial term for a mailing piece that is undeliverable as addressed and is returned to the mailer by the U.S. Postal Service; also called UNDELIVERABLE AS ADDRESSED mail. The addresses on nixies are retained so that they can be removed from the same LIST or from other mailing lists before being mailed again. This is an important function of the MERGE/PURGE process and is called *nixie elimination*.

**NO DEMAND STATE** *see* DEMAND STATES.

**NONCITY DELIVERY** RURAL ROUTE mail delivered to sparsely populated areas.

**NONDUPLICATION** prohibition by the FEDERAL COMMUNICATIONS COMMISSION (FCC) against identical programming by AM and FM facilities owned by the same company. Twin AM/FM stations must broadcast different programming on each station, according to this FCC regulation.

**NONDURABLE GOODS** *see* SOFT GOODS.

**NONMATCH** FULFILLMENT transaction, intended to change or otherwise adjust a RECORD on a computer FILE, that does not "find" the record to be changed. A nonmatch may occur if the name and address in the ADJUSTMENT transaction differs significantly from the name and address in the record. Using a MATCHCODE, if available, to locate records prevents most nonmatch situations. *See also* IDENTIFIED RENEWAL; INSERT-IF-ABSENT.

**NONMETALLIC COMPOSITION** method of COMPOSITION using film or photographic paper image carriers rather than a metallic carrier such as HOT TYPE. Nonmetallic composition is used primarily in LITHOGRAPHY and GRAVURE. It is inexpensive compared to metallic composition and suitable for print products, such as newspapers, for which fast MAKEREADY and printing is more important than print quality. In contrast to metallic composition, in which the image surface is raised above or engraved into the plate surface, nonmetallic composition uses a flat image surface, in which the image areas are distinguished chemically, or via black or transparent areas on film, from the nonimage areas. A more technologically advanced type of composition that does not use a metallic image carrier is COMPUTERIZED COMPOSITION.

**NONORDER MAIL** customer correspondence received by a direct mail marketer that does not include orders or payments. Nonorder mail generally consists of address change requests, complaints, and inquiries.

**NONPRICE COMPETITION** marketing approach whereby the cost of the product is minimized and other marketing factors are maximized by the creation of a distinctive quality about the product such as its design, performance, snob appeal, availability, or service guarantees. *See also* PRICE COMPETITION.

**NONPROFIT BULK MAIL** second-class and third-class BULK MAIL from nonprofit organizations charged a slightly discounted postage rate by virtue of the mailer's nonprofit status.

**NONPROFIT MARKETING** marketing that works to serve the public interest, as opposed to marketing purely for financial gain. Nonprofit marketing is conducted for organizations, such as relief agencies or charitable groups; individuals, such as political candidates; or ideas, such as the rights of freedom; as well as for goods and services, and it is more likely to promote social programs and ideas, such as highway safety, recycling, gun control, or energy conservation.

**NONRETURNABLE** agreement between a NEWSSTAND dealer and the WHOLESALER or DISTRIBUTOR that the cost of NEWSSTAND DRAW copies not sold must be borne by the dealer. Most newsstand agreements allow the return of unsold copies for a full refund. *See also* NEWSSTAND RETURNS; NEWSSTAND SALES.

**NONSTANDARD MAIL** mail with dimensions outside the specifications set by the U.S. Postal Service for mail it will handle. Nonstandard mail sizes can only be used if the mailer intends to use an ALTERNATE DELIVERY service. The USPS provides a free template for checking the size, dimensions, and thickness of a mailing piece against the standards. The minimum mail size is $3^1/2" \times 5"$ and at least .007" thick. Oversize first-class mail (weighing 1 ounce or less) and third-class mail (weighing 2 ounces or less) is longer than $11^1/2"$, higher than $6^1/8"$, and thicker than $^1/4"$, and has a ratio of height to length between 1:1.3 and 1:2.5 inclusive.

**NONSUBSCRIBING DONOR** subscription DONOR who does not have his own subscription to the periodical he has purchased for someone else. The name and address of the donor is kept for billing on CREDIT ORDERS and for refunds on canceled orders. Nonsubscribing donors will also be promoted to renew the gift subscriptions at the appropriate time and to give additional gifts.

**NONVERBAL COMMUNICATION** act of imparting or interchanging thoughts, opinions, or information without the use of spoken words. Nonverbal communication is used in MARKETING RESEARCH as a key VARIABLE to determine consumers' attitudes, values, and beliefs regarding a certain product or service. For example, an observer watching a focus group will pay special attention to the nonverbal cues of group interaction, such as body language, facial expressions, and eye contact, to identify group members' true feelings about an issue.

**NO-OP** outbound telemarketing call initiated by an automatic dialing device that is not picked up by an operator immediately after the call is answered by a live party. Some no-ops are expected when using a PREDICTIVE DIALING system but should be kept at a volume below 5% of the calls answered. A no-op becomes an *abandoned* call if the called party hangs up before an operator gets on the line. *See also* ABANDON RATE; AUTOMATIC DIALER.

**NO PAY** *see* DEADBEAT.

**NORC: A SOCIAL SCIENCE RESEARCH CENTER** nonprofit research organization affiliated with the University of Chicago, founded in 1941 and devoted to fostering the growth of survey, social science, and social policy research. NORC changed its name in 1983 from the National Opinion Research Center to reflect its growing commitment to behavorial and attitudinal studies. The Center's research activities include sociology, social psychology, ethnic group studies, and survey research methodology.

**NORTH-SOUTH LABELS** *see* -UP.

**NO-SCREEN EXPOSURE** *see* BUMP EXPOSURE.

**NOTCH** *see* MORTISE.

**NOTED SCORE** basic measure used by the research firm of DANIEL STARCH AND ASSOCIATES to represent the percentage of readers of a particular issue of a magazine who remember seeing a particular advertisement in that issue (AD-NOTERS).

**NOTIFICATION DATE** specific date that radio or television program sponsors must let a NETWORK know about their decision to cancel or renew their contract. Sponsors making firm commitments into the future are likely to get more favorable rates than are those who refuse to make such a commitment. On the other hand, advertisers willing to take unsold time on a flexible, last-minute, leftover basis, too, will have a favorable negotiating position for lower rates.

**N/S** *see* NEWSSTAND.

**N/S DRAW** *see* NEWSSTAND DRAW.

**N/S RETURNS** *see* NEWSSTANDS RETURNS.

**NTH-NAME SELECTION** extraction of a sample from a LIST of names on an interval basis. For example, a 7th-name selection would take every seventh name on the file based on whatever SEQUENCE the names are in. The size of the interval is based on the size of the sample needed and the size of the total file. For example, if the file has 80,000 names and 20,000 names are needed, a 4th-name selection would be made. Nth-name selection ensures that the sample is random, thereby representing the characteristics of the total file. A-B SPLITS also provide a RANDOM SAMPLE but cannot be used to provide a sample of a particular size.

**NUISANCE CALL** telemarketing call made to a consumer by a PREDICTIVE DIALING system that results in NO-OPS, ABANDONED calls, or calls that fail to disconnect promptly when the called party hangs up, thus tying up the phone line. Legislation at both the federal and state levels regulates practices that generate nuisance calls. *See also* CONSUMER PROTECTION TELEMARKETING ACT; TELEPHONE CONSUMER PROTECTION ACT.

**NUMBER-UP** see-UP.

**NUT**
**Broadcasting:** complete dollar amount reflecting an advertiser's entire sponsorship of a radio or television broadcast. A $700,000 advertising expenditure for a program sponsorship is an example of a nut.
**Printing:** allocation of horizontal space equivalent to $1/2$ EM in width, as used in the specification of type; also called *en quad.*

**NUTRITION LABELING** requirements of the 1990 federal Nutrition Labeling and Education Act (NLEA), which authorized the FOOD AND

DRUG ADMINISTRATION to enforce rules regarding food product labels. The NLEA also authorized the FDA to evaluate products making health claims, such as that they were *light* or *low-fat*, to ensure those claims adhere to federal definitions. The NLEA requirements went into effect in May 1994. The intent of nutrition labeling is to provide consumers with the information they need to make healthy food choices. Prior to this regulation, labels provided information on protein, vitamin, and mineral content relative to U.S. Recommended Dietary Allowances (RDA's). However, dietary deficiencies are no longer a concern for the majority of Americans who would gain more from information regarding calorie, fat, carbohydrate, protein, sodium, fiber, and cholesterol content. Under the NLEA, *Reference Values* replace RDA's, indicating for example that a product contains 30% of the recommended daily intake of fat for an adult consuming 2,000 calories and 65 grams of fat daily. The NLEA applies only to products regulated by the FDA and excludes U.S. Department of Agriculture regulated products, like fresh meat and poultry. Some food companies have complained that nutritional content testing expenses must be passed on to the consumer through higher prices. Others object to the amount of data that must fit on the label, leaving less room for promotional copy, art and preparation/storage instructions.

# O

**OBJECTIVE-AND-TASK METHOD** way of allocating funds to advertising based on the desired results, the steps that must be taken to achieve those results, and the projected costs of each. *See also* AFFORDABLE METHOD; COMPETITIVE PARITY; PERCENTAGE OF SALES METHOD.

**OBLONG** catalog, book, or periodical that is bound on the short side. Books of coupons are frequently bound in this manner to facilitate removal of the coupons.

**OBSCENE MAIL** according to federal statute 39 U.S.C. 3010, obscenity is in the eyes of the beholder. Individuals can use this statute to prevent the U.S. Postal Service, upon request, from delivering mail to them from any direct mail marketer, or other identifiable source, according to their own personal definition of obscenity.

**OCCASION** *see* SPOT.

**OCCUPANT MAILING** mailing piece that has an address but no name and is sent to all residents of a geographic area. Occupant mailings are frequently used to distribute items of immediate interest or value to the recipient, such as product samples or CENTS-OFF COUPONS or to advertise stores serving a particular geographic area. They are not widely used for direct-mail promotions, because direct marketers get higher response rates if they select individuals to receive their promotion based upon some indication of interest other than, or in addition to, place of residence, and because more personalized mailings get more attention and are therefore more effective sales tools.

**OFF CAMERA** describes action on the part of actors or an announcer that takes place beyond the range of the camera and is therefore not seen by the viewing audience, although the voice, or voices, may be heard.

**OFF-CAMERA ANNOUNCER** *see* OFF CAMERA.

**OFF CARD** special rate given to an advertiser for advertising time or space. The rate is said to be off card, because it does not appear on the medium's RATE CARD.

**OFFENSIVE WARFARE** marketing warfare strategy whereby a company in a second or third position will attack a competitive leader in the marketplace. Offensive warfare differs from DEFENSIVE WARFARE in that in defensive warfare, the market leader is protecting its position, whereas in offensive warfare, the market challenger is launching an attack on the market leader. There are five basic offensive strategies: (1) frontal attack, where the challenger attacks the competitor's strengths by matching the product, price, advertising, and distribution; (2) flanking attack, where the challenger attacks the leader's weakness by filling gaps not filled by the competitor and by developing strong products where the competitive products are the weakest; (3) encirclement, where the challenger attacks from all directions; (4) bypass attack, which is not really a direct attack but one where the challenger bypasses the competitor and targets an easier market, hoping that demand for its product will overtake the competitor's product; (5) guerrilla attack, where the challenger makes small periodic attacks with price cuts, executive raids, or concentrated promotional outbursts, hoping eventually to establish permanent footholds in the marketplace.

**OFFER** terms of a contractual agreement made by a seller pending acceptance by the buyer—for example, a magazine subscription offer of 12 issues for $9.95. The order form in this case becomes a legal contract once it is filled in and returned by the subscriber to the publisher. All advertising sales messages are offers and are governed by laws relating to legal agreements, such as the FEDERAL TRADE COMMISSION antitrust laws.

**OFFER TEST** promotion test that evaluates response to different prices and/or terms or quantities. It is critical in a direct-mail offer test that only the offer portion of the PACKAGE be changed, so that any difference in response to the test package versus the CONTROL package can be attributed to the different offer. Offer tests are especially important when introducing a new product to the market to evaluate how PRICE SENSITIVE the market is for that product. For example, a new magazine might have one offer of 12 issues for $15.95 and another of 12 issues for $19.95. For some products, a higher price generates more sales. For example, expensive perfume sells better than cheap perfume because the consumer believes expensive perfume is better. Small differences in price can sometimes generate big differences in response. In practice, consumers seem to prefer odd prices, ending in 9 or 5, over even prices. For example, $19.95 will probably produce a higher response than either $20.00 or $19.92.

**OFF-LINE** computer system that does not allow the user direct access to the MAINFRAME or stored files. Typically, information is stored on MAGNETIC TAPE and must be loaded onto the mainframe before information can be retrieved. New data entered to the system accumulates in temporary storage until a file UPDATE can be run that merges the new data into the existing file. For example, in a FULFILLMENT environment, DATA ENTRY information concerning orders, renewals, customer account adjustments, or payments is entered to a TRANSACTION bank and allowed to accumulate until an update is run. The update applies all of these transactions to the old file, thus creating a new file. From this updated file, output such as mailing labels, invoices, or LIST RENTAL selections can be generated. Off-line systems use CENTRAL PROCESSING UNIT time more efficiently than ON-LINE systems and are therefore more economical, but they do not offer the advantage of instant input and retrieval of information.

**OFF MIKE** in broadcast, describes sounds made or voices spoken in the background, away from the microphone, to give the illusion of noises in the distance.

**OFF-SALE DATE** date that NEWSSTAND RETURNS are tabulated and reported back to the WHOLESALER or DISTRIBUTOR. *See also* NEWSSTAND RETURNS; ON-SALE DATE.

**OFFSET GRAVURE** method of GRAVURE printing utilizing a print cylinder BLANKET that transfers ink from the gravure PLATE to the paper.

**OLIGOPOLY** marketing situation in which there are only a few competitors (usually large companies) for customers in a particular industry and where each of the competitors is sensitive to the others' marketing strategies, particularly in the area of product price. The automobile industry in the United States is an oligopoly because only six firms (General Motors, Ford, Chrysler, Honda, Toyota, and Nissan) account for almost 90% of U.S. automobile sales. *See also* MONOPOLY, MONOPSONY.

**ON-AIR TECHNIQUE** technique or test using audience feedback to evaluate the format, talent, and quality of a television or radio program or commercial that is projected for future broadcast. An on-air technique uses real broadcast material to test factors such as audience recall, preferences, purchasing motivations, and attitude change.

**ON CAMERA**  describes action that takes place in front of the camera and is therefore visible to the viewing audience. An actor, spokesperson, or announcer whose face appears in a television program or commercial is said to have been on camera.

**ONE-CENT SALE**  sales offer where two items are sold together for the price of one of the items and an additional penny. Usually this offer is made to consumers by the manufacturer of the products, through the dealer who sells the merchandise. Typically, a one-cent sale is offered to introduce a new product or to induce new customers to try a product. The reduced price of the merchandise is reflected in the dealer's cost or in the dealer's advertising allowance.

**ONE-SHOT**
**Advertising:**
1. stand-alone television program, such as a documentary or variety special, in contrast to a continuing series or a program shown in a limited number of parts over time. One-shots are usually heavily promoted before being aired and can give the advertiser greater EXPOSURE than a continuing program. Also, the content of the advertisement can be specially targeted to the context of the program.
2. television or motion picture shot of one subject, such as an announcer speaking directly to the camera with nothing in the background.

**Direct marketing:** sale completed in one step, such as the sale of a book, versus a sale that involves a series of steps over time, such as the sale of a subscription, that includes renewal of the subscription and delivery of each issue.

One shots are sometimes used to test a new publication. For example, a single issue of a new magazine may be published and offered on NEWSSTANDS. If sales are good, additional issues will be published annually, quarterly, or on a bimonthly basis as determined by the product development budget and the availability of advertising and editorial content.

**ONE-SIDED MESSAGE**  persuasive communication that presents only one point of view; also called *one-sided appeal*. Most mass media advertising messages are one-sided. A one-sided message is more appropriate for an audience that is favorably disposed toward the view being presented or is unlikely to be exposed to the other side. A religious fund-raising appeal is usually one-sided on the assumption that the targeted audience is favorably disposed toward the view being expounded and is unlikely to be receptive to other religious beliefs. With a more skeptical audience, a one-sided message is less effective than a TWO-SIDED MESSAGE, which presents both points of view and then arguments to counter the opposing view.

**ONE-TIME BUYER** customer on a LIST who has made only one purchase from the LIST OWNER since her initial order. *See also* MULTIBUYER.

**ONE-TIME USE OF LIST** standard condition of a LIST RENTAL agreement stating that the LIST USER is entitled to deliver only one PROMOTION to the individuals on the list. This maintains the LIST OWNER'S legal ownership of the list and future ability to derive revenue from renting the list. Although the user cannot be prevented from retaining the names without the owner's knowledge, the owner can monitor unauthorized usage via SALT NAMES placed on the list.

**ONE UP** *see* -UP.

**ONE-WAY MIRROR** glass that is transparent from one side and mirrored on the other. One-way mirrors allow marketers to observe a FOCUS GROUP INTERVIEW without being seen and without the intrusion of a video camera.

**ON-LINE** computer system that provides the user direct access to the MAINFRAME and to stored information from an input/output device such as a terminal. In an on-line environment, customer information may be entered directly to the customer file, customer records can be instantly accessed, and selections, such as LIST RENTALS, from stored files can be requested from and delivered to a terminal that communicates with the mainframe.

On-line systems usually store data on DISK for direct access to the information. In an OFF-LINE environment, the data is usually stored on MAGNETIC TAPE, and the system user must wait for a computer operator to load the correct tape onto the system before any data can be retrieved.

In contrast to off-line systems, stored files on an on-line system are always current, because they are UPDATED instantly when data is entered. The greatest disadvantage of an on-line system is that it requires significantly more CENTRAL PROCESSING UNIT time than comparable off-line systems.

**ON/OFF REPORT** FULFILLMENT file reconciliation report that shows all the changes made to the prior customer MAINFRAME resulting in the current customer mainfile. The types of transactions shown may be ADDS or DELETES that alter the number of RECORDS, or ADJUSTMENTS that alter the ACTIVE status of the records.

**ON-PACK PREMIUM** gifts or discount coupons that are a part of or attached to the outside of a package. The on-pack premium is designed to help promote sales of a product. When the premium is a gift or novelty item, it is typically one that has value as an impulse purchase item. Manufacturers must be careful, however, because sometimes the on-pack premium will make the package bulky and difficult to stack on shelves, in which case the retailer will not display it and the purpose of the premium will be defeated. Another disadvantage is that sometimes the on-pack premium will encourage theft. *See also* IN-PACK PREMIUM.

**ON-SALE DATE** date new issues of a periodical are scheduled to be delivered by the WHOLESALER or DISTRIBUTOR to NEWSSTANDS for sale to the public. The on-sale date drives the publication and printing process. Most wholesalers prefer to have monthly publications in hand within 10 days of the on-sale date, and weekly publications within 5 days. This schedule determines when the publication must be printed, when all COPY and ART must be submitted, and so forth. *See also* NEWSSTAND DRAW; NEWSSTAND RETURNS; NEWSSTAND SALES.

**ON SPEC** *see* ON SPECULATION.

**ON SPECULATION (ON SPEC)** describes work, such as advertising that is done for a client without a contract or job order, for which the client will pay only if the work is to be used. When a job is done on speculation, the person doing the work takes the risk in the hope of making a profit, gaining a valuable credit, or for some other reason. In the advertising business, creative talent will often work on spec in order to establish a name in the industry.

**OPACITY** characteristic of paper that can be printed on one side without the image showing through on the other side. The thicker the paper stock, the greater the opacity. Print products made with a relief (raised surface) PRINTING PLATE, that pushes ink onto the surface of the paper, must be printed on paper with a high degree of opacity. Opacity is important to the functioning of OPTICAL CHARACTER RECOGNITION scanners, since they are highly sensitive to light and any stray marks that may show through the paper.

**OPAQUE** *see* OPACITY.

**OPAQUE INK**
1. ink used to alter a printing NEGATIVE by covering unwanted transparent areas of the negative that would otherwise be seen in the printed image.
2. nontransparent ink that can be used to conceal printed images, such as the solution used to cover typing errors.

**OPEN ACCOUNT**
1. unpaid CREDIT ORDER also called *open credit*.
2. credit relationship between a buyer and a seller.

**OPEN DATING** consumer protection practice involving the use of "sell by" or other package dates that can be easily interpreted by the average consumer. Prior to open-dating, manufacturers used codes that could be interpreted only by the retailer or distributor. Open dating enables the consumer to evaluate the freshness or remaining useful life of the product.

**OPEN DISTRIBUTION** DISTRIBUTION of the same merchandise within a specified region or area by different dealers. In this type of distribution, dealers can carry competitive lines and there are no restrictions regarding the number of products a dealer can sell, offer for sale, or deliver to retailers. *See also* EXCLUSIVE DISTRIBUTION; SELECTIVE DISTRIBUTION.

## OPEN-END
### Broadcast:
1. ending to a network program or commercial that is left blank for local advertising. Leaving an open end gives local advertisers the opportunity to sponsor a national program, or to add their address and location to a national advertiser's product (*see* DEALER TAG). Commercial spots may also be left blank for local advertisements at a program's start or in its middle.
2. radio or television program with no specific scheduled completion time. For example, a radio talk show is sometimes scheduled to go on until the subject matter is exhausted, rather than rigidly adhere to the usual time schedule.
3. unscheduled termination of a television or radio program. A sudden cessation of programming may be due to a special news alert or may be caused by technical difficulties.

**Direct mail:** envelope that opens at the end, rather than at the side. This type of envelope is commonly used to mail books or catalogs, or any other material that can be more easily inserted at the end of an envelope. The envelope's flap may be gummed or fastened.

**OPEN-END TRANSCRIPTION** previously recorded radio or television broadcast in which provision is made for local commercial spots to be inserted throughout the program. After a direct CUE or announcement is given, the commercial spot is dropped into the scheduled program.

**OPENING BILLBOARD** list of credits appearing as the opening of a broadcast program. *See also* BILLBOARD.

**OPEN RATE** *see* BASE RATE.

**OPERATION MAIL** (MAIL is an acronym for *M*ail *A*ddressing *I*mprovement *L*ink) U.S. Postal Service program to assist mailers by providing an expert review of their mail preparation systems and procedures and offering suggestions for reducing undeliverable mail. To request a review, mailers should write to Operation MAIL, U.S. Postal Service, Washington, D.C. 20260-7233.

**OPERATIONS RESEARCH** application of scientific and mathematical principles to business decisions; also called *management science*. Operations research uses mathematical models and computer simulations to better understand and predict market behaviors. It is also used by industrial buyers to determine the optimal time to order additional inventory. Manufacturers use operational research techniques to schedule production processes, to schedule tasks necessary to complete complex projects, and to optimize production work flows. *See also* HEURISTICS; OPTIMAL ORDER QUANTITY.

**OPINION LEADER** individual whose ideas and behavior serve as a model to others. Opinion leaders communicate messages to a primary group, influencing the attitudes and behavior change of their followers. Therefore, in certain marketing instances, it may be advantageous to direct the communications to the opinion leader alone to speed the acceptance of an advertising message. For example, advertisers may direct a dental floss promotion to influential dentists or a fashion campaign to female celebrities. In both instances, the advertiser is using the opinion leader to carry and "trickle down" its message to influence its target group. Because of the important role opinion leaders play in influencing markets, advertisers have traditionally used them to give testimonials. *See also* SOCIAL CHANNEL.

**OPINION RESEARCH CORPORATION (ORC)** private firm founded in 1938 and located in Princeton, New Jersey, specializing in the survey research field. The ORC offers complete in-house facilities, which include questionnaire development, SAMPLING, interviewing, coding, computer processing, data analysis, reporting, GRAPHICS, and printing. In addition, the firm conducts interviews in person, by telephone, and by mail, and maintains a national probability sample. Custom-designed research studies and major research projects under shared-cost and multisponsor plans are performed by the ORC. The Public Opinion Index for Industry, a report measuring the opinions and attitudes of the general public and leadership groups on political, social, and economic problems that relate to business, is published by the firm.

**OPPORTUNITY COST** value given up as a result of not taking certain action. The revenue foregone as a result of being unable to supply enough product to meet demand is an opportunity cost. When choosing between two alternative courses of action, such as choosing which new product to take to market or which investment to make, the earnings that would have been generated by the investment not selected are an opportunity cost.

**OPTICAL CHARACTER RECOGNITION (OCR)** automatic computer input process whereby the computer SCANNER is able to read printed symbols, numbers, and letters, and convert them to electronic data. There are various types of scanners, such as fixed-head scanners that must have the scan line fed directly to them, or hand-held *wand* scanners that are manually passed in front of the scan line. Some scanners, such as those used in grocery stores or by the U.S. Postal Service, read a code consisting of vertical bars of varying height or width. Other scanners, such as those used by banks to process checks, can read ALPHANUMERIC characters. Wand scanners work best with BAR CODES, because it doesn't matter whether the position of the SCAN

HEAD along the height of each bar varies from one end of the code to the other. The scannability of alphanumeric characters is greatly affected by the position of the scan head, because the characters are not the same from top to bottom.

Scanning is a highly efficient form of DATA ENTRY that can read as many as 20,000 lines or documents an hour. Speed varies widely, depending on the type of scanner and the number of characters to be read.

Scanners are extremely sensitive to light and the reflectivity of ink and paper. They are also affected by the OPACITY of paper, the proximity of marks to the characters to be read, and the type FONT used.

Scanning enables retailers to maintain a "perpetual inventory," that is, an up-to-the-minute record of goods sold. The U.S. Postal Service scans ZIP codes and bar codes in order to process mail faster. Direct marketers use scanners to enter orders and to build computerized lists from HARD-COPY documents. Scanners are also used to accumulate statistics about redeemed CENTS-OFF COUPONS.

**OPTICAL PRINT** *see* COMPOSITE PRINT.

**OPTICALS** visual effects on film or videotape, such as DISSOLVES, CROSS FADES or a MONTAGE, which are added during the editing process. The opticals lend interest, mood, and continuity to the transitions in the basic footage and complete the effect established in the filming or videotaping.

**OPTICAL SCANNER** *see* OPTICAL CHARACTER RECOGNITION.

**OPTIMIZER** computer model that analyzes VARIABLES and determines the mix that will produce the most economical result. For example, in a mailing operation, the more SACKS used, the finer the level of PRESORT, and the higher the postage discount. However, with more sacks used, mail handling expense will increase.

A sacking optimizer determines the optimal number of PACKAGES to be placed in each sack to produce the most cost-effective number of sacks.

**OPTIONAL CITY** SACK of mail destined for a MULTICODED CITY, sorted to the FIVE-DIGIT ZIP CODE level. The U.S. Postal Service does not require that mail be sorted to the multicoded city level but, for certain cities, it does offer a second-class postage discount on optional CITY SACKS. A list of the discount-designated cities is in the DOMESTIC MAIL MANUAL, exhibit 122.63a.

**OPTIONAL ENDORSEMENT** computer-printed PRESORT-level indicator code printed on an address LABEL and used in lieu of COLOR-CODED ROUTING STICKERS to identify the presort level of each PACKAGE. Without optional endorsement, mail preparation is slowed by the manual application of the routing stickers. With optional endorsement, the information needed is on every label, so that the top piece in every package identifies the presort level of that package. Not all label presort systems are able to print an optional-endorsement code. The optional endorsement code is also needed by mailers who use the U.S. Postal Service ADDRESS CHANGE SERVICE. Under that program, the USPS picks up the name of the mailer from the optional endorsement code on undeliverable mailing pieces and gives the correct address for that addressee to the mailer.

**ORANGE GOODS** in merchandising, consumer goods, such as clothing, that will last for a period of time but will be replaced, at a moderate rate, because of wear and tear, desire to change, or change in season, or at the discretion of the consumer. *See also* RED GOODS; YELLOW GOODS.

**ORDER BLANK ENVELOPE** ORDER FORM printed on the inside of a SELF-SEALER envelope. This can be less expensive than providing a separate order form for enclosure in a REPLY ENVELOPE but has a more limited amount of space for copy and order information collection. *See also* BANGTAIL; WALLET FLAP.

**ORDER CARD** ORDER FORM printed on a BUSINESS REPLY CARD. *See also* BIND-IN; BLOW-IN.

**ORDER ENTRY** process of entering order information to a FULFILLMENT system. The most important objectives of order entry are speed and accuracy so that customers can receive what they have ordered as quickly as possible and marketers can determine which promotions are working best. In addition to product and customer information, order entry must also capture a KEY CODE and payment type (cash, credit, credit card). The order entry process may also include entry of DEMOGRAPHIC information gathered on the order form, such as occupation or age. If the order is taken over the telephone, the order entry clerk can act as a salesperson by trying to increase the size of the order. *See also* KEY ENTRY; SCAN ENTRY; TAPE ENTRY.

**ORDER FLOW PATTERN** volume of direct mail orders received at intervals over time, from the MAIL DATE till the last order is received. If receipts are plotted on a graph, the point at which the orders have peaked can be identified so that total orders can be projected. *See also* CATALOG SALES PROJECTION; DOUBLING DAY. *See next page.*

**ORDER FORM**
1. form used to request merchandise, usually from a wholesaler, manufacturer, or direct-mail retailer.
2. document provided by a DIRECT MARKETING firm to a customer so that order information can be communicated back to the marketer. It is essential that order forms capture all the information required by the seller without being difficult, time-consuming, or confusing for the buyer. Most order forms contain a KEY CODE so that the SOURCE of the order can be identified. For example, a key code may

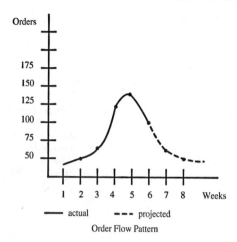

Order Flow Pattern

indicate the direct-mail PACKAGE that generated the order. *See also* CATALOG ORDER FORM; FINDER NUMBER

**ORDER MARGIN** total cost of goods sold—including product, selling, and delivery costs but not including promotion costs—subtracted from the total sales revenue generated, and divided by the number of UNITS sold. The promotion budget must not exceed the order margin and, in addition, must be small enough to leave a profit margin. For example, assume 100 units are sold by a retailer at a price of $20, yielding $2000 in revenue. The cost of the goods was $300, and all costs associated with warehousing, displaying, and selling the goods in the store totaled $1200. The order margin, therefore, is $15 per unit sold (1200 + 300 ÷ 100), leaving $500 for promotion expense and profit.

Direct marketers generally have a lower order margin than retailers, because they do not have the expenses associated with managing a retail outlet (leased space, salesclerks, electricity, furniture and fixtures, and so forth) and can sell goods at a lower price.

**ORDER NUMBER**
1. reference number used by a wholesaler, manufacturer, or retailer to identify a particular order, such as a reference number used by a LIST USER or LIST BROKER to identify a LIST RENTAL order.
2. reference number used in FULFILLMENT to link a customer RECORD on a computer FILE to the HARD-COPY order DOCUMENT that initiated the record. It usually consists of a document BATCH IDENTIFICATION number and the ORDER ENTRY date.

**ORDER REGULATION** NEWSSTAND distribution planning system that determines how many copies to distribute to a retailer based on his NEWSSTAND DRAW and NEWSSTAND SALES history.

**ORDERS PER THOUSAND (OPM)**  index used to measure the comparative success of direct-mail PACKAGES in terms of orders generated per thousand packages mailed. For example, a 200,000-piece mailing that generates 4500 orders has an OPM of 22.5. This is not an absolute measure of the success of a package unless NET orders are used rather than gross orders before payment, thus incorporating profitability into the equation.

**ORDINARY PAPERS**  periodicals such as fashion or photography magazines that do not have a time value and therefore do not require the U.S. Postal Service preferential delivery priority accorded red tag periodicals (periodicals that are issued at least weekly and contain news value information). According to USPS regulations, ordinary papers are distributed through the same PREFERENTIAL NETWORK as red tag mail but receive a lower priority.

**ORGANIZATIONAL MARKET**  all the individuals and companies who purchase goods and services for some use other than personal consumption. Organizational markets usually have fewer buyers but purchase in far greater amounts than CONSUMER MARKETS, and are more geographically concentrated. Organizational markets are divided into four components: industrial market, which includes individuals and companies that buy goods and services in order to produce other goods and services; reseller market, which consists of individuals or companies that purchase goods and services produced by others for resale to consumers; government market, which consists of government agencies at all levels that purchase goods and services for carrying out the functions of government; institutional market, which consists of individuals and companies such as schools or hospitals that purchase goods and services for the benefit or use of persons cared for by the institution.

**ORIGINAL ORDER**  first order received from a particular customer. It is important to track the SOURCES of original orders so that efforts to create new FIRST TIME BUYERS can be concentrated on the best sources. For example, if more original orders for a particular product per promotion dollar spent come from direct mail than from other sources and if direct-mail orders have a good PAY-UP history, then future promotional budgets should be allocated primarily to direct mail.

**ORIGINAL SOURCE**  *see* ORIGINAL ORDER.

**ORTHOCHROMATIC**  film that is insensitive to red light, reproducing only blue or green tones. *See also* PANCHROMATIC.

**OTC DRUGS**  *see* OVER THE COUNTER DRUGS.

**OUTBOUND TELEMARKETING**  *see* TELEMARKETING.

**OUTDOOR ADVERTISING**  advertising on signs that are located outdoors in public places. Outdoor advertising, one of the oldest and most enduring forms of advertising, can be broadly identified as any sign that publicly displays advertising or identifies something, such as a sign for a restaurant or other place of business. More specifically, though, the term has come to represent the advertising medium we casually call BILLBOARD advertising, which is a large standardized segment of the OUT-OF-HOME advertising media industry, with annual revenues exceeding one billion dollars. The medium is made up of some 270,000 standardized posters, PAINTED DISPLAYS and SPECTACULARS available to advertisers in more than 15,000 communities throughout the U.S. On a cost per thousand basis, it is actually the most economical of all media, with cost sometimes as low as $.50 per thousand.

The structures for placement of advertising posters, spectaculars, and painted displays are maintained by individual outdoor advertising companies called *plant operators*. The plant operators also own or lease the land on which the structures are built, primarily in commercial or business areas. The structures are scientifically located in places of heavy traffic volume along highways, alongside railroad lines, on rooftops, or on the outer walls of buildings so as to deliver an advertising message to the entire market in the community.

Outdoor advertising displays are an excellent reminder medium and are most commonly used in an advertising campaign to supplement other media.

**OUTDOOR ADVERTISING ASSOCIATION OF AMERICA (OAAA)** trade association of OUTDOOR ADVERTISING plant operators founded in 1891 to promote and increase the efficiency of outdoor advertising. The OAAA develops trade procedure standards, recommends standardized structures to insure uniformity in size, represents the industry in legislative activity, and performs market research and administrative functions. Members of the OAAA are standard poster advertising and PAINTED DISPLAY advertising plant operators. The INSTITUTE OF OUTDOOR ADVERTISING (IOA) coordinates and implements the OAAA's marketing activities. *See also* NATIONAL OUTDOOR ADVERTISING BUREAU.

**OUTDOOR SERVICE** performance of maintenance or repair functions to OUTDOOR ADVERTISING structures. Outdoor advertising plant operators are responsible for maintaining the outdoor advertising structures erected for advertisers, as well as making sure surrounding areas are clean and attractive. Some examples of typical maintenance functions or repairs are scraping poster boards, painting the structures that hold posters, checking and changing lights, and repainting boards displayed for a long duration. The NATIONAL OUTDOOR ADVERTISING BUREAU provides a field service for inspecting structures and maintains service control records for those advertising agencies using their services.

**OUTDOOR SPACE BUYER** *see* MEDIA BUYER.

**OUTER ENVELOPE** envelope used for a direct-mail PACKAGE to carry the package components to the addressee. The outer envelope is the first element of a direct-mail package that is seen by the recipient and determines the success or failure of the promotion by its ability to generate sufficient interest to get the package opened. Outer envelopes may be FULLFACE ENVELOPES or WINDOW ENVELOPES, and usually include teaser copy (CORNER CARD), graphic devices such as BURSTS or FLAGS, and/or ACTION DEVICES such as a PULL TAB. The color of the outer envelope and the weight of the paper used to make it contribute to the success of the overall design. The effectiveness of elaborate outer envelope designs, measured in terms of response to the promotion, must be weighed against the additional paper, printing, and production costs of the envelope. Some promotions use a simple white envelope without any copy, to avoid looking too much like a promotion. *See also* BANGTAIL; BARONIAL ENVELOPE; POLYBAG; REPLY ENVELOPE; SELF-SEALER.

**OUT-OF-FOCUS DISSOLVE** camera transition from one scene to the next effected by fading one shot out of focus while simultaneously fading the following one into focus. Out-of-focus dissolves are commonly used for SPECIAL EFFECTS or for transition points (such as just before commercial breaks).

**OUT-OF-HOME** term describing advertising media that must be viewed outside the household and is not available in the home, such as bus-shelter advertising, shopping-cart displays, BILLBOARDS, PAINTED DISPLAYS, TRANSIT ADVERTISING, and SKY WRITING. *See also* IN-HOME.

**OUTPUT** products of a computer system, such as PRINTOUTS, labels, reports, or LIST RENTAL selections. Output can be printed on paper, displayed on a cathode-ray tube screen (*see* CATHODE-RAY TUBE DISPLAY), punched onto KEYPUNCH cards, written onto MAGNETIC TAPES or DISKS, and so forth. The intended use of the output and the capabilities of the system generating it determine the FORMAT.

**OUTSERT**
1. separate piece of printed matter attached to the outside of a PACKAGE. An outsert is frequently used when an advertising message must be prominently viewed and the advertiser cannot risk inserting the message in an envelope that may or may not be opened. An outsert may also be used to highlight special offers or PREMIUMS.
2. separate cover used on the outside of a magazine or catalog. An outsert is frequently used in magazine marketing to inform advertisers of upcoming features, rate changes, advertising opportunities in special issues, and so on. In addition, it is used by catalog marketers to feature such things as special discount offers, product announcements or changes, or premiums.

**OUTSIDE BACK COVER** *see* BACK COVER.

**OVERALL EXPENSES METHOD** technique for evaluating the cost of goods sold by dividing the seller's total expense over time by the number of items sold during that time period. This prevents the seller from failing to include any relevant expenses in the calculation. It is also a useful measure of the change in expense realized relative to a change in the number of units sold. However, it is only accurate when the items sold are relatively homogeneous. It would not be accurate to attribute the same expense to selling a wool coat as to selling a fur coat that must be stored in a specially cooled area and kept under tight security.

**OVERFULL DEMAND STATE** *see* DEMAND STATES.

**OVERHANG COVER** cover on a book, catalog, or brochure that is larger than the page size; also called *extended cover, overlap*. Most hardcover books use an overhang cover, except for very wide books that would sag when placed upright on a shelf. *See also* FLUSH COVER.

**OVERHEAD** indirect expenses of running a business not directly associated with a particular item or service sold. For example, wages paid to factory workers and the cost of production materials are direct costs. Electricity, insurance, and benefits paid to workers are overhead expenses. By applying a factor called the *burden rate*, cost accounting attempts to allocate overhead, where possible, to the cost of goods sold.

**OVERKILL**
**In general:** expensive promotional effort that produces diminishing returns because it repels rather than attracts consumer interest.
**Direct marketing:** RECORDS on a LIST incorrectly identified as DUPLICATES by a computer program that doesn't accurately reflect the objectives of the LIST OWNER. For example, the program may be written to combine all records for the same household or business even though the list owner would like to send promotions to each individual.

**OVERLAY**
**In general:** unifying theme structure bringing together all elements of an advertising CAMPAIGN. Overlays are commonly used by advertising executives to help organize an entire promotion effort and/or as a tool to facilitate long-term planning.
**Broadcast:** acetate sheet used in television ANIMATION when producing COMMERCIALS. The sheet is used to draw motions that come after those in the original drawing.
**Outdoor advertising:** information sheet citing the name, address, and business hours of a retailer, affixed on the bottom of geographically dispersed outdoor advertising posters. Overlay sheets offer advertiser a flexible means of letting consumers know which retailers stock their products.
**Production:**
1. transparent or semitransparent covering used to protect artwork or photography, or as a means to surprint instructions, corrections, changes, copy variations, or comments on art, photography, text,

or an existing design. For example, color-breaking instructions for the photoengraver are usually marked on an overlay that is pasted on an original black-and-white piece of artwork. Since these instructions are not written directly on an original, the proper specifications are communicated without touching the original design. In addition, the original copy is protected from damage or smearing. Cellulose ACETATE or tracing tissue are most commonly used for overlay purposes.

**2.** shaped piece of paper, or thin sheets of paper, put on the tympan of a press to increase or equalize the impression. An overlay increases pressure on the dark portions of the plate, creating a pressure reduction on the plate's lighter portions.

**3.** separate transparent or semitransparent prints that can be combined to form a finished design. An overlay is used to assess how different changes in a design's individual elements can affect its overall design.

**Direct marketing:** Addition of data to a customer list by matching names on the data source list to names on the customer list. *See also* MODELED LIST.

**OVERPAYMENT**  money received from a credit buyer that exceeds the amount due. Unless the payment is for a continuous service that can be extended, such as a newspaper subscription, the amount of the overpayment must be refunded or must be credited to the buyer's account to be applied against future purchases.

**OVERPRINTING**

**1.** printing over already-printed images without obscuring the underlying image. This technique may be used to HIGHLIGHT elements of COPY, to add new copy, or to include some copy in only part of a print run. For example, two menus may be printed for a restaurant: one with prices and one without prices for the convenience of hosts who don't want their guests to be concerned with the cost of the meal. Overprinting is frequently used in catalogs to indicate that a particular item is temporarily unavailable or no longer offered, or to add a special "sale" price.

**2.** placing a LACQUER coating over a printed image to enhance the color of the underlying image.

**OVERRUN**  excess production. Printed material such as magazines, catalogs, and newspapers are frequently printed in quantities greater than the expected distribution in order to cover unexpected contingencies, such as damaged or lost copies, requests for BACK ISSUES, or distribution of copies as samples to prospective advertisers or buyers. *See also* OVERSET MATTER

**OVERSET MATTER**  excess typeset copy; also called *leftover matter*; *overmatter*. Overset matter is not part of the planned LAYOUT and is used on a contingency basis should space be left open at the last minute. For example, if an advertiser decides to pull an advertisement out of a magazine at the last minute, overset matter, such as a short article, can be used to fill the space that had been allocated to the advertisement.

**OVER-THE-COUNTER DRUGS** pharmaceutical products sold through retail channels without a physician's prescription. All products have been approved by the federal FOOD AND DRUG ADMINISTRATION, (FDA) and information describing any potential harmful side effects is provided on the product's PACKAGE and label. Advertising must accurately communicate the product's benefits without making false claims. Advertisers usually promote over-the-counter drugs to consumers year-round, even though certain products may be used for sporadic symptom relief at certain times of the year. Cold and allergy remedies, however, are usually heavily promoted during the winter and allergy season respectively.

**OVERWIRE HANGER** BANNER suspended from a wire or cord strung across the ceiling, used as advertising support primarily in retail store displays.

**OVERWORKED LIST** list made available too frequently for rental and/or for promotions. The individuals on the list will be less responsive to mailings if they get too many within a short period of time. LIST OWNERS attempt to prevent this by using ASSIGNED MAILING DATES.

**OVERWRAP** four-page attachment to a catalog cover that either is tailored to individual segments of the catalog mailing list or includes advertising for additional merchandise or COPY or OFFER tests for a sample segment. Overwraps are not necessary when SELECTIVE BINDING is available for binding special pages directly into the catalog or other publication.

**OWNERSHIP STATEMENT** statement by publishers granted SECOND-CLASS mail privileges that the U.S. Postal Service requires them to publish annually in the first issue of their periodical following September 30. The ownership statement lists the names and addresses of the principal owners of the periodical and shows CIRCULATION statistics.

**OZALID** process whereby a photograph, artwork, or other material can be duplicated from the original copy, in the same size as the original, without first making a negative. Ozalid prints are used in the process of reproducing original photographs, business forms, and architectural drawings. They will lack the sharp quality of the original but will be sufficient to check the accuracy of the copy before continuing the printing process.

# P

**PACING ALGORITHM** computer program that controls the number of calls made by a PREDICTIVE DIALING system, based on the maximum number of allowable NO-OPS.

**PACKAGE**
**In general:** set of items sold as one; also called package deal. *See also* PACKAGE TEST.
**Advertising:** television or radio programming available for purchase by advertisers either singly or as a discounted package deal.
**Direct mail:**
1. components constituting a direct-mail promotion piece. PACKAGES usually include the OUTER ENVELOPE, the REPLY ENVELOPE, the ORDER FORM, and a letter.
2. multiple pieces of mail, usually PRESORTED, batched by destination, and bound together for handling by the U.S. Postal Service.
**Merchandising:** container or WRAPPER used to present individual items of merchandise for sale or for shipping to buyers.

**PACKAGE BAND** advertisements, announcements, or special price offers printed on a strip of paper that forms a band around a package.

**PACKAGE CODE** code used in direct marketers' customer RECORDS to identify a particular mailing PACKAGE so that response to the package can be tracked. Package codes are especially important when testing a new package against a CONTROL package, so that response to each promotion can be compared. *See also* HOMOGENIZATION; KEY CODE; PACKAGE TEST.

**PACKAGE DESIGN**
**In general:**
1. planning and fashioning the complete form and structure of a product's package. In creating a new design or revamping an existing design, the following aspects of a product's package are usually reviewed: size and shape, color, closure, outside appearance, protection and economy, convenience, labeling, and the packaging material's effects on the environment. The best packaging system is then developed by careful evaluation of product, market competition, and existing product line. Generally speaking, package redesigning is done one element at a time, to preserve the brand loyalty of existing customers.
2. marketing support specialty embracing the planning, creation, and production of the entire physical presentation of a product's package. Trained designers specialize in this field, which encompasses the art and science of creating optimal product packages.

**Direct mail:** creating and developing the complete assemblage of a direct mail PACKAGE, including the envelope, letter, BROCHURE, LIFT LETTER, premium slip, and reply device.

**PACKAGED GOODS** consumer products packaged by manufacturers and sold through retail outlets. Food, tobacco, toiletries, health and beauty aids, and household products are typically involved in this product classification.

## PACKAGE ENCLOSURE
  **1.** *see* IN-PACK PREMIUM.
  **2.** *see* INSERT.

**PACKAGE FACING SLIP** tags attached to mail PACKAGES indicating the destination and PRESORT level of each package. *See also* PALLET TAG.

**PACKAGE INSERT** promotional material included in merchandise PACKAGES that advertises goods or services available from the same or different sellers; also called *package stuffer.* Catalog sellers frequently include a copy of their catalog in packages shipping an order from that same catalog. This gets the catalog into the buyer's hands again (like getting a retail buyer back into the store), provides a new order form, and replaces copies that may have been thrown away when the order was sent. The response rate will be lower than to the original catalog mailing, but the cost of including the catalog in the package is small, making any additional orders received profitable, and the buyer has already demonstrated a willingness to buy. *See also* BILL INSERT.

**PACKAGE PLAN** combination of SPOTS devised by networks or stations and offered to television or radio advertisers at a special price; also called *total audience plan.* For example, a radio station may offer an advertiser a special flat rate for several commercial TIME SLOTS over the broadcast day. Package plans are usually weekly or monthly buys.

**PACKAGE/SACK MARKS** BAR CODES printed on mailing labels to indicate the end of a SACK, PACKAGE, or PALLET, according to U.S. Postal Service regulations. Bar codes may be machine-read by a SCANNER or read by a worker on the mailing line, so that mail can be placed in sacks or packages or on pallets at the correct point. *See also* LOGICAL SACKING; OPTICAL CHARACTER RECOGNITION.

**PACKAGE STUFFER** *see* PACKAGE INSERT.

**PACKAGE TEST** DIRECT-MAIL ADVERTISING test of response to a new PACKAGE. To test a package, it is mailed to a sample of names from a LIST in conjunction with the mailing of a CONTROL package to another sample of names from the same list. The response to each of the packages is compared, to determine which package should be used in the future. To be complete, both gross (*see* GROSS AMOUNT) and NET

RESPONSE must be considered in the comparison. Net response includes CASH ORDERS and paid CREDIT ORDERS. A test package should differ from the control package in only one respect; if there is more than one difference, then the cause of the response difference cannot be identified. For example, a good package test might vary the color of the OUTER ENVELOPE. A poor package test might also add a LIFT LETTER to the package. The marketer will not know if the difference in response can be attributed to the envelope color or the lift letter. He also won't know if the difference would have been even greater if only one element had been changed. *See also* PACKAGE CODE; PANEL; TEST.

**PACKAGING** container or wrapper for a consumer product that serves a number of purposes including protection and description of the contents, theft deterrence, and product promotion. Innovative packaging may actually add value to the product if it meets a consumer need such as portion control, recyclability, tamper-proofing, child-proofing, easy-open, easy-store, easy-carry, and nonbreakability. The labels on packages are important components of the overall marketing mix and can support advertising claims, establish brand identity, enhance name recognition, and optimize shelf space allocations. When designing packaging, the cost to manufacture, ship and display the package must be considered. Packaging must be small enough to accommodate available shelf space and large enough to deter theft. It must also contain an adequate amount of product to keep the unit price competitive. Packaging should be designed to highlight product benefits and can be an integral part of the product itself, like facial tissue boxes. For some products, such as Pez Popper candy, the package *is* the product. Innovative packaging can create a whole new PRODUCT CLASS, like juice boxes. *See also* FAIR PACKAGING & LABELING ACT; NUTRITION LABELING.

**PACKING**
1. short for packing material; filler material included in a merchandise shipping package to cushion the merchandise from damage during shipping. *See also* AIR-BUBBLE PACKING.
2. shipping department function involving the placement of merchandise in boxes or other shipping containers.

**PACKING SLIP** form used in a warehouse PICK-AND-PACK operation that lists the items to be shipped and the recipient of the shipment. The packing slip may also include the amount due for a CREDIT ORDER and any shipping and handling charges, as well as a shipment control number. The packing slip travels with the shipment and, at the destination, is used to confirm that the shipment is complete. It is matched with the pertinent INVOICE before payment is made. *See also* COMPUTER-ASSISTED PICKING SYSTEM.

**PAD** add program material, ad lib, narration or music to a commercial or a broadcast show that has ended before its specific time allotment. For example, if a 30-second radio commercial ends instead in 25 seconds, a disc jockey may pad the commercial by playing background music or by making a 5-second comment about the weather.

**PAGE MAKEUP** *see* MAKEUP.

**PAGE PROOF** proof of typographic material and engravings set up to print an entire page. A printer will usually number page proofs in sequential order, as they are intended to appear in a book, magazine, or specialty publication. Corrections to page proofs are more expensive than corrections made on earlier GALLEY PROOFS.

**PAGINATION** COMPUTERIZED COMPOSITION and WORD PROCESSOR function that automatically breaks text into pages for printing. Page breaks may be inserted at the end of a fixed number of lines or at variable points, dependent upon the content of the text.

**PAID CANCEL** *see* COMPLETED CANCEL.

**PAID CIRCULATION** *see* CIRCULATION.

**PAID DURING SERVICE** SUBSCRIPTION AGENT payment agreement whereby the subscriber is billed in INSTALLMENTS as the subscription is serviced, and periodic payments are made by the agent to the publisher over the same time period; abbreviated *PDS*. PDS agents generally sell several magazines as a PACKAGE, with long terms of three to five years' duration. The average order can be as much as $300 to $400. Cancellations of PDS-sold orders are relatively high and renewal rates are low, since every bill is an opportunity to cancel and the sale is frequently made with a high-pressure telephone sales pitch. *See also* PAID IN ADVANCE.

**PAID IN ADVANCE** SUBSCRIPTION AGENT payment agreement whereby the publisher is paid in full by the agent when the subscription order is submitted to the publisher, and the subscriber is required to pay the agent in full when ordering. Most subscription agents are PIA agents. *See also* PAID DURING SERVICE.

**PAID STATUS** customer RECORD status that indicates whether and how the order was paid. Status types include CASH ORDER, paid CREDIT ORDER credit card order, CLAIMS-PAID COMPLAINT, unpaid credit order, complimentary subscription (*see* COMP), or MASS CANCEL.

**PAINTED BULLETIN** *see* PAINTED DISPLAY.

**PAINTED DISPLAY** form of OUTDOOR ADVERTISING where the advertising message is hand painted on the display. There are two types of painted displays: *painted walls* and *painted bulletins*.
    The painted bulletin is a freestanding steel or wooden structure, typically measuring approximately 50 feet long by 15 feet high, with a painting surface on its face surrounded by a molding that acts as a border for the artwork. Bulletins are generally found adjacent to highways and railroad lines, or on the roofs of buildings in high traffic areas.

The painted wall is also located in a heavy traffic area and is simply the outer surface of a building. The size of painted wall displays will vary according to the size of the wall available for painting. Conventionally, there are three classifications for painted walls: city walls, suburban walls, and town walls.

The cost of advertising on a painted display depends on the nature of the display, the amount of traffic passing by (circulation), the operational cost of the display, and the length of the advertising contract. Typically, contracts are for one year with periodical retouching and maintenance, although contracts can run for as long as three years.

**PAINTED WALL** *see* PAINTED DISPLAY.

**PALLET** small platform, also called a *skid*, usually made of wood and used to store and transport stacks of merchandise or materials. Pallets are moved with forklifts or pallet jacks. They can physically hold up to 2000 pounds of material, and measure 40 by 48 inches. The U.S. Postal Service permits the use of pallets in lieu of SACKS to transport mail. Unlike sacked mail, which earns PRESORT discounts based only on the presort level of sacks that carry a minimum number of packages, palletized mail earns presort discounts based on the presort level of each PACKAGE on the pallet, thus enabling mailers to qualify more packages for a discount. Other advantages of pallets over sacks are that palletized mail experiences less damage during transport and that pallets enable workers to transfer more mail in less time to and from mail trucks.

**PALLET CAP** lid placed on top of palletized material to secure the material during transport. Pallet caps are required by the U.S. Postal Service for palletized mailings weighing less than 1000 pounds.

**PALLET MARK** *see* PACKAGE/SACK MARK.

**PALLET TAG** label on a mail PALLET on which the pallet destination and PRESORT level are printed; also called *pallet placard*. The U.S. Postal Service requires that two 8½ by 11 inch tags be placed on adjacent sides of each pallet, and that the lettering on the tags be at least ½ inch in height. *See also* BAG TAG; PACKAGE FACING SLIPS.

**PALLET TAG REPORT** report produced in conjunction with mailing labels for a palletized mailing that includes PALLET TAG information, control information about the quantity of mail to be palletized, and ENTRY POINT information. It is used by the mailer when preparing pallets.

**PAN** rotation of a television camera up and down or from left to right to televise a panoramic scene or a moving subject. The camera remains in position but is swung from one angle to another without interruption to follow the subject.

**PANCHROMATIC** type of film that is sensitive to all shades of visible color.

**PANDER FILE NAMES** *see* DMA MAIL PREFERENCE SERVICE DELETE FILE.

**PANEL**
  1. sample taken from a LIST or group of people for testing purposes; also known as TEST PANEL. A test panel might be used to evaluate a direct-mail PACKAGE, an OFFER, a new or improved product, or other aspect of a marketing plan relative to the existing standard (CONTROL) package, offer, or product and so forth. *See also* KEY CODE.
  2. group of people brought together to discuss or offer opinions, such as a television talk-show panel. A market-research panel discussion would most likely be concerned with a product or a promotion, such as a panel of consumers doing a taste test or offering their opinion on a new commercial.
  3. outdoor advertising media VEHICLE, such as a BILLBOARD.
  4. faces of a folded brochure or mailing piece.

**PANTRY AUDIT** consumer research survey of household inventory kept on hand at any given time. PACKAGED GOODS manufacturers employ this research technique to gather data for new product development and packaging (*see* PACKAGE) strategies. In conducting a pantry audit, a RANDOM SAMPLE of the advertiser's target market is first selected. Questionnaires are then mailed or telephone solicitations are completed to determine what items are stocked in a consumer's kitchen. For example, if the pantry audit revealed that the majority of pantries sampled had half a box of spice that was a year old, it might result in a decision to package the spice in smaller quantities.

**PAR** present value of a CONTINUITY customer over the ACTIVE life of the customer. It is calculated by estimating the total revenue to be expected from the customer, less the total expenses expected to be incurred earning the revenue, discounted to arrive at the value that NET revenue would have if received in a lump sum payment today. The par value is used as a basis for evaluating various sources of new customers.

**PARAMETER** variable value; in a COMPUTER PROGRAM, the parameters are changed each time the program is run. List rental SELECTION parameters describe the criteria for selection applicable to each LIST RENTAL For example, the parameters may be set to select HOTLINES with male names and incomes over $50,000, or the parameters may be set for an NTH-NAME SELECTION.

**PARCEL POST** FOURTH-CLASS mail. Parcel post commonly refers to non-letter mail such as books and other boxed merchandise. In 1986, approximately 80% of parcel-post mail was delivered by ALTERNATE DELIVERY companies such as United Parcel Service, because the U.S. Postal Service did not provide a more competitive price and service.

**PARTICIPATION PROGRAM** *see* AUDIENCE-PARTICIPATION PROGRAM.

**PASS-ALONG CIRCULATION** publication's audience consisting of those readers who have not received a copy by purchase or request.

Pass-along readers may receive copies from the original subscriber or purchaser, such as a family member or the public library. The total audience of a publication is the sum of its paid and nonpaid subscribers and its pass-along readers.

**PASS CONSOLIDATION CODES** codes published in the PASS MANUAL (*Package and Sack/Skid Sequencing Manual for Publication Mailings*) that are endorsed by the U.S. Postal Service and used by periodical and catalog mailers on PACKAGE, SACK, and PALLET labels and tags to identify the PRESORT level of the mail.

**PASS MANUAL** (acronym for *Package and Sack/Skid Sequencing Manual for Publication Mailings*) manual published by the Graphic Communications Association (1730 North Lynn Street, Suite 604, Arlington, VA 22209-2085) that provides second- and third-class periodical and catalog mailers (LETTERSHOPS, FULFILLMENT service bureaus, PRINTERS, publishers) with standard industry guidelines for mail preparation that are in accordance with U.S. Postal Service and Canada Post regulations. The PASS manual describes the various PRESORT levels and presort qualification/preparation/identification requirements for packaged, sacked, and palletized (*see* PALLET) mail.

**PASTE DRIER** compound added to ink during ink manufacture to increase the speed with which it will dry. Paste driers consist of a metallic portion, such as cobalt, lead, or manganese, and an oil or resin portion. Cobalt-based driers are the strongest and are commonly used in WET PRINTING.

**PASTEUP** *see* MECHANICAL.

**PA SYSTEM** *see* PUBLIC ADDRESS SYSTEM.

**PATCH** correction or revision pasted on or stripped into an original and soldered into a printing plate. Patches are commonly used by printers to rectify last-minute mistakes and changes, so as to avoid the cost of having to create an entirely new piece of work.

**PATENT** government grant of exclusive rights to sell an item or to license its manufacture. U.S. patents are effective for 17 years, at which point the exclusivity is void. Patents are usually granted to the designer/inventor of the item if the patent is applied for and approved before knowledge of the design becomes part of the public domain. *See also* SERVICE MARK; TRADEMARK.

**PATENT MEDICINE** *see* OVER-THE-COUNTER DRUGS.

**PATRONAGE DIVIDEND AND REBATE** wholesaler vouchers issued to retailers and used as incentive builders by wholesalers to generate increased retailer sales and goodwill. A patronage dividend occurs when a wholesaler offers a retailer a pro rata share of earnings from one or many of the wholesaler's products. A patronage rebate, on the other hand, occurs when a wholesaler refunds part of a retailer's original payment for goods. In both cases, payment may be issued to retailers in the form of a bank check or a merchandise credit voucher.

**PATRONAGE PRICING** *see* PATRONAGE DIVIDEND AND REBATE.

**PAYLOAD**
1. cargo or freight producing revenue or income, usually expressed in weight. Any kind of merchandise that a carrier transports and that will be sold for profit is considered a payload.
2. returned merchandise transported by truck to a wholesaler, while en route to another merchandise delivery. Since the truck did not have to make an extra trip to return the unwanted products, its trip was not considered unprofitable.

**PAYMENT METHOD** means of payment employed by a customer, such as cash, check, money order, or credit card with order or upon invoicing; also called *payment type*. Customer RECORDS usually contain information regarding payment method and may include claims paid (*see* CLAIMS PAID COMPLAINT) as a payment method. LIST RENTAL selections are sometimes made by payment type if the marketer is interested in reaching a particular type of buyer, such as a credit card buyer, who can respond to a TELEMARKETING promotion by paying on order via credit card. Marketers can also improve response by offering similar payment terms on subsequent purchases, such as offering a CREDIT-ORDER option to previous credit buyers.

**PAYOUT** return on investment equal to the original marketing expenditure; also known as *payback*. When a company recovers its investment plus the expected built-in return from launching or reintroducing a new product or service, it has realized a profit from its original capital outlay. A company's payout, therefore, represents the minimum amount of dollar sales that must be generated to offset the cost of an advertising program. *See also* BREAK-EVEN ANALYSIS.

**PAY TV** *see* CABLE TELEVISION.

**PAY-UP** extent to which CREDIT ORDERS received in response to a promotion are paid at the point that billing of past-due accounts is stopped and unpaid accounts are written off. The pay-up percent is a good relative measure of the profitability of a promotion or product. For example, assume that product A sells for $10 and has a pay-up percent of 60% and that product B sells for $7 and has a pay-up percent of 90%. If 100 units of each are sold, Product A will generate $600 in revenue, and Product B, $630 in revenue. The pay-up speed is also important because of the time value of money—that is, $600 received today is worth more than $600 received a year from today.

**PDS AGENT** *see* PAID DURING SERVICE.

**PEEL-OFF LABEL** *see* PRESSURE-SENSITIVE LABEL.

**PENALTY MAIL** federal government mail, used only by government officials other than members of Congress, without prepayment of postage. The OUTER ENVELOPE or WRAPPER must say "OFFICIAL BUSINESS" and include the mailing agency's name. Penalty mail is intended to be used only for official government business. *See also* FRANKED MAIL .

**PENETRATION** measure of the degree to which a product or promotion has reached the individuals in a geographic area or MARKET. For example, an ethnic food product such as taco sauce would have a high penetration in Texas or New Mexico and a low penetration in New England. However, if it is a popular brand of taco sauce it could have a high penetration in the taco sauce market (consumers of Mexican food) within New England. Similarly, a Yiddish radio program would have a higher penetration in New York City than in upper New York State. The ultimate high-penetration advertising campaign is the one employed by Coca-Cola, which reaches a great number of people in virtually every region of the world. *See also* MARKET PENETRATION.

**PENETRATION MODELS** mathematical technique for projecting product ADOPTION levels over time based on the number of REPEAT SALES made during the early stages of product introduction and some assumptions as to the maximum probable penetration rate. Penetration models usually assume that 100% penetration of the market will never be reached. *See also* EPIDEMIC MODEL; PENETRATION.

**PENETRATION PRICING** pricing method of new product introduction to market that consists of pricing low and promoting heavily in order to gain a large market share and associated economies of scale as quickly as possible and before competition builds. This method assumes that consumers are price sensitive, that product awareness is low, and that competition will build quickly. *See also* SELECTIVE PENETRATION.

**PENETRATION STRATEGY** *see* MARKET PENETRATION.

**PEN NAME** pseudonym used by direct marketers to sign sales or service correspondence to customers. Pen names on customer service correspondence are frequently used to conceal the identity of individuals working for the marketer, who are thereby protected from receiving customer complaint calls at home. Some marketers, however, believe that the name should be genuine, and therefore use a product, promotion, or customer-service manager's name on all correspondence. When pen names are used, they are usually selected according to the type of product being sold. For example, a macho-sounding name like Scott Bullock would be a good pen name for a hunting supply catalog house, whereas a French name like Yves Printemp would be more appropriate to a cosmetic catalog house.

**PENNY-SAVER**
1. envelope with top flap sealed, and unopened flap tucked in for third-class mailing and postal inspection purposes; also known as *postage-saver*. Advertisers use penny-saver envelopes to create the impression that an envelope being mailed third class is sealed and is a first-class mailing. Since postal regulations specify that a sealed third-class mailing may be subject to inspection, some advertisers partially seal the envelope with a small spot of gum to keep their mailing intact.
2. name of local shopper's classified advertising guide distributed in the eastern and midwestern cities and towns in the U.S.

**PEOPLE METER**  device that resembles a remote control and is attached to a television set to measure consumer broadcast preferences, viewing frequencies, and viewer habits. A people meter usually is distributed to target households by a firm engaged in syndicated research in broadcast ratings, such as A. C. Nielsen Company. When the people meter is set up, each member of the family is assigned a button to push when viewing a television broadcast. The people meter also has buttons for visitors to press who may be watching a show with the family. From the signal transmitted from the people meter, the research firm is able to tell how long which family member or visitor is watching what program. Advertisers find this information helpful in targeting their advertising to a specific age, sex, and socioeconomic group of viewers watching their sponsored program. In addition, networks rely on people meters as a system to measure television audiences and, hence, to negotiate advertising contracts. People meters are newer and more accurate than the DIARY TECHNIQUE which relies on members of a television household to record who watched what show, and for how long.

**PERCEIVED RISK**  negative or unexpected consequences a consumer fears may occur as a result of making the wrong purchase decision. A high-priced, complex, DURABLE GOOD, like an automobile or personal computer, has a higher perceived risk than a low-priced, consumable commodity like hand soap. The greater the perceived risk, the more likely it is that the consumer will seek information about the product and the recommendations and experiences of peers before buying. Educated, self-confident, affluent consumers are less likely than others to perceive risk. In a situation with high perceived risk, the consumer is more likely to purchase the same brand repeatedly or to purchase a leading brand or one with performance guarantees and warranties; new products or brands will be avoided. *See also* INFORMED CHOICE; RISK REDUCTION THEORY.

**PERCEIVED VALUE**  benefit a consumer expects to gain from a product or service. Perceived value is derived from a combination of benefits that are tangible, like hunger abatement, and benefits that are psychosocial in nature, like status enhancement. The perceived value of a product has a direct effect on demand and should be one of the factors considered when establishing a price.

**PERCEIVED VALUE PRICING**  arbitrary pricing of a product based on its value as perceived by its buyers, as opposed to pricing based on the seller's costs of producing the product.

**PERCENTAGE-OF-SALES METHOD**  procedure used to set advertising budgets, based on a predetermined percentage of past sales or a forecast of future sales. This method of budget allocation is popular with advertisers because of its simplicity and its ability to relate advertising expenditures directly to sales. Management usually determines the budget's percentage figure, which is based on the industry average or the company's historical or previous year's advertising spending. For example, a firm expecting to do $50 million worth of business next year and choosing to allocate 5% of their sales to the advertising budget, would propose a $2.5 million advertising budget. A similar decision may be based on market share, with $2 million being allocated for every share point a brand holds. Many advertisers, however, shun this method because it is based on the theory that advertising results from sales, while the converse is true, that is, that sales result from advertising. In other words, advertisers feel that advertising communicates to prospective buyers the features and benefits of a product that are necessary to generate sales. In addition, the method does not recognize that as conditions change, advertising expenditures should change with them. Finally, using this method may erroneously lead to excessive spending for large established brands and inadequate budgeting for products that may profit from additional advertising, such as new or repositioned brands.

**PERCENT OF RETURN**  *see* RESPONSE RATE.

**PERCEPTUAL MAPPING**  process by which consumers' perceptions of an existing product are charted. Consumers answer questions about a given product based on their experience with the product and their thoughts about what the product should be. Answers are plotted on a graph, and the results are used to make improvements in the product or in the creation of new products. *See also* MULTIDIMENSIONAL SCALING.

**PER DIEM**  (Latin for "by day") daily allowance, usually for travel, entertainment, employee compensation, or miscellaneous out-of-pocket expenses while conducting a business transaction. The sum of money is always calculated on a daily basis, and may be paid in advance or after the expense is incurred. Employees are sometimes paid on a per diem basis.

**PERFECT BINDING**  method of binding magazines, books, and catalogs in which the pages are bound to the cover and held together by a thin strip of adhesive, forming a squared edge; also called *patent* *binding; adhesive binding.* Perfect binding is better suited than saddle stitching (*see* SADDLE STITCH) to a thick publication with many pages, such as *Vogue* magazine, since it makes it lie flatter when closed and the pages turn easily. Perfect binding is sometimes used to denote quality.

**PERFECTING PRESS** PRINTING PRESS that prints both sides of the paper, in one color, in one pass through the press; also called *perfector.* Perfecting presses save printing time and reduce paper usage. They are commonly used in offset LITHOGRAPHY and in LASER PRINTERS.

**PERFECT UNITARY ELASTICITY** ELASTICITY equal to one, such that a percentage change in one VARIABLE is balanced by a resultant percentage change in another. For example, a product would have perfect unitary elasticity of demand if an increase in price results in a decrease in demand (i.e., total units sold) without a change in total revenue. For example, a theater may be able to sell 100 tickets at $20 each and only 80 tickets at $25 each, but at either price/demand combination the total revenue is $2000. In most cases, perfect unitary elasticity does not occur. For example, small changes in the price of an item with a few substitutes, such as salt, show no change in demand.

**PERFORATION** row of unconnected cuts in a sheet of paper that make it easy to tear off a portion of the sheet, such as a CENTS-OFF COUPON or order form. *See also* BLIND PERF.

**PERGAMON AGB** British marketing research company, similar to AC NIELSEN COMPANY, that compiles data on television viewing audiences throughout the United Kingdom and Europe and sells the data to interested advertisers.

**PER INQUIRY DEAL** *see* PER-INQUIRY PAYMENT.

**PER-INQUIRY PAYMENT** payment based on a percentage of all money received from an advertiser's sales or inquiries, rather than on the published time or space rates. Per-inquiry (PI) payments occur when there is an agreement between an advertiser and a medium operator or between a LIST USER and a LIST OWNER for a specified amount of money to be paid for every order or inquiry received. This specified sum of money may or may not be higher than the rate published on the rate card, depending on the number of inquiries received. For example, if a station operator arranged a $5 per-inquiry deal with an advertiser, and 20 inquiries were received, the advertiser would be obligated to make a $100 per-inquiry payment to the station. To keep an accurate check on the number of inquiries received, some publishers or station owners require that all inquiries be directed to their headquarters. Per-inquiry deals are frequently made to introduce advertisers to new media.

**PERIODICAL** *see* PUBLICATION.

**PERIODICAL PUBLISHERS ASSOCIATION**  *see* MAGAZINE PUB-
LISHERS ASSOCIATION.

**PERMIT MAIL**  *see* INDICIA.

**PERPETUAL KILL FILE**  HOUSE list, similar to the DMA MAIL PREF-
ERENCE SERVICE DELETE FILE, listing individuals who have sent requests
to the marketer asking that additional promotions not be sent to them.
It is used in a MERGE/PURGE prior to any promotions being sent, to
eliminate those names from the promotion list. Deleting the names
saves the marketer the expense of promoting individuals who are not
likely to respond and assures compliance with direct-marketing-indus-
try ethical guidelines. *See also* CEASE ORDER.

**PERSONAL COMPUTER**  *see* MICROCOMPUTER.

**PERSONAL INFLUENCE**  power of individuals to sway or control the
purchasing decisions of others. Personal influence can be either external or internal. External personal influence involves social interaction
between two or more people, such as a neighbor, a mother, a father,
and a child. For example, a mother might seek advice from a neighbor about a product and convey this information to her family. Internal
personal influence occurs when decisions are influenced by mental
processes that have to do with other people or groups. For example,
a teenager may purchase a record album because he wants to be perceived as being "with it" to his friends. In both cases, identifying personal influences in a target market and turning these influences into
a positive force is important to advertisers because face-to-face
communication frequently has more impact than "nonpersonal" advertising in determining brand choice. *See also* OPINION LEADER; WORD-
OF-MOUTH ADVERTISING.

**PERSONAL INTERVIEW**  market research technique for gathering
information through face-to-face contact with individuals. Personal
interviews take place in a variety of settings—in homes, at shopping
malls, in a business office. This type of research is relatively costly,
because it requires a staff of interviewers, but it provides the best
opportunity to obtain information through probing for clearer expla-
nations. The personal style (tone of voice, rewording of a question) and
biases of each interviewer can affect how the participants respond
and how the responses are recorded. It is the best technique to use early
on in the research process when the researcher is not yet sure which
questions need to be asked, because new and better questions can come
out of the dialogue.

**PERSONALITY**
1. individual in the public eye, such as an athlete or a political or
   screen personality. The use of a personality by advertisers (or their
   agencies) as a SPOKESPERSON for their products or services in an
   advertising campaign is called *personality advertising*. The idea

behind personality advertising is that people may be more likely to use a product or service if they feel that some famous person recommends and uses it. *See also* TESTIMONIAL ADVERTISING.

**2.** *see* FORMAT.

**PERSONALITY ADVERTISING** *see* PERSONALITY.

**PERSONALIZATION** *see* COMPUTER PERSONALIZATION.

**PERSONAL PREFIX CODING** process of computer assigning a prefix such as Mr., Miss, or Mrs. to each name on a file according to the gender normally associated with that name. *See also* GENDER ANALYSIS.

**PERSONAL SELLING** delivery of a specially designed message to a prospect by a seller, usually in the form of face-to-face communication, personal correspondence, or a personal telephone conversation. Unlike advertising, a personal sales message can be more specifically targeted to individual prospects and easily altered if the desired behavior does not occur. Personal selling, however, is far more costly than advertising and is generally used only when its high expenditure can be justified. For example, the marketing of a sophisticated computer system may require the use of personal selling, while the introduction of a new product to millions of consumers would not. Two other forms of personal selling that are not used with high-end products are door-to-door selling and home demonstration parties. These two personal selling methods are primarily used for personal care products, cosmetics, cookware, encyclopedias, books, toys, food, and other items of special interest to homemakers. Ideally, personal selling should be supported by advertising to strengthen its impact.

**PERSON-TO-PERSON SALES** *see* PERSONAL SELLING.

**PERSPECTIVE**
   **1.** technique of visually suggesting a feeling of depth in a flat presentation, by using points or lines that vanish in relationship to pictured objects as the objects recede. Producers frequently use perspective to create illusions and special effects on stage sets. Color can also be used, along with linear graphic design, to create perspective in print advertisements.
   **2.** effect of space created by audio-matching the distance of a sound source. To achieve the desired perspective, audio technicians place sound sources and microphones at different distances.

**PERSUASION** act of inducing attitude changes and influencing a target market to action, by appealing to reason or emotion. Persuasion is a primary objective of modern advertising and can be achieved by creating advertisements with some combination of the following elements: effective attention-getting devices, a strong appeal to self-interest, a stimulation of desire for a product or service, and a powerful call-to-action response.

**PH** measure of the acidity or alkalinity of a substance, such as the solution used to develop film. The measurement range goes from 0 (acidic) to 14 (alkaline), with pH 7 being neutral. Paper with a pH of 7 tends to be longlasting.

**PHANTOM POST OFFICE BOX** LOCKBOX identification number provided to customers by a direct-mail organization or printed on reply envelopes, used to facilitate the sorting of large volumes of incoming mail. A phantom lockbox number does not represent a physical box; it indicates a type of mail the recipient wants to receive separately from other mail, such as mail for a special department within the company. Some local post offices will sort mail by phantom box number before delivering it to the recipient, but this service cannot always be relied upon consistently. The recipient pays the USPS for each phantom number as if it were a real box.

Most direct marketers purchase several phantom post office boxes to separate credit order payments from orders. They may also ask their customers to use a special post office box for all inquiries, complaints, and/or address change requests. It is easier for the marketer to distribute mail for processing when it is received by processing type.

**PHASING** U.S. POSTAL SERVICE privilege granted designated mailers enabling them to pay additional postage, when rates are increased by the POSTAL RATE COMMISSION on a phased basis over time, so that the full increase is not applied to their mail until the end of the phasing period.

**PHOTOCOMPOSITION** NON-METALLIC COMPOSITION technique using photographically created characters such as film or photographic paper rather than metal type slugs; also called COLD TYPE. *See also* HOT TYPES; PHOTOMECHANICAL.

**PHOTOCOPY** exact photographic reproduction, made directly on sensitized paper. Writings, printed material, drawings, and photographs are commonly photocopied in seconds with a cameralike machine called a photocopier. When copies are being made, the original may be reproduced to actual size or it can be enlarged or reduced many times. The copies are usually in black and white, although some photocopiers are equipped to render color reproductions. Strict laws govern the use of photocopying copyrighted material. Also, familiarly referred to as *Xerox,* after the xerographic machine manufactured by the Xerox Corporation.

**PHOTOMECHANICAL** print image carrier produced by photographically exposing a surface coated with light-sensitive material. Photomechanicals are used to reproduce CONTINUOUS TONE images such as photographs. The photomechanical process makes it possible to combine both type and picture images on the same image carrier. *See also* PHOTOCOMPOSITION.

**PHOTOMONTAGE**  MONTAGE designed exclusively with photographs and reproduced as a single photograph (usually blown up).

**PHOTOPOLYMER COATING**  photosensitive plastic applied to the surface of a flat printing plate. The plastic can be chemically altered to create a print image area receptive to ink and a nonimage area non-receptive to ink.

**PHOTOSTAT**  high-contrast photographic copy of any written, printed, drawn, typewritten, or photographed material in the form of paper negatives or positives; also called *stat*. Photostats are made on a machine called the Photostat and may be obtained quickly and at low cost. When making a photostat, the original is photographed through a lens with a prism and reproduced onto sensitized paper. A paper negative is made first, with the original values being reversed; that is, the print appears as white on black. Photostat negatives are frequently used when making a reverse photoengraving of a LINE COPY. To make a positive print, the negative print is simply shot again with the same Photostat machine. Because of the quality and affordability of copies, Photostats are frequently used for reproducing text, documents, and artwork, and for positioning layouts.

**PHOTOTYPESETTING**  *see* NONMETALLIC COMPOSITION.

**PHYSICAL SACKING**  *see* LOGICAL SACKING.

**PI**  in printing, individual type characters that have inadvertently become scrambled after having been set (*pi*); also called *pied type*.

**PI**  per inquiry. See PER INQUIRY PAYMENT.

**PIA AGENT**  *see* PAID IN ADVANCE.

**PICA**
1. unit of measure used in COMPOSITION equal to 1/6th of an inch.
2. 12 POINTS.
3. typewriter type font measuring 10 characters to the inch. *See also* ELITE.

**PICK-AND-PACK**  merchandise shipment process whereby items are selected (*picked*) from a warehouse according to what has been ordered by each customer, and then packed for shipment. Pick-and-pack is easy when every customer receives the same items but becomes complex when each customer orders various quantities and types of items from a variety of available merchandise. The different quantities and items require different sizes and types of packaging and increase the possibility of sending too much, too little, or the wrong items. The pick-and-pack process can be greatly simplified by a COMPUTER-ASSISTED PICKING SYSTEM. *See also* SHIPPING ORDER.

**PICKING**  *see* PICK AND PACK.

**PICK MODULE**  *see* COMPUTER-ASSISTED PICKING SYSTEM.

**PICKUP MATERIAL**  advertising material that is used again, in part or in entirety, in a different advertisement; also called *pickup*. Art or copy can be "picked up" by a printer or typesetter respectively, and placed on another advertisement. Since the same art and copy do not have to be created all over again for a different job, the use of pickup material saves both agencies and advertisers time and money.

**PICK-YOUR-OWN-TERM**  subscription promotion technique that allows subscribers to select the number of issues they want based upon a per copy price rather than forcing them to select a specific term, such as 6 or 12 months. Pick-your-own-term is often offered by news-weekly magazines, thus enabling them to avoid printing a high price on the order form (such as the price of a 12-month term), which might depress response. For example, "69¢ per copy" is much more appealing to a prospective subscriber than the equivalent "$36 per year." The subscriber receives the added benefit of a short-term trial-subscription option. *See also* HARD OFFER; TRIAL OFFER.

**PIECE**  *see* PACKAGE.

**PIECE RATE**  postage due per individual piece of mail, as distinguished from charges based upon the distance traveled. Mailing a FIRST-CLASS letter costs the same regardless of whether it is mailed across town or across the country. Periodicals mailed SECOND CLASS pay postage based upon a combination of ZONE CHARGES and piece rates. *See also* ADVERTISING WEIGHT.

**PIED TYPE**  *see* PI.

**PIGGYBACK COMMERCIAL**  two or more broadcast commercials aired one after the other, featuring different products of the same sponsor. Advertisers use piggyback commercials to get two or more unrelated advertising messages into the time allocated for one, without increasing commercial time. Advertisers generally purchase commercial spots from stations and network as a single unit.

**PIGGYBACK LABEL**  *see* PRESSURE-SENSITIVE LABEL.

**PIGMENT**  particles that are made of various natural and synthetic substances used to add color to solutions such as ink or paint. *See also* VARNISH; VEHICLE.

**PILOT**
**Broadcast:** sample television or radio program produced to introduce networks or prospective sponsors to the potential of an entire new series. The pilot affords advertisers the opportunity to become acquainted with the specific format, talent, and quality of the production, which in turn will help facilitate their sponsorship decision. For the producer, however, the creation of pilots is an expensive proposition. Producers must invest many hours in script editing, shooting, and hiring talent, and speculate large amounts of money that can be divided among programs only if the series is sold.

**Outdoor advertising:** BULLETIN used as a sample by agencies to plan an optimal way to display an advertising message. Artists use pilots to show advertisers the impact that different graphic variations of an advertising message can have on their strategy.

**PILOT STUDY** consumer-research study done on a trial basis to determine the potential of a larger and more in-depth survey of the same subject matter; also called *pilot survey*. A pilot study is used in SEGMENTATION product usage, and attitudinal, motivational, and other types of market research studies. For example, a market researcher may conduct a pilot study on a sample of 500 mothers to determine their attitudes about a certain type of diaper. If the study results show that the mothers responded favorably to the new brand, another study may be conducted with a larger sample size to determine other factors, such as diaper usage.

**PIMS (PROFIT IMPACT OF MARKETING STRATEGIES)** program that provides marketers with a database summarizing the financial and market performance of a few thousand business units representing several hundred companies. PIMS data describe the interaction between marketing factors, profitability, and cash flow, allowing a company to evaluate the potential effects of various marketing strategies on the performance of its products.

**PINFEED HOLES** rows of holes on each side of CONTINUOUS FORMS, used to mount the paper on pins that feed it through computer printers. The position of the pins and the rotation of the rollers on which they are mounted control the speed and alignment of the paper, keeping it in REGISTER for printing.

**PINK SHEET** *see* ABC STATEMENT.

**PIN REGISTER** technique for aligning two or more print impressions on a sheet of paper, or two or more pieces of film, by punching holes in the paper or film and mounting it onto pins that hold it in precise alignment.

**PIPELINE** manufacturer's inventory that has been sold to wholesalers and retailers, but has not been bought by consumers. When this inventory leaves the manufacturer's warehouse, the wholesaler or retailer must assume the carrying costs of the inventory. Some examples of inventory carrying costs are storage charges, the cost of capital, taxes, and insurance, and depreciation and obsolescence.

**PITCH**

**1.** presentation by one or more persons from an advertising agency to a prospective account. In this presentation, the agency will use a portfolio, slides, video, STORY BOARD or other devices to review its organizational setup, results for other clients, types of accounts, experience of personnel, specializations, extra fee charges, and any other information that is pertinent to winning the account. If the presentation is a *speculative pitch*, the agency will submit actual sample campaigns that include copy and LAYOUT to the prospective client. Since a speculative pitch is backed by an agency's research, art, typography, and other out-of-pocket expenses, it usually involves considerable expense. The industry generally objects to speculative pitches because it is felt that the speculative campaign is rarely based on a thorough knowledge of company policy, objectives, or competitive advantages.

**2.** presentation, sometimes high-pressure, to a prospect by a salesperson, to solicit an order or new business. In making a sales pitch to a prospective client, a salesperson usually begins with a positive opening line, demonstrates the features of the product while concentrating on selling its benefits, handles objections with a positive approach, and ends by asking for the order.

**PIX** informal term for pictures. *Pix* usually refers to still photographs used by art directors and photographers, such as shots of objects on a table.

**PLANNED OBSOLESCENCE** marketing practice whereby products are designed to become out of date long before they actually need replacement. Planned obsolescence capitalizes on such things as material wear-out, style changes, or functional changes and is said by its critics to increase waste, resource shortages, and environmental pollution. However, advocates of planned obsolescence consider it a means of satisfying changing consumer demands.

**PLANS BOARD** advertising agency executive committee that meets regularly to plan strategies and review proposed advertisements for clients. Senior management members representing the major departments of the agency are generally on an agency's plans board. After a meeting takes place, the departmental heads usually meet with their respective ACCOUNT EXECUTIVES to review the specific tactics to be used in a client's advertising.

**PLANT LOADING** *see* IN-PLANT LOADING.

**PLANT OPERATORS** *see* OUTDOOR ADVERTISING.

**PLATE** *see* PRINTING PLATE.

**PLATE CYLINDER** ROTARY PRESS device upon which the PRINTING PLATES are mounted.

**PLATE FINISH** uncoated paper surface that is smoother than that of all other uncoated papers, including calendared and supercalendared papers. The smooth finish is achieved by pressing the paper between smooth metal plates. *See also* CALENDAR ROLLS; SUPERCALENDAR.

**PLATTER** informal term for a phonograph record. Platters are used by advertisers to deliver promotional or educational messages about a product or service, or as a PREMIUM for those who respond to a special promotional offer.

## PLAYBACK

**Broadcasting:** reproduction of an audio or video recording, immediately after it has been made, in order to determine if the recording is of high standard. After viewing the playback, editing changes are usually made and problems that have been uncovered are rectified.

**Research:** respondent's verbatim account of answers to a market research survey or the details of an advertisement recently seen. A playback is generally used in qualitative market research studies to assess consumers' attitudes about a product and/or their specific recollection of an advertisement.

**PLOW-BACK METHOD** system of appropriating all money representing net profit received during a previous period to the advertising budget. The plow-back method is used by advertisers who want to invest maximum dollars in their promotions. A new-product promotion is an example of a situation where the plow-back method is usually used, since large up-front expenditures are usually required to generate consumer interest and overcome competitive restraints. Dollars may be "plowed back" into the advertising allocation every year until a stabilization point is reached.

## PLUG

1. favorable mention of a product, service, or personality on a radio or television show, at no charge to the advertiser. For example, a talk-show host may take time out from the program to discuss the merits of a new energy-saving product. In this specific example, the station would not charge the product's manufacturer for plugging the product on the show.
2. *see* COMMERCIAL.

**PMS COLORS** (acronym for *P*antone *M*atching *S*ystem colors) industry standards for various shades of ink color created by printing specified proportions and densities of primary color on paper. For example, a particular shade of blue may be 50% cyan and 5% magenta on a white surface. A printer's customer may request a particular shade, using a PMS identifying number taken from a PMS color chart.

**P.O. BOX** *see* LOCKBOX.

## POINT

**In general:**
1. unit of measurement.
2. *see* NET RATING POINT.
3. *see* GROSS RATING POINT.

**Advertising:** unit of measurement equal to $1/1000$-inch thickness of cardboard, used primarily in POINT-OF-PURCHASE ADVERTISING. For example, the thickness of an area of board used for a point-of-purchase display may be 50 points.

**Printing:** unit of measurement equal to 0.0138 ($1/72$) of an inch and $1/2$ of a PICA, used chiefly for designating type sizes. The point system is a standard measurement in typography used by typographers, compositors, and printers. Type is measured from the metal body bearing its typeface, and not from its actual character. When using this standardized method of measurement, 72-point type is approximately 1 inch high, and 36-point type is $^1/2$ inch high. Type can be created in any size, although the most popular cast sizes are 6, 8, 10, 12, 14, 18, 24, 30, 36, 42, 48, 60, and 72 point type.

**POINTER** *see* FLAG.

**POINT-OF-DELIVERY CODE**  code assigned to prospective customer or current customer RECORDS that identifies a type of address, such as business, single-family home, multifamily dwelling, and so forth. LIST RENTAL selections are frequently made by point-of-delivery code so that promotions appropriate to a particular address type will be sent only to those addresses. For example, a promotion for a lawn-care product should be sent to residents of single-family homes, not to tenants of apartment or office buildings.

**POINT-OF-PURCHASE ADVERTISING**  advertising that is built around impulse purchasing and that utilizes DISPLAY designed to catch a shopper's eye particularly at the place where payment is made, such as a checkout counter. There are various types of point-of-purchase displays, including window displays, counter displays, FLOOR STANDS, DISPLAY bins, BANNERS of any kind, and all types of open and closed DISPLAY CASES. Generally, these displays are created and prepared by the manufacturer for distribution to wholesalers or retailers who sell the manufacturer's merchandise. Often, a manufacturer will discount the cost of merchandise or in some other way compensate the retailer for using a point-of-purchase display.

**POINT-OF-PURCHASE ADVERTISING INSTITUTE (POPAI)** nonprofit organization founded in 1938 to promote more effective use of POINT-OF-PURCHASE ADVERTISING by providing advertisers, retailers, and producers with data on creating, producing, supplying, and purchasing this medium. Membership is composed of point-of-purchase display designers and manufacturers, suppliers, national advertisers, and retailers.

**POLITICAL ADVERTISING**  advertising whose central focus is the marketing of ideas, attitudes, and concerns about public issues, including political concepts and political candidates. The essential task of political advertising is to gain the confidence of the people for their acceptance of ideas and, in the case of political campaign advertising, to influence their vote. Political advertising differs from commercial advertising in that the product is either a person or a philosophy rather than goods and services, and, in addition, the advertising objectives must be met within a specific time frame. Also, political advertising carries a moral implication, because the results have potentially far-reaching effects on the population at large. Political advertising raises many controversial social questions concerning the funding of political campaigns, the truth or reality of political claims, and the likelihood of slanderous or libelous claims made by political candidates.

**POLITICAL ENVIRONMENT** *See* MACROENVIRONMENT.

**POLITICAL MARKETING** marketing designed to influence consumers about political issues, particular candidates for public office, or public issues. Although political marketing uses many of the same techniques that other forms of marketing do, it is actually used to promote a concept or an idea, rather than a specific product or service, and to motivate people to vote for that idea.

**POLYBAG**
**Direct Marketing:** polyethylene bag, heat sealed or open at one end, used to deliver one or more mailing pieces to an address. Polybags may be transparent or colorfully printed. They are the dominant carrier for CARD DECKS because of their low cost and attention-getting power, and usually have a tear strip at one end to open them easily.

Polybags have been used for many years by ALTERNATE DELIVERY services, who hang polybags carrying several promotional pieces, publications, product samples, and/or catalogs on doorknobs, instead of leaving the material in mailboxes, which are reserved for the exclusive use of the U.S. Postal Service.

Because of regulations passed by the USPS in 1986, second-class mailers, such as magazines, can mail promotional material such as brochures, reply cards, and catalogs inside the same sealed polybag as the magazine and pay second-class postage on everything. These are commonly referred to as *piggyback mailings, outserts, or ridealongs.* One thing that cannot be mailed at second-class rates is a product sample, which must mail third-class. In early 1987, the USPS considers anything that could not conceivably be bound into the magazine a product sample; therefore, fragrance strips and paper-embedded cosmetic samples can usually qualify for second-class treatment, while a bar of soap cannot. Stricter regulations were being considered at the time of publication that would disallow anything not relevant to the contents of the magazine.
**Merchandising:** polybags are also used to package retail merchandise such as groceries, hardware, and garments.

**PONY SPREAD** *see* JUNIOR PAGE.

**POOL PARTNER** *see* COMMERCIAL POOL.

**POOR TRAPPING** printing problem that occurs when additional layers of ink do not properly adhere to previous layers. This is usually controlled by using ink of progressively less TACK for each layer. *See also* TRAPPING.

**POP-IN** short paid announcement by a radio or television advertiser that may be of special interest to the viewer or listener. For example, during the holiday season a common pop-in by advertisers may be, "Company X wishes you and your family a very merry Christmas and a happy new year." In this example, there is no mention of the company's product, but the viewer or listener is informed that Company X is the sponsor of the message. Also called *image liner*.

**POP-OFF** quick and instantaneous movement of objects or information from on camera to off camera in a television program; also called *bump out*. In a popoff, new optical picture information, such as titles to a FRAME, are removed from the field of the camera.

**POP-ON** quick addition of new optical picture information in the field of a television camera; also called *bump in*. When objects or information such as titles to a FRAME are popped on, they appear suddenly on a television program's camera, as opposed to being popped off (*see* POPOFF), or removed from the field of the camera.

**POPULATION** *see* UNIVERSE.

**POP-UP** DIE-CUT brochure or other form of direct-mail or print advertising designed to rise or "pop up" when opened by a recipient. Pop-up mechanisms are used by graphic designers as attention-getting devices to add a "third dimension" to a certain element of a brochure. When a pop-up folder is opened, its pop-up mechanism is activated by a specially designed die-cut fold that will cause a specific graphic element to rise from the brochure's center. Pop-up folders are far more costly to produce than regular brochures and are generally used only when a special effect is desired.

**POROSITY** characteristic of paper that allows liquids or vapors to seep through it. The porosity of paper is used as a measure of the strength of the paper, because porosity is a function of loosely or closely bonded paper fibers. *See also* ABSORPTION.

**POSITION**
**In general:** place on page where an advertisement or insert appears, in relation to its placement on the page and/or the front, middle, or back of the publication. Because of a reader's viewing habits, the position of an advertisement plays an important role in determining its effectiveness. For example, certain positions, such as the back cover of a magazine or page 3 of a newspaper, frequently are desirable and command PREMIUM rates because studies have shown that they are almost always read. A publication's advertisement may be positioned on a right- or left-hand page, at the top of or below an editorial column, near or completely surrounded by editorial copy, adjacent to the GUTTER, or close to or enclosing around other advertisements. Most advertisers place print advertising on a RUN OF PAPER (ROP) basis; that is, the position of the advertisement is determined by the publisher, and the advertisement may appear anywhere within the run of the publication. However, some advertisers feel that a PREFERRED POSITION warrants the added expense and may request such a position on their

INSERTION ORDER. For example, sporting goods manufacturers may pay a preferred position rate to have their ads run in the sports section of a newspaper. On the other hand, some advertisers may elect to go with an ROP rate but will indicate a preference for a certain position on their insertion order (e.g., front forward, right-hand page, top of column, outside the column, adjacency to editorial matter) and will hope that the publication honors their request.

**Broadcast:** programs or time SPOTS felt by advertisers to be particularly desirable. In both radio and television, position is determined by time periods, with those spots watched and listened to by large audiences commanding high rates. For example, station-break spot announcements following programs with high ratings are sought after by advertisers and are offered at a PREMIUM price. *See also* ADJACENCY.

**Marketing:** marketing strategy that attempts to control the perception of a product or service relative to competitive products or services. For example: A particular brand of perfume is positioned, by the advertiser as the most expensive perfume in the world. And a computer company positions itself as the most reliable, service-oriented company. Statistical techniques such as MULTIDIMENSIONAL SCALING are used to identify the position of a product in the market according to the perception of consumers. Marketers attempt to control their position in the market as part of a total marketing strategy. The seller of the above-mentioned expensive perfume is employing a strategy that will cream the highest-price buyers off the top of the market. The computer company's positioning supports a strategy that is geared toward risk-averse buyers willing to pay extra for peace of mind. However, as computers become more commonplace, the sense of risk is reduced and the computer company will need to reevaluate its positioning strategy.

**POSITIONING**  *see* POSITION.

**POSITIVE**  photographic image that looks like the original, as distinguished from a NEGATIVE, which reverses the black and white (or high density and low density) areas of the original. Some printing is done from positives.

**POSITIVE APPEAL**  advertising copy approach that attempts to alleviate a person's anxiety about buying and using a product. The positive appeal stresses the positive aspects of a product and the positive gains for a person who purchases the product. *See also* NEGATIVE APPEAL.

**POSITIVE OPTION**  CONTINUITY or BOOK CLUB marketing technique that requires the customer to take some action prior to each regular merchandise shipment to indicate that the merchandise is wanted. This technique can be much less effective in terms of revenue per customer than NEGATIVE-OPTION programs, which ship the merchandise unless the customer takes some action to say no. However, customers can usually be recruited more easily for positive-option programs.

**POSTAL CODE** ALPHANUMERIC code assigned to groups of addresses by various national postal systems throughout the world to facilitate mail delivery. Since each country has its own coding system, international direct marketers find it difficult to maintain complete files of valid postal codes. The U.S. postal code is called the ZIP CODE; in Canada, the code is referred to as the CANADIAN POSTAL CODE (CPC).

**POSTAL CUSTOMER COUNCIL** group sponsored by the U.S. POSTAL SERVICE to give mailers a channel for communication with the Postal Service at a local level; abbreviated PCC. The PCC informs other mailers of new regulations and rates, organizes postal facility tours, and helps mailers to make the best use of postal services and products. Any mailer wishing to be on the local PCC may volunteer through his CUSTOMER SERVICE REPRESENTATIVE. Meetings are usually held monthly, during which new USPS regulations and services are explained and ideas are shared.

**POSTAL FILE** file maintained by direct marketers containing all necessary POSTAL CODES and the address areas to which they apply. It is used to supply missing postal codes and to validate those entered to a computer address file.

**POSTAL INSPECTION SERVICE** division of the U.S. POSTAL SERVICE responsible for the enforcement of laws regarding MAIL FRAUD. The Postal Inspection Service can criminally prosecute offenders and/or forcibly close their business. They may also protect consumers from a fraudulent offer by stamping "fraudulent," "refused," or "out-of business" on envelopes addressed to the company in question and returning them to the senders.

**POSTAL RATE COMMISSION** group appointed by the President of the United States, and approved by the Senate, to make recommendations regarding postage rate changes and mail classification policies; abbreviated *PRC*. The PRC increases rates periodically when the U.S. POSTAL SERVICE budget shows an expected or actual deficit that requires such a move. The process begins with a rate change request from the USPS, followed by a flurry of lobbying activity on the part of mailers. Because the objective of the USPS is to break even, it is possible, but unlikely, that the PRC will lower rates when a budget surplus is expected. It usually takes 10 months for the PRC to evaluate a rate case and make a recommendation.

**POSTAL SERVICE PROHIBITORY ORDER** legally binding order given by the U.S. Postal Service to a mailer, at the request of an individual, that the mailer no longer send any promotions to the individual; also called CEASE ORDER. *See also* DMA MAIL PREFERENCE SERVICE DELETE FILE.

**POSTAL SORT SEQUENCE** *see* PRESORT.

**POSTAL VERIFICATION** audit of a particular mailer, conducted by the U.S. Postal Service, to ensure that his mail is entitled to SECOND-

CLASS treatment. Second-class authorization is granted to publications that are either paid for, or requested, by the recipient; it is not intended to be used for promotional mailings. *See also* REQUESTOR.

**POSTCARD MAILER** *see* CARDPACK.

**POSTER** *see* BILLBOARD.

**POSTER ART**
1. artwork displayed on a poster.
2. technique of reproducing original artwork on a poster format. The original may be an oil painting, photograph, pastel drawing, pen and-ink sketch, watercolor or the like. Most posters are reproduced through a lithograph process (*see* LITHOGRAPHY), although, when the quantity to be reproduced is not large in volume, other techniques may be employed. In the reproduction process, the poster artist must plan the LAYOUT of sheets carefully so as not to change the effect of the design and must also reproduce the artwork without sacrificing any of the color values or other elements of the display.

**POSTING** physically placing or painting an advertisement on any kind of OUTDOOR ADVERTISING or TRANSIT ADVERTISING. The posting of an outdoor or transit advertisement can be done as frequently as once a month, depending upon the conditions outlined in the contract. PAINTED DISPLAYS, however, are usually posted no less than twice a year because of the additional time and expense entailed in creating this type of outdoor display.

**POSTING DATE** date on which display of an OUTDOOR ADVERTISEMENT begins. Usually, posting dates are every fifth day, starting with the first of the month. For example, an advertiser's posting date may be on either January 1, 5, 10, 15, 20, 25, or 30. However, PLANT OPERATORS have adopted this posting date system for flexibility and will, if necessary, arrange another posting date if it is specifically requested by an advertiser.

**POSTING PERIOD** duration of time that an outdoor or transit advertisement is scheduled to be displayed, as specified in a contractual agreement. A posting period is most commonly 30 days, but may also be as long as 12 months. Posting periods for PAINTED DISPLAYS, which are generally customized and have a long life, are usually longer than for other types of OUTDOOR ADVERTISING or TRANSIT ADVERTISING, and are almost always one, two, or even three years. To maximize flexibility, advertisers will generally try to keep their posting periods short and extend them if satisfied with results.

**POSTMARK** imprint stamped on mail delivered by the U.S. Postal Service showing when (A.M. or P.M. and the date) the mail was received by the USPS and the name of the receiving post office or SECTIONAL CENTER FACILITY. By monitoring the postmarks on incoming mail, direct-mail marketers can identify service delays. Postmarks sometimes incorporate small advertising messages. *See also* POSTMARK ADVERTISING.

**POSTMARK ADVERTISING**   advertising that is printed by a postage meter machine on an envelope as part of the postmark. Postmark advertising is used by business organizations, public utilities, service associations, retailers, hotels, and other institutions on their mailing envelopes and usually takes the form of a brief message, slogan, or design logo. Type and the PRINTING PLATE for postmark advertising are composed by the manufacturer of the postage-meter machine. Postmark advertising must meet certain U.S. Postal Service requirements. Advertising must be nonpolitical and noncontroversial, and the messages are not to contain any data or design that might be construed as regular postal markings.

**POSTMASTER**   U.S. POSTAL SERVICE official responsible for managing a particular region of the postal system. The total system is directed by the Postmaster General. *See also* U.S. POSTAL BOARD OF GOVERNERS.

**POST OFFICE BOX**   *see* LOCKBOX.

**POST OFFICE BOX SECTION**   *see* LOCKBOX.

**POST OFFICE BRANCH**   extension of a main city or town post office located outside the corporate boundaries of the city or town it serves. *See also* POST OFFICE STATION.

**POST OFFICE STATION**   extension of a main city or town post office located inside the corporate boundaries of the city or town it serves. *See also* POST OFFICE BRANCH.

**POUNCE PATTERN**   technique of creating a large PAINTED DISPLAYS from a much smaller sample of original artwork. In the painted display plant shop, an art master is photographically blown up and projected to full size and then traced on a stencil. The pictorial artist will then use this rendering to reproduce the design on the display. Using this method is exacting work and requires skill and attention to meticulous detail to faithfully reproduce the original artwork.

**POUND**   unit of measure of the weight and thickness of paper, such as 50-pound paper equal to the weight of one REAM of paper. *See also* BASIS WEIGHT.

**PRE-BILL**   common policy of magazine wholesalers, who bill the retailer in advance of delivery for each issue of a publication. The newsstand dealer can get a refund for unsold copies. See NEWSTAND RETURNS.

**PRECANCELED STAMPS**   postage stamps canceled in advance by the U.S. Postal Service and sold in large volumes to mailers who want to reduce the amount of time the USPS will spend processing the mail. Mailers apply the stamps to their mailings before submitting them to the USPS for delivery.

**PREDICTIVE DIALER** type of AUTOMATIC DIALER that uses a PACING ALGORITHM to adjust the timing of OUTBOUND TELEPHONE calls dialed, so as to deliver an answered call to every operator as soon as the operator becomes available. Timing is based on the number of operators on hand, the historical percentage of calls answered, and the average length of a call. If call lengths fall outside the expected range, operators may sit idle or calls may be lost, due to a shortage of available operators. Most telemarketers strive to maintain a NO-OP rate of less than 2%.

**PREDICTIVE MODELING** *see* CIRCULATION MODELING; FINANCIAL MODELING.

**PREEMPT**
1. withholding of regularly scheduled radio or television time by a network for the presentation of a special priority broadcast. For example, a network may preempt an entire program or a portion of a program to broadcast a presidential speech, sports event, documentary special, or emergency news broadcast.
2. Local broadcast time subject to change to accommodate NETWORK broadcasting. If a local advertiser purchases broadcast time that falls under the network preemption clause, the local advertiser may have to give up this period to a national advertiser, if the national advertiser elects to buy that time for its network broadcast. The terms of network option time are stated in the local advertiser's contract, and if a preemption occurs, the local advertiser usually has the option to move to another time period or cancel his program.

**PREEMPTIBLE RATE** discount rate charged advertisers in BROADCAST MEDIA for time that may have to be relinquished if another advertiser is willing to pay more. It is a gamble the advertiser takes in return for a low rate.

**PREFERENCE PATTERN** graphical representation of the product or brand preferences exhibited by the consumers in a market. A preference pattern is drawn on an X/Y chart with each axis representing a product characteristic such as sweetness or spice. Some consumers will be clustered around the high sweetness, low spice points while others will prefer a low sweetness, low spice point. Preference patterns may be homogenous (everyone prefers the same brand), diffuse (no pattern is evident), or clustered (two or more characteristics show a high degree of preference).

**PREFERENTIAL NETWORK** services and facilities of the U.S. Postal Service dedicated to SECOND-CLASS publications. Prior to 1986 changes in the regulations, the preferential network was reserved for *red-tag* publications—news-value publications, published at least weekly and containing information about current events, that would decline in value to the reader if not delivered promptly. To help the USPS recognize these periodicals among the rest of the mail, mailers used a red or pink SACK TAG; hence, these publications came to be known as red tag publications. Now, all second-class publications go through the preferential network, although the USPS still attempts to give some priority to the news-value publications as often as it can, given the volume of mail it must handle.

**PREFERRED POSITION** specific placement of advertisements in publications, as requested by an advertiser, usually for a higher rate than RUN-OF-PAPER placement of advertisements. Many advertisers consider certain locations in a newspaper or magazine as choice positions for advertising and will request these spaces; for example, a women's dress manufacturer may request the women's page, or a sporting goods manufacturer may request the sports page. In addition, some advertisers feel that a right-hand page, the top of a column, or a space surrounded by editorial matter is a preferred position. Each publication specifies its own preferred position rate (although some publications will attempt to honor a preferred-position request, without additional charge).

**PREFERRED START** periodical subscription begun with an issue other than that currently being assigned to new subscribers. An ADVANCE START (future issue) may be requested by a subscriber who has already purchased the current issue on the newsstand or who will not be at the subscription address until a later date—for example, a college student receiving her subscription at school who requests a September-issue start. A preferred start might also be a preview issue requested by a subscriber who wants to read a particular issue (*see* BACK DATING). The publisher may also assign a preferred start to better manage sack-issue inventories or to control the circulation by issue.

**PREMATURE** NEWSTAND copies returned to the publisher prior to the OFF-SALE DATE if, judging from sales to date, it appears that the NEWS STAND DRAW will exceed sales. *See also* NEWSSTAND RETURNS.

**PREMIUM**
1. special item, bonus, or award offered free or at a nominal price as an incentive to induce a target market to purchase or obtain for trial a product or service. Advertisers use premiums to attract consumers who would not normally buy a product or service, or to encourage more frequent buying by those already buying the product. In addition, premiums are used to introduce new products, provide extra appeal in special sales events, meet competitive prices, provide copy appeal, promote larger size units, and excite a company's sales force. Newspapers, magazines, radio broadcasts, packages, store displays, outdoor advertising, direct-mail, and package inserts are frequently used to promote premiums. An advertiser who elects to charge for a premium may offer an $8 can opener to its target group for $1 plus 10 box tops of the product. On the other hand, an advertiser may elect to offer the can opener free with 10 proofs of purchases. In both examples, the advertiser has used

the premium to boost sales. When premiums are used as an incentive to try a product, such as a magazine, it is important that the premium selected be attractive enough to get qualified prospects to respond, but not so desirable that consumers are more interested in the gifts than the product being sold. In fact, many advertisers believe that the most effective premium is the one that is closely related to the type of product offered. For example, a baby food manufacturer may offer a rattle as a premium with the purchase of baby food. It is also felt that the premium should be visually appealing and, if possible, serve as a constant, favorable reminder of the promoted product, since the more often the premium is used, the more often the customer is reminded of the product. For example, advertisers frequently imprint their name on their premium to reinforce the relationship between themselves and the premium. *See also* PROMOTION MARKETING ASSOCIATION OF AMERICA.

**2.** higher charge paid for a product, service, or special advertising request. For example, advertisers who want to assure that their advertisement will receive maximum impact will pay a premium price for a preferred position, such as page 3 of a publication. In addition, advertisers with deadlines to meet will pay a premium to get their production completed in a short period of time. Also called *premium price.*

**3.** highest-priced product or service in the competitive marketplace. Premium products have recently assumed an important market niche. For example, marketers have found that some consumers are willing to pay a premium price to purchase a quality product for items such as ice cream, cookies, and upscale food specialties.

**PREMIUM ADVERTISING ASSOCIATION OF AMERICA** *see* PROMOTION MARKETING ASSOCIATION OF AMERICA (PMAA).

**PRE-PRESS PROOF** proof made photographically, rather than on the actual PRINTING PRESS to be used, for the print buyer's approval prior to the full press RUN. This procedure is risky because the pre-press proof may not accurately represent the image that will be produced by the printing press. It does, however, save the expense of creating a PRINTING PLATE that may require changes. *See also* PRESS PROOF.

**PREPRINT**

**1.** duplicate of an advertisement before the advertisement is actually run in a publication. Preprints are often blown up and mounted on cardboard for retail display as sales promotional material or sent by the manufacturer to dealers or retailers as proof of advertising support.

**2.** *see* HI-FI.

**PRESCORE** recording of the sound or music track of a motion picture before filming or videotaping. Prescoring is performed prior to the actual production to check timing and determine how well the score works with the production's visuals. To prescore, a sound track is laid down on film in order to set up a basic "rough track" of the score. After the content of the sound or music track is finalized from the prescore trials, scoring for the production is then completed.

**PRESENTATION** setting forth in words and visuals a speech to enlighten an audience and/or persuade them to commit themselves to a course of action. An effective presentation is usually planned, organized, and tailored to a specific audience to help facilitate the behavior change, desired by the presenter. For example, presentations are frequently made by ADVERTISING AGENCIES when pitching (*see* PITCH) an account to communicate an agency's qualifications and experience. Presentations always involve face-to-face communication and can be made on a one-to-one basis or can be given to a very large group. For small presentations, blackboards, easel pads, prepared graphs, FLIP CHARTS, or overhead slides are common visual aids used to enhance a presentation. Films, slides, videos, or modern computer-graphics are examples of visual aids used for large group presentations.

**PRESORT** process of sorting mail by destination and type of handling prior to mailing in order to comply with U.S. Postal Service and Canada Post regulations for bulk MAIL preparation and, in most cases, to qualify for postage discounts. The U.S. Postal Service and Canada Post offer postage presort discounts to compensate mailers for doing some of the sorting work the postal service would otherwise have to do.

Discounts vary by the CLASS of mail, by the level of sort, and by the method of grouping: PACKAGE, SACK, or PALLET. For example, mail sorted to the CARRIER ROUTE level will earn a higher discount than mail sorted to the FIVE DIGIT ZIP CODE level. Mail sorted to a STATE level gets no discount. Palletized mailings usually earn more discounts than sacked mailings.

Each presorted package, sack, or pallet must meet minimum volume requirements in order to qualify for the discount; therefore, the larger the mailing or the more concentrated its distribution, the greater the potential for presort discounts. For example, 50 pieces going to each of the 50 states will not be eligible for discounts, but 50 pieces going to the same carrier route are eligible for a carrier-route discount in addition to a five-digit ZIP code discount. Fifty million pieces distributed nationwide are likely to meet enough minimum volume requirements to earn a substantial discount.

Details on the USPS and Canada Post presort requirements for second- and third-class mail are in the DOMESTIC MAIL MANUAL and the PASS MANUAL.

*See also* CONSOLIDATION LEVEL; SECOND CLASS; THIRD CLAS; THREE-TIER PRESORT.

**PRESORT LEVEL** *see* CONSOLIDATION LEVEL.

**PRESORT LOGIC** computer program used to PRESORT mailing addresses prior to the printing of address labels so that the labels can be printed in presort sequence. The mailing pieces will then automatically be presorted according to the sequence of the labels applied. Computer presorting is available as a service from direct-marketing service bureaus or may be purchased for in-house use from various software vendors. *See also* LOGICAL SACKING; PACKAGES/SACK MARKS; PRESORT PARAMETER.

**PRESORT PARAMETER** variable value in a PRESORT LOGIC program that establishes the criteria for presorting, such as the weight of the mailing piece and the pound capacity of the canvas mail SACKS being used. Presort parameters also identify the CLASS of mail and the level of sorting preferred, such as CARRIER ROUTE or FIVE-DIGIT ZIP CODE. *See also* PRESORT.

**PRESS**

1. manual or automatic machine that uses an inked surface to print words and images on paper or any other comparable surface. The platen press, FLATBED CYLINDER PRESS, ROTARY PRESS, and WEBB PRESS are examples of printing presses frequently used by printers. The platen press can print color or monotone on all types of thicknesses and is generally used for LETTERSHOP printing jobs requiring heavy pressure. The *flatbed cylinder press* contains a "flat-bed" support that holds the printing surface and is used both in LETTERPRESS and lithographic (*see* LITHOGRAPHY) printing. The *rotary press* features two CYLINDERS as its primary mechanism and is used for letterpress and GRAVURE printing (direct rotary) or lithographic printing (indirect rotary). The *web press* uses curved plates to print on a continuous roll of paper at unusually high speeds and is used in newspaper printing by letterpress and in rotogravure work. All presses contain a feeding device, which feeds each sheet to the printing unit; an inking mechanism, which sets forth ink to the cylinder; and a delivery system, which removes the sheets from the press and assembles them on top of each other.

2. informal term for publicity received for a product, service, accomplishment, or any activity surrounding corporate/marketing activities; also called *press coverage*. Press can be favorable or unfavorable, and it can either be done in coordination with a PUBLIC RELATIONS agency or be created by the medium in which it appears. For example, a company could receive favorable press coverage in a publication about the merits of a new product. On the other hand, a negative commentary could be written in a publication about the hazardous effects of a company's product.

3. informal term for the news media. An example of the press would be journalists at a news conference.

**PRESS KIT** collection of printed materials detailing various aspects of an organization, presented to members of the media to provide comprehensive information or background about the organization. A press kit may contain any one or all of the following: brief statements about the organization's personnel, a fact sheet about the organization's history, an annual report, copies of the organization's newsletter, a mission statement or fact sheet about the organization's policies, copies of publicity materials, photographs of products, listings of the organization's products or services, editorial materials concerning the organization, and copies of news releases that pertain to the organization.

**PRESS PROOF** prints made just before print production begins for a final quality check before the print run begins. Although it is advisable for the print buyer to review the press proof, in practice this task is often delegated for expedience to the printer. *See also* PRE-PRESS PROOF.

**PRESSURE-SENSITIVE LABEL** label with a gummed adhesive backing that can be peeled off the backing material and applied permanently to another surface simply by pressing. Pressure-sensitive address labels are more expensive than CHESHIRE LABELS costing as much as $3/M to $10/M, depending upon the volume purchased. They are useful, however, when the equipment to apply Cheshire labels is not available and labels must be applied by hand. This is only economical for small-volume mailings prepared well in advance of the MAIL DATE.

   Pressure-sensitive labels are sometimes included in direct-mail packages to perform the dual function of addressing the package through a WINDOW ENVELOPE and enabling the recipient to peel off the label and apply it to an order form (also called PIGGYBACK LABEL), making it easier for the recipient to complete the order form and increasing the likelihood of response.

**PRESTIGE ADVERTISING** advertising designed to enhance the prestige of a company or a company's products or services. *See also* CORPORATE ADVERTISING.

**PRESTIGE CITY** city or town with a famous name that is not officially recognized by the U.S. Postal Service as a delivery area. For example, the residents of Hollywood, California, must receive mail addressed to Los Angeles. Because most prestige cities have a high status level associated with them, the residents prefer that mail addressed *to* them and *from* them include the name of the prestige city instead of, or in addition to, the official city name. This presents a challenge to direct marketers, who must be able to identify the official city associated with orders and other correspondence coming from a prestige city as well as to produce address labels with both city names.

**PRESTIGE PRICING** selling at a high price in order to create an aura of superior quality and social status. Consumer studies have shown that for some products, such as perfume or cosmetics, the buyer believes price and quality are directly proportional.

**PRETEST** testing of copy, design, marketing strategies, research methodology, or any other element of a CAMPAIGN before launching. Pretesting is performed to determine which execution of a campaign is most productive and/or if the chosen research design is optimal. For example, an advertiser may pretest consumer reactions to a new product by displaying point-of-purchase samples in selected store locations, before a national campaign is launched. Pretesting is commonly used for methods of gathering data, since questionnaires, interviewer instructions, and interviewers' capabilities are frequently prone to subjective interpretation and may invalidly skew results. For example, how respondents would interpret and reply to questions is frequently pretested by using personal interviews.

**PREVIOUS MAIL SUPPRESSION** process of selecting names of individuals on a mailing list that have not already received a promotion from the LIST USER in the current campaign. This is especially important when a list user goes back to the same LIST OWNER for additional names after mailing to a SAMPLE of the names on that list. *See also* PYRAMIDING.

**PREVIOUS USAGE** *see* PREVIOUS MAIL SUPPRESSION.

**PRICE APPEAL** practical rather than emotional approach to advertising copy, where the promotion of a product or service is based on the price of the product or service.

**PRICE COMPETITION** marketing approach whereby products are differentiated according to how much they cost, and companies seek to attract customers solely on the basis of product price. In price competition, marketers seek to influence customer demand primarily through changing the prices of their products. *See also* NONPRICE COMPETITION.

**PRICE DISCRIMINATION** charging a different price for a different product or to a different buyer without any true cost differential to justify the different price. An agreement to charge a better price for the same product to one buyer versus another may constitute a violation of ANTITRUST LAWS. A marketer may charge more for one model of a product than for another in order to add perceived value to the product. For example, makers of designer jeans charge a premium price for a product that costs no more to manufacture than no-name jeans.

**PRICE LEADER** dominant competitor in a market whose price changes are matched by the rest of the competitors. The price leader usually has greater capital resources and economies of scale that enable it to risk sustaining lower prices than its competitors. The price leader may also have a distinct product advantage or enough advertising resources to sustain a higher price than its competitors. Price leadership is effective in the prevention of price wars and in reaching a consensus on pricing without collusion in violation of ANTITRUST LAWS. If the price leader is not followed by the rest of the market, the leader is at risk of losing market share.

**PRICE LINING** setting of prices by a seller in accordance with certain price points believed to be attractive to buyers. A men's store may have various styles and brands of ties that sell for $15; another line may sell for $22. Consumer decision making is made easier by holding constant one key variable. For example, a discount shoe store might offer three levels of quality at three prices, such as $9.99, $19.99, and $29.99, and display the shoes in three distinct areas within the store so that shoppers can go straight to the shoes in the range they can afford. Most merchandise catalogs offer goods within a price range representative of the catalog's image.

**PRICE POINT** standard retail price used by marketers for several items that vary slightly in wholesale cost but share a similar level of perceived value to the consumer. Not only do standard prices simplify bookkeeping and product pricing, they also simplify the consumer's purchase decision. In addition, they tend to have a psychological appeal for the consumer. For example, instead of basing the price of four hats on an absolute profit margin, resulting in prices such as $11.96, $11.23, $10.82, and $12.01, the marketer could price all of them at $11.95. Small differences in price, such as $11.95 versus $11.96, tend to have a disproportionate impact on sales. *See also* OFFER TEST.

**PRICE SENSITIVE** tendency of the demand for a product or service to vary according to variations in price. Some goods are more price sensitive than others, depending upon other factors that impact demand, such as need for the products (medicine vs. cosmetics), the availability of substitutes (salt vs. bread), and the relative size of the variation in price. Marketers of price-sensitive goods should test new prices before implementing them, to evaluate the impact on demand. *See also* ELASTICITY.

**PRICE WAR** attempt by a market competitor to drive one or more other competitors out of the market by pricing relatively lower. Before launching a price war, the initiator must be sure that it can survive a low price longer than the competitors can. The initiator is best positioned to sustain the low price if the lower price is a reflection of a true cost advantage and if competitive products have no perceived advantages. Strategies available to a competitor forced into a price war, other than matching the lower price, include adding perceived value to its product or targeting the nonprice sensitive segment of the market.

**PRIMARY ADVERTISING** also known as generic advertising, advertising for a general product category, as opposed to advertising for a specific brand in that category. *See also* GENERIC APPEAL.

**PRIMARY AUDIENCE**
1. targeted group for a specific advertising campaign. For example, the primary audience for new and improved diapers would be parents with babies. When an advertising strategy is being developed,

the characteristics and buying habits of a primary audience must be evaluated carefully.

**2.** targeted group for the editorial content of a publication. For example, the primary audience for an article on financial strategies would be investors. A publication will first identify its primary audience and then gear its editorial toward the wants and needs of this target group.

**3.** total number of a publication's primary readers. For example, if one hundred individuals either subscribed to, read, or purchased a publication, this figure would represent its primary audience.

**4.** individuals to whom, or places where, a publication is delivered or sold. For example, if one hundred copies of a publication are delivered among residences, newsstands, and libraries, this figure would be its primary audience.

**PRIMARY COLORS** three hues (red, yellow, blue) that together constitute all the colors in the visible SPECTRUM. In FOUR-COLOR PROCESS printing, the primary colors are commonly referred to as magenta (red), yellow, and cyan (blue), the fourth "color" being black. *See also* TINTS.

**PRIMARY DRIVES** internal motivator of human behavior that is instinctual, rather than learned, such as hunger, thirst, pain avoidance, and sex. Consumers make purchases to satisfy either LEARNED DRIVES or primary drives. CUES determine how a person will respond to a drive. Brand advertising cues a consumer to purchase a particular brand. If the purchase satisfies the drive, the purchase behavior will be reinforced and brand loyalty will begin to be established. *See also* HIERARCHY OF NEEDS MODEL.

**PRIMARY MARKET AREA**

**1.** newspaper or related publication's major area of editorial and advertising coverage. For example, XYZ newspaper may do a story on the XYZ fire department because it is situated in its primary market area. Similarly, retailers would place an ad in the XYZ newspaper if they were interested in reaching consumers living in XYZ's primary market area.

**2.** major area of sale and distribution for an advertiser's product or service; also called *heartland*. For example, the primary market area for woolen hats would be northern states or other cold-weather regions. Abbreviated PMA.

**PRIMARY METROPOLITAN STATISTICAL AREA (PMSA)** United States Bureau of the Census term for an area consisting of a large urbanized county or a cluster of counties that have strong economic and social links, as well as ties to neighboring communities in its CONSOLIDATED METROPOLITAN STATISTICAL AREA (CMSAS). Within the 20 CMSAS, there are 71 PMSAS. *See also* CONSOLIDATED METROPOLITAN STATISTICAL AREA, METROPOLITAN STATISTICAL AREA.

**PRIMARY SOURCE LIST**  collection of name and address records created by the list owner rather than purchased or rented from other sources. A primary source list might be derived from telephone directories, motor vehicle registrations, magazine subscriber lists, association memberships, or conference attendees. A primary source list may be made available to other marketers via LIST RENTAL arrangements.

**PRIME TIME**  in broadcast, that part of the day when the listening or viewing audience is the largest, as compared to other parts of the day. Programming during prime time is usually of a general nature designed to appeal to a wide demographic range. In radio, prime time is actually divided between two segments: MORNING DRIVE time, 6:00 A.M. to 10:00 A.M., and AFTERNOON DRIVE time, 3:00 P.M. to 7:00 P.M., Monday through Friday. Television prime time is 8:00 P.M. to 11:00 P.M. Monday through Saturday, and 7:00 P.M. to 11:00 P.M. on Sunday. Federal Communications Commission regulations limit the amount of prime-time network television programming to three hours per day Monday through Saturday. *See also* DAYPART.

**PRINT ADVERTISING**  *see* PRINT MEDIA.

**PRINT BAND**  *see* PRINT TRAIN.

**PRINT CHAIN**  string of type characters used on an IMPACT PRINTER. The print chain rotates, placing the appropriate character between a hammer device and an inked ribbon. The hammer presses the character against the paper, with the inked ribbon in between, creating a print impression. Print-chain text tends to space letters more widely and use more paper than computer-composed text. *See also* PRINT DRUM; PRINT TRAIN.

**PRINT DRUM**  barrel-shaped device on an IMPACT PRINTER with engraved type characters. The drum rotates, placing the appropriate character in front of a hammer device that presses the paper against the drum, with an inked ribbon in between, creating a print impression of the character. *See also* PRINT CHAIN; PRINT TRAIN.

**PRINTER**
   1. device used to apply inked images of ALPHANUMERIC or other symbolic characters to paper, or to duplicate an ILLUSTRATION; GRAPHIC DESIGN, or photographic image on paper. A printer may be manually operated, mechanically operated, or computer driven. There are many types of printers that vary in terms of the way the image is created and the type of paper and ink used. Some printers create a text image one character at a time; others can reproduce one full page at a time of both text and illustrations. Speed, quality, and cost also vary greatly. The best printer for a job depends upon the type of image to be created, the level of quality desired, and the speed required. *See also* GRAVURE; IMPACT PRINTER; INK-JET PRINTER; LASER PRINTER; LITHOGRAPHY; PRESS.

**2.** business or individual who performs printing services; a *print shop. See also* COMMERCIAL PRINTER.

**PRINTER'S ERROR (PE)** errors on a proof that are the fault of the printer, either through typographical error or imperfections caused by the machinery. Since these errors are the mistake of the printer, they will not be charged to the client. *See also* AUTHOR'S ALTERATION; EDITORIAL ALTERATION.

**PRINT IMAGE**
   **1.** image produced by a PRINTER.
   **2.** MAGNETIC TAPE formatted to print the data on the tape in a specific sequence and LAYOUT, using a tape-driven computer printer.

**PRINTING PLATE** device that carries the image to be printed and is applied directly to paper or to an intermediate image carrier, such as a print BLANKET, in order to transfer the image to paper. The image on the plate may be raised above the surface (*relief*), may be carved (*etched*—see ETCH) into the surface, or may be flush with the surface and differentiated chemically from the nonimage areas of the plate. Most printing plates are metallic. *See also* BIMETAL PLATE; DESENSITIZER; GRAVURE; LITHOGRAPHY.

**PRINTING PRESS** *see* PRESS.

**PRINT MEDIA** printed, as distinguished from broadcast or electronically transmitted communications. The print media include all newspapers, newsletters, booklets, pamphlets, magazines, and other printed publications, especially those that sell advertising space as a means of raising revenue. In the U.S., at present, there are 1745 daily and 7602 weekly newspapers, and 64,000 magazines. Most print media, with the exception of magazines, are local, although there are some national newspapers and trade publications that have become quite successful. Magazines, on the other hand, have always been national, although there is a trend today toward localization and specialization. Also included in print media category are directories, church and school newspapers and yearbooks, and programs at theater presentations and sporting events.

**PRINT ORDER** request given to a commercial printer describing the type of material to be printed and all necessary specifications, such as ink colors, paper weights and finishes, and quantity. A magazine print order would also have separate instructions for any special editions to be printed. Most print orders include a small print OVERRUN to allow for unexpected contingencies and waste.

**PRINTOUT** HARD-COPY output from a computer, such as selected information from or analyses of computer files or simply a printout of the information currently on the computer screen. Some printouts, such as statistical analyses, require special programs to tell the computer how to produce them. Others, such as a printout of the screen, are produced by the basic operating system programs. Printouts are usually produced on CONTINUOUS FORMS that vary in paper quality and color, depending upon the application. Accounting reports are usually produced on green bar paper that makes it easy to read a line of numbers across columns.

**PRINT QUALITY** characteristic of printed material evaluated in terms of color, REGISTER, clarity, and the degree to which it resembles the original image. Print quality is particularly important in FOUR COLOR PROCESS printing for magazine advertisements and catalogs. It is less important for newspaper printing, in which speed of distribution and legibility outweigh aesthetic considerations. Print quality is very important for information that will be machine read by an optical SCANNER.

**PRINT SHOP** *see* PRINTER.

**PRINT TAPE** MAGNETIC TAPE containing information to be printed, along with print format instructions such as line spacing and margins. The print tape is used to control a computer printer.

**PRINT TRAIN** device on an IMPACT PRINTER that holds the type characters needed for printing; also called *print band*. The print train rotates at high speed, bringing each character, in the appropriate sequence, into position between the ink ribbon and the paper. A hammer strikes the character on the print train, producing an image on the paper.

**PRIOR DONOR FILE** computer list of individuals who have purchased gifts from a marketer in a completed sale transaction, such as an expired gift magazine subscription that has been paid for in full. Prior donors are considered good prospects for additional gift promotions.

**PRIORITY** *see* PRIORITY LIST.

**PRIORITY LIST** table used in a MERGE/PURGE that controls the duplicate elimination (*see* DEDUPE) priority of each list, so that a name found on more than one list will remain on the higher priority list and will be purged from the lower priority list(s). A LIST USER'S own list, with which rented lists are merged, usually takes highest priority, so that LIST RENTAL charges will not be paid on names the list user already owns.

**PRIOR SOURCE** source of a previous order from a customer who has ordered again. For example, a magazine subscriber who originally subscribed via a SUBSCRIPTION SOURCE and is now renewing via the publisher's renewal promotion has an agency prior source and a renewal current source. It is important to track prior sources so that the long-term value of a customer can be evaluated in terms of SOURCE, enabling marketers to concentrate their resources on bringing in new customers from the most profitable sources—that is, those most likely to renew or to buy again.

**PRISM SHOT** photographic shot taken with a prism lens, used primarily for multiple-image effects. A prism lens arrests the image briefly and refracts light into a rainbow spectrum, reproducing the desired image again and again. For example, a prism shot is used in motion pictures to create a dreamlike image of a person's face. In this example, the prism lens is focused on the person's head, and the face repeats and rotates to give the feeling of disorientation.

**PRIVACY LAWS** laws passed by the United States Congress upon the recommendations of the Privacy Protection Study Commission established by the Privacy Act of 1974. The laws require LIST OWNERS who rent their list to other direct marketers to inform people on the list that the list is being rented and to give each individual "an opportunity to indicate to the organization that he does not wish to have his address. . . made available for such purposes." *See also* DMA MAIL PREFERENCE SERVICE DELETE FILE; TELEPHONE CONSUMER PROTECTION ACT.

**PRIVATE BRAND** *see* PRIVATE LABEL.

**PRIVATE EXPRESS STATUTES** laws that establish the U.S. Postal Service limited monopoly on first-class mail delivery. The statutes allow for overnight delivery of letter mail by ALTERNATE DELIVERY services and also for their delivery of books, magazines, and newspapers.

**PRIVATE LABEL** brand sponsored by a wholesaler, retailer, dealer, or merchant, as distinguished from a brand bearing the name of a manufacturer or producer; also called *private brand*. Manufacturers use either their own name, that of a middleman, or a combination of both when they are marketing their products. Private labeling occurs when middlemen, usually large retailers or wholesalers, develop their own brand. Since manufacturers' (producers') brands have large advertising expenditures built into their cost, a private labeler is able to buy the same goods at a lower cost and thus sell them at a lower price and/or at a better profit margin. In addition, private labelers have more control over pricing and are able to advantageously display their own brands for maximum impact. For example, a grocery store can quickly reduce the price of its own private-label brand in order to meet or beat a competitor's price. Or the grocery store can create a special POINT-OF-PURCHASE ADVERTISING display and/or give its brand predominant shelf space in order to boost sales. Private-label brands are usually priced lower than comparable manufacturers' brands and therefore appeal to bargain-conscious consumers. An example of a private-label brand would be a supermarket product bearing a store label with a product's name.

**PRIVATE MAIL** letter mail delivered by carriers other than the U.S. Postal Service, such as that delivered by ALTERNATIVE DELIVERY companies. Direct-mail marketers have a bit more flexibility with private mail because it is not governed by as many regulations as

USPS-delivered mail. For example, using private mail, marketers were delivering catalogs in POLYBAGS along with magazines well before USPS regulations permitted mailing these items together.

**PRIZE BROKER** arranger of the exchange of an advertiser's merchandise for free broadcast time or publicity PLUGS on a radio or television show; also called *barter broker*. A prize broker is employed by a company specializing in the "bartering" of merchandise for broadcast services, and is frequently called upon by game shows for these services. For example, a prize broker might arrange for a free refrigerator to be given away on a game show, in return for the program host's display and mention of the refrigerator's brand name, features, and benefits.

**PRIZM** Potential Rating Index by Zip Market (compiled by the Claritas Corporation of Alexandria, Virginia). This is a business information service subscribed to by marketers that relies on census data and examines consumer lifestyles by zip code. The PRIZM system has classified every United States neighborhood into one of 40 clusters, each of which has a unique combination of characteristics and is designated by a title that describes the prevailing lifestyle. Some examples of cluster titles are "blue blood estates" (describing consumers who have had wealth for generations), "money and brains," "furs and stationwagons," "shotguns and pickups," and "gray power" (senior citizens). After marketers have defined their target market for a particular product, they will use PRIZM data to improve their marketing efforts.

**PROBLEM-SOLUTION ADVERTISEMENT** advertisement that focuses on a consumer problem and offers a solution to the problem. For example, a problem-solution advertisement for a sunburn relief product will remind consumers of the problem of sunburn pain and promote its product as offering a fast, safe, and soothing solution to this pain. Product-solution advertisements are most effectively used when the consumer can readily identify with a problem, and when the solution to this problem is easily solved by purchasing the product.

**PROCESS COLORS** *see* FOUR-COLOR PROCESS.

**PROCESS PLATE** two or more color plates used together in FOUR-COLOR PROCESS printing to produce other colors and shades. Process plates are HALFTONE engravings made from COLOR SEPARATION negatives involving the application of the primary pigments of yellow, red (magenta), blue (cyan), and black to reproduce an original full-color design. A color separation is first prepared for an original's yellow, red, and blue values, and a final negative and plate is then made for the design's black value. A design using two colors, or one color and black, is called a "two-color process"; one using three colors is called a "three-color process." If a reproduction uses four colors, it is called "four-color process" or *full color*. Color photographs and colored drawings are created using process plates.

**PROCESS PRINTING** *see* FOUR-COLOR PROCESS.

**PROCESS SCREEN** *see* REAR-SCREEN PROJECTION.

**PRODUCER**
1. executive responsible for the creation, development, and supervision of a radio or television program, play, or motion picture. The producer usually works with the director, who is the artistic overseer of the production, to execute the direction of the show. Some examples of the producer's responsibilities may include securing money for a production, hiring personnel, and making purchasing decisions.
2. individual working on the staff of an agency or advertiser, or on a free-lance basis, who is in charge of the complete production of commercials. After a STORYBOARD is approved, a producer will begin duties that usually include preparing cost estimates, contacting vendors and evaluating bids, arranging for equipment and cast, conducting the recording session, scheduling screenings, and handling billings. In addition, the producer will be involved in editing, shooting, and acting as the sole communicator with the director, on behalf of the agency and the client.
3. manufacturer or creator of goods that are produced for consumers or for a specific TARGET MARKET. For example, a producer of widgets will assume full responsibility for producing or manufacturing the product but may or may not become involved in the product's marketing and sales.

**PRODUCER MARKET** buyers and sellers of services, finished goods, raw materials, product components, and equipment used in the manufacture or delivery of other products and services; also called BUSINESS MARKET. In contrast to the consumer market, the producer market revolves around personal service and selling, profit considerations, reliability, and customization to meet the needs of individual customers. Buyers in the producer market tend to make INFORMED CHOICES. The purchase decision is usually made by several persons with varying points of focus. *See also* INDUSTRIAL BUYER; INDUSTRIAL GOODS.

**PRODUCER PRICE INDEX (PPI)** formerly known as the wholesale price index, listing of the prices of approximately 3,000 basic items, such as raw materials or semifinished goods, published monthly by the United States Bureau of Labor Statistics. *See also* CONSUMER PRICE INDEX.

**PRODUCT** offering capable of satisfying a need or a want, that is offered to a TARGET MARKET for attention, acquisition, use, or consumption. A product can be an object, service, activity, person, place, organization, or idea. Each product has its own benefits, styling, quality, brand name, and packaging that gives it its own identity and distinguishing characteristics. An advertiser, though, will primarily concentrate on promoting a product's benefits, rather than its features. For example, the emphasis in an advertisement promoting a lipstick will be on the product benefit of beauty, with mention of its physical features, such as color and size, subordinate. In other words, the ad will try to appeal to a woman's desire to look beautiful and will promise the woman that wearing this lipstick will positively enhance her looks.

**PRODUCT BUNDLING** *see* BUNDLING.

**PRODUCT CLASS** group of similar products that fulfill the same need such as bar soaps; also called PRODUCT CATEGORY. There are variations between products within a class in terms of physical characteristics (color, fragrance, shape) or brand names. A single manufacturer may produce several brands within the same product class in order to appeal to different segments of the market. A product class has a longer life cycle than any one product within the class alone. *See also* INNOVATION; MULTIBRAND STRATEGY.

**PRODUCT DIFFERENTIATION** *see* DIFFERENTIATION STRATEGY.

**PRODUCT IMAGE** *see* BRAND IMAGE.

**PRODUCT LINE PRICING** establishing a single price for all products in a product line, such as having a price of $55 for the high-priced line of dress shirts, $45 for the medium-priced line, and $35 for the lower-priced line. Product line pricing factors in the impact of a product's price on demand for another product offered by that marketer. For example, if McDonald's offered a $12 sandwich, it would be far out of the price/value range established by other sandwiches in McDonald's PRODUCT LINE and demand would be minimal. The price of a complementary product such as software can directly impact demand for the hardware. The higher the price of the software, the lower the demand for the hardware. McDonald's could afford to offer a beverage at cost if the incremental sandwich sales revenue gained as a result outweighed the lost beverage revenue. The price of a product such as a compact car can impact demand for another compact car model that would serve as a substitute. The higher the price of one car, the greater the demand for the other. Variations in manufacturing costs across products are also a factor in product line pricing.

**PRODUCTION**
**In general:** process of physically preparing advertising in its completed form. Production entails the specification of typography, procuring paper for print jobs, securing printing, type, and engraving estimates from suppliers, and ordering printing plates and engravings. In addition, production involves checking a publication's mechanical requirements and closing dates and communicating this information to the agency to assure that scheduling deadlines are met and a quality advertisement is produced.

**Broadcast:**

**1.** preparation of television or radio program, motion picture, or play for its showing. Production involves determining the show's format, staffing, supervising script editing and rehearsing, coordinating camera men, securing a proper studio, and assuring that the entire program runs smoothly. *See also* PRODUCER.

**2.** dramatic entertainment that has been created and produced for an audience. For example, students may attend a production of a famous classic.

**Manufacturing:** process of physically creating an offering for a TARGET MARKET. For example, the production of widgets may be produced for target market XYZ.

**PRODUCTION DIRECTOR** individual responsible for the PRODUCTION activities of an advertising agency, advertiser, publisher, or broadcast station. A production director supervises the production department and staff, and has ultimate responsibility for the scheduling and quality of all advertising from the mechanical stage. A production director must have knowledge of the mechanical requirements of publications, engravings, printing, and typography, since he must evaluate printing bids, approve invoices, order photoengraving, and cost effectively produce four-color work. The production director's expertise has a great bearing on curtailing unnecessary expenses, since proper economy can be achieved by choosing the right suppliers, papers, and production methods. For example, when producing a four-color piece, the production director must select the lowest bidder with the highest quality work, prepare the work for reproduction by choosing the right methods and materials, and carefully check the specifications and quality of the finished advertisement before it is released to a publication.

**PRODUCT LIFE CYCLE (PLC)** theory that recognizes four separate developmental stages in the life span of a product, with each stage characterized by its own distinct marketing opportunities and restraints. In a product's *introductory* stage, growth is slow, with minimal profits, since consumers' purchases have merely been on a trial basis. If the product is successful, it goes into a *growth* stage, where its growth rapidly expands by new market entries, improved distribution channels, and shrewd pricing strategies. A *maturity* stage follows, where sales and profits stabilize. Finally, the product goes into a *decline*, where sales and profits decrease. The product life cycle theory states that a typical product's life cycle follows the form of an S-shaped curve, although some products may have a very rapid growth stage or an immediate decline. Also, some mature products can have their life cycle reversed. For example, when baking soda was launched, it was used only for cooking and quickly reached the maturity stage of its life cycle. When it was discovered that baking soda deodorized refrigerators, however, the product's sales soared and its new use put it back in the growth stage of its life cycle.

**PRODUCT LINE** group of products manufactured by a firm that are closely related in use and in production and marketing requirements. The *depth* of the product line refers to the number of different products offered in a product line. For example, General Foods has about a dozen different products in its coffee product line. Each of these items is promoted as distinctive, although they share the same distribution channels and similar manufacturing facilities. McDonald's has developed a food product line that includes several hamburger, fish, and chicken sandwiches. A product line may be targeted to a particular customer group, such as Skill home shop tools, or sold to various customer types through the same outlets, such as Ace Hardware Stores.

**PRODUCT MANAGER** *see* BRAND MANAGER.

**PRODUCT MIX** all of the products or PRODUCT LINES offered by a firm. Some companies have a wide product mix geared toward a diverse consumer group. For example, Procter & Gamble has a product mix that includes detergents, toothpaste, Procter bar soap, deodorants, disposable diapers, coffee, household paper goods, and food products. Some companies have a narrow product mix geared toward a particular market segment, such as the William Sonoma catalog that sells gourmet cooking accessories. Offering a wide product mix provides an opportunity to increase the amount of goods sold to each customer but has costs associated with the variety of resources (distribution, storage, marketing, etc.) required to support it.

**PRODUCT PRUNING** discontinuation of a product or brand in response to declining demand or insufficient financial returns. Product pruning enables the marketer to dedicate its resources to its best products or brands. The marketer must first evaluate whether a product or marketing mix modification could revive demand for the ailing product. Innovative and multibrand companies do a better job of product pruning than companies who have relied too much on one product or brand. A product may be pruned gradually by discontinuing all promotion expenditures and MILKING the market for any remaining demand. The declining product may also be sold to a competitor or sold in limited quantities to a market segment with self-sustaining demand.

**PRODUCT RESEARCH AND DEVELOPMENT (PR&D)** activity performed by a team of professionals working to transform a product idea into a technically sound and promotable product; also called *research & development (R&D)*. Corporate research and development (R&D) departments are found in both large and small companies and are generally responsible for product development and testing, researching brand names, and creating an effective packaging concept. For example, a cordless telephone manufacturer's R&D department may work on researching and developing a phone with even better voice quality and reach than its current model. Since the outcome of product R&D is frequently so uncertain, many companies find the prospect of budgeting very difficult and are constantly striving to allocate an optimal funding to the department.

**PRODUCT STRATEGY**  marketing plan for a product based on the characteristics of the target market, market share objectives, desired product positioning within the market, and profit objectives. Strategic plans for a product are based on decisions regarding the FOUR P's (product, place, price, promotion), financial targets and budgets, and tactical plans.

**PROFESSIONAL MAGAZINE**  magazine whose editorial content is designed for the benefit of members of a particular profession, such as the *New England Journal of Medicine*, which is compiled for the benefit of doctors. *See also* CONSUMER MAGAZINE; TRADE MAGAZINE.

**PROFESSIONAL SERVICES MARKETING**  marketing of advisory services offered by practitioners such as doctors, lawyers, or accountants. Professional services marketing is relatively new to the marketing industry, because until recently the professional associations governing each of these professions prohibited client solicitation, advertising, and price competition. In the early 1980s the U.S. Antitrust Division ruled that restraints such as those imposed by the professional trade associations were illegal.

**PROFIT MAXIMIZATION**  strategy whereby manufacturers work to achieve the greatest possible profit from the sales of their products and to secure an early recovery of the cash invested. A profit maximization strategy is in opposition to a strategy where the manufacturer is working toward achieving sales growth or a greater market share.

**PROFITABILITY CONTROLS**  measures maintained by manufacturers of the level of profit of their various products, territories, customer groups, distribution channels, or order sizes. Information gained from profitability controls will help the manufacturer determine whether any products or marketing activities should be expanded, reduced, or eliminated.

**PROFIT-TAKING STRATEGY**  *see* MILKING STRATEGY.

**PROGRAM**  *see* COMPUTER PROGRAM.

**PROGRAM ANALYZER**  voting-type machine used to analyze and continuously record the reactions of listeners or viewers to an entire broadcast program or a commercial. Program analyzers are used in test situations where research participants (chosen on the basis of sex, age, education, and geography) are gathered together to view or listen to a program. The participants are instructed to push the program analyzer's green button if they like what is being seen or heard and the machine's red button if they are not pleased with a portion of the program. If the participants are indifferent, they are told to push nothing. At the end of the program, a second-by-second analysis of the participants' reactions to the program is produced by the program analyzer in the form of a rising and falling curve. After the participants have completed their session, they are asked to give verbal opinions of the show to help substantiate the feedback that was just tabulated. The program analyzer is generally used to test a show before it is broadcast, but it can be used to earmark weaknesses in current programs. For example, researchers may use a program analyzer's data to examine the appeal and effects of serial programming for children (as well as analyzing its educational aspects), the typical program formula's ability to attract and hold listeners, and the characteristics of the shows' daily listeners.

**PROGRESSIVE PROOFS (PROGS)** set of proofs made during the four-color printing process; also called *color proofs*. Typically, there are seven different impressions in a set of progressive proofs: one for each color alone and then the combinations as succeeding colors are added. The final proof will show the finished color reproduction. An example of a progressive sequence follows: (1) impression of the red plate; (2) impression of the yellow plate; (3) impression of the yellow plate on the red plate; (4) impression of the blue plate; (5) impression of the blue plate on the yellow and red plate; (6) impression of the black plate; (7) impression of the black plate on the yellow, red, and blue plate. The progs serve as a guide and are used by the printer to match up inks in the four-color printing process. They also permit the customer to make any changes or corrections the need for which may become apparent as a result of the process.

**PROGS** *see* PROGRESSIVE PROOFS.

**PROJECTION**
1. estimate of future information on the basis of known current information, often done with numbers. For example, direct-mail advertisers may estimate the total returns from a mailing on the basis of returns received in the first few days or weeks.
2. attribution of an individual's own feelings, or attitudes to others.
3. process of displaying pictures through the use of a projector, as a slide or film projector.

**PROMO** in broadcast, a local or network spot offering a short promotional message about an upcoming broadcast program; also called *promotion spot*.

**PROMOTION** *see* SALES PROMOTION.

**PROMOTIONAL ALLOWANCE** reduction of the wholesale price as an incentive to retailers or middlemen. A promotional allowance compensates the retailer for expenditures made promoting the product. *See also* ALLOWANCE; BINDER ALLOWANCE.

**PROMOTION MARKETING ASSOCIATION OF AMERICA (PMAA)** organization founded in 1911 to foster the development, understanding, and usage of PREMIUMS in the marketing and advertising community. PMAA membership includes professionals from promotion and sales-incentive organizations as well as corporations using premium merchandise to increase sales. The organization conducts surveys and sponsors seminars on premium use in today's marketplace. Until 1977, it was called the *Premium Advertising Association of America.*

**PROMOTION MIX** four types of promotion that support marketing objectives, including advertising, personal (face-to-face) selling, publicity (nonpaid advertising such as news bulletins or magazine articles), and sales promotions (product displays, trade shows and other sales events, dealer allowances, coupons, contests, and a variety of other promotions that don't fit into the other three types). The relative importance of each varies, depending upon the market and the product. For example, personal selling is more important in business-to-business sales than in consumer sales.

**PROOF** copy of printed material that is inspected for errors and examined for fidelity to the original copy before the rest of the printing run is completed. If changes or corrections are necessary, they are made from the proof. The corrected proof is often used as a file copy.

**PROOF COPY** final sample of printed material created by the printer prior to the full print run to get final approval from the print buyer of the COPY and LAYOUT. *See also* BLUEPRINT; GALLEY PROOF; PAGE PROOF; PRE-PRESS PROOF; PRESS PROOF.

**PROOF-OF-PURCHASE** evidence that a product has actually been purchased. A boxtop or a label from a package is typically used as a proof-of-purchase. Often, manufacturers will sponsor sales promotions where the customer will receive a special premium in exchange for a proof-of-purchase.

**PROOFREAD** read copy, such as a PROOF or a typewritten text, for the purposes of checking for errors and making alterations, before the copy is submitted for further reproduction. A proofreader is a person who specializes in this process.

**PROOFREADER SYMBOL** universally recognized mark used to indicate changes and corrections to be made on printed copy. The proofreader symbol is typically placed next to the text in question, with a corresponding symbol in the nearer margin adjacent to the line or paragraph containing the correction.

**PROPAGANDA** message conveyed in order to support and spread a particular opinion or point of view, engaging both the intellect and the emotions of the audience. Propaganda may consist of an OVERT APPEAL, like most advertising copy, a nonovert appeal, such as the seller's participation in community events, company slogans and logos, and special employee benefits. Ben & Jerry's ice cream has benefited from public knowledge of their corporate commitment to environmental causes and employee empowerment, despite the lack of any direct relevance of those things to their products. Tobacco companies use sponsorships of sporting events to counter their unhealthy image. *See also* ONE-SIDED MESSAGE.

**PROPORTIONATE ALLOCATION**  MERGE/PURGE process of deleting DUPLICATE names from the lists in a merge/purge in proportion so that no one list is penalized more than the others for duplicates. For example, if List A represents 20% of the names input, then 20% of the duplicates between List A and List B will be deleted from List A. This is important to LIST OWNERS, who are paid by the list renters according to the number of names remaining on their list after the merge/purge. In some cases, the allocation is instead done according to preassigned list PRIORITY.

**PROPRIETARY DRUGS**  *see* OVER-THE COUNTER DRUGS.

**PROPRIETARY PHARMACEUTICAL**  *see* OVER-THE-COUNTER DRUGS.

**PRORATE**
**In general:** allocate proportionally.
**Magazines:** process of calculating the price or term of a subscription, based upon a payment or a period of time other than the standard one-, two-, or three-year term and price offers. For example, if a magazine costs $24 for 12 issues and only 6 issues are ordered, the prorated price is $12. Similarly, if $18 is sent by the subscriber in payment, the term of the subscription will be prorated to 9 issues. Marketers usually prorate the term of subscriptions for which an UNDERPAYMENT or OVERPAYMENT is received, rather than refund the difference or try to collect the remaining amount due.

**PROSPECT**  potential buyer of a product or service (who has not previously been a purchaser of that product or service). For example, a name on a mailing list is considered to be a prospect for the goods or services to be advertised by a mailing.

**PROSPECT LIST**  list of individuals qualified to purchase a product or service, maintained for promotion in the expectation that they will become customers. The size of the prospect list and the potential value of each customer figures into the promotion strategy. For example, if there are 50 prospects for a product worth $100,000, it would make sense to plan a personal sales call. On the other hand, if there are 50,000 prospects for a product worth $10, then a direct-mail promotion might be the best approach.

**PROTECTION** infrequent practice among LIST OWNERS, who guarantee to the LIST OWNER that, during a particular range of time before and after each user's mailing, the list will not be made available for rental by other mailers. This prevents the concurrent receipt of several promotional mailings that will compete for the recipient's attention. However, most mailers choose to mail during the same periods that seem to work best—that is, the Christmas buying season and June/July.

**PROTECTIONISM** strategy of imposing high tariffs or establishing quotas on foreign imports for the purposes of stemming the tide of foreign-made goods coming into the country and competing with domestic-made goods. Protectionism, however, is only a temporary solution to the flood of foreign-made goods on the market, and in the long run it will raise the cost of living for consumers while protecting inefficient domestic companies.

**PROTOTYPE** sample product INNOVATION manufactured on a small scale in order to test product performance and market response. If a prototype is successful, the marketer must determine how to produce it in large quantities in a cost-effective manner. A small group of targeted buyers might be selected to use the prototype on a test basis and participate in fine-tuning the product characteristics.

**PROVE** make a PROOF, sometimes spoken as "pulling a proof." Proving is designed to demonstrate the quality of a PRINTING PLATE and is typically done on a special small printing press, called a *proof press*, that has been designed exclusively for this purpose (in contrast to a press that is used for mass reproduction).

**PROVINCE** geographic division of Canada similar to a state in terms of its use for market research and postal PRESORTS.

**PSYCHIC INCOME** intangible benefits above and beyond the utilitarian value derived from a purchase. The greater the psychic income expected, the more a consumer is willing to spend on a purchase. For example, someone who would not spend more than $200 on an ordinary item of clothing may nevertheless spend as much as $1000 on a wedding dress because, in her mind, the importance of the occasion increases the benefit derived from looking her best. Similarly, people with very little DISCRETIONARY INCOME sometimes purchase expensive cars because the car enhances their feelings of self-worth.

**PSYCHOGALVANIC SKIN RESPONSE** *see* GALVANIC SKIN RESPONSE.

**PSYCHOGRAPHIC SEGMENTATION,** MARKET SEGMENTATION strategy whereby the intended audience for a given product is divided according to social class, lifestyle, or personality characteristics. Marketers segment markets by social class for the promotion of products such as cars, clothes, home furnishings, and leisure activities. When segmenting a market according to consumer lifestyles, marketers promote their products as expressions of those lifestyles, such as the promotion of natural fiber products as ideal for a natural, healthy, active life. Marketers use personality factors to segment markets by giving their products personalities that match consumer personalities. Typically this strategy is used to promote products such as women's cosmetics or liquor. *See also* BEHAVIOR SEGMENTATION, DEMOGRAPHIC SEGMENTATION, GEOGRAPHIC SEGMENTATION, PSYCHOGRAPHICS.

**PSYCHOGRAPHICS** criteria for segmenting consumers by LIFESTYLE, attitudes, beliefs, values, personality, buying motives, and/or extent of product usage. Psychographic analyses are used like geographic (place of residence or work) and DEMOGRAPHIC (age, income, occupation) criteria to describe and identify customers and prospective customers and to aid in developing promotion strategies designed to appeal to specific psychographic segments of the MARKET for a product. For example, the market for shampoo may consist of various psychographic segments described by their primary purchase motives (beauty, health, grooming), usage styles (daily, weekly, salon-only), or lifestyle (frequent travelers, parents with young children, empty-nesters).

The psychographic characteristics of the market affect not only advertising COPY but also packaging (travel size, child-proof, decorator pump) and channels of distribution (supermarkets, pharmacies, specialty stores).

Psychographic data can be gathered firsthand through PERSONAL INTERVIEWS, FOCUS GROUP INTERVIEWS, OR QUESTIONNAIRES, or purchased from research companies in the form of list OVERLAYS for direct marketers or MARKET PROFILES for general marketers. *See also* CUS-TOMER PROFILE.

**PUBLIC-ADDRESS (PA) SYSTEM** system of audio amplification used when addressing large crowds of people.

**PUBLICATION** any material that is published, in any format. For example, magazines and newspapers are referred to as publications.

**PUBLIC BROADCASTING SERVICE (PBS)** government-funded service founded in 1969 to provide educational, cultural, public affairs, and children's programming to noncommercial television stations. PBS was initially funded primarily by the Ford Foundation to oversee the interconnection process between stations, rather than to produce programs. PBS now is involved in compiling broadcast statistics, conducting audience research, and promoting public television through a weekly newsletter.

**PUBLIC DOMAIN (PD)** original material, such as art, literature, photographs, or music, that is available for use by anyone, without cost, because the material has not been copyrighted or because the copyright has expired.

**PUBLIC-PLACE SUBS** periodical subscription sold to places that make the periodical available to more than one reader, such as libraries, schools, and businesses. These subscriptions are of interest to advertisers in those periodicals because they usually have a higher number of READERS PER COPY sold than regular subscriptions.

**PUBLIC RELATIONS (PR)** form of communication that is primarily directed toward gaining public understanding and acceptance. It tends to deal with issues rather than specifically with products or services. Public relations uses publicity that does not necessitate payment in a wide variety of media and is often placed as news or items of public interest. Because public relations communications are placed in this manner, they offer a legitimacy that advertising does not have, since advertising is publicity that is paid for. The practice of PR is used to build rapport with the various publics a company, individual, or organization may have (i.e., employees, customers, stockholders, voters, competitors, or the general population). Publicity releases, employee-training seminars, and house organs are examples of instruments used in public relations. *Financial public relations*, a specialized branch of the profession, is concerned with corporate annual reports, stockholder communications, and the disclosure rules of the Securities and Exchange Commission.

**PUBLIC RELATIONS SOCIETY OF AMERICA (PRSA)** national professional organization, headquartered in New York City, for the benefit of public relations practitioners from all walks of the public relations industry. PRSA offers members research and job referral services and sponsors relevant seminars and symposiums.

**PUBLIC-SERVICE ADVERTISING** advertising with a central focus on the public welfare. Public-service advertising is generally sponsored by a nonprofit institution, civic group, religious organization, trade association, or political group. Typically, it is directed at some humanitarian cause, philosophical ideal, political concept, or religious viewpoint. Most public-service advertising involves the donation of time or space on part of the medium in which it is featured, although free time or space is not a prerequisite for this type of advertising. Groups such as the Red Cross, United Way, and International Ladies Garment Workers Union have sponsored a great deal of public-service advertising. *See also* ADVERTISING COUNCIL, INC.

**PUBLIC-SERVICE APPROPRIATIONS** funds provided to the U.S. Postal Service by Congress to ensure that postal services are uniformly provided throughout the country, regardless of postage revenue from each area.

**PUBLIC UTILITIES ADVERTISING ASSOCIATION** *see* PUBLIC UTILITIES COMMUNICATORS ASSOCIATION.

**PUBLIC UTILITIES COMMUNICATORS ASSOCIATION (PUCA)** international organization founded in 1921 to promote the development of utility advertising communications. PUCA members include advertising and public relations directors of electric, gas, transportation, steam, water, telephone, nuclear, and other utility companies and allied industries. PUCA's recent name change, from Public Utilities Advertising Association, reflects its expanding orientation toward the entire communication function.

**PUBLISHERS CLEARING HOUSE**  one of the largest SUBSCRIPTION AGENTS. PCH, located in Port Washington, New York, is known to the public for its SWEEPSTAKES promotions, first used in 1967, which make use of STAMP SHEETS, stickers, and other ACTION DEVICES. It is extremely advantageous for small magazines with small direct-mail budgets to be included in a PCH mailing because of the large number of orders generated by a large-scale mailing such as this. *See also* DIRECT-MAIL AGENCIES.

**PUBLISHERS INFORMATION BUREAU (PIB)**  organization founded in 1945 to monitor the advertising schedules and expenditures of advertisers in consumer publications. PIB issues reports on a monthly and cumulative basis on the measurement of advertising pages and revenue in general and farm magazines, newspaper sections, and newspaper supplements. Reported through magazines and industry classification and advertised products and services, this data is useful to firms needing to know more about a publication's advertisers and advertising revenue. PIB membership includes publishers of magazines and magazine sections of newspapers, and its service is prepared by LEADING NATIONAL ADVERTISERS, INC.

**PUBLISHER'S INTERIM STATEMENT**  CIRCULATION and distribution statement made to the AUDIT BUREAU OF CIRCULATIONS by a publisher at the publisher's option at a time other than when the semi-annual ABC STATEMENT is due. It is issued unaudited but is subject to audit at a later date. Advertisers use the interim statement to evaluate whether there has been a significant change in the circulation since the last statement.

**PUBLISHER'S LETTER**  *see* LIFT LETTER.

**PUBLISHER'S STATEMENT**  *see* ABC STATEMENT.

**PUB-SET**  in print advertising, an advertisement that is set in type by the publication in which it is to appear (as distinguished from an advertisement that is set by the advertiser or by a compositor of the advertiser's choosing and then supplied to the publication); also called *publication-set*. When an advertisement is pub-set, it is usually done without additional charge to the advertiser. However, the publication may not have the typeface or type size specified for the advertisement, or the publication's compositor may not take as much care with the layout as the advertiser might desire.

**PUFFERY**  advertising copy that indulges in subjective exaggeration in its descriptions of a product or service, such as "an outstanding piece of luggage." Puffery is always a matter of opinion on the part of the advertiser and often will use words such as "the best" or "the greatest" in describing the good qualities of a product or service. Sometimes puffery is extended into an exaggeration that is obviously untrue and becomes an outright parody, such as, "This perfume will bring out the beast in every man!"

## PULL
1. pull a proof; *see* PROVE.
2. public demand for a product or service as measured by the amount of sales in comparison to other products in the same category.

**PULL BACK** in film or video production, to dolly away from a subject or object; *see* DOLLY SHOT. A pull-back technique is often used to surprise the viewer by drawing back from a scene to reveal something that was formerly not in view.

## PULLING POWER
1. ability of an advertisement or commercial to sell a product or service or to evoke a response from readers, listeners, or viewers.
2. ability of a medium to draw an audience.

**PULL TAB** ACTION DEVICE used on an OUTER ENVELOPE, consisting of a perforated strip that, if pulled, will easily open the envelope. The pull tab is often cut in the shape of an arrow for greater dramatic emphasis.

**PULL TICKET** *see* COMPUTER-ASSISTED PICKING SYSTEM.

## PULP MAGAZINE
1. inexpensive publication featuring a collection of fictional stories. It derived its name from the low-grade, coarse paper that was initially used to economize on production costs. Pulp magazines are targeted to the mass market and usually feature one long story and several short ones about popular topics such as ambition, crime, and love. Although pulp magazines once boasted an impressive volume of advertisements, the magazines presently carry few advertisements and attain their revenues mainly from subscription and newsstand sales.
2. any publication printed on low-grade, coarse paper. Publishers of pulp magazines use inexpensive paper to economize on production costs.

**PUNCH CARD ADDRESSING** old-fashioned computer-addressing technique that utilizes name and address information stored on KEY PUNCH cards. Most address files today are stored on MAGNETIC TAPE or on DISKS, which make it easier and more cost efficient to store, transfer, and manipulate the information.

**PUPIL DILATION RESPONSE** measure of the amount of change in the size of a research subject's pupil in response to advertising or other images in order to measure the level of interest or amount of information absorbed. A pupillometer is used to measure pupil dilation. While pupil dilation does seem to have a correlation with retention (memory), there is considerable room for error when trying to establish a correlation between pupil dilation and product demand. *See also* EYE MOVEMENT ANALYSIS; GALVANIC SKIN RESPONSE.

**PURCHASE DECISION** *see* BUYING DECISION.

**PURCHASE FREQUENCY** number of occasions during a period of time that a consumer purchases a particular product or buys from a particular seller. Marketers can increase purchase frequency by promoting additional uses for the product such as a "not just for Thanksgiving" promotion for cranberry sauce. The higher the purchase frequency, the greater the opportunity for BRAND SWITCHING. Products with a high purchase frequency, like coffee, require a sustained, year-round advertising effort to avoid losing market share. Products with a low purchase frequency, like Christmas decorations, require seasonal advertising efforts. Consumable goods tend to have higher purchase frequencies than DURABLE GOODS. Direct marketers try to identify customers with high purchase frequency rates because they are usually the marketer's best prospects. An auto dealer uses knowledge of customer purchase frequency patterns to schedule mailings or phone calls to customers around the time of their next car purchase decision. *See also* RECENCY/FREQUENCY; REPEAT RATE; SYNCHROMARKETING.

**PURCHASE HISTORY** purchases made by a particular customer over time. Purchase history is frequently expressed in terms of the RECENCY/FREQUENCY/MONETARY VALUE ratio that defines the value of a customer.

**PURCHASE INTERVAL** average time lapse between occasions when a consumer purchases a particular product or buys from a particular seller. *See also* PURCHASE FREQUENCY.

**PURCHASE-PRIVILEGE PREMIUM** alternate name for SELF-LIQUIDATOR or SEMI-LIQUIDATOR.

**PURE RENEWAL** subscription RENEWAL received after the first renewal of a new subscription. The first renewal, called the *conversion renewal*, is typically harder to sell than a pure renewal. If a subscriber has purchased a conversion renewal and if the quality and price of the product or service remains constant, the purchase tends to become habitual, and thus less elaborate and expensive renewal promotion techniques can be used effectively to sell pure renewals.

**PURE STREAMING** CANADA POST mail-handling procedure that isolates each CLASS of mail during all phases of mail handling. Each class of bulk mail is identified by the unique color of the FACING SLIPS and SACK TAGS used by the mailer: green for third class, orange for second class.

**PURGE** *see* MERGE/PURGE.

**PUSH INCENTIVES** compensation, usually in the form of money, offered to retail salespersons to push the sale of a particular product; also called *spiffs*. For example: A salesperson in the leather goods department of a retail store may suggest a leather cleaner when completing the sale of a pair of leather gloves or a pocketbook. For each bottle of leather cleaner sold, the salesperson may receive a 25- to 50-cent spiff. Generally, spiffs are offered by the manufacturer, but they may also be offered as sales incentives by the head of a chain of stores or the management of a department store.

**PYLON**
1. tower or post supporting an OUTDOOR-ADVERTISING structure.
2. outdoor advertising structure.

**PYRAMIDING**
1. mailing-list testing technique that involves selecting and mailing progressively larger SAMPLES from a list until the total list is mailed, as long as the revenue from each mailing exceeds the costs; also called *continuation* mailing. This eliminates the risk of mailing a large volume of pieces to an unprofitable list. *See also* PREVIOUS MAIL SUPPRESSION.
2. fraudulent business practice in which the chain of distribution is artificially expanded by an excessive number of distributors selling to other distributors at progressively higher wholesale prices, ultimately resulting in unnecessarily inflated retail prices.

---

# Q

---

**Q&A FORMAT** *see* QUESTION-AND-ANSWER FORMAT.

**Q-RATING** research term used in compiling data about broadcast audience awareness. A Q-rating measures the amount of viewers or listeners who are familiar with a particular broadcast program or broadcast personality. Television and radio personalities often gauge their popularity by their Q-rating.

**QUAD** blank metal type SLUG used to create indentations (EM quad, EN quad) or other spaces on a typeset line. Quads fill the space remaining at the right end of a FLUSH left line when the words in that line do not fill the length of space allotted for each line on the page.

**QUALIFIED CIRCULATION** *see* CIRCULATION.

**QUALIFIED GRACING** periodical copies served after EXPIRE that qualify, according to AUDIT BUREAU OF CIRCULATIONS rules, as paid CIRCULATION. *See also* GRACE.

**QUALIFIED LEAD** prospective customer who has a demonstrated interest in the product or service being sold, the ability to pay, or the authority to make a purchase decision. For example, someone who has returned a reply card requesting a salesperson's call is a qualified lead, in contrast to someone who is contacted by a salesperson without any prior verification that he/she can pay, can make the decision to buy, or has any interest.

**QUALIFIED MAIL** part of a mailing that is eligible for PRESORT discounts. There are minimum volume requirements that must be met for each mail PACKAGE and SACK to qualify for a discount. The remaining mail presorted (*see* PRESORT) that does not meet the volume requirement is called *unqualified mail* or *unqualified sort*.

**QUALITATIVE RESEARCH** research that deals with the quality, type, or components of a group, substance, or mixture, whose methods are applied to advertising audience research in order to determine the quality of audience responses to advertising. Qualitative research is exploratory in nature and uses procedures such as in-depth interviews and focus group interviews to gain insights and develop creative advertising tactics.

**QUALITY CONTROL** controls placed on the manufacture, distribution, and/or sales of products and services to assure customers that the quality of the goods and services will remain at the industry's or manufacturer's standard for quality throughout all areas of production and sales. For example, in the printing industry, most reputable printers will take RANDOM SAMPLES from a run to check the consistency of quality throughout the run.

**QUANTITATIVE RESEARCH** research that deals with the quantities of things and that involves the measurement of quantity or amount, applied to advertising audience research to develop actual numbers of audience members in order to accurately measure market situations.

**QUANTITY PRINTS** multiple prints of a film, videotape, or photograph made at the same time from the original master.

**QUARTER SHOWING** in transit advertising, directive indicating that CAR CARDS or posters (see BILLBOARDS) are to be displayed in every fourth vehicle (or 25%) of a fleet. *See also* FULL SHOWING; SHOWING.

**QUERY** request from a customer or prospect for information about his account or about the product or service involved. *See also* CUSTOMER SERVICE; INQUIRY.

**QUESTION-AND-ANSWER FORMAT**
**In general:** meeting or interview format where information is given in the form of replies to questions.
**Advertising:** technique for writing copy where the advertiser or a spokesperson for the advertiser replies to questions posed by the customer or prospective customer.

**QUESTIONNAIRE** market research survey technique utilizing a list of questions answered separately by each survey participant. Questions may be *closed-ended* (answerable by checking one of several predetermined answers) or *open-ended* (requiring participants to answer in their own words). The answers to open-ended QUESTIONNAIRES are much more difficult to tabulate and analyze but provide more information than the surveyor might otherwise collect. Questionnaires are a good survey technique, because the cost (printing, distribution, collection, analysis) is low relative to that of other methods such as PERSONAL INTERVIEWS, because participants can respond at their own convenience, because no interviewer bias is introduced, and because responses can be kept completely confidential. The disadvantages are that the results may be biased toward the opinions of those who chose to respond to the questionnaire versus all those who had been asked to respond, and the results may be distorted if the questions were misunderstood.

**QUEUE** tasks fed to a computer and waiting to be processed in the sequence in which they were submitted.

**QUOTA**
1. predetermined goal in a sales program established as a total dollar amount, as a percentage of increase over sales from a previous time, or in quantities of merchandise sold.
2. predetermined goal in a media plan established in terms of money to be spent, gross rating points to be achieved, or number of insertions and spots to be bought.
3. *see* QUOTA SAMPLE.

**QUOTA SAMPLE** sample group of people used for research purposes who have been selected at the discretion of the interviewer. The interviewer will be instructed to make selections from a minimum number of persons who fulfill the researcher's QUOTA classifications. Classifications are usually based on census data and will correspond to the composition of the area under study. However, the field visits and choices are the responsibility of the interviewer, and often conditions will occur so that the sample will not be a true representation. For example: An interviewer may not choose people who live on high floors in non-elevator buildings because the interviewer may not want to walk up so many stairs. Consequently, the results of the research may not represent the actual picture, even though the researcher's quotas for each classification may have been filled.

# R

**RACK FOLDER** FLIER that has been folded so that it will fit into a rack designed for the display of such fliers.

**RADIO AREA OF DOMINANT INFLUENCE** term used by The Pulse, Inc., a radio audience measurement service, to indicate the total listening area served by a particular radio station.

**RADIO RATING POINT** *see* RATING.

**RAGGED LEFT OR RIGHT** describes typewritten or printed copy, with uneven margins at either the left side or the right side of a page as compared to FLUSH left or right. Ragged left refers to the margin at the left side of the page; ragged right, to the margin at the right. *See also* FLUSH LEFT OR RIGHT.

**RANDOM ACCESS UNIT** computer storage unit that allows for the access of information at random; also called *direct access storage*. With a random access unit, information can be called up by the computer operator from any position, no matter what order that information was input into storage. For example, if a particular group of information has been inputted in alphabetical order, information can be called up from any part of the alphabet at any time and does not have to be called in alphabetical order.

**RANDOM-DIGIT DIALING** method of obtaining respondents for telephone interviews whereby the exchange digits are dialed and then the rest of the digits are dialed at random. Random-digit dialing gives accessibility to unlisted as well as listed telephone numbers.

**RANDOMIZATION** *see* RANDOM SAMPLE.

**RANDOM SAMPLE** sample group of people to be used in a research testing situation where every person in the area under study had an equal chance of being included in the sample; also called *precision sample*. The process of selecting this sample on the basis of chance is called *randomization*.

**RATE** cost of advertising space or commercial time in a communications medium, as established by the management or ownership of the medium. The rate for advertising space or time as based on the circulation of a publication or the size of the listening audience, the quality of the medium's audience, and various other factors. Media will allow advertisers discounts from the basic rate structure when advertisers exceed a certain dollar volume in INSERTION ORDERS or exceed a certain number of specified insertions, or when payment of advertising costs is made within a specified time period. The cost of media for advertising after discounts have been applied is called the *net rate*. *See also* RATE BOOK; RATE CARD.

**RATE BASE** guaranteed AVERAGE NET PAID CIRCULATION of a periodical set by the publisher according to the number of copies he believes he can sell on a consistent basis. It is used by advertisers to evaluate the benefit of advertising in that periodical. Space advertising prices are based upon the rate base, and if the rate base guarantee is not set, the publisher must compensate advertisers for the difference.

Copies sold in excess of the rate base, commonly called BONUS CIRCULATION, are free.

## RATE BOOK

1. reference volume of RATE CARD information, such as the CONSUMER MAGAZINE AND AGRI-MEDIA RATES AND DATA, which is published monthly and issued on a subscription basis to advertisers, advertising agencies, and others interested in costs of advertising.
2. manufacturer's book that lists products and their prices, for use by the manufacturer's sales representative.

**RATE CARD** pamphlet, brochure, or single sheet that tells the costs for advertising on or in a communications medium. The rate card is usually designed to give the advertiser all the pertinent data relative to advertising with the medium. In addition to the unit costs for time or space, the card will list any and all of a medium's regulations governing the use of said time or space, restrictions on the time or space as set up by the medium, requirements to be met for CAMERA-READY copy (in the case of print media), copy regulations, facilities available from the medium, various discount plans, and kinds of products or services that are not acceptable for advertising in the medium. Production studios and editing facilities also publish rate cards listing their facilities and costs on a per hour or per day basis.

**RATE DIFFERENTIAL** difference between local and national advertising rates. The local media typically charge local advertisers at a lower rate than they charge national advertisers. Because of this fact, many national companies offer COOPERATIVE ADVERTISING money to their local dealers or distributors.

**RATE HOLDER** advertisement, usually measuring the smallest space a publication will allow, that has been placed by an advertiser to "hold" a contracted discount rate offered by the publication for a minimum number of lines or a minimum number of insertions. In broadcast, advertisers will purchase a 10-second spot for this same purpose.

**RATE PROTECTION** agreement between an advertising medium and an advertiser that the advertiser's contracted rate will be guaranteed even if the medium raises its rates during the time of the contract. Rate protection is generally guaranteed from three months to a year from the date of signing the contract.

**RATES AND CLASSIFICATIONS** department within the U.S. Postal Service responsible for interpreting and enforcing postage rate and classification regulations and for working with mailers to explain how the postal system can be used most economically.

## RATING

**Broadcast:** size of an actual listening or viewing audience for a particular program or commercial as compared to the size of the *potential* audience. The potential audience consists of all households in a geographic area that have broadcast receivers (radios and televisions), whether or not these broadcast receivers are turned on. One rating point represents 1% of the households making up the potential audience. Thus, if a program had a rating of 10 (10 rating points), it would mean that 10% of all households in a particular geographic area had sets tuned in to that program. Ratings and rating points are an integral part of the broadcast evaluation system, particularly television, and are used in the planning of broadcast media schedules for advertising campaigns. A program with a high rating will deliver a large audience to advertisers for their commercials.

**Outdoor advertising:** estimate of the number of persons exposed to an outdoor sign. Each outdoor structure is rated in terms of the number of persons who pass by on a daily basis as compared to the entire population in the area where the structure is located. If a structure located in an area with a population of 1000 has 100 passersby on a daily basis, that structure has a 10% rating and each rating point is equal to 10 passersby. These numbers play an important role in determining the COST PER THOUSAND for outdoor advertising.

**RAW NAMES** name and address information on customers or prospects that is in HARD-COPY form prior to conversion to a computer storage medium such as MAGNETIC TAPE or DISK. Raw names are usually on the original data collection documents, such as coupons, application forms, warranty cards, or conference rosters.

**R&D** research and development. *See* PRODUCT RESEARCH AND DEVELOPMENT.

**REACH** *see* CUMULATIVE AUDIENCE.

**REACH AND FREQUENCY** components used to figure out the GROSS RATING POINTS obtained by a broadcast media schedule. *Reach* tells how many households will be exposed to the schedule, and FREQUENCY tells how often each household will be exposed. The two numbers multiplied together will indicate, by percentage, the total potential audience exposure in a given market. Some measure of reach and frequency must be determined in planning a broadcast media advertising campaign, and the MEDIA PLANNER must decide upon the balance between the two. For some campaigns, reach will be more important, particularly in a new product introduction, where the primary goal is to gain awareness of the product. However, a campaign whose advertising contains many product details will most likely require a great many exposures, making the Frequency Factor more important in the media plan.

**READABLE MAIL** letter mail with optically scannable addresses or ZIP codes. The U.S. Postal Service uses machines to read addresses and sort the mail by destination. *See also* OPTICAL CHARACTER RECOGNITION.

**READER CONFIDENCE** publisher's confidence that a publication will have a regular readership who will continue to purchase and/or subscribe to the publication.

**READER IMPRESSION STUDY** study by DANIEL STARCH AND ASSOCIATES the intention of which is to find out what a particular advertisement in a publication meant to respondents who noted the ad (*see* ADNOTER). A reader impression study is done after the regular readership study.

**READER INTEREST** readers' expression of interest in advertisements they have seen in publications. Reader interest may be evaluated by unsolicited mail, or by researching the numbers of people who can remember being interested in the advertisement when they read it, or by the measurement of the number of readers expressing interest in one advertisement as compared to those expressing interest in other advertisements.

**READER RESPONSE** measurement of advertising and editorial readership based on information requests, letters received, and orders placed as a result of advertisements or editorial copy.

**READER SERVICE CARD** *see* BINGO CARD.

**READERSHIP**
1. total number of readers of a publication.
2. in audience measurement, percentage of audience who recall reading a print advertisement.

**READERS PER COPY** number of persons who read a particular issue of a periodical. The readers-per-copy number is calculated by dividing the total audience (including primary and pass-along readers) of the publication by the circulation of an average issue of the publication.

**READING TIME** average length of time that the readers of a publication devote to each issue. When comparing similar publications, advertisers may find the publication with the most reading time attractive because the TARGET AUDIENCE will have more time to read their advertisements.

**READ-MOST** person or category of persons who read more than 50% of a specific print advertisement. The term was originated by the research firm of DANIEL STARCH AND ASSOCIATES.

**REAL PEOPLE** persons used in advertisements to represent actual consumers rather than actors. They generally have greater believability than paid performers.

**REAL SEEDS** SALT NAMES of actual persons voluntarily participating in a salt, versus fictitious names created for the purpose of salting.

Mailers and list owners sometimes enlist friends, associates, and employees at addresses throughout the mailing area to help them monitor delivery time as well as list usage. These individuals report what mail they receive and when they have received it. A slight change in their name is usually made on each list to identify mailing pieces that used that particular list. For example, "Jane" might be changed to "Jayne." The recipients might also return the mailing piece to the mailer so he can inspect it.

**REAM** 500 sheets of paper. The BASIS WEIGHT of paper is the weight of one ream cut to the standard dimensions for that type of paper.

**REAR PROJECTION** *see* REAR-SCREEN PROJECTION.

**REAR-SCREEN PROJECTION**
1. method of creating a background scene by projecting images behind a translucent screen; also called *background plate, process screen*, and *rear projection*. This method is commonly used in television and motion pictures. For instance, when filming a movie on a set, rear-screen projection would be used to project a moving background behind a stationary car to create the appearance of a car in motion.
2. method of film or television projection where the projection apparatus is behind the projection screen.

**REASON-WHY ADVERTISING** copywriting approach to print advertising whose format is to state a fact about a product or service in a headline and then explain why the fact is true in the copy text. The idea behind this type of advertising approach is to give a reason why a customer should buy the product or service. Reason-why advertising works better in print than in broadcast, because the reader has more time to consider the message. Broadcast presents a time limitation, and the viewer may very well miss the opening headline or the reasons why the opening headline is true.

**REASON-WHY COPY** *see* REASON-WHY ADVERTISING.

**REBATE**
**In general:** refund of a payment.
**Media:** refund given to an advertiser by a media vehicle. A rebate is usually given when the advertiser places more advertisements than originally contracted, therefore earning a larger discount. For example, the XYZ Company contracts to place a full-page ad in a periodical every week for three weeks, earning a 10% media discount. Later, the company decides to extend the campaign to six weeks, which would normally earn a 15% discount. The periodical would issue a 5% rebate to the XYZ Company.
**Sales promotion:** refund given to a consumer for sending in proof-of-purchase after a sale.

**RECALL RESEARCH** techniques used to judge the effectiveness of an advertisement by testing the respondent's ability to remember the advertisement or any of its specifics. *See also* AIDED RECALL, UNAIDED RECALL.

**RECEIVER**

**Broadcast:** device used to transform electromagnetic waves into images or sounds. For example, a television or stereo would be considered receivers.

**Communications:** person or group of people to whom a communications message is transmitted. The receiver perceives and responds to the message in terms of his own background and psychological processes. In mass communications, the receiver is the audience.

**RECENCY/FREQUENCY** measure of the value of a customer or group of customers in terms of the number of purchases made and the length of time between purchases as well as the length of time since the last purchase. The higher the degree of recency and frequency, the more valuable the customer. For example, a customer who made 20 purchases last year is more valuable than a customer who made 20 purchases three years ago. They are both more valuable than a customer who made one purchase three years ago. *See also* RECENCY/FREQUENCY/MONETARY VALUE.

**RECENCY/FREQUENCY/MONETARY VALUE** three measures considered jointly to determine the value of a customer or group of customers in terms of the time since the last purchase was made, the number of purchases made during a period of time, and the dollar value of the purchases made. For example, a customer who purchases $100 worth of goods over a two-month period is more valuable than a customer who purchases $100 worth of goods over a two-year period.

Although difficult, it is possible to quantify the value of recency and frequency by using a system that assigns a value from 1 to 10 to various recency/frequency values. For example, the frequency rating for a customer who purchases five times in a six-month period may be rated an 8. The recency of his last purchase was one week ago, and that is a 10, for a total customer rating of 18. Another customer made one purchase in the last six months, earning a frequency rating of 2. His purchase was five months ago, which earns a recency rating of 2, for a total customer rating of 4. A rating scale can also be used for the monetary value of the purchases, which, added to these recency/frequency ratings, will produce an overall relative rating for the customer.

**RECIPROCITY** arrangement between two participants in the PRODUCER MARKET who are both buyer and seller to each other. For example, a company providing services to a trade journal may pay for advertising space in the journal with their services. A reciprocity opportunity may persuade a company to choose a less desirable vendor in exchange for sales made to that vendor.

## RECOGNITION

1. formal acknowledgment granted by the various publications or broadcast media to an advertising agency after the agency has proven financially able, competent, ethical, and bona fide. Recognition, which is also known as *agency recognition*, entitles the agency to receive commissions for the time and space it sells and also entitles the agency to make purchases on credit.

2. consumer awareness of having seen or heard an advertising message. When it is not possible to determine directly the effectiveness of the advertising message, because several media have been used and a direct correlation between sales and an advertising medium cannot be established, advertisers will sometimes run recognition tests. If the tests provide a high degree of consumer recognition of the advertising message, then the advertiser can assume that the advertising is doing its job. *See also* AIDED RECALL.

**RECOMMENDED DAILY ALLOWANCE (RDA)** amount of a particular vitamin, mineral, or nutrient required by an individual each day, in order to maintain good health. Recommended daily allowances are established independently by the Food & Drug Administration and the National Academy of Sciences.

**RECORD** subset of a FILE consisting of all relevant data about each individual item in the file. For example, the information about one particular customer in a customer file represents a record. Customer and prospect file records usually contain a minimum of the information required to contact the customer in order to make additional sales, deliver the goods ordered, or collect for unpaid orders: for example, name, address, item ordered, quantity, and price. Customer file records also frequently contain marketing information concerning how the sale was made, so that future sales resources can be concentrated on the most successful strategies.

LIST RENTAL selections can be made from a file that excludes any proprietary information in the records such as payment status and SOURCE KEY. *See also* FIELD; FIXED FIELD; KEY CODE.

**RECORD RETENTION** logic in a COMPUTER PROGRAM indicating how DUPLICATE records should be combined into one. *See also* PRIORITY LIST; PROPORTIONATE ALLOCATION.

**RECORD STATUS** characteristic of a file RECORD. The record status may be active, and eligible for service on a subscription or CONTINUITY, or paid and eligible for additional credit purchases.

**RED BOOK** *see* STANDARD ADVERTISING REGISTER.

**REDEMPTION**
1. exchanging a coupon, trading stamp, or similar device for a discount or premium.
2. percentage of coupons or trading stamps actually turned in; also called REDEMPTION RATE.

**REDEMPTION RATE** *see* REDEMPTION.

**RED GOODS** consumer goods, such as food products, that are consumed and replaced at a fast rate and have a low profit margin. *See also* ORANGE GOODS; YELLOW GOODS.

**RED TAG** *see* PREFERENTIAL NETWORK.

**REDUCED RATE**
1. *see* DISCOUNT.
2. *see* ALLOWANCE.
3. periodical subscription or newsstand-sold copy sold at a price less than the BASIC RATE. Most new subscriptions are sold at reduced rates as an incentive for new customers. When the subscriptions are renewed the publisher attempts to get the full price. Subscriptions are usually not profitable until renewed at the full rate.

**REDUCING GLASS** double concave lens of ophthalmic glass mounted in a frame used to reduce the apparent size of photographs and illustrations. By using a reducing glass, an artist or engraver can judge how a particular piece of artwork would look if reduced to a smaller size.

**REDUCTION PRINT** film or photographic print reduced from the size of the original negative. For instance, it might be necessary to reduce 35mm film to 16mm.

**REENROLLMENT MAILING** direct-mail promotion to former members of a CONTINUITY (or book club, record club, etc.) asking them to again become members. The COPY and the PACKAGE are different from those used for NEW MEMBER MAILINGS. The copy may refer to some of the membership benefits the recipient has enjoyed before and may include an EMOTIONAL APPEAL that says "We want to welcome you back" or "We miss you."

**RE-ETCH** further etch a halftone printing plate in order to enhance contrasts. *See also* FINE ETCHING.

**REFERENCE GROUP** group, class, or category of people to which individuals believe they belong, whether or not they actually do. Their relationship to their reference group may influence their buying behavior. For example, if a man buys a more expensive car than he normally would because his neighbors drive that particular model, his buying behavior is seen to be influenced by his reference group.

**REFERENCE MEDIA** sources of statistical, demographic, or commercial information published periodically for use by advertisers and other businesses.

**REFERRAL** name of a prospective customer (or member, donor) acquired from a current customer or other third party. Most referral programs offer the customer an incentive award for referrals, particularly for referrals that become customers. For example, air travel clubs offer bonus mileage. Referrals generally respond to promotions at a much higher rate than other prospects, but the response rate decreases as the average number of referrals per customer increases. Studies show that customers who give many referrals tend to include people with little or no likelihood of interest in the product. *See also* FRIEND-OF-A-FRIEND; MEMBER-GET-A-MEMBER.

**REFLECTION COPY** image to be printed that is highly reflective of light and must therefore be photographed in special lighting. Examples include glossy photographs, oil paintings, or varnished surfaces.

**REFUND** money returned by a seller of a product or service in exchange for the return of some portion of a product or service. For example, stores will issue a refund for the return of empty soda bottles or cans.

**REFUND OFFER**
1. manufacturer or sales-promotion strategy that promises to refund part of the retail sales price to the consumer upon receipt of PROOF OF PURCHASE; also called REBATE offer. Although the purpose of the refund is to motivate buyers, the sellers assume most buyers will not go to the trouble of requesting a refund.
2. sales-promotion strategy that guarantees the buyer a refund if not satisfied. *See also* HARD OFFER; TRIAL OFFER.

**REGION** U.S. BUREAU OF THE CENSUS term for one of four large divisions of the United States, including the Northeast, North Central, South, and West. *See also* GEOGRAPHIC CENSUS DIVISION.

**REGIONAL EDITION** national publication with a specific advertising section for advertisers in a particular geographic location. Many publications publish regional editions so that they may offer local advertisers opportunities for advertising in their own geographic area. The editorial content in such a publication remains the same in all editions, but a section of the space allocated to advertising is reserved for regional advertisers. Distribution of regional editions is limited to the specific geographic area involved in the advertising.

**REGISTER**
**Business:** record a trademark, patent, copyright, etc., with a government agency in order to claim exclusivity.
**Printing:** align color plates correctly in order to print a perfect color reproduction of artwork. The print is "in register" when it is faithful to the original. When it is "out of register," it may be blurry and look like a 3-D comic book picture.

**REGISTER MARKS** crossed or perpendicular lines used to align COLOR SEPARATIONS when printing, or to align cuts, folds, or overprinted (*see* OVERPRINTING) images on a sheet of paper.

**REINSTATEMENT** placement of a customer record in ACTIVE status after having been suspended (*see* SUSPEND), canceled, expired, or otherwise inactivated. Reinstated subscriptions have usually been canceled for nonpayment and are reinstated when a late payment is received. A subscription renewal that is received after EXPIRE, but in enough time to provide unbroken service, will be reinstated rather than treated as a new subscription with no prior customer history.

**REJECT**
**Data processing:**
   1. transaction entered to a computer file that cannot be processed; for example, a customer change-of-address request for which the computer cannot find a record with the old address. In most cases, a person who reviews the rejects can resolve problems the computer could not and can then successfully reenter the transactions for processing.
   2. machine-processed item that cannot be processed, such as a damaged bar-coded (*see* BAR CODE) document that cannot be machine read and is rejected by the SCANNER.
**Manufacturing:** incorrectly manufactured item that fails to meet quality control standards or that a retailer will not accept for sale to consumers. Rejects are sometimes sold at discounted rates, particularly if the flaws are minor.

**RELATED-ITEM APPROACH** *see* CROSS MERCHANDISING.

**RELAUNCH** reintroduction of a product or marketing campaign after it has been discontinued for a period of time and then undergone some sort of improvement or change.

**RELEASE**
   1. legal authorization by a person to allow someone else to use that person's likeness, name, writings, or other property for advertising, film copy, trade or marketing purposes, or any other stated purpose in exchange for remuneration of some kind.
   2. agreement by the proposed seller of creative material or a creative concept not to hold the proposed buyer responsible for payment should the material be unusable.
   3. news item, such as a change of personnel in a company or a fund raising event sponsored by a community service organization, that has been written by the company or organization and delivered to the media to be inserted into their publications or broadcasts for public relations purposes; more properly called a *publicity release* or a *press release*.

**RELEASE DATE** a specific date and time when a new product, promotional campaign, or news story will be announced to the media.

Release dates are set by public relations professionals to maximize media coverage and gain the attention of the broadest possible audience.

**RELIABILITY** in research, probability that a measurement is free from random error and yields consistent results; that is, the same results can be expected at another time. For example, a reliable promotion test means that a similar promotion will yield similar results. *See also* CONFIDENCE LEVEL; VALIDITY.

**REMAINDER** merchandise that remains unsold at its original price due to lack of demand; also called *overstock*. The remainder is usually then sold at a lower price. Calendars sold months after the year has begun would be considered remainder merchandise and thus sold at a substantial discount.

**REMARKETING** marketing efforts to spur demand for a product that is experiencing declining demand by marketing it as though it were a new product. The success of a remarketing effort depends on a good understanding of what market changes have caused demand to decline so that the remarketing strategy can be based upon the current market environment. The nonpower lawnmower has benefited from remarketing that positioned it as a quieter, environmentally friendly alternative to power lawnmowers that is both a lawn tool and an exercise machine.

**REMINDER ADVERTISING**
1. brief messages designed chiefly to keep a product in the mind of the consumer once the product is already familiar. Reminder advertising usually follows an extensive advertising campaign, and therefore does not elaborate on the reasons to buy the product. Common examples of reminder advertisements are those found on matchbooks and pencils and in skywriting, as well as the more traditional media vehicles.
2. advertising designed to remind consumers of the benefits of a product or service, or of their current need for those benefits. For instance, the XYZ Company may seek to remind consumers of their need for XYZ anti-freeze when the weather begins to turn cold.

**REMIT RATE** remittance rate; portion of a periodical subscription sales price remitted to the publisher by a SUBSCRIPTION AGENT after deduction of the agent's commission. The remit rate is usually 10% to 40% of the selling price.

**REMITTANCE** *see* REMIT RATE.

**REMOTE** broadcast production that takes place outside the studio. The simplest remote production is the type seen nightly on local or network news where a newscaster reports about an event from the place where it is taking place. The most complex remote productions are the elaborate large-scale types used to cover sports and entertainment events, such as the Super Bowl or the Thanksgiving Day Parade.

**RENEWAL** subscription order from a current subscriber received prior to EXPIRE or within six months after expire. Most publishers do not make any profit on a subscription until it has been renewed. A high renewal rate of 50% to 75% is essential to the economic survival of periodicals that do not derive most of their revenue from selling advertising space (such as children's or consumer magazines that don't accept advertising, or magazines that are sold only by subscription). Most renewals are sold at the full undiscounted BASIC RATE, in contrast to new subscriptions that are sold at discounted rates. The PRIOR SOURCES of subscribers who renew at a high rate are carefully tracked so that efforts to recruit new subscribers will be concentrated on those sources. Renewal orders may be received from sources of business other than the publishers own RENEWAL PROMOTIONS, resulting in lower renewal revenues. For example, a subscriber may use a BIND-IN card with a discount offer to renew. *See also* CONVERSION RENEWAL PERCENTAGE; IDENTIFIED RENEWAL; PURE RENEWAL.

**RENEWAL-AT-BIRTH** ADVANCE RENEWAL of a subscription ordered at the same time that payment for the current subscription is sent; abbreviated *RAB*. Many publishers offer RABs at special rates to increase cash flow and to extend the term of the subscriptions sold. RAB offers usually include wording such as "pay $12 for one year, or double your savings and get two years for only $18." RABs are not a major source of business relative to other sources such as COLD MAIL PROMOTIONS, because relatively few customers will accept the offer to double their purchase. However, their cost is so minimal as to make them one of the most profitable.

**RENEWAL PROMOTION** promotional mailing sent to current subscribers soliciting RENEWAL of those subscriptions. Renewal promotions consist of a series of promotions called EFFORTS that begin about seven months prior to EXPIRE and continue for two or three months after expire. They may also include ADVANCE RENEWAL offers and/or RENEWAL-AT-BIRTH offers. The renewal promotion COPY usually begins with a soft-sell approach such as "Renew now before our price increase is effective" and ends with an approach such as "We don't want to lose you, but this is your last chance." Renewal promotions usually are direct-mail packages utilizing many of the traditional DIRECT-MAIL ADVERTISING techniques, but the series may include a telephone effort as well. Renewals received in response to a renewal promotion are called IDENTIFIED RENEWALS. Most renewals require cash with order, but credit offers are also used successfully.

**RENEWAL RATE** proportion of the subscribers scheduled to EXPIRE during any one cycle who renew their subscriptions. *See also* RENEWAL; RENEWAL PROMOTION.

**RENEWAL SERIES** *see* RENEWAL PROMOTION.

**RENEWED BEFORE** complaint from a subscriber responding to a RENEWAL PROMOTION and stating she has already renewed. These complaints are often treated as renewal orders rather than complaints, without the expense of sending a letter of apology or explanation to the subscriber. This generally satisfies the subscriber.

**RENT** *see* LIST RENTAL.

**REP**
1. CUSTOMER SERVICE REPRESENTATIVE.
2. short for *sales representative.*

**REPEAT MAILING** second mailing of the same PACKAGE made to the same list after a short period of time, such as six weeks. Repeat mailings can generate as much as half the response of the original mailing, because the repetition enhances the persuasiveness of the message.

**REPEAT PURCHASE** consumer purchase of the same brand purchased on the previous purchase occasion; also called REPURCHASE. BRAND LOYALTY may be deduced by a pattern of repeat purchases. *See also* REPEAT RATE.

**REPEAT RATE** number of times a product is purchased by an individual consumer within a period of time. For example, soap has a higher repeat rate than automobiles, because it is used up more quickly. A high repeat rate for a particular brand indicates a high degree of customer satisfaction. Repeat rates are particularly important in the evaluation of a new product. The time needed to conduct a product test is proportionate to the length of time between purchases, because the marketer must evaluate whether that product or brand is selected again by the same consumer.

   The results of a repeat-rate measurement can be used to determine future promotional strategies. A high repeat rate after little introductory advertising indicates that additional advertising will provide disproportionately great returns. A low repeat rate indicates that the product might benefit from being promoted more heavily. If, after heavy promotion, repeat rates remain low, this suggests that the product should be redesigned or abandoned.

**REPEAT SALE** purchase of a product by a consumer to replace a prior purchase that has been consumed; also called REPLACEMENT SALE. *See also* REPEAT RATE.

**REPETITION** multiple consumer EXPOSURES to an advertisement over a period of time. Repetition has been proven to increase recall and comprehension, particularly if the message is complex. However, a message may lose effectiveness if the consumer is overexposed to the advertisement through excessive repetitions, causing the consumer to lose interest in the message.

**REPLACEMENT FILE** list of names and addresses provided by a list owner for substitution by the list user for other names and addresses on a rented list. A replacement file may be provided if a rented list has an excessive number of undeliverable addresses making it unusable.

**REPLACEMENT SALE** *see* REPEAT SALE.

**REPLY ENVELOPE** self-addressed envelope provided by a direct marketer for the return of orders or other replies. The ease of using a reply envelope increases the likelihood of getting a response. BUSINESS REPLY ENVELOPES are also postage paid by the direct marketer, to remove one more barrier to response. Most direct-mail PACKAGES include a reply envelope, but these envelopes are also inserted into magazines and catalogs and are distributed in a variety of other ways as well. Some reply envelopes include an order form on the envelope flap. *See also* BANGTAIL; ORDER BLANK ENVELOPE; SELF-MAILER; SELF-SEALER; WALLET FLAP.

**REPLY FORM** document provided by a direct marketer or other organization for the collection of information from individuals. Examples are ORDER FORMS, applications, and QUESTIONNAIRES. Reply forms should include a request that the information be printed or typed to make it easier to read. The reply form should also collect all the necessary information without becoming a complex task for the responder. The best rule of thumb is to keep it simple.

**REPORT GENERATOR** computer program that is used to create statistical reports based upon the information in a computer file. Most report generator programs are written for use by people other than programmers. The simplest report generators create reports that illustrate the relationship between only two VARIABLES in the DATABASE. For example, a report generator might plot gross responses to a catalog mailing against mailing lists, showing the relative performance of each list used.

**REPOSITIONING** modification of consumer perception of a product or service relative to competitive products or services. Repositioning is necessary when the preferences of the market shift. For example, a premium brand of shampoo that sold at a relatively high price with advertising that emphasized its superior performance may need to be repositioned as consumers become more price sensitive. One way would be to position it as the best value brand with price cuts and advertising emphasizing that a little bit goes a long way. The costs associated with repositioning a brand, in terms of product, price or promotion modifications, must be weighed against the added revenue potential. *See also* POSITION.

**REPRINT**
 1. reproduction of an advertisement after the advertisement has appeared in a publication. Reprints are used in the same manner as

PREPRINTS—to show advertising support and as point-of-purchase promotional displays.

**2.** duplication of a favorable article that has appeared in a magazine or newspaper, used in an advertising display, as a direct-mail piece in conjunction with a promotion, and for public relations.

**REPRODUCTION PROOF**  high-quality, CAMERA-READY proof of type copy made for PHOTOMECHANICAL reproduction; also called *repro proof*, SLICK. The reproduction proof or a photograph of it becomes the print image carrier.

**REPRO PROOF**  camera-ready proof intended for photographic reproduction on a printing plate. *See also* ENAMEL PROOF, SLICK.

**REPURCHASE RATE**  *see* REPEAT RATE.

**REQUEST CANCEL**  subscriber request to cancel a CREDIT ORDER before payment has been made. Soft-offer promotions usually generate a high proportion of request cancels that come in after customers have reviewed the product and decided it is not what they expected. Some people will respond to a soft offer, with the intention of canceling to get a free sample of the product. New products or publications are especially susceptible to request cancels because customers are not familiar with what they will be getting. This is especially true if the promotion misrepresents or exaggerates attributes of the product.

**REQUEST EXPIRE**  subscriber request that the subscription be allowed to expire without additional RENEWAL PROMOTIONS being sent.

**REQUEST FOR PROPOSAL**  document sent by a potential buyer to potential vendors soliciting price quotes; also called Request for Quotation. Commonly referred to as an RFP, it includes all of the buyer's product or service requirements as well as a description of the required format, timing, and content of the price quotes to be submitted. RFPs enable the buyer to ensure that all vendors have an equal understanding of the requirements and that the bids can easily be compared. This is especially important for highly complex products and services that require customization to meet the unique needs of the buyer. *See also* COMPETITIVE BID.

**REQUESTOR**  free publication designated by the U.S. Postal Service to be eligible for second-class treatment normally reserved for paid publications. A requestor publication must show proof, in the form of a signed request form, of the recipient's interest in receiving the publication. Publications other than paid or requestor publications are considered promotional material eligible only for third-class treatment.

**REROUTE**  computer file maintenance REJECT that has been adjusted as necessary and is now being resubmitted for entry to the computer system.

**RERUN**  repeat RUN of a machine such as a computer or printing press that was previously interrupted because of a problem or mistake, or was run incorrectly. If the problem was created by the computer service customer, print buyer, or the like, the cost of the rerun may be billed back to the customer.

**RESCALE** *see* RESIZE.

**RESEARCH**
1. scientific method of systematically gathering, recording, and analyzing data important to advertisers. Research information is used to plan, create, and execute more effective advertising and marketing campaigns.
2. department within a company whose primary responsibility is conducting these types of investigations.

**RESEARCH AND DEVELOPMENT** *see* PRODUCT RESEARCH AND DEVELOPMENT.

**RESEARCH DIRECTOR** *see* CONSUMER RESEARCH DIRECTOR.

**RESELLER MARKET** buyers who purchase with the intent of selling those products to others. The reseller market includes wholesalers, retailers, and distributors. Resellers may restrict their purchases to one product or brand or offer a variety of products and brands. *See also* CHANNEL MANAGEMENT; PRODUCER MARKET; TRADE PROMOTION.

**RESIDUAL** fee paid to a performer for repeat performances of a broadcast commercial or program; also called *re-use fee*, *SAG fee*, *talent charge*. The residual may be paid by the advertiser or television or radio station, depending on the nature of the program. Rates are generally established by AFTRA (American Federation of Television and Radio Artists) or SAG (Screen Actors Guild) contract.

**RESIDUAL MAIL** mail pieces remaining from the total mailing after a computer PRESORT of addresses has identified this portion as being ineligible for postage discounts—usually because the volume of mail going to any one destination is too small to meet minimum volume requirements. The U.S. Postal Service permits the combination of residual first-class and third-class mailing pieces from several mailers. to be combined for presort discounts, but the mailer or service performing the combination must have prior approval.

**RESIST** chemical used to protect the nonprinting areas of a copper PRINTING PLATE from exposure to the etching solution. *See also* STAGING.

**RESISTOR** individual who has a history of not responding to direct-mail promotions. Resistors should be deleted from promotional mailing lists during a MERGE/PURGE.

**RESIZE** modify the size of a print advertisement to conform to the space units of different publications; also called *rescale*. For example, the XYZ Company usually runs a full-page advertisement in magazines. However, to run the same full-page ad in a newspaper, it would have to be resized to the newspaper's specifications.

**RESPI SCREEN** fine mesh CONTACT SCREEN that produces a high-quality HALFTONE print with smooth gradations in tone due to the large number of very small halftone DOTS.

**RESPONDENT** individual who participates as a subject and provides information in a poll, study, or other research-gathering service.

**RESPONSE**
1. replies and reactions to stimuli, such as those responses in a research study that account for the findings of the study. *See also* RESPONSE ANALYSIS; RESPONSE RATE.
2. *see* ACTION.
3. *see also* READER RESPONSE.

**RESPONSE ANALYSIS** statistical analysis of the response to a direct mail promotion showing how the various elements of the promotion (LIST, PACKAGE, OFFER) performed. The response analysis usually includes gross response by list, package, and offer and may also include NET response information, such as the number of cash orders, unpaid credit orders, and paid credit orders. A thorough response analysis is the key to successful direct marketing. *See also* GROSS AMOUNT, HOMOGENIZATION; KEY CODE; PACKAGE TEST; RESPONSE RATE.

**RESPONSE DEVICE** *see* REPLY FORM.

**RESPONSE PROJECTION** forecast of total expected response to a PROMOTION based on the number of responses received to date or based upon previous experience with this promotion, LIST, or product. A marketer might use the response projection to decide whether an additional promotion is necessary or to plan order FULFILLMENT work volumes. *See also* DOUBLING DAY.

**RESPONSE RATE** gross or NET responses received as a percentage of total PROMOTIONS mailed or contacts made. The response rate to a direct-marketing promotion rarely exceeds 5%. The objective of most promotion tests is to increase the response rate by varying some element of the promotion. KEY CODES are used to identify each variation, and the response rate is then tabulated by key code. In most cases, a response is an order, but it may also be an INQUIRY, an answer to a survey, or an entry to a SWEEPSTAKES. *See also* GROSS AMOUNT; NET AMOUNT; RESPONSE ANALYSIS; RULE OF 300.

**RESTORE** final step in a MERGE/PURGE process that produces the OUTPUT list based upon the remaining names.

**RETAIL DISPLAY ALLOWANCE** decrease in the amount paid by a retailer to a manufacturer in exchange for a more prominent display of the product in the store or on the shelf. *See also* FULL-COVER DISPLAY.

**RETAILER'S SERVICE PROGRAM** advertising, promotion, or similar sales enhancement services designed specifically to help independent retailers be more competitive. As part of retailer's service program, a producer or wholesaler may provide COOPERATIVE ADVERTISING, display material and/or advertising LAYOUTS in order to help the retailer reduce the cost of selling the product.

**RETAIL RATE**  media advertising rate offered to local retailers.

**RETENTION CYCLE**  length of time an INACTIVE customer record will be kept on a computer file, expressed in terms of cycles, such as six issues of a magazine or three months of a cable television service. The retention cycle is used to automatically delete expired or canceled records after a predetermined amount of time or to delete a DONOR record at the same time that the DONEE record is due to expire. Most publishers retain expired or canceled records on the file for a period of time in case the record becomes a REINSTATEMENT.

**RETOUCHING**  process of correcting or improving artwork, particularly photographs (either positives or negatives), by means of an AIRBRUSH, or by hand, using a pencil, crayon, paintbrush, or other means, in order to remove imperfections or add new qualities to the work. The commercial artist who specializes in this process is known as a *retoucher.*

**RETURN AFFIDAVIT**  document used by NEWSSTAND dealers to inform the publisher, wholesaler, and/or distributor of the number of unsold copies for which the dealers are entitled to a refund. The affidavit is used as an alternative to returning the actual magazines or covers. *See also* NEWSSTAND DRAW; NEWSSTAND RETURNS; NEWSSTAND SALES.

**RETURN PERCENTAGE**  *see* RESPONSE RATE.

**RETURN POSTAGE GUARANTEED**  endorsement printed on an OUTER ENVELOPE that authorizes the U.S. Postal Service to return undeliverable mail to the mailer at the mailer's expense. This is used primarily on third-class BULK MAIL. First-class mail will be returned automatically at no cost to the mailer. *See also* ADDRESS CORRECTION REQUESTED.

**RETURN POSTCARD**  self-addressed postcard used in a direct-mail package to offer recipients a convenient way to request information or order merchandise. The advertiser is responsible for the postage on a return postcard. In a large mailing, the advertiser can purchase a permit from the post office and imprint the return cards with the permit number, which will identify the advertiser and guarantee that the postage will be paid.

**RETURN RECEIPT CARD**  card sent with registered or CERTIFIED MAIL for the recipient's signature. The card is returned to the sender by the U.S. Postal Service to confirm receipt of the item.

**RETURNS**
   **1.** responses to a direct-mail promotion. *See also* REPLY ENVELOPE; REPLY FORM; RESPONSE RATE.

**2.** merchandise returned to a supplier for credit. *See also* NEWSSTAND RETURNS.

**RE-USE FEE** *see* RESIDUAL.

**RIDE-ALONGS** *see* INSERT.

**RIFLE APPROACH** promotional strategy wherein the promotional campaign is directed toward a select target audience, and promotional materials are distributed only within that target audience. With the rifle approach, members of the target audience are selected based on their demonstrated interest in a product and their ability to purchase. See also SHOTGUN APPROACH.

**RIGHT-ANGLE FOLD** method of folding paper so that each fold is made at a right angle to the previous fold. Right-angle folds are usually used when creating SIGNATURES for a magazine or catalog from a single printed sheet or cut portion of a paper roll (WEB). The folded edges are then cut to create pages.

**RISER** small, portable platform or box used to elevate a camera, object, or person in order to improve a television shot; also called *apple*. A *half apple* is used when the desired height is lower than that achieved by use of a riser or apple.

**RISK REDUCTION THEORY** theory of consumer behavior that purchase choices are made in order to minimize the perceived risks associated with a wrong choice. Products such as deodorants, hair colors, and baby foods have a high perceived risk and consumers usually choose established national brands. There is less perceived risk with products such as paper towels or napkins, and consumers tend to switch brands in response to price promotions or choose lower priced private label brands more readily. Purchase of a product INNOVATION in the place of a familiar product contains a greater element of perceived risk and requires a greater degree of persuasion on the part of the seller. The most persuasive argument for an innovation is that significant benefits will be missed if the product is not purchased. The consumer will seek more information about a high-risk product than a low-risk product in order to minimize the risk of a wrong choice. *See also* INFORMED CHOICE.

**ROADBLOCK** describes a method of scheduling broadcast commercial time on local stations or networks. On local stations, a local roadblock will present the same commercial on all stations at the same time on a given day in a given area. A network roadblock would air the same commercial at the same time on the same day on all networks. Advertisers will request roadblock scheduling when they want fast, broad coverage for their product or service,

**ROBINSON-PATMAN ACT** 1936 federal amendment to the CLAYTON ACT that prohibited specific forms of price discrimination not adequately addressed by the Clayton Act. Large volume buyers who might use their buying power to extract special deals, including quantity discounts, free promotional materials, or purchase allowances, were targeted by the Robinson-Patman Act. Another target is sellers who offer price discounts not based on true cost differentials. The Robinson-Patman Act imposes limits on these practices without prohibiting them entirely. The Act is enforced by the Federal Trade Commission in conjunction with the Department of Justice. *See also* MILLER-TYDINGS ACT.

**ROLLER STRIPPING**  problem in offset printing caused by an inking roller that becomes ink repellent.

**ROLL IDENTIFICATION**  information printed on a 1-UP roll of mailing labels to ensure that the labels are applied to the appropriate mailing pieces and to provide control information, such as the number of rolls in the mailing and the sequence in which they should be applied to maintain the postal PRESORT sequence; also called *roll tag*. For example, magazine label rolls include the name of the publication and the issue, edition name, and ENTRY POINT.

**ROLLING BILLBOARD**  outdoor advertising medium consisting of a panel truck that can electronically produce digital images on its exterior or that carries a printed BILLBOARD on its exterior. The rolling billboard can either park in a visible area or move around a city. Some magazines have parked rolling billboards outside advertising agency offices to get the attention of MEDIA BUYERS.

**ROLLOUT**
**Direct mail:** main or largest mailing EFFORT in a direct-mail CAMPAIGN sent to the names remaining on the promotion list after either one or more test mailings to a SAMPLE of the list have shown positive results. *See also* PYRAMIDING.
**Merchandising:** full introduction of a new product to the entire market after a successful test introduction.

**ROLL TAG**  *see* ROLL IDENTIFICATION.

**ROTARY PRESS**  PRINTING PRESS that utilizes plates mounted on a rotating CYLINDER that come into contact with paper mounted on another rotating cylinder. Rotary presses are the best choice for high-volume print RUNS because they are fast, but they can be more expensive because duplicate plates must be created from flat plates to fit the curve of the cylinder. Rotary presses may be web-fed or SHEET-FED, but most magazines and catalogs are printed on web-fed rotary presses (*see* WEB PRESS).

**ROTOGRAVURE**
**1.** magazine supplement to a newspaper (usually part of the Sunday edition) that is printed using the GRAVURE process.
**2.** rotogravure printing. *See* GRAVURE.

**ROUGH CUT**  *see* WORK PRINT.

**ROUTE** *see* CARRIER ROUTE.

**ROUTED** address on a mailing list that can be assigned a CARRIER ROUTE CODE according to the coding file being used by the mailer. Not all records that are routed will be qualified for a CARRIER ROUTE PRESORT discount; that is dependent upon satisfying the minimum volume requirement for pieces going to each carrier route. *See also* CARRIER ROUTE QUALIFIED.

**ROUTE TYPE** U.S. Postal Service designation for different kinds of CARRIER ROUTES, such as RURAL ROUTE, *lockbox section* (see LOCK-BOX), and CITY DELIVERY.

**ROUTING STICKER** *see* COLOR-CODED ROUTING STICKER.

**RUBBER CEMENT** smooth, transparent adhesive used to mount ARTWORK. Rubber cement forms a bond with the artwork but will not wrinkle, shrink, stain, or tear the material used for the mounting.

**RUBBER STAMP**
**In general:**
1. hand-held printing device with a raised print surface on a rubber block. The image surface is rubbed with ink and then stamped onto paper. Rubber stamps are used when a short message must be repeatedly added to a number of documents, such as stamping "paid" onto invoices, "confidential" onto envelopes, or "approved" onto purchase orders.
2. term used to refer to individuals who, with little thought, approve everything that crosses their desks (e.g., rubber-stamp executives or politicians).
**Direct marketing:** graphic device used in direct-mail packages that simulates the appearance of a hand-stamped message, lending a tone of urgency and/or personalization. A typical rubber-stamp message is "Preferred Customers Only: Open Immediately!"

**RULE LINE** straight line used as a border or divider line in an advertisement. A rule line may be employed to define a box, panel, or other component of an advertisement, as well as to separate the entire advertisement from its surroundings. A decorative rule line may be used to enhance the design of the advertisement.

**RULE OF 300** direct-mail-testing rule of thumb that, to be valid, a SAMPLE mailing must be large enough to generate 300 responses based upon the expected RESPONSE RATE. For example, if a test mailing is to be compared to a CONTROL package that usually generates a 5% response, the test sample must have at least 6000 pieces, so that about 300 responses will be received. A smaller sample would not be expected to produce *reliable* results—that is, a response rate with a high probability of being consistent across several mailings of the same test package.

**RUN**

**In general:** completed process done on a computer or other electronic or mechanical device.

**Data processing:** processing of data by a computer, such as a *file update. See also* ABEND; RERUN.

**Printing:** number of copies printed for an order; also called *press run* or *print run.*

**RUNAROUND** type copy set with some of the lines indented or shortened to fit around for an illustration or other graphic element.

**RUN CHARGE** computer-service fee based upon jobs processed or file names passed. For example, a run charge for a LIST RENTAL selection may be a fixed rate for the selection job or may be based upon the number of names on the file from which the selection was made. List rental agreements usually include a per name run charge that applies to any names for which a rental fee is not paid. For example, if the mailer agrees to pay a list rental fee for 70% of the names, a run charge is applied to the remaining 30%. This charge protects the LIST OWNER from the cost of running a very large file of which only a small portion is rented. *See also* NET NAME ARRANGEMENT.

**RUNNING HEAD** caption or title that is repeated across the top of each page in a book or magazine. In a magazine, the running head is usually the name of the publication, whereas, in a book, the running head is usually the book title, a chapter title, or a subhead.

**RUNNING TEXT** main body of text on a printed page in a book or magazine.

**RUNNING TIME** total length of time that a film, program, or commercial actually runs. For example, the running time of a particular film may be 78 minutes.

**RUN-OF-PAPER ADVERTISING** *see* RUN OF PAPER.

**RUN OF PAPER (ROP)** newspaper publisher's option to place advertisements anywhere in the newspaper that space allows, at the sole discretion of the publisher. If an advertiser requests a PREFERRED POSITION within a newspaper, most publishers will try to place the advertisement in the requested position if possible.

In broadcast, this same option is called *run of schedule* or *run of station*, the former allowing a television station to position commercials anywhere in the schedule that it is convenient, and the latter allowing a radio station to do the same. Run-of-schedule and run-of-station commercial positions are charged at the lowest rate on the RATE CARD.

**RUN OF PRESS** see RUN OF PAPER.

**RUN OF SCHEDULE/STATION (ROS)** *see* RUN OF PAPER.

•

**RURAL CARRIER** U.S. Postal Service mail carrier assigned to a rural area without easy access to a post office, who provides many of the collection and delivery services of a post office for residents of that area.

**RURAL DELIVERY SERVICE** delivery and collection route operated by a RURAL CARRIER.

**RURAL DIRECT** CANADA POST presort level for mail PACKAGES going to the same rural six-digit POSTAL CODE area. Rural areas are assigned a 0 in the second position of the Canadian postal code. In second class, six or more pieces for the same rural postal code area must be made into a rural direct package. In third class, ten or more pieces must be made into a rural direct package.

**RURAL ROUTE** CARRIER ROUTE in a rural area, served by a mail carrier who uses a truck to get from one household to another.

**RUSHES** see ASSEMBLY DAILIES.

# S

**SACK** canvas mail bag containing one or more PACKAGES of mail for a common destination. Sacks vary in size and capacity. The most common sack sizes are a #2, which holds 70 pounds, and a #3, which holds 45 pounds. In practice, some amount less than the maximum capacity is placed into the sack. *See also* OPTIMIZER; PRESORT; SACK TAG.

**SACK LABEL** *see* SACK TAG.

**SACK OPTIMIZER** *see* OPTIMIZER.

**SACK SECTIONING** SAMPLING technique used by direct-mail advertisers that draws a SAMPLE based on mail SACKS rather than on an nth name basis or A-B SPLIT of the mailing list. This allows mailers to break a mailing into test PANELS, without creating several smaller mailings and thus reducing the PRESORT discount on postage.

**SACK TAG** identifying label placed on a mail SACK containing information about the sack contents; also called BAG TAG. The sack tag information includes the CONSOLIDATION LEVEL, the postal facility at which the mail will be turned over to the U.S. Postal Service for delivery, the ZIP code or ZIP code prefix, the class of mail, and identifying information about the mailing piece itself, such as "Spring Catalog."

**SADDLE STITCH** method of binding a small booklet by stitching it through the center fold of the sheets that comprise its pages. Saddle stitching allows the booklet to open flat but can only be done through a minimum thickness. When the booklet is too thick for saddle stitching, a different stitch must be used. Saddle stitching can be done with regular binding thread, saddle wire, or staples.

**SADDLE WIRE** *see* SADDLE STITCH.

**SAFELIGHT** special lamp used in photography darkrooms that will not affect film which is exposed to it. Different types of film require different types of safelight. The correct safelight to use is usually printed on the film package by the manufacturer.

**SAFETY** in a magazine advertisement, space between the perimeter of the advertisement and the edge of the page. The safety permits binding the pages without losing the boundaries of the advertisement. Television commercials also must be edited within a specific dimension, called a safety, to account for the various sizes of television screens.

**SAG FEE** *see* RESIDUAL.

**SALES AREA MARKETING, INC.** marketing research company (owned by Time, Inc.) which provides syndicated reports to retailers and manufacturers on the shipment of food, beauty, and household products from warehouses to chain stores; abbreviated SAMI.

**SALES CONVERSION RATE** the number of sales made relative to the number of contacts made. In telemarketing, if the sales conversion rate does not meet expectations, the marketer may revise the sales script, choose different prospect list sources, or make changes in the sales force.

**SALES DECAY** decrease in the volume sold over time. Some sales decay is an inevitable part of the PRODUCT LIFE CYCLE. Marketers can delay or minimize decay through product innovations and aggressive brand advertising. Sales decay may be the result of heightened competition that spurs BRAND SWITCHING, a decline in demand for that PRODUCT CLASS, or the result of decreased advertising expenditure.

**SALES EFFECTIVENESS TEST** testing designed to judge the ability of an advertising campaign, promotion, or communications medium to sell a product.

**SALES FORECAST** prediction of the future sales of a particular product over a specific period of time based on past performance of the product, inflation rates, unemployment, consumer spending patterns, market trends, and interest rates. In the preparation of a comprehensive marketing plan, sales forecasts help the marketer develop a marketing budget, allocate marketing resources, and monitor the competition and the product environment.

**SALES FORCE** persons selling products or services via direct contact with the customer. Sales force members may be paid a fixed salary regardless of sales volume or may receive a small base salary plus commissions calculated as a percentage of revenue sold. Noncommissioned sales forces are appropriate when selling requires the involvement of a team of individuals or when there is an extremely long sales cycle. For example, some complex industrial services may require several years of effort before the prospect is sold. Salespeople may be full-time employees of the seller or may be independent, nonexclusive agents. Members of the sales force are assigned a SALES TERRITORY that may be segmented by exclusive or nonexclusive geographic or market segments, product or product lines, or by specific customers or prospects. *See also* SALES QUOTA.

**SALES INCENTIVE** remuneration offered to a salesperson for exceeding some predetermined sales goal. Sales incentives are offered by manufacturers as part of a promotion for the sale of their goods. The incentive may be in cash, or it may take the form of a special prize, such as a trip to an exotic or exciting vacation place.

**SALES LETTER** letter used to introduce the selling effort of a direct-mail package. Sales letters may be individually typewritten, typeset and printed, fully computer typed, or printed as a form letter and then completed by inserting the names and addresses of prospects.

**SALES PORTFOLIO** book of sales data used as a reference tool by a salesperson. The sales portfolio contains information about terms, special deals, prices, types of discounts, and available merchandising material.

**SALES PROMOTION**
1. activities, materials, devices, and techniques used to supplement the advertising and marketing efforts and help coordinate the advertising with the personal selling effort. SWEEPSTAKES are among the most well-known sales promotion tools, but other examples include special DISPLAYS, COUPONS, promotional discounts, contests, and gift offers.
2. casually, combined activities employed to sell a product or service.

**SALES QUOTA** minimum sales volume goal established by the seller. A sales quota may be expressed in terms of dollars or units sold. Quotas may also be set for sales activity (number of calls per day), sales costs and profitability in addition to sales volume. A sales quota may be required of a salaried or commissioned salesperson or may be a goal set for a brand, a product line, or a company division. Sales quotas are used to ensure that company sales goals are met even though they may exceed an individual salesperson's personal goals or abilities. Sales quotas also ensure that the volume sold will cover the fixed costs of producing the product or service. Sales quotas should be high enough to encourage excellence but not so high as to be unachievable, thereby discouraging the sales force. Failure to meet sales quotas is an immediate call for action on the part of the seller. If a salesperson fails to meet quota, the salesperson may be given a smaller or less desirable prospect territory or may be terminated. A salesperson may receive a bonus for exceeding the sales quota. *See also* INCENTIVE PROGRAM.

**SALES TERRITORY** segment of the market for which a salesperson is responsible. Territory assignments may be exclusive, meaning no other salesperson can sell in that territory, or nonexclusive. Territories may be defined in terms of geographic or market segments, product or product lines, size of customer, or by specific customers or prospects. The best territories with the greatest revenue potential are usually assigned to the best salespeople. The individual talents or characteristics of the salespeople can also be used to determine territory assignments. It takes a different skill set to make sales to large corporations than to small retailers. Geographic territory assignments should be made so as to minimize the travel expenses incurred by any one salesperson. When creating geographic territories, the density of the prospect base will determine the size of the territory. For example, New York City alone may offer as many prospects as several Northwestern states combined. *See also* HOUSE ACCOUNT; SALES FORCE.

**SALT NAME** name planted on a list by a LIST OWNER to monitor use of a rented list and to detect unauthorized usage; also called *decoy name*, DUMMY, *seed name*. Promotions sent to the salt name are reported to the list owner. The salt name may be that of a real person (*see* REAL SEEDS) or may be a false name created for this purpose.

Salts can also be used for other purposes: for example, (1) to monitor delivery time by including salts from various geographic locations who report the date of receipt; (2) to monitor the accuracy of LETTERSHOP work, allowing the lettershop user to check whether the package COMPONENTS were inserted correctly; and (3) to monitor the efficiency of a FULFILLMENT operation, to see if orders are filled correctly and customer questions are answered. Cash salts are also sometimes placed in LETTER TRAYS of incoming mail to monitor whether mail-opening clerks are handling cash receipts correctly.

**SAMPLE**
**Market research:** subset of a population drawn for testing purposes under the assumption that the results derived from, or the behavior of, a randomly drawn sample can predict the results or behavior of the

population. For example, a sample may be selected from a mailing list to which a test PACKAGE is sent. If response to the test mailing is good, it is assumed that the RESPONSE RATE of the entire mailing list to that package would be good, and a larger mailing is then sent to the names remaining on the list. The method used to select a sample and the size of the sample both play a key role in the RELIABILITY of the test results. If a sample is biased toward a particular part of the population, then the test results will be representative only of that portion and not of the entire population. For example, if a sample of U.S. car buyers was drawn only from the Detroit area, the results of a buying-pattern survey might be biased toward American-made cars and not reflect the popularity of foreign-made cars in other areas of the country. Similarly, the behavior of a sample of 2 people would not accurately predict the behavior of a population of 20,000 people. *See also* A-B SPLIT; CONFIDENCE LEVEL; NTH NAME SELECTION; RULE OF 300; SAMPLING.

**Merchandising:**
1. item used by a salesperson to enable buyers to examine the goods available for purchase.
2. *see* TRIAL SIZE.

**SAMPLE BUYER** individual who purchases at a special introductory rate or obtains at no cost a sample of a product, such as a travel-size bottle of shampoo or a box of detergent big enough for one washload. *See also* TRIAL SIZE.

**SAMPLE PACKAGE**
1. *see* TRIAL SIZE.
2. mock-up, or actual sample, of a direct-mail PACKAGE submitted to a LIST OWNER by a LIST USER for approval. CUSTOMER-LIST owners sometimes require sample packages to verify that list users are not sending packages that may be objectionable to individuals on the list.

**SAMPLING**
**Marketing research:** studying a small group of people who are representative of a larger group. If the research is correctly conducted, conclusions drawn from the sample can be applied to the larger group without incurring exorbitant costs.
**Sales promotion:** offering a product or a small portion of it to consumers at little or no cost in order to stimulate regular usage.

**SANDWICH BOARD** form of OUT-OF-HOME media hung from the shoulders of an individual with signs in front and back used for announcements or advertisements for products or services.

**SANS SERIF** *see* GOTHIC.

**SATISFICING** settling for less than the optimal solution in order to reach a satisfactory solution as quickly and cheaply as possible. In theory, consumers would select the optimal product or service to meet their needs. However in reality, a full evaluation of the multitude of choices available is not practical. Consumers therefore settle for a satisfactory choice in the interest of expediency. *See also* HEURISTICS.

## SATURATION
**Media:** strategy for achieving maximum impact by increasing advertising coverage and frequency above standard levels. For instance, a retailer would schedule more advertisements during a sale.
**Printing:** degree to which a color is chromatically pure and free of dilution from white, black, or gray. The less dilution, the more intense the color appears. *See also* CHROMA; HUE.

**SCALING** process of reducing or enlarging copy or artwork to a desired size for printing.

## SCAN
1. use of a mechanical or electronic device to check for recorded data (as on a punch card or magnetic tape).
2. casually look from item to item in search of a specific item. *See also* OPTICAL CHARACTER RECOGNITION SCANNER.

**SCAN DOCUMENT** document that can be read by an OPTICAL CHARACTER RECOGNITION machine, commonly referred to as a SCANNER. Most scan documents are REPLY FORMS or TURNAROUND DOCUMENTS printed according to the requirements of the scanner that will be used. Documents to be scanned must meet various specifications, including paper weight, paper reflectivity, ink reflectivity, print quality, size, and so forth. Most scan documents are preprinted in a special machine-readable FONT or BAR CODE; however, some hand-printed documents can also be scanned.

**SCAN ENTRY** method of entering data to a computer via an OPTICAL CHARACTER RECOGNITION machine commonly referred to as a SCANNER. Scan entry is a much faster and more accurate type of DATA ENTRY than KEY ENTRY. Usually, the fewer the number of characters to be read, the more accurate the scan entry is and the fewer REJECTS there are. Scan entry makes it possible to enter orders, payments, and some types of customer complaints at a rate of 12,000 to 18,000 documents per hour. Scan entry is also used to record product and price information at store checkout counters. Coupon clearing houses use BAR CODE scanners to tabulate coupon REDEMPTION RATES. The U.S. Postal Service uses bar code and ZIP code scanners to sort mail. *See also* BAR CODE SORTER; FINDER NUMBER; SCAN DOCUMENT.

**SCAN HEAD** device on a SCANNER that receives the scannable images. It is analogous to the human eye, which receives light images, subsequently translated by the brain into a recognizable object. The brain performs the same function for the eye that a computer processor performs for the scan head. A scan head may be fixed in place, requiring that the SCAN DOCUMENT be placed in front of it or it may be on a hand-held device called a wand, which is placed in front of the scannable image. The scan head embedded in some supermarket checkout counters is a fixed head. Wand scanners are frequently used in department stores to read item and price information printed on the price tag.

**SCANNER** OPTICAL CHARACTER RECOGNITION machine consisting of a SCAN HEAD, a computer processor, and an OUTPUT device. The scan head reads a scannable image which is then interpreted by the computer and output in a usable format. For example, a direct-mail marketer might use a scanner to read invoices that have been returned with payment checks. The scanner picks up a code on the invoice that indicates which customer is making the payment and how much was owed. The computer then formulates an instruction to the customer file that the customer's record should be marked paid.

Scanners come in a variety of forms capable of reading preprinted ALPHANUMERIC characters in specific FONTS, BAR CODES, or handprinted letters or symbols. Payment scanners, called *encoders*, can scan an alphanumeric scan line on invoices and can encode and endorse the checks at the same time. Document scanners that can read at speeds of 18,000 documents per hour are used to enter responses to direct-mail promotions. Wand scanners are used to read bar-coded merchandise information such as stock number and price. With the use of bar codes, prices can be changed, without changing price tags, merely by changing the instructions in the computer system that interprets the bar codes. *See also* SCAN DOCUMENT; SCAN ENTRY.

**SCATTER PLAN** broadcast media plan that schedules advertising announcements to run during a variety of radio and/or television programs. This schedule gives an advertiser a wider audience for the advertising dollar than would be achieved by being a SPONSOR of a single program. *See also* MAGAZINE PLAN.

**SCHEME** list of addresses, by street name, number, and directional, that constitute a CARRIER ROUTE. *See also* CARRIER ROUTE INFORMATION SYSTEM.

**SCHOOL AGENCY** SUBSCRIPTION AGENT that works in cooperation with schools, using students as salespersons for magazine subscriptions. The subscriptions are sold at the BASIC RATE, and the school earns a commission that may be as high as 40% of the selling price. The publisher receives a small portion of the price, averaging 20%. The students receive no direct compensation other than prizes for various sales levels. Most school agents have two campaigns a year, coinciding with the fall and spring semesters, and each campaign lasts only a few days. The average sales per student are low, but cancellations are also relatively low and the orders are sold on a cash-with-order basis. This is a profitable source of business for the publisher.

**SCIENTIFIC METHOD** marketing research technique that employs principles commonly used in other scientific research disciplines, in which a postulate or theory is hypothesized and then either proven or disproven based on observation of causes and effects in a controlled environment. For example, a blind taste test to measure consumer preferences for various soft drink formulas is a scientific approach. A nonscientific approach to the same problem would be a shopping mall questionnaire that asked consumers to rate their preferences for various brand name soft drinks. In this example, the consumer's expressed preference can be caused by a number of factors unrelated to the contents of the beverage. In the taste-test environment, the contents of the beverage are the only relevant variable affecting the consumer's choice.

**SCOOP** television FLOODLIGHT; also called *basher*. The scoop is the most commonly used floodlight. It emits a very soft light that evens out the areas of highlights and shadows, and thus smoothly blends all the illumination on a set. The scoop consists of a lamp mounted in a semicircular housing surrounded by a matte-surfaced reflecting material. The most frequently used scoop is about 18 inches in diameter and is equipped with either a 1000- or 1500-watt lamp.

**SCORE** impression made along the fold line on paper to facilitate even folding. Scoring is necessary when folds must be made in heavy paper stock or against the paper grain.

**SCRATCH** process of erasing the data on a computer-storage device, such as a MAGNETIC TAPE or DISK, before reusing it. Ample controls must be in place to ensure that any unneeded information be scratched, because data cannot be restored to a scratched tape.

**SCRATCH AND SNIFF** ACTION DEVICE used in advertising and direct-mail promotion consisting of an area impregnated with a fragrance that is released by lightly scratching the surface.

**SCRATCH OFF** ACTION DEVICE used in direct-mail PACKAGES consisting of an opaque substance that can be scratched away with a fingernail or coin to reveal a hidden message. The substance is usually a metallic silver or gold. Scratch offs are frequently used for instant winner LOTTERY tickets or SWEEPSTAKES entry forms to conceal the winning (or losing) number.

**SCRATCH TRACK** unfinished and unedited sound track used to give a rough idea of the sound of the completed recording.

**SCREEN**
**In general:** select or eliminate names or items from a list or group based upon some SELECTION CRITERIA, such as income, occupation, or gender. In direct marketing, screening is used to identify QUALIFIED LEADS and to make LIST RENTAL selections.
**Advertising:**
**1.** surface on which a commercial or other film can be projected.
**2.** view a commercial or other film prior to release to ascertain audience reaction.

**Fulfillment:** CATHODE-RAY TUBE DISPLAY in a predetermined format that provides or requests the information needed for a specific purpose. For example, an order-entry screen will request the customer's name and address, as well as the item(s) ordered, the quantity, and the price. A change-of-address screen will show the old address and leave blank space for input of the new address.

**New product development:** process of ruling out some new product ideas and choosing others for further development. This is necessary in order to concentrate the marketer's resources on those new product concepts with the most potential for success. The screening process should consider a variety of factors including potential market demand, manufacturing expense, and technical and managerial requirements. Screening errors consist of eliminating good concepts and failing to eliminate poor concepts.

**Printing:** grid device used in HALFTONE and FOUR-COLOR PROCESS printing to create an image, as photographed through the screen, consisting of DOTS that can be reproduced more easily than a CONTINUOUS-TONE image. Screens vary in size from 55 to 300 lines per inch, depending primarily on the level of detail required in the print. *See also* CONTACT SCREEN; RESPI SCREEN.

**SCREEN ACTORS GUILD (SAG)** national union of actors that negotiates collective bargaining agreements for both motion picture and television actors. It was founded in 1933 and is headquartered in Hollywood, California.

**SCREEN ANGLE** angle, expressed in degrees, of the grid on a print SCREEN through which HALFTONE images are photographed. In FOUR-COLOR PROCESS printing, cyan, magenta, and black are photographed 30° apart and yellow is photographed 15° from either the magenta or the cyan. The angle of the screen impacts the REGISTER of the various color images.

**SCREENER** individual who views television shows before they are aired and reports on the degrees of sex, violence, profanity, drug or alcohol abuse, and nudity for the benefit of prospective advertisers. Advertisers will hire screeners and use their reports to determine whether advertising during a particular program (or series of programs) will project the appropriate or desired image of their product.

**SCREEN RULING** number of lines per inch in a HALFTONE printing SCREEN.

**SCRIM**
1. gauzelike curtain used in theater, motion picture, and television presentations to give special lighting effects. When illuminated from one side, the material is translucent; when illuminated from the other side, it is opaque. Therefore, a scrim can be used to give the illusion of a wall; then, with a change in lighting, the audience can see the action going on behind the wall.

**2.** translucent material used to diffuse or decrease the light intensity from a lighting instrument. Scrims are frequently used on SCOOPS or other FLOODLIGHTS to heighten their soft light quality.

**SCUMMING** *see* CATCHING-UP.

**SEALED-BID PRICING** price quotes solicited by governmental and other public agencies to ensure objective consideration of COMPETITIVE BIDS. Interested vendors are formally notified in advance of the request for a bid and must meet a bidding deadline as well as stringent bid format requirements. Sealed bids are sometimes opened publicly in the presence of all bidders. The lowest bid is awarded the order.

**SEAL OF APPROVAL** documentation offered by such organizations as Good Housekeeping Institute or Underwriter's Laboratories that a product has been tested by these organizations and has been found to meet the standards set by the organization in order to gain the seal of approval. Usually, a manufacturer will pay a fee to have a product tested. In some cases, the testing organization is affiliated with a particular publication, and the publication will require the manufacturer to advertise the product in the publication for a minimum amount of insertions. Seals of approval provide an independent endorsement of a product, although the testing organization administering the seal will usually retain jurisdiction over the way a manufacturer may use it in advertising. *See also* GOOD HOUSEKEEPING SEAL.

**SEASONAL DEMAND** consumer interest in purchasing particular products only during a specific period within the calendar year. For example, Christmas ornaments and snow ski equipment are subject to seasonal demand.

**SEASONALITY** characteristic of a market, product, or promotion that shows a pattern of variation with changes in seasons. For example, in northern states the hot chocolate market is most active in winter and relatively inactive in summer. Most magazine promotions achieve their highest RESPONSE RATE during the Christmas buying season, because many people give subscriptions as Christmas gifts. Certain mailing lists also perform better at different times of year. A mailing to residents of large cities will not do well in July or August, because many people leave the city for vacation or for weekends.

**SECOND CLASS** U.S. Postal Service designation for a level of mail service reserved for publications such as magazines and newspapers that are published at predetermined intervals on a continuous basis and have been paid for or requested by the recipient. Second-class mail accounts for almost 10% of total U.S. mail volume. ALTERNATE DELIVERY services for second-class mail are growing but are still outweighed by those for first-class and fourth-class mail.

The USPS requires that second-class mail be packaged (*see* PACKAGE) and sacked or palletized to the finest mandatory CONSOLIDATION

LEVEL possible for each mailing. Second-class mail sorted to optional consolidation levels is awarded a postage discount. Under second-class PRESORT regulations, six or more copies destined for the same mandatory consolidation level must be packaged, and four or more packages must be sacked. If the mailer is using PALLETS, a pallet must be made up if there are 650 pounds destined for a mandatory consolidation level. The total number of mailing pieces per SACK or pallet depends upon the weight of the mailing piece.

The mandatory consolidation levels are FIVE-DIGIT ZIP CODE, UNIQUE THREE-DIGIT CITY, STATE, and MIXED STATES. The optional consolidation levels are FIRM PACKAGE, CARRIER ROUTE, CITY, SECTIONAL CENTER FACILITY, and STATE DISTRIBUTION CENTER. Presorting to optional levels facilitates fast and accurate mail delivery.

*See also* PASS MANUAL; PRIVATE EXPRESS STATUTES.

**SECOND COVER** *see* INSIDE FRONT COVER.

**SECTIONAL CENTER FACILITY** U.S. Postal Service mail-handling facility that serves a group of post offices sharing a common THREE-DIGIT ZIP CODE area. *See also* PRESORT; SECOND CLASS.

**SEED NAME** *see* SALT NAME.

**SEEN/ASSOCIATED** term used by the research firm of DANIEL STARCH AND ASSOCIATES to describe research participants who not only say they have seen a certain advertisement, but also recognize the advertiser.

**SEGMENT** *see* LIST SEGMENT.

**SEGMENTATION STRATEGY**
1. *see* DIFFERENTIATION STRATEGY.
2. marketing plan where all marketing efforts are directed at one particular market segment. For example, all advertising efforts on behalf of Piaget watches position the watch as a luxury item, and the advertising is targeted toward an upscale audience.

**SEGUE** in broadcast, transition from one sound source to the next without interruption, from the Italian, meaning *"there follows"*; pronounced *segway*.

**SELECTION** extraction of a SAMPLE or subset of a group based upon certain SELECTION CRITERIA. *See also* LIST SELECTION; PARAMETER; SCREEN.

**SELECTION CRITERIA** basis for extraction of a subset from a group. Selection criteria most often pertain to a LIST SELECTION made on the basis of some characteristic of the individuals on the list, such as income, age, occupation, purchase history, SOURCE, geographic location, LIFE-STYLE, number of children, gender, education level, and so forth. List selection criteria are chosen according to the marketer's experience that certain criteria are better predictors of positive response to a mailing or other promotion. For example, if most of a marketer's current customers live in Texas, she will select only Texan addresses. If she wishes to test non-Texan addresses, she will select based upon a criterion that will exclude Texan addresses, such as a list of ZIP code areas outside of Texas.

LIST RENTAL selection charges are frequently based upon the number of selection criteria. As the number increases, the UNIVERSE of available names decreases—that is, there are only so many blue-eyed, left-handed piano players in any one state.

**SELECTION PARAMETER** VARIABLE in a LIST SELECTION program that defines the SELECTION CRITERIA.

**SELECTIVE ATTENTION** tendency of a consumer to pay attention only to messages that address a need or interest or are consistent with the consumer's attitudes, opinions, and beliefs. Selective attention is why consumers make more impulse purchases when they go to the grocery store on an empty stomach than when they go after a meal. A marketer can bypass selective attention by delivering its message in the absence of competing stimuli such as to the captive audience in a doctor's waiting room. *See also* COGNITIVE DISSONANCE.

**SELECTIVE BINDING** binding technique that selects and binds various publication segments into various finished print products for different intended recipients in one binding RUN. For example, a catalog can be selectively bound so that pages advertising women's fashions will be sent only to women, or pages advertising gardening tools will go only to people living in single-family dwellings. The selective binding process is driven by a code in the address file that indicates which sections each individual in the file should receive. That same address file provides the address information for the mailing label. Substantial cost savings are achieved by printing, binding, and mailing all versions at once. The selective binding process can also be used to insert special reply forms, to attach different covers to newsstand and subscription magazine copies, or to conduct price or other promotional tests. This process was developed by R. R. Donnelley & Sons under the trademark name "Selectronic Gathering."

**SELECTIVE DEMARKETING** *see* DEMARKETING.

**SELECTIVE DISTRIBUTION** DISTRIBUTION of products only to those wholesalers or retailers who (a) agree to sell the product for no less than a certain price, (b) patronize the distributor on a regular basis or for at least a certain dollar amount annually, or (c) meet specific requirements established by the distributor as outlined by the manufacturer. Selective distribution is used primarily for HARD GOODS, such as appliances, stereo equipment, or furniture. It allows manufacturers to maintain more control over the way their products are sold and minimizes price competition among sellers of the products. *See also* EXCLUSIVE DISTRIBUTION; OPEN DISTRIBUTION.

**SELECTIVE RECEPTION** ignoring, distorting, or discounting a message that is inconsistent with the recipient's attitudes, opinions, or beliefs. People use selective reception on a subconscious basis to avoid COGNITIVE DISSONANCE. Selective reception presents a challenge to advertisers trying to change strongly held beliefs. For example, a health-oriented consumer will probably discount any medical research claims made by a tobacco company on the assumption the claims are biased. *See also* TWO-SIDED MESSAGE.

**SELF-COVER** cover on a book, magazine, catalog, or brochure that is printed along with the rest of the pages and may be on the same paper stock.

**SELF-IMAGE** psychological term referring to individuals' concepts of themselves and their roles in relation to others; also known as *self-concept*.

**SELF-LIQUIDATOR** premium offer paid for by the consumer rather than the advertiser; also known as a *purchase-privilege premium*. In this way, an advertiser can offer something of value that enhances the product image without incurring any cost. For example, the XYZ Company sells sugar. On the boxes, a special offer is highlighted for a set of commemorative spoons costing only $3.95. Because the spoons are sold at cost, they may be inexpensive enough to induce the consumer to buy the box of sugar. When, and if, the consumer sends away for the spoons, the cost to the advertiser is fully recovered by the $3.95 payment. *See also* SEMI-LIQUIDATOR.

**SELF-MAILER** REPLY FORM that is addressed to the marketer and can be mailed without an envelope. *See also* BUSINESS REPLY CARD; SELF-SEALER.

**SELF-SEALER** REPLY FORM that has scored (*see* SCORE) or otherwise marked fold lines and a strip of adhesive, and that can be folded and sealed, like an envelope, for mailing. Self-sealers save the addressee the expense of REPLY ENVELOPES but are difficult to open on automated mail-opening equipment.

**SELL-IN** manufacturers' efforts to persuade retailers to distribute and stock their products. For example, if the XYZ Company wants to convince a retailer to feature its product on the store's shelf, it might offer special discounts or promotions that compare more favorably than its competitors. *See also* SELL THROUGH.

**SELLING AREA MARKETING, INC.** (SAMI) *see* SALES AREA MARKETING, INC.

**SELL OFF** reselling advertising space and time that has already been contracted for to another advertiser.

**SELL THROUGH** manufacturer's effort to increase the sales of its product at the retail level. *See also* SELL-IN.

**SELVAGE** straight-edge margin area on a STAMP SHEET. A brief sales message is sometimes printed on the selvage.

**SEMI-LIQUIDATOR** premium offer paid in part by the consumer; also known as a *semi-self-liquidator* or *purchase-privilege premium*. *See also* SELF-LIQUIDATOR.

**SENTENCE COMPLETION TEST** test used in consumer research where respondents are asked to complete a sentence that has been started by the examiner. The sentence completion test will tap into the respondents' cognitive resources and will reveal predetermined attitudes, feelings, and emotions all of which will help to gain insight into consumer behavior.

**SEPARATION MARKS** *see* PACKAGE/SACK MARKS.

**SEPIA**
1. film whose color tends toward brown tones rather than shades of gray, giving the image an old-fashioned and sometimes dreamlike quality. Sepia also refers to the brownish color itself, as in sepia tones.
2. brown color (as in sepia tones) resembling sepia, a brown pigment derived from the inky secretion of a cuttlefish.

**SEQUENCE** order in which computer file RECORDS are sorted. The sequence is based on a FIELD in the record, such as ZIP code or customer number. The ZIP code is used most often to sequence records because it facilitates LOOKUP from the name and address information on customer correspondence and the printing of mailing labels in ZIP CODE SEQUENCE.

**SERIF** short, delicate, decorative cross lines or tails at the ends of the main strokes in many letters and symbols in some typefaces.

**SERIGRAPHY** color printing method in which ink is forced through a stencil placed over a screen; also called *silk screen*. A stencil is created for each color. Then, one at a time, each stencil is placed on a fine wire or silk screen. A squeegee is passed over the stencil so that the ink goes on the surface below, except where the stencil prevents the flow of ink. Because this process can be used on any surface, it is ideal for printing messages on T-shirts. Serigraphy is also usually the most economical method of printing small runs of posters and signs.

**SERVE** send magazine issues due to a subscriber. An individual who subscribes for a 12-issue term is served 12 issues.

**SERVICE**
1. work done by one person that benefits another.
2. type of business that sells assistance and expertise rather than a tangible product. For example, the field of management consulting is a service industry.
3. after-purchase assistance that is offered by the manufacturer to maintain the quality of the product during its use. Service is often the main selling point for big-ticket items such as cars, washing machines, and television sets.

**SERVICE BUREAU** service business that makes its resources (computers, people) available to others for a fee—for example, a MERGE/PURGE, LIST MAINTENANCE, or FULFILLMENT service. In practice, most service bureaus offer a variety of related services at a lower cost than individual users could achieve, because the service bureau has the advantage of economies of scale.

**SERVICE FEE** money paid to an advertising agency by an advertiser. In most cases, the agency is paid a retainer for general services. Any services beyond those are compensated at special rates.

**SERVICE MAGAZINE** *see* WOMEN'S SERVICE MAGAZINE.

**SERVICE MARK** word, name, or symbol that represents a service company or a service provided by a company that differentiates it from the competition and establishes it as unique. The service mark may be legally registered for the exclusive use of that company. For example, "Cluster Plus" is a service mark of Donnelley Marketing, representing the demographic CLUSTER ANALYSES that the firm does. *See also* TRADEMARK.

**SET**
**Advertising:** props and/or setting for the filming of a commercial.
**Printing:**
1. arrangement of type for printing. *See also* COMPOSITION.
2. series of books on a common theme, sold as a package in one sales transaction.
3. length of a line of type or the width of each type CHARACTER expressed in POINTS, such as a character set-size of 12 points.

**SETS IN USE** *see* HOUSEHOLDS USING TELEVISION.

**SEX CODING** *see* GENDER ANALYSIS.

**SHADOW** darkest areas of an image, such as a HALFTONE print area with the highest density of DOTS, or the darkest area of an original image, or the lightest area of a continuous-tone NEGATIVE. *See also* HIGHLIGHT.

**SHADOW BOX** boxes suitable for displaying small items in retail stores.

**SHARE**
1. percentage of households in a specific geographic area with television sets tuned to a particular program as compared to the percentage of households with television sets turned on (HUT—*see* HOUSEHOLDS USING TELEVISION). In an area where only 10 television sets are turned on and 5 are tuned to a particular program, the program would have a share of 50. However, a program share of 50 means nothing without knowing the possible size of the audience. The program RATING will tell this information. If there are 100 television households in this same geographic area, the rating for this particular program would be 0.5, indicating that 5 out of

a possible 100 households have their sets tuned in to the program. Advertisers need to know both the program share and rating in order to determine the most effective placement of their commercials. Therefore, share and rating are key concepts in understanding the planning of broadcast media for advertising.

**2.** *see* AUDIENCE SHARE.

**3.** *see* BRAND SHARE.

**SHARED MAILING** direct-mail promotion from several mailers sent to the same list of individuals in order to share the costs of LIST RENTAL and PROMOTION. Shared mailings include COOPERATIVE MAILINGS, JOINT MAILINGS, CARD PACKS, PROMOTION INSERTS, and PACKAGE INSERTS. The participating mailers must share the same TARGET MARKET but not be in direct competition. *See also* SOLO MAIL.

**SHARE OF AUDIENCE** *see* AUDIENCE SHARE.

**SHARE OF MARKET** *see* BRAND SHARE.

**SHARE OF MIND** *see* BRAND ASSOCIATION.

**SHARE OF VOICE (SOV)** percentage of advertising for one brand in a particular product category as compared to other brands in the same category. If five different brand names advertise in one product category and the percentage of advertising for one of them is 60% of the total volume of advertising in that product category, that brand will have the greatest share of voice (in that product category).

**SHEET** piece of paper to be printed.

**SHEET-FED** type of printing press utilizing sheets of cut paper instead of paper rolls (*webs*). A sheet-fed press is used primarily for low-volume, high-quality print jobs. *See also* STREAM FEEDER; WEB PRESS.

**SHEETWISE** *see* IMPOSITION.

**SHELF TALKER** printed advertisement that is hung from the shelf in a retail store, supermarket, or variety store.

**SHELTER MAGAZINE** *see* HOME SERVICE BOOK.

**SHERMAN ANTITRUST ACT** federal legislation passed in 1890 prohibiting "monopolies or attempts to monopolize" and "contracts, combinations, or conspiracies in restraint of trade" in interstate and foreign commerce. The major purpose of the Sherman Antitrust Act was to prohibit monopolies and sustain competition so as to protect companies from each other and to protect consumers from unfair business practices. The act was supplemented by the CLAYTON ANTITRUST ACT in 1914. Both acts are enforced by the Federal Trade Commission (FTC) and the Antitrust Division of the U.S. Attorney General's office.

**SHIPPING AND HANDLING** warehouse costs associated with filling a direct-mail order, such as postage and PICK-AND-PACK expense.

Shipping and handling charges are frequently charged back to the customer, based on the weight of the items ordered. Direct marketers are required by law to clearly state on the order form that shipping and handling charges will be added, although the precise amount of the charges need not be stated.

**SHIPPING ORDER**  inventory control document that is used to identify what should be shipped from the warehouse and to whom and where it should be shipped. The shipping order usually accompanies the shipment, so that the recipient can verify that the items listed were received. The shipping order can then be used to prepare an invoice or, in the case of a COLLECT ON DELIVERY (COD) order, can serve as the invoice. The information included on a shipping order is typically an order number and date, shipping and receipt dates, a customer purchase order number, special shipping instructions such as "UPS" or "overnight," the buyer's name and address, the shipping address (if different), and a list of the items ordered, shipped, and/or BACK-ORDERED (*see* BACK ORDER), including quantity and warehouse storage location. The shipping order may also include a space for the recipient's signature.

**SHOEHORN**  informal term for adding copy or visuals to an already existing advertisement. Many times, at the last minute, the client will ask the advertising agency to squeeze in additional information where there is no space for it.

**SHOOT**
1. filming or videotaping of scenes to be used in a motion picture, television program, or commercial. The term is used both as a verb and a noun and encompasses all of the work and personnel involved in a production, including camera crew, talent, lighting and sound technicians, and equipment, as well as the caterer for any food served while the filming or videotaping is in progress.
2. operate a camera or cause a camera to operate in a film, videotape, or photographic session.

**SHOPPER**  locally distributed newspaper, usually free-of-charge, that advertises local stores, restaurants, and shopping centers; also called *shopping newspaper*. Shoppers usually include sale announcements and discount coupons for local stores.

**SHOPPER PROFILE**  CUSTOMER PROFILE based on the typical patrons of a retail outlet.

**SHOPPING SERVICE**
1. service provided by independent businesses who send representatives to stores to comparison shop for specific products. A shopping service is hired by contract and will compare competitive prices or prices for the same item in competitive stores, depending on the requests and needs of the client.

**2.** service offered to cable television subscribers where consumers can buy products (usually at discounts) that are displayed on a special shopping service channel.

**3.** service offered to subscribers of personal information services for home computer use. For example: CompuServe Consumer Information Service provides on-line information to subscribers. Among the many services offered by this company is one called Products, Guides, Etc. from which consumers may shop and select purchases right from their own computer terminals.

**SHORT TERM** periodical subscription sold for a duration of less than one year. TRIAL OFFERS are frequently made on a short-term basis, encouraging high order rates but placing a financial burden on the publisher, who must spread the cost of the subscription sale across fewer issues.

**SHOT**
**1.** particular style or angle of a photograph—for example, a BEAUTY SHOT, CLOSE-UP, LONG SHOT, or COMPOSITE SHOT.
**2.** unedited, uncut strip of exposed film or videotape taken by one camera without interruption.
**3.** informal photograph, usually taken by an amateur, without any attention to technique; a snapshot.

**SHOTGUN APPROACH** promotional strategy wherein the promotional campaign is a broad-based one, and promotional materials are distributed to as wide and diverse an audience as possible in the hope of obtaining the greatest possible sales of a product. See also RIFLE APPROACH.

**SHOWING**
**Outdoor advertising:** term used to indicate the number of display units bought for placement of advertisements. Units are offered in showings, such as a 50, 75, or 100 showing. A 100 showing means that the combination of units purchased will be exposed to the entire population of a MARKET at least once during any given day. A 50 showing means that half the population will pass by the advertising at least once during any given day, and so on. With the exception of PAINTED DISPLAYS, showings are usually purchased on a monthly basis.
**Transit advertising:** term used to indicate the exposures in the purchase of CAR CARDS for advertising in a transit system, such as buses, subway cars, or the like. A FULL SHOWING means that car cards will be displayed in every vehicle in the fleet; a half showing, in only half of the vehicles; and so on. Posters on the outside of transit vehicles are purchased in the same way as outdoor advertising units (i.e., 100 showing, 50 showing, etc.).

**SHOW-THROUGH** printing problem where the image printed on one side of the paper can be seen on the other side. Show-through is caused by using overly thin paper.

## SHRINKAGE
**Merchandising:** gradual loss of inventory over time due to damage, misplacement, or theft. Retailers must allow for some shrinkage in their financial planning. Shrinkage is especially high during the Christmas season, when temporary employees, with little experience, are hired and inventory levels are at capacity. Shoplifting is a major cause of shrinkage in the United States.

**Printing:** reduction in size from the original of a mold used to cast PRINTING PLATES. *See also* MATRIX.

**SHRINK WRAP** clear, plastic protective covering used on product packages that can be shrunk by heat to fit tightly around the package. Large-volume shrink-wrap operations use a conveyor belt system. The shrink wrap is placed loosely around each shipment and is carried on the belt into an oven for shrinking. *See also* BUBBLE WRAP.

**SIC CODE** *see* STANDARD INDUSTRIAL CLASSIFICATION CODE.

**SIDE GUIDE** device used to align paper on one side as the paper is automatically fed into a machine such as a PHOTOCOPY machine or a SHEET-FED press.

**SIDE WIRE** binding technique that stitches the pages together along one side with wire staples; also called *side stitching*. The stitching is usually about 5/16 of an inch from the edge. Side-wire-bound books do not lie open as flat as books using SADDLE-STITCH binding, but make it possible for a single sheet of paper, such as a special advertising insert, to be bound in along with the SIGNATURES.

**SIGNAL** communication transmitted and received over the airwaves, as radio and television signals. Particularly in radio, people often speak of a strong or weak signal when referring to the clarity and audibility with which the sound is heard. In radio, the signal is actually an electrical impulse made by changing audible sounds of various frequencies into electrical waves of the same frequencies for broadcasting. In television, light waves are also produced along with the audio signal, so that an image is received along with the audio portion.

## SIGNATURE
**1.** folded sheet of printed paper constituting a set of pages in a publication. All signatures constitute a number of pages in a multiple of 4, such as 4, 8, or 16 pages. Signatures are gathered and bound, and the folds are trimmed away to produce a finished magazine, catalog, or book.

**2.** song associated with a television or radio show or a product or service; also called *theme song*.

**SILHOUETTE HALFTONE** HALFTONE print image from which the background surrounding the central image has been removed, usually through etching or masking; also called outline halftone. *See also* ETCH; MASK.

**SILK SCREEN** *see* SERIGRAPHY.

**SIMMONS MARKETING BUREAU, INC.** market research firm located in New York City that provides audience composition information about the readers of magazines, newspapers, and newspaper supplements and about the viewers of national television programming. The information is broken down into demographic categories as well as product usage data and is published in a syndicated series, the *Simmons Selective and Mass Media Studies*. The series is available by subscription to advertising agencies, advertisers, media planners, and the various media. An advertiser of vodka, for example, would use the series to determine those periodicals or national television programs whose audiences purchase the highest quantities of vodka.

**SIMULATION** type of *statistical modeling*, using a computer, that attempts to mathematically predict the results of an action or series of actions, based on assumptions about how different VARIABLES affect each other. The values of certain variables are set to simulate a particular circumstance, so that the effect on the variable of interest can be measured. For example, the effect of a price change on a market can be simulated by making assumptions about the behavior of competitors and consumers in response to a price change.

**SIMULCAST** synchronization of an FM radio signal with the usual video and audio signal of a television program for the simultaneous broadcast of the program on FM radio and television stations. Simulcasts are usually used to improve the quality of the sound in the television broadcast.

**SINGLE COPY** periodical issue sold to a retail customer as distinguished from a subscriber. Single-copy sales are heavily influenced by the DISPLAY, the position in a display, the type of retail outlet, and the illustrations and copy on the cover. Some periodicals are sold exclusively on a single-copy basis without offering subscriptions.

**SINGLE-FAMILY DWELLING** residence housing one family or household; also called a HOUSE. Residents of single-family dwellings are the best prospects for certain types of products, such as lawn care and insulation, and for certain types of promotions such as door-to-door sales. *See also* DWELLING UNIT; MULTIFAMILY DWELLING.

**SIPHON** term used in broadcast to describe the act of relaying a free television program via PAY-TV.

**SITCOM** situation comedy; weekly radio or television show focusing on the humorous side of real-life situations, often centered around a family or family situation. Among the first sitcoms to appear on television were "Ozzie and Harriet," "Father Knows Best," "Leave It to Beaver," and "I Love Lucy," each of which dealt with everyday occurrences within the family about which the show was centered.

Typically, the sitcom is a 30-minute program, where the situation is presented in the first 10 minutes, developed in the next 10 minutes, and then resolved in the last 10 minutes. The television format presents the perfect medium for the sitcom because of the visual opportunities it allows. The format has been extremely successful over the years, particularly during PRIME TIME.

**SITE SELECTION** process of choosing the optimal location for a business based on accessibility to and availability of customers as well as considerations as to space costs, size, and other physical characteristics, zoning regulations, investment tax credits, and the quality of the available workforce. The greater the perceived value of the goods offered, the greater the effort a consumer is willing to expend in order to reach the seller's place of business. For example, a grocery store in a rural area with limited competition does not have to worry about accessibility as much as a dry cleaner in an urban area with numerous competitors. Sophisticated computer modeling tools can be used to evaluate site alternatives based on the number and characteristics of consumers in each prospective location. *See also* COGNITIVE MAPPING.

**SITUATIONAL ANALYSIS** examination of the internal strengths (S), weaknesses (W), external opportunities (O), and threats (T) affecting an organization. Also called *SWOT Analysis*, a situational analysis is a basic element of the marketing plan and is used to make projections for the proposed marketing activities. Typically the analysis seeks to answer two general questions: Where is the organization now? and, In what direction is the organization headed? Factors studied in order to answer these questions are the social and political developments impacting on marketing strategy, competitors, technological advances, and other industry developments that may affect the marketing plan.

**SIXTEEN MILLIMETER** (16MM) width of film used for moving pictures. Sixteen millimeter film is the industry standard for local television and film production and is also used in some commercial filming. It runs at a speed of 36 feet per minute, and shoots and projects 24 frames per second. *See also* EIGHT MILLIMETER; THIRTY-FIVE MILLIMETER.

**:60** scriptwriter notation for 60 seconds, often used to indicate the length of a commercial. *See also* COMMERCIAL MINUTE.

**SIZING**
1. substance applied to paper to make it more resistant to moisture damage.
2. substance applied to paper to prepare it for gilding with gold leaf or foil.
3. substance applied to paper to coat the surface, producing a smooth, nonporous finish.

**SKEW**
1. to introduce bias into a research situation leading to false results. For example, an interviewer who nods or smiles when a positive response is given to a question about a product will encourage the respondent to respond favorably on other questions.
2. printed information that is out of alignment with the target area of the paper or envelope. On a direct mail piece, a skewed address may not show through the envelope window.

**SKID** *see* PALLET.

**SKIMMING** pricing strategy usually used in the early stages of the PRODUCT LIFE CYCLE that targets a small number of consumers who are willing to pay a relatively high price for the product. Over time, the price may be reduced to take advantage of production economies of scale achieved by selling higher volumes. A skimming strategy can attract competitors to the market if the product or technology can be easily duplicated. Luxury perfumes use a skimming strategy that takes advantage of the high perceived value, enabling them to sell perfume at hundreds of dollars per ounce. The term is derived from the concept of "skimming the cream" off a bottle of milk. In this case, the marketer is skimming the cream, or the best consumers, off the market. *See also* MILKING STRATEGY.

**SKIM PRICING** establishing a relatively high price for a product or service; also called HIGH-PRICE STRATEGY. This usually works for product INNOVATIONS with limited competition and a low or negative price ELASTICITY of demand. Skim pricing enables the seller to more rapidly recover the costs of development and introduction. This strategy carries some risk in that it will attract more competitors to the market and may antagonize consumers. A skim pricing strategy also works well with prestige products such as perfume. *See also* LOW-PRICE STRATEGY; PRESTIGE PRICING.

**SKIN SACK** mail SACK with too few packages in it to be handled efficiently. The creation of skin sacks is avoided, because the PRESORT discounts are not enough to offset the cost of handling.

**SKYWRITING** OUT-OF-HOME advertising medium where a brief message is written in the sky by an airplane using a chemical substance to emit small puffs of smoke that form the letters of the message. Since the puffs of smoke dissipate very quickly into the atmosphere, the message is usually limited to a one- or two-word reminder of a product, brand name, or service. Skywriting is employed in areas where large crowds congregate, such as beaches, open sports stadiums, amusement areas, or large metropolitan areas. It is used essentially as a supplementary medium in an extensive advertising campaign.

There is also a companion medium known as skytyping, which uses a fleet of seven radio-equipped planes that fly in formation and electronically "type" out a 13-letter message in block form. The sky-typed message is 15 miles long and a mile deep and, on a clear day, can be seen in a 40-mile radius for approximately 10 to 30 minutes, depending on atmospheric conditions.

**SLICE-OF-LIFE** *see* SLICE-OF-LIFE ADVERTISEMENT.

**SLICE-OF-LIFE ADVERTISEMENT** advertising-copy technique where a real-life problem is presented in a dramatic situation and the item being advertised becomes the solution to the problem. This advertising format is relied upon heavily by detergent manufacturers.

**SLICK** high-quality, CAMERA-READY proof of an advertisement printed on glossy paper, which is sent to newspapers and magazines for reproduction. *See also* ENAMEL PROOF; REPRODUCTION PROOF.

**SLIDE** color photograph set in a frame and made on transparent film that may be projected and enlarged onto a screen for viewing by a group of people. Slides are usually made from 35mm film.

**SLIPPAGE**
1. term referring to people who purchase a product intending to redeem a coupon, request a REBATE, or send in for a PREMIUM, but fail to do so.
2. ratio between people who actually take advantage of the type of promotion defined above and those who don't. This ratio is usually calculated as a percentage of total purchases. Most advertisers project a certain degree of slippage in their promotions in order to forecast the promotion's results; also known as *slippage rate*.

**SLITTING** process of cutting paper. Slitting devices are attached to some printing presses and folding machines to cut large sheets of paper into pages as printing and folding are completed. Automated slitters are also used to open envelopes on mail-opening machines, so that the contents can be easily extracted.

**SLOGAN** phrase or sentence used repeatedly in the advertising of a product or service that, through its repetition alone, eventually comes to identify the product or service. Essentially, slogans serve one of two basic functions: either to communicate an idea that manufacturers want associated with the product or service, such as "The Science of Sound" by Technics stereo equipment, or to retain continuity within an advertising campaign. A famous example of the latter is "Ask the man who owns one," associated with the Packard automobile of the 1930s. This particular slogan has been remembered throughout the years, long past the life of the product, and is often used in other contexts.

**SLUG**
**Advertising:** signature of an advertiser on a print advertisement. The slug can be a distinctive LOGO, TRADEMARK, or simply the name of

the advertiser (with or without the address) placed in the advertisement for identification.

**Printing:**
1. a one-piece line of type that is cast by machine, rather than by hand.
2. piece of metal usually measuring six points in thickness used for spacing between lines of type.

**Television production:** blank footage inserted into a film or videotape to represent a program or portion thereof that is still to come. The slug will be the exact length of the forthcoming piece so that the RUNNING TIME of the footage will be the same as that of the finished product.

**SMALL CAPS** smaller of two capital-letter sizes in a roman typeface. Small caps are slightly larger than the lowercase letters in that typeface. They are used primarily for subheadings and running heads or to highlight certain words, such as the cross-referenced words in this dictionary.

**SNIPE** sheets containing extra information that are pasted at the bottom of an outdoor poster. For example, a poster for a national chain may have room for sheets giving the addresses of individual franchises. *See also* OVERLAY.

**SOAP OPERA** serialized melodramatic presentations on broadcast television of true-to-life circumstances centering around romance and family life and its problems and tragedies. Begun as 15-minute segments on radio in the 1930s, the presentations were affectionately named "soaps" (which later became "soap operas"), because they were sponsored by soap manufacturers, particularly Procter & Gamble. The creator of the format was a woman named Irna Phillips, who began the genre in Chicago in 1930 with "Painted Dreams," the story of an Irish widow and her family. The longest-running soap opera (actually the longest-running drama in broadcast history) is "Guiding Light," which began on radio in 1937 and continues today as a full-color one-hour drama on the CBS Network. Many famous actors and entertainers have made their way to stardom through the ranks of soap operas.

Today these dramas appear on daytime television on all networks, as well as some local stations, in at least three different languages, and are primarily sponsored by soap manufacturers and companies specializing in home-care products. Additionally, the soap opera format has been adapted for prime-time programming in shows such as "Dallas" and "Dynasty."

**SOCIAL CHANNEL** person who exerts influence over the BUYING DECISIONS of an individual or group within a TARGET MARKET through a personal relationship such as a friend, relative, OPINION LEADERS, or coworker; *also called* WORD-OF-MOUTH ADVERTISING. *See also* ADVOCATE CHANNEL; EXPERT CHANNEL.

**SOCIAL MARKETING** promotion of social programs and ideas such as recycling, highway safety, family planning, energy conservation, and use of libraries. Social marketing typically relies on donated funds and may be engaged in by public, nonprofit, or for-profit institutions.

**SOFT DOT** *see* HARD DOT.

**SOFT GOODS** merchandise that is soft to the touch, such as clothing and other textile goods; considered in the merchandising industry to be nondurable goods. *See also* HARD GOODS.

**SOFT OFFER** *see* HARD OFFER.

**SOFTWARE** COMPUTER PROGRAM that controls the functions of a computer.

**SOLO MAIL** direct-mail promotion for one product or service. It is the opposite of a SHARED MAILING and represents the majority of direct-mail promotions.

**SORT**
**Computer file maintenance:** process that arranges records in the appropriate SEQUENCE.
**Direct mail:** process of batching mail by its destination prior to mailing, or batching documents for distribution and/or handling. For example, incoming direct-mail orders are usually sorted by cash and credit orders so that the cash orders can receive special handling.

**SOUND EFFECTS (SFX)** sounds, such as footsteps, ocean waves, or the squealing of automobile brakes, that are heard in a radio or television program or commercial in accompaniment to the script and that add to the mood or atmosphere of the presentation. Sound effects are produced by playing a recording of the actual sound that has been made previously wherever the sound actually occurred, or by recreating the sound by approximating the conditions under which it actually happens, or by using special devices and props to approximate the sound itself (such as crinkling cellophane to simulate the sound of fire).

**SOURCE** channel of sale that generated an order or customer. SOURCE EVALUATION is an essential part of direct marketing that enables marketers to concentrate their promotion expenditures on the best sources. Sources are evaluated not just by number of orders generated, but also in terms of profitability, taking into account the long-term purchase and payment history of each customer by source. Sources for magazine subscription orders include insert cards (*see* BIND-IN; BLOW-IN), gifts, direct-mail promotions, WHITE MAIL, SUBSCRIPTION AGENTS, and RENEWALS. Sources may be broken into subsets by key codes that indicate the LIST, promotion CAMPAIGN, PACKAGE, or OFFER that generated an order from a particular source. *See also* KEY CODE. *See also* PRIOR SOURCE.

**SOURCE COUNT**  tally of the number of customers on a file generated by each SOURCE of business.

**SOURCE CREDIBILITY**  perception of trustworthiness an individual imparts to other people. Factors that influence source credibility are expertise and reputation for honesty.

**SOURCE EVALUATION**  process of analyzing the long-term profitability of each SOURCE of business, taking into account all revenue generated and various elements of expense, depending upon the method of source evaluation being used. Source evaluation enables marketers to concentrate their resources on the sources that best suit their long-term strategies, which may include growth, maintenance of present sales levels, or reduction in sales levels. *See also* DEPLETION METHOD; MAINTENANCE METHOD; STEADY-GROWTH METHOD.

**SOURCE INCONGRUITY**  in communication, a situation in which the consumer's attitudes or opinions about the source of the message are in conflict with attitudes about the message itself. People subconsciously attempt to reduce source incongruity. For example, if a celebrity the consumer does not like endorses a product the consumer does like, the consumer's perception of the celebrity will become more positive and the consumer's perception of the product will become less positive. *See also* COGNITIVE DISSONANCE.

**SOURCE KEY**  code used for the statistical reporting and tracking of direct-marketing RESPONSES that combines SOURCE information with data pertaining to CAMPAIGN, LIST, PACKAGE, OFFER, and so forth. The source key is printed on REPLY FORMS and is entered into a computer along with the order information. Order and customer volumes and other statistics are then tracked and tabulated by source key. Source keys vary in size, but most are four to six digits long. Although they provide essential information, marketers prefer to keep source keys as short as possible, in the belief that long code numbers on a reply form discourage response. *See also* HOMOGENIZATION.

**SOURCE MIGRATION**  order pattern made over time by a customer who orders in response to various types of promotions. An example is a FIRST-TIME BUYER who purchases through the mail something advertised in a SPACE advertisement, makes a second purchase from a catalog sent to new customers, and then makes a third purchase from a catalog sent to current customers. In magazine subscriptions, the source migration typically begins with a direct-mail promotion, becomes a CONVERSION RENEWAL, and then a PURE RENEWAL. Marketers track source migration patterns to best know how to generate repeat sales and to monitor whether repeat sales are coming from the most profitable sources. For example, magazine publishers want to verify that most renewals are made in response to their own renewal promotions rather than SUBSCRIPTION AGENT promotions or other less profitable sources. Publishers will reevaluate renewal promotion strategy if agents are renewing subscribers before they themselves have tried.

**SPACE** area in a PRINT ADVERTISING medium, such as a magazine, newspaper, or BILLBOARD, that is sold to advertisers at a price based upon the size of the area, the position of the area within the advertising VEHICLE (such as the inside front cover or CENTER SPREAD), and the number of people expected to see the advertisement (such as the CIRCULATION of a magazine). *See also* POSITIONING; RATE CARD; TRANSIT ADVERTISING.

**SPACE ALLOCATION** amount of shelf space in a retail outlet, reserved for display of a product.

**SPACE BUYER** *see* MEDIA BUYER.

**SPACE POSITION VALUE** measures of effectiveness and visibility of outdoor advertisements. It is based on four factors: the distance from where the advertisement can first be seen, the speed of traffic approaching it, the angle from where it can be seen, and the number of competing advertisements in its vicinity. Space positions value is expressed as a percentage ranging from zero to 100, with zero representing zero visibility.

**SPACING-IN (SPACING-OUT)** composition technique for keeping line lengths uniform by reducing or increasing the width of the space between words in the line. In metal type composition, blank SLUGS of varying widths are placed between the type characters. *See also* COMPOSING STICK; LETTERSPACING.

**SPEC** *see* ON SPECULATION.

**SPECIAL** broadcast program that is not part of the regular broadcast schedule and is presented on a one-time basis. Usually the program is of special interest to the listening or viewing community. It may also be a dramatic showcase for known talent, or a spectacular production such as an awards presentation or a musical variety show. Because of the special nature of the program, a large audience is usually expected by the producer and sponsor. Therefore, commercial time will sell at a premium throughout the length of the presentation. *See also* ONE-SHOT.

**SPECIAL CAP ROUTINES** COMPUTER PROGRAM logic used for addressing mailing labels or pieces that controls where capital letters are used, such as at the beginning of names or, in some cases, in the middle of certain names such as McMahon.

**SPECIAL EFFECTS (FX)** those visual elements in movies and television such as fog, smoke, lightning, breaking furniture, snow, or the like, that are used to effect reality in the picture or videospace and that are either impossible or impractical to produce firsthand. Special effects also account for those visual elements that are produced electronically and that create an imaginative reality in motion pictures such as *Star Wars* or the *Star Trek* series. In television, electronic effects such as DISSOLVES, FREEZE FRAMES, MONTAGES, and others requiring auxiliary electronic equipment are also categorized as special effects.

**SPECIALTY GOODS**  consumer products that are unique or special enough to persuade the consumer to exert unusual effort to obtain them. For example, the work of a particular artist or designer may be offered in only one gallery but interested consumers will go out of their way to get there.

**SPECIFICATIONS**  documented requirements for a process, service, system, or product. For example, the specifications for a LIST RENTAL selection would include the number of names desired, the SELECTION CRITERIA, the format for the OUTPUT, such as address LABELS or MAGNETIC TAPE, and the desired delivery date. It is always important that specifications be comprehensive and accurate. The specifications for a computer system or program would describe the available INPUT and the required output, as well as any processes that should take place in between.

**SPECS**  *see* SPECIFICATIONS.

**SPECTACULAR**
1. elaborate television show, motion picture, or live stage presentation that usually features a very large cast, unusual costuming, and many SPECIAL EFFECTS, and costs vast sums of money to produce.
2. OUTDOOR ADVERTISING display that features neon or electric lighting, some moving parts, lavish colors, and/or unusual special effects as a part of the advertisement. Located in or around large metropolitan areas, spectaculars are usually custom-made to fit special high-traffic locations and are the costliest of all outdoor advertising displays. Typically, they are leased by an advertiser on some long-term arrangement.

**SPECTRUM**  range of radiant energy (light) wavelengths. Within the visible spectrum, various light wavelengths are perceived as colors ranging from red to blue, depending upon the length of the wave. White light is a combination of all visible colors mixed in equal proportions. This characteristic of light, which enables it to be combined, so that the resultant light is equal to the sum of its constituent wavelengths, is called *additive color mixing. See also* COLD COLOR; SUBTRACTIVE PRIMARIES; WARM COLOR.

**SPEEDBALL**  trademarked name of a variety of broad-nibbed pens used for creating lettering strokes of various thicknesses.

**SPIFF**  see PUSH INCENTIVES.

**SPINE**  side where SIGNATURES of a book or catalog are bound together and attached to the cover; also called *binding edge.*

**SPINOFF** television program derived from situations or characters in another television program. For example, the show "Laverne and Shirley" was derived from characters who first appeared on the show "Happy Days."

**SPIRAL BINDING** *see* WIRE-O BINDING.

**SPIRIT ADDRESSING** addressing technique utilizing a reusable carbon-impregnated address card that is moistened with a solution and applied to a label or envelope, leaving a carbon impression of the address. This is an old-fashioned method rarely used today.

**SPLIT RUN** technique used to test the effectiveness of advertising copy. Two different versions of the same advertisement are printed in the same press RUN of an issue of a particular publication, so that some of the copies contain one version of the ad and the others contain the other version. The publication is distributed normally, but the distribution of the advertisements is split according to the request of the advertiser. Some advertisers split their run in alternate bundles; (*see* ALTERNATE BUNDLES RUN) others prefer to split by geographic location or by subscription versus newsstand sales. The purpose of the split run is to compare the effectiveness of the two alternate ad copies. Advertisers will take advantage of this option when they desire to learn which of two elements used in the advertising will achieve the desired objectives. Elements that are often tested are prices, copy appeal, layout, type of illustration, coupon offered or no coupon offered, or premium or rebate offered or not. The results of split-run testing are revealed by the number of responses to each advertisement. The split-run option is offered as a convenience to advertisers. However, not all publications offer this option.

**SPLIT SCREEN** *see* COMPOSITE SHOT.

**SPLIT STATES** densely populated states serviced by more than one STATE DISTRIBUTION CENTER.

**SPLIT TEST** direct-marketing test utilizing RANDOM SAMPLES drawn from a single list. *See also* A-B SPLIT; AREA SAMPLE; NTH NAME SELECTION.

**SPOKESPERSON** individual who speaks on behalf of a product or service and whose name becomes associated with the product or service, as, for example, Red Buttons has become the spokesperson for a real estate development in Florida. A spokesperson may be a celebrity or someone who begins as an unknown and who gains a measure of celebrity through association with the product. *See also* PERSONALITY; TESTIMONIAL ADVERTISING.

**SPONSOR** advertiser who pays for part or all of a television or radio program by running one or more advertisements during the program. Sponsorship entitles the advertiser to a mention as the program's sponsor, and to a specific amount of commercial time throughout the program, depending on the time of day, the type of program (local vs. network), and the station's regulations.

**SPONSOR SALES** subscriptions sold on behalf of a charitable or civic organization that earns a commission on each subscription sold, with the remaining amount going to the publisher and any SUBSCRIPTION AGENT utilized. *See also* SCHOOL AGENCY.

**SPORTS MARKETING** marketing products through the sponsorship of sporting events or the sponsorship of teams or equipment for sporting events. *See also* EVENTS MARKETING.

**SPOT**
1. broadcast time slot set aside to be filled by either a commercial advertisement or a public service message; also called *occasion.*
2. in a technical production sense, casual name for a spotlight.
3. commercial time on local television stations, as distinguished from commercial time on a network. Within this context there are two types of spot purchases that can be made: (1) *local spot*—handled by an individual television station, with time bought in one market only, for the benefit of the audience in that particular market; (2) *national spot*—handled by a local television sales representative, with time bought by a national advertiser on an individual basis in more than one market.

**SPOT ANNOUNCEMENT**
1. *see* SPOT.
2. *see* ANNOUNCEMENT.
3. announcement made in a spot commercial time slot.

**SPOT GLUE** adhesive applied to a form or page to allow the fastening of another piece of paper or to seal a folded form for mailing. *See also* SELF-SEALER; TIP-ON.

**SPOT RADIO** local radio time set aside for SPOT commercials. When advertisers speak of spot radio, they are speaking of the purchase of commercial time in a MARKET-BY-MARKET BUY.

**SPOT TELEVISION** local television time set aside for SPOT commercials. When advertisers speak of spot television, they are referring to the purchase of commercial time in a MARKET-BY-MARKET BUY.

**SPREAD**
**Broadcast:**
1. in television filming, to focus the lens on a lighting instrument to its widest opening in order to give maximum width to the light distribution, as, for example, in opening the fresnel spotlight (spotlight with an adjustable lens that allows for the variation of transmitted light) to its flooded capacity.
2. to stretch a live broadcast to fill the entire time slot allotted it.
**Printing:** type that runs across a page, rather than type that is set in columns.
**Publishing:** article or advertisement that appears on two facing pages in a publication. If the two facing pages are in the center of the magazine, the piece is said to appear as a *center spread.*

**STAGING**

   **Advertising:**

1. planning the location, floor plan (including sets and props), and/or actions to be executed for a commercial being filmed in a studio or on location.
2. presentation or show performed for filming or in front of an audience.
3. arrangement of audiovisual equipment and screens in the various locations in which a program will be presented, such as a slide presentation of a new line of clothing to be shown to buyers throughout the country.

   **Direct marketing:** preparation of equipment and materials for a process or a machine run.

   **Printing:** coating the nonprinting areas of a plate with a substance resistant to the etching solution. *See also* RESIST.

**STAMP SHEET** page of adhesive-backed stamps that are surrounded by perforated edges and applied to a REPLY FORM to indicate a choice. Stamp sheets are most often used by direct-mail SUBSCRIPTION AGENTS. Each stamp contains a magazine title and offer. Subscribers choose stamps to paste onto the reply form to indicate the magazine(s) they want. Stamp sheets are a classic ACTION DEVICE.

**STANDARD ADVERTISING REGISTER** two companion directories, the *Standard Directory of Advertising Agencies* and the *Standard Directory of Advertisers*, which have become an invaluable tool of the advertising industry. The books are referred to as the Red Books because of their red covers. *The Standard Directory of Advertising Agencies* acts as a guide to the industry in that it lists the names and addresses of most of the nation's agencies by state, the associations to which they belong (if any), and the media associations that recognize (*see* RECOGNITION) them for credit purposes. It also lists each agency's annual billing by media classification, the names and titles of its executives, and the names of its current accounts. *The Standard Directory of Advertisers* lists the names of approximately 17,000 corporations that advertise nationally, and the names and titles of their executives. It also gives the names of their agencies, their total annual advertising budget, and the principal media used. Both directories are published by the National Register Publishing Company, which is part of the Standard Rate and Data Service.

**STANDARD ADVERTISING UNIT (SAU)** uniform measures of COLUMN INCHES established by print media for advertisements that are carried in publications on a national level. The establishment of SAUs has simplified the purchase of advertising space in that marketers need to create only one size advertisement for publication in a variety of markets, which eliminates the cost of designing various sizes for each separate print purchase.

**STANDARD CONSOLIDATED STATISTICAL AREA** *see* CONSOLIDATED METROPOLITAN STATISTICAL AREA.

**STANDARD DEVIATION** statistical calculation of the difference between an average and the individual values included in the average. For example, it would be useful to know how much variation there is in response to a direct-mail package across several mailing lists. The standard deviation, represented by the Greek letter sigma ("Σ"for a population and "*s*" for a sample) is equal to the square root of the variance. The formula is:

$$ s = \sqrt{\frac{\sum (x - x)^{-2}}{n - 1}} $$

where   $n$ = number of values in the sample,
   $x$ = each value in the sample,
   $x$ = mean (average) value of the sample.

The greater the degree of difference of a value from the average, the larger the standard deviation. The advantage of a standard deviation calculation over a variance calculation (*see* ANALYSIS OF VARIANCE) is that it is expressed in terms of the same scale as the values in the sample. For example, if the standard deviation of a sample group of automobile prices is calculated, a standard deviation of 500 is equal to $500. That means that most of the prices are within ± $500 of the average price. A standard deviation calculation indicates the degree to which values are clustered around the average. For example, the standard deviation of a group of compact automobile prices might be $500, meaning that there is relatively little price difference in that automobile market—the prices are all within $500 of each other. However, the standard deviation of the entire United States automobile market might be $5000, indicating a large variation in prices.

**STANDARD DIRECTORY OF ADVERTISERS** *see* STANDARD ADVERTISING REGISTER.

**STANDARD DIRECTORY OF ADVERTISING AGENCIES** *see* STANDARD ADVERTISING REGISTER.

**STANDARD INDUSTRIAL CLASSIFICATION CODE** (SIC CODE) four-digit numeric code established by the U.S. government to designate various industries as defined by their functions and products. SIC codes are used by direct marketers to SEGMENT lists and to target promotions. The government uses them to report and track business-related census data. The first two digits indicate a major industrial classification; the second two digits, an industrial subgroup. For example SIC code 2300 represents a manufacturer of clothing; code 2352, a manufacturer of hats and caps. What the code cannot tell the direct marketer is whether a business is engaged only in that activity defined by the SIC code or whether the code represents only a primary business activity. If the latter is the case, there may be other marketing opportunities pertaining to that firm not identified by the SIC code.

**STANDARD METROPOLITAN STATISTICAL AREA (SMSA)** *see* METROPOLITAN STATISTICAL AREA.

**STANDARD RATE AND DATA SERVICE** *see* CONSUMER MAGAZINE AND AGRI-MEDIA RATES AND DATA; DIRECT MAIL LIST, RATES, AND DATA.

**STAR** *see* GROWTH-SHARE MATRIX.

**STARCH, DANIEL, AND ASSOCIATES** *see* DANIEL STARCH AND ASSOCIATES.

**STARCH RATINGS** *see* DANIEL STARCH AND ASSOCIATES.

**STAR ROUTE** *see* HIGHWAY CONTRACT ROUTE.

**START** cycle at which a SUBSCRIPTION or CONTINUITY begins, such as the first issue served on a magazine subscription or the first book served in a continuity series. Marketers monitor the start of new customers so that adequate inventory will be produced to fill their orders. Starts are of particular interest to periodical publishers, who monitor the number of new subscribers that start with each issue and can be relied upon to replace those who will EXPIRE or CANCEL each issue, thus maintaining RATE BASE. *See also* ADVANCE START; BACK DATING; PREFERRED START.

**STAT**
  **1.** *see* PHOTOSTAT.
  **2.** medical term meaning *immediately*, which has come into common usage.

**STATE** in the language of direct marketing, one of the 50 geographic and governmental units of the United States (i.e., the 50 states), as well as Washington, D.C., and all U.S. territories. Every state has its own laws regarding various aspects of marketing. For some products and in some states, direct-mail marketers are required to collect sales tax on purchases made by residents of those states. SECOND-CLASS and THIRD-CLASS mail must be sorted by state into state SACKS and PACKAGES according to U.S. Postal Service regulations. There is no postage discount offered for this level of PRESORT. PALLETS of mail sorted only to the state level are not accepted by the USPS. *See also* MIXED STATES.

**STATE COUNT** tally of the number of RECORDS on a file by STATE. This number is of interest to direct marketers who wish to identify those geographic areas in which their product sells best, by analyzing a state count of their customer file. State counts of periodical subscription files must be reported to advertisers in accordance with AUDIT

BUREAU OF CIRCULATIONS regulations, so that advertisers can evaluate whether the publication reaches their TARGET MARKET.

**STATE DISTRIBUTION CENTER (SDC)** main post office(s) in a STATE that receives and distributes all mail for that state to and from the various other post offices within the state. *See also* SECOND CLASS; THIRD CLASS.

**STATEMENT**
1. summary document outlining the status of an open credit account showing amounts due and paid. The term is commonly used interchangeably with "INVOICE" or "bill" by direct marketers.
2. *see* ABC STATEMENT.

**STATEMENT STUFFER** *see* BILL INSERT.

**STATE SACK** *see* STATE.

**STATES MAIL** *see* MIXED STATES.

**STATIC NEUTRALIZER**
1. mechanical device or floor mat used to reduce or absorb static electricity around static-sensitive electronic equipment, such as some computers.
2. device placed on paper-handling devices, such as PRINTING PRESS feeder mechanisms, folders, or joggers (*see* JOG), to reduce static electricity. Static electricity makes paper sheets cling together, thereby interfering with the smooth flow of paper.

**STATION ID** *see* STATION IDENTIFICATION.

**STATION IDENTIFICATION** in broadcast, public announcement of the call letters, channel number (where applicable), and city of origin of a broadcast station, as required by the Federal Communications Commission, on the hour and half hour. Also known as *station ID*.

**STATION POSTER** advertising BILLBOARDS displayed in bus stations, commuter service stations, subway stations, or railroad and airline terminals. Generally, station posters are characterized by attention-getting devices such as moving parts, flashing lights, three-dimensional scenes, island or floor displays, or clocks with special illumination, and are custom designed to meet the needs of the advertiser.

**STATISTICAL MODELING** *see* SIMULATION.

**STEADY-GROWTH METHOD** subscription SOURCE EVALUATION technique that estimates the cost and impact on profitability of building the RATE BASE over time via various sources of business. The cost of acquiring, billing, and renewing subscriptions is taken into account, as well as expected PAY-UP, cancellation, and RENEWAL rates. *See also* CHANNEL OF SALES; DEPLETION METHOD; MAINTENANCE METHOD

**STEP-UP** *see* UPGRADE.

## STEREOTYPE

**Printing:** duplicate PRINTING PLATE cast from a paper MATRIX used in letterpress. Newspapers or other print media who use the letterpress printing method require advertisers to provide a plate of their ad. This is done by creating a metal mold of the ad. A papier-maché mold is then made by pressing the paper material against the metal plate under pressure so that a matrix forms a mirror image. The paper matrix is then mailed (at a low cost) to the newspaper, where another metal mold is created by pouring metal over the matrix. This duplicate mold is called a stereotype.

**Psychology:** general mental image that is held of a group or class of people that is usually oversimplified. An advertiser may feature a stereotypical user of his product in order to encourage the audience to identify with the user. For example, housewives are often used in advertisements for cleaning products.

**STET** proofreader's or editor's direction to the printer or typesetter indicating that material marked for correction should remain as it was before the correction. The work to remain is underscored with a series of dots, and the word *stet* is written in the margin. The term is Latin for "let it stand."

**STILL** photograph, slide, or painting showing an individual or a scene frozen in time.

**STING** distinctive background music used to add emphasis to an important moment in a motion picture or television program; also called *stinger*.

**STINGER** *see* STING.

**STITCHING** binding method that sews (staples) all SIGNATURES together in one step, using either the SADDLE-STITCH or SIDE-WIRE method. It produces a strong but inflexible binding that is best used for relatively thin books, catalogs, or magazines that will open easily despite the inflexible binding. *See also* PERFECT BINDING.

## STOCK

1. various grades or types of paper used for printing, with different BASIS WEIGHTS and FINISHES.
2. material in INVENTORY, such as preprinted forms and envelopes in a lettershop inventory, or store merchandise.

**STOCK-KEEPING UNIT (SKU)** inventory control count that represents one or more items that will be sold together. For example, a retail bed store would consider one bed frame with four wheels equal to one SKU (even though the frame and the wheels come from different suppliers), because a frame is never sold without wheels, and wheels are never sold alone. Conversely, a frame, a box spring, and a mattress would be considered three SKUs, because any of the three items might be sold separately.

**STOCK SHOT** photograph or filmed footage of an action, scene, or special effect, such as a sunrise, that is stored in a production studio library or special effects library and can be borrowed from the library and inserted into a film, program, or commercial where the script calls for such a scene; also called *library shot*. The use of a stock shot does not require a credit line nor an additional payment to models or talent who appear in the shot.

**STONE** flat surface or table originally made of stone, hence the name; used in manual COMPOSITION to compose type.

**STOP AND HOLD** INACTIVE customer RECORD status used when the address in the record is known to be undeliverable or when a temporary cessation in service to the customer is required or requested for other reasons, such as when a magazine subscriber is away on extended vacation. By placing a record in stop and hold, service can be suspended without canceling the record or allowing it to EXPIRE. Customer records associated with UNDELIVERABLE BILLING DOCUMENTS are placed in stop and hold until the customer contacts the marketer and supplies a correct address. *See also* SUSPEND.

**STOP MOTION** *see* FREEZE FRAME.

**STORECAST** broadcast of radio programming in a retail store. A storecast may be an actual radio station broadcast over loudspeakers positioned throughout the store, or it may originate from a wired service that simulates radio broadcasting. Special announcements of sales or featured items may also be considered storecasts.

**STORE CHECK** review of merchandise in a retail store by non-sales personnel whose specific responsibilities are to run such in-field examinations. Store checks are done to see how the merchandise is displayed, how it is handled by the sales staff, and how it is selling. The information gathered in a store check will aid the manufacturer in the marketing of products.

**STORE-DISTRIBUTED MAGAZINE** magazine not offered by subscription whose circulation depends primarily on sales in retail outlets. *Family Circle* and *Woman's Day*, magazines sold from POINT-OF-PURCHASE ADVERTISING displays at retail grocery stores, are examples of store-distributed magazines.

**STORE-REDEEMABLE COUPON** merchandise discount certificate that can be redeemed in any store where the merchandise is sold, as distinguished from a certificate that can be redeemed through the mail. *See* COUPON.

**STORYBOARD** visual display of the action elements in a script prepared in conjunction with the script, particularly for commercials, to add the dimension of sight to the script. The storyboard is a sequential series of illustrations depicting the key action called for by the script. Used as a visualization of the commercial for client approval, it also helps in estimating costs for the commercial. Additionally, it will also point out flaws in the script or weaknesses in the concept, and can act as a guide in the actual shooting of the commercial.

**STRATEGIC ALLIANCE** *see* JOINT VENTURING.

**STRATEGIC BUSINESS UNIT (SBU)** company division, product line within a division, or single product or company brand that has an objective and mission different from other company business and that can be marketed independently from the rest of the company. The organizational structure of an SBU is typically less disciplined than the organizational structure of the parent company, allowing the SBU to respond more quickly to market changes and opportunities. See also GROWTH-SHARE MATRIX.

**STRATEGIC PLANNING** determination of the steps required to reach an objective that make the best use of available resources. In marketing, a strategic plan involves selecting a TARGET MARKET segment or segments and a POSITION within the market in terms of product characteristics, price, CHANNELS OF DISTRIBUTION, and SALES PROMOTION. For example, consider the case of a firm or manufacturer that decides to select the New York gourmet delicatessen market. The firm's strategic plan would include a gourmet-quality PRODUCT LINE that is high-priced, that is purchased from New York area wholesale distributors and sold in various small retail outlets in wealthy areas of the city, and that is promoted in local SHOPPERS and regional publications or on local TV. The company's long-term strategy might include diversifying into the direct-mail business with a gourmet-food gift catalog.

Part of a strategic plan involves deciding whether to enter a new untapped market, to grow an existing market, to dominate an existing market, or to dominate a small segment of an existing market by replacing competitors or by filling an unmet need. Advertising plans are an important part of strategic planning that must support the overall objective of the seller. For example, the firm or manufacturer in our example would not profit from purchasing commercial television time on a national basis but might benefit greatly from a regular spot on a local TALK SHOW or from a local newspaper advertisement.

**STRATEGIC WINDOW** short time period between specific events during which there is an opportunity to capitalize on a marketing situation.

**STRATEGY** any plan for achieving goals or objectives. *See also* CREATIVE STRATEGY; MARKETING PLAN.

**STREAM FEEDER** device that delivers sheets of paper to a PRINTER, moving the sheets in an overlapping flow rather than leaving space between each sheet as in a SHEET-FED press. This method feeds paper to the printer at a higher speed without requiring a proportionately higher feeder speed.

**STRIPPING**   process of applying film negatives (or positives) of illustrations and COPY onto a support base in an arrangement that comprises a complete page; also called *image assembly*. This will be used to create a PRINTING PLATE for that page.

**STRIP PROGRAMMING**   *see* ACROSS-THE-BOARD.

**STRIP RECORD**   abbreviated version of a computer RECORD, which contains only those FIELDS necessary for a particular process. Computer memory and time are saved by using a strip record. For example, the name and address field might be all that is needed to do a GENDER ANALYSIS by STATE. *See also* TALLY RECORD.

**SUBHEAD**   line of copy that is secondary in importance to the HEADLINE of an advertisement, but that adds a new idea or expands the theme presented by the headline to further encourage reader interest. Subheads may appear above or below the headline or within the text of the advertisement. Generally, they are set in smaller type than the headline but in larger type than the body text; however, they may also be in boldface type or in different-color ink than the body text, so that they stand out.

**SUBLIMINAL ADVERTISING**   advertising messages presented below the level of consciousness, such as words flashed across a television or movie screen at intervals of no more than 10 seconds in length, during the presentation of regular programming or a feature film. Some amount of subliminal advertising was done in the 1950s, but it has since been declared illegal.

**SUBLIMINAL PERCEPTION**   attention paid to a message without conscious awareness of the message. Although this has never been proven to exist, the theory is that the recipient of a subliminal message cannot erect mental barriers against the message and is thus more susceptible to the message's influence. *See also* SUBLIMINAL ADVERTISING.

**SUBSCRIPTION**   contractual agreement between a seller and a buyer to provide the buyer with a service or product to be delivered (served) over a period of time specified in the contract at a total price that is dependent upon the duration of the service. For example, one might subscribe to a magazine or newspaper for a set term (number of issues) or to a television cable service for a set term (number of months). Marketers who sell on a subscription basis expend considerable efforts attempting to attract new subscribers, to renew subscriptions, and to sell subscriptions of long duration. Discounts are frequently offered to new subscribers and for long-term subscriptions, but not for renewed subscriptions.

**SUBSCRIPTION AGENT**   business that sells periodical subscriptions to the public in return for a commission from the publisher, which is expressed in terms of a percentage of the subscription selling price. There are various types of subscription agents, who earn commissions ranging from 100% to 5% of the selling price, depending upon how badly the publisher needs them and the subscriptions they bring in. Most subscription agents handle more than one publication. Publishers employ subscription agents because the publishers may not have the financial resources to sell as many subscriptions as agents can or as quickly as agents can or because a publisher may not want to spend money up front to sell subscriptions. *See also* CASH FIELD AGENT; CATALOG AGENCY; DIRECT-MAIL AGENCY; PAID DURING SERVICE; PAID IN ADVANCE; SCHOOL AGENCY; TELEPHONE AGENCY.

**SUBSCRIPTION TV (STV)** television programming that is transmitted over the airwaves through a scrambler. Subscription TV can be viewed only by households subscribing to the service. For a monthly fee, subscribers receive a special device that is attached to their television sets and decodes the signal, allowing viewers to see the programming. STV broadcasts over standard broadcast channels that, for the most part, are independent stations featuring regular syndicated or local programming during the day, switching over to STV programming in the evening.

**SUBSTANCE**
**In general:** physical material in solid, liquid, or gaseous form, composed of one or more chemical elements derived from animal, mineral, or vegetable sources.
**Printing:** BASIS WEIGHT of paper.

**SUBTRACTIVE PRIMARIES** yellow, magenta, and cyan inks used in FOUR-COLOR PROCESS printing. They are subtractive in the sense that when they are combined, the color, or radiant energy, that results from the combination is of a lower wavelength than the sum of the wavelengths of the three colors. Therefore, by overlapping equal amounts of cyan, yellow, and magenta ink, black is produced. *Subtractive color mixing* is achieved in four-color process printing by overlapping successive layers of ink DOTS. Nonoverlapped dots produce additive color mixes when viewed at a reading distance. Both overlapped and nonoverlapped dots constitute most four-color process images. *See also* SPECTRUM.

**SUBTYPE** subscription RECORD code indicating the kind of subscription it is, according to the needs of the marketer. In many cases, subtype refers to whether the subscription is a nongift subscription, Christmas gift subscription, non-Christmas gift subscription, complimentary subscription, or employee subscription. Different types of RENEWAL promotions may be sent, based upon subtype. Subtype is not the same as SOURCE, which identifies the promotion that sold a subscription. For example, a subscriber who purchases a subscription for herself using a gift promotion form has a gift source but a nongift subtype. A subscriber who was given a subscription by a friend who used a BIND-IN card to submit the order has a bind-in source and a gift subtype.

**SUGGESTED RETAIL PRICE** selling price suggested by the manufacturer of merchandise. The suggested retail price is not mandatory, although manufacturers may hope that retail outlets maintain a price within the range of the suggested retail price.

**SUGGESTIVE SELLING** *see* CROSS-SELL.

**SULFATE PULP** inexpensive, brown, durable paper that is not bleached, so that wood-pulp fibers are highly visible. Sulfate pulp is used primarily for making bags and cardboard boxes.

**SUNDAY SUPPLEMENT** *see* SUPPLEMENT.

**SUPER** superimpose, superimposition; words, phrases, or images from one video source that are imposed over an image from another video source. The two sources are combined and presented as one composite image. A super may be a special price announcement, a headline, a disclaimer, a brand or product name, or any other visual element used to identify or promote interest in the product or service being advertised.

**SUPERCALENDERING** passing paper through steel and cotton or steel and paper CALENDER ROLLS after the papermaking process is complete, at sufficient pressure to produce a smooth, glossy FINISH. Supercalendered uncoated paper approximates the smoothness of COATED PAPER. Calendered paper passes through rollers attached to the papermaking machine, producing a less glossy, less smooth finish. Both coated and uncoated papers may be supercalendered, depending upon the finish desired.

**SUPERETTE** retail grocery store whose volume is not as large as a supermarket but that carries a variety of products and operates similarly to a supermarket (i.e., with island displays, self-service, checkout counters). Guidelines of the U.S. Department of Commerce suggest that, in order for a store to qualify as a superette, it must do a minimum of $75,000 in annual sales. If annual sales exceed $1 million, the store is classified as a supermarket.

**SUPERIMPOSE** *see* SUPER.

**SUPERSTATION** *see* CABLE TELEVISION.

**SUPPLEMENT** section added to a newspaper, particularly the Sunday edition, that enhances the content of the newspaper. Supplements are typically composed in a MAGAZINE FORMAT and contain fiction and nonfiction articles of a general or family appeal. Some supplements specialize in their content—for example, comic supplements, book supplements, or the broadcast-schedule supplement. Others may be marked "supplement," but are actually printed by an advertiser and inserted in the paper as a form of advertising. Supplements may be locally edited or nationally syndicated, but are never sold separately from the newspapers that carry them. Two examples of nationally syndicated MAGAZINE SUPPLEMENTS are *Family Weekly* and *Parade*, which are sold to and carried by local newspapers throughout the country. The syndications edit and print their supplements, and then imprint each with the MASTHEAD of the individual newspapers that will feature them (as per newspaper postal requirements).

The advantages of advertising in a supplement are (1) the longer ad life, due to the fact that people tend to keep something in magazine format longer than the rest of the paper, and (2) the fact that the limitations on the closing dates are not as stringent nor as long in advance as those of most magazines. In addition, advertisers in a syndicated supplement are afforded the capability of reaching a mass audience.

**SUPPLEMENTAL LABEL**  periodical-subscription address label produced at a point in time between main label-printing RUNS. Supplemental labels are produced to provide new subscribers with their first issue as quickly as possible, rather than to make them wait until labels are printed for the next issue. For example, if the September-issue labels are printed August 20 and the October-issue labels September 20, supplemental labels for the September issue will be printed between August 20 and September 20 to provide copies of the September issue to new subscribers who submitted subscription orders during that period of time.

**SUPPLEMENT LINE**  extra FIELD in a computer file RECORD used for additional address information beyond that required for most residential addresses, such as company name, TITLE, or apartment-building name. Without a supplement line, the additional information would have to be omitted, at some risk of undeliverability, or fitted into the record by abbreviating elements of the name and address. It has been found that many people object to receiving mail addressed with a shortened version of their name.

**SUPPRESSION**  deletion of records from the OUTPUT of a MERGE/PURGE accomplished by matching records input to the merge/purge with the records on a suppression file. Names most commonly suppressed include those of current customers when the output will be used for a COLD-MAIL PROMOTION or for BAD-PAY LIST names.

**SURPRINT**  superimpose one photographic negative over another and print the assemblage as one piece. This is most commonly done when an advertisement calls for a line of type to run across a picture, such as an image of a product with the headline "Final Sale!" running across it.

**SURVEY AREA**
1. geographic location represented by a sample group in a study.
2. geographic area in a radio market. The radio listening audience is spoken of as either the Total Survey Area (TSA) or the Metro Survey Area (MSA). The TSA represents a radio station's total

listening audience in a geographic area, and areas in a TSA can and do overlap (because a number of geographic areas can receive programming from different originating stations in different cities). MSAs do not overlap and are used when making purchases for radio broadcast commercial time.

**SUSPEND** customer-file RECORD status used to temporarily stop SERVICE to the customer while continuing other activity, such as billing. Customers who purchase a subscription on credit but fail to pay in response to the first few INVOICES are usually suspended until payment is received. A suspend status differs from a STOP AND HOLD status, in which all activity is discontinued.

**SWEEPS** specific time period when television network audience sizes are calculated in order to determine advertising rates for the following season. Sweeps start mid-week and end mid-week, and run for a four-week period in February, May, November, and July. Typically the networks program highly popular and new shows during sweeps to attract larger audiences, since advertising rates are based on number of viewers. The name derives from the networks' desire to sweep up the entire available audience.

**SWEEPSTAKES** popular type of SALES PROMOTION where lavish prizes are offered to entrants who have only to submit entries with their name and address by return mail or at a location determined by the sweepstakes sponsor, usually in a retail outlet where the sponsor's products are sold. Winners are chosen at random from among the entries, and no purchase is required in order to enter (a legal condition of a sweepstakes, allowing it to avoid the laws regulating state lotteries). The idea of a sweepstakes is to create consumer involvement with a brand or product and thus encourage consumption of the product.

**SWOP** (acronym for *S*pecifications for *W*eb *O*ffset *P*ublications) recommended specifications, published every few years by a committee of representative publishers, printers, advertising agencies, color separators, and advertisers (known as the SWOP industry review committee), that establish quality standards for magazines printed on high-speed WEB PRESSES. The SWOP manual includes various aspects of color reproduction and printing, and of text printing. For example, SWOP states that DOT GAIN from film to print should not exceed 17% +/– 4%. The SWOP committee encourages industry members to self-monitor the quality of the work they produce and to work only with organizations adhering to the quality standards set forth in SWOP. Copies of SWOP are available from the AAAA (American Association of Advertising Agencies), the ABP (American Business Press), and the Magazine Publishers Association.

**SWOT ANALYSIS** *see* SITUATIONAL ANALYSIS.

**SYMPATHETIC FORWARDING** delivery of improperly addressed mail to the correct party by a U.S. Postal Service employee not required by regulations to do so. This service is frequently performed by experienced postal carriers who are familiar with the households on their route and who recognize the intended recipient of the mail.

**SYNCHROGRAPHICS** data about a consumer related to the timing of significant life events such as marriage, birth of a child, college graduation, or purchase of a home. This information is useful to direct marketers because the need for a related product or service can be predicted to occur in conjunction with these events. For example, a new parent will frequently be sent promotions for various baby care products, furniture, and parenting publications. New home buyers are good prospects for lawn and garden tools, major appliances, and repair/renovation services. *See also* DEMOGRAPHICS; PSYCHOGRAPHICS.

**SYNCHROMARKETING** marketing efforts aimed at trying to bring inconsistent or seasonal demand levels in synch with supply levels. Restaurants use early-bird dinner specials to bring in customers during the slow period between normal lunch and dinner hours. Ski resorts promote summer activities and festivals to bring in tourists during the summer months.

**SYNDICATE**
1. sell or distribute a television program or series to one or more local stations. Syndicated programs include reruns of former network presentations, made-for-TV movies, and film presentations.
2. group of newspapers, such as the Hearst chain, owned or managed by the same person or company.
3. sell or distribute a newspaper SUPPLEMENT or feature column to a number of publications for release at the same time.
4. offer for sale the findings of a research company. Syndicated research services conduct research in the areas of consumer and product information, broadcast audience composition, magazine and newspaper readership, and product usage, and then sell their results to various clients on a subscription basis.
5. sell or distribute MAILING LISTS. (Syndicated mailings are used by a company that will prepare letters, brochures, and pamphlets about its products and then turn over these materials to another company that specializes in mailing materials to prospects from its own prepared lists.)
6. sell or distribute artwork to advertisers, advertising agencies, or others who use artwork in their advertising; a syndicated art service.

**SYNDICATION** *see* SYNDICATE.

**SYNECTICS** idea-generating technique, similar to BRAINSTORMING, where the discussion is centered around a general idea that is related to a problem, rather than the problem itself (as in brainstorming); also called *blue sky*. Synectics is often used by the creative department of an advertising agency when designing an advertising campaign.

The method is based on four concepts: (1) the identification of a specific leader, (2) the knowledge of a common understanding of the problem or situation, (3) the common belief that all ideas have some good qualities, and (4) the equal importance of all participants and their ideas.

# T

**TABLE LOOKUP** step in a manual process or a COMPUTER PROGRAM that involves matching a value (number or word) to another value in a list of paired values and following a prescribed action as dictated by the matched pair. For example, when you look up a telephone number in a directory, you are performing a table lookup. In this case, the person you want to call is the value that you match against a name in the directory. The telephone number is the value paired to the name, and the action is to call that telephone number. The process is the same in a computer environment except that the table is stored electronically rather than on paper.

A table lookup can be used to assign a particular edition of a magazine or catalog to a customer based on his address. For example, in the table that follows, a range of three-digit ZIP code prefixes is paired with various editions of a catalog. The ZIP code in a new customer address is then matched against the prefixes in the table, and the appropriate edition is assigned. For example, a customer living in the 06905 area would be assigned the Northeastern edition.

| | |
|---|---|
| 010-196 | Northeastern |
| 197-339 | Southeastern |
| 350-884 | Regular |
| 890-999 | Western |

**TABLOID** newspaper with a page size smaller than that of the standard newspaper. Approximate page dimensions are 14" deep by 10" to 12" wide, with five or six columns each 2" wide. A tabloid typically contains news in condensed form, with a great many photographs—for example, the NEW YORK DAILY NEWS. A tabloid has the appearance of an unbound magazine and is sold flat, rather than folded in half, as is the standard-size newspaper.

**TACK** property of ink describing its stickiness as measured by an INKOMETER. Tack controls the amount of force necessary to press an inked surface, such as a print BLANKET or PLATE, against another surface, such as paper, to transfer ink and then to separate the surfaces. Ink with too much tack damages the paper surface. Tack control is especially important in OVERPRINTING (layering printed images onto the same sheet), which requires the bottom-layer ink to have the greatest degree of tack and each sucessive layer to have less tack. Generally, the faster the PRINTING PRESS used, the less tack the ink should have.

**TACKOSCOPE** *see* INKOMETER.

**TAG**

1. card used as a supplement to advertising that is hung from a product. It may identify the manufacturer; give care instructions for the product; explain additional features; list the materials from which the product is made; tell the size, price, style, or color of the product; or bear the product guarantee.
2. short announcement, that may almost seem an afterthought, made at the end of a broadcast program or commercial.
3. *see* DEALER TAG.

**TAG LINE** closing line of a program intended to emphasize the dramatic or humorous intent of the preceding dialogue.

**TAKE**

1. variation of SHOT.
2. turn off a video source by the director's command, as in "Take one."
3. individual scene or pose used in the final print of a film, program, or commercial. Every scene is assigned a take number as it is being shot, which is later used to locate the scene for editing or screening. The take number usually agrees with the number of times the scene has been shot before the director feels that it is the way it should be.
4. in retailing, amount of money in the cash register(s) of a retail outlet at the close of business on a given day.

**TAKE-ONE** transit advertising display in which a pad or envelope containing additional information and a return request form is attached to a CAR CARD for transit system riders to take. A take-one car card may be the same size as a standard car card (11" × 14", 11" × 28") but is die cut to hold the pad or envelope. Usually, the advertising space for take-ones is offered by the transit system at additional charge, to cover maintenance.

**TAKE-UP REEL** blank reel used in conjunction with a reel of film or audio tape in a projection or playback system. The take-up reel actually pulls the tape through the system and holds the film or audio tape that has already been played.

**TALENT CHARGE** price paid to actors used in a broadcast commercial or program. *See also* BUYOUT; RESIDUAL.

**TALENT PAYMENT** *see* RESIDUAL.

**TALK SHOW** broadcast show with a format arranged around interviews conducted by a host. The interviewees may be celebrities, or members of the viewing or listening audience. NBC's *Tonight Show* is a familiar example of a television talk show.

**TALLY RECORDS** group of duplicate computer file RECORDS used in computer counts and containing a portion of the information in the original records. Tally records are created for the purpose of generating computer counts without using as much computer time and memory as would be required if the complete record were used. For example, the FIELDS in a tally record for a direct-mail promotion might include customer name, LIST of origin, PACKAGE sent to that customer, and ZIP code. Counts can then be produced by list, package, or ZIP code. Tally records are usually created during a MERGE/PURGE. *See also* STRIP RECORD.

**TAPE**
1. strip of magnetized plastic used in the recording of audio signals (audio tape) and video signals (videotape).
2. record on audio or video tape.
3. casual reference to a cash register receipt.

**TAPE COPY** process of creating a duplicate MAGNETIC TAPE file. Tape copies are made to prevent the loss of data due to damage, loss, or theft of the MASTER copy or to transfer data from one computer system to another, such as for a subscription file CONVERSION or a LIST RENTAL.

**TAPE DRIVE** computer HARDWARE device used to read MAGNETIC TAPE data and transfer it to the CENTRAL PROCESSING UNIT (CPU), or to write magnetic tape data from the CPU onto a magnetic tape.

**TAPE DUMP** HARD-COPY printout of the data on a MAGNETIC TAPE, produced without converting the data to a report format. Tape dumps are usually used as a visual check of the data and format on the tape. *See also* DUMP.

**TAPE ENTRY** method of DATA ENTRY utilizing a MAGNETIC TAPE to input data to a computer system. Tape entry is more efficient and accurate than KEY ENTRY or SCAN ENTRY, because it involves no document handling and no clerical processing that might introduce human error. In direct marketing, tape entry is the preferred means of entering orders to a FULFILLMENT system but is only possible when the orders are prepared for entry by an intermediate organization such as a TELEPHONE AGENCY or SUBSCRIPTION AGENT. Orders received directly from customers are almost always in HARD-COPY form. *See also* TAPE-TO-TAPE.

**TAPE LIBRARY** facility used to store and maintain MAGNETIC TAPES. Tapes are usually stored on racks from which they hang vertically. A serial number and identification information is placed on each tape. Many facilities use computerized systems to assign serial numbers and tape locations. Random assignment can be used to make it more difficult for an intruder to find and steal a particular tape.

**TAPE-TO-TAPE** TAPE ENTRY system that stores on MAGNETIC TAPE the data entered to the system. For example, a direct-marketing firm that stores its customer file on tape might receive new orders on tape from a TELEPHONE AGENCY. Those orders can be added to the marketer's customer file, using tape-to-tape entry. *See also* KEY-TO-DISK; KEY-TO-TAPE.

**TAPE TRANSFER** *see* FILM TRANSFER.

**TARGET AUDIENCE**  audience to whom the advertising is directed. The target audience is defined in terms of DEMOGRAPHIC (and sometimes PSYCHOGRAPHIC) characteristics, such as age, sex, education, income, buying habits, and the like.

**TARGET GROUP INDEX (TGI)**  syndicated reports published by the Axiom Market Research Bureau that detail information about national broadcast or magazine audiences. TGI is offered to interested parties by subscription. It is used by MEDIA PLANNERS to help identify the national media sources for heavy and light users of a product or brand, and to select media that offer the largest audience of HEAVY USERS.

**TARGET MARKET**  group of persons for whom a firm creates and maintains a PRODUCT MIX that specifically fits the needs and preferences of that group. For example, the furniture market can be divided into segments described as Early American, contemporary, or traditional. A marketer may choose to target the entire furniture market with the generalized product, promotion, distribution, and pricing strategy meant to appeal to everyone, or may go after one segment of the furniture market with a customized strategy or several segments of the furniture market with more than one strategy.

Market segments can be defined in several other ways besides product types—for example, consumer types, CHANNELS OF DISTRIBUTION, or price levels. Consumer market segments are defined in terms of geographic (place of purchase or use), DEMOGRAPHIC (age, income, occupation of consumer), and PSYCHOGRAPHIC (buying motives, product usage level, LIFE-STYLE) criteria.

Selecting a TARGET MARKET segment for a product rather than attempting to sell to the entire market can be a more efficient use of promotion dollars, because a greater MARKET SHARE can be achieved by capturing most or all of a segment via a carefully directed marketing plan that reaches precisely the right people with the right message than by trying to capture market share with a generic approach. It is also a better use of production resources if they can be concentrated on a single product and/or package, thus experiencing economies of scale. For example, a factory that only makes metal bed frames can operate with less equipment, expertise, and materials than a similar size company that makes metal bed frames, sofa beds, dining room tables, and office furniture.

Target marketing makes better use of distribution dollars as well, enabling marketers to concentrate on developing working relationships with department-store chains or on developing a business-to-business sales force, but not both.

**TARGET MARKETING** choosing a market and developing a product for that market. *See also* MARKET TARGETING; TARGET MARKET.

**TARGET PRICING** pricing method whereby the selling price of a product is calculated to produce a particular rate of return on investment for a specific volume of production. The target pricing method is used most often by public utilities, like electric and gas companies, and companies whose capital investment is high, like automobile manufacturers. Essentially, the selling price is calculated according to the following formula:

$$\text{Selling price} = \frac{\text{investment costs} \times \text{target return (\%)}}{\text{\# of units to be produced}} + \text{unit cost}$$

Target pricing is not useful for companies whose capital investment is low because, according to this formula, the selling price will be understated. Also the target pricing method is not keyed to the demand for the product, and if the entire volume is not sold, a company might sustain an overall budgetary loss on the product.

**TARGET-PROFIT PRICING** *see* TARGET PRICING.

**TARGET-RETURN PRICING** *see* TARGET PRICING.

**TEAR SHEET** page clipped from a newspaper or magazine and sent to the advertiser or advertising agency as proof that an ad was inserted as ordered. Generally, a tear sheet accompanies the invoice for the advertisement, as many advertisers will not pay their bill without evidence that the ad ran as ordered. *See also* ADVERTISING CHECKING BUREAU; CHECKING COPY.

**TEASER AD** brief advertisement designed to tease the public by offering only bits of information without revealing either the sponsor of the ad or the product being advertised. Teaser ads are the frontrunners of an advertising campaign, and their purpose is to arouse curiosity and get attention for the campaign that follows. In order for a teaser campaign to be effective, the ads must have great visibility in print, broadcast, and OUT-OF-HOME media so as to reach a great many people. Teaser ads are often used in the introduction of a major motion picture or a new product.

**TEASER COPY** *see* CORNER CARD.

**TECHNOLOGICAL ENVIRONMENT** see MACROENVIRONMENT.

**TELECOLLECTIONS** use of outbound telemarketing to contact debtors and collect debts. Some marketers have found that a telecollections effort in place of a mailed invoice during the normal billing cycle is a strong payment incentive. Other marketers use telecollections at the end of their regular mailed billing series. Because telecollections are often perceived to be a "strong-arm" tactic, telecollection calls early in the billing cycle have to be carefully scripted to avoid antagonizing good customers.

**TELEMARKETING** use of the telephone as an interactive medium for promotion or promotion response; also know as *teleselling*. Telemarketing, a response vehicle, includes receiving orders, inquiries, and donation pledges in response to print and broadcast advertising, catalogs, and direct-mail promotions, and also receiving customer inquiries and complaints. Incoming telephone callers are usually given access to an IN-WATS number but may also call collect or call at their own expense. Outbound telemarketing is used to FOLLOW-UP on inquiries, to sell products or services, to clarify or UPGRADE an order, or to gather information about consumers or other aspects of the market.

Unlike other promotion mediums, outbound telemarketing calls interrupt the consumer by demanding immediate attention and are not identifiable as a promotion before the consumer is interrupted. Therefore, telemarketers must be particularly careful not to antagonize the consumer. For example, calls should not be made at inconvenient hours such as dinnertime or early morning. A carefully written script should be utilized by every caller to get the most value from the time and money spent on each call and to avoid angering or annoying the person receiving the call. Some elaborate calling scripts include answers to every objection a prospective buyer might mention. In contrast, a few telemarketers have utilized a prerecorded message rather than a "live" caller; the consumer can respond to the recording by pressing numbers on a touch-tone telephone dial. Telephone numbers can be dialed at random by a computer that relays the call to an operator when a contact is made. Calls are frequently made to preselected individuals such as current or prior customers or likely prospects selected from a rented list.

Telemarketing is used heavily by business-to-business marketers to identify QUALIFIED LEADS, avoiding travel and other costs associated with personal sales calls. One telemarketing call can cost four times as much as a direct-mail piece but can generate as much as two to six times the response. The success of a telemarketing program is measured in terms of contacts made (reaching the right person), attempts made (calls that do not reach the right person, busy signals, or no-answers), and CONVERSIONS (completed sales, surveys, etc.).

The DIRECT MARKETING ASSOCIATION has established guidelines for telemarketing, concerning issues such as calling hours, use of unlisted telephone numbers, and recording of conversations. *See also* TELEPHONE AGENCY.

**TELEPHONE AGENCY** business that makes and/or receives TELEMARKETING calls for another organization or individual. Telephone agents frequently specialize in either incoming or outbound calls and in either consumer or business products and services. Telephone agencies are usually paid on a commission basis as some percentage (usually 15%) of the gross or NET revenue generated, or they may be paid a fee based on the number of calls, contacts, or completed calls made. Agencies paid on a net basis usually take responsibility for collecting payments from the buyers. A telephone agent will generally work with its clients to develop a script to be followed by each caller that fulfills the objectives of, and represents the style of, each client.

**TELEPHONE AUCTION** fund-raising campaign technique pioneered by local public television stations. Donated merchandise and services are displayed to the television viewing audience. Viewers can then contact the station by telephone to bid on the items. The highest bid is accepted, with all proceeds going to the television station.

**TELEPHONE CONSUMER PROTECTION ACT** 1991 rules and regulations enforced by the Federal Communications Commission concerning the use of AUTOMATIC DIALERS, prerecorded telemarketing messages, unsolicited facsimile transmission advertising, and other telephone marketing techniques. The TCPA protects the rights of residential consumers to restrict unwanted telephone solicitations. Tax-exempt, nonprofit organizations, and marketers who have an established business relationship with the consumer are exempted from the regulations. TCPA regulations concerning automatic dialers restrict access to emergency and medical office/facility numbers. Prerecorded calls to residences are prohibited with some exceptions. When a prerecorded message is used, the caller must be identified at the beginning of the recording. Rules were also established by the TCPA for calling hours (8:00 A.M.–9:00 P.M.) and the maintenance of do-not-call lists as requested by consumers. Direct marketers supported the passage of the act because it allows them to maintain individual do-not-call lists rather than requiring them to purchase access to a federally controlled list.

**TELEPROMPTER** instrument used in television production, in place of CUE CARDS, that works as a prompter for the on-camera performers. The TelePrompTer is usually mounted on the camera and uses either a closed-circuit television receiver or a long roll of paper with the dialogue imprinted in large letters to display the script to the performers.

**TELESELLING** *see* TELEMARKETING.

**TELETEXT** system for broadcasting text information. A teletext system usually consists of a television and a KEYBOARD. By hitting a key, the viewer can select and view a specific text item from those available. Teletext is used to broadcast stock quotes, news, weather, sports results, and so forth. Teletext systems are not capable of broadcasting charts, illustrations, or other pictorial images. *See also* ELECTRONIC CATALOG; VIDEOTEX.

**TELETHON** *see* MEGATHON.

**TELETYPE (TELEX, TWX)** machine capable of delivering and receiving typewritten messages to or from other places having a Teletype terminal. The Teletype system is a worldwide network and is available through a subscription service. More than 200,000 businesses in the United States, Canada, and Mexico have Telex terminals on their premises, and there are more than 1.5 million subscribers throughout the world. Subscribers from one network can communicate with subscribers from any other network through the use of Telex numbers. Western Union is one of the companies offering a Telex subscriber network.

**TELEVISION (TV)** medium of communication that operates through the transmission of images and sounds over a wire or through space by means of an electronic system that converts light and sound into electrical waves and then reconverts them into visible images and audible sounds. Television was first broadcast to the public in 1941 and has grown rapidly ever since. In the top 50 geographic television markets in the United States, households with televisions increased from 6 million in 1950 to 40 million in 1970, and to almost 60 million in 1986.

In its first decade, television proved to be extremely powerful in its ability to sell concepts, ideas, goods, and services to the public. During this time, entire shows were sponsored by advertisers whose names became identified with their shows. For example, the Milton Berle show, which premiered in 1948 and dominated the ratings for years, was identified with Texaco products, and was, in fact, titled "Texaco Star Theater." As the industry developed, new avenues for television station revenue were opened up through the sale of commercial time.

As an advertising medium, television is the youngest and has grown faster than any other in history. No other medium has the unique creative capabilities of television. The combination of sight, sound, and movement, the opportunities for demonstration and the believability of seeing something happen right before one's eyes, the potential for special effects—all these have contributed to television's successful impact. Television, the second largest advertising medium in terms of total dollars spent by advertisers, also attracts the largest volume of national advertising, more than $11 billion in 1984. *See also* CABLE TELEVISION.

**TELEVISION HOUSEHOLD** standard of measurement used by audience rating companies; a home with at least one television set. *See also* HOUSEHOLDS USING TELEVISION.

**TELEVISION SUPPORT** advertisement broadcast on television to serve as a secondary part of a MULTIMEDIA campaign. For example, the television medium is sometimes used to announce a newspaper INSERT and/or to remind the viewer to read the insert. The insert will contain detailed information on the product or promotion not provided in the television broadcast and may include a REPLY FORM. Television-support advertisements are usually broadcast in specific areas that correspond with the locations where the newspaper insert will be distributed. *See also* SPOT TELEVISION.

**TELEX** *see* TELETYPE.

**TEMPORARY CHANGE OF ADDRESS** request from customers that the mailing or billing address in their RECORD be changed for a temporary period of time. Temporary changes of address are frequently used by college students who live off-campus between semesters and by people with vacation homes or summer houses. These address changes present a problem for the FULFILLMENT system if it cannot automatically start and stop a temporary address change. Most systems are equipped to handle only one address at a time and cannot store a second address for later use.

**:10** scriptwriter notation for 10 seconds, often used to indicate a 10-second broadcast commercial.

**TENT CARD** card used for the display of an advertisement. A tent card is imprinted and folded so that it is readable on either side of the fold and can stand free on a table top, counter, or other flat surface. Often, tent cards are used in restaurants to advertise the specials or a new wine or liquor that patrons may wish to try.

**TERM**
1. duration of a subscription, continuity, membership, or other agreement, usually expressed in terms of a number of months, issues, cycles, or years. Long-term agreements are valued by sellers, because these agreements postpone the costs and risks associated with renewing or replacing a customer. Buyers prefer long-term agreements in an inflationary market, because they prevent the seller from raising the price for the term of the agreement. In a market with declining prices, buyers prefer short-term agreements, which enable them to renew or replace the product or service at a lower price at the end of the term.
2. condition of an agreement, such as a payment term specifying that all invoices are payable within 30 days.
3. word or phrase that defines a thing, concept, or process, such as the terms in this dictionary.

**TERMINAL** *see* VIDEO DISPLAY TERMINAL.

**TEST**
**In general:** means used to evaluate the behavior of a person, the characteristics of a person or thing, or the effect of an action. Tests require a method and scale of measurement and a controlled environment in which to observe or measure. For example, to test a light bulb, the method used might be to place it in a lamp that is plugged into a socket and turned on. The scale of measurement relates to the increase in light

seen coming from the light bulb. The control involves using a lamp that works, has access to electricity, and is visible to the observer.

**Advertising:** introduction of a new product or promotion on a small scale to measure consumer response. Testing of this nature is usually limited to consumer marketing. In business-to-business marketing, reactions are usually gathered through PERSONAL INTERVIEWS conducted before a product is introduced to the market. A product test may include the initial in-factory assessment of the product, a small test by a group of potential users, and, finally, a MARKET TEST, which is a simulation of a national launch.

The design of an effective market test includes decisions regarding where to test, how long to test, and what to do in response to test results. A test location is generally chosen based upon the presence of demand for that product and the degree to which consumers in that location/city are representative of the total market. The duration of the test depends upon the money budgeted, the length of time it usually takes for a consumer to make a second purchase (or first purchase if the test sample was free), and the probability of a competitor's entering the market. *See also* TEST MARKET.

**Direct marketing:** evaluation of one or more elements of a marketing strategy or promotion on a small scale prior to full-scale introduction. Tests usually consist of a standard element called the CONTROL (such as a control package or offer, etc.) and a test element. The control represents the PACKAGE that has outperformed every other package used to date. The objective of the test package is to assess its ability to beat the control. The control and the test are sent to SAMPLE groups of prospects or customers selected using a statistical SAMPLING technique. The validity of a test is dependent upon the degree to which the sample selected is representative of the promotion UNIVERSE.

The elements most frequently tested are product, OFFER, LIST, COPY, and package; however, virtually every aspect of a direct-marketing promotion gets tested at one time or another, from the tilt of the address label to the taste of the glue on the reply envelope.

Direct marketing is uniquely well-suited to testing, because the results of a promotion change are easily measured in terms of RESPONSE. Most direct marketers include a test of some sort in every mailing or promotion they do. One basic rule of testing is that only one element at a time should be changed, so that a difference in response can be clearly attributed to that change. It is commonly understood that what doesn't work for one marketer might work for another; therefore, the results of a test should not be universally applied across all marketers. *See also* A-B SPLIT; DRY-TESTING; KEY CODE; NTH NAME SELECTION; PANEL; PYRAMIDING; ROLLOUT; RULE OF 300.

**TESTIMONIAL ADVERTISING** advertising copy approach using an individual who has tried a product and been satisfied with it to favorably endorse the product. The endorsement may be in the form of a statement or a letter, and the individual may be a well-known personality, such as an actor or athlete, or a satisfied customer appearing as an impartial "person in the street." The idea behind testimonial advertising is that a prospective customer may be favorably influenced to try a product when it has been praised by another impartial consumer, or by a known personality whom the consumer may wish to emulate.

**TEST MARKET** geographic location selected for the introduction of a new product, new advertising campaign, or both. The use of a test market allows the advertiser or manufacturer to evaluate the product performance on a small scale, and to evaluate the MARKETING PLAN for the product before embarking on a national introduction of the product. The test market location generally includes an area that has at its center at least one city that is the heart of all commercial and media activity, as well as the surrounding counties that are served by the city. The introduction of a product or campaign in a test market is the final step in the testing process and allows the manufacturer or advertiser to evaluate all the components of the advertising and marketing strategy.

**TEST MARKETING** one of the final stages in NEW PRODUCT DEVELOPMENT, where the product and the marketing program are introduced on a small scale into one or more selected cities or market areas. Test marketing provides the marketer the opportunity to observe consumer behavior toward the product in a real market situation, gain experience with the marketing program, and assess potential problem areas before launching a full-scale product introduction. Test marketing provides a great deal of information about the future success of the product and is often used to make profit and SALES FORECASTS.

**TEST PANEL** *see* PANEL.

**TEST TAPE** MAGNETIC TAPE produced by a computer system, consisting of a sample of the data on a system file, in order to test whether the data can be read, analyzed, or processed by another computer system. A test tape is usually generated when a computer FILE will be converted to a new system. A test tape may also be used when a SUBSCRIPTION AGENT or TELEPHONE AGENCY is preparing to submit orders on magnetic tape to its client's FULFILLMENT system. A test tape may also be used prior to a MERGE/PURGE of several LIST RENTAL tapes, to verify that the merge/purge system can read and process all the tapes. *See also* CONVERSION.

**TEXT**
1. wording in an advertisement, brochure, or other printed document. Generally, the more complex a purchase decision is, the more effective text can be in an advertisement. For example, the more information an advertiser provides about the features of a videocassette

recorder, the better; but, for an item like ice cream, informational text is less persuasive. *See also* BODY COPY.
2. class of type, including roman, italic, script, gothic, and text.

## THEME
1. primary topic, subject, or idea around which an advertising campaign, book, motion picture, television show, recording, or the like is organized. In an advertising campaign, the theme is most likely to be a product feature or a sales point that will have maximum impression on the intended prospective consumers.
2. recurring melody that characterizes a personality, television show, movie, radio broadcast, or theatrical presentation. *See also* SIGNATURE.

**THERMO-MECHANICAL PULP** steam-treated GROUNDWOOD PULP used to make a more durable newsprint than ordinary groundwood pulp.

**THINNER** liquid, such as turpentine, added to paint to make the paint more fluid. Thinners may also be added to ink, glue, or the like, for the same purpose.

**THIRD CLASS** mail delivery service provided by the U.S. Postal Service for BULK MAIL such as CATALOGS and other direct-mail promotions weighing less than one pound. It is the primary class of mail used by direct marketers. Special discounted postage rates are available for bulk third-class mailings meeting certain quantity (200 pieces or 50 pounds minimum) and PRESORT requirements. A different rate structure applies to nonprofit bulk mailers. Third-class mail may be prepared in SACKS or PALLETS. The mandatory CONSOLIDATION-LEVEL requirements apply to 125 or more pieces or 15 pounds going to the same FIVE-DIGIT ZIP CODE, THREE-DIGIT ZIP CODE prefix, STATE, and MIXED STATES destinations. FIRST-CLASS and SECOND-CLASS mail receive a higher priority service than third-class mail. Mailers must have a permit (*see* INDICIA) to send mail third class.

**THIRD COVER** *see* INSIDE BACK COVER.

**THIRD-PARTY SALE** sale made by an agency acting as an intermediary between a buyer and a seller. *See also* LIST BROKER; SUBSCRIPTION AGENT.

## THIRTY
1. symbol used by newscasters and newspaper editors to indicate the end of a news broadcast or article. It is written as -30-.
2. *see* COMMERCIAL.

**:30** scriptwriter notation for 30 seconds, often used to indicate a 30-second broadcast commercial.

**30-DAY DELAYED DELIVERY RULE** Federal Trade Commission rule, usually referred to as the Thirty-Day Rule, stating that if mail order goods will not be delivered within the time promised, or within

30 days of receipt of a properly completed order if no time frame was specified, the buyer must be given the option of canceling for a full refund. The seller must notify the buyer that delivery will not be made within 30 days and must provide the buyer with a means, such as a postpaid postcard, to cancel the order or to extend the time for shipment. If the order is not canceled, the seller has another 30 days to deliver the merchandise. Failure to deliver within that 30-day period requires reconfirmation of the order by the buyer. In addition, sellers are prohibited from making delivery commitments, other than 30 days, that they aren't reasonably likely to meet. For magazines, delivery refers to shipment of the first issue only. The 30-day period on credit subscriptions does not begin until the first bill is mailed. The rule does not apply to photofinishers, sellers of seeds or plants, COD sales, and NEGATIVE OPTION sales.

**THIRTY-DAY RULE**  *see* 30-DAY DELAYED DELIVERY RULE.

**THIRTY-FIVE MILLIMETER (35MM)**
   **1.** 2" × 2" slides used in a slide chain (35mm slide projection).
   **2.** film format used in the production of most motion pictures. It is also used in the production of network television shows and for some nationally produced commercials. However, only the networks and the largest television stations are equipped to project 35mm film; therefore, it is rarely used in other television productions. Thirty-five millimeter film has a running and projection speed of 90' per minute, 24 frames per second. Because of its size, the film produces exceptionally beautiful pictures.
   **3.** print film used in 35mm cameras.

**THREE-DIGIT SACK**  presorted mail, destined for an area designated by a common THREE-DIGIT ZIP CODE prefix, that is delivered to the U.S. Postal Service in canvas mail SACKS. This PRESORT level is required by the USPS for SECOND-CLASS and THIRD-CLASS mail; however, it applies only to three-digit prefixes representing an area comprised of two or more cities. It does not refer to three-digit ZIP code prefixes that identify one particular city (*see* UNIQUE THREE-DIGIT CITY).

   In second class, 6 or more pieces with the same three-digit ZIP must be made into a PACKAGE, and 4 or more packages must be sacked, but the sack may contain fewer than 4 packages. In third class, 10 or more pieces must be packaged, and 12 or more packages must be sacked. *See also* UNIQUE THREE-DIGIT CITY.

**THREE-DIGIT ZIP CODE**  first three digits of a ZIP code, which designate either a SECTIONAL CENTER FACILITY or a main post office; also called ZIP *code prefix*. The numbers range from East to West, starting with 010-027 in Massachusetts and ending with 995-999 in Alaska. *See also* FIVE-DIGIT ZIP CODE; NATIONAL ZIP CODE AREA; THREE-DIGIT SACK.

**3541 FORM**  U.S. Postal Service form used by mailers to compute the postage due on second-class mailings (magazines, newspapers). It is sent to a USPS office that will be receiving some of the mailing for final distribution. The amount due is based upon the weight of that issue of the periodical, the proportion of the weight made up by advertising, the number of copies mailed, the distance the mail must travel, and the level to which it has been presorted (*see* PRESORT) prior to entering the postal system.

**3579 FORM** form used by the U.S. Postal Service on second-class mail to inform the mailer the addressee has moved. If the new address is known, it will be noted on the 3579 form. Mailers with the ability to process address changes in MAGNETIC TAPE format can opt to utilize the USPS ADDRESS CHANGE SERVICE in lieu of receiving 3579 forms. *See also* NATIONAL CHANGE OF ADDRESS.

**THREE-SHEET POSTER** BILLBOARD used in OUTDOOR ADVERTISING and TRANSIT ADVERTISING. A three-sheet poster measures 80" to 84" high by 40" to 43" wide and is displayed on panels on subway platforms, in bus shelters, or at ground-level locations on the outside of retail outlets. The primary purpose of three-sheet poster advertising is to attract pedestrian traffic.

**THREE-TIER PRESORT** three levels at which THIRD-CLASS mail may be presorted. The levels are called basic, FIVE-DIGIT, and CARRIER ROUTE, and they correspond with different PRESORT postage discounts. Basic is the lowest level of presort, for which there is no discount. Five-digit and carrier-route presort levels both offer a discount, with carrier route offering the highest because it is also the most precise level of presort, thus saving the U.S. Postal Service considerable handling expense. Both basic and five-digit have mandatory and optional presort levels, but a presort for carrier route is optional.

The basic presort level includes three-digit, SECTIONAL CENTER FACILITY, STATE DISTRIBUTION CENTER, STATE, MIXED STATES, CITY, and UNIQUE THREE-DIGIT CITY. The five-digit level includes five-digit zip and mixed directs (pieces going to the same five-digit zip within a unique three-digit city). The carrier-route level includes carrier-route-sorted mail and FIRM PACKAGES.

Similar presort levels of mail are required for SECOND-CLASS mail and are referred to as levels A, B, and C.

**THROUGHPUT** processing speed of a machine measured by the user in terms of the amount of output it produces under normal operating conditions in a set period of time (usually one hour). It differs from the manufacturer's rated speed of the machine, which defines the output capabilities under optimum conditions. Throughput speed allows for operator-caused delays and other irregularities in actual processing and is a better measure of the time needed to complete a job. For example, a mail-opening machine may have a rated speed of 1000 envelopes per hour but may have a throughput of only 800 per hour due to paper jams, incompletely opened envelopes, time needed for the operator to remove the envelope contents, and so forth. Computers generally have high throughput rates, because they can process several jobs simultaneously.

**THROUGH-THE-BOOK METHOD** research method used by Simmons Market Research Bureau, Inc. to tabulate the actual readers of an issue of a publication. In a personal one-on-one interview, respondents who have declared themselves to be readers of a particular issue of a magazine are taken through the magazine and asked questions about the various articles. Upon completion of this close examination of the book, the respondent is then asked if he/she is sure that he/she read the magazine. After this rather burdensome process, only those who answer yes are counted as readers of the issue. The timing on the through-the-book technique is important because, if testing is done too soon after publication, later readers of the issue will be missed. However, if it is done too late, a forgetting factor will apply. Simmons Market Research Bureau conducts through-the-book interviews with a sample of approximately 15,000 people each year, for all the issues of approximately 40 to 50 magazines.

**THROWAWAY** *see* HANDBILL.

**THUMBNAIL** small rough sketch of a proposed advertising LAYOUT that is used to try out various arrangements of the elements that may appear in the advertisement. *See also* ESQUISSE.

**TIEBREAKER** digit randomly added to a MATCHCODE to prevent duplication; also called *unique character*. Since most matchcodes are derived from various elements of the name and address FIELDS in a RECORD, it is possible to create a duplicate. However, it is highly unlikely that the same tiebreaker would be randomly assigned to two such similar matchcodes. For example, without a tiebreaker, a matchcode consisting only of the first, third, and fourth characters of the last name, the first three characters of the street address, and the ZIP code would be identical for the following individuals (the matchcode here is CHE12E10017; the tiebreakers are 8 and 3):

Samuel Cohen 12 E 12th Street, New York 10017=CHE12E100178
Winston Cahern 12 E. Edwards Ave., New York 10017= CHE12E100173

    *See also* CHECK DIGIT.

**TIE-IN ADVERTISEMENT** print advertisement that relates to other advertising. A tie-in advertisement may be run by a retail store owner in conjunction with a manufacturer's advertisement for a product carried in the store. It may also be an advertisement for several different products (involving several different manufacturers) that ties in with a local sales promotion. A tie-in advertisement is paid for by the retailer who sponsors it.

**TIE-IN PROMOTION** special marketing displays and gimmicks that relate to an ongoing advertising campaign. A tie-in promotion will carry the same basic theme as the campaign and may be in the form of a SWEEPSTAKES offering, a POINT-OF-PURCHASE ADVERTISING display, a PREMIUM giveaway, or anything else that will create immediate sales, help to introduce a product, or otherwise enhance the advertising campaign.

**TIER** person or machine that ties mail or finished print products into bundles, using string, rubber bands, or plastic strips, for easier handling.

**TIGHT CLOSE-UP** *see* CLOSE-UP.

**TILL-FORBID** standing order for goods or services, such as a request to run an advertisement in a space or time slot, until told to stop. Many advertisers utilize till-forbid agreements to reserve space or time uniquely well suited to their advertising message, such as the BOOK CLUB advertisements on the back page of the *New York Times Review of Books*. *See also* AUTOMATIC RENEWAL; CONTINUITY; NEGATIVE OPTION.

**TILT SHOT** camera angle that looks up or down at the object being photographed, instead of being on the same level. Tilt shots are usually more dramatic than straight-angle shots. A downward tilt shot is used to observe action over a large area such as a football field; to create a kaleidoscope effect, such as that achieved when looking down at the movements of a water ballet; or to create a psychological impression of inferiority or weakness—for example, by looking down at a small child. Conversely, an upward tilt shot lends an impression of superiority, awe, or size—for example, by looking up at the "Jolly Green Giant" or the spires of a cathedral. *See also* ANGLE SHOT.

**TIME BUYER** *see* MEDIA BUYER.

**TIME-SERIES ANALYSIS** stage in preparing a SALES FORECAST in which the past performance of the product is analyzed in order to predict future sales. In some situations the time-series analysis is considered sufficient for the sales forecast.

**TIME-SHARING**
1. shared use of a MAINFRAME computer by various individuals or organizations who do not have the need or resources to own and operate their own computer. The mainframe is usually accessed via a REMOTE terminal—that is, a terminal in a separate location from the mainframe, typically located in the user's office. Time-sharing is made possible by the computer's ability to process several jobs simultaneously. The fee for a time-sharing service is usually based upon some combination of a flat fee for the service, a variable fee for the number of times the computer is accessed, and a variable fee for the duration of each access. *See also* CPU TIME.

   **2.** real estate sales agreement in which the buyer contracts for ownership of a property during a specified portion of each year.
   Timesharing is commonly used to sell vacation and resort
   properties.

**TIME SIGNAL** in broadcast, a public service announcement of the
exact time, sometimes accompanied by a buzzer, beep, bell, or other
sound that signals the exact moment of the time. Some stations will
offer the time signal for sponsorship by an advertiser. In that case, the
time would be announced and an announcement would be made that
the time signal was "brought to you by XYZ Company" followed
by a TAG LINE or slogan that represents the company.

**TIME SLOT** in broadcast, a period of time slated for a particular program or commercial.

**TINT PLATE** printing surface used for printing a light, flat color (even
area without texture, design, or gloss). A tint plate may be used to add
a touch of color to the background of a one-color reproduction. It may
also be used when the copy calls for a prominent area of color in the
reproduction.

**TINTS**
   **1.** different colors derived from a single color, such as powder blue
   from blue or rose from red, that are created by varying the amount
   of white mixed into the color or showing through the color. Ink
   color charts, which are used to order color printing, provide samples of various standard tints, with quantified strengths of color,
   such as 50% or 25% of full color. The charts include tints composed
   of one primary color or combinations of two PRIMARY COLORS.
   **2.** lithographic printing problem that occurs when the FOUNTAIN SOLU-
   TION and the ink form an emulsion (oil- and water-based solution),
   causing the nonimage areas of the plate to pick up a small amount
   of ink that will lightly color (tint) the paper.

**TIP-IN** insert placed in a publication, such as an extra page of advertising or a subscription return card.

**TIP-ON** item attached with SPOT GLUE or a glue strip to a promotion
piece or to a page in a catalog, magazine, or book. Examples of tip-ons
are REPLY FORMS, product samples, CENTS-OFF COUPONS, or subscription renewal notices. Tip-ons are frequently confused with TIP-INS,
which become an integral part of the bound product, requiring more
complex application devices.
   When renewal notices, which usually mail THIRD CLASS, are tipped
onto magazine covers in lieu of an address label, care must be taken
to PRESORT the renewal documents in accordance with SECOND-CLASS
regulations, so that the magazines can be mailed second class.
RENEWAL PROMOTIONS are often used as EXPIRE issue tip-ons, with COPY
that clearly announces this is the last issue. *See also* TIPPING.

**TIPPING** process of attaching a TIP-ON or TIP-IN to a page in a magazine, catalog, or book. There are two types of tipping; outside and inside. Outside tipping involves attaching the item to the beginning or end of a SIGNATURE. Inside tipping involves attaching the item to the inside of a signature. Outside tipping is less costly because it can be done by machine. Inside tipping must be done by hand.

**TISSUE OVERLAY** *see* LAYOUT PAPER.

**TITLE**

1. name of a specific publication or film or, generically, any publication or film, such as the titles carried by a NEWSSTAND or by a film distributor.
2. prefix used before or suffix used after an individual's name to properly address the individual according to standards of etiquette, such as Mr., Miss, Mrs., Jr., Sr., and so forth. *See also* GENDER ANALYSIS.
3. designation for the functional responsibilities of individuals in their occupations, such as sales manager, teacher, president. Titles are used to select from a LIST the best prospects for a DIRECT-MARKETING promotion. Counts by title of the individuals who read a publication are used to characterize that group of readers for potential advertisers. These advertisers can then place advertisements in publications that reach individuals in a position to buy what the advertisers are selling.
4. brief text shown at the beginning or end of a film or television program, such as the CREDITS indicating who produced the film. A title may be used to identify the primary sponsor/advertiser of a program.
5. ownership of an entity, such as title to a house, or the legal document showing ownership of an entity.
6. caption describing an illustration.

**TOLL-FREE** *see* IN-WATS.

**TOMBSTONE AD** casual reference to an advertisement for a professional individual—such as a doctor, lawyer, or banker—or an organization—such as a banking institution, medical association, or brokerage house—that must meet specific legal requirements and regulations imposed on the industry represented in the advertising. For example, in the securities industry, an advertisement for a public offering of securities, sponsored by an investment banking firm, must follow certain guidelines as outlined by the Securities and Exchange Commission (SEC).

**TONER**

1. pigment used to lend color, OPACITY, or body (VISCOSITY) to ink.
2. chemical used in ELECTROPHOTOGRAPHY (photocopy) machines.

**TONING** *see* CATCHING-UP.

**TOOTH** characteristic of paper with a slightly rough texture, making it more receptive to ink.

**TOP CAP**  *see* PALLET CAP.

**TOP-DOWN PLANNING** strategy used in corporate planning whereby the top management personnel set the goals and control planning activities for all the lower levels of management. Top-down planning provides a consistent direction for the marketing effort. See also BOTTOM-UP PLANNING.

**TOP OF MIND** in advertising research, phrase used to describe the first brand name, product name, or advertising campaign that a respondent mentions in answer to an appropriate question.

**TOTAL AUDIENCE RATING (TA)** percentage of the population in a given geographic area that has viewed a particular television station for a given interval of time, or a specific program on a given station for a minimum of six minutes. Typically, the total audience rating is higher than the AVERAGE AUDIENCE RATING, which is measured on a minute-by-minute basis. *See also* NIELSEN RATING.

**TOTAL MARKET POTENTIAL** calculation of the greatest amount of potential sales of a particular product in that product industry in a specific time period. The total market potential is calculated by multiplying the number of buyers in the market by the quantity purchased by the average buyer, by the price of one unit of the product. For example, if there are one million potential buyers of a particular product in the market and the average buyer buys four units each year at a price of one dollar per unit, the total market potential for that product for the year is one million times four, times one, or four million. Total market potential may be stated in dollars or units.

**TOTAL NET PAID** total purchased copies of an issue of a publication, including subscription circulation and retail sales. The standards for inclusion in the total net paid are determined by the AUDIT BUREAU OF CIRCULATIONS. Issues involved in bulk sales, as well as issues given away at the discretion of the publisher, are not included.

**TOTAL PAID** paid CIRCULATION of an issue of a periodical, including paid subscription copies, newsstand and other single-copy sales, graced copies (*see* GRACE), and other copies considered to be paid according to AUDIT BUREAU OF CIRCULATIONS or BUSINESS PUBLICATIONS AUDIT OF CIRCULATIONS regulations governing paid-copy reporting; also called *total net paid.* The number of total paid copies is used to determine the price of advertising SPACE in the publication, because it measures the size of the AUDIENCE that advertisers can REACH through that publication. Some advertisers also include pass-along circulation (copies read by more than one person) in their calculation of the total available audience. Paid circulation is considered to be worth more to advertisers than nonpaid circulation, since readers actually paid to obtain the periodical.

**TOUCH SCREEN VIDEO** VIDEO SYSTEM whose monitors are designed to allow viewers to touch a designated section on the screen to access information that is then displayed on the screen. Often used by companies who produce electronic catalogues, touch screen video systems are usually located in high pedestrian traffic areas, such as convention centers, railway/bus stations, airports, or shopping malls. If a viewer is interested in knowing more information about a particular product listed in the electronic catalogue, he or she is instructed to touch a portion of the screen and more specific information about the product will be displayed.

**TOWN MARKER** predecessor, currently not in use, to PACKAGE/SACK MARKS that indicated on mailing labels or addressed mailing pieces the beginning or end of that portion of the mailing addressed to the same town. These portions had to be packaged and sacked separately according to the U.S. Postal Service regulations. Today, FIVE-DIGIT ZIP codes and other geographic areas are used in lieu of towns.

## TRACKING

**In general:** monitoring a process or the results of an action.

**Direct marketing:** process involving post-promotion FOLLOW-UP, consisting of tabulating and analyzing the performance of various elements of a promotion CAMPAIGN. Tracking looks at four stages in the life cycle of a promotion: early response, response at the halfway point, final response, and long-term results. Early-response tracking involves FLASH COUNTS and WEIGH COUNTS, which give a quick estimate of gross response. Response at the halfway point is measured in terms of both gross and NET paid response to the promotion as a means of projecting the total expected response, so that budgets and subsequent promotions can be adjusted accordingly and so that production and FULFILLMENT departments can be prepared for the total volume expected. The final analysis looks at NET RESPONSE in terms of the number of cash orders and paid CREDIT ORDERS that were sold without cancellation or returns, and determines the profitability of the campaign. The long-term analysis looks at long-term results, such as whether FIRST-TIME BUYERS created by the promotion have made subsequent purchases from the marketer.

In each of these four stages, various elements of the campaign are tracked separately, such as the different LIST, OFFERS, and PACK-AGES used. Effective tracking is critical to the success of future promotions, because they are designed according to the results of past promotions. Tracking can best be accomplished by assigning KEY CODES to each of the elements to be tracked so that statistical tabulations can be made.

It is this ability to track and measure the results of a promotion that most differentiates direct marketing from advertising. The direct marketer knows, via key codes, who received which promotion and whether that individual ordered, paid, and/or ordered again. A limited amount of tracking is possible in advertising, such as monitoring changes in product sales volumes following an advertising campaign, but the advertiser is not able to clearly and definitely attribute those changes to the advertising campaign.

**Advertising:**

**1.** making an audio recording (*sound track*), by moving a stylus along a track in a record.

**2.** making a film recording (*video track*), by moving the camera along a straight path as on a track.

**Merchandising:** monitoring inventory received, sold, and ordered, to maintain optimum levels.

**TRADE ADVERTISING** consumer-product advertising designed to stimulate wholesalers or retailers to purchase products for resale to their customers. An example of trade advertising would be a Coca-Cola advertisement placed in a TRADE MAGAZINE, such as *Progressive Grocer*, in order to promote Coca-Cola to food store managers. The primary objective of trade advertising is to promote greater distribution of the advertised product. This can be done by opening up new outlets for products or by increasing the volume among present outlets.

**TRADE BOOK** *see* TRADE MAGAZINE.

**TRADE CHARACTER** people, animals, animated characters, objects, or the like that are used in advertising a brand and that come to be identified with the brand, in much the same way that a trademark is identified with a brand. The Keebler Elves for Keebler cookies and the Pillsbury Doughboy for Pillsbury products are examples of trade characters, as is Betty Crocker for General Mills.

**TRADE MAGAZINE** magazine with editorial content of interest only to persons engaged in a particular industry, occupation, or profession; also called *business publication*. A trade magazine may be as wide in scope as manufacturing management or sales, or as narrow in scope as patio-furniture manufacturing or used-car sales. Trade magazines are frequently, but not always, controlled CIRCULATION magazines, because the publishers derive more revenue from selling advertising space that reaches a large audience of targeted readers than by selling single copies or subscriptions to the readers. *See also* BUSINESS PUBLICATIONS AUDIT OF CIRCULATIONS; CONSUMER MAGAZINE.

**TRADEMARK (TM)** identification mark, as defined by the Lanham Trade-Mark Act of 1946 (effective 1947): "names, symbols, titles, designations, character names, slogans, and distinctive features emphasized in advertising . . . " used by manufacturers, advertisers, and merchants to identify products and to distinguish them from competitive products. Registration of trademarks is handled by the United States Patent Office subject to the provisions of the Lanham Trade Mark Act. Under this Act, trademarks are protected from infringement by competitors. Trademarks also protect the public, so that consumers can feel confident that, in purchasing a particular product with a known trademark, they will receive the product they desire. There are three basic types of trademarks: brand names, corporate or store names, and symbols. Some other marks, such as certification marks (that certify quality), service marks (that identify services rather than products), and collective marks (that signify organization membership), are also considered trademarks, since they are essentially identifying marks as well, and these are also protected.

**TRADE MARKETING MIX** elements of the marketing mix that relate to building demand at the MIDDLEMAN (wholesaler, retailer, distributor) level. For example, a marketer might offer special display allowances and promotional support to retailers in exchange for additional display space. Other elements of the trade marketing mix include advertising, personal selling and service, wholesale pricing, and payment/return options. *See also* TRADE ADVERTISING.

**TRADE PROMOTION** marketing techniques used to build demand at the MIDDLEMAN level as part of the TRADE MARKETING MIX. Trade promotions include special pricing and sales incentives, discounted or free display fixtures, trade shows, demonstrations, and no-obligation gifts such as tickets to sporting events or novelties (pens, paperweights, calculators). *See also* TRADE ADVERTISING.

**TRADE RATE** special price offered to retailers by wholesalers, manufacturers, or distributors or by a seller to individuals or organizations in a related industry. For example, some publications offer special trade rates to businesses that will make the publications available to prospects for subscription or single-copy sales; this is commonly done by fashion and beauty magazines, which offer a trade rate to beauty-salon operators who will display the magazines in a reception room. Trade shows and conventions offer special admission rates to business people that might buy from the trade-show exhibitors. A marketer introducing a new product or selling a product in a competitive market might offer a trade rate to individuals with influence on buyers outside the trade. For example, an over-the-counter drug might be sold at a special trade rate to physicians who will dispense it to their patients.

**TRADE SHOW** exhibit of goods and services for the benefit of individuals or companies involved in a particular trade. Generally, a trade show is held in an exhibition hall, and each exhibitor is allowed to rent space to display goods and services. Many trade shows are accompanied by seminars and lectures where the newest trade information can be presented and new trade ideas and concepts may be exchanged. The annual Consumer Electronics Show held for the benefit of those in the consumer electronics industry, as well as those interested in the industry, is an example of a trade show.

**TRAFFIC AUDIT BUREAU (TAB)** nonprofit organization, headquartered in New York City, with a membership composed of advertisers and outdoor advertising plant operators whose primary functions are to conduct research on the number of people who pass outdoor advertising structures, to establish a method for evaluating this traffic, and to measure the potential size of a market.

**TRAFFIC CODE** six-digit code used to represent a customer's city and state of residence. It corresponds with the codes assigned to each city and state in the CITY-STATE MASTER and is used as part of the KEYLINE or MATCHCODE to identify a particular RECORD on a customer FILE.

**TRAFFIC DEPARTMENT** advertising agency department responsible for the coordination of all phases of production. The traffic department keeps track of the various stages of all work so that at any given time the status of a particular job can be determined. This department is also responsible to see that production deadlines are met and that the work is delivered or shipped on schedule, particularly advertisements and commercials that must be received by the media by certain dates in order to be inserted in publications and broadcast schedules.

**TRAILER** section of a computerized customer file RECORD that represents a particular order; also called *contract*. In some file systems, a BASE RECORD, containing information pertinent to each customer (such as name and address), is supplemented by trailers containing information pertinent to each order from that customer, such as SOURCE KEY, product name, quantity, and price and payment status. Trailers accumulate as additional orders are received. In subscription files, trailers accumulate as subscriptions are renewed and are deleted as subscriptions expire.

**TRANSACTION**
**In general:** process performed with a single objective or end result, such as a purchase transaction.
**Computer file maintenance:** process performed against a FILE with the objective of altering the file in some way. The basic file transactions are *adds* (addition of a record), *delete*s (deletion of a record), and *changes* (alteration of the information in a record). These basic transactions may be further defined according to the characteristics of each transaction. For example, an add may be a CASH ORDER, a CREDIT ORDER, a CREDIT-CARD ORDER, or an INSERT-IF-ABSENT transaction. A delete may be an EXPIRE, a cancellation (*see* CANCEL), or a DEADBEAT record. Transaction codes are usually assigned to each transaction to direct the operations of the computer system and to accumulate statistics about the transactions applied to a file.

**TRANSCRIBED PROGRAM** prerecorded radio or television program available for SYNDICATION (meaning that it can be sold to any number of sponsors and stations throughout the country, although, in any one market, it will be sold on an exclusive basis). *See also* SYNDICATE.

**TRANSCRIPTION** *see* ELECTRICAL TRANSCRIPTION.

**TRANSFER CIRCULATION** subscribers to a magazine or periodical who are acquired by another magazine. Subscription lists are sold or given free-of-charge when a magazine ceases publication so that the publisher's liability to the subscribers is met. Also, a publisher may offer to purchase the subscribers of a successful competitive publication to eliminate the competitor. When acquiring transfer circulation, the publisher must be certain that the list of subscribers comes from a publication with similar editorial content, price, FREQUENCY, and AUDIENCE, so that the publisher has a high expectation of retaining and renewing the subscriptions. It is also important to consider the costs associated with meeting a higher RATE BASE commitment versus the additional advertising-space revenue expected.

**TRANSFER HUB** U.S. Postal Service mail-routing facility within the PREFERENTIAL NETWORK that distributes mail to various STATE DISTRIBUTION CENTERS and BULK MAIL CENTERS within its service area. The transfer hub does not SORT or otherwise break apart the mail it receives; it only forwards it on for processing elsewhere.

**TRANSIENT COPY RATE** SECOND-CLASS postage rate applied to bound printed material that is not prepared in accordance with U.S. Postal Service regulations for BULK MAIL. This rate usually applies to copies mailed by nonpublishing individuals and is higher than that for presorted (*see* PRESORT) mailings.

**TRANSIENT RATE** fee paid for a single nonrepeated advertisement.

**TRANSIT ADVERTISING** OUT-OF-HOME advertising on transportation vehicles such as buses, taxicabs, subways, commuter trains, rapid transit trains, and ferries, as well as in transportation vehicle terminals. There are three major types of transit advertising: CAR CARDS, found inside the vehicles in a fleet; outside posters, located outside the vehicles in a fleet; and STATION POSTERS, located in carrier terminals. Transit advertising is offered at relatively low cost, with cost per thousand approximating $.50 inside vehicles and $.10 to $.15 outside. Additionally, transit advertising reaches a mass audience with a high rate of repetition and can be geographically selective. Approximately $150 million is spent annually on transit advertising in more than 75,000 vehicles in approximately 400 urban markets.

**TRANSPARENCY**
**Advertising:** advertising and covered with a sticky, gelatinous substance that may be pasted onto a window for display.
**Photography:** positive color photographic image on a sheet of film or glass that represents the actual color values of the original subject.

**TRANSPARENT** characteristic of paper that is thin enough for an image printed on the reverse side or lying below to show through; also called SHOW-THROUGH. *See also* TISSUE OVERLAY.

**TRANSPARENT COPY** illustration or text printed on a transparent medium such as plastic or film through which light must be projected for the image to be seen; also called *transparency.*

**TRANSPARENT INK** ink used in printing that allows the color of other inks layered under it to SHOW-THROUGH. Transparent ink is used in FOUR-COLOR PROCESS printing that reproduces all the colors of the original image by printing two or three PRIMARY COLORS in layers. *See also* OPAQUE INK; TRAPPING; WET PRINTING.

**TRANSPORTATION MANAGEMENT OFFICE (TMO)** department within the U.S. Postal Service responsible for planning how the service transports mail. Mailers usually inform the local TMO if they are planning a large mailing, so that the TMO can prepare. The TMO may tell the mailer what sequence to use in loading the mail onto USPS trucks for easier dispatching later.

**TRANSPOSE** typesetting error in which the positions of two characters are reversed—for example, "transpose," where the "p" and the "s" are reversed.

**TRAPPING** method of printing by layering various colors of ink on the same sheet of paper. This is used in multicolor printing (creating a printed image with as many colors as the colors of ink used) and FOUR-COLOR PROCESS printing (creating a printed image with a full SPECTRUM of color created from three colors of ink). It is important that each successive layer of ink have less TACK than the previous layer, so that the ink can be applied smoothly without damage to the previous layer of ink. *Dry trapping* is the application of ink to a dry ink surface. *Wet trapping* is the application of ink to a wet ink surface. *See also* TRANSPARENT INK; WET PRINTING.

**TRAVEL AND ENTERTAINMENT (T&E)** budget allocation for traveling and entertaining expenses incurred as part of normal business routine. Travel and entertainment covers all employee meals, lodging, travel, and costs for entertaining clients.

**TRAY** *see* LETTER TRAY.

**TRAY PACK** POINT-OF-PURCHASE ADVERTISING display wherein the top of a case of merchandise can be opened and folded back or removed so that the case becomes a display tray that fits on a shelf or counter in a retail store.

**TRENDEX** company headquartered in New York City that specializes in the sale of syndicated research services.

**TRIAL BUYER** *see* TRIAL OFFER; TRIAL SUBSCRIBER.

**TRIAL OFFER** soft-offer (*see* HARD OFFER) technique that allows a FIRST-TIME BUYER to examine, use, or test a product for a short period of time before deciding to purchase or return it; also called *free trial offer, free examination offer.* A trial offer may also be a special reduced rate for first-time buyers and/or may be in a special reduced quantity or TERM. Trial offers are particularly important in direct marketing, because the buyer has the disadvantage of not being able to see or handle the actual product as he would in a store. Trial usage is a good stimulant for word-of-mouth advertising.

Products best suited to a direct-mail trial offer are those that are easiest to ship, have a long shelf life, and are not likely to be damaged in transport. For example, print products are well suited to trial offers. The product must also be one that can be produced at a low-enough cost to offset losses incurred when prospective customers do not return or pay for goods shipped on trial. To keep the loss small, a trial version of the product can be developed—for example, a food sample that is enough to provide a taste, an excerpt from an audio or video recording, or a computer disk that demonstrates a software product without providing the complete program. *See also* TRIAL SIZE; TRIAL SUBSCRIBER.

**TRIAL RATE** speed and extent to which consumers in a market make a first time purchase of a new product or new brand. The trial rate is looked at in conjunction with the REPEAT RATE to measure consumer satisfaction and the sales potential of the brand. A high trial rate with a low repeat rate indicates consumers have a need for the product but the brand does not meet their expectations.

**TRIAL SIZE** smaller than usual size of a package. A trial-size package of a product may be used as a sample to be given away or may be sold at a low price to attract prospective customers.

**TRIAL SUBSCRIBER** FIRST-TIME BUYER of a subscription at a special reduced rate and/or for a short TERM. *See also* TRIAL OFFER.

**TRIAL USAGE** *see* TRIAL OFFER.

**TRIM**
1. final process in book, catalog, or brochure production that involves cutting off folded edges to make separate pages or cutting off excess or uneven edges to produce pages that match the desired dimensions. In some cases, trimming is necessary to separate two or three magazines or catalogs that are printed and bound 2-UP or 3-UP. CONTINUOUS FORMS may be trimmed to remove the PINFEED HOLES and perforated edges. There are various types of automated or manual trimming devices that may trim one stack or two or more stacks of print products at a time on one or several sides. *See also* GUILLOTINE.
2. strip that forms the edges or frame of an outdoor advertisement.
3. removal of a scene, or take, from the final film; also called EDIT, *outtake.*

**TRIM MARKS** *see* REGISTER MARKS.

**TRUTH-IN-ADVERTISING** requirement by the Federal Trade Commission as well as various state and local government agencies, that advertisements not make misleading, false, or deceptive claims. An advertisement can be deceptive without being an outright lie depending upon the perception it creates in the mind of the consumer. For example, a product that calls itself "light" may be nothing more than a slightly lower calorie version of its regular formula but will be perceived to be a low-calorie product. Or a beverage called an "orange juice drink" may contain primarily sugar and water with a minuscule juice content. Deceptive advertising can be accomplished with pictures as well as with words. In one famous case, a soup manufacturer placed marbles in the bottom of the bowl so that the contents of the soup rose to the surface in a photograph taken for their advertisements. An advertisement can also be considered deceptive if it makes a claim that is true but also leads the consumer to believe falsely that the same claim could not be made by competitive brands. For example, using "fat free" claims on a bottle of maple syrup might lead consumers to believe that other syrups contain fat. *See also* FAIR PACKAGING AND LABELING ACT; WHEELER-LEA ACT.

**TRUTH IN LENDING ACT** also called the Consumer Credit Protection Act, legislation enacted in 1968 requiring money lenders to be explicit about the true costs of credit transactions. The Truth in Lending Act outlaws the use of threatened or actual violence to collect debts and restricts the amount of garnishments. The act also established a National Commission on Consumer Finance.

**TURNAROUND DOCUMENT** computer-created form that will be used to enter data to the computer. For example, some INVOICES or subscription RENEWAL PROMOTIONS are created by first selecting names and addresses from a computerized customer file along with any relevant information, such as amount due and/or customer MATCHCODE. This information is then printed onto a turnaround document, which is sent to the customer. The customer submits a payment or indicates his decision to renew, and returns the document to the sender. The document is then used to enter a payment or renewal TRANSACTION to the computer file. Turnaround documents that include a matchcode or KEYLINE identifying the customer and the type of transaction can be scan entered (*see* SCAN ENTRY) rather than key entered (*see* KEY ENTRY), saving time and expense.

**TURNAROUND TIME** time it takes to get a job done and deliver the OUTPUT, once the job is submitted for processing. Turnaround may be as simple as unloading and reloading a delivery truck before sending it out again, or as complex as completing a MERGE/PURGE of several rented lists, getting a product into the buyer's hands once it is ordered, or receiving approval on a PROOF that has been submitted to the print buyer. In most cases, a short turnaround time is economically advantageous, making the most efficient use of time and materials.

**TURNOVER**
1. speed of sale of a product measured in terms of the quantity purchased during a period of time. For example, if the owner of a list of one million names rents a total volume of five million names over one year's time, it has a turnover rate of 5. It is important in both retail and direct marketing to evaluate product turnover and price so that selling space, whether it is on a shelf or in a catalog, is used to best advantage. For example, assume Product A has a retail price of $10 and a turnover rate of 100 and Product B has a retail price of $12 and a turnover rate of 70. For the amount of space expended, Product A produces $1000 in revenue and Product B produces $840 in revenue. This indicates that, despite its lower price, Product A, with a high turnover, should be displayed, instead of Product B. On the other hand, if a third product with a turnover of only 1 earns $1500 in revenue, the third product is a better use of the selling space.
2. number of people tuned to a television or radio program at any one time, divided by the total number of people who tuned to it at all. For example, if 100 people watched part of a television program but only 50 watched it at one point in time, the program has a turnover rate of 50%, indicating that it was not able to hold the viewers' attention to any great extent.

**:20** scriptwriter notation for 20 seconds, sometimes used to indicate a 20-second broadcast commercial.

**24-SHEET POSTER** sheet with an 8'8" by 19'6" printing area surrounded by a border, used in OUTDOOR ADVERTISING on poster displays. A 24-sheet poster represents 24 multiples of a standard one-sheet poster, which is 28" high by 41" long. When assembled, the 24-sheet is 4 sheets high by 6 sheets wide. In the early days of outdoor advertising, each of the 24 sections was pasted on the poster panel, or BILLBOARD, by hand, but printing presses are larger today and a 24-sheet now usually consists of only 10 to 12 sections to be pasted on the panel.

**TWIN PACK** retail product package made up of two containers of the same product packaged together under the same wrapping or in the same container. A twin pack is usually offered at a discount price that is less than the price of the two containers combined but more than the price of a single container. The special price is advertised on the wrapping of the twin pack. *See also* BONUS PACK.

**TWIN-WIRE MACHINE** type of fourdrinier papermaking machine, named after the family that sponsored its development in the early 1800s, that has two *wires* (fine mesh screening) instead of one, giving both sides of the paper a similar surface texture. The wires, which are made of nylon, bronze, or brass cloth, hold the paper pulp during the time that it is converted from groundwood (which consists of 99% water) to a continuous web (roll) of paper containing very little moisture. With single-wire machines, the paper produced has a somewhat rough WIRE SIDE and a relatively smooth FELT SIDE. Twin-wire machines are most often used to produce NEWSPRINT. *See also* TWO-SIDEDNESS.

**TWO-COLOR PROCESS** printing process utilizing two colors of ink. Two-color printing is less costly than FOUR-COLOR PROCESS printing. The two-color combinations most often used include yellow-MAGENTA, yellow-CYAN, cyan-magenta, yellow-black, magenta-black, and cyan-black. The colors are combined in varying proportions to achieve different hues. *See also* FOUR-COLOR PROCESS.

**2 PERCENT RULE** AUDIT BUREAU OF CIRCULATIONS rule stating that subscriptions sold at a rate within 2 percent of the BASIC RATE may be reported as sold at the basic rate. This allows publishers with a basic rate of $15.00, for example, to sell at rates as low as $14.70. Common practice, however, is to take advantage of the rule to gain a psychological advantage with a minimal discount; thus a publisher with a basic rate of $15.00 would offer a price of $14.95 or $14.97.

**TWO-SHEET DETECTOR** device on a PRINTING PRESS used to determine if more than one sheet at a time is fed through the press in error; also called *two-sheet caliper, choke*. The two-sheet detector is usually equipped with a device that automatically shuts off the press.

**TWO-SIDED MESSAGE** persuasive communication that presents two points of view and then presents arguments to counter the opposing view; also called *two-sided appeal*. A two-sided message for a service bureau might acknowledge that a competitor is located closer to the prospect and then assert that proximity is irrelevant if the service bureau is doing a good job. A two-sided message is more appropriate to an audience that is favorably disposed toward the opposing view or is likely to be exposed to strong arguments for the other side. An audience that favors another brand or point-of-view must be persuaded to abandon that view before a new view can be accepted. Two-sided messages work best with an educated audience that tends to make INFORMED CHOICES, like INDUSTRIAL BUYERS. The order in which the views are presented in a two-sided appeal can affect the impact of each message depending upon the audience characteristics.

**TWO-SIDEDNESS** characteristic of paper having both a smooth FELT SIDE and a rough WIRE SIDE, affecting the printability of each side, depending upon the type of papermaking machine used. Paper made on a fourdrinier single-wire MACHINE is printed on the felt side. Paper made on a CYLINDER machine is printed on the wire side. The rougher wire side can be identified by folding over the paper so that both sides can be seen together for comparison, or by wetting the paper. The wire side can be seen more clearly on wet paper. *See also* TWIN-WIRE MACHINE.

**TWO-STEP FLOW OF COMMUNICATION** theory stating that the nonpersonal marketing message is really passed on to an OPINION LEADER who then passes it on to the individual consumer. Believers in this theory attempt to base their marketing strategy on identifying opinion leaders and communicating their marketing message to them. *See also* COMMUNICATION CHANNELS.

**TYING AGREEMENT** sales practice forbidden by Section 3 of the CLAYTON ACT in which a marketer uses economic dominance over the supply of one product to force customers to purchase another product, thereby competing unfairly. For example, the sole manufacturer of a patented pharmaceutical who restricts sale of that drug to customers who also purchase another nonpatented drug. In the absence of a monopoly, it has been difficult for the courts to prove that economic dominance exists and the mere existence of a patent is not adequate evidence. *See also* BUNDLE.

**TYPEFACE** particular style and design of alphabetic letters, numerals, and symbols that make up a FONT. Typefaces are designed by artists and usually named by them, with some faces bearing the name of the artist, such as Bodoni type.

Times Roman

*Times Italic*

**Times Roman Bold**

***Times Bold Italic***

**TYPE GAUGE** device used by typographers (*see* TYPOGRAPHY) and in COPYFITTING to measure the size of the type in terms of PICAS and POINTS; also called *pica gauge, line gauge.*

**TYPE HIGH** size of a type SLUG measured from the nonprinting back surface to the front printing surface; usually 0.918 of an inch. Slugs used to create spaces between letters or words are less than type high so that no impression is made by them when placed along with type high slugs against the printing surface.

**TYPE MECHANICAL** *see* KEYLINE.

**TYPESETTING** *see* COMPOSITION.

**TYPO** typographical error; mistake in copy made by a word processor, printer, or typist when transcribing copy.

**TYPOGRAPHY** art of selecting and spacing TYPEFACES appropriate to the content of the material to be printed and to the ink and paper used, in order to produce a legible, aesthetically appealing printed piece. Typographers or book designers decide upon line length, spacing between lines, combinations of typefaces, type size, ink color, and paper color and texture. Advertising typography tends to be difficult, because a prescribed amount of text must be copyfitted (*see* COPY-FITTING) into a fixed amount of space in a manner acceptable to representatives of both the advertiser and the advertising agency. Advertising typography requires that a series of LAYOUTS (called rough, comprehensive, and final) be produced for approval by advertising agency account executives and product and promotion managers.

# U

**U & L**  *see* LOWERCASE; UPPERCASE.

**ULTRAHIGH FREQUENCY (UHF)**  bands of television channels from 14 to 83 on the television dial, operating at frequencies assigned by the Federal Communications Commission (FCC) from 470 to 890 MHz (MEGAHERTZ). UHF channels were first assigned by the FCC in 1952 when 70 additional channels were authorized for increased television transmission. In 1965, a law was passed requiring all new television sets to be equipped to receive UHF programming. Today, there are 250 UHF stations in existence.

**UNAIDED RECALL**  research technique used to test the effectiveness of advertisements and commercials and to learn whether respondents are familiar with a particular brand, slogan, or other facet of an advertising campaign. Respondents are asked questions such as "What program did you watch last night?" or "What commercials or advertisements do you remember seeing?" and their answers are noted. In this technique, respondents are not prompted in their responses as they are in AIDED RECALL. However, it should be noted that unaided recall is really a relative term, since recall seldom, if ever, happens spontaneously and some amount of cueing is necessary to conduct the research.

**UNCOLLECTIBLE**  *see* DEADBEAT.

**UNDELIVERABLE AS ADDRESSED**  mail that has an invalid, incomplete, or illegible address. Undeliverable-as-addressed mail is costly for direct marketers, not only because it involves wasted PACK-AGE and postage expense, but also because a high undeliverable-as-addressed volume can negatively impact RESPONSE to such an extent that the marketer incorrectly assumes the package was unsuccessful. Undeliverable first-class mail is automatically returned to the sender by the U.S. Postal Service. For a small fee (30¢ in 1986), the USPS will return other classes of mail. Direct marketers should track undeliverable-as-addressed volumes by LIST, so that lists with a high proportion of bad addresses will not be used or rented again.

**UNDELIVERABLE BILLING DOCUMENT (UBD)** INVOICE that is UNDELIVERABLE AS ADDRESSED. Since invoices are mailed first class, undeliverable billing documents will automatically be returned to the sender by the U.S. Postal Service. The mailer should then verify that the address that was used MATCHES the one in the customer RECORD and, if so, inactivate that record so that no further merchandise shipments, promotions, or invoices are mailed until a corrected address is received from the customer.

**UNDERCOLOR REMOVAL (UCR)** variation of GRAY COMPONENT REPLACEMENT that reduces the amount of colored ink printed in areas where all three of the colors used in FOUR-COLOR PROCESS printing will be layered (*see* TRAPPING). This is accomplished by reducing the DENSITY of the individual COLOR SEPARATIONS. Black ink is substituted for the colored ink in an amount equal to the amount of colored ink reduced, because using too much ink would interfere with the trapping of the inks. Black ink costs less; therefore, UCR reduces ink expense. The primary benefit, however, is a sharper image with darker shadow areas and lighter HIGHLIGHTS.

**UNDERLYING SERVICE** issues of a periodical due to be served a subscriber with the exception of issues remaining on the order currently being served. For example, if a subscriber has 4 issues remaining on a current subscription, has submitted an early renewal order for 12 additional issues, and has been given a gift subscription for 12 issues, the underlying service on the subscription is 24 issues. A high volume of underlying service across a subscriber group means that a publisher will not have to spend as much to bring in new subscribers or to renew current subscribers in order to maintain the current CIRCULATION level; on the other hand, the publisher has less opportunity to benefit in the short run from a subscription price increase. Some publishers also exclude from the underlying service calculation issues due on a renewal order received prior to a second renewal.

**UNDERPAYMENT** INVOICE payment that is less than the amount billed. The seller may either bill again for the remaining amount, accept the amount received as full payment, or proportionately reduce the service or goods to be delivered. The option chosen depends upon the percentage of difference, the dollar value of the difference, and the seller's objectives. Many buyers write checks to the nearest dollar to avoid making cent calculations in their checkbooks. These payments are usually accepted as full payment, because the cost of billing for the remainder exceeds the amount still owed. Magazine and newspaper publishers frequently will make it a policy to accept underpayments as payment in full if the advertising sales revenue derived from the additional CIRCULATION is worth more than the payment differential. Other publishers will reduce the term of the subscription in proportion to the per copy value of the underpayment.

**UNDIFFERENTIATED MARKETING** MARKET COVERAGE strategy whereby a company ignores differences within a market and attempts to appeal to the whole market with a single basic product line and marketing strategy. Undifferentiated marketing relies on mass distribution and mass advertising, aiming to give the product a superior image in the minds of consumers. It is cost effective because there is only one product line to be produced, inventoried, distributed and advertised. Also the absence of segmented market research lowers the costs of CONSUMER RESEARCH and product management. *See also* CONCENTRATED MARKETING; DIFFERENTIATED MARKETING; MASS MARKET.

**UNDISCOUNTED** goods or services sold at the full established price without ALLOWANCES or DISCOUNTS. Undiscounted pricing protects CATALOG HOUSES and other direct marketers from the cost of reprinting price sheets and promotions each time a price is changed. It also reduces the possibility that a customer will be annoyed to discover someone else paid less for the same thing. Undiscounted pricing works best for goods and services with stable demand and little price ELASTICITY.

**UNDUPLICATED AUDIENCE** *see* CUMULATIVE AUDIENCE.

**UNIDENTIFIED RENEWAL** *see* IDENTIFIED RENEWAL.

**UNIDENTIFIED TRANSACTION** *see* IDENTIFIED TRANSACTION.

**UNIQUE CHARACTER** *see* TIEBREAKER.

**UNIQUE RECORDS** RECORDS on a FILE or LIST that do not DUPLICATE any other records. The objective of list management is to maintain only unique records on a particular list. Unique records identified during a MERGE/PURGE of several lists represent individuals who have purchased from (or donated to) only one LIST OWNER and are therefore of less value to marketers than a MULTIBUYER.

**UNIQUE SELLING PROPOSITION** concept developed by Rosser Reeves, one of the founders of Ted Bates advertising agency, which says that advertising must offer the consumer a logical reason for buying a product that separates the product from its competitors. According to this concept, all successful advertising campaigns are based on a product's unique selling proposition. There are three basic tenets to the concept: (1) each advertisement or commercial must offer a special benefit to the consumer; (2) the benefit must be unique to the advertised brand (something the competition does not offer); and (3) the benefit must be strong enough to pull customers toward the brand.

**UNIQUE THREE-DIGIT CITY** large city that is assigned its own THREE-DIGIT ZIP CODE prefix. According to U.S. Postal Service regulations, 6 or more pieces of SECOND-CLASS or THIRD-CLASS mail destined for a unique three-digit city must be made into a PACKAGE. In second class, 4 or more packages destined for the same unique three-digit city must be in SACKS. In third class, 12 or more packages must be sacked. The complete list of unique three-digit cities can be found in the DOMESTIC MAIL MANUAL, exhibit 122.63a.

## UNIT
**In general:**
1. single thing, person, or group of things or persons treated as a whole.
2. one business engaged in a single activity in one location.
3. mechanical device performing a single function, such as one automobile, consumer, restaurant, or focus group.

**Marketing:** standard package size or quantity in which a product is sold, such as one case of soda or one page in a print advertising medium.

**Printing:**
1. combination of devices used to perform a single function, such as each combination of PLATE IMPRESSION, and inking devices used for each color of ink in FOUR-COLOR PROCESS printing.
2. measure of the width of a letter or space. One EM equals 18 units. Units are used for SPACING IN (OUT) according to the width in units of the letters and spaces on each line.

**UNITARY FALLOFF** percentage reduction in response or sales volume equal to the percentage increase in price. For example, a 50% decrease in response to an offer at a 50% increase in price represents a unitary falloff in sales. A 25% decrease in response to a 50% increase in price would be a half unitary falloff. *See also* PERFECT UNITARY ELASTICITY.

**UNIT PRICING** translation of a consumer product price into the cost per standard size or weight. Unit pricing helps the consumer to make price/value comparisons between brands. Unit prices are usually displayed on supermarket shelf tags along with the package price. Unit pricing has contributed to the decline in popularity of NATIONAL BRANDS over their lower-priced PRIVATE LABEL brand counterparts.

**UNIVERSAL PRODUCT CODE (UPC)** number used to identify a product. Translated into BAR CODES consisting of a series of vertical parallel bars, the UPC can be used for SCAN ENTRY, by an electronic cash register, of information for product sales and inventory TRACKING. NEWSSTAND wholesalers use the UPC code to record magazine returns; each code identifies the magazine TITLE and ISSUE. Grocers and other retailers use the UPC code to identify products and prices and to maintain a record of goods sold.

The code is assigned by the Uniform Code Council (UCC), in Dayton, Ohio, upon receipt of an application from a manufacturer. The first six digits are the same for all of the manufacturer's products and represent the name of the manufacturer; they are assigned by the UCC. The next five digits refer to the product itself and are assigned by the manufacturer to the product of his choice. Retailers use this portion of the code to reference a computerized table of prices when the UPC code is entered to an electronic cash register. The correct price is automatically pulled from the table and recorded on the register. The last digit of the UPC code is a CHECK DIGIT.

**UNIVERSE** total population, MARKET, or group of interest. For the purpose of market research, a subset of the population called a SAMPLE is selected from the universe to be investigated. In merchandising, all buyers of ski equipment would represent the total universe for ski equipment sales. In direct marketing, however, the universe represents only the available names on lists of buyers or other individuals who represent good prospects or mailing. The total universe of buyers is irrelevant for a direct marketer who has no way to identify and therefore reach them.

Some products will not be sold via direct mail if the universe of mailable names is not large enough to generate adequate sales volumes, even though the universe of buyers is enormous. For example thousands of people buy flowers from street vendors, but a product designed for those buyers could not be profitably marketed through the mail because their names are not collected.

**UNKEYED** direct-mail promotion lacking a *source key* identifier that prevents the marketer from TRACKING the results of a promotion. *See also* HOMOGENIZATION.

**UNQUALIFIED MAIL** *see* QUALIFIED MAIL.

**UNQUALIFIED SORT** *see* QUALIFIED MAIL.

**UNROUTED** RECORD on a file after the CARRIER-ROUTE CODING assignment process has been completed that did not match any of the addresses on the carrier route file and remains uncoded. Unrouted addresses can be mailed but are not eligible for a carrier route discount.

**UNTAPPED MARKET** demand that has not been met by an existing product or brand, or a market that could use an existing product in an innovative way. An untapped market is often the impetus for product INNOVATION or customization. For example, the personal hygiene market was an untapped market for the makers of baking soda until they developed a baking soda toothpaste. There was an untapped market for athletic brassieres until the first jogging bra was developed.

**-UP** forms (such as invoices), LABELS, or SIGNATURES printed in sequence across or down the page. This method reduces print time by taking advantage of the full capacity of the PRINTER.

Name and address labels are printed in ZIP code or other postal presort sequence l-Up, 2-Up, 3-Up, 4-Up, or 5-Up (1 across, 2 across, 3 across, etc.). The sequence runs either East-West (horizontally) or North-South (vertically) down the page.

Signatures are printed and folded in pairs head to head or head to tail. The signatures are then split apart and trimmed on three sides to book size.

**UP-AND-OVER** direction given to the sound effects person to bring up the volume on the sound so that it plays over the dialogue, rendering the latter inaudible.

**UPDATE**
1. computerized file maintenance process in an OFF-LINE system that applies all necessary TRANSACTIONS against the old file, producing a new file reflecting all ADDS. DELETES, and CHANGES that have become necessary since the last update. It is necessary to update a file before producing any OUTPUT, to ensure the accuracy and completeness of the output. Most updates are conducted on a regular schedule, corresponding with the required frequency of the output. Regular updates are not necessary for ON-LINE systems that are continuously updated.
2. provide current information to an individual or group of persons, or revise printed information according to the most current information available.

**UPGRADE** increase the value of an order either at the time of purchase/order or when a credit order is paid or when a second order is made. Order forms might include an upgrade option such as leather trim instead of vinyl on a suitcase. Invoices sometimes include an upgrade option such as a subscription offer for two years at a lower per copy rate than the one-year subscription ordered. Fund-raisers also attempt to upgrade donations, asking for a larger donation during the current campaign than that made previously or requesting a larger donation than was pledged for the current campaign. RENEWAL PROMOTIONS usually upgrade the subscriber to a higher-price subscription than the introductory order. Upgrade offers generally do not negatively impact response but vary greatly in their degree of success. *See also* COLLECTION EXTENSION.

**UPPERCASE** capital letters of the alphabet, as compared to the small or LOWERCASE letters.

**UPSCALE** persons at the high end of a demographic characteristic range, such as people with high incomes, high levels of education, or professional status. For some advertisers and products, such as luxury cars or jewelry, upscale individuals are the best prospects. Many advertising-media VEHICLES specialize in reaching these individuals. COMPILED LISTS may be created for direct marketers from lists of high-priced-item buyers, theater sponsors, charity ball attendees, and so forth.

**UPWARDLY MOBILE** description of a segment of the population that is attempting to move up on the socioeconomic class scale. Upwardly mobile describes a trend toward higher status in terms of income, material goods, and life-styles. The YUPPIES are an example of this upwardly mobile trend.

**URBAN DIRECT** Canadian PRESORT level consisting of mail destined for a particular urban FORWARD SORTATION AREA. Urban-direct mail may be identified by a POSTAL CODE with the same first three digits and a number from 1 to 9 in the second position. According to second-class regulations, 6 or more urban-direct pieces must be made into a PACKAGE. In third class, 10 or more pieces must be packaged. The urban-direct presort level is roughly equivalent to the THREE-DIGIT ZIP CODE level in U.S. mail in terms of its usefulness for identifying a LIST SEGMENT.

**URBANIZED AREA** U.S. Bureau of the Census term for a portion of a *metropolitan statistical area* (MSA) that includes a city with at least 50,000 people and a total population, including both city and suburban area people, of 100,000. It differs from rural areas, which represent less densely populated portions of an MSA and which rely upon agricultural employment.

**U.S. BUREAU OF THE CENSUS** federal government agency (part of the Department of Commerce) that creates and publishes CENSUS DATA. Most census data is available free of charge in public libraries. Special tabulations and raw data are available for a small fee, provided no data is traceable to particular individuals or organizations. A quarterly *Bureau of Census Catalog* is published, listing all the data files and tabulations available. The most widely utilized census is the population census conducted every 10 years. It surveys the entire U.S. population regarding marital status, age, gender, race, household head, place of birth, mobility, education, employment, occupation, income, and so forth, organized by various geographic areas of residence. Other surveys conducted cover housing, agriculture, transportation, business, manufacturing, mineral industries, commercial fisheries, and local governments. *See also* BLOCK GROUP; CENSUS COUNTY DIVISION; CENSUS DESIGNATED PLACES; CENSUS TRACT; CONSOLIDATED METROPOLITAN STATISTICAL AREA; COUNTY; ENUMERATION DISTRICT; MINOR CIVIL DIVISION; STANDARD CONSOLIDATED STATISTICAL AREA; STANDARD METROPOLITAN STATISTICAL AREA.

**U.S. POSTAL BOARD OF GOVERNORS** controlling board of the U.S. Postal Service. The board includes nine governors, who are appointed by the President of the United States and approved by the Senate; the Postmaster General, who is appointed by the Board of Governors; and the Deputy Postmaster General, who is appointed by the Postmaster General and the governors.

**U.S. POSTAL SERVICE (USPS)** semi-autonomous organization established by the Reorganization Act of 1972, which created it from a federal government department. The USPS is headquartered in Washington, D.C., and is responsible for the collection, distribution, and delivery of mail. The regulations, procedures, and policies of the USPS are detailed in the FUNCTIONAL MANUALS, including the DOMESTIC MAIL MANUAL and the INTERNATIONAL MAIL MANUAL. The USPS provides several levels of service, known as CLASSES, primarily including FIRST CLASS (letter mail), SECOND CLASS (magazines and newspapers), THIRD CLASS (catalogs and direct-mail PACKAGES), and FOURTH CLASS (books and parcels). Other services provided include EXPRESS MAIL, ELECTRONIC COMPUTER-ORIGINATED MAIL, and MAILGRAMS. The Postal Service provides mailers with a CUSTOMER SERVICE REPRESENTATIVE who assists them in utilizing the services of the USPS to best advantage. The USPS is managed by the U.S. POSTAL BOARD OF GOVERNORS, headed by the Postmaster General. *See also* ALTERNATE DELIVERY; MAILER'S TECHNICAL ADVISORY COMMITTEE; POSTAL INSPECTOR; POSTAL RATE COMMISSION; PRIVATE EXPRESS STATUTES.

**UTILITY MAXIMIZATION** economic theory that when making a purchase, the consumer attempts to get the greatest value possible from the least amount of expenditure in order to maximize the total value derived from the consumer's available dollars. *See also* DIMINISHING MARGINAL UTILITY.

**UTILITY PROGRAM COMPUTER PROGRAM** that performs one of the routine operating functions of a computer, such as file storage.

# V

**VACUUM FRAME** device used in making CONTACT PRINTS that holds both the NEGATIVE (or POSITIVE) and the light-sensitive material that will receive the image from the negative (or positive).

**VALIDITY** in research, degree to which a statistical technique accurately measures or predicts a value—a valid SAMPLE will exhibit the characteristics of the population. For example, a valid sample drawn from a mailing list will respond to a promotion at a rate equal to the predicted RESPONSE RATE of the total mailing list. One measure of buying intentions that may lack validity is the *gift method*. Respondents are told that a drawing will be held at a future time for a year's supply of a certain product. Respondents report which of several brands they would prefer to receive if they win. The choice made may have been a more expensive brand than a respondent actually would buy. *See also* RELIABILITY.

**VALID ZIP FILE** computer-file listing of all FIVE-DIGIT ZIP CODES used to check the accuracy of the ZIP code on a customer or promotion file. Valid ZIP files may be purchased on MAGNETIC TAPE, MICROFICHE, or HARD COPY from companies licensed by the U.S. Postal Service. *See also* ZIP CODE CORRECTION.

**VALS** acronym for *Values and Life-styles*, a system for grouping consumers according to psychological and sociological theories in order to predict their behavior in the purchase decision process. There are three main categories: *need-directed*—consumers who make purchases based solely on need; *outer-directed*—consumers who make purchases based on their perceptions of the way others view them; and *inner-directed*—consumers who make purchases out of some inner need. VALS can aid in defining targets for products and are also helpful in the development of advertising copy and media strategies. The concept was introduced in 1978 by the California consulting firm of SRI International.

**VALS 2** newer version of VALS. It describes American market segments in terms of demographic and lifestyle factors and classifies consumers in eight basic lifestyle groups: actualizers, fulfillers, believers, achievers, strivers, experiencers, makers, and strugglers. Each group is based on two major dimensions: self-orientation and resources. Self-orientation comprises the attitudes affecting consumer buying approaches and resources including income level, education, self-confidence, health, eagerness to purchase, and energy level. Resources increase from youth to middle age and decline with old age. VALS 2 is an extremely useful classification system for segmenting consumers.

**VALUE ANALYSIS** technique used by an industrial buyer to identify the least costly combination of raw materials or components required to produce a product, without any reduction in the quality of the finished good. Value analysis enables the buyer to identify unnecessary features or components that can be eliminated in order to reduce the cost, without any reduction in the performance quality of the finished product. For example, a baked goods company may determine through a value analysis that imitation vanilla extract can be used instead of natural vanilla without any loss of flavor or texture.

## VARIABLE

**In general:** value that changes.

**Market research:** value that changes as a result of direct intervention (INDEPENDENT VARIABLE) or a change in another variable (DEPENDENT VARIABLE). A variable may be numerical or classificatory, such as *gender*. In market research, key variables must be identified. For example, an airline might wish to measure its competitive position according to the attitudes of air travelers. The key independent variables that might influence their attitudes (attitude being the dependent variable) would include reservation service, baggage handling, check-in procedures, seat comfort, and so forth. These would have varying values, depending upon consumer opinion of them. In a direct-mail package or advertisement, both the characteristics of the promotion and consumer response to it are variables. To test a promotion, one or more variables such as OFFER or COPY are changed, to measure resultant changes in response. In this example, offer and copy are independent variables, and response is the dependent variable. It is best, when testing, to change only one independent variable per test, so that differences in the dependent variable can clearly be attributed to that change. If more than one independent variable is changed, it will not be clear whether the difference in response is caused by one or more of the changes or, also, whether the change caused by each variable is in the same direction. One change may increase response; the other may decrease it.

**VARIABLE COST**  business expense that varies in proportion to the quantity of goods sold or manufactured such as packaging materials or product components. Variable costs tend to decline on a per unit basis as the quantity manufactured or sold increases, due to economies of scale. However, at some point, additional savings can not be realized and variable costs will begin to rise. For example, a marketer might have to spend increasingly greater amounts on advertising and promotion to sustain an artificially high demand level.

**VARIABLE FIELD**  *see* FIXED FIELD.

**VARIABLE-LENGTH RECORD**  computer-file RECORD that may vary in the number of CHARACTERS or FIELDS it includes from one record to another. Although a variable-length record may have a maximum size, its length is otherwise determined by the amount of information necessary to establish the record. For example, a name and address record might require as few as four fields and as many as six or even more. Variable-length records give the file owner added flexibility but may consume more computer time than fixed-length records.

**VARIABLE PRICING**  marketing strategy that allows a different price to be charged to different customers or at different times. This type of pricing is common among street vendors, antique dealers, and other small, independently owned businesses but is not practical for direct marketers, who rely upon preprinted promotion forms. Variable pricing risks the loss of customer goodwill when one customer discovers another paid less. Federal and state laws protect competing retailers from discriminatory pricing that gives competitors an unfair advantage. *See also* ALLOWANCE; UNDISCOUNTED.

**VARIETY STORE**  retail store that sells a wide assortment of low-priced, popular merchandise.

**VARNISH**
1. solution (VEHICLE) sometimes used as the base component of ink. The varnish used determines the ink TACK, gloss, resistance to wear and drying speed. Varnish may be composed of linseed oil or other natural or synthetic oils.
2. coating applied to paper to protect the surface from wear and to give it a glossy FINISH.

**VEHICLE**
**Advertising:** specific medium for advertising, such as *Time* magazine, rather than the magazine medium in general.
**Printing:** base solution from which ink is produced. Pigments are added to the vehicle to give it color. The vehicle determines other ink

properties such as TACK, gloss, resistance to wear, and drying speed. There are a variety of synthetic and natural substances used in vehicles, and there may be more than one vehicle in a particular ink, lending it different characteristics. *See also* VARNISH.

**VELLUM FINISH**  uncoated paper with a slightly rough-textured surface similar to an eggshell or ANTIQUE FINISH. Vellum-finish paper is highly absorbent and works well in high-speed printing.

**VELOX**  commercially prepared photographic paper that is sensitized so as to offer unique reproduction capabilities (such as the reproduction of HALFTONE copies as LINE COPIES) at low cost. Velox is available in standard sizes as well as in rolls.

**VERBATIMS**  research reports that are word-for-word duplications of interviews, without editorial comment.

**VERTICAL CONTIGUITY**  *see* CONTIGUITY.

**VERTICAL DISCOUNT**  special reduced rate for the purchase of several radio or television time slots to be broadcast at intervals within a set period of time such as a day. It is called a *vertical* discount because the time slots on a media schedule are listed with hours vertically and days horizontally. *See also* ACROSS THE BOARD; CONTIGUITY.

**VERTICAL HALF PAGE**  magazine advertising space that divides the page in half vertically rather than horizontally, thus making the long dimension of the advertisement vertical. Whether the advertisement is for a vertical or a HORIZONTAL HALF PAGE, the space is sold at the half page rate.

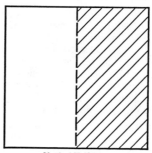

Vertical Half Page

**VERTICAL MARKET**  circumstance where the market for a particular product is limited (narrow), but the majority of consumers within the limited market need the product. For example, in the computer industry there exist certain pieces of technological equipment that all manufacturers of computers must purchase in order to build computers.

**VERTICAL MARKETING SYSTEM** joining producers, wholesalers, and retailers in the production and distribution of products. There are three major types of vertical marketing systems, and each uses different means for setting up leadership and power in the system: (1) corporate, where coordination and conflict management are attained by common ownership; (2) contractual, where coordination and conflict management are attained through contractual agreements among members of the system; (3) administered, where leadership is assumed by one dominant system member. The purpose of a vertical marketing system is to eliminate conflicts arising from each company's pursuit of its own financial objectives. *See also* HORIZONTAL MARKETING SYSTEM.

**VERTICAL PUBLICATION** publication whose editorial content is written for the benefit of a single business, industry, trade, or profession. Examples of vertical publications are *Retail Baking Today* for the benefit of the retail baking industry, *Chain Store Age* for chain store operators, owners, and suppliers, or *National Petroleum News* for the petroleum industry. Every industry has several of these publications available for interested parties and for advertisers. *See also* HORIZONTAL PUBLICATION.

**VERTICAL THIRD PAGE** print advertising SPACE equal to one-third of a page that is divided vertically (from top to bottom) into three parts. Vertical third-page advertisements placed on the outer edge of the page are easily spotted when a reader flips through a publication, but requests for this position are inconsistently honored. Positioning along the GUTTER or middle of the page can be especially awkward if a coupon is included in the advertisement, because it is difficult for the reader to remove. Vertical half-page space is also sold to advertisers.

**VERY HIGH FREQUENCY (VHF)** television channels 2 through 13 assigned by the Federal Communications Commission (FCC) to operate on the very high frequency band of the electromagnetic spectrum (wavelengths over which all electronic over-the-air communication takes place). Up until 1952 all television stations were VHF, but the demand for new stations was so great that the FCC assigned more stations on the ULTRAHIGH FREQUENCY (UHF). At present, there are approximately 500 VHF television stations across the United States.

**VIDEOCASSETTE RECORDER** magnetic tape machine that when attached to a television set, can record television broadcasts on video tape cassettes to be viewed later. The machine is also capable of playing prerecorded videotape cassettes, such as movies or concerts, that have been made professionally and are available for sale or rent. The videocassette recorder was first introduced for the home market by Sony in 1976 (Betamax) and was closely followed by Matsushita with the VHS (video home system). The formats for these two machines are mutually incompatible but remain as the two principal formats for the unit. Only 3% of American households had purchased videocassette recorders by 1982, but as of 1986, 40% of television households were equipped with the machines.

**VIDEO COMMERCIAL** advertisements produced specifically for presentation at the beginning of a rented videotape movie. Video commercials are designed for universal appeal and are often featured in conjunction with a special promotion involving the movie on the videotape.

**VIDEODISC** professionally recorded disc, similar to a phonograph record, which has both audio and visual playback capabilities. Videodiscs are played on a laser-operated videodisc recorder. A videodisc system is similar to a videocassette system except that the videodisc system has no recording capacity and can be used only for playback. Videodiscs generally have better fidelity (due to the use of lasers) than videocassettes, and the system is far less expensive than the videocassette system. *See also* VIDEOCASSETTE RECORDER.

**VIDEODISC KIOSK** viewing station providing public access to a VIDEODISC recording and operated by the viewer. Videodisc kiosks advertise goods available for sale from one or several sellers and may include a KEYBOARD or telephone for ordering the goods via credit card. Videodisc kiosks are placed in a variety of locations including the public areas in shopping malls and other retail areas, inside stores, and in other locations likely to draw consumers of the products advertised. For example, a major shoe manufacturer displays its entire product line via videodisc kiosks set up inside its retail stores. If a particular shoe is not in stock, customers can order it, using the kiosk, for delivery to their home. This medium can be expensive (ranging from $250,000 to several million dollars) if owned and operated by one advertiser, but suppliers will provide the equipment on a leased basis at a significantly lower cost. *See also* ELECTRONIC CATALOG; TELETEXT; VIDEOTEX.

**VIDEO DISPLAY TERMINAL** computer input/output device consisting of a KEYBOARD and a CATHODE-RAY TUBE DISPLAY, and either including a MICROCOMPUTER or having a communication link to a separate computer. *See also* MODEM.

**VIDEO ENGINEER** individual in a television studio who is responsible for the video portion of all television broadcasts.

**VIDEOGRAPH** address-label printing machine once in common usage that produced l-UP labels electrostatically at a rate of about 135,000 labels per hour. This technology has been surpassed by the MEAD printer.

**VIDEOLOG** *see* CATALOG MARKETING.

**VIDEO NEWS RELEASE (VNR)** public relations material (often about an organization or a new product) produced in a video newscast format and distributed to the news departments of television stations to be aired as a news item in a regularly scheduled newscast. VNR's are scrutinized by news directors, 80% of whom will edit the production in keeping with the particular news broadcast format. Undocumented material will not be accepted, and material that is too biased, too promotional, or too controversial will not be aired. A typical VNR for a new product, for example, runs about two to three minutes and features interviews with corporate executives, shots of the new product in production, and historical shots of the company and its background. *See also* RELEASE (3).

**VIDEO SYSTEMS** marketing tools that offer sales or product information through the use of video monitors. There are two basic types of video systems: electronic catalogues and video networks. Electronic catalogues offer visual images and information about a company's product line. They are usually found in high pedestrian traffic areas. Video network systems are usually found in supermarkets or department stores and are composed of several closed-circuit video monitors that feature advertisements, special promotions, or information about items for sale within the confines of the network. *See also* TOUCH SCREEN VIDEO.

**VIDEOTAPE** 2" magnetic tape used for the recording of television programs and commercials. There is often controversy over the use of videotape versus film, but usage is really a matter of personal taste. Videotape can be played back immediately after shooting and is easier to edit. Theoretically, a videotape commercial can be shot one day and be on the air the next. This is particularly beneficial to retailers who plan their advertising with very little advance notice and whose advertised products change very frequently.

**VIDEOTEX** interactive system for transmitting text and graphic information to consumers via a personal computer system, consisting of a KEYBOARD, MODEM, CATHODE-RAY TUBE DISPLAY, and telephone line. This system has been extremely successful in France, where the HARDWARE is provided to users at no cost, but it is growing slowly in the United States. Videotex systems are also available for public access via videotex kiosks in airports, shopping malls, and so forth. Videotex can be used to bank, shop, receive news and stock market quotations, send and receive mail, make travel and theater arrangements, review restaurant listings, run credit checks, and for a variety of other applications. Home access to videotex services is usually sold to consumers on a SUBSCRIPTION basis, with an additional charge based on the amount of usage. Advertisers pay a fee based upon the quantity of information and GRAPHICS they have available for viewing on the system. *See also* ELECTRONIC CATALOG; TELETEXT; VIDEODISC KIOSK.

**VIEWER**
1. individual who views a television broadcast.
2. optical instrument designed to aid in the viewing of artwork, slides, photographs, transparencies, or the like.

**VIEWER IMPRESSION** attitude or reaction of an individual who has seen a commercial in the context of normal, at-home television watching. Viewer impression studies are done periodically by the research firm of DANIEL STARCH AND ASSOCIATES and are offered by subscription, along with other data about television commercials. The studies are conducted to determine the communication effectiveness of commercials.

**VIEWERS PER VIEWING HOUSEHOLD (VPVH)** estimated number of individuals who comprise the viewing audience within any one household where the television is tuned to a particular program or station, or where the television is turned on during a given time period. The viewers per viewing household are usually classified by sex and age, such as women, 18 to 34.

**VIGNETTE**
1. illustration, photograph, or halftone print in which the outer edge or background gradually and irregularly fades off until it blends into the unprinted paper.
2. camera lens covering that will fade off the edges or background of a camera shot.
3. technique used in commercial production where several situations that emphasize the qualities of a product are shown in rapid sequence. Each situation shows a scene of people enjoying the product as they enjoy life, sometimes accompanied by lively music.
4. small drawing or illustration that appears in the body text of an advertisement.

**VIRTUAL CORPORATION** cooperative agreement between two or more business entities to combine their resources in order to achieve a shared goal. It is called a *virtual* corporation because by bringing in additional partners, unlimited skills and resources can be pooled. Virtual corporations are usually temporary, and the partnership dissolves once the shared goal is reached. For example, several computer hardware and computer software manufacturers might form a virtual corporation in order to produce a product that exploits a particular market niche such as a PC system for the real estate industry. Computer, cable television, telephone, and communications industry companies have formed virtual corporations to exploit interactive television technologies known as the *electronic highway.*

**VISCOSITY** characteristic of ink or other fluids that describes its thickness. Different levels of ink viscosity are required for different printing equipment and speeds. Viscosity can be reduced by adding solvents to the ink.

**VISUAL**
**Advertising:** one of the first rough LAYOUTS for an advertisement. The visual is merely a sketch that shows the relative positions of the elements to be included in the ad.
**Motion picture or television production:** visible element in a motion picture or television scene.

**VO** voice-over. *See* ANNOUNCER VOICE-OVER.

**VOICE MAIL** automated electronic touch-tone telephone system that is answered by a recorded message that directs callers to press specific numbers as codes to access information, place orders, or leave messages.

**VOICE-OVER** *see* ANNOUNCER VOICE-OVER.

**VOICE-OVER CREDITS** acting and production credits presented by an announcer whose voice is heard but who is not on camera. Voice-over credits are an alternative to an opening or closing BILLBOARD and are used solely at the discretion of the producer or director. The movie version of M.A.S.H. is an example of a film using voice-over credits.

**VOLUME MERCHANDISE ALLOWANCE** manufacturer's discount offered to a retailer or wholesaler for buying large volumes of merchandise.

# W

**WAFER SEAL** gummed foil or paper device, usually circular or BURST-shaped, imprinted with a sales message such as "Look Inside For Special Offer." It is used on direct-mail package COMPONENTS such as the OUTER ENVELOPE, and on SELF-MAILERS and folded sheets to hold them closed. Wafer seals attract the recipient's attention and heighten interest in the promotion.

**WAIT ORDER** instructions to a publication, usually a newspaper, to wait until subsequently notified to insert an advertisement. The advertisement referred to in the wait order has already been typeset and is ready to go, upon further notification. A rainwear manufacturer might use a wait order with an ad for raingear and then notify the newspaper to run the advertisement on a date when the forecast calls for rain.

**WALK-OFF** printing problem involving a slow deterioration of the image area of the PRINTING PLATE during printing.

**WALL BANNER** advertising BANNER suspended from a wall.

**WALLET FLAP** envelope with a large straight-edged flap that almost covers one side of the envelope, sealing at the bottom edge with a wide glue strip that produces an especially strong seal. The average size ranges from $3^3/8" \times 5^3/8"$ to $3^7/8"$ by $7^1/2"$.

**WARM COLOR** HUE at the red-yellow end of the color SPECTRUM, such as pink, orange, or coral. Colors are the way we perceive light of varying wavelengths that emit energy in the form of heat to an extent depending upon the length of the wave. For example, hot metal appears to turn red to the human eye. Warm colors emit more energy than COLD COLORS such as blue or green, and are used in advertising to evoke sensations of warmth, sexuality, and youth.

**WARM-UP** three-to-five-minute period prior to a live television (or radio) show when someone affiliated with the upcoming broadcast spends time with the audience telling jokes, relating information about the show, or explaining some production elements in the show. A warm-up is done to make an audience more at ease and to make them feel as if they are part of the production, so that they will be in a responsive mood when the show comes on.

**WARRANTY** guarantee given by a seller to a buyer that the goods or services purchased will perform as promised, or a refund will be given, an exchange made, or a repair done at no charge. Warranties usually become effective when the manufacturer receives a warranty application from the buyer (not at the date of purchase) and are effective for a limited period of time. Warranties usually include limitations that exclude defects not caused by the manufacturer.

The warranty application form typically contains requests for DEMOGRAPHIC and other marketing information about the buyer such as marital status, occupation, age, income, where and when the item was purchased, and why that brand was selected. Direct marketers maintain lists of individuals who have completed warranty applications, and use the data for promotion LIST ENHANCEMENT.

**WASH DRAWING** illustration made from highly diluted ink or paint that produces pale, transparent colors. Wash drawings can be used to produce many variations in tone and shading, using only one color of ink or paint and making this type of illustration uniquely well-suited to one-color printing.

**WASHUP** process of cleaning a PRINTING PRESS at the end of the work day or when inks are changed. Washup includes cleaning the PLATE or other printing surfaces, CYLINDERS, rollers, and DOCTOR BLADES, and emptying the INK FOUNTAIN. Some presses have automatic washup devices. Three different cleaning solutions are used to dilute and then emulsify residual ink and to then remove any remaining ink and cleaning solutions.

## WASTE CIRCULATION

1. persons in an advertiser's audience who are not prospects for the production or service being advertised. For example: A menswear manufacturer may choose to place advertising in a general publication whose readership consists of 60% men and 40% women. Since women are not users of the product, there is a 40% waste circulation for that advertiser in that publication. (Of course, this 40% waste figure is not 100% accurate, because some purchases may be influenced by women or may even be made by women as gifts. However, that factor cannot be measured.) Waste circulation for one advertiser is not necessarily waste circulation for another; thus, each advertiser must decide the degree of waste that is acceptable. Since advertising rates for any media are based on the size of the audience and since advertisers pay to reach every reader, viewer, or listener, waste circulation is an important consideration.
2. advertising for a product in a medium in an area where the product is not distributed.

**WATERMARK**  graphic design IMPRESSION made in paper during the papermaking process, consisting of an area that is slightly thinner and more translucent than the rest of the paper. The watermark is produced by a wire design on a roller called the DANDY ROLL that is pressed against newly formed paper before most of the water content of the paper is removed. Watermarks are best viewed when the paper is held against light. They are used in high-grade paper to show the paper manufacturer's TRADEMARK or the grade of paper, or to show the paper user's LOGO or trademark, making the paper appear more distinctive and rich.

**WAVE**  *see* FLIGHT.

**WEAROUT FACTOR**  condition that may apply to the point at which an advertisement or advertising campaign is no longer effective. The wearout factor depends on the frequency of communications, the target market, the quality of the advertising copy, the novelty of the campaign, and the variety of messages used. Some ads or campaigns wear out in a relatively short time, while others seem to last for years.

**WEB**  *see* WEB PRESS.

**WEBER'S LAW**  psychological concept applied to consumers' purchasing patterns that holds that consumers are more likely to purchase products based on the perceived differences *between* products than they are to purchase based on the attributes of one product or another.

**WEB PRESS ROTARY**  PRESS that prints on a continuous roll of paper or other material called a *web*, rather than on individual sheets of cut paper. Web paper is less expensive than cut paper, and web presses are suited to any type of large-volume and/or high-speed printing. They are most commonly used to print newspapers, magazines, and catalogs. Unlike SHEET-FED presses, web presses can also print on plastic or foil surfaces for package and label printing. Web presses may differ in the number of rolls that are held at one time and ready to be fed into the press, the speed with which the webs can be fed, how the webs are spliced together, and how WEB TENSION is controlled. After printing, the web may be cut into sheets, folded, or rewound for printing on the opposite side, or it may be combined with other webs for folding and cutting. *See also* FLYING PASTER.

**WEB TENSION** force used to pull a paper web through a WEB PRESS. Too much web tension can cause a tear or break in the web. Too little tension allows excessive paper movement and will result in a blurred or poorly registered image, as well as incorrectly placed folds and cuts. Precise web-tension control is especially important in FOUR-COLOR PROCESS printing that requires exact print REGISTER. Web tension may be controlled manually, mechanically, or electronically, depending upon the press used.

**WEIGH COUNT** count of documents or forms, such as returns received to a direct-mail promotion, based upon the weight of a batch of documents placed on an electronic scale. They are typically done on a daily basis when returns to a promotion start to come in, to give the marketer a "quick and dirty" view of the response and to relieve some of the anxiety associated with a direct-mail CAMPAIGN that took many months and dollars to implement. Weigh counts are much faster than the alternative method of manually counting the documents piece by piece, but are not as precise as counts that will be produced by a computer system after mail opening and ORDER ENTRY sort out the orders from the nonorder mail and unprocessible orders.

Weigh counts are also used to verify the volume of incoming shipments from forms suppliers. The U.S. Postal Service uses weigh counts to calculate postage due on BUSINESS-REPLY-ENVELOPE mail.

**WEIGHT**
**Advertising:**
**1.** number of exposures of an advertising message.
**2.** number of GROSS RATING POINTS an advertiser wants to place in a market (ADI [AREA OF DOMINANT INFLUENCE] or DMA [DESIGNATED MARKET AREA]).
**3.** *see* MEDIA WEIGHT.
**Paper stock:** *see* BASIS WEIGHT.
**Print advertising:** size as well as color, shape, and degree of blackness of an element in an ad (as a TYPEFACE).

**WEIGHT OF TYPE** variations in the darkness of type images created by the width of the lines that make up each character. Weight is usually described in terms of light, medium, heavy, bold, and black.

Medium is very effective in terms of legibility and readability for BODY COPY, while bold is more appropriate to HEADLINES and/or small portions of COPY that should stand out from the rest.

**WET PRINTING** FOUR-COLOR PROCESS printing technique that layers ink over previously printed surfaces that have not yet dried. Most WEB PRESSES and a few SHEET-FED presses operate too quickly to allow drying time between ink color impressions. If wet printing is to be used, the PROOFS should also be created using wet printing, to accurately represent the appearance of the final product. Four-color process printing can also be done with a combination of wet and dry printing on a two-color press that allows drying time during WASHUP and press preparation for the next two colors. *See also* TRANSPARENT INK.

**WHEELER-LEA ACT** 1938 amendment to the FEDERAL TRADE COMMISSION Act that authorized the FTC to restrict unfair or deceptive acts; also called the ADVERTISING ACT. Until this amendment was passed, the FTC could only restrict practices that were unfair to competitors. This broadened the FTC's powers to include protection for consumers from false advertising practices. *See also* CLAYTON ACT; ROBINSON-PATMAN ACT; TRUTH-IN-ADVERTISING.

**WHIP SHOT** *see* BLUE PAN.

**WHITE-COAT RULE** ruling handed down by the Federal Trade Commission stating that it is deceptive advertising to use actors dressed in white laboratory coats, to look like members of the medical profession, as spokespersons for a product in advertisements and commercials.

**WHITE GOODS** in retailing, all those heavy household appliances that were originally manufactured with a white enamel finish, such as refrigerators, freezers, washers and dryers, or stoves. Today the term applies to all such goods, even though they are available in a variety of decorator colors and finishes.

**WHITE MAIL** correspondence received from customers in their own envelope rather than in an envelope provided by the marketer. White mail generally contains address-change requests, complaints, inquiries, and orders. Customers sometimes want to send payment along with a BUSINESS REPLY CARD or SPACE ad order and will therefore enclose the card in an envelope along with their check. White mail typically takes two to three times longer to process than REPLY ENVELOPE mail, because the variety of envelope sizes makes machine opening slow and the variety of items enclosed must be sorted according to the type of processing required.

**WHITE SPACE** empty or open space in a print advertisement. Manufacturers of expensive or prestige products will sometimes use a lot of white space in their ads in an attempt to create a concept of luxury or elegance. Conversely, advertisements for discount products sold at discount variety stores seldom contain any white space.

**WHIZ PAN** *see* BLUE PAN.

**WHOLESALE PRICE INDEX** *see* PRODUCER PRICE INDEX.

**WHOLESALER** business that buys goods from manufacturers and that sells goods, usually in large quantities to retailers, who in turn sell them to the end user. Virtually everything sold on a retail basis can be purchased from a wholesaler, who acts as middleman between the manufacturer (or owner, as in the case of LIST RENTALS) and the retailer. Wholesalers help manufacturers by absorbing some of the costs of sales and distribution, and allow manufacturers to concentrate their resources on manufacturing. *See also* MARKUP.

**WIDE-ANGLE LENS** camera lens whose point of focus is a short distance from its optical center, so that it has a wide horizontal field of view. These lenses are available in different sizes and some can actually cover an area wider than the eye can see. Wide-angle lenses also provide a deep perspective, or DEPTH OF FIELD, so that all the elements seen through the lens will appear in sharp focus.

**WIDE-AREA TELEPHONE SERVICE** *see* IN-WATS.

**WIDOW** word, part of a word, or short phrase of two or three words, that is the last line of a paragraph in a body text of editorial matter or that ends up on the top of a page. Publishers often consider a widow to be awkward and will change the spacing or edit the line or the preceding copy, so as to eliminate it.

**WILD SHOT** shot taken by a television or motion picture camera that has not been synchronized with sound. Sometimes in the making of a motion picture, television show, or commercial, directors will have the camera crew take a series of wild shots that will be viewed during the editing process and used as the director and editor see fit.

**WILD TRACK** nonsynchronous sound that has been recorded for a motion picture, television show, or commercial, for much the same reason as a WILD SHOT.

**WINDOW ENVELOPE** envelope with one or more openings through which part of the contents can be seen. Windows may be completely open or may have a transparent plastic or paper covering. Most window envelopes, especially those used to mail invoices, are used to display the name and address of the recipient on a form inside the envelope, thus saving the expense of addressing an envelope. However, many window envelopes used for direct-mail promotions display other portions of the package COMPONENTS, adding (or changing) color, copy, and graphics on the OUTER ENVELOPE or personalizing the outer envelope for each recipient, without the expense of printing special envelopes. For example, some of the copy elements shown through windows are "reply by" dates; tokens with copy imprinted on them, such as "FREE"; curiosity-arousing portions of the copy or graphics inside, such as the question portion of a multiple-choice quiz; or portions of what resembles a bank check.

The cost of a window envelope depends upon the size of the envelope, the type (standard or nonstandard), and the number of windows. In most cases, a window envelope will cost slightly more than a similar-size FULLFACE ENVELOPE.

**WINDOW STREAMER**  advertising BANNER hung in a store window; also called *window strip*.

**WINDOW STRIP**  *see* WINDOW STREAMER.

**WIPE**  in film or videotape production, transition where one image appears to wipe the preceding image from the screen. Wipes are used most frequently and most effectively when a rapid succession of scenes is desired. There are several different types, including a *flip wipe* (in which the entire scene appears to turn over like the front and back of a postcard), a *horizontal wipe* or *vertical wipe* (in which an image moves from side to side, or from top to bottom or bottom to top), a *diagonal wipe* or *closing door wipe* (in which an image moves in from both sides), a *circle wipe* or *iris wipe* (in which a new image comes in, in a circle that grows bigger and bigger, or an old image moves out, in a circle that grows smaller), or a *clock wipe* (in which images sweep around the screen in a clockwise or counterclockwise motion).

**WIRE-O BINDING**  bookbinding technique that winds a circular double-wire strip through prepunched holes along the binding edge of the pages; also called spiral binding. Wire-o bound books lie flat when open and are useful for manuals or notebooks that people will write in or put down open in order to keep their hands free while performing tasks described by the manual.

**WIRE SIDE**
1. side of uncoated paper that is formed against the wire. For paper made on a fourdrinier machine, the wire side is rougher and is generally not the side printed. For paper made on a cylinder machine, the wire side is the smoother, printing side. The wire side of COATED PAPER cannot be distinguished from the FELT SIDE.
2. woven brass, nylon, or bronze cloth used in papermaking machines. *See also* TWIN-WIRE MACHINE.

**WITH THE GRAIN**  direction parallel to the paper fibers; also called *machine direction*. Tears and folds can be made more easily with the GRAIN, but paper is more susceptible to dimensional distortion, caused by moisture damage, with the grain. *See also* AGAINST THE GRAIN.

**WOMEN'S SERVICE MAGAZINE**  magazine the editorial contents of which are designed to appeal to homemakers; also called *service magazine*. Articles contain information about child rearing, cooking, household management, home decorating, and other home-related subjects. *Good Housekeeping* and the *Ladies' Home Journal* are examples of women's service magazines.

**WOODCUT** ancient printing technique utilizing a carved wooden block or board as a relief image carrier; also called *black-line engraving*. In a wood engraving, the image areas are recessed below the surface of the board; in a woodcut, the nonimage areas are carved away. Woodcuts can be used with one or several colors of ink. Although they have largely been replaced by modern photographic and printing techniques, woodcuts are still in use as an artist's medium and are employed in advertising to evoke "the olden days," and for their unique character as a fine art form.

**WORD ASSOCIATION TEST** in research testing, verbal communication test where the test given will say a word and the test taker is asked to reply with the first thing that comes to mind. Word association tests are used, particularly in advertising, to determine attitudes and to test cognitive knowledge in the hope of achieving understanding of human behavior.

**WORD-OF-MOUTH ADVERTISING** advertising communicated from one satisfied customer of a product or service to a family member, friend, or acquaintance who may be a prospective customer for the same product or service. Strictly speaking, this is not really advertising, since advertising communications are usually paid for by an advertiser. However, word of mouth, according to research studies, is the most important source of information for consumers (outside their own experience, of course), and in some cases plays a more important role than the mass media in determining certain purchases. This is particularly true of some food and personal or small domestic items.

**WORD PROCESSOR** programmable typewriter or computer program used to compose, format, sort, and rearrange text upon command and sometimes perform other related functions such as correcting misspelled words. Word processors are commonly used to compose COPY and to create personalized computer letters to customers or prospects using standard formats with spaces for inserting information specific to that customer.

**WORK-AND-TUMBLE** IMPOSITION layout; also called *print-and-tumble, work-and-roll, work-and-flop*. The work-and-tumble layout produces the same image on both sides of a sheet with one image carrier or plate. However, with work-and-tumble, it is difficult to control the print REGISTER because, unlike WORK-AND-TURN and SHEETWISE layouts, the side used as the GRIPPER EDGE is changed when the sheet is turned. Therefore, work-and-tumble layouts are used only when work-and-turn or sheetwise impositions will not work with the dimensions of the paper being used.

**WORK-AND-TURN**  IMPOSITION layout; also called *print-and-turn*. The work-and-turn layout prints the same image on both sides of a sheet with one image carrier or plate. The first side is printed; then, keeping the GRIPPER EDGE constant, the side edges are reversed, turning the unprinted side toward the image carrier. This is less expensive than using two image carriers, although a separate PLATE is still needed for each color printed. *See also* WORK-AND-TUMBLE.

**WORK-AT-HOME**  growing business practice in which an employee or entrepreneur works at home instead of in a company office. The development of personal computers (*see* MICROCOMPUTER) has broadened the scope of work-at-home applications to include white-collar workers who can communicate electronically with a central office, sending and receiving memoranda, reports, and research material.

   Several common MAIL FRAUD practices include work-at-home schemes in which an advertisement promises the victim an opportunity to make impossible amounts of money at home and asks the individual to send the advertiser an employment application or referral fee. For example, the advertisement might promise that a person can earn $100 per day stuffing envelopes. In return for a fee, the individual receives a list of companies that have used at-home workers in the past but that may or may not be hiring now.

**WORKED MAIL**  outgoing mail that has been through all the necessary LETTERSHOP processes, including PRESORT, and is ready for mailing.

**WORK-IN-PROCESS**
   **Manufacturing:** inventory at a stage between raw materials and finished goods. Work-in-process must be accounted for when valuing inventory for accounting purposes.
   **Fulfillment:** cash orders received and cashiered (*see* CASHIER) but not entered to the FULFILLMENT system at the time reports are generated. Work-in-process creates an imbalance between cash-deposit reports and order-volume (production) reports.

**WORK PRINT**
   **Film production:** DUB of an original film that is used for editing so that the MASTER will remain intact.
   **Television commercial production:** assemblage of scenes that have been selected from the ASSEMBLY DAILIES and placed in proper sequence without the opticals (DISSOLVES, WIPES, etc.), titles, or any SUPERS; also called *rough cut*. As the name implies, this is the print to which scenes will be added, deleted, or substituted and on which other changes will be made until the director feels that the footage is right and the other elements can be added. When the work print is complete to the director's satisfaction, a COMPOSITE PRINT will be made. *See also* ANSWER PRINT; FINAL PRINT; INTERLOCK.

**WOVE PAPER** rough-textured uncoated paper FINISH created during the papermaking process by pressing a woven wire cloth, wrapped around the dandy roll, into the newly formed paper before the water content of the pulp has been removed. *See also* LAID PAPER; WATERMARK.

**WRAP**
1. in motion picture or television production, conclusion of a day's shooting or conclusion of shooting (*see* SHOOT) for the entire production. The expression "It's a wrap" means that the shooting is finished and everybody connected with it can leave.
2. *see* BUBBLE WRAP.
3. *see* SHRINK WRAP.

**WRAPAROUND** advertising BANNER that is wrapped around a display case of retail items.

**WRAPAROUND PLATE** cylindrical relief (raised image area) plate used in *direct* (to paper) and *indirect* ROTARY PRESS printing. Wraparound plates reduce preparation time and expense, compared to other relief printing methods in which a cylindrical duplicate has to be made from a flat plate. Wraparound plates do not have to be etched as deeply as other plates, also saving expense. They are most often used for long press runs, such as for newspaper and magazine printing.

**WRAPPER**
**Advertising:** *see* LABEL.
**Direct mail:** paper cover wrapped around, or bound to the front and back cover of, a magazine, newspaper, or catalog. Wrappers may be as big as the cover and include an address label or may cover only the middle section; also called BELLY BAND. KRAFT-paper wrappers are used to protect publications from damage while in transit or, in the case of some "adult entertainment" titles, to conceal the name of the publication. Wrappers made of CARD STOCK with a perforated REPLY FORM are used to attach RENEWAL PROMOTIONS, subscriber surveys, and so forth to magazines. Wrappers are frequently used on last issue and next-to-last issue copies to let subscribers know their subscriptions are about to EXPIRE. Wrappers may also be used to mail supplementary material along with the publication as permitted by the U.S. Postal Service for POLYBAG-carried materials.
**Printing:** paper jacket for a hard-cover book. Wrappers frequently include promotional COPY about the book and author, including positive critical reviews, lists of other books written by that author, and/or the name of a book club that featured the book.

**WRINKLES** print problem caused by a crushed or irregular paper surface that can ruin the print product. Wrinkles can be caused by many factors, including moisture damage, sloppy packing or handling, or incorrect paper feed to the PRINTER.

**WRONG FONT (WF)** type character from a different FONT that has been set by mistake in a body of copy. *WF* or *w.f.* is a proofreader's mark indicating that the compositor has made such a mistake and that the character should be changed to the font that was specified.

# X

**XEROGRAPHY** electrophotography technique that produces an image on paper, using electrically charged particles. Electricity is projected onto the paper in the form of the image to be printed. Particles of pigment bond to the charged area. The pigment is then made permanent by the application of heat. *See also* LASER PRINTER.

**XEROX** trade name of the Xerox Corporation or trademark for any of its products, such as copy machines, duplicators, and copy paper.

# Y

**YELLOW** with red and blue, one of three ink colors used in FOUR-COLOR PROCESS printing. Yellow is printed from the blue COLOR SEPARATION negative, which acts as a filter, blocking all color except yellow.

**YELLOW GOODS** in merchandising, nonconsumable household goods, such as refrigerators or ovens, that are expensive and are usually replaced only after many years of service. Generally, yellow goods have a high profit margin. *See also* ORANGE GOODS; RED GOODS.

**YELLOW PAGES ADVERTISING** advertisements placed in a telephone yellow pages directory. Yellow pages advertising revenue is estimated at approximately $4.6 billion annually, $560 million of which is spent by national advertisers. *See also* DIRECTORY ADVERTISING.

**YES/NO OPTION** response option on a reply form that allows the recipient to say no or yes to the offer. Some yes/no options provide a slot for inserting one of two tokens marked either yes or no. Other promotions use check boxes, stamps, or seals. "No" responses are usually entered to a computer-file system for later use as a promotion and rental list. Another type of yes/no option includes a "maybe" response, which the marketer considers an order with full cancellation and/or refund privileges.

Yes/no options are used primarily in SWEEPSTAKES promotions, which legally must allow the recipient to enter the sweepstakes regardless of whether a purchase is made. Most sweepstakes promotions receive three times as many noes as yesses.

**YUPPIE** term derived from *y*oung, *u*rban *p*rofessional, a designation that came into vogue in the 1980s. The yuppie population consists of that group of people in their thirties whose life-styles are UPWARDLY MOBILE and who represent a TARGET AUDIENCE for some advertisers, such as BMW automobiles or Fila sportswear. The term has come to have a somewhat pejorative connotation, particularly when applied to a specific individual.

# Z

**ZIP + 4** *see* NINE-DIGIT ZIP CODE.

**ZIP-A-TONE** device used for applying shades of tonal values to line reproductions without the use of a screen (as in a HALFTONE process). Zip-a-tone is an economical means of preparing printing plates and represents a savings on art costs.

**ZIP CODE** abbreviation for Zoning *I*mprovement *P*lan code established by the U.S. Postal Service to identify numerically the destination of a mailing piece for easier sorting and dispatching. The original FIVE-DIGIT ZIP CODE has been expanded by four digits and is now called the ZIP + 4 code (*see* NINE-DIGIT ZIP CODE) . *See also* ZIP CODE ANALYSIS.

**ZIP CODE ANALYSIS** analysis technique used by direct marketers to determine where their best and worst prospects are and/or to determine how a promotion has performed according to a FIVE-DIGIT ZIP CODE or ZIP+4 area (*see* NINE-DIGIT ZIP CODE); also called *ZIP code count.* Direct marketers believe that ZIP CODE-based purchase patterns can be identified, because people with similar consumption habits reside (or work) near each other. For example, assume 100,000 direct-mail pieces are mailed, of which 50,000 go to residents of the 06905 area and 50,000 to residents of the 10104 area. A ZIP code analysis might reveal that 2500 responses were received from the 06905 area and only 30 from the 10104 area. This indicates that future mailings should be made to residents of 06905 and not to residents of 10104. A ZIP code analysis of a current CUSTOMER LIST can be used to measure the PENETRATION a marketer has achieved in various ZIP code areas. For example, if there are 2500 customers in a five-digit ZIP code area with a population of 250,000, then the penetration level is 1%. A ZIP code analysis of a mailing list can also show how many names are available to be mailed from each ZIP code area. ZIP code analysis of a BAD DEBT file can be used to identify, by ZIP code, groups of prospects most likely to be bad credit risks.

**ZIP CODE CORRECTION**    data-processing technique that adds missing ZIP codes, or identifies and corrects invalid ZIP codes in a list of name and address RECORDS according to a MASTER list of valid ZIP codes; also called *ZIP validation*. ZIP code correction is necessary before a mailing to ensure that all mailed pieces are deliverable, but is generally not necessary for a list that has already been ZIP code corrected prior to a previous mailing. ZIP code correction may be completed as part of the DATA ENTRY function when new names are added to a file and is routinely performed during a MERGE/PURGE to ensure that DUPLICATE records can be identified by ZIP code. Some ZIP code correction systems can also identify incorrect city and state combinations, such as Los Angeles, Texas. ZIP code correction SOFTWARE and services are available for purchase.

**ZIP CODE COUNT**    *see* ZIP CODE ANALYSIS.

**ZIP CODE OMISSION**    process of deleting from a promotion file or list, by ZIP code, those groups of RECORDS that the direct marketer expects, based upon a ZIP CODE ANALYSIS, to be poor prospects for a promotion. This is done during the MERGE/PURGE process. *See also* ZIP SELECT.

**ZIP CODE SEQUENCE**    computerized file-maintenance technique that numerically sorts the name and address RECORDS in a FILE by ZIP code; also called *ZIP sequence; ZIP sort*. Direct marketers sort mailing lists by ZIP code to facilitate the printing of address labels or mailing pieces in ZIP code sequence as required by the U. S. Postal Service for second-class and third-class BULK MAIL. Sorting a customer file by ZIP code sequence makes it easier to locate a record based on the customer's address, which, unlike customer account numbers or MATCH-CODES, appears on most order forms and correspondence. *See also* PRESORT.

**ZIP PAN**    *see* BLUE PAN.

**ZIP SELECT**    process of selecting RECORDS from a promotion file or list, based upon the ZIP code area in which the individuals reside (or work). Direct marketers often select records that, based upon a ZIP CODE ANALYSIS of current customer addresses, are expected to respond best to a promotion. ZIP selects are also made to test response to a promotion by individuals residing in a particular ZIP code area. ZIP selects are usually performed during a MERGE/PURGE. *See also* ZIP CODE OMISSION.

**ZIP SORT**    *see* ZIP CODE SEQUENCE.

**ZIP VALIDATION**    *see* ZIP CODE CORRECTION.

**ZONE** geographic region used to define sales territories, market test areas, or delivery areas. The U.S. Postal Service identifies neighborhood delivery zones by the last two digits of the FIVE-DIGIT ZIP CODE. Some direct-mail merchandise pricing is based upon zones for which there are predetermined SHIPPING AND HANDLING charges, depending upon the distance between each zone and the shipping point. *See also* ZONE CHARGES.

**ZONE CHARGES** postage charges applied to various classes of mail by the U.S. Postal Service based upon the weight of the mailing piece and the number of zones traveled from ENTRY POINT to delivery. In SECOND CLASS, there are per piece charges applied to each mailing, in addition to zone charges. Second-class mailers sometimes use DROP SHIPPING to truck mail across zones before entering the postal system to reduce zone charges. *See also* ADVERTISING WEIGHT.

**ZONE PRICING** strategy of setting selling prices according to the geographic area (zone) in which the product will be sold, allowing for the costs of product shipping and handling to the zone. Zone pricing provides a uniform delivered price to all buyers within a geographic area. However, selling prices are incrementally higher as the zones get further away from the place of product manufacture.

**ZOOMAR LENS** *see* ZOOM LENS.

**ZOOM IN (OUT** in television or motion pictures, camera move (sometimes rapid) from a long shot to a close-up (in) or from a close-up to a long shot (out), without blurring or without changing cameras, effected by a ZOOM LENS.

**ZOOM LENS** camera lens that can focus at varied distances from its optical center, from the short distance of a WIDE-ANGLE LENS to the length of a telephoto lens, without ever losing focus; also called *zoomar/lens*. Because of its variable focal length, it is the most popular lens used in television production.

# APPENDIX

## ABBREVIATIONS AND ACRONYMS

### A

**AA** author's alteration

**AAAA, 4A's** American Association of Advertising Agencies

**AAF** American Advertising Federation

**A&M** art and mechanical

**AAW** Advertising Association of the West

**ABC** American Broadcasting Company; Audit Bureau of Circulations

**ABEND** abnormal end (refers to erroneous termination of a computer program)

**ABMPS** Automated Business Mail Processing System

**ABMS** Audit Bureau of Marketing Service

**ABP** American Business Press, Inc.

**ACB** Advertising Checking Bureau

**ACD** associate creative director

**ACG** address coding guide

**ACI** Advertising Council, Inc.

**ACK** acknowledgment

**ACORN** A classification of residential neighborhoods (used in direct mail)

**ACS** Address Change Service

**AD** art director

**ADC** area distribution center

**ADI** area of dominant influence

**ADRMP** automatic dialing and recorded message player

**AE** account executive

**AFA** Advertising Federation of America

**AFM** American Federation of Musicians (of the U.S. and Canada)

**AFP** American Family Publishers

**AFTRA** American Federation of Television and Radio Artists

**AGMA** American Guild of Musical Artists

**AID** Arbitron Information on Demand, Automatic Interaction Detector

**AIDA** awareness, interest, desire, action

**AIO** activities, interests and opinions

**AM** amplitude modulation

**AMA** American Marketing Association

**AMF** airport mail facility

**ANA** Association of National Advertisers

**ANPA** American Newspaper Association

**AOR** agency of record

**APA** Agricultural Publishers Association

**APO/FPO** Army & Air Force Post Office/Fleet Post Office

**ARB** American Research Bureau. Inc.

**ARF** Advertising Research Foundation

**ASA** American Statistical Association

**ASCAP** American Society of Composers, Authors and Publishers

**ASF** auxiliary service facility

**ATR** awareness, trial, repeat

**A/W** alternate weeks

### B

**B&W, B/W, b&w** black and white

**B/W**

**BAPSA** Broadcast Advertising Producers Society of America

**BAR** Broadcast Advertisers Reports

**BC** back cover

**BCG** Boston Consulting Group

**BDI** Brand Development Index

**BG** background

**BIPAD** Bureau of Independent Publishers and Distributors

**BIT** binary digit

**BMC** bulk mail center

**BMI** Broadcast Music, Inc.

**BNF** Brand Names Foundation

**B of A** Bureau of Advertising

**BPA** Business Publications Audit of Circulations

**BPAA** Business/Professional Advertising Association

**BPI** brand potential index

**BPI** buying power index

**BPO** blanket purchase order agreement

**BRC** Broadcast Rating Council; business reply card

**BRE** business reply envelope

**BRM** business reply mail

**BTA** best time available

### C

**C/A** change of address

**CAD/CAM** computer-aided design/computer-aided manufacturing

**CAPS** computer-assisted picking system

**CATV** cable TV; community antenna television

**CBC** Canadian Broadcasting Corporation

**CBS** Columbia Broadcasting System

**CCA** controlled circulation audit

**CCD** census county division

**CCTV** closed-circuit television

**CD** creative director

**CDP** census-designated place

**CMSA** consolidated metropolitan statistical area

**COD** collect on delivery

**COMSAT** Communications Satellite Corporation

**CPB** Corporation for Public Broadcasting

**CPC** Canadian Postal Code

**CPGRP** cost per gross rating point

**CPI** cost per inquire

**CPI** Consumer Price Index

**CPM** cost per thousand

**CPO** cost per order

**CPS** cost per subscription; cycles per second

**CPU** central processing unit

**CRIS** Carrier Route Information System

**CRT** cathode-ray tube

**CTV** Canadian TV network

**CU** close-up

**D**

**DAR** day-after recall

**DASD** direct access storage device

**db** decibel

**DB** delayed broadcast

**DGA** Directors Guild of America

**DIS** distribution at

**DJ** disc jockey

**DMA** designated market area; Direct Marketing Association

**DMLRD** Direct Mail Lists, Rates, and Data

**DMM** Domestic Mail Manual

**DMMA** Direct Mail Marketing Association

**E**

**EA** editorial alteration

**EBC** Educational Broadcasting Corporation

**EC or EEC** European Economic Community

**ECOM** electronic computer-originated mail

**ECU** extreme close-up

**EDP** electronic data processing

**EFTA** European Free Trade Association

**EMRC** Electronic Media Rating Council

**ET** electrical transcription

**F**

**FCC** Federal Communications Commission

**FDA** Food and Drug Administration

**FEP** fast evening person's (report)

**FIM** facing identification mark

**FIPS** Federal Information Processing Standards

**FM** frequency modulation

**FS** full shot

**FSA** Forward Sortation Area (Canada)

**FTC** Federal Trade Commission

**FX** special effects

## G

**GATT** General Agreement Tariffs and Trade

**GCR** gray component replacement

**GMF** general mail facility

**GMS** general mail system

**GNH** gross night hour

**GPO** general post office

**GRP** gross rating point

## H

**HABA** health and beauty aids

**HBA** health and beauty aids

**HPRP** homes per rating point

**HUT** households using television

## I

**IABC** International Association of Business Communicators

**IBC** inside back cover

**ID** identification

**IMM** International Mail Manual

**INAME** International Newspaper Advertising and Marketing Executives

**INTELSAT** International Telecommunications Satellite Organization

**IN-WATS** Incoming Wide-Area Telephone Service

**IOA** Institute of Outdoor Advertising

**ISAL** International Surface Air Lift

**ISBN** International Standard Book Number

**ISSN** International Standard Serial Number

## L

**LDU** local delivery unit

**LED** light-emitting diode

**LNA** Leading National Advertisers, Inc.

**LOH** lady of the house

**LP** long play

**LS** long shot

## M

**M** thousand

**mm** millimeter

**MM** million

**MAB** Magazine Advertising Bureau

**MC** master of ceremonies

**MCU** medium close-up

**MGM** member-get-a-member

**MHz** megahertz

**MIS** Marketing Information System

**MOB** mail-order buyer

**MPA** Magazine Publishers Association

**MRCA** Market Research Corporation of America

**MRI** Mediamark Research, Inc.

**MS** manuscript (plural, MSS); medium shot

**MSA** metropolitan statistical area

**MSC** management sectional center

**MTAC** Mailer's Technical Advisory Committee

### N

**NAB** National Association of Broadcasters

**NAC** net advertising circulation

**NARB** National Advertising Review Board

**NASA** Newspaper Advertising Sales Association

**NBC** National Broadcasting Company

**NBP** National Business Publications

**NCOA** national change of address

**NCTA** National Cable Television Association

**NDG** National Distribution Guide

**NEA** National Editorial Association

**NET** National Educational Television

**NFI** Nielsen Food Index

**NIAA** National Industrial Advertisers Association

**NOAB** National Outdoor Advertising Bureau

**NORC** National Opinion Research Center

**NRP** net rating point

**N/S** newsstand

**NSI** Nielsen Station Index

**NTI** National Television Index

### O

**OAAA** Outdoor Advertising Association of America

**OBC** outside back cover

**OC** on camera

**OCR** optical character recognition

**OPM** orders per thousand

**ORC** Opinion Research Corporation

**OTC** over-the-counter

### P

**PA** public address (system)

**PAAA** Premium Advertising Association of America

**P&L** profit and loss

**PBS** Public Broadcasting System

**PCC** Postal Customer Council

**PCH** Publishers Clearing House

**PD** public domain

**PDS** paid during service

**PE** printer's error

**PGSR** Psychogalvanic Skin Response

**P.I.** per inquiry

**PIA** paid in advance

**PIB** Publishers' Information Bureau

**PIMS** Profit Impact of Marketing Strategies

**PLC** product life cycle

**PMA** primary market area

**PMS** Pantone Matching System

**POPAI** Point-of-Purchase Advertising Institute

**PPA** Periodical Publishers Association

**PPI** Producer Price Index

**PR** public relations

**PR&D** product research and development

**PRC** Postal Rate Commission

**PUAA** Public Utilities Advertising Association

**PUCA** Public Utilities Communicators Association

**R**

**R.®** registered trademark

**RAB** renewal at birth

**R&D** research and development

**RDA** recommended daily allowance; retail display allowance

**RDD** random-digit dialing

**RFM** recency/frequency/ monetary (value)

**RFP** Request For Proposal

**ROP** run of paper

**ROS** run of schedule; run of station

**S**

**SAG** Screen Actors Guild

**SAMI** Sales Area Marketing, Inc

**SAU** standard advertising units

**SCF** sectional center facility

**SCSA** standard consolidated statistical area

**SDC** state distribution center

**SFX** sound effects

**SIC** Standard Industrial Classification (Code)

**SITCOM** situation comedy

**SKU** stock-keeping unit

**SMSA** standard metropolitan statistical area

**SOV** share of voice

**SRDS** Standard Rate & Data Service

**STV** subscription TV

**SWOP** Specifications for Web Offset Publications

## T

**TA** total audience (rating)

**TAB** Traffic Audit Bureau

**T&E** travel and entertainment

**TELEX, TWX** Teletype

**TGI** Target Group Index

**TM** trademark

**TMO** Transportation Management Office

## U

**U&L** uppercase and lower-case

**UBD** undeliverable billing document

**UCR** undercolor removal

**UHF** ultrahigh frequency

**UPC** universal product code

**USP** unique selling proposition

**USPS** U.S. Postal Service

## V

**VALS** values and life-styles

**VCR** videocassette recorder

**VHF** very high frequency

**VNR** video news release

**VO** voice-over

**VOC** voice-over credits

**VPH** viewers per household

**VPVH** viewers per viewing household

## W

**WATS** Wide-Area Telephone Service

**WF, wf** wrong font

## PROOFREADING MARKS

PROOFREADING MARKS

| | | | |
|---|---|---|---|
| ℒ | Delete | **em /** | Insert em dash |
| ℒ̃ | Delete and close up | **en /** | Insert en dash |
| Ɔ | Reverse | ⌃ | Insert semicolon |
| Ↄ | Close up | ⊙ | Insert colon and en quad |
| # | Insert space | ⊙ | Insert period and en quad |
| Ↄ/# | Close up and insert space | ?/ | Insert interrogation point |
| ¶ | Paragraph | ⓦ | Query to author—in margin |
| ☐ | Indent 1 em | ⌒ | Use ligature |
| ⊏ | Move to left | **SP** | Spell out |
| ⊐ | Move to right | **tr** | Transpose |
| ⊔ | Lower | **wf** | Wrong font |
| ⊓ | Raise | **bf** | Set in boldface type |
| ⋀ | Insert marginal addition | **rom** | Set in roman type |
| **VⲀ** | Space evenly | **ital** | Set in *italic* type |
| ✗ | Broken—letter used in margin | **caps** | Set in CAPITALS |
| | | **sc** | Set in SMALL CAPITALS |
| ↓ | Push down space | **lc** | Set in lower case |
| ⇒ | Straighten line | **ℓ** | Lower-case letter |
| ‖ | Align type | **stet** | Let it stand; restore words crossed out |
| ⋀ | Insert comma | | |
| ⋁ | Insert apostrophe | **no ¶** | Run in same paragraph |
| ⋎ | Insert quotation mark | **ld in⟩** | Insert lead between lines |
| =/ | Insert hyphen | **hr #** | Hair space between letters |

## PRINT FONTS

Avant Garde Gothic Book

abcdefghijklmnopqrstuvwxyz
ABCDEFGHIJKLMNOPQRSTUVWXYZ
1234567890 .,;:"&!?$

Avant Garde Gothic Book Oblique

abcdefghijklmnopqrstuvwxyz
ABCDEFGHIJKLMNOPQRSTUVWXYZ
1234567890 .,;:"&!?$

Avant Garde Gothic Medium

abcdefghijklmnopqrstuvwxyz
ABCDEFGHIJKLMNOPQRSTUVWXYZ
1234567890 .,;:"&!?$

Baskerville

abcdefghijklmnopqrstuvwxyz
ABCDEFGHIJKLMNOPQRSTUVWXYZ
1234567890 .,;:"&!?$

Baskerville Italic

abcdefghijklmnopqrstuvwxyz
ABCDEFGHIJKLMNOPQRSTUVWXYZ
1234567890 .,;:"&!?$

Baskerville Bold

abcdefghijklmnopqrstuvwxyz
ABCDEFGHIJKLMNOPQRSTUVWXYZ
1234567890 .,;:"&!?$

Helvetica

abcdefghijklmnopqrstuvwxyz
ABCDEFGHIJKLMNOPQRSTUVWXYZ
1234567890 .,;:"&!?$

Helvetica Italic

abcdefghijklmnopqrstuvwxyz
ABCDEFGHIJKLMNOPQRSTUVWXYZ
1234567890 .,;:"&!?$

Helvetica Bold

abcdefghijklmnopqrstuvwxyz
ABCDEFGHIJKLMNOPQRSTUVWXYZ
1234567890 .,;:"&!?$

Kabel Demi

abcdefghijklmnopqrstuvwxyz
ABCDEFGHIJKLMNOPQRSTUVWXYZ
1234567890 .,;:"&!?$

Kabel Bold

abcdefghijklmnopqrstuvwxyz
ABCDEFGHIJKLMNOPQRSTUVWXYZ
1234567890 .,;:"&!?$

Kabel Ultra

abcdefghijklmnopqrstuvwxyz
ABCDEFGHIJKLMNOPQRSTUVWXYZ
1234567890 .,;:"&!?$

Old English Text

abcdefghijklmnopqrstubwxyz
ABCDEFGHIJKLMNOPQRSTUVWXY̧
1234567890 .,::"&!?$

Park Avenue Script

Aa Bb Cc Dd Eε Ff Gg Hh Ii Jj Kk Ll
Mm Nn Oo Pp Qq Rr Ss Tt Uu Vv Ww X
Yy Zz 1234567890 .,::"&!?$

Peignot Bold

abcdefghijklmnopqrstuvwxyz
ABCDEFGHIJKLMNOPQRSTUVWXYZ
1234567890 .,;:'&!?$

Souvenir Light

abcdefghijklmnopqrstuvwxyz
ABCDEFGHIJKLMNOPQRSTUVWXY
1234567890 .,;:'&!?$

Times Roman

abcdefghijklmnopqrstuvwxyz
ABCDEFGHIJKLMNOPQRSTUVWXYZ
1234567890 .,;:"&!?$

Windsor

abcdefghijklmnopqrstuvwxyz
ABCDEFGHIJKLMNOPQRSTUVWX
YZ1234567890 .,;:"&!?$

# TITLES THAT
# GENERATE SUCCESS!

## Business Success Series

Eleven titles comprise Barron's innovative series designed to help the business person succeed! Seasoned professionals offer commonsense advice and facts on how to master job techniques that will generate success. Each book: Paperback, $4.95, Can. $6.50, 96 pp., 4³/₁₆" x 7"

**Conduct Better Job Interviews** (4580-7)
**Conquering Stress** (4837-7)
**Creative Problem Solving** (1461-8)
**Delegating Authority** (4958-6)
**How To Negotiate a Bigger Raise** (4604-8)
**Making Presentations With Confidence** (4588-2)
**Maximizing Your Memory Power** (4799-0)
**Motivating People** (4673-0)
**Projecting a Positive Image** (1455-3)
**Running a Meeting That Works** (4640-4)
**Time Management** (4792-3)
**Using the Telephone More Effectively** (4672-2)
**Winning With Difficult People** (4583-1)
**Writing Effective Letters and Memos** (4674-9)

Prices subject to change without notice. Books may be purchased at your bookstore or by mail from Barron's. Enclose check or money order for total amount plus sales tax where applicable and 10% for postage and handling (minimum charge of $1.75, Canada $2.00). ISBN PREFIX: 0-8120

**Barron's Educational Series, Inc.**
250 Wireless Blvd., Hauppauge, NY 11788
In Canada: Georgetown Book Warehouse
34 Armstrong Ave., Georgetown, Ont. L7G 4R9

# More selected BARRON'S titles:

**DICTIONARY OF COMPUTER TERMS, 3rd EDITION**
*Douglas Downing and Michael Covington*
Nearly 1,000 computer terms are clearly explained, and sample programs included. Paperback, $8.95, Canada $11.95/ISBN 4824-5, 288 pages

**DICTIONARY OF FINANCE AND INVESTMENT TERMS,**
**3rd EDITION,** *John Downs and Jordan Goodman*
Defines and explains over 3000 Wall Street terms for professionals, business students, and average investors.
Paperback $9.95, Canada $13.95/ISBN 4631-5, 544 pages

**DICTIONARY OF INSURANCE TERMS, 2nd EDITION**
*Harvey W. Rubin*
Approximately 3000 insurance terms are defined as they relate to property, casualty, life, health, and other types of insurance.
Paperback, $9.95, Canada $13.95/ISBN 4632-3, 416 pages

**DICTIONARY OF REAL ESTATE TERMS, 3rd EDITION**
*Jack P. Friedman, Jack C. Harris, and Bruce Lindeman*
Defines over 1200 terms, with examples and illustrations. A key reference for everyone in real estate. Comprehensive and current.
Paperback $10.95, Canada $13.95/ISBN 1434-0, 224 pages

**ACCOUNTING HANDBOOK,** *Joel G. Siegel and Jae K. Shim*
Provides accounting rules, guidelines, formulas and techniques etc. to help students and business professionals work out accounting problems.
Hardcover: $24.95, Canada $33.95/ISBN 6176-4, 832 pages

**REAL ESTATE HANDBOOK, 3rd EDITION**
*Jack P. Friedman and Jack C. Harris*
A dictionary/reference for everyone in real estate. Defines over 1500 legal, financial, and architectural terms.
Hardcover, $29.95, Canada $39.95/ISBN 6330-9, 700 pages

**HOW TO PREPARE FOR REAL ESTATE LICENSING**
**EXAMINATIONS-SALESPERSON AND BROKER, 4th EDITION**
*Bruce Lindeman and Jack P. Friedman*
Reviews current exam topics and features updated model exams and supplemental exams, all with explained answers.
Paperback, $11.95, Canada $15.95/ISBN 4355-3, 340 pages

**BARRON'S FINANCE AND INVESTMENT HANDBOOK,**
**3rd EDITION,** *John Downes and Jordan Goodman*
This hard-working handbook of essential information defines more than 3000 key terms, and explores 30 basic investment opportunities. The investment information is thoroughly up-to-date. Hardcover $29.95, Canada $38.95/ISBN 6188-8, approx. 1152 pages

**FINANCIAL TABLES FOR MONEY MANAGEMENT**
*Stephen S. Solomon, Dr. Clifford Marshall, Martin Pepper, Jack P. Friedman and Jack C. Harris*
Pocket-sized handbooks of interest and investment rates tables used easily by average investors and mortgage holders. Paperback
Real Estate Loans, $6.95, Canada $8.50/ISBN 1618-1, 336 pages
Mortgage Payments, 2nd, $5.95, Canada $7.95/ISBN 1386-7, 304 pages
Bonds, 2nd, $5.95, Canada $7.50/ISBN 4995-0, 256 pages
Comprehensive Annuities, $5.50, Canada $7.95/ISBN 2726-4, 160 pages
Canadian Mortgage Payments, 2nd, Canada $8.95/ISBN 1617-3, 336 pages
Adjustable Rate Mortgages, $6.95, Canada $8.50/ISBN 1529-0, 288 pages

All prices are in U.S. and Canadian dollars and subject to change without notice. At your bookseller, or order direct adding 10% postage (minimum charge $1.75, Canada $2.00), N.Y. residents add sales tax.   ISBN PREFIX: 0-8120

Barron's Educational Series, Inc.
250 Wireless Boulevard, Hauppauge, NY 11788
Call toll-free: 1-800-645-3476
In Canada: Georgetown Book Warehouse
34 Armstrong Ave., Georgetown, Ontario L7G 4R9
Call toll-free: 1-800-247-7160

# More selected BARRON'S titles:

**DICTIONARY OF ACCOUNTING TERMS**
*Siegel and Shim*
Nearly 2500 terms related to accounting are defined.
Paperback, $10.95, Can. $14.50 (3766-9)

**DICTIONARY OF MARKETING TERMS**
*Imber and Toffler*
Nearly 3000 terms used in the marketing and ad industry are defined.
Paperback, $11.95, Can. $15.95 (1783-8)

**DICTIONARY OF BANKING TERMS**
*Fitch*
Nearly 3000 terms related to banking, finance and money management.
Paperback, $10.95, Can. $14.50 (3946-7)

**DICTIONARY OF BUSINESS TERMS, 2nd EDITION**
*Friedman, general editor*
Over 6000 entries define business terms.
Paperback, $11.95, Can. $15.95 (1530-4)

**BARRON'S BUSINESS REVIEW SERIES**
These guides explain topics covered in a college level business course.
Each book: paperback
ACCOUNTING, 2nd EDITION. *Eisen.* $11.95,Can.$15.95 (4375 8)
BUSINESS LAW, 2nd EDITION. *Hardwicke and Emerson.* $11.95,
Can. $15.95 (1385 9)
BUSINESS STATISTICS, 2nd EDITION. *Downing and Clark.* $11.95,
Can. $15.95 (1384-0)
ECONOMICS, 2nd EDITION. *Wessels.* $11.95, Can. $15.95 (1392 1)
FINANCE, 2ndEDITION. *Groppelli and Nikbakht.* $11.95,
Can. $15.95 (4373 1)
MANAGEMENT, 2nd EDITION. *Montana and Charnov.* $11.95,
Can. $15.95 (1549 5)
MARKETING, 2nd EDITION. *Sandhusen.* $11.95, Can. $15.95 (1548-7)
QUANTITATIVE METHODS. *Downing and Clark.* $10.95,
Can. $14.95 (3947 5)

**BARRON'S FOREIGN LANGUAGE BUSINESS DICTIONARIES**
Six bilingual dictionaries translate about 3000 terms not found in most
foreign phrasebooks:
Each book, paperback: $9.95, Can. $11.95
FRENCH FOR THE BUSINESS TRAVELER, ISBN 1768-4
GERMAN FOR THE BUSINESS TRAVELER, ISBN 1769-2
ITALIAN FOR THE BUSINESS TRAVELER, ISBN 1771-4
KOREAN FOR THE BUSINESS TRAVELER, ISBN 1772-2
RUSSIAN FOR THE BUSINESS TRAVELER, ISBN 1784-6
SPANISH FOR THE BUSINESS TRAVELER, ISBN 1773-0

All prices are in U.S. and Canadian dollars and subject to change without notice.
At your bookseller, or order direct adding 10% postage (rninumum charge $1.75,
Canada $2.00) N.Y. residents add sales tax. ISBN PREFIX 0-8120

Barron's Educational Series, Inc.
250 Wireless Boulevard, Hauppauge, NY 11788
Call toll-free: 1.800.645.3476
In Canada: Georgetown Book Warehouse
34 Armstrong Ave., Georgetown, Ontario L7G 4R9
Call toll-free: 1-800-247-7160